6th Edition

HEALTH ECONOMICS
Theory, Insights, and Industry Studies

Rexford E. Santerre

Professor of Finance and Healthcare Management
Department of Finance
School of Business
University of Connecticut

Stephen P. Neun

Vice President for Academic Affairs
Antioch University New England

SOUTH-WESTERN
CENGAGE Learning·

Australia • Brazil • Japan • Korea • Mexico • Singapore • Spain • United Kingdom • United States

SOUTH-WESTERN
CENGAGE Learning

Health Economics: Theory, Insights, and Industry Studies, Sixth Edition
Rexford E. Santerre and Stephen P. Neun

Senior Vice President, LRS/Acquisitions & Solutions Planning: Jack W. Calhoun

Editorial Director, Business & Economics: Erin Joyner

Editor-in-Chief: Joe Sabatino

Senior Acquisition Editor: Steven Scoble

Developmental Editor: Clara Goosman

Editorial Assistant: Elizabeth Beiting-Lipps

Marketing Manager: Nathan Anderson

Senior Marketing Communications Manager: Sarah Greber

Art and Cover Direction, Production Management, and Composition: PreMediaGlobal

Media Editor: Anita Verma

Rights Acquisition Director: Audrey Pettengill

Rights Acquisition Specialist, Text and Image: Amber Hosea

Senior Manufacturing Planner: Kevin Kluck

Cover Images: © George Paul/iStockphoto; © Ash Waechter/iStockphoto; © Olena Timashova/iStockphoto

For product information and technology assistance, contact us at
Cengage Learning Customer & Sales Support, 1-800-354-9706

For permission to use material from this text or product,
submit all requests online at **www.cengage.com/permissions**
Further permissions questions can be emailed to
permissionrequest@cengage.com

Library of Congress Control Number: 2012936155

ISBN-13: 978-1-111-82272-9

ISBN-10: 1-111-82272-7

Student Edition ISBN 13: 978-1-111-82274-3

Student Edition ISBN 10: 1-111-82274-3

South-Western
5191 Natorp Boulevard
Mason, OH 45040
USA

Cengage Learning products are represented in Canada by Nelson Education, Ltd.

For your course and learning solutions, visit **www.cengage.com**

Purchase any of our products at your local college store or at our preferred online store **www.cengagebrain.com**

Printed in the United States of America
2 3 4 5 6 7 16 15 14 13

To All the Girls in Our Lives:
Alexis
Jessica
Joan
Laurie
Lorraine
Mabel
Pamela
Patricia
Paula
Stephanie
Veronica

The health care sector, now representing more than one-sixth of the U.S. economy in terms of economic activity, continues to change in unimaginable ways. Sweeping transformations in the organizational arrangements of health care providers, newly developed medical technologies, the creation of new health insurance products, and the development and evaluation of various public policy initiatives all make the health care sector a dynamic and exciting area for applying the lens and tools of economic analysis. Indeed, not a day goes by without the unfolding of a medical event that requires the insights of economics to unravel the depths of its implications.

Our textbook, now in its sixth edition, is written expressly to capture the excitement generated by the health care field. As in the earlier editions, we take a fresh, contemporary approach to the study of health economics. We present the material in a lively and inviting manner by providing numerous and timely real-world examples throughout the text. At the same time, we resist the temptation of becoming overly encyclopedic and avoid purely technical issues that interest only academics and not students.

As a result of the approach taken, our book has wide appeal. Many business schools; liberal arts colleges; medical schools; and schools of public health, pharmacy, and health administration, at both the undergraduate and graduate levels, have chosen to use our textbook. The mix of adopters attests to the relevance and practicality of the material and the consistent and inviting manner in which various principles and concepts of health economics are presented throughout the text.

What's New in the Sixth Edition?

In addition to updating all of the statistics to the most recent year available, adding many new empirical studies, and thoroughly rewriting and condensing numerous chapters, several major changes have been made in this edition.

- We now discuss, at the end of most chapters, various provisions of the Patient Protection and Affordable Care Act (PPACA) of 2010 that apply to the material in those chapters. For example, comparative effectiveness analysis, the health insurance mandate, accountable care organizations, various health care taxes and subsidies, different health insurance regulations, and how the PPACA may affect the three-legged stool of medicine are discussed at the end of Chapters 3, 6, 7, 9, 11, and 16, respectively. These discussions not only benefit the students in terms of updating them on the scope and breadth of PPACA but also provide students with the opportunity to apply the theories and empirical lessons from the text to a better understanding of the potential economic effects of the PPACA.
- An appendix, written by Dhaval Dave of Bentley University, is offered at the end of Chapter 2 which fully develops Grossman's model of the demand for health. Faculty will now have a choice of separately discussing health status determinants (Chapter 2) and the demand for medical care (Chapter 5) within a commodities framework or relate these two theories within the more integrated time allocation model introduced in Appendix 2.
- An examination of the health care system in Switzerland, which relies partly on managed competition, has been added to Chapter 4.
- The material on agency and transaction cost theories has been moved from Chapter 13 to the end of Chapter 7. As a result, students have an earlier

understanding why health care organizations may merge horizontally or vertically. Some other cost concepts, such as learning-by-doing and sunk costs, have also been added to Chapter 7.

- A section, written by Austin Frakt of the Veterans Administration and Boston University, discusses competition between traditional Medicare and Medicare Advantage plans in Chapter 10.
- Chapter 11 has been greatly rewritten to reflect various empirical studies showing that health insurers likely possess market power in many regions of the United States. In addition, the discussion on the monopsony power of health insurers has been expanded significantly.
- Chapter 16 now compares the health care system in the United States to those in other industrialized countries in terms of the three-legged stool of medicine. Also, the efficiency status of the U.S. health care system is illuminated within a supply and demand model of a health economy. Finally, the chapter now discusses the proposed single-payer system in Vermont.

Organization of the Textbook

The textbook contains four parts: Part I, which contains Chapters 1 through 8, deals with basic health economic concepts, such as trade-offs, the production of health, health care systems and institutions, the demands for medical care and health care system, the health care system product, production and cost theories, cost-effectiveness and cost-benefit analyses, and market analysis. Specifically, Chapter 2 theoretically and empirically examines the different factors that help to produce health. Not surprisingly, the role of medical care in producing health is given particular attention in this chapter.

Chapter 3 covers cost-benefit and cost-effectiveness analyses, among other topics. Knowledge of these two evaluation methods helps policy makers determine efficient and effective ways to keep people healthy at minimum cost. An overview of health care system elements and an introduction to the U.S. health care system are provided in Chapter 4. A general model of a health care system and the role of financing, reimbursement, and delivery in a health economy are some of the issues discussed in this chapter.

Chapters 5 and 6 provide theoretical and empirical material on the demands for medical care and medical insurance. This information becomes important, for example, when asking questions concerning the utilization of medical care and why some people lack health insurance. Chapter 7 provides basic instruction on production and cost theories. These theories are crucial for understanding the behavior of any type of medical firm, regardless of its ownership type and how much competition it faces in the marketplace. Lastly, tools of market analysis are provided in Chapter 8. In this chapter, different market structures, such as perfect competition and monopoly, are discussed and compared in the context of a medical care industry.

In Part II, Chapters 9 and 10 focus on the important role of government in health matters and medical care markets. In particular, Chapter 9 provides an overview of government functions, such as regulation, antitrust, and redistribution, as applied to health and medical care issues. Chapter 10 discusses government's ever-increasing role as a producer of health insurance and examines the Medicaid and Medicare programs in considerable detail.

Part III includes Chapters 11 through 15. These chapters use the concepts and theories developed in the earlier chapters to extensively analyze specific health care industries by applying the structure, conduct, and performance paradigm of industrial organization. The private health insurance, physician, hospital, pharmaceutical, and nursing home industries are covered in great depth, and the analysis is kept as current as possible. Various health care topics and issues are examined in these chapters.

Finally, Part IV, or Chapter 16, deals with health insurance reform. Some of the more debated plans for reforming the U.S. health insurance system at the federal and state levels are discussed and evaluated. The book ends with a glossary.

In most colleges and universities, a course in health economics is offered on a one-semester basis. Within one semester, it is difficult to cover all of the material in this text. The business curriculum at the University of Connecticut offers the typical health economics course in two semesters at both the undergraduate and MBA/MPH levels. (Not all students always take both courses, however.) The first-semester course is titled Health Insurance. This first course covers Chapters 4 (Health Care Systems and Institutions), 6 (The Demand for Medical Insurance), 10 (Government as Health Insurer), 11 (The Private Health Insurance Industry), and 16 (Health Care Reform). Parts of Chapter 2 (Health and Medical Care) are also covered before Chapter 6, and Chapter 8 (Structure, Conduct, Performance, and Market Analysis) is briefly reviewed before introducing Chapter 11 in this first semester Health Insurance course.

The second-semester course is titled Health Care Economics, which covers Chapters 1 (Introduction), 2 (Health and Medical Care), 3 (Cost and Benefit Analysis), 5 (The Demand for Medical Services), 7 (Medical Care Production and Costs), 8 (Structure, Conduct, Performance, and Market Analysis), 9 (Government, Health, and Medical Care), and the four remaining industry chapters (12–15). Supplemental readings are assigned in both courses, and typically student presentations or point/counterpoint debates are assigned. Spreading the material over two courses means less rushing from topic to topic and provides more time to explore individual issues in greater detail. The students seem to appreciate the two-course approach and our book is written in such a manner as to accommodate this approach.

Supplements

Economic Applications: Economic Applications includes South-Western's dynamic Web features: EconNews, EconDebate, and EconData Online. Organized by pertinent economic topics and searchable by topic or feature, these features are easy to integrate into the classroom. EconNews, EconDebate, and EconData all deepen students' understanding of theoretical concepts through hands-on exploration and analysis of the latest economic news stories, policy debates, and data. These features are updated on a regular basis. For more information, visit http://www.cengage.com/economics/infoapps

InfoTrac: With InfoTrac College Edition, students can receive anytime, anywhere online access to a database of full-text articles from thousands of popular and scholarly periodicals, such as *Newsweek, Fortune,* and *Nation's Business.* InfoTrac is a great way to expose students to online research techniques, with the security that the content is academically based and reliable. For more information, visit http://www.cengage .com/economics/infoapps

Web Site: The support site for *Health Economics* can be accessed at www.cengage .com/economics/santerre and contains chapter-by-chapter web links, term paper tips, instructor resources, and other teaching and learning resources.

If a 1pass access card came with this book, you can start using many of these resources right away by following the directions on the card. One username and password gives you multiple resources. Get started today at www.cengage.com/ economics/santerre/

Web-Based Instructor's Manual: The *Health Economics* support site (www .cengage.com/economics/santerre) contains password-protected material for instructors only, including answers to end-of-chapter questions in the text, teaching notes for the case studies, a sample syllabus with web links, a list of readings for each chapter, and ideas for course projects.

PowerPoint™ Slides: PowerPoint slides are also located on the support site and are available for use by instructors for enhancing lectures. Each chapter's slides include a lecture outline illustrated with key tables and graphs.

Instructor's Resource CD-ROM: Get quick access to the Instructor's Manual and PowerPoint slides from your desktop via one CD-ROM.

Acknowledgments

Our goal is to create the best possible learning device for students and teaching tool for professors. We are profoundly grateful to all of the reviewers of this textbook and the talented and dedicated staff at Cengage Learning for helping us bring this goal closer to fruition.

For reviewing the fifth edition and providing numerous comments and suggestions for improving the sixth edition, we thank Doris Bennett, Jacksonville State University, Karen Buhr (University of Maine), Jie Chen (College of Staten Island/CUNY), Joey Crosby (Armstrong Atlantic State University), Atilla Cseh (Valdosta State University), Diane Dewar (University at Albany), Debra Dwyer (Stony Brook University), Bianca Frogner (George Washington University), Warren Greenberg (University of Maryland), Vivian Ho (Rice University), Latoya Jackson (Albany State University), David Latif (University of Charleston), Ricky Leung (University of Missouri-Columbia), Haiyong Liu (East Carolina University), Christina Marsh (University of Georgia), Neil Meredith (West Texas A&M University), Claudia Pereira (National School of Public Health), John Perry (Centre College), Jessica Wolpaw Reyes (Amherst College), Patrick Richard (George Washington University), Katie Showman (Florida State University), Christine Spencer (University of Baltimore), Karen Travis (Pacific Lutheran University), Yavuz Yasar (University of Denver), and Mustafa Younis (Jackson State University).

We also appreciate the reviewers of past editions and others who have provided us with comments for improving the text over the years, including:

Mir Ali	Partha Deb	Vivian Ho
Steven Andes	Derek DeLia	Ashley Hodgson
Jay Bae	Diane Dewar	Robert Jantzen
Mary Ann Bailey	Eric Doremus	Juan Kelly
Mark Barabas	Randall Ellis	Donald Kenkel
Laurie Bates	Alfredo Esposto	Timothy Leslie
Richard Beil	Maya Federman	Dong Li
Sylvester Berki	Andrew Foster	Mindy Marks
Jay Bhattacharya	A. Mark Freeman	Amalia Miller
David Bishai	Linda Ghent	Frank Musgrave
Stacey Brook	Stephan Gohmann	John Nyman
Bruce Carpenter	Glenn Graham	Albert Oriol
Sewin Chan	Darren Grant	Gabriel Picone
Chris Coombs	Dennis Heffley	Irene Powell
Guy David	Jim Hilliard	Keith Rayburn

Jeffrey Rubin	Leon Taylor	Gary Wyckoff
Windsor Westbrook	James Thornton	Aaron Yelowitz
Sherrill	Marie Truesdell	Donald Yett
Jessica Wolpaw Reyes	Kay Unger	Nicole Yurgin

As mentioned in the previous editions, if you have any comments or suggestions for improving the text, please bring them to our attention. Also please alert us to any theoretical or empirical articles that should be cited and/or discussed in our text. We are only an email message away. We thank you in advance.

Rex Santerre
rsanterre@business.uconn.edu

Stephen Neun
sneun@antioch.edu

CONTENTS

Basic Health Care Economic Tools and Institutions

PART ONE

CHAPTER 1

Introduction

Like millions of Americans at some point in their lives, Joe awoke one night feeling a crushing weight on his chest. As the pain spread down his arm, he realized he was experiencing his worst dread: a heart attack. His wife, Angela, called the paramedics. While the ambulance rushed Joe to the hospital, she anguished over the kind of care he would receive. Angela's anxiety starkly illustrates the basic questions any health care system faces:

1. Who should receive medical goods and services? Would a person like Joe receive care merely because he is a citizen, or would he receive care only if he worked for a large company that provides health insurance for its employees?
2. What types of medical goods and services should be produced? Should the most expensive tests (such as angiograms) be performed without regard to cost? What treatments (such as balloon angioplasties) should be provided?
3. What inputs should be used to produce medical goods and services? Should the hospital use high-tech medical equipment, a large nursing staff, or both?[1]

All health care systems face questions such as these, but sometimes choose to answer them differently. When responding to health and health care questions, societies around the world take into account important moral, cultural, legal, economic, and other considerations. Addressing all of these concerns simultaneously and thoroughly is a daunting task, in part because one concern often conflicts with another, but also because this task involves a substantial amount of time, effort, and knowledge. Indeed, the intellectual resource commitment would be so great that no one book could adequately cover all of the pertinent issues.

This textbook focuses solely on the economic aspects of questions involving health and health care. The general objective of this textbook is to develop a set of analytical and conceptual tools that can be used to gain valuable insights into a host of health care issues and problems from an economic perspective. This chapter takes the first step in accomplishing this important objective. In particular, this chapter:

- introduces the discipline of health economics
- discusses resource constraints, trade-offs, efficiency, and equity
- highlights the state of the health economy in the United States and sets the stage for the material in the remaining chapters.

---

1. We are indebted to Gary Wyckoff of Hamilton College for providing us with this example.

What Is Health Economics?

For many of you, this textbook provides your first exposure to the study of health economics. Perhaps the ongoing controversy regarding health care reform or the prospect of a career in the health care field motivated you to learn more about health economics. Or perhaps you need only three more credits to graduate. Whatever the reason, we are sure you will find health economics to be challenging, highly interesting, and personally rewarding.

The study of health economics involves the application of various microeconomics tools, such as demand or cost theory, to health issues and problems. The goal is to promote a better understanding of the economic aspects of health care problems so that corrective health policies can be designed, proposed, and implemented. A thorough understanding of microeconomic analysis is essential for conducting sound health economics analyses. If you lack a background in microeconomics, don't worry. This textbook is intended to help you learn and apply basic microeconomic theory to health economics issues. Before long, you will be thinking like a health economist!

The tools of health economics can be applied to a wide range of issues and problems pertaining to health and health care. For example, health economics analysis might be used to investigate why 13 of every 1,000 babies born in Turkey never reach their first birthday, whereas all but 2 of every 1,000 babies born in Japan live to enjoy their first birthday cake. The tools of health economics analysis might also be used to examine the economic desirability of a hotly contested merger between two large hospitals in a major metropolitan area. The burning question is: Will the merger of the two hospitals result in lower hospital prices due to overall cost savings or higher prices because of market power?

Health economics is difficult to define in a few words because it encompasses such a broad range of concepts, theories, and topics. The *Mosby Medical Encyclopedia* (1992, p. 361) defines *health economics* as follows:

> **Health economics** … *studies the supply and demand of health care resources and the impact of health care resources on a population.*

Notice that *health economics* is defined in terms of the determination and allocation of *health care resources*. This is logical, because medical goods and services cannot exist without them.[2] Health care resources consist of *medical supplies*, such as pharmaceutical goods, latex rubber gloves, and bed linens; *personnel*, such as physicians and lab assistants; and *capital inputs*, including nursing home and hospital facilities, diagnostic and therapeutic equipment, and other items that provide medical care services. Unfortunately, health care resources, like resources in general, are limited or scarce at a given point in time, and wants are limitless. Thus, trade-offs are inevitable and a society, whether it possesses a market-driven or a government-run health care system, must make a number of fundamental but crucial choices. These choices are normally couched in terms of four basic questions, discussed next.

The Four Basic Questions

As just noted, resources are scarce. Scarcity means that each society must make important decisions regarding the consumption, production, and distribution of goods and services as a way of providing answers to the four basic questions:

1. What mix of nonmedical and medical goods and services should be produced in the macroeconomy?

---

2. Even health care services produced in the home, such as first aid (therapeutic services) or home pregnancy tests (diagnostic services), require resources.

2. What mix of medical goods and services should be produced in the health economy?
3. What specific health care resources should be used to produce the chosen medical goods and services?
4. Who should receive the medical goods and services that are produced?

How a particular society chooses to answer these four questions has a profound impact on the operation and performance of its health economy.

The first two questions deal with **allocative efficiency:** What is the best way to allocate resources to different consumption uses? The first decision concerns what combination of goods and services to produce in the overall economy. Individuals in a society have unlimited wants regarding nonmedical and medical goods and services, yet resources are scarce. As a result, decisions must be made concerning the best mix of medical and nonmedical goods and services to provide, and this decision-making process involves making trade-offs. If more people are trained as doctors or nurses, fewer people are available to produce nonmedical goods such as food, clothing, and shelter. Thus, more medical goods and services imply fewer nonmedical goods and services, and vice versa, given a fixed amount of resources.

The second consumption decision involves the proper mix of medical goods and services to produce in the health economy. This decision also involves trade-offs. For example, if more health care resources, such as nurses and medical equipment, are allocated to the production of maternity care services, fewer resources are available for the production of nursing home care for elderly people. Allocative efficiency in the overall economy and the health economy is achieved when the best mix of goods is chosen given society's underlying preferences.

The third question—what specific health care resources should be used?—deals with **production efficiency**. Usually resources or inputs can be combined to produce a particular good or service in many different ways. For example, hospital services can be produced in a capital- or labor-intensive manner. A large amount of sophisticated medical equipment relative to the number of patients served reflects a capital-intensive way of producing hospital services, whereas a high nurse-to-patient ratio indicates a labor-intensive process. Production efficiency implies that society is getting the maximum output from its limited resources because the best mix of inputs has been chosen to produce each good.

Production and Allocative Efficiency and the Production Possibilities Curve

The most straightforward way to illustrate production and allocative efficiency is to use the **production possibilities curve (PPC)**. A PPC is an economic model that depicts the various combinations of any two goods or services that can be produced efficiently given the stock of resources, technology, and various institutional arrangements. Figure 1–1 displays a PPC. The quantities of maternity services, M, and nursing home services, N, are shown on the vertical and horizontal axes, respectively.[3] Points on the bowed-out PPC depict the various combinations of maternity and nursing home care services that can be efficiently produced within a health economy assuming the amounts of health care resources and technology are fixed at a given point in time.

Every point on the PPC implies production efficiency, since all health care resources are being fully utilized. For example, notice points A, B, C, D, and E on the PPC. At each of these points, medical inputs are neither unemployed nor underemployed (e.g., a nurse involuntarily working part time rather than full time) and are being

---

3. We assume society has already made its choice between medical and nonmedical goods.

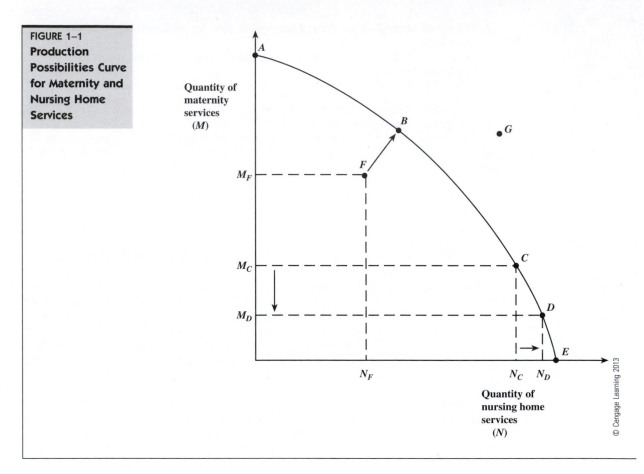

FIGURE 1–1

Production Possibilities Curve for Maternity and Nursing Home Services

The PPC shows the trade-off between any two goods given a fixed stock of resources and technology. Any point on the PPC, such as points *A* through *E*, reflects efficiency because units of one good must be given up to receive more of the other. A point in the interior, such as *F*, reflects inefficiency because more of one good can be attained without necessarily reducing the other. A point outside the PPC, such as *G*, is not yet attainable but can be reached with an increase in resources or through institutional or technological changes that improve productivity.

used in the most productive manner so that society is getting their maximum use. If a movement along the curve from one point to another occurs, units of one medical service must be forgone to receive more units of the other medical service.

Specifically, assume the health economy is initially operating at point *C* with M_C units of maternity care services and N_C units of nursing home services. Now suppose health care decision makers decide that society is better off at point *D* with one more unit of nursing home services, $N_D - N_C$. The movement from point *C* to point *D* implies that $M_C - M_D$ units of maternity care services are given up to receive the additional unit of nursing home services. Because medical resources are fully utilized at point *C*, a movement to point *D* means that medical inputs must be drawn or reallocated from the maternity care services market to the nursing home services market. As a result, the quantity of maternity care services must decline if an additional unit of nursing home services is produced. The forgone units of maternity care services, $M_C - M_D$, represent the **opportunity cost** of producing an additional unit of nursing home services.[4] Generally, opportunity cost is the value of the next best alternative that is given up.

_____

4. As economists are fond of reminding noneconomists, "There is no such thing as a free lunch!"

The bowed-out shape of the PPC implies that opportunity cost is not constant but increases with a movement along the curve. Imperfect substitutability of resources is one reason for this so-called **law of increasing opportunity cost**. For example, suppose the nursing home services market expands downward along the PPC. To produce more nursing home services, employers must bid resources away from the maternity care services market. Initially, the least productive inputs in the maternity care services market are likely to be bid away, because they are available at a lower cost to nursing home employers. Consequently, very few maternity care services are given up at first. As the nursing home services market continues to expand, however, increasingly productive inputs in the maternity care services market must be drawn away. The implication is that society gives up ever-increasing units of maternity care services. Thus, the law of increasing opportunity cost suggests that ever-increasing amounts of one good must be given up to receive successively more equal increments of another good.

If medical inputs are not fully utilized because some inputs are idle or used unproductively, more units of one medical service can be produced without decreasing the amount of the other medical service. An example of an underutilization of resources is indicated by point F in the interior of the PPC. At point F, the health care system is producing only M_F units of maternity services and N_F units of nursing home services. Notice that by moving to point B on the PPC, both maternity care services and nursing home services can be increased without decreasing the other. The quantities of both goods increase only because some resources are initially idle or underutilized at point F. Health care resources are inefficiently employed at point F.

A point outside the current PPC, such as G, is attainable in the future if the stock of health care resources increases; a new, productivity-enhancing technology is discovered; or various economic, political, or legal arrangements change and improve productive relationships in the health economy. If so, the PPC shifts out and passes through a point like G. For example, technological change may enable an increased production of both maternity and nursing home services from the same original stock of health care resources. Alternatively, a greater quantity of maternity and nursing home services can be produced and the PPC shifts outward if more people enter medical professions (possibly at the expense of other goods and services).

Production efficiency is attained when the health economy operates at any point on the PPC, since medical inputs are producing the maximum amount of medical services and no unproductive behavior or involuntary unemployment exists. Allocative efficiency is attained when society chooses the best or most preferred point on the PPC. All points on the PPC are possible candidates for allocative efficiency. The ideal, or optimal, point for allocative efficiency depends on society's underlying preferences for the two medical services.

Of course, the real world is much more complex than the example depicted here by the PPC. Rather than only two goods, an unimaginable number of goods and services are produced in a society. The PPC is a model because it offers a simplification of reality. As pointed out in more depth in Appendix 1, models are useful in the field of economics because they serve as conceptual devices or tools for organizing our thoughts about a topic. The PPC provides a good example of a simple but powerful model because it sheds light on a number of important lessons including: (1) the all-important economic role of scarcity; (2) the significance of economic choices; (3) the costs of inefficiency; and (4) how growth takes place in an economy.

The Distribution Question

The answer to the fourth question—who should receive the medical goods and services?—deals with **distributive justice** or **equity**. It asks whether the distribution of services is equitable, or fair, to everyone involved. In practice, countries around the world have chosen to address this medical care distribution question in many different ways.

When thinking about the distribution question, it is sometimes useful to consider two theoretically opposite ways of distributing output: the **pure market system** and a **perfect egalitarian system**. Goods and services are distributed in a pure market system based solely on each person's willingness and ability to pay because decisions concerning the four basic questions are answered on a decentralized basis within a system of markets. That is, goods and services are distributed, or rationed, to only those people who are both willing and able to purchase them in the marketplace. Thus, those who value goods the greatest are the ones to purchase and receive them. Also, because people face an incentive to earn income to better afford goods and services in a pure market system, they tend to work hard and save appropriately for present and future consumption. Consequently, productive resources tend to be allocated efficiently in a pure market system. In other words, the incentives associated with a pure market system typically mean that the economy operates on the PPC.

In many cases, differences in ability to pay among individuals reflect that some have consciously chosen to work harder and save more than others. Unfortunately, differences in ability to pay may also indicate that some people have less income because of unfortunate life circumstances such as a mental, physical, or social limitation. Regardless of the specific reason, it follows that people without sufficient incomes face a financial barrier to obtaining goods and services in a pure market system in which price serves as a rationing mechanism. Given income disparities, some people may be denied access to needed goods and services. Consequently, the pure market system is typically viewed as inherently unfair by many when it comes to the distribution of important goods and services such as health care.

In direct contrast, an administrative body, such as a federal or subnational unit of government, may answer the distribution question by ensuring everyone receives an equal share of goods and services. That is, a certain amount of income or goods and services is guaranteed in the absence of any productive activities. In an egalitarian system of this kind, everyone has access to the same goods and services without regard to income status or willingness to pay. Therefore, no one is denied access to needed goods and services. But an incentive may exist for people to choose to work and save less because the consumption decision is divorced from the distribution of earned income. Because of this inefficient allocation of resources, fewer goods and services may be available for distribution in an egalitarian system. In this case, the economy may operate inside the PPC.

In practice, most countries have adopted a mixed distribution system, with the reliance on central versus market distribution varying by degree across countries. For example, in the United States, many goods and services are distributed by both the market and the government. The Supplemental Nutrition Assistance Program (commonly known as food stamps), Temporary Assistance for Needy Families, and Medicaid programs represent some of the many policies adopted by the U.S. government to redistribute goods and services. Some people applaud these programs, whereas others argue that they worsen both efficiency and equity among individuals. They argue that efficiency and equity are compromised when those who choose to commit fewer resources to production are rewarded through redistributive programs and productive individuals are penalized via taxation. The efficiency and equity implications of various redistributive policies are constantly debated in the United States and elsewhere. In the context of health care, the consequence of this debate regarding distribution might determine who lives and who dies. For this reason, among others, more discussion on the redistributive function of government is taken up in Chapters 9 and 10.

Implications of the Four Basic Questions

Given scarcity of economic resources, a society generally wishes to produce the best combination of goods and services by employing least-cost methods of production. Trade-offs are inevitable. As the PPC illustrates, some amount of one good or service must be given up to increase the production and consumption of another good or service. As a result, each society must make hard choices concerning consumption and production activities because scarcity exists. Choices may involve sensitive trade-offs, for example, between the young and the old, between prevention and treatment, or between men (prostate cancer) and women (breast cancer).

In addition, some individuals lack financial access to necessary goods and services such as food, housing, and medical care. Because achieving equity is a desirable goal, a society usually seeks some redistribution of income. Normally, the redistribution involves taxation. However, a tax on labor or capital income tends to create a disincentive for employing resources in their most efficient manner.[5] Inefficient production suggests that fewer goods and services are available in the society (production inside the PPC). Thus, a trade-off often exists between equity and efficiency goals, and, consequently, hard choices must be made between the two objectives. The design of a nation's health care system normally reflects the way the society has chosen to balance efficiency and equity concerns.

Taking the Pulse of the Health Economy

A health economy, like a macroeconomy, involves the production and consumption of goods and services and the distribution of those goods and services to consumers. A health economy differs from a macroeconomy because it distinctly considers production, consumption, and distribution activities that directly relate to population health. More will be said about that difference in Chapters 2 and 4. Another difference concerns the way in which economists take the pulse of the macroeconomy and health economy. While economists are really concerned with efficiency and equity, the unemployment, inflation, and gross domestic product (GDP) growth rates are also considered when gauging the performance of a macroeconomy. If you recall from ECON 100, GDP captures the total market value of all goods and services produced in an economy during a particular period.

For a health economy, the analogous performance indicators are the components that make up the three-legged stool of medical care: costs, access, and quality. Again, although health economists are more concerned about efficiency and equity, many often use some variation of the three-legged medical stool to gauge the performance of a health economy. We discuss and provide some historic and contemporary data for each of these components in the following sections. The discussion not only introduces the various legs of the medical stool, but also motivates and acts as a road map for the remaining material in this textbook.

Medical Care Costs

Although the topic of medical care costs is taken up more formally in Chapter 7, recall from our earlier discussion that medical care resources, like resources in general, are scarce at a given point in time. It follows that an opportunity cost, or a price, is associated with each and every medical care resource because of scarcity. Thus, we can think of medical care costs as representing the total opportunity costs when using various societal resources such as labor and capital to produce medical care rather than other goods and services.

Each year since 1960, actuaries at the Centers for Medicare & Medicaid Services (CMS) have collected and reported data on the uses, sources, and costs of medical care in the United States. The data can be compared across various industries in the health care sector, like hospital, physician, and nursing home services, examined in a

5. This point is discussed in more detail in Chapter 9.

particular year, or tracked over time. Funding sources including consumers, insurers, or government can also be examined for various types of medical care, and over time. Hence, the CMS data yield important insights with respect to how health care funds are used, where the funds come from, and how much money in total is spent on medical care in the United States.

Uses of Medical Funds

Figure 1–2 provides a percentage breakdown of the uses of health care funds in 2010. These statistics offer insight into the mix of medical goods and services actually produced and consumed in the U.S. health economy. Recall that the second basic question is "what mix of medical care 'should be' produced?" Also recall that more of one type of medical care means less of the other types for a given size of the medical care pie.

According to the figure, 31 percent of medical care funds is spent on hospital services. The "big ticket" nature of hospital services should not be too surprising. Acutely ill individuals typically stay for a fairly long time in a hospital at some point in time. Physician services make up the next largest use of funds with 20 percent of the total. The dominant role of physicians makes sense because physicians are the primary care gatekeepers and patients must often first pass through them before accessing other types of medical care, including hospitals and prescription drugs. In addition, specialty physicians, such as heart surgeons, provide important services that maintain, improve, and extend human lives. Their reimbursement reflects, in part, the value placed on remaining healthy, which is discussed in Chapter 3.

Collectively, hospital and physician services account for more than half of all health care spending, not only in 2010 but over time as well. We will learn more about the structure, conduct, and performance of the physician and hospital services markets in Chapters 12 and 13, respectively. Finally, prescription drugs (10 percent), nursing home care (6 percent), dental services (4 percent), and home health care (3 percent) represent four other major areas where medical care funds are directly spent on patient care. The prescription drug industry is taken up in Chapter 14, whereas the home health and nursing home care industries are discussed in Chapter 15.

FIGURE 1–2
Uses of Health Care Funds in the United States, 2010

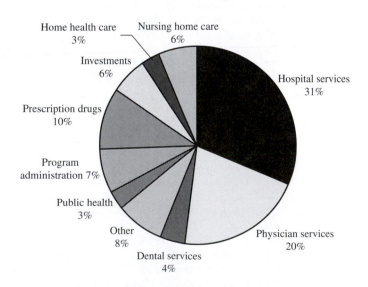

SOURCE: Centers for Medicaid & Medicare Service, http://www.cms.hhs.gov. Accessed January 10, 2012.

Sources of Medical Funds

The percentages of medical funds coming *directly* from consumers, private insurers, and government are shown in Figure 1–3. We emphasize the word *directly* because all funds ultimately come from consumers in the form of out-of-pocket payments, premiums, foregone wages, and/or taxes. In 2010 about 53 percent of all funds spent on national health care came from the private sector, down from approximately 76 percent in 1960. The bulk of this decrease took place in the mid-1960s when two public health insurance programs—the Medicare and Medicaid programs—were first introduced.

The mix between private insurance and out-of-pocket payments has also changed in recent years. In particular, private insurance has expanded its role as a source of funds and substituted greatly for out-of-pocket payments. In 1980, for example, private health insurance provided funds for 29 percent of all health care costs in the nation and out-of-pocket payments provided another 17 percent. By 2010, about one-third of national health care expenditures came from private insurers while consumer out-of-pocket payments fell to 12 percent. The greater reliance on private insurance funding reflects both a greater number of individuals and more types of medical care (e.g., pharmaceuticals and dental) covered by medical insurance. Business payments to provide health care services directly to employees, philanthropic sources, private construction, and nonpatient revenue sources (such as revenues from hospital gift shops) help to account for 7 percent of all health care spending in 2010.

Data also suggest that roughly 47 percent of all national health spending in 2010 came from the government. Most of the government funds were spent by the Medicare and Medicaid public health insurance programs. Given that the government funds less than half of all health care spending in the nation, the United States is often looked upon as possessing a privately financed health care system. However, Woolhandler and Himmelstein (2002) offer an alternative view of the relative share of health care spending financed through private and public sources. In particular, they scrutinize the method used by CMS to measure government spending in the national health accounts and show that the government has much more responsibility than the private sector with respect to financing the U.S. health care system.

FIGURE 1–3

Sources of Health Care Funds in the United States, 2010

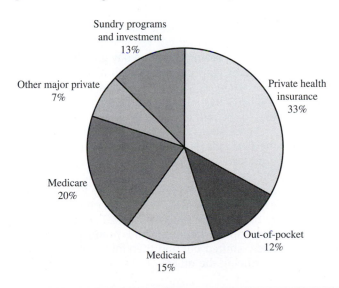

SOURCE: Center for Medicaid & Medicare Services, http://www.cms.hhs.gov. Accessed January 10, 2012.

Woolhandler and Himmelstein explain that CMS includes only direct purchasing of medical care for programs such as Medicare, Medicaid, and government-owned hospitals in its measure of government spending. Consequently, public employee benefits, such as those through the Federal Employees Health Benefits Program and various state employee health insurance programs, are missing from CMS's reported figures. Although the government supports these public health insurance programs with tax financing, private insurers administer the programs on behalf of the government and are responsible for writing the actual checks. In addition, Woolhandler and Himmelstein point out that employer-sponsored health insurance premiums are exempted from various federal, state, and city taxes. (We take this up later in Chapter 6.) Thus, the government also implicitly helps to finance employer-sponsored health insurance through these tax preferences.

To get a better idea about the extent to which health insurance is tax-financed, Woolhandler and Himmelstein add together the direct purchasing of medical care by government with expenditures on public employee health benefits that are tax-financed but administered by the private sector plus the value of the health insurance premium tax preference. Woolhandler and Himmelstein report that the direct spending of government equaled 45 percent of all health care costs, while public employee benefits accounted for another 5 to 6 percent, and the tax subsidy for health insurance premiums amounted to an additional 9 percent or more. Thus, government, at all levels, was responsible for financing around 60 percent of all health care costs in the United States. Thus, one might rightfully argue that, similar to other countries around the world, the government largely finances the health care system in the United States.

These estimates of Woolhandler and Himmelstein are certainly provocative. They show that tax financing represents the major source of health care funds in the United States. Indeed, tax financing accounts for an even greater share of health care costs, considering that not-for-profit health care organizations such as hospitals, behavioral health care organizations, and nursing homes are also granted preferences on income, property, and sales taxes. (We also take this up in later chapters.)

Amount of Medical Care Spending

Only someone living in entire seclusion, perhaps a World War II Japanese soldier hiding somewhere on a Pacific island or someone raised in a nuclear fallout shelter of the 1950s, would be unaware of the situation involving medical care costs in the United States.[6] Indeed, it seems that not a day goes by without a radio, television, or popular press commentator pointing, with much alarm, to the high and continually rising costs of health care. There is certainly no need to dispute those facts. According to CMS figures, the United States spent $2.6 trillion on health care or $8,400 per person in 2010. Compare that to the figures of $26.9 billion and $141, respectively, in 1960.

These figures are potentially alarming because trade-offs may be involved. That is, the PPC tells us that high health care costs translate into lower amounts of other goods produced and consumed. Certainly, high health care costs could reflect more and better medical care, but high spending may also involve the sacrifice of other equally important goods and services like food, clothing, and shelter. However, the productive capacity of the U.S. health economy has changed over time—the situation may not be as bleak as the statistics show. For example, the economy may now possess more labor and capital resources and productivity-improving technologies. Thus, the PPC has likely shifted out and therefore more of one good or service can be produced without sacrificing the others.

---

6. One of the authors of this textbook was stationed in Guam during the Vietnam conflict, where a World War II Japanese soldier was rumored to be hiding on the island. View the movie *Blast from the Past* starring Brendan Fraser to learn how growing up in a fallout shelter can affect one's knowledge of current events.

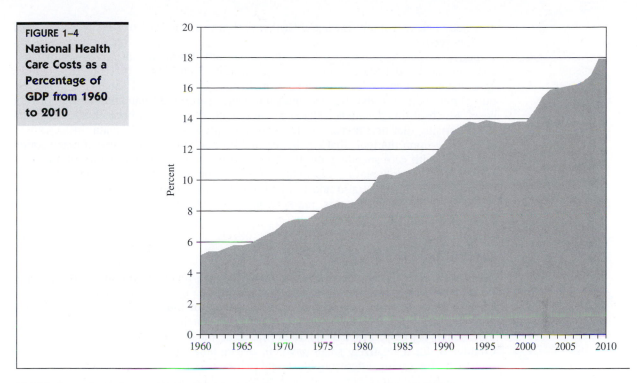

FIGURE 1–4

National Health Care Costs as a Percentage of GDP from 1960 to 2010

SOURCE: Centers for Medicare and Medicaid Services, http://www.cms.gov. Accessed January 10, 2012.

One way of controlling for differences in the underlying productive capacity of an economy or economies is by dividing, in this case, the amount of health care spending by GDP. Greater productive capacity, resulting from higher amounts of resources and better technology, generally means a larger level of GDP and therefore more goods and services in general. With that notion in mind, Figure 1–4 shows health care spending as a percentage of GDP from 1960 to 2010.

Figure 1–4 shows that health care spending as a percentage of GDP has grown tremendously over time in the United States. Standing at 5.2 percent in 1960, that same ratio of health care spending to GDP is now about 17.9 percent, which means instead of spending $1 out of every $20, we now spend nearly $1 out of every $5 on health care. However, even the rising percentage of GDP devoted to health care does not necessarily indicate other goods and services have been sacrificed. The GDP of $14 trillion in 2010 is much greater than the GDP of $526 billion in 1960. Given the health care spending to GDP ratios in the two years, spending on all other goods amounted to nearly $12 trillion in 2010 compared to $495 billion in 1960. Simply put, the greater productive capacity of the U.S. economy allowed for greater amounts of both health care and all other goods to be produced. In fact, productivity-enhancing technologies in the rest of the economy may have freed up resources for use in the health economy where the labor intensity of medical services doesn't allow us much productivity improvement. Of course, the relative mix of goods has certainly favored the health care sector since 1960.

Figure 1–4 also shows that health care spending has not increased at the same continuous rate throughout the years. For example, health care spending grew more quickly relative to GDP prior to the 1990s. In contrast, notice that after the 1990s, the ratio of health care spending to GDP remained relatively stable during the 1993 to 1999 period. The ratio of health care costs to GDP grew quickly for several years after 2000, especially because of the slowing of GDP growth due to the 2007 to 2009 recession and its slow recovery.[7]

Policy makers continue to debate the cause and desirability of rising health care costs in the United States and in other countries. Some argue that the U.S. health care system contains a lot of production inefficiency that can and should be squeezed out. Others point out that the benefits from health care more than compensate for the costs. Much of this debate is covered in various chapters of this book. It shouldn't be too surprising that health economists are heavily involved in this debate. In fact, they often draw upon the tools that can be learned in this book when trying to make some sense of health care spending and the health care economy. The structure of a health care system certainly plays a role so that topic is taken up in Chapter 4. The material in Chapters 5, 6, 7, and 8 also add to our understanding of health care costs and how consumers, providers, insurers, markets, government, and economic incentives help to shape health care spending.

Medical Care Access

Medical care access, another leg of the medical stool, relates to the distribution question. That is: Does everyone have reasonable access to medical care on a timely basis? Timely access is often measured by the percentage of individuals with health insurance. For most people, the cost of catastrophic care, such as organ transplants and cardiovascular surgery, lies beyond their financial means. But, as explained fully in Chapter 6, for a relatively small payment or premium, insurance provides access to high-cost, life-saving interventions if and when people experience severe illnesses. Thus, health insurance may be an important factor in terms of ensuring timely access to medical care. Figure 1–5 offers some information on the percentage of people without health insurance in the United States since 1940.

Before discussing the data in Figure 1–5, it should be noted that the health insurance product has changed considerably over time. Prior to the 1970s most people

FIGURE 1–5
Percentage of the U.S. Population without Health Insurance from 1940 to 2010

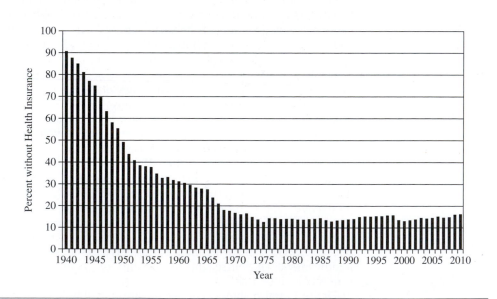

SOURCE: Santerre (2007) and DeNavas-Walt, Proctor, and Smith (2011).

---

7. To examine the efficiency consequences of medical spending we must consider the benefits of medical goods and services in addition to their costs. That topic is taken up in Chapter 3.

purchased only hospital insurance. Today people purchase health insurance for other types of medical care, as mentioned previously. Also, the amount of medical care expenditures covered by insurance has increased over the years. Thus, for the sake of consistency, it may be best to think of Figure 1–5 as showing the percentage of the U.S. population without hospital insurance.

In any case, the data in the figure show that great strides have been taken in terms of more people insured in the United States. In 1940, only 10 percent of the U.S. population possessed health insurance, purchased almost entirely in the private marketplace. Even before public health insurance programs, beginning with the Medicare and Medicaid Acts of the mid-1960s, many people began purchasing private health insurance in the United States following the 1940s. By 1975, the uninsured rate in the United States dipped to about 13 percent because of both private purchases and public expansions. However, beginning around 1980, further persistent declines in the uninsured rate have not materialized. In 2010, the uninsurance rate in the United States stood at 16.3 percent. While we take up the causes, types, and social costs of uninsurance in Chapters 6 and 11, it suffices to note that a sizeable percentage of the U.S. population currently lacks timely access to medical care because of their uninsured status. In addition, severe racial disparities exist with respect to uninsured status, as noted in Chapter 11.

However, the potentially good news, in this regard, is that the Patient Protection and Affordable Care Act (PPACA) of 2010 mandates that all but truly poor individuals purchase insurance or pay a penalty. Subsidies and tax credits will be provided to individuals, families, and small businesses to aid in the purchasing of health insurance. In addition, the Medicaid program, the public health program for certain segments of the poor, will be greatly expanded. Public authorities anticipate that all of the health insurance reforms will help increase health insurance coverage to an additional 30 million people in the United States. We discuss the reasoning behind a health insurance mandate and its potential implications on the health care sector of the United States in the remaining chapters of the book.

Medical Care Quality

The final leg of the medical stool we consider is medical care quality. As discussed more fully in Chapter 2, quality represents a complex and multidimensional concept. In keeping with the other two legs of the medical stool, we confine our discussion to a single measure of quality that is easily understandable and important from a societal point of view, and for which data can be obtained over time for comparative purposes. The chosen measure is the infant mortality rate (IMR) that tells us the number of children below 1 year of age that died as a percentage of all live births in that same year. The IMR for the United States from 1960 to 2009 is reported in Figure 1–6.

Like the uninsured rate, the IMR has improved significantly over time in the United States falling from a height of over 25 infant deaths per 1,000 live births in 1960. Although it stands to reason that rising health care spending and increased insurance coverage contributed to the decline, Chapter 2 discusses the theoretical framework and empirical findings regarding the many factors influencing health status outcomes such as infant mortality. Despite the vast improvements that have taken place over time, Figure 1–6 suggests that slightly more than 6 out of every 1,000 live babies in the United States do not live beyond 1 year of age. Also, the United States lags far behind when compared to other industrialized countries like Belgium, France, Italy, Japan, and the United Kingdom, which have IMRs below 5 deaths per 1,000 live births. Finally, the figure does not capture the vast variations in health outcome measures, such as infant mortality, among different income, racial, and ethnic groups. Once again, the tools of health economics can prove useful for analyzing health outcomes and proposing ways of improving societal health.

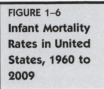

FIGURE 1–6
Infant Mortality Rates in United States, 1960 to 2009

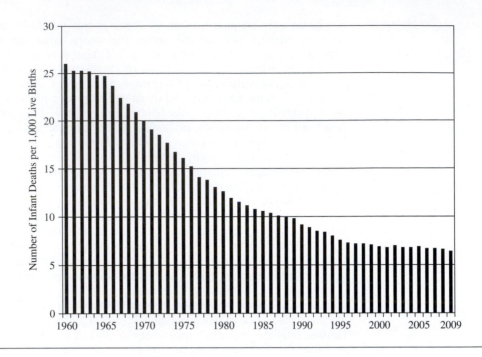

SOURCE: OECD (2011).

A Note on the Relation between System Structure and Performance

Many theories and empirical findings pertaining to health economics are introduced and developed in this text. Sometimes theories and empirical findings are of interest for their own sake, particularly for academicians such as the authors. But the main reason for their introduction and development is that we wish to obtain a better grasp of the operation and performance of the real-world health economy around us. If the health economy does not perform in a socially efficient and equitable manner, then we would hope that solutions would be proposed and policies could be changed to alter that undesirable performance.

An understanding of the link between structure and performance is essential when crafting new policies. Structure plays a role in determining how people behave or conduct themselves in the health economy. Figure 1–7 shows the complex interaction between structure and performance. A health economy is structured in a particular way, and this health economy structure is discussed in great detail in Chapter 4. Structure shows up in the ways various organizations are designed in terms of their size and scope, the mix of market activities and government involvement in the health economy, and financing and reimbursement mechanisms, among other considerations.

This underlying structure helps to establish the prevailing incentives in a health economy and thereby influences how people, organizations, and government itself behave. If incentives are distorted because of structural defects, then suboptimal performance likely results in terms of inefficient and inequitable outcomes. Given the suboptimal performance, solutions can be proposed and public policies can be designed to remedy the situation. In particular, policies can be changed to either indirectly affect behavior through a restructuring of the system or directly by introducing conduct remedies.

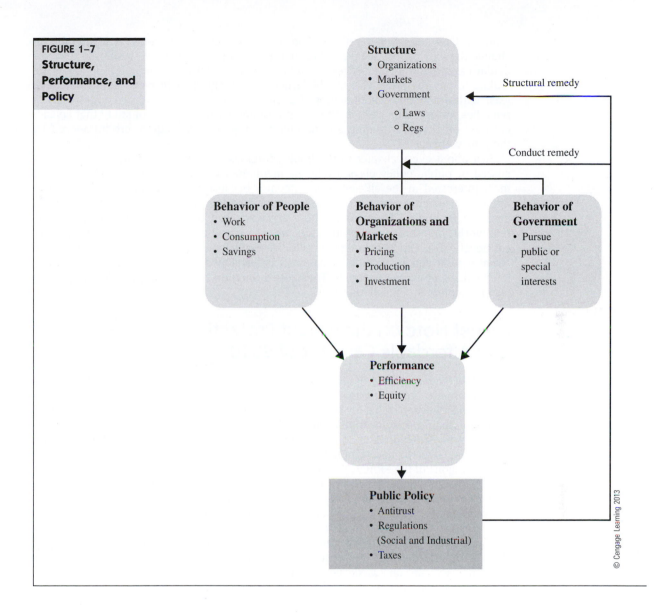

FIGURE 1–7
Structure, Performance, and Policy

An example may highlight the difference between a structural and conduct remedy when it comes to health or medical care. One important issue faced by public health authorities is childhood obesity. In fact, current estimates suggest the obesity rate among children and adolescents aged 2 to 19 is approximately 17 percent.[8] The major concern is that obesity is related to diabetes, health disease, and other illnesses.

Removing vending machines containing sugary beverages and candy from local public schools is a structural remedy that has been adopted by various communities throughout the United States as a way to reduce childhood obesity. Out-of-sight, out-of-mind may be one consideration behind this remedy. In contrast, some authorities have proposed a "fat" tax as a way of incentivizing children (and their parents) to spend less money on sugary items—not only within but also outside the public

---

8. http://www.cdc.gov/obesity/data/trends.html

schools. This latter policy reflects more of a conduct remedy because it attempts to change the way people behave rather than their set of actual choices. Note, in this particular case, that the conduct remedy allows the behavior to continue if individuals are willing to pay the price whereas the structural remedy outright bans the behavior—at least within a public school setting. Figuring out the best remedy or combination of remedies, even in this case, is difficult at best and requires a careful study that considers how efficiency, including any unintentional effects, and equity are influenced by the policy change.

Just about every chapter in the book addresses an issue where incentives are discussed or public policy plays a role. As mentioned previously, health economists are most interested in the efficiency of outcomes because resources are scarce. Unfortunately, efficiency is often difficult to gauge or measure in practice. An alternative is to design a theoretical benchmark where efficiency can be attained; then compare the real world, in terms of the existing incentives because of its structure, to that theoretical benchmark. Our benchmark for allocative efficiency (the point at which marginal social benefit equals marginal social cost) is developed in Chapter 3. This benchmark is expanded upon in Chapter 8. The most discussion concerning public policy shows up in Chapters 9, 10, and 16.

A Brief Note on the Patient Protection and Affordable Care Act of 2010

In 2010, Congress passed the Patient Protection and Affordable Care Act (PPACA) that contains many provisions that should monumentally alter the financing, reimbursement, and delivery of health care in the United States. No sector of the health care economy should remain untouched. At the time of producing this sixth edition, it is unclear if the U.S. Supreme Court will uphold or invalidate this new health care reform legislation. Given its uncertain nature, we decided to address at the end of each chapter any provisions of the PPACA that may relate to topics discussed in that particular chapter. That way, if some provisions of the health care legislation are struck down by the Supreme Court, the flow of the material in the rest of the chapter remains unscathed.

For example, we take up comparative effectiveness research at the end of Chapter 3. At the end of Chapters 5 and 6, we discuss how PPACA will likely impact the demands for health care and health insurance in the United States. In Chapter 7, the effects of PPACA on the delivery and costs of health care are highlighted. Other provisions affecting Medicare and Medicaid, physician manpower, insurance markets, and pharmaceuticals are taken up at the end of those respective chapters.

Summary

Health economics is concerned with the determination and allocation of health care resources and distribution of medical services in a society. Because resources are scarce, society must determine what amounts of medical services to produce, what kinds of medical services to produce, what mix of health care resources should be used, and who should receive the output of health care services. Answering these four basic questions involves tough trade-offs.

A health economy, like a macroeconomy in general, can be analyzed with respect to its performance. We discussed how the health economy can be assessed with regard to medical care cost, access, and quality and learned that the tools of health economics can and will be used to explore more thoroughly these components of the three-legged medical stool in subsequent chapters of this book. Controlling medical costs, access, and quality also involves trade-offs.

Finally, economic analysis can help us better understand the causes of problems relating to health and health care. The tools and concepts of health economics can also be used to find solutions and offer public policy prescriptions. The public policy prescriptions may involve structural and/or conduct remedies.

Review Questions and Problems

1. Draw a bowed-out PPC with an *aggregate* measure of medical services, Q, on the horizontal axis and an *aggregate* measure of all other goods (and services), Z, on the vertical axis. Discuss the implications of the following changes on the quantities of medical services and all other goods.
   A. A movement down along the curve.
   B. A movement from the interior of the curve to a northeasterly point on the curve.
   C. An increase in the quantity of labor in the economy.
   D. A technological discovery that increases the production of Z.
   If it were your choice, where would you choose to produce on the PPC? Why?
2. Congratulations! Upon graduating, you accept a well-deserved job with XER Consulting. Your first job involves a consulting gig with a state subcommittee on health care issues. The Senate health care subcommittee is considering the expansion of two existing public health programs. One program concerns additional funding for nursing homes around the state. The other program involves additional funding for community health centers around the state. In both cases, the funding is supposed to be used to attract more nurses for expansion purposes. Your job involves the following four tasks:
   A. Draw and use a PPC to graphically show and verbally explain to the subcommittee members the opportunity cost at a point in time of expanding any one of the programs, assuming that both of them are initially operating efficiently. Be sure to correctly label the axes and all points. Refer to the points on the graph in your explanation.
   B. Use the PPC to graphically show and verbally explain how one or both programs could be expanded at a lower opportunity cost if some inefficiency or slack initially exists in the overall public health system. Refer to various points on the graph in your explanation.
   C. Use the PPC to graphically show and verbally explain how both programs could be expanded at a lower opportunity cost if growth is expected for the public health care system. Refer to points on the graph in your explanation.
   D. Verbally explain to the subcommittee members what factors might cause the public health care system to grow.
3. Identify the three legs of the medical stool. Explain how trade-offs might take place among the three legs. If you had to choose one of the three to improve upon at the neglect of the others, which would you choose? Why?
4. Does the U.S. health care system possess a privately or publicly financed health care system? Explain.
5. What are two major uses of medical funds? How do the two major uses relate to the four basic questions?
6. At this point in the book, do you think the United States spends too much on medical care? Explain your reasoning using the PPC.
7. Explain the change in the percentage of the U.S. population with health insurance from 1940 to 1980. Can you think of any economic factors that may have caused that change? Explain the change in the percentage insured since 1980.
8. Explain the change in the IMR in the United States since 1960. Do you think the IMR is too high in the United States? Why? What is the implication of a reduction

in the IMR if we treat IMR reductions as one good on one axis of the PPC and all other goods on the other axis? What is the implication of an IMR reduction if we assume that some production inefficiency initially exists in the U.S. health care system? Why?

9. In your own words, explain the general link between system structure, performance, and policy.

10. As you know, the U.S. government implemented a variety of policies to limit smoking over the last few decades. Can you provide an example of a structural remedy? How about a conduct remedy?

References

DeNavas-Walt, Carmen, Bernadette D. Proctor, and Jessica C. Smith. "Income, Poverty, and Health Insurance Coverage in the United States: 2010." U.S. Census Bureau, Current Population Reports, P60-239, U.S. Government Printing Office, Washington, DC, 2011.

The Mosby Medical Encyclopedia. New York: C. V. Mosby, 1992.

Organization for Economic and Cooperative Development. OECD Health Data 2011. June 2011.

Santerre, Rexford E. "Tracking Uninsurance and Inflation in the U.S. Health Economy." University of Connecticut, Center for Healthcare & Insurance Working Paper 2007–05 (September 2007).

Woolhandler, Steffie, and David U. Himmelstein. "Paying for National Health Insurance—and Not Getting It." *Health Affairs* 21 (July/August 2002), pp. 88–98.

Economic Models and Empirical Testing

Health economics can be considered as both a social science and a science.[1] As a social science, the field of health economics studies people in their everyday lives and addresses issues such as obesity, alcohol abuse, and abortion. As a science, health economics offers testable hypotheses. For example, a health economist might explore empirically if people purchase more whiskey or fast food when their prices decline—the law of demand. In either case, models and empirical methods are used in health economics. This appendix offers an introduction to both of these tools of health economic analysis.

Economic Models

As mentioned earlier, the PPC is an example of an **economic model**. Models are abstractions of reality and are used in economics to simplify a very complex world. Economic models can be stated in descriptive (verbal), graphical, or mathematical form. Usually an economic model like the PPC describes a hypothesized relation between two or more variables. For example, suppose the hypothesis is that health care expenditures, E, are *directly* (as opposed to *inversely*) related to consumer income, Y. That hypothesis simply means that expenditures on health care services tend to rise when consumer income increases. Mathematically, a health care expenditure function can be stated in general form as

(A1–1)
$$E = f(Y).$$

Equation A1–1 implies that health care spending is a function of consumer income. In particular, health care expenditures are expected to rise with income.

An assumption underlying economic models is that all factors, other than the variables of interest, remain unchanged. For example, our hypothesis that health care expenditures are directly related to income assumes that all other likely determinants of health care spending, such as prices, tastes, and preferences, stay constant. As another example, notice in the previous analysis that the stock of resources and technology are held constant when constructing the PPC. Indeed, economists normally qualify their hypotheses with the Latin phrase *ceteris paribus*, meaning "all other things held constant." By holding other things constant, we can isolate and describe the pure relation between any two variables.

---

1. In fact, economics, of which health economics is a subdiscipline, touches upon history, psychology, sociology, philosophy, mathematics, and statistics.

The expenditure function in Equation A1–1 is expressed in general mathematical form, but a hypothesis or model is often stated in a specific form. For example, the following equation represents a linear expenditure function for health care services:

(A1–2)
$$E = a + bY,$$

where a and b are the fixed parameters of the model. This equation simply states that health care expenditures are directly related to consumer income in a linear (rather than nonlinear) fashion. Mathematically, the parameter a reflects the amount of health care expenditures when income is zero, whereas b is the slope of the expenditure function. The slope measures the change in health care expenditures that results from a one-unit change in income, or $\Delta E / \Delta Y$.

For example, let us assume the parameter a equals $1,000 per year and b equals one-tenth, or 0.1. The resulting health care expenditure function is thus

(A1–3)
$$E = 1,000 + 0.1Y.$$

Equation A1–3 implies that health care expenditures rise with income. In fact, the slope parameter of 0.1 suggests that each $1,000 increase in consumer income raises health care spending by $100.

The health care expenditure function in Equation A1–3 is represented graphically in Figure A1–1. Yearly consumer income per household is shown on the horizontal axis, and annual health care spending per household is shown on the vertical axis. According to the function, health care spending equals $3,000 when household income is $20,000 per year. Consumers earning $50,000 per year spend $6,000 per year on health care services. Note that the expenditure function clearly represents our hypothesis concerning the direct relation between income and health care spending.

FIGURE A1–1

Health Care Expenditure Function

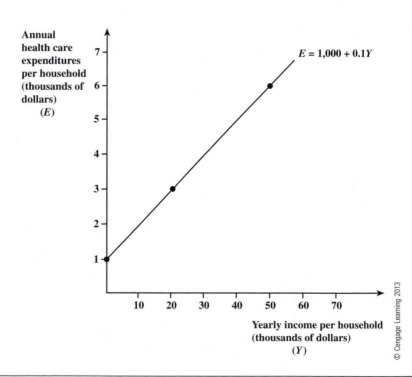

According to the expenditure function, health care spending increases with income. For example, health care spending equals $3,000 when household income equals $20,000 per year and $6,000 when household income equals $50,000 per year.

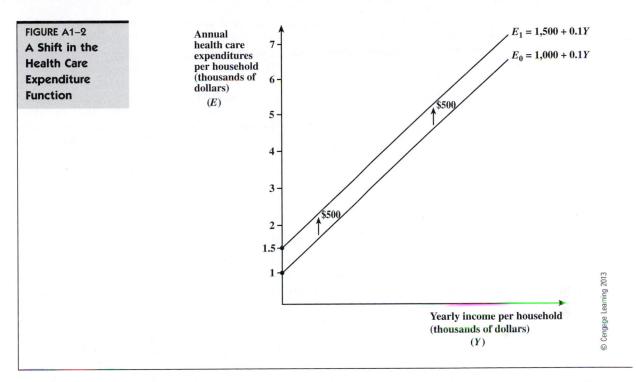

FIGURE A1-2

A Shift in the Health Care Expenditure Function

Yearly health care spending is assumed to increase by $500 for a reason other than a change in income. Thus, the expenditure function shifts upward at each level of income by $500 to E_1.

Now suppose some other determinants of health care expenditures change. Although this assumption violates our implicit *ceteris paribus* condition, we can incorporate changes in other factors into the health care expenditure model fairly simply. For example, suppose people generally become sicker than before, perhaps because households have become older on average. Obviously, this change tends to increase health care spending. Assuming that the "aging" effect influences only the intercept term and not the value of the slope parameter, the expenditure function shifts upward by the yearly increase in health care spending due to the aging population. Figure A1–2 shows an example of this effect.

Yearly medical costs are assumed to increase by $500 for the typical household. Thus, the health care expenditure function shifts upward at each level of income by $500 to E_1. If the aging effect also influences the percentage of additional income that people spend on health care services, the slope of the function changes as well. An increase (decrease) in the marginal propensity to spend out of income raises (lowers) the slope and rotates the expenditure function to the left (right).[2]

As you can see, a model, such as this expenditure function or the PPC, is useful because it helps simplify an otherwise complex world. We can better and more easily understand the relation among key variables. Models are also useful because they often offer valuable insights into the necessity or relative effectiveness of various public policies. For example, we saw from the PPC that policy changes typically involve trade-offs that public policy makers should heed.

In the case of our health care expenditure function, suppose that some government agency, such as the U.S. Government Accountability Office or Congressional Budget

---

2. Problem 2 at the end of the chapter asks you to complete an exercise of this type.

Office, determines that $4,000 of annual household spending on health care is necessary to maintain the health of family members in a typical household. Further suppose that a study by this same government agency finds that our health care expenditure model, as reflected in Equation A1–3, represents the true relation between household income and health care spending. If so, our model suggests that households with incomes less than $30,000 tend to spend less than the necessary amount on health care. The government might use this information to determine the subsidy needed at each level of family income to reach the targeted amount of $4,000. For example, a household with $10,000 of income would require a $2,000 subsidy to reach the targeted amount of health care spending whereas a household with $28,000 would need only $200.

Consequently, economic models are useful because they help simplify complex situations so we can more easily understand how things fit together. Models also are of great use for policy purposes.

Positive versus Normative Analysis

Health economists perform two types of analysis. **Positive analysis** uses economic theory and empirical analysis to make statements or predictions concerning economic behavior. It seeks to answer the question "What is?" or "What happened?" For example, we might investigate the exact relation between income and health care spending. Because positive analysis provides explanations or predictions, it tends to be free of personal values.

Normative analysis, on the other hand, deals with the appropriateness or desirability of an economic outcome or policy. It seeks to answer the question "What ought to be?" or "Which is better?" For example, an analyst might conclude that households with incomes less than $30,000 per year should be subsidized by the government because they are unable to maintain a proper level of health care spending. Naturally, this implies that the analyst is making a value judgment. Because opinions vary widely concerning the desirability of any given economic outcome and the role government should play in achieving outcomes, it is easy to see why normative statements generally spark more controversy than positive ones. For instance, when 518 health economists were asked whether the Canadian health care system is superior to the U.S. health care system, there was much disagreement. Fifty-two percent of the economists agreed and 38 percent disagreed with the statement. The remaining 10 percent had no opinion or lacked the information needed to respond to the question (Feldman and Morrisey, 1990).

The following sets of positive and normative economic statements should give you a better understanding of the difference between the two. Notice that the positive statements deal with what is or what will be, whereas the normative statements concern what is better or what ought to be.

> *Positive:* According to Becker and Murphy (1988), a 10 percent increase in the price of cigarettes leads to a 6 percent reduction in the number of cigarettes consumed.
> *Normative:* The government should increase the tax on cigarettes to prevent people from smoking.
> *Positive:* A study by Heidenreich et al. (2011) estimates the direct cost of cardiovascular disease in the United States equals $272.5 billion in 2010.
> *Normative:* It is in our country's best interests that the federal government take a more active role in the prevention of AIDS.
> *Positive:* National health care expenditures per capita are higher in the United States than in Canada.
> *Normative:* The PPACA of 2010 was enacted because every citizen of the United States should have access to quality health care at a reasonable cost.

Empirical Testing

Empirical testing of economic theories is important for two reasons. First, economic hypotheses require empirical validation, especially when a number of competing theories exist for the same real-world occurrence. For example, some people believe medical illnesses occur randomly whereas others believe medical illness is largely a function of lifestyle. The "random" and "lifestyle" explanations represent two competing theories for medical illnesses. Empirical studies can potentially ascertain which theory does a better job of explaining illnesses.

Second, even well-accepted theories are unable to establish the magnitude of the relation between any two variables. For example, suppose we accept the theory that lifestyle is a very important determinant of health status. A question remains about the magnitude or strength of the impact lifestyle has on health status. Does a young adult who adopts a sedentary lifestyle face a 10, 20, or 50 percent chance of dying prematurely compared to an otherwise comparable but more physically active individual? Empirical studies can help provide the answer to that question.

There are many different ways for researchers to conduct an empirical analysis. The method we emphasize in this book, which most economists also use, is **regression analysis**. Regression analysis is a statistical method used to isolate the cause-and-effect relation among variables. Our goal is to provide the reader with an elementary but sufficient understanding of regression analysis so the regression results discussed in this book can be properly interpreted. Regression analysis is explained through an example.

The example used concerns the relation between health care expenditures, E, and consumer income, Y. Suppose we hypothesize that health care expenditures rise with household income and want to test our theory. Health care expenditures represent the dependent variable, and income is the independent variable. Furthermore, suppose we expect a linear (or straight-line) relationship between income and health care expenditures, or

(A1–4) $$E = a + bY,$$

where a is the constant or intercept term and b is the slope parameter. If you recall, the slope parameter in this case identifies the change in health care expenditures that results from a one-unit change in income.

Because we are interested in the actual or real-world magnitudes of the parameters a and b, we will now collect a random sample of observations relating information on both medical expenditures and income. The data might be series observations on income and expenditures for a particular household over time or cross-sectional observations on income and expenditures across different households at a particular point in time. In this case, the household represents the unit of analysis, but the unit of analysis could be an individual or a town, county, state, region, or country. Suppose we collect cross-sectional data on income and medical expenditures from a random survey of 30 households.

Exhibit A1–1 shows a scatter diagram illustrating our random sample of observations (only 5 of the 30 observations are illustrated for easier manageability). Notice that the scatter diagram of observations does not automatically show a linear relation between income and health care expenditures because of omitted factors that also influence spending on health care, some randomness to economic behavior, and measurement error. Our objective is to find the line that passes through those observations and provides the best explanation of the relation between Y and E. One can imagine numerous lines passing through the set of observations. What we want is the line that provides the best fit to the data.

A criterion is necessary to determine which line constitutes the best fit. One popular criterion is ordinary least squares, or OLS. OLS finds the best line by minimizing the

EXHIBIT A1–1
Scatter Diagram of Income and Health Care Expenditures

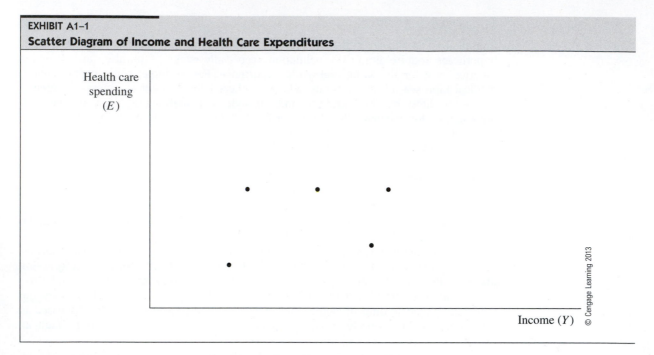

A scatter diagram showing the actual relation between household income and health care spending for five observations.

sum of the squared deviations, e_i, from the actual observations and a fitted line passing through the set of observations, or

(A1–5) $$\text{Minimize } \sum e_i^2 = \sum (E_a - E_f)^2 = \sum (E_a - \hat{a} - \hat{b}Y)^2,$$

where E_a is the actual observation on medical expenditures and E_f is fitted (or predicted) expenditures from the estimated regression line, $\hat{a} + \hat{b}Y$. In Exhibit A1–2, we show an example of a fitted line and the resulting deviations between actual and fitted expenditures. Based upon the sample of observations, a computer program (such as SAS, STATA, or EVIEWS) searches for the best line using the OLS procedure. In the process of finding the best line, the intercept and slope are determined, and thus we estimate the best magnitudes for a and b that minimize the sum of the squared deviations from the actual observations. Let's suppose the following results are obtained from the regression analysis:

(A1–6) $$E = 2,000 + 0.2Y.$$

The results would tell us that the best fitted line to the data has an intercept of $2,000 and a slope of 0.2. Although the fitted or estimated regression line provides the "best" fit compared to all other lines, we do not know yet whether it represents a "good" fit to the actual data. Fortunately, the computer estimation procedure also provides us with some goodness-of-fit information that we can use to determine if the best fit is also a reasonably good one.

The two most common and elementary goodness-of-fit measures are the coefficient of determination, R^2, and the t-statistic, t. The coefficient of determination identifies the fraction of the variation in the dependent variable that is explained by the independent variable. Thus, the R^2 ranges between 0 and 1. Researchers tend to place more faith in a regression line that explains a greater proportion of the variation in the dependent variable.

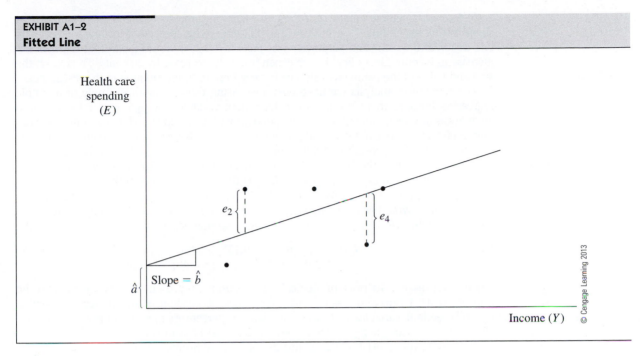

EXHIBIT A1–2
Fitted Line

The fitted line resulting from OLS and the associated deviations between the fitted and actual values.

The values for the parameters $\hat{a}$ and $\hat{b}$ are average estimates rather than true values because they are based on a sample instead of all possible observations; thus, they are associated with some error. Accordingly, there will be some deviations around the average estimate for a and also around the average estimate for b. In fact, if the deviations are very large, we cannot place much faith in the estimated value for the parameters. Indeed, the true value for b may be zero. If so, no relation exists between income and health care expenditures.

The computed t-statistic, which equals the estimated parameter divided by its standard error, helps us identify how much deviation occurs around the estimated average value for the parameters of the model. A t-statistic of 2 or more means that the value of the estimated parameter was at least twice as large as its average deviation. A rule of thumb is that when the t-statistic is 2 or more, we can place about 95 percent confidence in the estimated average value for the parameter, meaning that only a 5 percent likelihood exists that the relation could have occurred by chance. Another rule of thumb is that when the t-statistic is 3 or more, we can place 99 percent confidence in our estimated value for the parameter. In this case, only a 1 percent likelihood exists that the relation occurred by chance.

Regression results are generally reported similar to the following:

(A1–7)
$$E = 2{,}000 + 0.2Y \qquad R^2 = 0.47$$
$$ (2.52) \quad (3.40) \qquad N = 30$$

The t-statistics are reported in parentheses below the parameter estimates. Because the t-statistic associated with income is greater than 3, we can place a high degree of confidence in the parameter estimate of 0.2. Also, according to the regression results, income explains about 47 percent of the variation in health care expenditures. The number of observations, N, is 30.

Before we move on, we need to interpret the parameter estimates for Equation A1–7. The intercept term of 2,000 tells us the level of health care expenditures when income is zero. The parameter estimate of 0.2 on the income variable is much more telling and suggests that expenditures on health care will increase by 20 cents if income increases by one dollar. If the estimated parameter was instead −0.2, it would mean that a one-dollar increase in income causes health care expenditures to decrease by 20 cents. Thus, both the sign and value of the parameter estimate convey important information to the researcher.

The regression analysis we have been discussing thus far is an example of a simple regression because there is only one independent variable. Multiple regression refers to an analysis in which more than one independent variable is specified. For example, theory might tell us that price or tastes and preferences should also be included in an expenditure equation. The OLS procedure behind multiple regression is the same as that for simple regression and finds the best line that minimizes the squared deviations between the actual and fitted values. The computed R^2 identifies the variation in the dependent variable, say, health care expenditures, explained by the set of independent variables, which in our example would be price, income, and tastes and preferences. Each independent variable would be associated with an estimated parameter and t-statistic. For example:

(A1–8)
$$E = 1,000 - 0.2P + 0.13Y + 0.8A \quad R^2 = 0.75$$
$$(2.32) \quad (0.42) \quad (3.23) \quad (4.00) \quad N = 30$$

where P represents the price of medical services and A represents the average age in the household as a proxy for tastes and preferences. According to the regression results, the independent variables collectively explain 75 percent of the variation in health care expenditures. Also, the regression results suggest that both income and age have a statistically significant direct impact on health care expenditures. Price, on the other hand, has no impact on health care expenditures according to the regression findings.

Association versus Causation

As mentioned previously, the intent behind multiple regression analysis is to establish a cause-and-effect relation among variables. Sometimes, however, multiple regression analysis simply captures an association or correlation among variables rather than a true causal relationship. That happens most often for observational studies that involve either cross-sectional or time series data but contain no correction for the circumstances behind the observed relationship. The association, but inability to draw a causal relation, reflects that the underlying observations have not resulted from a randomized process involving both a control and a treatment group. Figure A1–3 helps to show why an observational study may be hindered by its inability to distinguish between a causal relationship and an association.

The figure illustrates a simple relation between physical health status (say a self-reported index ranging from poor to excellent physical health) and the number of physician visits (as a measure of medical care). All other measurable factors affecting physical health status, like age, gender, and income, are collapsed and captured in the variable X. Suppose we are investigating if more office visits help to improve, or cause, better health. However, even if the multiple regression analysis yields a statistically significant relation between the number of physician visits and more favorable health, we cannot be certain if the evidence supports a causal relationship. The uncertainty holds for two reasons.

First, a third unobservable and therefore immeasurable factor, Z, that cannot be included in X, may simultaneously affect both the number of physician visits and physical health status and thereby produce the observed association. For example, suppose we cannot properly and completely measure mental health status (e.g., the severity of depression), and mental health status influences both the self-reported physical health index and the likelihood of visiting a physician. Perhaps, severely depressed individuals simultaneously downgrade their physical health status and become more reclusive so they fail to visit their physician. If so, any observed correlation between

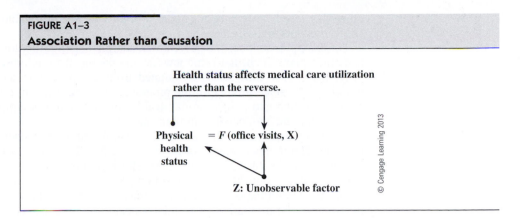

FIGURE A1–3

Association Rather than Causation

Office visits are associated with physical health status because an unobservable factor, such as mental health status, affects both or physical health status affects the number of office visits.

physician visits and physical health status, in the presence of this important omitted unobservable variable, may not reflect causation.

Second, reverse causality may pose a problem when attempting to draw inferences about the direction of causal relationships from regression results. That is, physical health status, the dependent variable in Figure A1–3, may influence the number of physician visits, the independent variable. For example, state governments may pursue policies to encourage more doctors per person in areas with the highest IMRs. Or, pregnant mothers may be more likely to seek out physicians when they suspect the health of their infants may be at greater risk. Hence, the regression results from an observational study would actually reflect a reverse effect—health status causes visits.

As a result, investigators often use various methods to identify or isolate causal relationships. Basically, some type of identification strategy is necessary to distinguish a causal relationship from an association. One strategy randomly assigns people or households to different situations or categories and conducts a controlled behavioral experiment. Following our same example, on a random basis, various individuals might be required to visit the doctor a certain number of times per year. Some individuals may not be allowed any physician visits at all, and others may be forced to visit their doctor ranging from one to ten times per year, regardless of their income, observable mental health status, or other personal characteristics. The random assignment of households corrects for any self-selection bias that results when individuals with different (unobservable) mental health states are allowed to choose the number of doctor visits.

The analyst then studies the relation between the number of office visits and physical health status, while controlling for other observable measures that may also affect health status using a technique such as multiple regression analysis. The hypothesis is that physical health status improves with more office visits—*ceteris paribus*. As you might expect, randomized **social experiments** of this kind offer valuable insights but are very expensive to conduct. In addition, the health of some individuals might be seriously compromised if they are not permitted to visit the doctor a reasonable number of times per year. Hence large social experiments are rarely conducted. In Chapter 5, we will discuss the RAND Health Insurance Study of the 1970s, which randomly assigned households to different health plans and investigated various hypotheses relating to health and health care.

A **natural experiment**, an alternative identification strategy, arises when some type of external global policy, unrelated to other determinants of physical health status, produces an uncontrollable shock in the medical care received by a treatment group. Changes in the health outcomes of this treatment group are then compared to health outcomes of the control group that did not experience that same external shock but otherwise faced fairly similar circumstances. The uncontrollable nature of the policy shock prevents self-selection.

For example, suppose the government sharply cuts funding for various public health insurance plans such that some low-income people are randomly terminated from the programs. Those individuals terminated from the programs represent the treatment group and those continuing in the programs represent the control group. After a given period, we then gather data on physical health status and other determinants of health status including age, gender, and income.

In the multiple regression analysis, physical health status serves as the dependent variable. The independent variables include a 0 or 1 dummy variable identifying if the individual was subjected to the policy shock or not, and other measurable determinants of physical health status. Assuming 1 represents an individual in the treatment group, we would expect a negative coefficient on the dummy variable because termination from the programs causes poorer health, all other factors held constant.

Several natural experiments have studied the effect of medical care program terminations (such as veteran or maternal health benefits) on the health outcomes of a treatment group compared to an otherwise similar control group for which the termination did not occur (Levy and Meltzer, 2001). While this method offers a valuable way of identifying the existence of causal relationships, various drawbacks exist. First of all, not many policy shocks occur in practice for testing various hypotheses. Even when they do, the treatment and control groups may not be randomly selected. For example, in some of the studies just cited, only those individuals with less severe illnesses were terminated from the medical care programs.

The third identification strategy is called the **instrumental variables approach**. To conduct the instrumental variables approach, in the context of our example, a variable (i.e., an instrument) or a set of variables must be found that affect the number of office visits but not physical health status. For instance, the distance of each household from the physician's office might be used as an instrument because it could be argued that distance helps to determine the number of office visits (i.e., convenience), but not physical health status.

If so, a multiple regression technique called two-stage least squares can be employed to examine the extent to which distance affects the number of physician visits in the first stage of the estimation procedure and then the effect of physician visits on physical health status is studied in the second stage. This technique essentially purges some of the association between the actual number of physician visits and physical health status resulting from the third-variable problem or reverse causality. That is, we can identify any change in physical health that results from a change in the number of office visits simply because of less or greater convenience and not because of a reverse causality or third-variable problem.

The instrumental variables approach is one of the more popular methods for identifying causal relationships. However, in practice, it is often difficult to find a suitable set of instruments. This is particularly true for health economic analyses where many variables are highly correlated with one another such as the consumption of medical care, health insurance status, income, and health status—it is very hard to find a factor of set of factors that affect one but not the others.

The final method to identify a causal relationship is referred to as the **fixed effects model**. A panel data set, which combines both cross-sectional and time series data, is necessary to use a fixed effects model. The same 100,000 people over 10 years or 50 states over 20 years represent examples of panel data sets. Because of the time dimension and the repeated observations, we can track how the same cross-section of observations reacts to changes in various factors over time. More importantly, a 0/1 dummy variable for each cross-section observation in the sample can be specified in the multiple regression equation to control for unobservable heterogeneity (i.e., unobservable differences among the cross-section observations).

Recall from our running example that we are unable to control for the severity of mental depression and that omitted variable creates a third-variable problem. Assuming each individual's state of mental depression is fairly constant over time, the set of cross-section dummy variables or fixed effects essentially helps to control for mental health status differences as well as any other unobservable differences among the individuals in the sample. This reduces the likelihood of a third-variable problem and allows the researcher to better identify a causal relationship.

For that reason, most of the statistical research today in health economics involves a fixed effects model. There are a couple of shortcomings associated with the fixed effects approach, however. First, data requirements are much greater. Data for the same cross-section of observations must be obtained and inputted for a number of years. But with greater amounts of data available on-line and in predetermined formats, that shortcoming is becoming less troublesome. Second, the fixed effects model assumes that the unobservable heterogeneity—for example, severity of mental depression—is relatively constant over time. If the unobservable variable changes over time, then the third-variable problem may not be eliminated and the empirical results may reflect an association instead of a causal relationship. When a social or natural experiment cannot be performed, a preferred identification strategy combines an instrumental variables approach along with a fixed effects model.

Summary

Economic models and empirical testing of hypotheses are important for making sense of the real world, for advancing knowledge, and for public policy purposes. Economic models help to organize our thoughts about the relation among key variables by helping to simplify an otherwise complex world. Positive analysis cannot be performed without economic models and normative analysis should be based on solid positive theory.

Empirical evidence should also be based on sound economic theory. That is, the variables specified in a multiple regression equation should be based on economic reasoning rather than on ad hoc notions. Knowing the quantitative magnitude of the relation among variables provides important insights into the relative effectiveness of various policies. As a result, choosing the best policy often requires hard empirical evidence.

We recognize that learning the material in this appendix does not make the reader an econometrician. Econometrics is way too complex for that to happen. The material does, however, introduce the reader to the general idea behind the empirical testing of health economic hypotheses. It also exposes the reader to some of the pitfalls involved and several techniques for dealing with these pitfalls. The basic idea is that all multiple regression models are not created equally; some are clearly better than others. We invite you to learn more about the theory and practice of econometrics.[3]

Review Questions and Problems

1. Determine whether the following statements are based on positive or normative analysis. Be sure to substantiate your answers.
   A. Prices of physician services should be controlled by the government because many citizens cannot afford to pay for a visit to a physician.
   B. According to Tosteson et al. (1990), a 25 percent drop in the number of people who smoked in 1990 would reduce the incidence of coronary heart diseases by 0.7 percent by the year 2015.

---

3. Studenmund (2006) offers a good introduction to econometric issues. Also, Dowd and Town (2002) offer a worthwhile discussion of causation versus association in the context of health care research.

    C. Rising health care costs have forced numerous rural hospitals to close their doors in recent years.

    D. According to government statistics, in 2009, the number of alcohol-induced deaths was roughly 20 per 100,000 residents between the ages of 45 and 64. To decrease this number, the government should impose higher taxes on alcohol.

2. Suppose a health expenditure function is specified in the following manner:

$$E = 500 + 0.2Y,$$

where E represents annual health care expenditures per capita and Y stands for income per capita.

    A. Using the slope of the health expenditure function, predict the change in per capita health care expenditures that would result from a $1,000 increase in per capita income.

    B. Compute the level of per capita health care spending when per capita income takes on the following dollar values: 0; 1,000; 2,000; 4,000; and 6,000.

    C. Using the resulting values for per capita health care spending in part B, graph the associated health care expenditure function.

    D. Assume that the fixed amount of health care spending decreases to $250. Graph the new and original health care functions on the same graph. What is the relation between the original and new health care expenditure functions?

    E. Now assume that the fixed amount of health care spending remains at $500 but the slope parameter on income decreases to 0.1. Graph both the original and new health care expenditure functions. Explain the relation between the two lines.

3. Victor Fuchs (1996) lists the following questions in an article in the *Wall Street Journal*. Identify whether the following questions involve positive or normative analysis. All the questions deal with a Republican plan to reform Medicare, the public health insurance program for the elderly.

    A. How many Medicare beneficiaries will switch to managed care?

    B. How much should the younger generation be taxed to pay for the elderly?

    C. Should seniors who use less care benefit financially, or should they subsidize those who use more care?

    D. How many Medicare beneficiaries will switch to medical savings accounts (see Chapter 16)?

    E. What effect will these changes have on utilization?

    F. How much should society devote to medical interventions that would add one year of life expectancy for men and women who have already passed the biblical "three score and ten"?

    G. Will senior citizens' choices about types of coverage depend on their health status?

    H. If the rate of spending growth is reduced to 6 percent from 10 percent a year, what will happen to the growth of medical services? To physician incomes?

4. Identify two purposes of empirical testing.

5. Suppose you are explaining the technique behind OLS to a statistically challenged but otherwise intelligent uncle of yours. Further suppose the statistical relationship concerns one between the number of physician visits and physical health status. Don't worry about drawing causality but only explaining the OLS technique itself. Explain to him how OLS fits a line to a set of observations. You might want to use a scatter diagram and an equation for a line to make your point.

6. Suppose you are presented with the following regression equation involving health care expenditures and its determinants, where all of the variables have been defined previously.

$$E = 500 - 25P + 0.20Y - 1.2A \qquad R^2 = 0.30$$
$$\quad (1.21) \ (2.45) \ (0.43) \quad (4.13) \qquad N = 1{,}000$$

   A. What percentage of the variation in health care spending is explained by the various independent variables?
   B. Which of the independent variables possesses a statistical significant impact on health care spending? What do the results suggest about the relation between income and health care spending?
   C. Supposing that both P and E are measured in dollars, interpret the coefficient estimate on P.
   D. What does the coefficient estimate on A suggest about the relation between age and health care spending?
   E. Can you think of any omitted variables that might cause our estimates to be suspect?
7. Some years ago, several researchers found a correlation between cigarette smoking and suicides. Do you think this correlation reflects an association or a causal relationship? Why? If it reflects an association, can you think of a plausible third variable?
8. What are meant by the third-variable problem and reverse causation?
9. In your own words, explain the difference between a social experiment and a natural experiment.
10. In your own words, explain how the instrumental variables and fixed effects approaches deals with the third-variable problem.
11. As you know, the U.S. government implemented a variety of policies to limit smoking over the last few decades. Can you give an example of a structural remedy? How about a conduct remedy?

References

Becker, Gary S., and Kevin M. Murphy. "A Theory of Rational Addiction." *Journal of Political Economy* 96 (August 1988), pp. 675–700.

Dowd, Bryan, and Robert Town. "Does X Really Cause Y?" AcademyHealth, Washington, D.C., September 2002.

Feldman, Roger, and Michael A. Morrisey. "Health Economics: A Report on the Field." *Journal of Health Politics, Policy and Law* 15 (fall 1990), pp. 627–46.

Fuchs, Victor R. "The Tofu Triangle." *The Wall Street Journal*, January 26, 1996, p. A16.

Heindenreich, Paul A. et al. "Forecasting the Future of Cardiovascular Disease in the United States." *Circulation* (March 2011), pp. 933–44.

Levy, Helen, and David Meltzer. "What Do We Really Know about Whether Insurance Affects Health." Mimeo, University of Chicago, 2004.

Studenmund, A. H., *Using Econometrics: A Practical Guide*, Addison-Wesley, 2006.

Tosteson, Anna, et al. "Long-Term Impact of Smoking Cessation on the Incidence of Coronary Health Disease." *American Journal of Public Health* 80 (December 1990), pp. 1481–86.

CHAPTER 2

Health and Medical Care: An Economic Perspective

The disintegration of the Soviet Union, which many Americans viewed on their televisions with the collapse of the Berlin Wall on November 6, 1989, emerged as a major turning point in the twentieth century and radically changed the lives of millions of people. As a case in point, in just five short years, from 1989 to 1994, the life expectancy of men in Russia fell by 6.6 years. For women over the same time period, life expectancy fell by 3.3 years. Brainerd and Cutler (2005) investigate five reasons why these mortality rates may have increased in Russia: (1) the deterioration of the health care system; (2) the increase in traditional risk factors for cardiovascular disease such as smoking; (3) the increase in alcohol consumption; (4) changes in diet; and (5) material deprivation. Overall, they find that about half of the increase in mortality in Russia was brought about by increased alcohol consumption and the stress that accompanied the transition to a market economy. According to their statistical analysis, the other three major trends did not impact the observed increase in mortality rates.

This study by Brainerd and Cutler illustrates the important roles that medical care, lifestyle, socioeconomic conditions, and the environment may play in the overall health of the people in a country. This chapter explores these relationships more deeply by establishing the theoretical and empirical connection between health and various factors such as medical care. In particular, this chapter:

- discusses the concepts of health and medical care
- introduces utility analysis to explain why people desire health
- utilizes production theory to explain the making of health
- reviews the empirical results concerning the factors that influence health
- discusses the historical impact of public health on health outcomes
- analyzes the implications of the Patient Protection and Affordable Care Act (PPACA) of 2010 on issues relating to medical care and health.

What Is Health?

The *Mosby Medical Encyclopedia* (1992, p. 360) defines **health** as "a state of physical, mental, and social well-being and the absence of disease or other abnormal conditions." Somewhat similar, the World Health Organization (WHO) defines health as a "state of complete physical, mental, and social well-being, and not merely the absence of disease" (see the WHO.org website). Economists, in contrast, take a radically different approach by viewing health as a durable good, or type of capital, that provides services to an individual. The services flowing from the stock of health "capital" are consumed continuously over an individual's lifetime (see Grossman, 1972a, 1972b). Each person is assumed to be endowed with a given stock of health at the beginning of a period, such as a year. Over the period, the stock of health may depreciate, particularly as a person ages, but the loss of health capital may be augmented through investments in medical services. Death occurs when an individual's stock of health falls below a critical minimum level.

Naturally, the initial stock of health, along with its rate of depreciation, varies from individual to individual and depends on many factors, some of which are uncontrollable. For example, a person has no control over the initial stock of health allocated at birth, and a child with a congenital heart problem begins life with a below-average stock of health. However, we learn later that medical services may compensate for many deficiencies, at least to some degree. The rate at which health depreciates also depends on many factors, such as the individual's age, physical makeup, lifestyle, environmental factors, and the amount of medical care consumed. For example, the rate at which health depreciates in a person diagnosed with high blood pressure is likely to depend on the amount of medical care consumed (is this person under a doctor's care?), environmental factors (does he or she have a stressful occupation?), and lifestyle (does the person smoke or have a weight problem?). All these factors interact to determine the person's stock of health at any point in time, along with the pace at which it depreciates.

Regardless of how you define it, health is a nebulous concept that defies precise measurement. In terms of measurement, health depends as much on the quantity of life (i.e., number of life-years remaining) as it does on the quality of life. Quality of life has become an increasingly important issue in recent years due to the life-sustaining capabilities of today's medical technology. This issue has captured national attention on several occasions over the years with the tragic events that left Karen Ann Quinlan, Nancy Beth Cruzan, and most recently Terri Shiavo in permanent vegetative states. Because the quality of life is a relative concept that is open to wide interpretation, researchers have wrestled with developing an instrument that accurately measures health. In Chapter 3, we discuss some of these measures.

Why Good Health? Utility Analysis

As mentioned earlier, health, like any other durable good, generates a flow of services. These services yield satisfaction, or what economists call **utility**. Your tablet computer is another example of a durable good that generates a flow of services. It is the many hours of enjoyment you receive from accessing the world-wide web, managing a social media account, watching a film, or playing an electronic game that provides utility, not the computer itself.

As a good, health is desired for consumption and investment purposes. From a consumption perspective, people feel better when they are in a state of good health. They want to jump up and kick their heels! Healthy people feel great and are in a wonderful position to enjoy their lives. The investment element concerns the relation between health and use of time. If you are in a state of good health, you allocate less time to sickness and therefore have more healthy days available to work and enhance your income or to pursue leisure activities. Economists view education from a similar

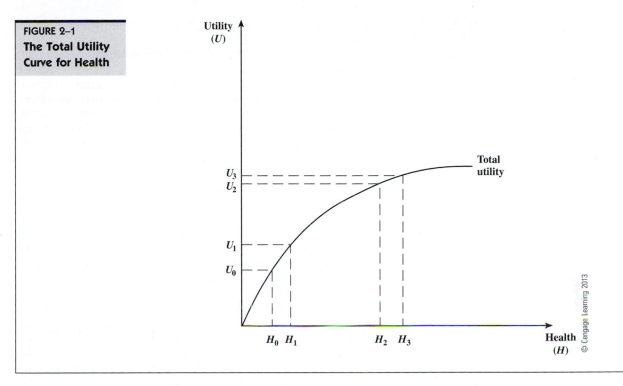

FIGURE 2–1

The Total Utility Curve for Health

The total utility curve is upward sloping and depicts the relation between an individual's stock of health and utility. The positive slope indicates that total utility increases as an individual's stock of health improves; the bowed shape of the curve captures the impact of the law of diminishing marginal utility. This law is a fundamental principle of economics stating that each additional improvement in health generates an ever smaller increase in utility. Notice that the increase in health from H_0 to H_1 causes utility to increase from U_0 to U_1, while an equal increase in health from H_2 to H_3 results in a smaller increase in utility from U_2 to U_3.

human capital perspective. Much as people invest in education to enhance their potential to earn a higher wage, people invest in health to increase their likelihood of having more healthy days to work and generate income.

The investment element of health can be used to explain some of the lifestyle choices people make. A person who puts a high value on future events is more inclined to pursue a healthy lifestyle to increase the likelihood of enjoying more healthy days than a person who puts a low value on future events. A preference for the future may explain why a middle-aged adult with high cholesterol orders a salad with dressing on the side instead of a steak served with a baked potato smothered in sour cream. In this situation, the utility generated by increasing the likelihood of having more healthy days in the future outweighs the utility received from consuming the steak dinner. In contrast, a person who puts a much lower value on future events and prefers immediate gratification may elect to order the steak dinner and ignore the potential ill effects of high cholesterol and fatty foods.

Naturally, individuals choose to consume that combination of goods and services, including the services produced from the stock of health, which provides the most utility to them. The isolated relation between an individual's stock of health and utility is captured in Figure 2–1, where the quantity of health, H, is measured on the horizontal axis and the level of utility, U, is represented on the vertical axis.[1] The positive slope of the curve indicates that an increase in a person's stock of health directly enhances total utility. The shape of the curve is particularly important because

---

1. To simplify matters, we ignore the intermediate step between the health stock, the services it provides, and the utility received from these services and assume that the stock of health directly yields utility.

it illustrates the fundamental economic principle of the **law of diminishing marginal utility**. This law states that each successive incremental improvement in health generates smaller and smaller additions to total utility; in other words, utility increases at a decreasing rate with respect to health.

For example, in Figure 2–1 an increase in health from H_0 to H_1 causes utility to increase from U_0 to U_1, while an equal increase in health from H_2 to H_3 generates a much smaller increase in utility, from U_2 to U_3. In the second case, the increase in utility is less when the stock of health is greater because of the law of diminishing marginal utility. The implication is that a person values a marginal improvement in health more when sick (i.e., when having a lower level of health) than when healthy. This does not mean every individual derives the same level of utility from a given stock of health. It is possible for two or more people to receive a different amount of utility from the same stock of health. The law of diminishing marginal utility requires only that the addition to total utility decreases with successive increases in health for a given individual.

Another way to illustrate the law of diminishing marginal utility is to focus on the marginal utility associated with each unit of health. Marginal utility equals the addition to total utility generated by each successive unit of health. In mathematical terms,

(2–1)
$$MU_H = \Delta U / \Delta H,$$

where MU_H equals the marginal utility of the last unit of health consumed and Δ represents the change in utility or health. In Figure 2–1, MU_H represents the slope of a tangent line at each point on the total utility curve because it represents the rise over the run (see Equation 2–1). The bowed shape of the total utility curve implies that the slope of the tangent line falls as we move along the curve, or that MU_H falls as health improves.

Figure 2–2 captures the graphical relation between marginal utility and the stock of health. The downward slope of the curve indicates the law of diminishing marginal utility holds because each new unit of health generates less additional utility than the previous one.

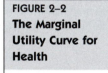

FIGURE 2–2
The Marginal Utility Curve for Health

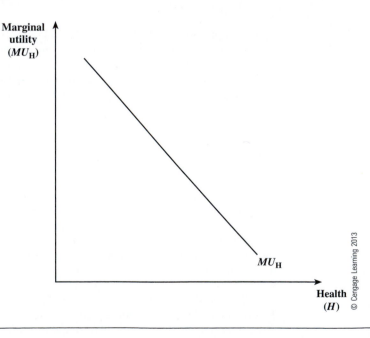

The MU_H curve illustrates the relation between marginal utility and the stock of health, and it is downward sloping because of the law of diminishing marginal utility. The shape of curve reflects the notion that each additional improvement in health results in a smaller increase in utility than the previous one.

What Is Medical Care?

Medical care reflects the myriad goods and services that maintain, improve, or restore a person's health. For example, a young man might have shoulder surgery to repair a torn rotator cuff so that he can return to work, an elderly woman may have hip replacement surgery so she can walk without pain, or a parent may bring a child to the hygienist for an annual teeth cleaning to prevent future dental problems. Prescription drugs, wheelchairs, and dentures are examples of medical goods, while surgeries, annual physical exams, and visits to physical therapists are examples of medical services.

Because of the heterogeneous nature of medical care, units of medical care are difficult to measure precisely. Units of medical care are also hard to quantify because most represent services rather than tangible products. As a service, medical care exhibits the four *I*s that distinguish it from a good: intangibility, inseparability, inventory, and inconsistency (Berkowitz et al., 1989).

The first characteristic, **intangibility**, means that a medical service is incapable of being assessed by the five senses. Unlike a new car, a steak dinner, or a new CD, the consumer cannot see, smell, taste, feel, or hear a medical service. To evaluate a service, it must be experienced.

Inseparability means that the production and consumption of a medical service take place simultaneously. For example, when you visit your dentist for a checkup, you are consuming dental services at the exact time the dentist is producing them. In addition, a patient often acts as both producer and consumer. Without the patient's active participation, the medical product is likely to be poorly produced.[2]

Inventory is directly related to inseparability. Because the production and consumption of a medical service occur simultaneously, health care providers are unable to stockpile or maintain an inventory of medical services. For example, a dentist cannot maintain an inventory of dental checkups to meet demand during peak periods.

Finally, **inconsistency** means that the composition and quality of medical services consumed vary widely across medical events. Although everyone visits a physician at some time or another, not every visit to a physician is for the same reason. One person may go for a routine physical, while another may go because he needs heart bypass surgery. The composition of medical care provided or the intensity at which it is consumed can differ greatly among individuals and at different points in time.

The quality of medical care is also difficult to measure. Quality differences are reflected in the structure, process, and/or outcome of a medical care event (Donabedian, 1980, 1988). **Structural quality** is reflected in the physical and human resources of the medical care organization, such as the facilities (level of amenities), medical equipment (type and age), personnel (training and experience), and administration (organizational structure). **Process quality** reflects the specific actions health care providers take on behalf of patients in delivering and following through with care. Process quality might include access (waiting time), data collection (background history and testing), communication with the patient, and diagnosis and treatment (type and appropriateness). **Outcome quality** refers to the impact of care on the patient's health and welfare as measured by patient satisfaction, work time lost to disability, or postcare mortality rate. Because it is extremely difficult to keep all three aspects of quality constant for every medical event, the quality of medical services, unlike that of physical goods, is likely to be inconsistent.

---

2. Educational services, like medical services, require the consumer's active participation; that is, education is likely to be poorly provided when the student plays a passive role in the process.

As you can see, medical care services are extremely difficult to quantify in practical terms. In most instances, researchers measure medical care based on availability or use. If medical care is measured on an availability basis, such measures include the number of physicians or hospital beds available per 1,000 people. If medical care is measured in terms of use, the analyst employs data indicating how often a medical service is actually delivered. For example, the quantity of office visits or surgeries per capita is often used to represent the amount of physician services rendered, whereas the number of inpatient days is frequently used to measure the amount of hospital or nursing home services consumed. Sometimes researchers use medical care expenditures because it may not only reflect the amount of utilization but also the quality of services received.

The Production of Good Health

Health economists take the view that the creation and maintenance of health involves a production process. (Alternatively, health can be analyzed within a demand framework using a time allocation model, as presented in Appendix 2.) Much as a firm uses various inputs, such as capital and labor, to manufacture a product, an individual uses medical care inputs and other factors, such as a healthy lifestyle, to produce health. The relation between medical care inputs and output can be captured in what economists call a production function. A **health production function** indicates the maximum amount of health that an individual can generate from a specific set of health-related inputs in a given period of time. In mathematical terms, it shows how the level of output (in this case, health) depends on the quantities of various health-related inputs, such as medical care. A generalized short-run health production function for an individual takes the following form:

(2–2)   Health = H(Profile, TECH, Environment, SES, Lifestyle, Medical Care)

where, at a point in time, *health* reflects the person's level of health; *profile* captures the individual's mental, social, and physical profile at the beginning of the period in addition to uncontrollable factors like age, race, and gender; *TECH* refers to the state of medical technology; *environment* stands for a variety of environmental factors, including air and water quality along with any public health measures; *SES* reflects the joint effect of social and economic factors, such as education, income, and poverty; *lifestyle* represents a set of health-related choices such as diet and exercise; and *medical care* equals the quantity and quality of medical care consumed. Note that these six health-related inputs have been listed from left to right in terms of those inputs the individual has the least to most control over (although some ambiguities and overlap may exist).

Our point, for now, is to focus on how medical care relates to the production of health. To focus on that relation, we assume initially that all other factors in the health production function remain constant. Figure 2–3 depicts this graphical relation, where q is a hypothetical measure of medical care and H represents the level of health. The intercept term represents the individual's level of health when no medical care is consumed. As drawn, the **total product curve** implies that an individual's level of health is positively related to the amount of medical care consumed.[3] The shape of the curve is very similar to that in Figure 2–1 and reflects the **law of diminishing marginal productivity**. This law implies that health

---

3. However, we should not rule out the possibility that poor health status or an illness might be created by additional medical services. An illness created by a medical care encounter is referred to as an *iatrogenic disorder*, "a condition caused by medical personnel or procedures or through exposure to the environment of a health-care facility" (*Mosby Medical Encyclopedia*, 1992, p. 401). For example, a physician may accidentally harm a patient by prescribing the wrong medicine for a given medical condition.

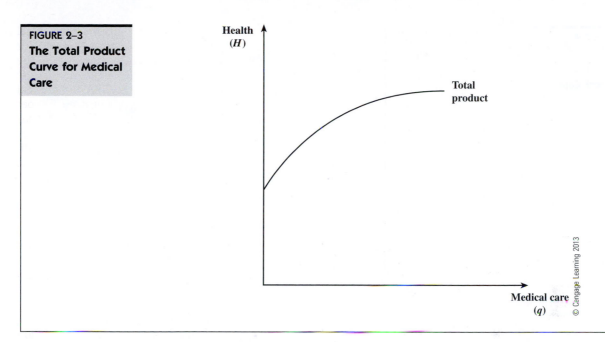

FIGURE 2–3

The Total Product Curve for Medical Care

The total product curve is upward sloping and indicates that as an individual consumes more medical care, overall health improves. The positive intercept term represents the individual's level of health when no medical care is consumed and is a function of other factors such as lifestyle and the environment. The law of diminishing marginal productivity accounts for the bowed shape of the curve. This law is a fundamental principle of production theory and it implies that health increases at a decreasing rate when additional units of health care are consumed, holding constant all other inputs in the health production process.

increases at a decreasing rate with respect to additional amounts of medical care, assuming other health-related inputs are held constant. For example, suppose an individual makes an initial visit and several follow-up visits to a physician's office for a specific illness or treatment over a given period of time. It is very likely that the first few visits have a more beneficial impact on the individual's stock of health than the later visits. Thus, each successive visit generates a smaller improvement in health than the previous one.

The relation between health and medical care can also be viewed from a marginal perspective, where the marginal product of medical care represents the incremental improvement in health brought about by each successive unit of medical care consumed, or

(2–3) $$MP_q = \Delta H / \Delta q,$$

where MP_q equals the marginal product of the last unit of medical care consumed. The law of diminishing marginal productivity states that the marginal product of medical care diminishes as the individual acquires more medical care. A graph of this relationship appears as a negatively-sloped curve in Figure 2–4.[4]

The other variables in the health production function can also be incorporated into the analysis. In general terms, a change in any one of the health-related inputs in the production function may alter the position of the total product curve. The total product curve may shift in some instances and/or rotate in others. In the latter case, the curve

---

4. As in utility analysis, the marginal product of medical care equals the slope of a tangent line drawn to every point on Figure 2–3.

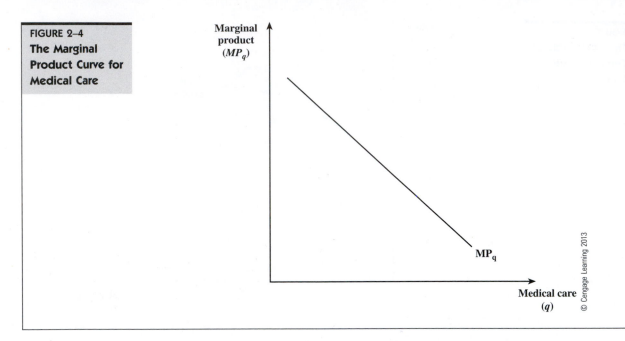

FIGURE 2–4
The Marginal
Product Curve for
Medical Care

The MP_q curve establishes the relation between the marginal product of medical care and the amount of medical care consumed. The curve is downward sloping because the marginal product of the last unit of medical care consumed decreases as the individual consumes more medical care, reflecting the law of diminishing marginal productivity.

rotates because the marginal productivity of medical care has changed in response to the change in the other health-related inputs.

For example, new medical technologies have profoundly affected all aspects of the production of medical care. In the broadest of terms, examples of new technologies include the development of sophisticated medical devices, the introduction of new drugs, the application of innovative medical and surgical procedures, and most recently, the use of computer-supported information systems, just to name a few. According to Cutler and Huckman (2003) and Cutler and McClellan (2001), technological change can result in *treatment expansion, treatment substitution,* or some elements of both. Treatment expansion occurs when more patients are treated by a new medical intervention, perhaps because of a higher success rate or lower risks to health than was previously the case. Treatment substitution occurs when the new technology substitutes for or replaces an older one.

In the context of our health production model, the development and application of a new medical technology may cause the total product curve to shift upward in a parallel fashion if the same amount of medical care, say a visit to a doctor's office, can now produce a greater improvement in a person's health and the marginal productivity of medical care remains unaffected. In that case, proportionately more health can now be generated from a physician visit because of the new technology. For example, the physician clinic may find a way to reduce waiting times so each patient spends more time actually meeting with the physician during the allotted time for each and every visit. The curve may also pivot upward if, for some reason, the marginal productivity of each unit of medical care consumed also improves. For example, repeated visits to a doctor's office may better ensure that patients take their newly-prescribed medicines. In this case, the marginal productivity of medical care increases because the physician makes sure that the medical technology (i.e., a new pill) is repeatedly applied. Of

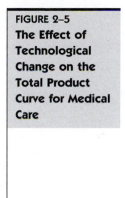

FIGURE 2–5

The Effect of Technological Change on the Total Product Curve for Medical Care

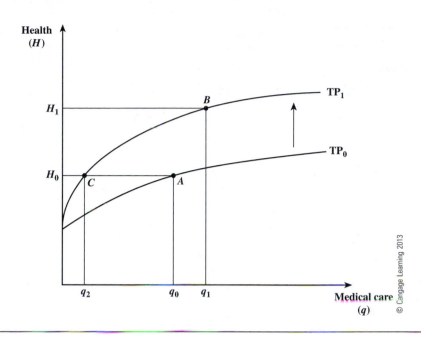

The total product curve shifts upward with the development and application of new medical technology because of an increase in the marginal product of medical care. A movement from point A to point B illustrates the case in which a new technology results in a simultaneous increase in the amount of medical care consumed and improvement in health. A movement from point A to point C depicts the case in which the new medical technology has no impact on health but results in less consumption of medical care.

course, a new medical technology may also involve both a shifting and pivoting of the total product curve upward.

Figure 2–5 shows the situation where the marginal productivity of medical care improves because of a new medical technology. Notice that the total product curve rotates upward from TP_0 to TP_1 and each unit of medical care consumed now generates a greater amount of health both in total and at the margin. The movement from point A to point B in Figure 2–5 illustrates the case in which the improvement in medical technology brings about an increase in the amount of medical care consumed from q_0 to q_1 along with an improvement in health from H_0 to H_1. This movement represents the treatment expansion resulting from the new medical technology. Movement from point A to point C illustrates the situation in which the new technology has no impact on health but results in less consumption of medical care from q_0 to q_2. In this case, the new technology is cost saving, everything else held constant. It should be noted that the increase in the marginal product of medical care brought about by the new medical technology also causes the marginal product curve to shift to the right.

The profile variable in Equation 2–2 depends on a host of variables and controls for such items as the person's genetic makeup, mental state, age, gender, and race/ ethnicity as of a given point in time (such as the beginning of the year). Any change in the profile variable potentially affects both the intercept term and the slope of the health production function. For example, an individual's genetic makeup may make that person a candidate for cancer. If this individual gets cancer, then the total product curve shifts downward. That is because overall health has decreased regardless of the amount of medical care consumed. The total product curve also rotates downward at the same time if the marginal product of medical care also decreases as profile worsens. The total product curve may rotate downward because an otherwise healthy person is likely to respond more favorably to medical treatments *for a given*

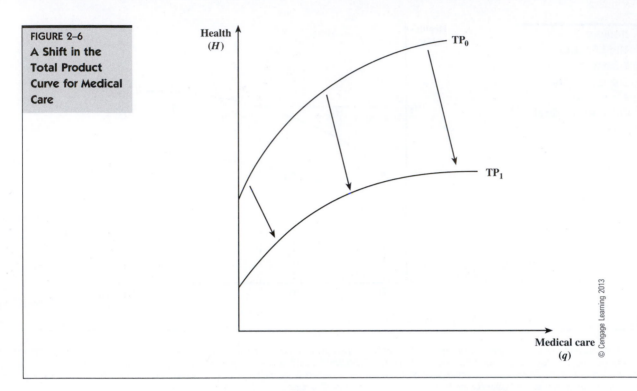

FIGURE 2–6
A Shift in the Total Product Curve for Medical Care

The graph illustrates what happens to the total product curve when an individual gets an illness such as cancer for a reason other than improper medical care. The curve shifts downward because at each level of medical care consumed the individual is less healthy than previously was the case. The curve also rotates downward and becomes flatter, reflecting the likelihood that the now ill individual is going to respond less favorably to a given amount of medical care consumed, such as an office visit, than previously was the case when she was healthy.

medical complication than one who is less healthy. Both of these changes are represented in Figure 2–6, where the total product curve shifts and rotates downward at the same time from TP_0 to TP_1. The marginal product curve for medical services also shifts to the left, because each incremental unit of medical care now brings about a smaller improvement in health.

The effect of age on the production of health is relatively straightforward. Age affects health through the profile variable. As an individual ages and deteriorates physically, both health and the marginal product of medical care are likely to fall. In addition, the rate at which health depreciates over the period is also likely to increase with age. This causes the total product curve to shift downward and flatten out. The decrease in the marginal product of medical care also causes the marginal product curve to shift to the left.[5]

Lifestyle variables consider the impact of personal health habits on the production of health. Personal habits include such things as whether the person smokes, drinks excessively, leads a sedentary lifestyle, is overweight, or has an improper diet. For example, consider a newly health-conscious individual who decides that a change in lifestyle is in order. After a regimen of diet and exercise, this person loses some weight and improves his or her physical conditioning. As a result of this change in lifestyle, the individual's level of health and the marginal product of medical care should increase. This causes the total product curve to shift and rotate upward.

---

5. The impact of gender on the total and marginal product curves is left to the reader and is the focus of a review question at the end of this chapter.

As is the case with improvements in personal habits, improved socioeconomic conditions may cause the intercept term and the marginal product of medical care to increase. For example, since education is likely to make the individual a more efficient producer of health independently of the amount of medical care consumed, the total product curve shifts upward. An individual with more education is likely to better understand the positive impact of a healthy diet on health. The total product curve also steepens, or the marginal product of medical care increases, because education allows the person to utilize each unit of medical care consumed more effectively. For example, an educated individual may be more inclined to understand and follow a physician's advice concerning diet and exercise after undergoing a heart bypass operation. In addition, she or he may be able to recognize a medical problem early and seek medical care quickly when the effectiveness of medical treatment is generally at its maximum.

However, we cannot rule out the reverse effect that health may influences education, particularly during childhood. Take the case of a child with chronic asthma where an asthma attack can be brought on by any number of events such as exposure to allergies or viral infections, and physical exertion. As a result, a child with chronic asthma is more likely to miss school, learn less while attending school, and in the end acquire less education. Over time, what the researcher may observe is a less healthy adult with only a modest level of education.

Some analysts have hypothesized that the relation between education and health is far more complex. For example, Fuchs (1979) argues that the acquisition of education and health depends on the value people place on future events, or the rate at which they discount future events. Individuals who place a high value on future benefits and are willing to postpone gratification are inclined to acquire more education and pursue a healthier lifestyle when they are young. This is because they want to reap the rewards of a higher income and a longer life that more education and a healthier lifestyle can bring. On the other hand, individuals who place a low value on future events and desire immediate gratification are not likely to acquire significant amounts of education or to follow a healthy lifestyle because they have adopted a "live for today" attitude. Thus, according to Fuchs, higher levels of education may be associated with better health not because there is a direct link between the two variables but because both variables are directly correlated with a third factor, the degree to which future events are valued.

The impact of income on health is also complex and is referred to as the "income gradient" in the literature "to emphasize the gradual relationship between the two: health improves with income throughout the income distribution" (Deaton, 2002, p. 14). Income is likely to indirectly impact health through a number of pathways. An increase in income provides the individual the means to consume more medical care. In addition, a more affluent individual is likely to be more educated, pursue a healthier lifestyle, and live in a safer environment, all of which contribute to improved health. For example, a more affluent individual may live in a suburban community where the crime rate is low, access to drugs and alcohol is limited, and quality medical care is available just around the corner. Income may also have a direct impact on health, although the net effect is far from clear. On the one hand, a wealthier individual may be employed in a safer work environment where the risk of a work-related accident or illness is slim. On the other hand, a wealthier individual may be employed in a more stressful occupation, which can adversely impact health.

In recent years, an extensive body of literature has developed that examines whether the distribution of income impacts health, and the income-health hypothesis has taken on a variety of forms. According to the literature (Lynch et al., 2004; Wagstaff and van Doorslaer, 2000), the various hypotheses that have been offered over time can be classified into four broad categories: the absolute income hypothesis, the relative income or deprivation hypothesis, the relative position hypothesis, and the income inequality hypothesis.

The absolute income hypothesis simply states that an individual's absolute income is positively related to health for the reasons discussed previously. The relative income or deprivation hypothesis posits that an individual's income relative to some social group average impacts overall health. Put in more definable terms, it is a person's income relative to some critical level such as the poverty line in the United States that matters. The presumption is that anyone with an income below the poverty line lacks the ability to acquire the basic necessities, such as health care.

The relative position hypothesis emphasizes that one's social position in the income distribution also impacts health. For example, those at the bottom of the income scale in the United States may become frustrated and feel left behind by the "American dream" despite the fact that they have enough income to live in reasonable housing and receive adequate health care. Out of a sense of discouragement, these people may tend to give up and pursue a lifestyle detrimental to their health that could involve increased alcohol consumption, smoking, and obesity.

Finally, the income inequality hypothesis states that the distribution of income itself directly impacts health. For example, greater income inequality may create an incentive for government to limit spending on social programs that have a direct bearing on health in an attempt to lower taxes. Greater income inequality may also lead to an erosion of social capital, defined as "those features of social organizations—such as the extent of interpersonal trust between citizens, norms of reciprocity, and vibrancy of civic organizations—that facilitate cooperation for mutual benefit" (Kawachi and Kennedy, 1999, p. 221). As a result, the poor may find their public health needs largely ignored by society at large.

An adjustment in a person's physical environment is also likely to affect the total product curve. For example, an individual with an asthmatic condition might move from Los Angeles, where smog is intense, to a community on the far outskirts of the city. Or the person's spouse may give up smoking to decrease the level of secondhand smoke in the home. As a result, the probability that this person will succumb to a respiratory ailment diminishes. Both of these changes cause the total product curve to shift and rotate upward.

In short, health production theory suggests that a variety of factors, such as the individual's profile, medical care, state of medical technology, lifestyle, socioeconomic status, and environment, interact to determine health. The theory also suggests that health increases at a diminishing rate with respect to greater amounts of medical care consumed, provided all other inputs remain constant. If any other inputs in the production process change, the impact of medical care on health is also likely to change. The effect of any one nonmedical input on health is also likely to exhibit diminishing returns—all other inputs held constant. For example, running two miles a day may reduce someone's weight by 15 pounds over a six-month period. It is doubtful, however, that an additional two miles per day of running could produce additional 15 pounds of weight loss during the next six-month period.

Before we conclude this section, you should be aware that Jacobson (2000), Bolin et al. (2002), and others have extended the Grossman model and developed a number of sophisticated mathematical models that focus on the family rather than the individual as the main producer of health. While these models are beyond the scope of this book, they represent a valuable addition to the literature. The common theme is that individual decisions to invest in health are made within the context of a family and that any decision on the part of one family member regarding investments in health may impact the health investment decisions of others in the family. For example, a learning-disabled child may provide an incentive for a mother to invest more in her own health to ensure that she will have the time to aid her child. These theoretical developments provide a number of challenges to researchers as they strive to understand the complex relationships between family members and individual health-related decisions.

Empirical Evidence on the Production of Health in the United States

Health economists have long been trying to understand the complex nature in which medical care and other factors interact to improve, maintain, and restore health. That quest has led researchers to develop a variety of sophisticated estimation models that find their theoretical underpinnings in Equation 2–2 to empirically examine the production of health. Using the literature as our guide, we review the empirical evidence concerning the characteristics associated with the production of health for adults, infants, and the elderly.

The Determinants of Health among Nonelderly Adults

Medical Care and Health. Some debate exists in the literature regarding the impact of medical care on the health of nonelderly adults. Early observational studies such as Auster et al. (1969) and Hadley (1982) found that medical care had only a small quantitative impact on the health of nonelderly adults. Even the Rand Health Insurance social experiment of the late 1970s found that households in low coinsurance plans received more medical care yet possessed virtually the same level of health as those households in high coinsurance plans, *ceteris paribus* (Newhouse, 1993). (In Chapter 5, the Rand Health Insurance study is discussed in more detail). Studies such as these, led Enthoven (1980) to point to the small marginal impact of medical care services on the health status of adults as "flat-of-the-curve" medicine. In the context of Figure 2–3, Enthoven meant the typical adult consumes medical services at the point where the slope of the total product curve or marginal product of medicine is near zero. That could happen because of overly generous health insurance coverage or because the marginal medicine reflects custodial "caring" rather than actual "curing."

However, some argue the earlier observational studies may have confused association with causation (see Appendix 1). Others point out that the Rand Health Insurance study only compared people with different amounts of health insurance coverage and not those who are insured and uninsured. As a result, Freeman et al. (2008) surveyed the literature regarding the impact of health insurance coverage on the utilization of medical services and health outcomes among nonelderly adults. Freeman et al. argue that the only pathway through which health insurance coverage could affect health status is through medical care. They confine their analysis to causal studies using fixed effects, instrumental variables, or quasi-experimental approaches (see Appendix 1) and find 14 studies analyzing the causal effect of health insurance coverage on the health status of nonelderly adults. Their review consistently shows that health insurance increases physician and preventive services, improves self-reported health status, and lowers mortality conditioned on injury and disease. Thus, the surveyed studies clearly show that the marginal product of medical care is positive.

Unfortunately, the surveyed studies offer no direct estimates of the magnitudes of the marginal productivity of medical care among nonelderly adults. As a result, we do not know empirically if the marginal product of medical care is any greater than the marginal product of other types of health-related inputs such as lifestyle or physical environment. With that limitation in mind, we review studies examining the impact of other health-related inputs on the health status of nonelderly adults.[6]

Education and Health. The positive relation between education and health is well documented in the literature (Woolf and Braverman, 2011). For example, Lleras-Muney (2001) finds a significant relation between education levels and health. In particular, she finds that one more year of schooling decreases the probability of dying within 10 years by 3.6 percent. More recently, Cutler and Lleras-Muney (2006)

---

6. A discussion of the impact of technology on health is postponed until Chapter 3.

estimate that an additional year of education increases life expectancy somewhere between 0.18 and 0.6 years.

Income and Health. Like education, there are a large number of empirical studies that have documented a positive connection between income and health. Ettner (1996) finds that increases in income enhance both mental and physical health, while Lantz et al. (2001) find that income and education are both associated with improved health. More specifically, they find that people with less than a high school education and incomes below $10,000 are between two and three times more likely to have functional limitations and poorer self-rated health than their more advantaged counterparts.

While the positive relation between income and health is well established in the literature, a question remains concerning how temporary changes in the macroeconomy impact health. In other terms, what is the relationship between cyclical changes in the macroeconomy and overall health? Your first inclination is to assume that a procyclical relationship holds between the state of the economy and health. In other words, as an economy emerges from a recession and the unemployment rate begins to fall, overall health should improve. You might argue that higher per capita incomes should translate into improved health as people have more discretionary income to spend on medical care. In addition, as more people acquire jobs with employer-financed health insurance, the out-of-pocket price of medical care should drop, causing people to consume more health care. An improved economy may also be associated with healthier lifestyles because as unemployed workers find employment, stress levels are likely to fall along with declines in alcohol consumption and smoking.

Ruhm (2000, 2003) argues that just the opposite may occur: an improved economy may be linked to poorer health. He cites three reasons why health may decline during a cyclical economic expansion. First, the opportunity cost of time is likely to increase with an improved economy. As workers find employment, the amount of leisure time they have to perform what Ruhm refers to as health-producing activities (such as exercise and eating right) diminishes. In fact, in another paper Ruhm (2005) finds that a one-percentage-point decrease in the number employed reduces the frequency of smoking (−0.6 percent), obesity (−0.4 percent), and physical inactivity (−0.7 percent). Second, the act of work may adversely impact the production of health. As the economy improves and more workers find employment, the number of work-related accidents and work-related stress cases increase. Third, an economic expansion may cause an increase in other causes of mortality such as traffic fatalities, homicide, and suicide.

To test the relationship between cyclical conditions and health, Ruhm estimates the impact that various economic indicators such as unemployment and personal income have on a number of health indicators. Among the measures of health included in the analysis were overall mortality rates, age-based mortality rates, and deaths due to specific causes such as cardiovascular diseases, chronic liver disease and cirrhosis of the liver, motor vehicle accidents, and suicide.

The results are illuminating and suggest an inverse relationship between the strength of the economy and health in the short run. Overall, Ruhm finds that a 1 percent drop in the unemployment rate (i.e., a stronger economy), relative to the state historical average, results in an increase in the total mortality rate of between 0.5 and 0.6 percent. In addition, Ruhm finds that the impact of changes in the unemployment rate on mortality rates appears to be concentrated among the relatively young, between ages 20 and 44. This makes intuitive sense, given this age group is likely hit hardest by temporary changes in economic conditions. Ruhm also finds that fluctuations in state unemployment rates are inversely related to a number of specific causes of death. For example, Ruhm finds decreases in state unemployment rates to be associated with increased fatalities from auto accidents, other types of accidents, homicides, cardiovascular disease, and influenza. Ruhm (2003) also finds that a one-percentage-point decrease in the unemployment rate is associated with acute morbidity and ischemic heart disease increases of 1.5 and 4.3 percent, respectively. Ruhm's empirical results are compelling because they suggest that cyclical, or temporary, changes in economic activity inversely impact health.

Income Inequality and Health. Lynch et al. (2004) and Wagstaff and van Doorslaer (2000) provide two excellent reviews of the literature regarding the relation between income inequality and the health of nonelderly adults. Both papers agree that there is significant support in the literature for the absolute income hypothesis. The same cannot be said for the other alternative hypotheses, however. According to Wagstaff and van Doorslaer, there is "no support for the relative-income hypotheses and little or no support for the income-inequality hypothesis" (p. 543). They conclude that there is no empirical support for the relative position hypothesis. These results were largely reaffirmed by Lynch et al. (2004) and Lorgelly and Lindley (2008). However, Lynch et al. (2004) find some support for the hypothesis that greater income inequality worsens health outcomes at the state level in the United States.

Lifestyle and Health. The literature abounds with studies that illustrate the important role lifestyle plays in determining health. Among the risky lifestyle behaviors found to negatively impact health are smoking, excessive alcohol consumption, lack of physical activity, and poor diet. For example, Ostbye and Taylor (2004) find that smoking is empirically linked to the loss of life-years. In particular, male heavy smokers (more than one pack a day) between the ages of 50 and 54 can expect to live two less years compared to those of the same age group who never smoked. For females of the same age group the difference between heavy and never smokers is 1.44 life-years. Strum (2002) analyzes the impact of obesity, being overweight, smoking, and problem drinking on health and the consumption of health care for a sample of adults between ages 18 and 65. He finds that all four risk behaviors impact health to some degree, with obesity having the greatest impact. In fact, Strum estimates that obesity has the same impact on health as 20 years of aging when health status is measured by the number of 17 common chronic conditions present. Finally, Balia and Jones (2008) find that lifestyle, particularly smoking and sleep patterns, plays a significant role in predicting mortality. Using some rather sophisticated modeling and econometric techniques that focus on the distribution of health inequality, they estimate that predicted mortality rates may be much more sensitive to lifestyle factors, and less sensitive to socioeconomic factors and aging, than previously thought.

In the context of Figure 2–6, these results collectively suggest that adverse lifestyles cause the total product curve for medical care to shift downward and possibly flatten out. To compensate for the loss in health, a person may opt to slide up the total product curve by consuming more medical care. For example, Strum (2002) finds that obesity is related to an average increase in expenditures on inpatient and ambulatory care of $395 per year.

Environment and Health. The relation between environmental factors and health is very complex in terms of both the types of pollution (e.g., air, water, soil) and their impacts on health. For example, if we confine our discussion to just air pollutants we must consider the four basic categories: gaseous pollutants, persistent organic pollutants, heavy metals, and particulate matter. When considering the health effects we must establish, for example, whether the pollutant is impacting the respiratory system, the cardiovascular system, the nervous system, or the urinary system (Kampa and Castanas, 2008). For expository purposes, we focus on two studies that examine the impact of fine particulate matter on health. According to the Environmental Protection Agency (EPA) (www.epa.gov), fine particulate matter is defined as a mixture of solid and liquid droplets in the air with a diameter of less than 2.5 micrometers. To put this in perspective, according to the EPA, the average human hair is approximately 70 micrometers in diameter. What makes these particulates so dangerous is that they can easily be absorbed in the lungs. Pope et al. (2009) examine the impact of changes in fine-particulate air pollution on life expectancy in a sample of urban areas across the United States during the latter part of the twentieth century. They find that "reductions in air pollution accounted for as much as 15 percent of the overall increase in life expectancy" over the period in question (p. 376). Miller et al. (2007) find that long-term exposure to fine-particulate air is related to cardiovascular disease and death among postmenopausal women.

These two studies are examples of a vast body of literature linking environmental factors to health outcomes. Recent environmental disasters such as the massive 2010 oil spill in the Gulf of Mexico or the 2012 nuclear disaster in Japan brought on by a tsunami point to the need for a more detailed understanding of the interplay between environmental changes and health outcomes.

Other Determinants and Health.   Other variables found to contribute to health are age and marital status. The impact of marital status on health is interesting and merits a brief discussion. Married adults appear to experience better health than their single counterparts, everything else held constant. Most likely, this is because a spouse augments the production of health within the home. Marriage may also have a positive effect on health by altering preferences for risky behavior. Manor et al. (2000) find the mortality rate of married women to be lower than unmarried women for a sample of Israeli adult women, while Kravdal (2001) finds that married people have a higher chance of survival from 12 common forms of cancer in Norway than their unmarried counterparts.

The Determinants of Health among Children

Numerous studies have investigated the factors that influence health among children. This body of literature is important because it illustrates the lasting impact of childhood health into adulthood. For example, Case et al. (2005) find that childhood health has a long-term impact on adult health, education, and social status. Such information is valuable when crafting public policies aimed at improving lifetime health.

Case et al. (2002) focus on the impact of socioeconomic status on children's health.[7] To no one's surprise, Case et al. find a strong positive relation between the education of the parents and the health of their children. For example, the health of children is directly related to the education of mothers for children living with a mother. Education, in this case, is measured by whether the mother did not complete high school, had a high school diploma, or had more than a high school education. The education of fathers is also found to positively contribute to improved health among children, implying that parental education positively impacts the production of a child's health at all age levels.

The study also finds that household income is a strong predictor of children's health. More specifically, Case et al. find that when household income doubles, the probability that a child 3 years old or younger is in excellent or very good health increases by 4 percent. Comparable income-induced improvements in health for children between ages 4 and 8, 9 and 12, and 13 and 17 are 4.9 percent, 5.9 percent, and 7.2 percent, respectively. Just as interesting, Case et al. find that permanent income is a strong determiner of children's health. In particular, they find that family income before a child is born is positively related to the child's health for all ages.

Finally, Case et al. find that healthier parents tend to have healthier children. Why that is the case, however, remains to be determined. The authors do estimate a series

---

7. Consult Case and Paxson (2002) for a nontechnical overview of the study.

of equations for children with adoptive and biological parents and find that the impact of income on health is not significantly different across the two populations. While this evidence is not definitive, it does suggest that genetics may explain only part of the reason why healthier parents have healthier children. Could it be that the production of health takes place at the household level and that healthier parents are simply more efficient producers of health for all members of the household? Clearly, more research needs to be done before we fully understand how parental behavior coupled with socioeconomic factors impacts children's health.

Two articles point to the significance of environmental factors on infant health. Mohai et al. (2011) find that children in Michigan who attend schools located in areas with high air pollution levels have lower attendance rates (an indicator of poor health) and are more likely to fail to meet the state's education testing standards. Currie and Neidell (2005) find that reductions in carbon monoxide also impact infant mortality. In particular, they find that reductions in carbon monoxide in California throughout the 1990s saved approximately 1,000 infant lives. These studies are part of a growing body of literature that illustrates the importance of environmental factors in determining the health of infants.

The literature concerning uninsured versus insured status and health outcomes offers additional insights into the effect of medical care on infant health as well as on other groups. However, we couch the discussion in terms of the relation between medical care and health because the only plausible pathway from insurance to health outcomes is through medical care as mentioned previously. In a series of articles, Currie and Gruber (1996a, 1996b, and 1997), using a quasi-experimental design, examine the expansion of Medicaid eligibility by Congress on birth-related health outcomes. The authors exploit the fact some states expanded Medicaid eligibility more than others did and at different times. By correlating the magnitude and timing of eligibility expansions with the magnitude and timing of changes in health outcomes, it is possible to determine if a causal effect of insurance on health holds. Currie and Gruber conclude that a significant increase in health inputs and a corresponding reduction in low infant birthweight and child mortality relative to a baseline results from an expansion in Medicaid eligibility. They also find that the magnitude of the Medicaid expansion's impact on infant mortality depends upon the proximity to high-tech hospitals.

The Determinants of Health among the Elderly

Several studies have examined the medical care utilization and health of individuals who suddenly become Medicare-eligible at age 65 but previously uninsured to otherwise comparable individuals who were continuously insured.[8] Lichtenberg (2002) analyzes the effect of Medicare on the health of elderly individuals by looking for sudden discontinuities in medical care utilization and health outcomes at age 65, when people typically become eligible for the federal program. Notice that chronological age is an external factor that cannot be altered by nonmedical determinants of health or influenced by health status. He finds evidence that the utilization of ambulatory and inpatient care increases sharply at age 65. Lichtenberg also finds evidence that people spend less time in bed and face a reduced probability of dying compared to what would have occurred in the absence of Medicare. His results suggest that medical care has a relatively large marginal productivity when applied to the elderly population.

---

8. Even among the elderly, the production of health literature has debated the "flat-of-the-curve" argument and its applicability to the U.S. health care system. The empirical debate centers around the degree to which variations in health care spending are related to differences in the quality of care. For example, after reviewing a number of studies Fisher et al. conclude that "higher spending does not result in better quality of care." (2009, p. 2). Chandra and Staiger (2007) and Kaestner and Silber (2010) conclude otherwise. In particular, after studying the relation between inpatient spending and the 30-day mortality rate for Medicare patients, Chandra and Staiger question the relevance of the "flat-of-the-curve" hypothesis.

These results are reaffirmed by Card et al. (2007). Using data between 1992 and 2002, they examine the mortality rates of 400,000 elderly patients who were discharged from California hospitals before and after their 65th birthday when they become eligible for Medicare. To control for the possibility that some of the elderly may postpone medical care until they become eligible for Medicare, the authors compare Medicare-eligible people to uninsured individuals who were admitted to the emergency room for medical conditions that require immediate attention. Card et al. find that Medicare eligibility is associated with more medical spending and procedures and a reduction in the mortality rate of elderly individuals.

Using a nationally representative data set, McWilliams et al. (2007) provide a quasi-experimental analysis of longitudinal data for 5,006 adults who were continuously insured and 2,227 adults who were persistently or intermittently uninsured. Individuals ranged from 55 to 64 years of age. The authors find that acquisition of Medicare coverage is associated with improved trends in self-reported health for previously uninsured adults, particularly for those with cardiovascular disease or diabetes.[9] Considering these three studies and others, the empirical evidence appears to suggest that medical care likely has a significant impact of the health of elderly individuals.

The Role of Public Health: An Historical Approach

Thus far our discussion has revolved around the production of good health at the micro, or individual, level. Recall that the health production function, as specified in Equation 2–2, is taken from the perspective of the individual in terms of the various inputs needed to produce health. We cannot ignore, however, the tremendous impact improvements in public health have had on health over time through an impact on the environmental and technology factors in Equation 2–2. Public health places the emphasis on improving health at the community level and looks to such things as improving health education, controlling communicable diseases, improving sanitation, and monitoring and controlling environmental hazards. The fact that almost every municipality, county, and state in the country has a department of public health attests to the importance of public health on our everyday lives.

To illustrate the importance of public health, we discuss two very important public health interventions in the United States. The first health intervention deals with the development of clean water in the United States during the first half of the twentieth century. It coincides in our history with a number of improvements in nutrition and public health that caused infectious-disease mortality rates to decrease significantly. The second intervention deals with the development of a polio vaccine, which corresponds with the growth in modern medicine in the United States starting in the 1930s with the development of sulfa drugs, or antibiotics (Cutler and Lleras-Muney, 2006).

During the first part of the twentieth century the United States witnessed an almost unprecedented advancement in health as measured by a drop in the overall mortality rate. Cutler and Miller (2005) provide a compelling case that a majority of this decrease in the mortality rate can be attributed to improvements in water quality brought about by public investments in clean water technologies. Their study uses historical data for 13 cities where dates were available for four clean water interventions: water filtration, water chlorination, sewage treatment, and sewage chlorination. The dependent variables in the study include alternative measures of mortality. The empirical results suggest that improvements in water quality could explain 43 percent of the reduction

---

9. However, Finkelstein and McKnight (2005) find that the introduction of Medicare in 1965 had no measurable impact on elderly mortality during the first decade of the program. That is probably because many high-powered medical technologies such as angioplasty and stents were not available at that time. Finkelstein and McKnight did find the Medicare substantially reduced the exposure of the elderly to the out-of-pocket costs of medical care. Thus, while not initially reducing mortality, Medicare did offer a substantial amount of utility for elderly individuals because of the greater financial security.

in mortality rates from 1900 through 1936 across the cities in the sample. Even more convincing, cleaner water explained 62 percent of the drop in infant mortality and 74 percent of the decline in child mortality over the same time period.

Poliomyelitis, or polio, was one of the most dreaded epidemics to hit the United States in the mid-twentieth century. It is a highly infectious virus that generally afflicts children and can lead to paralysis or death. The most celebrated case occurred in 1921 when Franklin Delano Roosevelt, then a relatively unknown politician from New York, contracted polio while vacationing with his family. The disease left his legs paralyzed and he was largely wheelchair bound for the remainder of his life. While his disability was not hidden from the public, reporters were discouraged from taking pictures of him in his wheelchair while he was the governor of New York and later the president of the United States.

While polio had been around for many years, the number of new polio cases began to accelerate in the United States in the 1940s and early 1950s, reaching epidemic proportions in 1952 with 21,000 new cases. In 1955 the American public received news that Jonas Salk had developed a polio vaccine. The news was received nationally with much fanfare and Salk became a national hero overnight. With the support from the federal government and the March of Dimes organization, a plan was developed to distribute the vaccination across the country with priority given to young children. Within two years the number of reported polio cases fell by approximately 90 percent (Oshinsky, 2005).

This public health intervention is rather extraordinary because for the first time in our history a private philanthropic organization played a vital role in eradicating a major health problem. Much of the medical research and distribution of the vaccine was funded by the National Foundation for Infantile Paralysis, or the March of Dimes, which was started in 1938. Support for the foundation in terms of volunteers and funds was unprecedented and in 1954 alone the foundation raised an excess of $66 million.[10]

The polio vaccine has improved over the years. Today states require students in licensed day care or kindergarten to be immunized for polio, with few exceptions. In many communities, local public health departments, or school clinics, provide vaccinations free of charge for those families who cannot afford to be vaccinated by a private health care provider.

These two examples illustrate the significant impact public health has had on reducing infectious diseases in the United States in the twentieth century. In the context of the total product curve, both public health initiatives caused the curve to shift and rotate upward as illustrated in Figure 2–5. Enhanced water sanitation improved the physical environment, while the polio vaccination is an example of a new medical technology. Needless to say, public health can impact the production of health in a variety of ways. Other examples may include a statewide anti-smoking campaign aimed at improving lifestyle or a teenage pregnancy prevention program in the local high schools directed at enhancing sex education.

The 10 Major Causes of Death in the United States in 2010

As mentioned previously, individual choices, socioeconomic status, and environmental factors play a significant role in the production of health. If so, one might suspect that national disease-specific mortality rates would reflect the importance of these variables. That is, mortality rates should be high for diseases that are more sensitive to adverse lifestyles, low socioeconomic status, or unhealthy environments. With this in mind, Table 2–1 lists the top 10 causes of death in the United States for 2010. Over the course of the year, more than 2.4 million individuals died in the United States. Of this number,

---

10. Some of our older readers may remember as a young school child being asked to donate a shiny new Roosevelt dime to the March of Dimes to help eradicate polio.

TABLE 2–1
The 10 Leading Causes of Death in the United States in 2010

Cause	Number of Deaths
1. Diseases of the heart	595,444
2. Malignant neoplasms	573,855
3. Chronic lower respiratory diseases	137,789
4. Cerebrovascular diseases (stroke)	129,180
5. Unintentional injuries	118,043
6. Alzheimer's disease	83,308
7. Diabetes mellitus	68,905
8. Nephritis, nephritic syndrome, and nephrosis (kidney disease)	50,472
9. Influenza and pneumonia	50,003
10. Intentional self-harm (suicide)	37,793
TOTAL	2,465,932

SOURCE: National Center for Health Statistics. www.cdc.gov/nchs/fastats/deaths.htm.

approximately 75 percent succumbed to the 10 most common causes of death listed in the table. By far the number one cause of death is diseases of the heart, accounting for 24 percent of all deaths in the United States in 2010. Although researchers are still unclear as to what determines an individual's risk for heart disease, they are certain that the blood level of cholesterol, smoking, level of physical activity, stress, and obesity play a major role in determining the risk of heart disease. Each of these factors is influenced by lifestyle choices, socioeconomic status, and environmental settings.

The second leading cause of death is malignant neoplasms, or cancers. Lifestyle choices often have an impact on this type of illness as well. Evidence indicates that more than 80 percent of all lung cancer deaths, the most common form of cancer, can be attributed to smoking. Socioeconomic status and environmental factors also come into play in determining the likelihood of contracting lung cancer through exposure to such items as asbestos and radon. The third leading cause of death is chronic lower respiratory diseases, which includes chronic obstructive pulmonary disease, emphysema, and chronic bronchitis. Air pollution plays a critical role in the progression of these diseases. The fourth leading cause of death is stroke and the medical community is in agreement that lifestyle, such as whether a person follows a proper diet and exercises, impacts the chances of having a stroke.

It is interesting to note that two of the ten categories, accidents and suicide, deal with deaths related to individual behavior rather than natural causes. A total of 155,836 died from violent deaths in 2010. Together these causes represent the number three reason for deaths in the United States.

This rather simple exercise underscores the importance that lifestyle choices, socioeconomic status, and environmental factors play in determining deaths in the United States. It is worth noting that the information in Table 2–1 can also be used to illustrate the importance that an individual's mental and physical profile play in the making of health. For example, age is a critical factor in determining the onset of Alzheimer's disease, while the environment, genetics, and age contribute to the development of diabetes.

Empirical Evidence on the Production of Health: A Summary

Health production theory suggests that medical care, lifestyle factors, environmental surroundings, and socioeconomic status all influence health conditioned upon the state of medical technology and an individual's medical profile. Clearly, the total impact of medical care on health is significant and many people would die without proper medical care attention. But from a practical economic perspective, it is important to know which factors contribute more to improved health at the margin so cost-effective policies can be designed. Given limited resources, society's goal is to implement least-cost methods of improving population health.

In terms of adult health, evidence seems to suggest that medical care matters but nonmedical factors also play an important role in maintaining wellness. For example, a better lifestyle and improved socioeconomic and environmental conditions seem to make a substantial difference for adult health. Medical care also appears to be important at the margin for the health of infants, especially for low-income infants. But as we saw in this chapter, socioeconomic and environmental conditions are also important for infant health. In fact, even lifestyle is important for infants. While at first blush that statement may sound odd, low birthweight and greater infant mortality have been linked to adverse maternal lifestyle behaviors such as tobacco, alcohol, and drug abuse. For the elderly, particularly those without health insurance coverage prior to becoming Medicare-eligible, medical care is also important at the margin. But even in this case, nonmedical factors, such as exercise and diet, likely play an important role.

These empirical findings have some rather interesting policy implications. They suggest that any public policy initiative aimed at improving health should also consider raising education levels, reducing the amount of poverty, and encouraging improved lifestyles rather than simply providing additional medical care. Naturally, the specifics of any policy should be based on sound cost-benefit analysis.

Implications of the Patient Protection and Affordable Care Act (PPACA) of 2010

PPACA may influence the health of the U.S. population in several ways. First and foremost, government studies anticipate that the combination of health insurance mandate, tax credits, and subsidies will lead to an additional 30 million people in the United States with health insurance coverage. As discussed in this chapter, various empirical studies have found that the transition from uninsured to insured status typically results in an increase in medical care utilization and a meaningful improvement in health status. Thus, the health of the U.S. population is expected to improve with the PPACA as long as capacity constraints are absent in the medical care production process.

Second, the PPACA may impact the production of health through its emphasis on wellness and prevention. The act calls for the establishment of the National Prevention, Health Promotion, and Public Health Council to coordinate activities at the federal level regarding prevention, wellness, and health promotion practices. The council is composed of the heads of various federal agencies and chaired by the surgeon general and will be responsible for developing a National Prevention and Health Promotion Strategy. The act also creates a Prevention and Public Health Fund to invest in wellness and public health activities such as prevention research and health screening and calls for the establishment of a grant program to support the delivery of evidence-based prevention and wellness services at the community level.

Third, grants and technical assistance to employers will be provided to establish wellness programs for workers. Employers will also be permitted to offer rewards to those employees who participate in any wellness programs and meet certain criteria.

Finally, chain restaurants and food sold in vending machines will be required to provide information regarding the nutritional content of each item sold. Finally, the establishment of accountable care organizations (see Chapter 7) may help to replace the fragmented health care system in the United States with a more integrated one. An integrated system that can better coordinate medical care among different levels of primary and specialty care may lead to better health.

Summary

Health, like any other good or service, is desired because it generates utility. Also like other goods and services, health is subject to the law of diminishing marginal utility. This law stipulates that each additional unit of health provides less marginal utility than the previous unit.

The making, or production, of health is influenced by a variety of factors, including the amount of medical care consumed. The positive relation between health and medical care, however, is nonlinear due to the law of diminishing marginal productivity. This law underlies a fundamental production relation stating that health increases at a decreasing rate with additional amounts of medical care, holding other inputs constant. Some of the other factors determining health are the state of medical technology, the individual's initial health profile, socioeconomic status, lifestyle, and environmental factors.

The empirical evidence for adults indicates that good health may depend not only on medical care but also socioeconomic status and lifestyle choices. Changes in health appear to be more sensitive to changes in the consumption of medical care among vulnerable segments of the population such as low-income young and elderly individuals. Early in the twentieth century, health improved sharply in the United States in large part because the number of deaths from infectious diseases decreased because of advances in public health.

Review Questions and Problems

1. Describe the factors that make it difficult to measure output in medical care markets.
2. As mentioned at the beginning of the chapter, the life expectancy rate in Russia fell significantly from 1989 through 1994. Use health production theory to explain what would happen to the relationship between good health and medical care in Russia if alcohol consumption diminished and the market economy strengthened. Provide a graph to illustrate your explanation.
3. Use health production theory to explain the role gender plays in the production of health during pregnancy. Provide a graph to illustrate your answer.
4. Use production theory to graphically illustrate the case in which a medical innovation improves health without any change in the consumption of medical care.
5. In your own words, use utility analysis to explain why people demand health. How does the law of diminishing marginal utility fit into the analysis?
6. Explain how an increase in income may affect the level of health in a relatively affluent country like the United States compared to a relatively poor country like Haiti.
7. You have just been appointed to the post of surgeon general of the United States. The president wants you to develop an advertising campaign called "A Healthy America by the Year 2020" that encourages Americans to lead a healthier lifestyle. What types of behavior would you try to influence? Why?

8. A recent study (Sheffield et al., 2011) links fine-particulate air pollution to respiratory illness among infants. Explain these findings in the context of the total product curve for medical care.
9. Explain how a change in each of the following factors would alter the shape of the total product curve for medical care.
   a. An increase in education.
   b. An improvement in lifestyle.
   c. An improvement in the environment.
10. Some people believe that cigarette and alcohol advertisements should be banned completely in the United States. If this were the case, what would likely happen to the shapes of the total and marginal product curves for medical care?
11. Explain why a researcher must be careful when interpreting findings from a survey that finds a positive association between education levels and health outcomes.
12. Consult the website of your state or county Public Health Department. Are there any public policy initiatives currently in place that are aimed at improving lifestyles, enhancing access to health care, or impacting the environment? Explain the intent of these policies in the context of health production theory.
13. In a 1991 issue of the *Cato Journal*, Santerre et al. estimate an infant mortality equation using a sample of 20 countries belonging to the Organization for Economic Cooperation and Development (OECD) during the six adjacent half decades from 1960 to 1985 and a fixed effects model. They obtained the following (abbreviated) results:

$$IMR = 3.93 - 0.069TIME - 0.892RGDP - 0.539PHYS + 0.707^*URBAN - 0.004FLFPR - 0.135ED$$
$$(2.60)(1.112) \quad (6.83) \quad (6.89) \quad (4.21) \quad (1.21) \quad (2.34)$$

$$\text{Adjusted } R^2 = .954, N = 110$$

All of the variables have been converted to logarithms so the coefficient estimates can be treated as elasticities. The numbers below the estimated coefficients represent t-statistics.

IMR = infant mortality rate in each country for each year
TIME = a time trend from 1 to 5 (1960 to 1985) capturing changing technology and knowledge
RGDP = real gross domestic product per capita in each country for each year
PHYS = number of physicians per capita in each country for each year
URBAN = percentage of the population in urban areas in each country for each year
FLFPR = female labor force participation rate in each country for each year
ED = level of education in each country for each year.

Based upon these findings answer the following questions:

a. What percentage of the variation in the infant mortality rate is explained by the independent variables? How do you know that?
b. Using health production theory as much as possible, provide a hypothesis or theory about the relationship (direct or inverse) between the first three independent variables and the infant mortality rate.
c. Are those three hypotheses supported by the regression results? Explain.
d. Given that the estimated coefficients are also elasticities, interpret the coefficients on the number of physicians and real GDP.
e. Should we expect the physician elasticity to remain constant if increasingly more physicians are employed in the typical health economy? Why or why not?
f. Based upon those findings explain why the infant mortality rate may be so much higher in Turkey than Japan?

Online Resources

To access Internet links related to the topics in this chapter, please visit our website at **www.cengage.com/economics/santerre**.

References

Auster, Richard, Irving Leveson, and Deborah Sarachek. "The Production of Health: An Exploratory Study." *Journal of Human Resources* 9 (fall 1969), pp. 411–36.

Balia, Silvia, and Andrews M. Jones "Mortality, Lifestyle, and Socioeconomic Status." *Journal of Health Economics* 27 (2008), pp. 1–26.

Berkowitz, Eric N., Roger A. Kerin, and William Rudelius. *Marketing*, 2nd ed. Homewood, Ill.: Richard D. Irwin, 1989.

Bolin, Kristian, Lena Jacobson, and Bjorn Lindgren. "The Family as the Health Producer—When Spouses Act Strategically." *Journal of Health Economics* 21 (May 2002), pp. 475–95.

Brainerd, Elizabeth, and David M. Cutler. "Autopsy on an Empire: Understanding Mortality in Russia and the Former Soviet Union." *Journal of Economic Perspectives* 19 (winter 2005), pp. 107–130.

Card, David, Carlos Dobkin, and Nicole Maestas. "Does Medicare Save Lives?" *National Bureau of Economic Research*, Working Paper No. 13683, November 2007.

Case, Anne, Angela Fertig, and Christina Hall. "The Lasting Impact of Childhood Health and Circumstance." *Journal of Health Economics* 24 (2005), pp. 365–389.

Case, Anne, Darren Lubotsky, and Christina Paxson. "Economic Status and Health in Childhood: The Origins of the Gradient." Center for Health and Wellbeing Working Paper. Princeton University: February 2002.

Case, Anne, and Christina Paxson. "Parental Behavior and Child Health." *Health Affairs* 21 (March/April 2002), pp. 164–78.

Chandra, Amitabh, and Douglas Staiger. "Productivity Spillovers in Health Care: Evidence From the Treatment of Heart Attacks." *Journal of Political Economics* (2007), pp. 107–140.

Currie, Janet, and Jonathan Gruber. "Health Insurance Eligibility, Utilization of Medical Care, and Child Health." *Quarterly Journal of Economics* 111 (1996a), pp. 431–466.

Currie, Janet, and Jonathan Gruber, "Saving Babies: The Efficiency and Cost of Recent Changes in Medicaid Eligibility on Pregnant Women." *Journal of Political Economy* 104 (1996b), pp. 1263–1296.

Currie, Janet, and Jonathan Gruber. "The Technology of Birth: Health Insurance, Medical Interventions, and Infant Health." *National Bureau of Economic Research*, Working Paper No. 5985, 1997.

Currie, Janet, and Matthew Neidell. "Air Pollution and Infant Health: What Can We Learn from California's Recent Experience?" *Quarterly Journal of Economics* 120 (August 2005), pp. 1003–30.

Cutler, David M., and Robert S. Huckman. "Technological Development and Medical Productivity: The Diffusion of Angioplasty in New York State." *Journal of Health Economics* 22 (2003), pp. 187–217.

Cutler, David, and Adriana Lleras-Muney. "Education and Health: Evaluating Theories and Evidence." *National Bureau of Economic Research*, Working Paper No. 12352, June 2006.

Cutler, David M., and Mark McClellan. "Is Technological Change in Medicine Worth It?" *Health Affairs* 20 (September/October 2001), pp. 11–29.

Cutler, David, and Grant Miller. "The Role of Public Health Improvements in Health Advances: The Twentieth-Century United States." *Demography* 42 (February 2005), pp. 1–22.

Deaton, Angus. "Policy Implications of the Gradient of Health and Wealth." *Health Affairs* 21 (March/April 2002), pp. 13–30.

Donabedian, Avedis. *The Definition of Quality and Approaches to Its Assessment*. Ann Arbor, Mich.: Health Administration Press, 1980.

Donabedian, Avedis. "The Quality of Care: How Can It Be Assessed?" *Journal of the American Medical Association* 260 (September 23–30, 1988), pp. 1743–48.

Enthoven, Alain C. *Health Plan*. Reading, Mass.: Addison-Wesley, 1980.

Ettner, Susan L. "New Evidence on the Relationship between Income and Health." *Journal of Health Economics* 15 (1996), pp. 67–85.

Finkelstein, Amy, and Robin McKnight. "What Did Medicare Do (And Was it Worth it)?" *National Bureau of Economic Research*, Working Paper No. 11609, September 2005.

Fisher, Elliot et al. "More Isn't Always Better." *A Dartmouth Atlas Project Topic Brief*. The Dartmouth Institute for Health Policy and Clinical Practice (February 27, 2009).

Freeman, Joseph D., Srikanth Kadiyala, Janice F. Bell, and Diane P. Martin. "The Causal Effect of Health Insurance on Utilization and Outcomes in Adults: A Systematic Review of U.S. Studies." *Medical Care* 46 (October 2008), pp. 1023–32.

Fuchs, Victor R. "Economics, Health and Post-Industrial Society." *Millbank Memorial Fund Quarterly* 57 (1979), pp. 153–82.

Grossman, Michael. *The Demand for Health: A Theoretical and Empirical Investigation*. New York: National Bureau of Economic Research, 1972a.

Grossman, Michael. "On the Concept of Health Capital and the Demand for Health." *Journal of Political Economy* 80 (March–April 1972b), pp. 223–55.

Hadley, Jack. *More Medical Care, Better Health*. Washington, DC: Urban Institute Press, 1982.

Jacobson, Lena. "The Family as Producer of Health—An Extended Grossman Model." *Journal of Health Economics* 19 (September 2000), pp. 611–37.

Kaestner, Robert, and Jeffrey Silber. "Evidence on the Efficacy of Inpatient Spending on Medicare Patients." *The Millbank Quarterly* 88 (2010), pp. 560–94.

Kampa, Marilena, and Elias Castanas. "Human Health Effects of Air Pollution." *Environmental Pollution* 151 (2008), pp. 362–67.

Kawachi, Ichiro, and Bruce P. Kennedy. "Income Inequality and Health: Pathways and Mechanisms." *Health Services Research* 34 (April 1999, Part II), pp. 215–27.

Kravdal, Oystein. "The Impact of Marital Status on Cancer." *Social Science and Medicine* 52 (2001), pp. 357–68.

Lantz, Paula M., et al. "Socioeconomic Disparities in Health Change in a Longitudinal Study of U.S. Adults: The Role of Health-Risk Behaviors." *Social Science and Medicine* 53 (2001), pp. 29–40.

Lichtenberg, Frank. "The Effects of Medicare on Utilization and Outcomes." *Frontiers in Health Policy Research* 5 (January 2002), pp. 27–52.

Lleras-Muney, Adriana. "The Relationship between Education and Adult Mortality in U.S." *Center for Health and Wellbeing Working Paper*. Princeton University: May 2001.

Lorgelly, Paula A., and Joanne Lindley. "What is the Relationship Between Income Inequality and Health? Evidence From BHPS." *Health Economics* 17 (February 2008). pp. 249–65.

Lynch, John, et al. "Is Income a Determinant of Population Health? Part 1. A Systematic Review." *Milbank Quarterly* 82 (2004), pp. 5–99.

Manor, Orly, Zvi Elsenbach, Avi Israeli, and Yechiel Friedlander. "Mortality Differentials among Women: The Israel Longitudinal Mortality Study." *Social Science and Medicine* 51 (2000), pp. 1175–88.

McWilliams, J. Michael, Ellen Meara, Alan M. Zaslavsky, and John Z. Ayanian. "Health of Previously Uninsured Adults After Acquiring Medicare Coverage." *Journal of the American Medical Association*. 24 (December 26, 2007), pp. 2886–94.

Miller, K. A. et al. "Long-Term Exposure to Air Pollution and Incidence of Cardiovascular Events in Women." *The New England Journal of Medicine* 356 (February 1, 2007), pp. 447–58.

Mohai, Paul et al. "Air Pollution Around Schools is Linked to Poorer Student Health and Academic Performance." *Health Affairs* 30 (May 2011), pp. 852–62.

Mosby Medical Encyclopedia, 2nd ed. New York: C. V. Mosby, 1992.

Newhouse Joseph P. *Free for All? Lessons from the RAND Health Insurance Experiment*. A RAND Study, Cambridge and London: Harvard University Press, 1993.

Oshinsky, David M. *Polio: An American Story.* Oxford, New York: Oxford University Press, 2005.

Ostbye, Truls, and Donald H. Taylor Jr. "The Effect of Smoking on Years of Healthy Life (YHL) Lost Among Middle-Aged and Older Americans." *Health Services Research* 39 (June 2004), pp. 532–51.

Pope, C. Arden, Majid Ezzati, and Douglas Dockery. "Fine-Particulate Air Pollution and Life Expectancy in the United States." *The New England Journal of Medicine* 360 (January 22, 2009), pp. 376–86.

Ruhm, Christopher J. "Are Recessions Good for Your Health?" *Quarterly Journal of Economics* 115 (May 2000), pp. 617–50.

Ruhm, Christopher J. "Good Times Make You Sick." *Journal of Health Economics* 22 (2003), pp. 637–58.

Ruhm, Christopher J. "Healthy Living in Hard Times." *Journal of Health Economics* 24 (2005), pp. 341–64.

Santerre, Rexford et al. "Government Intervention in Health Care Markets and Health Care Outcomes: Some International Evidence. *The Cato Journal* 11 (spring/summer 1991), pp. 1–12

Sheffield, Perry, et al. "Fine Particulate Matter Pollution Linked to Respiratory Illness in Infants and Increased Hospital Costs." *Health Affairs* 30 (May, 2011) pp. 871–78.

Strum, Roland. "The Effect of Obesity, Smoking, and Drinking on Medical Problems and Costs." *Health Affairs* 21 (March/April 2002), pp. 245–53.

Wagstaff, Adam, and Eddy van Doorslaer. "Income Inequality and Health: What Does the Literature Tell Us?" *Annual Review of Public Health* 21 (2000), pp. 543–67.

Woolf, Steven H., and Paula Braverman. "Where Health Disparities Begin: The Role of Social and Economic Determinants—And Why Current Policies May Make Matters Worse." *Health Affairs* 30 (October 2011), pp. 1852–59.

Demand for Health Capital[1]

Individuals regularly invest in their human capital, for instance through education, on-the-job training, or even just by reading the daily newspaper. Our investments, however, are not necessarily confined to our stock of knowledge. We also regularly make decisions that affect our health—either positively or negatively. We visit the doctor, receive flu shots, take prescription drugs and vitamin supplements, and obtain diagnostic screening for various ailments. We exercise and diet, though at the same time, we also engage in risky behaviors such as smoking, excessive drinking, and consumption of high-caloric and high-fat foods. This notion that consumers actively invest (or disinvest) in their health through a conscious allocation of resources was advanced by Michael Grossman's seminal work on the demand for health (Grossman, 1972), and helps us better understand the determinants of health.

A few economists, going back to the 1960s, had recognized that health can be viewed as a component of human capital (Becker, 1964; Fuchs, 1966). However, health was still primarily viewed as being externally determined by factors such as genetics, medical technology, microbial agents, accidents, and the general environment. Very little role was attributed to rational individual choices and health behaviors. Grossman formally integrated this role into his study of the demand for health. He broadened the definition of human capital to include not just knowledge capital but also the investments that we make toward our own health. In Grossman's model, individuals choose their level of health similar to choosing consumption levels of other commodities, and therefore have some control over their health. For instance, we choose how much to spend on cars and clothes, and Grossman's point is that we also choose to some extent how healthy we want to be based on the decisions that we make. That this view of the consumer presented a departure from convention was evidenced by an editorial of Grossman's model, which argued that "it seems a trifle obscure to talk about people 'choosing their level of health.'"[2]

In retrospect, the intuition behind the insight that individuals have control over their own health is hard to dispute. Mokdad and colleagues (2004; 2005) analyzed the various causes of mortality in 2000 for the United States, and concluded that modifiable behavioral risk factors constitute leading causes. Tobacco consumption, poor diet, physical inactivity, and alcohol consumption were at the top of the list. (Also note the discussion on the 10 major causes of death in Chapter 2.) In his classic work, *Who Shall Live?*, health economist Victor Fuchs recounts "A Tale of Two States,"

1. The authors are especially grateful to Dhaval M. Dave, associate professor of economics at Bentley University and research associate at the NBER, for contributing this wonderfully concise and insightful review of the Grossman model and its applications. Dave thanks Michael Grossman for his helpful comments on an earlier draft of this review.

2. The editorial appeared in the December 13, 1972, issue of *Financial World*: America's Investment and Business Weekly. Seeing the silver lining in the cloud, in reference to the editorial, Grossman later quipped in a speech that "... bad publicity is always better than no publicity" (Grossman 2004).

comparing contiguously situated Nevada and Utah. While the residents of Utah were found to be among the healthiest in the United States, those in Nevada were at the opposite end of the spectrum. At the time of the study, the infant mortality rate and the adult mortality rates were 40 to 50 percent higher in Nevada relative to Utah. Yet, both states were similar with respect to their levels of income, education, climate, urbanization, number of physicians and hospital beds per capita, and many other factors commonly associated with differences in health. Fuchs (1974) posited "What, then, explains the huge differences in death rates?" and found that the answer lied mostly in the different lifestyles of the residents of both states. Utah, for instance, is primarily populated by Mormons, who generally lead stable lives and do not use tobacco or alcohol.[3]

Grossman's Model of the Demand for Health

Grossman (1972; 2000) captured this insight, of people having some say over how healthy they are, when he integrated the theory of human capital and household production to study the demand for health. The main ways in which the demand for health differs from the demand for other goods and services can be encapsulated in the following conditions that set up the basic model.

(A2–1)
$$U_t = U(H_t, Z_t)$$

Equation A2–1 denotes the individual's utility (U) function at a given time t. Utility, or satisfaction, increases with the individual's health status (H) and with other commodities (Z)—such as entertainment, meals and nutrition, and shelter.[4] Individuals desire health because they enjoy being in good health. Thus health in this model is a consumption commodity, similar to sleep, entertainment, or eating; it directly enters the individual's preferences since illness and sick days are distasteful and diminish utility.

The individual is assumed to be forward-looking and to maximize their lifetime utility at each point in time. Due to the scarcity of resources and other limitations, however, the individual is subject to various constraints while trying to maximize their utility.

(A2–2)
$$H_{t+1} = H_t - \delta_t H_t + I_t$$

Health, in addition to being a consumption good, is also a capital good. It has durable aspects, which is reflected in Equation A2–2. Thus, health in the next period (H_{t+1}) depends on the current stock of health (H_t), though just like any other capital good such as a car or a computer, health depreciates over time (with δ_t representing the rate of depreciation). Individuals can also add to their health stock by actively investing in health, for instance through regular doctor check-ups, exercise, or a healthy diet. The above condition then says that the health stock in the following period equals the current level of health less any depreciation ($\delta_t H_t$) plus any investments (I_t).

The main point that individuals have some active control over their health is reflected in the production function for health investments in Equation A2–3.

(A2–3)
$$I_t = I(M_t, TH_t; E)$$

At each period t, individuals can make investments (I_t) in health by investing resources, namely medical care or other market inputs (M) and their time devoted to health-producing activities (TH). For instance, suppose individuals wish to invest in

3. The picture is not much different today, almost 30 years later. Across multiple ranking schemes, Utah is consistently among the healthiest states in the union, and Nevada is typically among the least healthy states. See for instance: Agency for Healthcare Research and Quality's 2010 State Snapshots (http://statesnapshots.ahrq.gov/snaps10/); United Health Foundation's State Health Stats (http://www.americashealthrankings.org/); and Commonwealth Fund's State Scorecard (http://www.commonwealthfund.org/Maps-and-Data/State-Data-Center/State-Scorecard.aspx).

4. With respect to health, utility can increase at an increasing or decreasing rate. That is, it is not necessary to assume that there is diminishing marginal utility of health, as we typically assume for other goods and commodities.

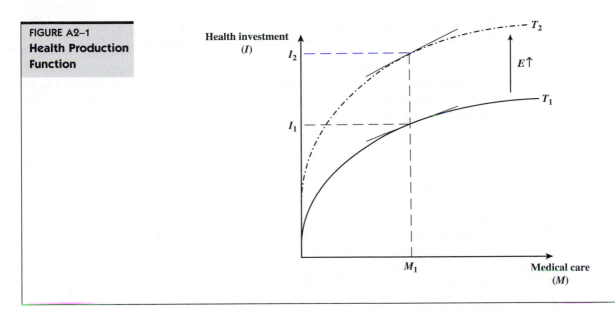

FIGURE A2–1
Health Production Function

The shape of the total product curve reflects the law of diminishing marginal productivity, meaning that higher levels of medical care improve health at a diminishing rate. The total product curve shifts upward with an improvement in efficiency from T_1 to T_2. For example, with higher levels of education the health production function shifts upward because an educated individual is more capable of processing information regarding the production of good health. For the same level of inputs (M_1), a higher-educated individual is capable of producing more health (I_2 as opposed to I_1).

their health by maintaining healthy levels of good and bad cholesterol. They might be able to do so in various ways. One way might be to use medical care (M)—regularly screen cholesterol by visiting the doctor and take prescription drugs such as statins (e.g., Lipitor or Zocor) to reduce high levels of bad cholesterol. Another way might be to use time inputs (TH) and engage in regular exercise and physical activity, or use time and store-bought ingredients to cook healthy meals at home. Figure A2–1 is similar to Figure 2–3 and denotes this health production function. Similar to a firm, individuals can "produce" health by combining and using various market, medical, and time inputs. Thus, a second key point underscored by the Grossman model is that individuals are both consumers and producers of health.

As reflected in the concave shape of T_1 in Figure A2–1, higher levels of medical care or market inputs (M) raise health, though at a diminishing rate. For instance, the first visit to the doctor in a given year may be highly beneficial; it may uncover illness conditions that the individual is not aware of, lead to treatment options, and the physician may provide the individual with health-promoting information such as the importance of quitting smoking or regular exercise. The second visit to the doctor may also yield health benefits, though not necessarily as great as the first visit. Similarly each subsequent visit to the physician leads to ever smaller and smaller increases in healthy days, consistent with diminishing marginal returns.

In addition to market and time inputs, an individual's production of health also depends on efficiency (E). For instance, Grossman contended that education makes individuals more efficient in producing health. Similar to the role that technology plays in a firm's production process, higher levels of education shift the health production function upward (from T_1 to T_2). Thus, for the same level of inputs (M_1), an educated individual is able to produce more health (I_2 vs. I_1). Educated persons may be more capable of processing information regarding what promotes health. For instance, educated persons may make the most of their visit to the doctor because they know what questions to ask and remember to adhere to the doctor's recommendations. Education thus raises the marginal product of health inputs; for the same extra amount of inputs, higher-educated individuals are able to obtain more health. This is reflected in the higher slope at each point on the new production function (T_2).

Similar to a production function for health, individuals also produce other commodities (Z) in their utility function. Equation A2–4 denotes this production function for these other commodities, which are also produced using market inputs (denoted by X) and time inputs (denoted by TZ). Education (E) may also raise the individual's efficiency for this type of production.

(A2–4)
$$Z_t = Z(X_t, TZ_t; E)$$

One example of Z might be meals. Different individuals may produce meals using different inputs. Some people may choose to buy raw ingredients in the market (X) and spend a greater amount of time (TZ) preparing foods at home. For these individuals, their meals are produced using relatively time-intensive inputs. Other individuals may instead produce their meals with greater market inputs than with time inputs—for instance, just eating out at a restaurant or a fast-food establishment rather than cooking at home.

These production functions for health and other commodities capture the fact that individuals have some control over the production process, and they can determine what quantity and mix of resources to use in producing their health, meals, entertainment, transportation, etc. Broadly speaking, individuals are combining inputs bought in the marketplace with their time. However, just like any other resource, these resources are scarce and constrained by the individuals' total income and their total time. Thus, the individual faces two additional constraints in these respects at time *t*.

(A2–5)
$$W \cdot TW = P_M \cdot M + P_X \cdot X$$

Equation A2–5 shows the individual's income constraint. The individual's income, denoted by the product of the wage rate (W) and work time (TW), is expended on market goods M and X.[5] The right-hand side of the equation represents expenditures on the market goods, denoted by the product of the respective price (P) and quantity of M and X.

(A2–6)
$$TT = TW + TH + TZ + TL$$

Equation A2–6 captures the individual's time constraint. Total time (TT), measured over some interval such as a day or year, is exhausted on work (TW), time spent on health (TH), time spent on other commodities such as meals and socializing (TZ), and time lost due to illness and sick days (TL).

The final condition captures another important aspect of health capital. Any capital good generally exhibits two characteristics. It is durable and adjusts over time due to depreciation and investments, as reflected in Equation A2–2. A second aspect of capital goods is that they also provide some return over time. In this respect, an increase in the health stock (H) reduces an individual's time lost to illness (TL) and raises the individual's total effective time. With less time being sick, the individual can work more and earn a greater income and/or use some of the freed-up time to engage in other activities that the individual enjoys (e.g., vacation, socializing, sleeping, watching a movie, etc.). This higher income-generating capacity due to more available time is the return to investing in health.

(A2–7)
$$\text{Healthy Days} = (365 - TL) = F(H)$$

Suppose that time is measured as days per year. Then, the individual's total healthy days in a given year equals 365 − TL, or 365 days minus the days that he or she loses

---

5. Since individuals maximize their utility over their lifetime, saving or borrowing on the aggregate over their lifetime horizon is not allowed. That is, individuals can save or borrow at a period in time; however, over their lifetime the present value of their income stream must equal the present value of their expenses. (Typically individuals save when young and while working, and rundown on their savings when older to finance their retirement.)

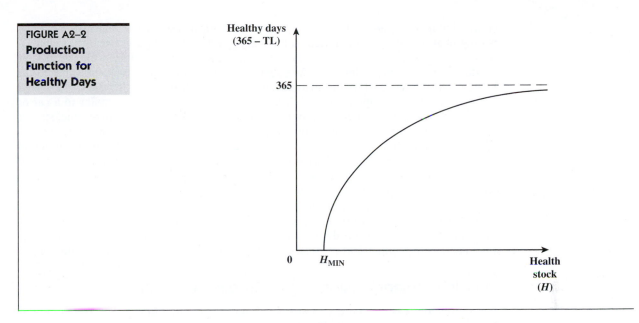

FIGURE A2–2
Production Function for Healthy Days

The graph captures the relation between healthy days and health stock. The curve's bowed shape indicates the number of healthy days increases at a decreasing rate with improvements in the stock of health. H_{MIN} represents the minimum stock of health such that death occurs if health falls below that level. The number 365 represents the maximum number of healthy days an individual has in a given calendar year.

because of illness. Equation A2–7 says that the number of healthy, productive days (365 − TL) that the individual has is a function of their underlying health stock (H). The greater is the individual's health stock, the more healthy and productive days he has in a given year. This is graphed by the production function for healthy days in Figure A2–2. Grossman defines a minimum level of subsistence health stock (H_{MIN}), such that death occurs if health falls below this level. Beyond H_{MIN}, total number of healthy days increases with the individual's health stock. As the individual actively invests in health and becomes healthier, he gains more productive time during the year.[6] By definition, this increase occurs at a decreasing rate since the individual's total number of healthy days in a given year cannot exceed 365. Thus, the marginal product of health is positive but diminishing. As the health stock increases, the marginal product or the slope of the production function in Figure A2–2 gets smaller.

The seven conditions (Equations A2–1 through A2–7) capture the key features of Grossman's framework and summarize the aspects of health that make it different from other commodities. First, the individual is both the consumer and producer of health. The individual consumes health for two reasons: she enjoys feeling healthier, and health also raises her productive capacity by raising her available productive time which can potentially be used to earn more income. For most goods (e.g., cars or computers or a textbook), there is a separation between the consumer and the producer. However, with respect to health, the individual consumes health not by simply passively purchasing it in the market. Indeed, "health" cannot be purchased. The individual is also a mini-firm who produces health by combining inputs such as medical care, diet, exercise, smoking, and their time.

Second, health is both a consumption commodity as well as an investment commodity. Similar to watching a movie or taking a car-ride in the countryside on a

---

6. Health may also directly affect people's wages. All else equal, healthier individuals tend to be more productive and therefore earn a higher wage. For simplicity, Grossman (1972) abstracted from this wage effect, though the general predictions of the model are not affected if wage is allowed to depend on health.

sunny day in June, we desire and consume health for its own sake—because we enjoy feeling healthy. At the same time, health is also an investment good because it yields a return. Thus, we desire health because it means fewer lost days due to illness, greater productivity, and higher incomes. We spend current money and time investing in our health, and this yields a higher income capacity in the future.

Third, health is a capital stock. It has features of a durable good, similar to a car or computer. Health can depreciate over time, but we can also invest in it over time, similar to doing regular tune-ups on a car or investing in antivirus software for a computer.

Finally, note that it is health that belongs in the individual's utility function (Equation A2–1), not medical care (M). The implication of this is that we do not directly demand or desire medical care. It is health that we ultimately want. We only consume medical care due to our underlying demand for health. In other words, we do not particularly enjoy going to the doctor or getting a flu shot for its own sake; these are simply inputs that we demand in order to produce better health. Our demand for medical care is akin to the demand for steel by an automobile manufacturer; health (like cars) is the output and medical care (like steel) is an input into its production.

Pure Investment Version of the Grossman Model

For simplicity, it is convenient to abstract from the consumption aspect of health and focus instead only on the investment aspect of health. This pure investment framework retains many of the key insights and predictions from the full model. Thus, in this version of the model, we assume that individuals consume and demand health because of its investment features: it provides a return over time in the form of more productive days due to less illness.

Suppose we have the following function relating an index of health stock (H) to healthy days (365 − TL), as shown in Table A2–1. As the individual invests more in their health stock (H), their days lost due to illness (TL) are reduced, which in turn raises their total availability of healthy days in the year (365 − TL).

The increase in healthy days occurs at a decreasing rate, however, due to diminishing returns. This was shown earlier in Figure A2–2, which graphed the production function between the health stock and healthy days. For instance, raising the health stock from 10 to 11 units raises healthy days from 253 to 293 days—an increase of 40 days, which is the marginal product of health (MPH). Raising the health stock from 11 to 12 units though yields an increase in healthy days by only 25 days. Each subsequent increase in the health stock yields ever smaller and smaller increments to the total number of healthy days. Hence, the marginal product of health is diminishing as the health stock increases.

Assuming that the wage is the opportunity cost of time, the individual values this marginal product—the number of extra days that they gain—at the wage rate. Suppose that the individual can earn a daily wage of $100. In this case, investing in the health stock from 10 units to 11 units, which results in 40 extra healthy days, is worth $4000 to the individual. This is known as the marginal efficiency of capital (MEC), shown in the final column of Table A2–1 as the product of the marginal product of health and the wage rate.

(A2–8) $MEC = MPH \cdot Wage$

The MEC captures the value of the additional healthy days gained from a one-unit increase in the health stock.[7] Figure A2–3 graphs the MEC (final column of Table A2–1) with respect to the health stock (first column of Table A2–1). As the

---

7. Grossman (1972) defines the MEC in percentage terms, as (MPH · W)/Cost of Health Investment—which would be interpreted as the percent return on health investment. We define it in monetary $ terms for convenience of exposition. The conditions are equivalent, except for the units of comparison.

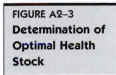

FIGURE A2–3
Determination of Optimal Health Stock

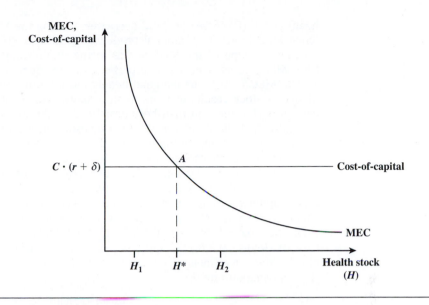

The figure MEC captures the value to a typical consumer/patient of an additional healthy day gained from a one-unit increase in the stock of health. The curve is downward sloping because the marginal efficiency of capital decreases due to the diminishing marginal product of health. Remember that the marginal efficiency of capital equals the marginal product of health multiplied by a constant wage, and that the marginal product of health decreases with investments in health because of the law of diminishing marginal productivity. As such, the MEC represents the demand for health capital. The cost-of-capital curve is horizontal and equals the cost of health investment (C) multiplied by the sum of the real interest rate (r) plus the rate of depreciation (δ). This curve represents the supply curve of health capital. Point A equals the optimal level of health stock (H*) where the marginal efficiency of capital equals the cost-of-capital. Any level of health stock less than H* is not optimal because the marginal efficiency of capital exceeds the cost-of-capital and it is in the individual's best interest to invest in more health capital. Any investments beyond the amount H* are not optimal because the cost-of-capital exceeds the marginal efficiency of capital.

TABLE A2–1
Marginal Efficiency of Capital

Health Stock (H)	Illness Days (TL)	Healthy Days (365 – TL)	Marginal Product of Health (MPH)	Marginal Efficiency of Capital (MEC = MPH * W)
10	112	253	–	–
11	72	293	40	$4000
12	47	318	25	$2500
13	32	333	15	$1500
14	22	343	10	$1000
15	16	349	6	$600
16	11	354	5	$500
17	7	358	4	$400
18	4	361	3	$300
19	2	363	2	$200
20	1	364	1	$100

health stock (H) increases, MEC decreases, making the MEC curve downward sloping. Since MEC is just the marginal product of health (MPH) times a constant wage, the downward slope of the MEC is due to the diminishing marginal product of health. The MEC curve can be interpreted as the demand curve for health capital.

The MEC reflects the marginal benefits to investing in health. Each additional unit of health stock results in more healthy days, which raises the individual's earnings capacity. The question then becomes: What is the optimal level of health stock that the individual should invest in? Since investing in health requires resources, the individual needs to compare the benefits (MEC) to the cost of investing in health capital. The cost of health capital is similar to the cost of any durable good. Consider, for instance, the cost of owning a house for a year. Part of the cost comes from the opportunity cost or the borrowing cost of funds, which is typically the real interest rate.[8] Since capital goods depreciate over time, the cost should also include this depreciation. Thus, if the real interest rate is 5 percent and the depreciation rate is 3 percent, then the cost of owning a $300,000 home for a year is approximately $2,400: Cost of Home $\cdot$ $(r + \delta)$. Similarly, the cost of an additional unit of health stock is the cost of this investment (C) multiplied by the sum of the real interest rate (r) and the depreciation rate (δ).

(A2–9) $$\text{Cost-of-capital} = C \cdot (r + \delta)$$

The first term in the cost-of-capital, the cost of health investment (C), includes the price of the resources used to invest in an additional unit of health. This would include, for instance, the price of medical care and the foregone wages (since investing in health also requires time). Suppose that raising the health stock by one unit requires the following resources:

a. Three visits to the physician (at a cost of $300 each, plus a full day off from work for each visit valued at a daily wage rate of $100)
   Total Cost = $1,200
b. Prescription medications (at a cost of $200)
   Total Cost = $200
c. Daily exercise (total of seven days in a year, valued at a daily wage rate of $100)
   Total Cost = $700
d. Vitamin supplements (at a cost of $400)
   Total Cost = $400

The cost (C) of the resources needed for increasing the health stock by one unit in this example is therefore $2,500.[9] (This is similar to the cost of buying the home for $300,000, mentioned earlier.) Assuming that the individual faces a real interest rate (r) of 7 percent and a depreciation rate (δ) of 5 percent, the cost-of-capital would be $2500 \cdot 12$ percent or $300. The extra unit of health stock is a durable good—it lasts and depreciates over multiple periods. Thus, similar to the cost of owning a home for one year, the *marginal cost of "buying" an additional unit of health stock for one year* is $300.

The cost-of-capital curve is also graphed in Figure A2–3. It can be interpreted as the supply curve of health capital. It is shown as a horizontal line since the individual is assumed to be a price taker, similar to a firm in a perfectly competitive market. That is, the individual typically does not have control over the market prices or the real interest rate. Regardless of how many times he may visit the doctor or how many

---

8. The real rate of interest is the nominal rate adjusted for inflation.

9. The marginal cost of the resources depends on the relative mix of time versus market inputs used in the health investment. For instance, exercising may be relatively more time-intensive and thus its cost is more likely to reflect the opportunity cost of time (wage rate), whereas taking vitamin supplements do not require a lot of time but do require market purchases and therefore their costs are more likely to reflect the price of the market-purchased inputs.

medications he may buy, the individual generally faces a constant price which is independent of his actions. The depreciation rate in Grossman's model is also more reflective of genetics and the biological progression of health over the life cycle, and therefore assumed to be independent of the health stock. Thus, the cost-of-capital is constant for the individual.[10]

Going back to our original question: What is the optimal level of health stock that the individual should invest in? The rational individual will invest up to the point where the marginal efficiency of capital (MEC) equals the cost-of-capital. In Figure A2–3, this occurs at a health stock of H*.[11] Any level of health stock to the left of H* (e.g., H_1) would not be optimal because the benefits to increasing health (MEC) still exceeds the cost of the additional health capital. Thus, the individual should continue investing in health beyond H_1. Any level of health stock to the right of H* (e.g., H_2) would also not be optimal since at this point the individual has "over-invested" in health; the costs (cost-of-capital) are exceeding the benefits (MEC). Thus, the individual should reduce their investment in health from H_2. The optimal health stock is therefore H* where the costs of investment equal the benefits. In our previous example, we noted that the cost-of-capital is $300 for this individual. Thus, referring to Table A2–1, the optimal health stock for the individual would be 18 units—where MEC = Cost-of-capital = $300. Investing in 14 units of the health stock is suboptimal because additional investment (going from 14 units to 15 units) costs only $300 but will yield benefits of $600. Investing in 20 units is also suboptimal because this investment (going from 19 to 20 units) costs $300 but yields only $100 in benefits.[12]

Shifts in Equilibrium

The pure-investment version of Grossman's model can be used to predict changes in health investment in response to various factors, such as age, wage rate, education, and the price of medical care. These factors affect investments in health by affecting either the cost-of-capital and/or the MEC.

Age. Grossman allows the depreciation rate (δ) to depend on age. He notes that after some point in the life cycle it is highly likely that the depreciation rate increases with age due to the biological processes of aging. For instance, the individual's physical strength and memory capacity diminish with age, consistent with an increase in depreciation over the life cycle. Our joints wear out with age. Each year that we grow older, the time it takes for our heart muscles to squeeze and relax grows longer, by 2 to 5 percent on average.[13] Figure A2–4 shows the effects of a higher depreciation rate, because of age, on the health stock. Specifically, an increase in the depreciation rate (from δ_1 to δ_2 to δ_3) with age raises the cost-of-capital and shifts this supply curve of health capital upwards. Thus, the pure-investment model predicts that the optimal health stock will decline (from H_1^* to H_2^* to H_3^*) as the equilibrium shifts from point A to point B to point C. At some point, as the depreciation rate continues to rise, the health stock will fall below H_{MIN}, and death occurs. In this sense, the optimal life span

---

10. The cost-of-capital would be a positively sloped curve if there are rising costs associated with greater and greater investments in health. Grossman (2000) and Ehrlich and Chuma (1990) consider this possibility.

11. This equilibrium of H* is based on individuals demanding health purely for its investment aspects. In general, individuals demand health both for its investment aspect (it reduces sick time and raises earnings) and for its consumptive aspects (individuals enjoy feeling healthy, and health raises utility). In a general model with both consumption and investment effects, the equilibrium level of health stock would be to the right of H*.

12. Grossman (1972) compares the MEC, in percentage terms, to the supply cost-of-capital, in percentage terms: $(MPH \cdot W)/C = (r + \delta)$. For convenience of exposition, we compare the MEC, in monetary $ terms, to the supply cost-of-capital, in monetary $ terms: $MPH \cdot W = C \cdot (r + \delta)$. Note that, except for the units of comparison, both conditions are equivalent.

13. See: http://www.hopkinsmedicine.org/news/media/releases/aging_heart_changes_shape_shrinks_and_loses_pumping_function_too

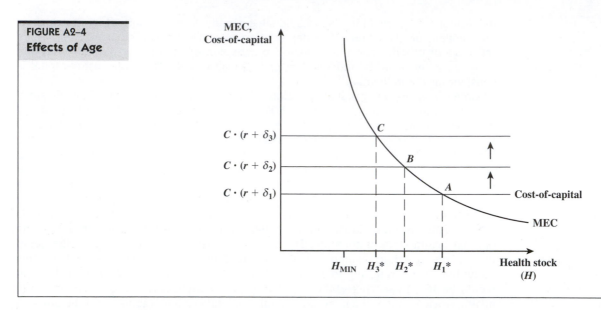

FIGURE A2–4
Effects of Age

This figure illustrates what happens to the optimal health stock as an individual ages and physical strength and memory diminish. As an individual ages, the depreciation rate (δ) increases causing the cost-of-capital to shift upward. As a result, the optimal health stock declines form H_1^* to H_2^* to H_3^*. At some point in the aging process, the optimal health stock falls below H_{MIN} and death occurs.

is to some extent controlled by the individual through his or her decisions over the life cycle that affect health (Grossman 2000). For instance, the choice to remain a lifelong smoker reduces life expectancy on average by about 10 years relative to a never-smoker[14]. Studies that seek to explain differences in health status across individuals therefore typically take into account differences in age; regardless of how health is measured (whether it be self-reported health, activity limitations, measures of specific illness conditions, or mortality), these studies find that after some point health generally deteriorates with age.[15]

Since the increase in the depreciation rate is a biological aging-related phenomenon, individuals have an incentive to partly offset the higher depreciation with an increase in their health investments, all else equal. Recall Equation A2–2, which suggests that tomorrow's stock of health capital depends on depreciation as well as investments undertaken today. Under reasonable assumptions, the model therefore predicts that individuals will raise their investment in health as they age.[16] Thus, older (unhealthy) individuals will make larger investments in health than younger (healthier) individuals.

One way to invest in health, especially as one gets older, is through medical care inputs. Thus, another prediction of the model is that older individuals demand more medical care, which accords well with what we observe. The average person between the ages of 55 and 64 years spent $7,787 on health care in 2004, compared to persons between the ages of 45 and 54 who spent $5,210, and persons between the 19 and 44 years of age who spent $3,370.[17]

---

14. Doll et al. (2004). Every cigarette smoked reduces average life expectancy by 11 minutes (http://www.medical newstoday.com/releases/9703.php).

15. See for instance Dave et al. (2008) and Strauss et al. (1993).

16. Specifically, Grossman shows that a sufficient condition for gross investment in health to rise with age is an inelastic demand curve for health capital. Thus, if the MEC schedule has an elasticity magnitude (in absolute value) below unity, then investment in health rises with age even as the optimal level of health falls.

17. Source: https://www.cms.gov/NationalHealthExpendData/. Individuals over the age of 65 years spent $14,797, though this partially includes the effect of obtaining insurance through Medicare at age 65.

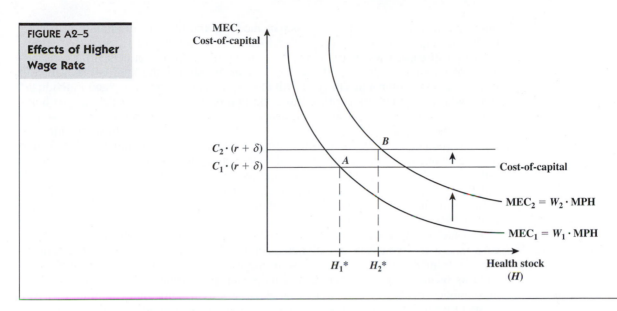

FIGURE A2–5

Effects of Higher Wage Rate

Recall the MEC equals the marginal product of health times the wage rate. As the wage rate increases and the opportunity cost of being sick increases, the MEC shifts upward from MEC_1 to MEC_2. The increase in the wage rate also causes the cost-of-capital curve to shift upward because time is an input in the production process. Notice that the optimal stock of health stock increases from H1* to H2* with an increase in the wage rate. This is because the shift of the health capital demand curve is greater than the shift in the cost-of-capital curve. In this case, the individual now invests more in health because on net the returns to health investment are greater.

Wage. Figure A2–5 shows the effects of a higher wage rate (from W_1 to W_2). Note that the MEC equals the wage rate (W) times the marginal product of health (MPH): $MEC = W \cdot MPH$. Thus, higher wages lead to a higher marginal efficiency of investment. In other words, an individual with a higher wage rate has a higher opportunity cost of being sick; since investments in health reduce time lost to illness and this extra time can be used to earn income, higher wages raise the return to health. This shifts the MEC or the demand curve for health capital upwards (from MEC_1 to MEC_2). The higher wage rate will also raise the cost of producing health (from C_1 to C_2), since time is an input into health production. Thus, the supply cost-of-capital curve will also shift upward. However, as long as health is produced using both time and market inputs (and not solely time), then the upward shift in the MEC curve will exceed the upward shift in the supply curve.[18] Thus, the individual now invests more in health since the net returns to health investment are higher. A person making $1000 a day has more to lose from getting the flu in terms of foregone earnings, relative to someone who earns the minimum wage. The equilibrium shifts from point A to point B, and the optimal health stock is higher for higher-wage individuals (H_2^* vs. H_1^*).

This prediction of the Grossman model that, all else equal, higher-wage individuals are healthier is consistent with empirical research.[19] A related prediction of the

---

18. In the extreme case, if health is produced using only time, then both curves shift by the same amount and there is no change in health status. However, this is not realistic since generally all forms of health investment require some combination of time and market inputs. Even exercising requires a lot of time combined with the proper attire and sneakers, for instance!

19. Lee (1982) accounts for the joint causality between wages and health (e.g., higher wages can lead to better health, as predicted by the Grossman model, but better health can also raise productivity and wages), and concludes that wages have a strong positive effect on the demand for good health. Bolin et al. (2002) account for the dynamic properties of the demand for health and also largely find support for the predictions of the Grossman model with respect to the effects of age, wage, and education (discussed next). The prediction that higher wages lead to better health because of greater health investments can also potentially explain part of the income-health gradient, which is the empirical observation that higher income and better health go hand-in-hand (Cutler et al., 2011).

pure-investment version of the Grossman model is that retirement should also affect health through its effect on wages. Specifically, since retirement is associated with a reduction in earned wages (to zero), the returns to health investment drop considerably postretirement. This would lead to a downward shift in the MEC curve, which in turn lowers the optimal health stock. All else equal, comparing same-aged individuals, those who are retired are predicted to be in poorer health. This prediction also holds when we allow for the consumption aspects of health in addition to the investment aspects, as long as the consumption value of health does not sufficiently increase after retirement. That is, as long as retired and nonretired individuals enjoy feeling healthy about the same, then the model predicts a decline in health status due to retirement. There has also been some empirical support for this prediction. Dave et al. (2008) study physical and mental health status for the same individuals over a 13-year period and find that retirement leads to about 4 to 6 percent increase in illnesses and 6 to 9 percent decline in mental health.

Given that wages lead to better health, how do wages affect the demand for medical care? There are two effects at play here. The first is the scale effect. Since the demand for health increases due to an increase in the wage rate, the demand for health inputs such as medical care also increases. This is similar to saying that if the demand for automobiles increased, and producers wish to manufacture more output, then the demand for inputs such as steel will also increase. The second effect is the substitution effect. A higher wage rate raises the opportunity cost of time. Since health can be produced using both time and market-purchased inputs such as medical care (as shown in Equation A2–3), the individual will substitute away from time and toward medical care since time is now more costly. Thus, for instance, a high-wage individual may decide to control their cholesterol using prescription drugs rather than with daily exercise since the opportunity cost of time is higher. Both the scale effect and the substitution effect reinforce each other and predict that an increase in the wage rate will increase the demand for medical care.[20]

Education.   A stylized fact in health economics is the strong positive correlation between education and health. In terms of just about all measures of health, persons with higher levels of schooling tend to be in better health. Furthermore, this effect persists even after controlling for income which on average is higher among educated persons. A 25-year-old who did not go beyond high school is expected to live up to 74.6 years on average, whereas a 25-year-old with at least some college education can look forward to an extra 7 years in life expectancy.[21] There are several reasons that may explain the association between education and health. Victor Fuchs (1982) proposed that this association reflected an underlying "third factor"—namely time preference, or how present- or future- oriented a person is.[22] Fuchs noted that individuals who are forward-looking are more likely to invest in their schooling as well as in their health, hence leading to a positive correlation between schooling and health.[23] According to Fuchs, there is no causal relationship between schooling and health; the correlation is being driven by some other third factor. Other possible "third factors" also include parental investments and parental education, which may affect both their

20. See, for instance, Coffey (1983), who shows that the time price is a significant determinant of the probability of seeking medical care, as well as the probability of seeking a public versus private provider.

21. See Meara, Richards, and Cutler (2008).

22. Also see Farrell and Fuchs (1982) for an application of this hypothesis to cigarette smoking.

23. An alternative interpretation is that time preference is "endogenous," that is, time preference itself may be a function of factors such as schooling (Becker and Mulligan 1997). Higher levels of schooling may lead individuals to become more future-oriented, and thereby increase their investments in health. An individual, who makes greater educational investments, also has a stronger incentive to make investments in his or her health to prolong life expectancy so as to maximize the period over which the returns from the higher education can be realized. According to this interpretation, education is causal on health by affecting an individual's time preference and planning horizon.

children's education and health. Another reason for the positive association between health and schooling may reflect causality from better health to more schooling. For instance, healthier children and youths (perhaps due to genetic reasons or parental upbringing) may be more productive at school; they may be less likely to miss school due to illnesses and may be better able to process information. This may lead them to become more educated and healthy adults.

Grossman (1972, 2000) suggested a different explanation: it is education which causes better health. He proposed that education raises an individual's efficiency in health production. Schooling plays a similar role for the individual that technology plays for the firm—they both enhance the efficiency of the production process. As shown in Figure A2–1, higher levels of education shift the health production function upwards and raise the marginal product of health. For the same expenditures on inputs, a more educated person can derive more health output. For instance, even if a higher- and lower-educated individual visit a doctor for the same amount of time, the higher-educated individual may be using their time with their doctor more efficiently— knowing the right questions to ask, better translating their doctor's advice into better health, remembering to take their medications on time, and instituting changes in lifestyle.[24]

Figure A2–6 shows the effects of an increase in education on health capital. Education raises the marginal product of health (from MPH_1 to MPH_2); this reflects an increase in efficiency in the production of health. The higher MPH raises the marginal benefits or returns to health investment, and shifts the MEC curve upwards (from MEC_1 to MEC_2). The new equilibrium now occurs at point B, representing an increase in the optimal health stock.

FIGURE A2–6 **Effects of Higher Education**	

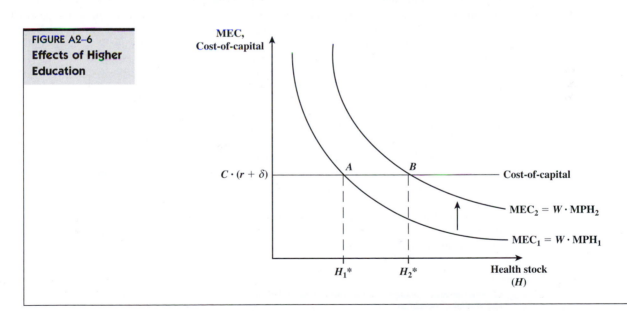

Education causes the marginal product of health to increase because the individual is now a more efficient producer of health. Since the marginal efficiency of capital equals the marginal product health times the wage rate, the MEC shifts upward from MEC_1 to MEC_2. As a result, the optimal health stock increases from H_1^* to H_2^*.

---

24. Goldman and Smith (2002) show that higher-educated HIV patients are more likely to adhere to their medication therapy, including the highly active antiretroviral treatments that became available in the mid-1990s. Such adherence to therapy in turn leads to improvements in health. They conclude that adherence to therapy by higher-educated persons appears to be an important mechanism through which schooling can improve health among those with a new illness condition when a new treatment regime is introduced.

Several studies have tested this prediction of the Grossman model and conclude in support of the hypothesis that higher education causes better health. Lleras-Muney (2005), for instance, uses U.S. compulsory education laws, which have raised years of schooling, to show that higher education causes lower mortality. Specifically, her estimates indicate that an additional year of schooling lowers the probability of dying in the next ten years by 3.6 percentage points. Educated individuals also tend to have better lifestyles, including lower rates of alcohol and cigarette consumption and higher rates of exercise. About 20 percent of the increase in life-expectancy among higher-educated individuals relative to those who are lower-educated between 1981 and 2000 can be explained by the lower prevalence of smoking among the former (Meara et al., 2008). Kenkel (1991) finds that part of the reason that schooling helps people choose such healthier lifestyles is "by improving the knowledge of the relationships between health behaviors and health outcomes." Educated individuals are more *allocatively* efficient at producing health, meaning that they choose a different and more health-promoting mix of health inputs relative to low-educated individuals.[25] In support of this allocative efficiency hypothesis, Kenkel (1994) also finds that educated persons have a higher demand and utilization of preventive care.

The model unambiguously predicts that educated individuals will be healthier; however, the effect of higher education on the demand for medical care is mixed, depending on which of two effects dominate. The scale effect suggests that since education raises the demand for health capital, it will also increase the demand for health care inputs such as medical care. However, education makes persons more efficient at producing health—therefore, they do not need as many resources. This efficiency effect suggests that education reduces the demand for medical care. Consider a parallel scenario wherein new technology substantially raises the fuel efficiency of cars. This will increase the overall output of cars. However, effects on the total demand for gasoline are ambiguous. On the one hand, more cars mean a higher demand for gasoline (scale effect). But, on the other hand, each car uses less gasoline since it is more fuel-efficient; this would reduce the demand for gasoline, all else equal (efficiency effect). Thus, how education affects the demand for medical care depends on whether the scale or the efficiency effect is greater.[26]

Price of Medical Care. An increase in the price of medical care raises the cost (C) of investing in health. This raises the cost-of-capital $[C \cdot (r + \delta)]$, and results in an upward shift of the horizontal supply curve.[27] Hence, there is a decrease in the optimal health stock. With respect to the demand for medical care, there are again two effects at play—and both predict that an increase in medical care prices will reduce the demand for medical care. The scale effect indicates that, since the individual's optimal health output is lower, he needs and therefore demands less medical care to produce the lower level of health. The substitution effect relates to the optimal mix of inputs to be used in producing a given output. Since the price of medical care is now higher, and wages (and all other factors) are assumed to remain unchanged, it is cheaper for individuals

---

25. See Grossman (2006) and Grossman and Kaestner (1997) for a summary of the evidence bearing on this question of whether education causes health.

26. The empirical evidence on the association between education and medical care is somewhat mixed, depending on the type of care being studied. Pohlmeier and Ulrich (1995), for instance, find that higher levels of schooling reduce visits to a general practitioner but raise visits to a specialist. They note that since education correlates with medical knowledge, higher-educated persons may favor specialists over general practitioners (GPs). Also, since a higher education can improve individuals' health more efficiently, they may need less contact with a general practitioner (which would suggest that the efficiency effect dominates the scale effect for GPs). Kenkel (1994) finds that higher levels of education lead to a higher demand for preventive services such as a breast exam and a pap test, consistent with educated individuals wanting to invest more in their health and being more allocatively efficient in health production. He notes that schooling effects for curative care are not consistent in other work.

27. The graph is similar to Figure A2–4, except that the supply curve is shifting upwards due to an increase in C (rather than an increase in δ, which was considered there).

to produce health using their time rather than with medical care. For instance, if the price of a doctor visit or prescription drugs increases, an individual might find it cheaper to produce health with exercise and diet rather than through medications and doctor visits.

The Grossman model thus predicts that the demand for medical care is downward sloping—higher prices lead to lower demand due to reinforcing scale and substitution effects. While this may seem like a conventional demand function, a key insight from the framework is that individuals do not demand medical care for its own sake. We do not enjoy taking prescription drugs or receiving flu shots; we demand these medical services because of our underlying demand for health. Hence, the demand for medical care in Grossman's theory is a demand for an input derived from the underlying demand for the output being produced, which is health. In other words, the demand for medical care is akin to an automobile manufacturer's demand for steel—an input whose demand is dictated by the underlying demand for cars. The notion that the demand for medical care is inversely related to its price is supported by a vast array of studies (e.g., see the discussion on the RAND Health Insurance Experiment in Chapter 5). For instance, the RAND Health Insurance Experiment found that individuals who were randomly assigned to more generous insurance plans (lower cost of medical care to the individual) used more healthcare services; the price elasticity estimates were negative in the inelastic −0.1 to −0.2 range (Manning et al. 1987). This is referred to as *ex post* moral hazard—the notion that more generous insurance raises health care utilization by reducing the consumer price of medical care.

The substitution effect relating to the price of medical care has also been studied. Specifically, one implication of the health production function (Equation A2–3) is that a decrease in the price of medical care may lead to the substitution of medical care for healthy behaviors and a healthy lifestyle. This is referred to as *ex ante* moral hazard. For instance, health insurance may give individuals less of an incentive to engage in a healthy lifestyle since having insurance reduces the cost of medical care and thereby reduces the cost of treatment if the individual gets sick, all else equal. Dave and Kaestner (2009) find evidence of such *ex ante* moral hazard among older adults. Individuals in the United States become eligible to receive health insurance through the government at age 65, which is known as Medicare. Dave and Kaestner find that individuals who were previously uninsured engage in more unhealthy behaviors—they are less likely to quit smoking, more likely to consume alcohol daily, and less likely to exercise—upon obtaining Medicare coverage at age 65.

Applications of the Grossman Model

Since the Grossman model offers insights into the determination of health, it provides a useful theoretical framework for empirically analyzing a wide range of policy issues relating to the individual and socioeconomic influences on health and health behaviors. The following section is meant to give a flavor of some of the areas of empirical study that have applied a Grossman-type framework. The reader is referred to Grossman (2000, 2006) and Bolin (2011) for more comprehensive surveys on theoretical extensions and empirical applications of the model.

Health Production Function. A vast literature has studied the effects of various inputs on health status, using both aggregate data as well as individual-level micro data. Many of these studies acknowledge the multi-dimensional nature of health production and analyze the effects of various market-based inputs and lifestyle choices. Thornton (2002), for instance, estimates a health production function for the United States, based on state-level information for 1990, considering the effects of medical care, socioeconomic status (education and income), lifestyle factors (cigarette and alcohol consumption), environmental factors (urbanization, crime, manufacturing), and demographics (race and gender) on the mortality rate. He finds that medical care spending in a state does not have any significant effects in terms of lowering mortality. This suggests that the marginal product of medical care is close to zero, and that the average state is likely located on the flat-of-the-curve of the production function shown in Figure A2–1. The largest effects, on the other hand, are found for lifestyle factors and socioeconomic status. Cigarette consumption raises the mortality rate, whereas higher levels of income and education in a state are associated with a lower mortality rate. Balia and Jones (2008) use individual-level longitudinal data from the British Health and Lifestyle Survey to study the determinants of premature mortality and the determinants of the socioeconomic inequality in premature mortality. They find significant effects of lifestyle factors such as smoking, sleep patterns, and obesity on health outcomes, and conclude that differences in these factors across socioeconomic groups contribute strongly to health inequalities. Llena-Nozal et al. (2004) estimate a production function for mental health, also based on longitudinal individual-level data. They find that the depreciation rate for mental health is lower when individuals are employed, and especially for females, they find large effects of occupation on mental health.

Another strand of related studies has estimated production functions for infant health. Rosenzweig and Schultz (1983) study the production of birthweight and fetal growth based on a sample of about 10,000 births in the United States. They account for biases resulting from unmeasured heterogeneity (for instance unobserved health endowments) and unmeasured determinants of efficiency across mothers. Their estimates suggest that maternal smoking and delaying prenatal care have substantial negative effects on birthweight. Corman et al. (1987), using county-level data, consider the effects of various health inputs including prenatal care, neonatal intensive care, abortion, environmental factors such as community health centers and family planning clinics, and the WIC (Women, Infants, and Children) Program on the production of race-specific neonatal mortality rates.[28] Their results point to the importance of abortion, prenatal care services, WIC, and neonatal intensive care in affecting birth outcomes, with black neonatal mortality rates being especially sensitive to the use of these basic health inputs. Reichman et al. (2009) use individual-level data on about 3,500 births in 19 U.S. cities to study production functions for birthweight and abnormal infant health conditions, based on a richer specification of health inputs than typically observed in other studies. Their estimates suggest that prenatal illicit drug use and smoking, pre-existing maternal health conditions and a sexually transmitted disease (STD) during pregnancy, pre-pregnancy maternal underweight status, maternal history of mental illness, and the wantedness of the pregnancy (whether the mother had considered an abortion) are significant inputs into infant health.

Recent studies have incorporated the effects of the macroeconomy, business cycle, and job-loss into health production functions. These studies seek to answer the question: "Are Recessions Good for Your Health?" (see the discussion on Ruhm, 2000 and 2003, in Chapter 2).While the results from this literature are generally mixed, the studies typically invoke Grossman's framework in discussing the potential pathways through which a recession may impact health and health behaviors. For instance, job-loss leads to a reduction in income (the income constraint in Equation A2–5 becomes tighter), an increase in the available time (the time endowment constraint in Equation A2–6 becomes looser), and a reduction in the opportunity cost of time due to a decrease in wages and market work opportunities. Thus, activities which are relatively time-intensive may increase during a recession. The *ex ante* moral hazard effect also suggests that if job-loss is associated with a loss of health care coverage, then individuals may be more incentivized to take better care of themselves, including

---

28. The neonatal mortality rate is defined as the number of infant deaths within the first 27 days of life per thousand live births.

exercising more. Xu and Kaestner (2010) and Colman and Dave (2011) both find that recreational exercise does indeed increase when the unemployment rate goes up.[29] Since time-intensive health inputs are relatively cheaper for an unemployed individual (due to the greater availability of time) and market-purchased inputs are now more constrained due to the reduction in income, individuals may also shift from more expensive market-based inputs to time-based inputs or toward other cheaper market inputs. Dave and Kelly (2011) find that individuals substitute away from the consumption of fruits and vegetables toward cheaper snacks and fast food during a recession, with this effect being driven primarily due to a decrease in real income and an increase in depression and stress associated with job-loss.

Risky Behaviors. The Grossman framework can also shed light on some of the determinants of risky behaviors such as smoking, illicit drug use, and obesity. For instance, cigarette consumption enters the production function (Equation A2–3) as a negative input into one's health. Yet, there are still many individuals who smoke. Grossman's framework assumes that individuals are rational, utility-maximizing individuals. Thus, if individuals are aware of the health costs of smoking, then the benefits of smoking (increase in utility) must be exceeding the costs of smoking (the monetary price and the health costs) for those who continue to smoke. The demand for cigarettes therefore includes both a consumption aspect (some individuals enjoy smoking and this experience raises utility) and also represents a derived input demand (demand for smoking is derived from an individual's underlying demand for health since smoking is a health input). Several studies have analyzed the demand for cigarettes, finding price elasticity estimates in the range of −0.3 to −0.5.[30] Evidence, based on U.S. data, also suggests that cigarettes are an inferior good, whose demand declines with income.

Becker and Murphy (1988) formalize a theory of rational addiction, wherein rational forward-looking individuals consume addictive substances because they derive utility from their consumption even though consumption may have adverse health effects. This contrasts with models of myopic addiction, wherein the future consequences are ignored when making current decisions.[31] In the Becker and Murphy framework, current utility depends on three commodities: (1) current consumption of the addictive good (A); (2) stock of the addictive good built up through past cumulative consumption (S); and (3) other non-addictive consumption (NA). They formally model the three traits of addiction, including reinforcement, tolerance, and withdrawal. The reinforcement effect is modeled by allowing the marginal utility of current addictive consumption to be affected by past consumption. Marginal utility denotes, for instance, the additional utility a person might derive from smoking one extra cigarette. This marginal utility depends positively on past consumption (S). Thus, the more cigarettes one has consumed in the past, the higher is their extra enjoyment (utility) from consuming one more cigarette today. By definition, a smoker would thus have a higher marginal utility from smoking an extra cigarette than a nonsmoker who has never consumed cigarettes. This "reinforcement" effect leads past and present consumption of addictive goods to be positively correlated for addictive goods; the more cigarettes one has consumed in the past, the more he is likely to consume today. Past consumption of addictive goods (S) also has an adverse effect on current health, and thus reduces current utility. This recognizes the fact that certain addictive substances

29. Colman and Dave (2011) find though that the total level of physical exertion during the day declines during a recession due to a decrease in work-related physical activity; the increase in exercise is not large enough to compensate for the decrease in work-related exertion.

30. See Chaloupka and Warner (2000) for an excellent survey on the economics of smoking, including theoretical and empirical extensions of economic models of addiction. Many of these issues relate to all addictive substances, including alcohol and illicit drugs.

31. A myopic agent takes account of the past but not the future. Thus, a rational forward-looking agent is maximizing a lifetime utility function, whereas a myopic individual is maximizing a current-period utility function.

(e.g., cigarettes and alcohol) are inputs into the health production function with a negative marginal product of health—they reduce the health stock. The reduction in current utility from higher levels of past consumption also represents a tolerance effect; a person would need to consume more cigarettes today than in the past to obtain the same level of utility. Finally, withdrawal is captured since total utility falls with the cessation of addictive consumption.

The rational addiction model makes several testable predictions, which have generally found support in empirical studies (Gruber and Köszegi, 2001; Chaloupka and Warner, 2000; Becker et al., 1994). For instance, consumption displays "intertemporal complementarity" due to the reinforcement effect. Past, present, and future levels of consumption of addictive goods are complements and therefore positively correlated. This also implies that the current consumption of an addictive good will be inversely related to the current price and also inversely related to the past as well as future prices. Thus, a higher cigarette excise tax today (which would raise cigarette prices) would lower the demand for cigarettes not only today, but also in the future. If this increase in excise tax was anticipated, it would also reduce the demand for cigarettes prior to when the actual increase takes place. Furthermore, the long-run effect of a permanent change in price (a change in price in all periods) will exceed the short-run effect.

Many researchers have also studied the determinants of obesity within a Grossman-type framework.[32] During the past three decades, the number of obese adults has more than doubled to about 34 percent of the population.[33] Since obesity is a function of the difference between calories consumed and calories expended over one's lifetime, a behavioral model of obesity needs to consider the determinants of caloric consumption and expenditure. As Chou et al., (2004) note, no one desires to be obese; rather obesity is a by-product of other factors that the individual desires such as health, palatable eating, and other activities. In other words, the following extensions can be built into the Grossman model: (1) Palatable eating (high calorie/high fat consumption) raises utility but also raises obesity. (2) Exercise may reduce utility for some individuals (some persons do not enjoy exercising per se), but also reduces obesity. (3) Obesity is a direct negative input into the production of one's health. Thus, certain experiences, such as a palatable meal or lack of rigorous exercise, directly raise utility because they are enjoyable but also indirectly reduce utility because they adversely affect one's health by increasing obesity.

This extension of the model highlights several factors that may have contributed to the higher prevalence of obesity. Higher real wage rates have raised the opportunity cost of time and also raised real income. More women have entered the labor force in the past three decades, which has reduced total available nonwork time for the household. All else equal, this would predict a decline in exercise (a relatively time-intensive activity). Furthermore, the production of meals would also substitute market inputs for time inputs, since income is higher but time is now more expensive and scarcer for the household. Thus, households are more likely to obtain their meals at restaurants and in the market rather than buying the ingredients and cooking at home. Restaurant-bought meals tend to be richer in calories and fat. There have also been changes in the monetary and nonmonetary price of certain health inputs. For instance, there are now more fast-food and full-service restaurants per capita, and the price per calorie at a fast-food restaurant has increased at a much lower rate than overall inflation. Thus, both the monetary and convenience costs of eating at fast-food restaurants have decreased, which would lead individuals to eat more at such establishments rather than cooking at home. In general, real food prices have trended downwards, which

---

32. See Chou, Grossman, and Saffer (2004), Dave and Kelly (2011), and Colman and Dave (2011) for instance.

33. Obesity is defined based on the body mass index (BMI). BMI is computed as weight in kilograms divided by height in meters squared. Based on the BMI, a person is classified as underweight (BMI < 18.5), normal-weight (BMI 18.5–24.9), overweight (BMI 25.0–29.9), and obese (BMI of 30 or above).

also contributes to greater food intake and in turn increased caloric consumption and obesity. Cigarette consumption is also an input into the production of obesity, since smoking has been found to suppress appetite and reduce bodyweight. Thus, the decline in smoking rates (partly due to the diffusion of information regarding the hazards of smoking and partly due to higher cigarette taxes) has also been found to contribute to the rise in obesity. This result points to an unintended consequence of the anti-smoking campaign.

Summary

Michael Grossman's model for the demand for health capital recognizes that individuals are not passive consumers of health. While our health certainly depends on genetics and certain random shocks, we have, and indeed exercise, active control over our health through decisions that we make everyday—getting a flu shot, keeping a doctor's appointment, forgoing a hamburger for a salad, stopping at the gym on the way home from work, putting an extra layer of clothes when the temperature drops, postponing the decision to quit smoking, and so on. This insight that individuals demand and produce health, and that health is a capital good that yields returns in the form of higher potential earnings, allows us to study this commodity health through the use of standard economic tools and principles. Indeed, empirical studies have investigated the determinants of the demand for health (e.g., wages, medical care prices, education, age, and depreciation rates) and how various inputs affect the production of health capital for both adults and infants (e.g., medical care services, risky behaviors such as smoking, drinking, illicit drug use, and obesity, environmental factors such as crime and neighborhood effects, unemployment, and such). Grossman's model also frames the demand for medical care as the demand for a derived input, based on our underlying demand for health. Since a given level of health may be produced using different combinations of inputs, our demand for health is affected by changes in the opportunity cost of time, changes in the prices of various inputs, and changes in technology and efficiency in health production.

The Grossman model assumes that individuals are rational, forward-looking, and have full information. Rationality implies that individuals weigh all costs and benefits associated with their actions. While such a comparison may not be made mechanically in all cases, individuals typically do consider the costs and benefits when making major decisions, for instance those relating to schooling, occupational choice, and health. Are individuals forward-looking? That is, do they consider not just the current costs and benefits, but also those realized in the future? While individuals can certainly differ from one another with respect to the rate of time preference, there is indeed evidence that on average they do have a time horizon beyond just the present. Gruber and Köszegi (2001), for instance, find strong evidence that individuals' consumption of cigarettes drops when there are announced future tax increases. This implies forward-looking behavior. Individuals also regularly invest in activities that typically yield little current benefits but substantial future benefits such as schooling and preventive care. Perfect information and certainty are abstractions, often invoked to keep our models simple and tractable.[34] Even if the individual has an incentive to make decisions based on all available information, gathering information sometimes entails costs. And, especially in healthcare, there are strong informational asymmetries between consumers and providers, and a great deal of uncertainty with respect to health-related decisions and outcomes. Individuals are never quite sure about the actual costs and benefits of their actions—how much will consuming this extra pack of cigarettes hurt my health (not the average person's health, but *my*

34. See Grossman (2000) for a survey of studies that have extended the model to incorporate uncertainty.

personal health)?; how will this prescription medication affect me personally?; how effective will be the angioplasty, that the doctor is recommending, in preventing a heart attack? While all of these are undoubtedly strong assumptions, they make the economic models less complex and yield predictions that can then be tested empirically.[35]

Review Questions and Problems

1. Discuss how health can be classified as a "consumption" good as well as an "investment" good?
2. Explain the basic structure of the Grossman model, based on the seven equations that comprise the model.
3. With the help of a graph, discuss the concept of a health production function. In what sense is the individual considered a "producer" of health in the Grossman model?
4. Explain the education-health causality debate in the context of the Grossman model. What does the model say about the education-health relationship—that is, how does education affect the optimal health stock in the model? What are some other explanations of the observed positive relation between education and health?
5. Discuss how the optimal demand for health is determined in the Grossman model based on the MEC and cost-of-capital.
6. What is the effect of an increase in education on the demand for medical care?
7. What is the effect of an increase in wages on the demand for medical care?
8. Using the Grossman model, discuss what happens to the demand for health and the demand for medical care when the price of medical care (P_m) increases.
9. Using the Grossman model, discuss two factors that may have led to the increase in obesity in the United States.
10. Using the Grossman model, discuss two factors that may explain why individuals in less developed nations have a lower life expectancy relative to those in more developed nations.

References

Balia, S., and Jones, A. "Mortality, Lifestyle, and Socio-economic Status." *Journal of Health Economics* 27 (2008), pp. 1–26.

Becker, G. S. *Human Capital.* New York: Columbia University Press, 1964.

Becker, G. S. "Nobel Lecture: The Economic Way of Looking at Behavior." *Journal of Political Economy* 101 (1993), pp. 385–409.

Becker, G. S., Grossman, M., and Murphy, K. M. "An Empirical Analysis of Cigarette Addiction." *American Economic Review* 84 (1994), pp. 396–418.

Becker, G. S., and Mulligan, C. B. "The Endogenous Determination of Time Preference."

Quarterly Journal of Economics 112 (1997), pp. 729–58.

Becker, G. S., and Murphy, K. M. "A Theory of Rational Addiction." *Journal of Political Economy* 96 (1988), pp. 675–700.

Bolin, K. "Health Production." In *Oxford Handbook of Health Economics*, eds. S. Glied and P. C. Smith. New York: Oxford University Press, 2011, pp. 95–123.

Bolin, K., Jacobson, L., and Lindgren, B. "The Demand for Health and Health Investments in Sweden." In *Individuals Decisions for Health*, eds. B. Lindgren. London: Routledge, 2002, pp. 93–112.

---

35. See Becker's Nobel Lecture (1993) for a discussion of the economist's view of the individual and the assumptions under which he/she makes decisions. Becker notes that "no approach of comparable generality has yet been developed that offers serious competition to rational choice theory."

Chaloupka, F., and Warner, K. "The Economics of Smoking." In *Handbook of Health Economics,* Volume IB, eds. A. J. Culyer and J. P. Newhouse. Amsterdam: Elsevier Science, 2000, pp. 1539–627.

Chou, S., Grossman, M., and Saffer, H. "An Economic Analysis of Adult Obesity: Results from the Behavioral Risk Factor Surveillance System." *Journal of Health Economics* 23 (2004), pp. 565–87.

Coffey, R. "The Effect of Time Price on the Demand for Medical Care." *Journal of Human Resources* 18 (1983), pp. 406–24.

Colman, G. and Dave, D. "Exercise, Physical Activity, and Exertion over the Business Cycle." National Bureau of Economic Research (NBER) Working Paper No. 17406. NBER: 2011.

Corman, H., Joyce, T. J., and Grossman, M. "Birth Outcome Production Function in the United States." *Journal of Human Resources* 22 (1987), pp. 339–60.

Cutler, D., Lleras-Muney, A., and Vogl, T. "Socioeconomic Status and Health: Dimensions and Mechanisms." In *Oxford Handbook of Health Economics,* eds. S. Glied, S., and P. C. Smith. New York: Oxford University Press, 2011, pp. 124–63.

Dave, D., and Kaestner, R. "Health Insurance and Ex Ante Moral Hazard: Evidence from Medicare." *International Journal of Health Care Finance and Economics* 9 (2009), pp. 367–90.

Dave, D., and Kelly, I. "How does the Business Cycle Affect Eating Habits?" *Social Science and Medicine*, Novermber 19, 2011, http://www.sciencedirect.com/science/article/pii/S0277953611006460, accessed April 1, 2012.

Dave, D., Rashad, I., and Spasojevic, J. "The Effects of Retirement on Physical and Mental Health Outcomes." *Southern Economic Journal* 75 (2008), pp. 497–523.

Doll, R., Peto, R., Boreham, J., and Sutherland, I. "Mortality in Relation to Smoking: 50 Years' Observations on Male British Doctors." *British Medical Journal* 328 (2004), pp. 1519–528.

Ehrlich, I., and Chuma, H. "A Model of the Demand for Longevity and the Value of Life Extensions." *Journal of Political Economy* 98 (1990), pp. 761–82.

Farrell, P., and Fuchs, V. "Schooling and Health: The Cigarette Connection." *Journal of Health Economics* 1 (1982), pp. 217–30.

Fuchs, V. "The Contribution of Health Services to the American Economy." *Milbank Memorial Fund Quarterly* 44 (1966), pp. 65–102.

Fuchs, V. *Who Shall Live? Health, Economics, and Social Choice*. New York: Basic Books Inc., 1974.

Fuchs, V. "Time Preference and Health: An Exploratory Study." In *Economics Aspects of Health,* eds. V. Fuchs. Chicago: University of Chicago Press, 1982, pp. 93–120.

Goldman, D. P., and Smith, J. P. "Can Patient Self-Management Help Explain the SES Health Gradient?" *Proceedings of the National Academy of Sciences of the United States* 99 (2002), pp. 10929–934.

Grossman, M. "On the Concept of Health Capital and the Demand for Health." *Journal of Political Economy* 80 (1972), pp. 223–55.

Grossman, M. "The Human Capital Model." In *Handbook of Health Economics*, Volume IA, eds. A. J. Culyer and J. P. Newhouse. Amsterdam: Elsevier, 2000, pp. 347–408.

Grossman, M. "The Demand for Health, 30 Years Later: A Very Personal Retrospective and Prospective Reflection." *Journal of Health Economics* 23 (2004), pp. 629–36.

Grossman, M. "Education and Non-market Outcomes." In *Handbook of the Economics of Education*, Vol. 1, eds. E. Hanushek and F. Welch. Amsterdam: North-Holland, Elsevier Science, 2006, pp. 577–633.

Grossman, M., and Kaestner, R. "Effects of Education on Health." In *The Social Benefits of Education,* eds. J. R. Behrman and N. Stacey. Ann Arbor: University of Michigan Press, 1997, pp. 69–123.

Gruber, J., and Köszegi, B. "Is Addiction 'Rational'? Theory and Evidence." *Quarterly Journal of Economics* 116 (2001), pp. 1261–303.

Kenkel, D. S. "Health Behavior, Health Knowledge, and Smoking." *Journal of Political Economy* 99 (1991), pp. 287–305.

Kenkel, D. S. "The Demand for Preventive Medical Care." *Applied Economics* 26 (1994), pp. 313–25.

Lee, L. E. "Health and Wage: A Simultaneous Equation Model with Multiple Discrete Indicators." *International Economic Review* 23 (1982), pp. 199–221.

Llena-Nozal, A., Lindeboom, M., and Portrait, F. "The Effect of Work on Mental Health: Does Occupation Matter?" *Health Economics* 13 (2004), pp. 1045–62.

Lleras-Muney, A. "The Relationship between Education and Adult Mortality in the U.S." *Review of Economic Studies* 72 (2005), pp. 189–221.

Manning, W. G., Newhouse, J. P., Duan, N., Keeler, E. B., and Leibowitz, A. "Health Insurance and the Demand for Medical Care: Evidence from a Randomized Experiment." *The American Economic Review* 77 (1987), pp. 251–77.

Meara, E., Richards, S., and Cutler, D. "The Gap gets Bigger: Changes in Mortality and Life Expectancy by Education: 1981–2000." *Health Affairs* 27 (2008), pp. 350–60.

Mokdad, A. H., Marks, J. S., Stroup, D. F., and Gerberding, J. L. "Actual Causes of Death in the United States, 2000." *Journal of the American Medical Association* 291 (2004), pp. 1238–245.

Mokdad, A. H., Marks, J. S., Stroup, D. F., and Gerberding, J. L. "Correction: Actual Causes of Death in the United States, 2000." *Journal of the American Medical Association* 293 (2005), pp. 293–94.

Pohlmeier, W., and Ulrich, V. "An Econometric Model of the Two-Part Decisionmaking Process in the Demand for Health Care." *Journal of Human Resources* 30 (1995), pp. 339–61.

Reichman, N. E., Corman, H., Noonan, K., and Dave, D. "Infant Health Production Functions: What a Difference the Data Make." *Health Economics* 18 (2009), pp. 761–82.

Rosenzweig, M. R., and Schultz, T. P. "Estimating a Household Production Function: Heterogeneity, the Demand for Health Inputs, and their Effects on Birth Weight." *Journal of Political Economy* 91 (1983), pp. 723–46.

Ruhm, C. J., "Are Recessions Good for Your Health?" *Quarterly Journal of Economics* 115 (2000), pp. 617–50.

Strauss, J., Gertler, P., Rahman, O., and Fox, K. "Gender and Life-Cycle Differentials in the Patterns and Determinants of Adult Health." *Journal of Human Resources* 28 (1993), pp. 791–836.

Thornton, J. "Estimating a Health Production Function for the U.S.: Some New Evidence." *Applied Economics* 34 (2002), pp. 59–62.

Xu, X., and Kaestner, R. "The Business Cycle and Health Behaviors." National Bureau of Economic Research (NBER) Working Paper No. 15737. NBER: 2010.

CHAPTER 3

Cost and Benefit Evaluation Methods

Every day decisions are made in the health care sector concerning the best or most efficient amount of medical care to provide. At some juncture in the decision-making process, the all-important question becomes: At what point does the added costs of providing more medical care outweigh the benefits in terms of improved health? In practice, the answer to this question is complex because costs and benefits depend on such factors as the availability of medical resources, patient preferences, and the severity of illnesses.

Consider an adult who complains to a physician about chest pains during an annual physical exam. The first thing the physician must do is determine the seriousness of the problem. The pain could simply be the result of stress or could be a sign of more serious trouble, such as an impending heart attack (remember Joe at the beginning of Chapter 1?). When confronted with a patient's chest pains, a physician faces several options. For example, one clinical professor of medicine says,

> To assess chest pain … we can take a history and a physical examination for $100; do an exercise test for $500; perform a nuclear stress test for $1,500; or do coronary angiography for $5,000. Each escalation in diagnostic approach improves the accuracy of diagnosis from 50 percent to 60 to 80 to 100 percent. (Rubenstein, 1994)

Basically, a cost effective medical procedure is chosen by comparing the incremental costs of progressively more expensive medical tests with the benefits of additional medical information provided by greater diagnostic capabilities.

This chapter examines how costs and benefits affect medical decisions from the point of view of a health policy maker who is attempting to make informed choices concerning the production or allocation of medical care services. The information provided will make you more knowledgeable about such important concepts as costs, benefits, and efficiency. Specifically, this chapter:

- introduces cost identification analysis
- reviews the theory underlying cost-benefit analysis
- illustrates how cost-benefit analysis can be used to make health care decisions
- explains the concept of discounting to take into account those costs and benefits resulting from health care decisions that occur over time
- discusses the monetary value of a life using the human capital and willingness-to-pay approaches
- introduces cost-effectiveness analysis as an alternative to cost-benefit analysis
- introduces cost-utility analysis and the concept of a quality-adjusted life-year (QALY)
- analyzes the implications of the Patient Protection and Affordable Care Act (PPACA) of 2010 with regard to the material provided in this chapter.

Cost Identification Analysis

The first type of analysis we consider is cost identification. Generally speaking, **cost identification studies,** or cost of illness studies, measure the total cost of a given medical condition or type of health behavior on the overall economy. The total cost imposed on society by a medical condition or a health behavior can be broken down into three major components:

1. Direct medical care costs
2. Direct nonmedical costs
3. Indirect costs

Direct medical care costs encompass all costs incurred by medical care providers, such as hospitals, physicians, and nursing homes. They include the cost of all necessary medical tests and examinations, the cost of administering medical care, and the cost of any follow-up treatments. An abbreviated list of the specific costs considered are inpatient and outpatient hospital care, nursing home care, hospice care, rehabilitation care, diagnostic equipment, and drugs.

Direct nonmedical costs represent all monetary costs imposed on any nonmedical care personnel, including patients. For the patient, direct nonmedical costs include the cost of transportation to and from the medical care provider, in addition to any other costs borne directly by the patient. For example, the patient may require home health care or have specific dietary restrictions. Other costs may also be influenced by the specific treatment delivered. For example, the cost of instituting a substance abuse program in the workplace includes not only the direct medical costs of drug and alcohol rehabilitation but also any nonmedical costs the firm incurs while implementing and overseeing the program. Family members may be financially affected as well.

Indirect costs consist primarily of the time costs associated with implementation of the treatment. Indirect costs include the opportunity cost of the patient's (or anyone else's) time that the program affects, especially because many health behaviors and medical conditions result in lost productivity due to injury, disability, or loss of life. Consider the substance abuse program previously discussed. Costs should reflect the opportunity costs of the time needed to educate workers about the potential dangers of substance abuse. The time cost is borne by the employer and equals the value of forgone production.

By and large, cost identification studies consider the direct medical care and indirect costs associated with medical actions or adverse health behaviors. For example, a study sponsored by the Society of Actuaries (Behan and Cox, 2010) estimated the total cost of being overweight and obese in the United States and Canada at $300 billion in 2009. Of that total, 42 percent can be attributed to the cost of medical care while the remaining 58 percent results from excess mortality and disability. Dall et al. (2010) put the annual cost of pre-diabetes and diabetes at $218 billion in 2007, with $153 billion attributed to direct medical costs and the remaining $65 billion to indirect expenses such as reduced productivity. Finally, the American Heart Association (2011) sets the cost of cardiovascular diseases and stroke at $286.6 billion in 2007.

Cost identification studies like these are enlightening because they provide a sense of the total costs associated with various medical conditions or health behaviors and can be used to demonstrate which diseases may require additional medical resources. However, they provide little guidance for decision making. For example, what is the best, or most efficient, method to treat Alzheimer's disease? To answer questions like this, we must turn to other types of decision-making techniques, such as cost-benefit and cost-effectiveness analysis.

Cost-Benefit Analysis

As we learned in Chapter 1 with the introduction of production possibilities curve analysis, resource scarcity forces society to make choices. For example, an entire economy must collectively decide how much medical care to produce and who will receive it, while each health care provider must determine the most appropriate method to produce health care services. Even the consumer who has complete medical insurance coverage faces scarcity and choices because time is a finite commodity. The consumer must decide whether the time needed to make a doctor's appointment, travel to the physician's office, and receive medical services is worth the value of foregone activities. Thus, scarcity necessitates choice. As you are well aware, economics is the social science that analyzes the process by which society makes these choices.

Economists treat people as *rational* decision makers. **Rationality** means people know how to rank their preferences from high to low or best to worst. It also means that people never purposely choose to make themselves worse off. Consequently, it stands to reason that people will make choices based on their self-interests and choose those activities they expect will provide them with the most net satisfaction. Pursuing self-interest does not mean people are always selfish, however. For example, giving money to a charity, or volunteering one's time at a local hospital, gives even the most devout and good samaritan a considerable amount of pleasure.

The decision rule followed when choosing activities is straightforward and involves an assessment of the expected benefits and costs associated with each choice. If expected benefits exceed expected costs for a given choice, it is in the economic agent's best interest to make that choice. In formal terms, the optimizing rule looks like this:

(3–1)
$$NB^e(X) = B^e(X) - C^e(X)$$

where X represents a particular choice or activity under consideration, B^e stands for the expected benefits associated with the choice, C^e equals the expected costs resulting from the choice, and NB^e represents the expected net benefits.

If NB^e is larger than zero, the economic agent's well-being is enhanced by choosing the activity. The fact that you are reading this textbook indicates the book's expected benefits outweigh its expected costs (unless, of course, your professor forced you to buy and read it). That is, you expect this book to provide benefits in excess of the money you spent on it, plus the forgone use of your time. Nonreaders of this book obviously believe the costs outweigh the benefits, or that NB^e is negative.

Formal cost-benefit analysis utilizes the same net benefit calculus to establish the monetary value of all the costs and benefits associated with a given health policy decision. Such information is invaluable to policy makers who are under pressure to utilize scarce resources to generate the most good for society. To illustrate this point, let's suppose that an all-knowing benevolent dictator, called the "surgeon general," is responsible for ensuring the economic happiness of the people in some hypothetical society. The surgeon general realizes that people possess unlimited wants and that numerous goods and services, such as food, clothing, housing, medical care, and automobiles, provide them with satisfaction. The surgeon general also knows that scarcity of resources involves tradeoffs; that is, more of one good means less of the others.

The surgeon general's task is to maximize the social utility of the population by choosing the best aggregate mix of goods and services to produce and consume.[1]

---

1. In the context of the production possibilities curve, the surgeon general is trying to find the specific point that maximizes the collective well-being of the population. The surgeon general is assumed to accept the current distribution of income.

To accomplish this objective, the surgeon general has the power to allocate land, labor, and capital resources to any and all uses. Consistent with the maximization of the social utility received from all goods and services, we can think of the surgeon general as trying to maximize the **total net social benefit (TNSB)** from each and every good and service produced in the economy. The TNSB derived from a good or service is the difference between its total social benefit (TSB) in consumption and its total social cost (TSC) of production. The difference represents the net benefit, or gain, that the society receives from producing and consuming a particular amount of some good or service. The TSB can be treated as the money value of the satisfaction generated from consuming the good or service. The TSC can be looked at as the money value of all the resources used in producing the good or service.

For example, the TNSB from medical services can be written as

(3–2)
$$\text{TNSB}(Q) = \text{TSB}(Q) - \text{TSC}(Q).$$

Equation 3–2 allows for the fact that the levels of benefits, costs, and net social benefit depend on the quantity of medical services, Q. The surgeon general maximizes TNSB by choosing the quantity of medical services at which the difference between TSB and TSC reaches its greatest level. Figure 3–1 presents a graphical representation of this maximization process.

Notice in the figure that TSBs increase at a decreasing rate with respect to the quantity of medical services. This shape reflects an assumption that people in society experience diminishing marginal benefit with respect to medical services and indicates that successive incremental units generate continually lower additions to social satisfaction. TSCs increase at an increasing rate and reflect the increasing marginal costs of producing medical services.

FIGURE 3–1
Determination of the Efficient Level of Output

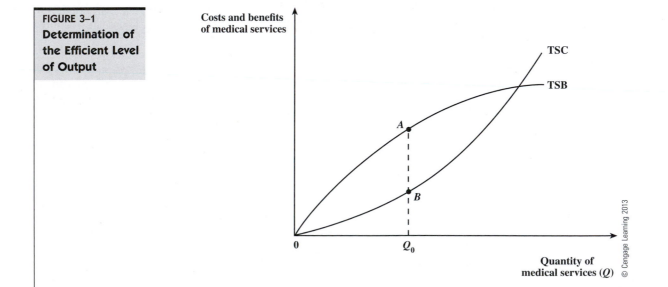

The TSB curve represents the monetary value of the total social benefit generated from consuming medical care. The curve is positively sloped to reflect the added monetary benefits that come about by consuming more medical care. The curve bows downward to capture the fact that society experiences diminishing marginal benefit with regard to medical care. The TSC curve represents the total social cost of producing medical care and is upward sloping because total costs increase as more medical care is produced. The curve bows toward the vertical axis because the marginal cost of producing medical care increases as more medical care is produced. TNSB is maximized when the vertical distance between the two curves is greatest and that occurs at Q_0 level of medical services.

The slope of the TSB curve can be written as

(3–3) $$\text{MSB}(Q) = \Delta\text{TSB}/\Delta Q,$$

where MSB stands for the marginal social benefit from consuming a unit of medical services. Obviously, MSB decreases with quantity since the slope of the TSB curve declines due to diminishing marginal benefit. Similarly, the slope of the TSC curve is

(3–4) $$\text{MSC}(Q) = \Delta\text{TSC}/\Delta Q,$$

where MSC represents the marginal social cost of producing a unit of medical services. MSC increases with output as the slope of the TSC curve gets steeper due to increasing marginal cost.

TNSB is maximized where the vertical distance between the two curves is the greatest at distance AB. A common principle in geometry is that the distance between two curves is maximized when their slopes are equal. That condition holds at output level Q_0 and implies that allocative efficiency, or the best quantity of medical services, results where

(3–5) $$\text{MSB}(Q) = \text{MSC}(Q).$$

Thus, the surgeon general chooses output Q_0 because it maximizes TNSB.

To illustrate this point in a slightly different manner, Figure 3–2 graphs the MSB and MSC curves. Notice that the negatively sloped MSB and the positively sloped MSC reflect diminishing marginal benefit and increasing marginal cost, respectively. The efficient amount of medical services is at Q_0 in Figure 3–2 because MSB equals MSC. Let us consider why Q_0 is the efficient or best level of medical services by examining the figure more closely.

In the figure, units of medical services to the left of Q_0, such as Q_L, imply that too few medical services are being produced because MSB (point E) is greater than MSC (point F). At Q_L, an additional unit of medical services generates positive additions to TNSB because the net marginal social benefit, the difference between MSB and MSC, is positive. Society is made better off if more medical services are produced. At Q_0, where MSB equals MSC, the net marginal social benefit is equal to zero and TNSB is maximized.

In contrast, output levels to the right of Q_0 suggest that too many medical services are being produced. For example, at Q_R, MSC (point G) exceeds MSB (point H) and net marginal social benefit is negative, subtracting from maximum total net social benefits. The cost of producing unit Q_R exceeds the benefits at the margin, and society could be made better off by not producing this unit. This same argument applies to all units of medical services to the right of Q_0.

TNSB is represented by the area below the MSB curve but above the MSC curve in Figure 3–2. This is because TNSB is equal to the sum of the net marginal social benefits, or the difference between MSB and MSC for every unit of medical services actually produced. Thus, in Figure 3–2, the area ABC represents the maximum TNSB that society receives if resources are allocated efficiently. (Conceptually, this area is equal to the vertical distance AB in Figure 3–1.)

If the surgeon general decides to produce Q_L instead of Q_0 units of medical services, society fails to receive the part of the TNSB indicated by area ECF. In economics, the lost amount of net social benefits is referred to as a **deadweight loss**. In this example, it measures the cost associated with an underallocation of resources to medical services. Similarly, if the surgeon general chooses to produce Q_R units of medical services, a deadweight loss of area GCH results. Area GCH indicates the net cost to society from producing too many units of medical services and therefore too few units of all other goods and services.

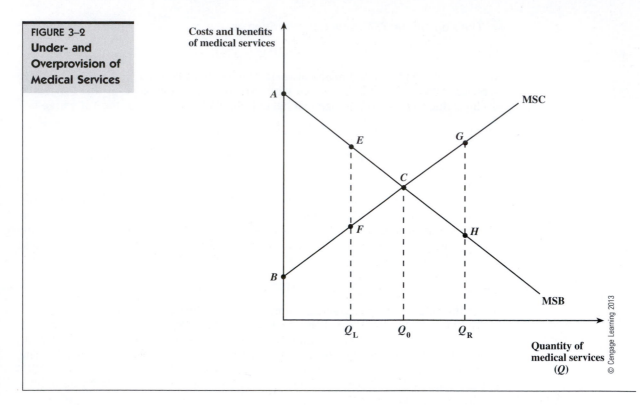

FIGURE 3–2
Under- and Overprovision of Medical Services

The MSB curve stands for the marginal social benefit generated from consuming medical care and is downward sloping because of the notion of diminishing marginal benefit. The MSC curve stands for the marginal social cost of producing medical care and is upward sloping because of increasing marginal costs. TNSB is maximized at Q_0 level of medical care where the two curves intersect. At that point, the MSB of consuming medical care equals the MSC of production. If Q_L amount of medical care is produced, then the MSB exceeds the MSC and society would be better off if more medical services were produced. If Q_R amount of medical care is produced, then the MSB is less than the MSC and too much medical care is produced.

The preceding discussion can be easily couched in terms of the net benefit calculus in Equation 3–1. For example, if we solve Equation 3–5 for the difference between the MSB and the MSC, we get

(3–6)
$$\text{NMSB}(Q) = \text{MSB}(Q) - \text{MSC}(Q),$$

where NMSB equals the net marginal social benefit the society derives from consuming a unit of the good. If NMSB is larger than zero, total net social benefit increases if an additional unit of the good is consumed. Naturally, if NMSB is negative, the society is made worse off if an additional unit of the good is produced and consumed.

The Practical Side of Using Cost-Benefit Analysis to Make Health Care Decisions

Public policy makers concerned with formulating health policies that affect the overall well-being of society, or TNSB, must wrestle with the problem of operationalizing Equation 3–6. That is no easy task, as it requires they establish the monetary value of all the costs and benefits associated with a given health policy decision. The problem is complicated by the fact that some of the costs and benefits may be of an indirect nature and therefore difficult to quantify. For example, suppose you are responsible for estimating the net benefits associated with a rehabilitation program that requires one hour of exercise a day for people who recently had a heart bypass operation. One of the costs you will have to measure is the opportunity cost of the patients' time. Your first inclination may be to base your estimate on the average hourly wage of the people in the program. But what if the people conduct their daily exercise regime on their own time rather than while at work? You now face the problem of determining the opportunity cost of leisure time.[2] As you can see, indirect costs or benefits may be hard to quantify. The benefits, or diverted costs, of a medical intervention fall into four broad categories:

1. The medical costs diverted because an illness is prevented.
2. The monetary value of the loss in production diverted because death is postponed.
3. The monetary value of the potential loss in production saved because good health is restored.
4. The monetary value of the loss in satisfaction or utility averted due to a continuation of life or better health or both.

The first benefit is usually the easiest to calculate and involves estimating the medical costs that would have been incurred had the medical treatment not been implemented. The next two benefits involve projecting the value of an individual's income that would be lost due to illness or death.

The last benefit is the most subjective and therefore the most difficult to quantify, because it involves estimating the monetary value of the pleasure people receive from a longer life and good health. For example, how does one attach a dollar value to the decrease in pain and suffering an individual may experience after hip replacement surgery? Or what is the monetary value of the satisfaction a parent receives from watching a child grow up? Given the difficulty involved in measuring the pleasure of life, many studies simply calculate the other three types of benefits. The resulting figure is considered to reflect a lower-bound estimate of total benefits.[3]

Discounting

The costs and benefits of any medical decision are likely to accrue over time rather than at a single point in time. For example, the benefits of a polio vaccination are felt primarily in terms of allowing children who might otherwise have been afflicted with polio to lead normal, healthy, active lives. The benefits in this case accrue over many decades. Therefore, an adjustment must be made to account for the fact that a benefit received (or a cost incurred) today has more value than one received at a future date. That is, the net benefit of an activity yielding a stream of future returns must be expressed in **present value (PV)** terms before proper comparisons can be made.

In simplest terms, PV means that an individual prefers $100 today rather than a year from now. Even if the individual wants to spend the money a year from now, he or she is still made better off by accepting the money today. For example, $100 deposited in a savings account offering a 4 percent annual return yields $104 a year later. We say that the PV of $104 to be received a year from now at a 4 percent rate

---

2. Although no hard-and-fast rule exists, the opportunity cost of leisure time is most often estimated at some fraction, usually one-half, of the average hourly wage.

3. In this simple example, we considered the costs and benefits associated with a new medical treatment where one never existed before. As a result, we considered the total costs and benefits experienced by society. In some instances, however, that approach is not appropriate. Consider a new medical treatment that potentially displaces, or complements, an existing one. In this situation, the appropriate practice is to focus on the incremental, or marginal, costs and benefits associated with the new treatment rather than the total costs and benefits. As such, only the added costs and benefits of the new treatment are considered.

of interest equals $100. In more formal terms, we can state PV using the following equation:

$$(3\text{–}7) \qquad \text{PV} = \frac{F}{(1+r)}$$

where F equals a fixed sum of money and r represents the annual rate of interest, or the rate at which the sum is discounted. In our example, F equals $104 and r is 4 percent, or 0.04, so PV equals $100. Notice that a higher interest rate means the PV of a fixed sum falls. For example, if the rate of interest increases to 5 percent, the PV of $104 decreases to $99.05. Thus, the PV of a fixed sum is inversely related to the rate at which it is discounted.

When referring to sums of money received over a number of periods, the PV formula becomes slightly more complicated. If different sums of money, or net benefits, are to be received for a number of years, n, at the close of each period, the formula looks like the following:

$$(3\text{–}8) \qquad \text{PV} = \frac{F_1}{(1+r)^1} + \frac{F_2}{(1+r)^2} + \frac{F_3}{(1+r)^3} + \cdots + \frac{F_r}{(1+r)^T}$$

where F_t $(t = 1, 2, 3, \ldots, T)$ equals the payment, or net benefit, received annually for T years. For simplicity's sake, we normally assume the discount rate is fixed over time. Each annual payment is expressed in today's dollars by dividing it by the discounting factor. The discounting factor equals 1 plus the rate of interest raised to the appropriate power, which is the number of years in the future when the payment is to be received. The sum total, or PV, represents the present value of all annual payments to be received in the future.

If Equation 3–8 is rewritten in summation form and specifically in terms of benefits and costs over time, it looks like the following:

$$(3\text{–}9) \qquad \text{NB} = \sum_{t=1}^{T} \frac{(B_t - C_t)}{(1+r)^t}$$

where NB equals the PV of net benefits.

In every cost-benefit study in which the effects of a medical treatment or project occur over time, careful consideration must be given to choosing the discount rate. That is because the rate at which future payments are deflated can profoundly affect the present value of a project, especially when the costs or benefits do not accrue until far into the future. The earlier polio vaccination example is a case in point. A cost-benefit analysis of a polio vaccination project involves taking the PV of benefits potentially received 70 years into the future (the average American can expect to live about 75 years). Selecting an interest rate that is too high may result in the choice of medical interventions that offer short-term net benefits. Conversely, choosing an interest rate that is too low could lead to the choice of medical projects that provide long-term net benefits.

Theoretically, the chosen interest rate should equal the rate at which society collectively discounts future consumption, or society's time preference. In an industrial economy, however, there are many interest rates to choose from, including the prime business lending rate, the residential mortgage rate, and the U.S. government bond or T-bill rate. So naturally, the "correct" interest rate is open to interpretation. Most studies choose a discount rate of between 3 and 5 percent or look to private financial markets for guidance. In the latter instance, the interest rate on government bonds is the typical choice. The T-bill interest rate is chosen because it supposedly represents a risk-free rate of return and therefore reflects the rate at which the private sector discounts future streams of income in the absence of risk. Some studies approach this problem by presenting a range of estimates based on alternative rates of interest. It is then left to the ultimate decision maker to choose the appropriate rate of discount.

The Value of Life

To properly estimate the total benefits of a medical intervention, we must be able to measure the value of a human life, because many medical interventions extend or improve the quality of life. The most common method used to determine the monetary worth of a life is the human capital approach.[4] The **human capital approach** essentially equates the value of a life to the market value of the output produced by an individual during his or her expected lifetime. The technique involves estimating the discounted value of future earnings resulting from an improvement in or an extension of life.

Figure 3–3 provides some average estimates of the PV of lifetime earnings (including fringe benefits) by age and gender, discounted using a 3 percent discount rate. Notice that the discounted value of lifetime earnings initially increases with age and then decreases. The PV figures increase at first because as an individual ages beyond infancy, the value of lifetime earnings that accrue mainly in the middle adult years are discounted over a shorter period of time. For both males and females, the discounted value of lifetime earnings peaks between the ages of 20 and 24, and amounts to $1.52 million for males and $1.09 million for females. Eventually, lifetime earnings

FIGURE 3–3
Present Value of Lifetime Earnings for Males and Females, 2000

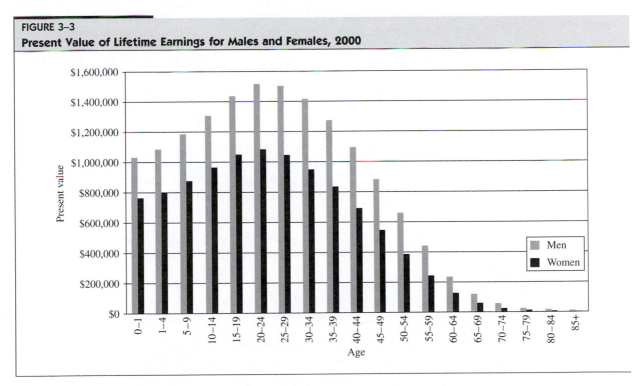

SOURCE: Max, Wendy et al. "Valuing Human Life: Estimating the Present Value of Lifetime Earnings," 2000. Center for Tobacco Control Research and Education. University of California, San Francisco, 2004, Table 2.

---

4. Economists view expenditures on education and health as personal investments that enhance an individual's ability to command a higher salary in the marketplace; hence the term *human capital*.

decrease with age as productivity and the number of years devoted to work decrease. The estimates are also sensitive to the discount rate. For example, if the figures were discounted at a 5 percent rate rather than a 3 percent rate (earnings figures not shown in Figure 3–3), the present value of lifetime earnings for males between the ages of 20 and 24 falls to $1.06 million and for women in the same age group they fall to $775,711. Naturally, the higher the discount rate the lower the discounted value of lifetime earnings.

Although the human capital approach is the most widely accepted method for determining the value of a life, the technique is not without shortcomings. One concern is that the approach is unable to control for labor market imperfections. For example, from Figure 3–3, it is apparent that the discounted value of lifetime earnings for males is substantially greater than that for females. Gender discrimination in the workplace may account for a portion of the difference. As a result, women may be penalized and assigned a lower value of life because of their gender. Also, racial and other forms of discrimination may result in inappropriate estimates of the value of life when the human capital approach is used.

The human capital approach can also be criticized because it fails to consider any nonmarket returns individuals might receive from other activities, such as leisure. As such, it does not reflect the value of any pain and suffering averted because of a medical treatment, nor does it consider the value an individual receives from the pleasure of life itself. For example, take an extreme view. According to the human capital approach, a chronically unemployed person has a zero or near-zero value of life.

An alternative approach used to measure the value of a human life is the willingness-to-pay approach. The **willingness-to-pay approach** is based on how much money people are willing to pay for small reductions in the probability of dying. This kind of information is revealed when, for example, people install or fail to install smoke detectors in their homes, wear or do not wear automobile seat belts, or smoke or do not smoke cigarettes. For example, assume that people in society choose to spend $100 per person per year on some device that improves environmental quality and reduces the probability of a person dying by 1 in 10,000. In this case, the imputed value of the average person's life equals $1 million ($100 ÷ 1/10,000).

To understand how the willingness-to-pay approach works, consider a person who is deciding whether to purchase a potentially life-saving medical service. The benefit of the life-saving medical service equals the reduced probability of dying, π, times the value of the person's life, V. Using a cost-benefit approach, the "marginal" person purchases the medical service if the benefit, $\pi \times V$, just compensates for the cost, C, or

(3–10)
$$\pi \times V = C,$$

although "inframarginal" consumers might perceive greater benefits because they value their lives more highly. Dividing both sides by π results in

(3–11)
$$V = C/\pi.$$

Equation 3–11 implies that a lower-bound estimate can be calculated for the value of a human life by dividing the cost of a life-saving good or service by the reduced probability of dying.

The advantage of the willingness-to-pay approach is that it measures the total value rather than just the job market value of a human life. The imputed value of life generated by the willingness-to-pay approach includes the value of forgone earnings plus the nonmarket value received from life and good health. As a result, the willingness-to-pay approach generally estimates the value of a life to be higher than that generated by the human capital approach. For example, based on a survey conducted in 1999, Alberini et al. (2002) estimate the mean value of a statistical life to equal $933,000 in Canada and $1.5 million in the United States for a 5 in 1,000 reduction in risk. The mean estimates jump to $3.7 million in Canada and $4.8 million in the United States for a 1 in 1,000 reduction in risk. Viscusi and Aldy (2003) review the findings of more than 60 studies and find the estimates to range from $5.0 to $6.2 million in 2000, while Mrozek and Taylor (2002) reviewed more than 40 studies and find the statistical value of a life to be between $1.5 and $2.5 million in 1998 dollars. All indications are that the willingness-to-pay estimates are higher than the human capital estimates.

Keeler (2001) illustrates how the human capital approach can be reconciled with the willingness-to-pay approach by estimating the discounted value of life and considering the monetary value of all time, not just work time. As such, he estimates the value of a life by assuming that all time is valued at the market wage rate and by controlling for the total number of hours remaining for an individual at a given age, rather than simply the remaining number of work hours. Given that the average worker under 50 years of age is likely to spend only one-tenth to one-fifth of future hours working, you can imagine how this increases the discounted value of a remaining life. For a 30-year-old male, Keeler estimated the value of all future hours to equal slightly more than $2.6 million in 1990 dollars, which is more than 5 times the discounted value of future earnings, and in line with willingness-to-pay estimates. While his figures are crude, they illustrate that people place a significant monetary value on the amount of time spent outside work, and that researchers need to consider that when estimating the value of a human life.

An Application of Cost-Benefit Analysis— Should College Students Be Vaccinated?

An increase in the number of reported cases of meningococcal disease in the United States prompted a discussion as to whether college students should be vaccinated for the disease. Jackson et al. (1995) utilize a cost-benefit analysis to determine if such a policy is an appropriate use of scarce health care resources. The analysis compares the benefits that would result from a decrease in the number of cases of meningococcal disease to the cost of implementing a vaccination program for all college students.

The cost of this medical intervention equals the cost of the vaccine multiplied by the number of doses needed plus the estimated cost of any side effects occurring because of the vaccine. The total cost of the vaccine was assumed to equal $30 per dose, which accounted for the actual cost of the vaccine plus the cost of administering the vaccine. Jackson et al. also assume that 2.3 million freshmen would enter college every year and that 80 percent of those would receive the vaccine. Regarding side effects, Jackson et al. assume that there would be one severe reaction to the vaccine per 100,000 students vaccinated, which would cost $1,830 per case. Based on these factors, Jackson et al. calculate that it would cost $56.2 million a year to administer a vaccination program among college students.[5]

The benefits include the medical costs diverted plus the estimated value of the lives saved because of the vaccine. Treatment costs per case were assumed to equal $8,145, which included seven days of hospitalization and one physician visit per day, and costs for cases occurring in the second, third, and fourth years of college were discounted at a rate of 4 percent. Because there is no way of knowing the rate at which college students contract meningococcal disease, Jackson et al. used varying multiples of the baseline rate (the national average for that age group) to calculate the benefits. A total of 58 cases would be prevented at 2 times the baseline rate for a savings of $500,000 in direct medical costs. The cost savings equal $3.1 million at 15 times the baseline rate.

---

5. The $56.2 million figure comes from the study of Jackson et al. However, the calculation actually comes out to $55.2 million.

TABLE 3–1

Estimated Benefits and Costs for the Vaccination of College Students against Meningococcal Disease (in millions of dollars)

	Baseline Times 2	Baseline Times 15
Cost of the vaccination program	$56.2	$56.2
Total benefits	9.3	63.8
Direct medical benefits	0.5	3.1
Indirect benefits—value of lives saved	8.8	60.7
Net benefits—(benefits − cost)	−46.9	7.6

SOURCE: Lisa Jackson et al. "Should College Students Be Vaccinated against Meningococcal Disease? A Cost-Benefit Analysis." American Journal of Public Health 85 (June 1995), Table 1.

The human capital approach was used to determine the value of lost earnings, and it was assumed that each life saved was worth $1 million. The total benefit from lives saved was $8.8 million for 2 times the baseline rate and $60.7 million for 15 times the baseline rate.

Table 3–1 summarizes the findings for the scenarios where students contract meningococcal disease at 2 times and 15 times the national average. According to the estimates, the net benefit for vaccinating college students is − $46.9 million, assuming a baseline rate of 2 times the national average for that age group. In other words, the estimated costs of this program outweigh the benefits by more than $46 million. Under the assumption that students contract the disease at 15 times the national average, the net benefits equal $7.6 million. In fact, a student rate of 13 times the national average must be employed before the estimated benefits generated by a vaccination program equal the costs. Using a rate of 2.6 times the national average for that age group, which is the maximum possible rate for students, Jackson et al. conclude that the costs of any vaccination program are likely to far outweigh the benefits. Thus, while one cannot ignore the fact that lives would be saved through a vaccination policy, the estimates indicate that such a policy may not be the most efficient way to spend scarce medical care dollars.

The Costs and Benefits of New Medical Technologies

Most analysts would agree that advances in medical technology have been the driving force behind rising medical costs in the United States over the last few decades. A cursory look at health statistics also appears to confirm that these new technologies have had a profound effect on the health and well-being of millions of people. For example, overall mortality and disability rates in the United States have fallen consistently since World War II. New surgical and diagnostic techniques, medical devices, pharmaceutical products, and the like are introduced each year and recent advances in such areas as biomedical research and information technology almost ensure that the pace of technological development will not abate anytime soon.

The impact of medical technology on health can best be illustrated by the total product curve for medical care discussed in the previous chapter. Recall that the total product curve as depicted in Figure 2–5 shows the relationship between health and amount of medical care consumed. Also recall that any new medical technology that improves health causes the total product curve for medical care to rotate upward.

The curve rotates upward because each unit of medical care consumed now has a greater impact on overall health. For example, take the person who is suffering from emphysema and depression. Now assume that this individual begins taking a new anti-depressant drug far more effective at combating depression and has fewer side effects than her previous medication. In this case the total product curve rotates upward, capturing the enhanced ability of the new drug to counteract depression and the fact that the medical care she is consuming as a result of her emphysema now becomes that much more effective.

Some have argued that new expensive technologies are developed and adopted with little regard to whether the benefits justify the costs. While that is clearly a debatable premise, Cutler and McClellan (2001) analyzed the costs and benefits associated with technological change for five specific health conditions: heart attack, low-birthweight infants, depression, cataracts, and breast cancer. In all cases they found that the benefits of technological change are not less than the costs.

For example, from 1984 through 1998 technological advances in treatment of heart attacks increased the life expectancy for the average heart attack victim by one year. Assuming each added year of life is worth $100,000 and subtracting out the yearly cost of consumption at $25,000, because most heart attack victims cease to work, the added benefit to society of an additional year of life is $75,000, or $70,000 in present value terms. Given that the costs of treating heart attacks increased by approximately $10,000 from 1984 to 1998 in present value terms, the net benefit of enhanced technology in the treatment of heart attacks is roughly $60,000 per patient. In other words, there is a 7 to 1 payoff in terms of benefits to costs. This finding supports a convincing argument that the increase in spending brought about by technology is more than justified in terms of health benefits.

As another example, Cutler and McClellan found that in the case of low-birthweight infants, the net benefits equal $200,000 per infant with a payoff of approximately 6 to 1. To further bolster their claim concerning the value of medical technology, Cutler and McClellan state that "if one takes just the medical component of reduced mortality for low-birthweight infants and ischemic heart disease, medical care explains about one-quarter of overall mortality reduction" (p. 24).

While one should be careful not to overgeneralize from their results, it is fair to say that Cutler and McClellan developed a compelling case for the positive net benefits associated with new medical technologies. In most cases, the benefits of technological change in recent years appear to justify the costs. Cutler and McClellan concluded their article with a word of caution concerning cost containment policies. While everyone benefits when resources are used efficiently in the production of health, any policy change that halts or slows the rate of technological innovation should be examined with a skeptical eye. That is, serious attempts at cost containment may come at the expense of new medical technologies and thereby compromise the quality and longevity of future lives.

Cost-Effectiveness Analysis

The difficulty of measuring benefits is one major drawback of cost-benefit analysis. The problem is even more pronounced in the health care field because the benefits associated with the adoption of a new technology or medical intervention are often in terms of intangible long-term benefits such as the dollar value of prolonging life or an enhancement in the quality of life. As we learned earlier, considerable debate surrounds the most appropriate way to determine the value of a human life. When the benefits that accrue from a particular policy are clearly defined and deemed desirable, cost-effectiveness analysis (CEA) is often employed.

McGuigan and Moyer (1986, pp. 562–563) suggest that the primary difference between cost-benefit and CEA lies in the basic question being asked: "Cost-benefit analysis asks the question: What is the dollar value of program costs and benefits, and do the benefits exceed the costs by a sufficient amount, given the timing of these outcomes to justify undertaking the program?" In contrast, the question asked in CEA, "Given that some prespecified object is to be attained, what are the costs associated with the various alternative means for reaching that objective?"

With CEA, the analyst estimates the costs associated with two or more medical treatment options or clinical strategies for a given health care objective, such as life-years saved, to determine the relative value of one medical treatment or technology over another.[6] In most cases, the comparison is done through the calculation of an **incremental cost effectiveness ratio (ICER)**. For example, assume that a new medical treatment, *new*, is being compared to an existing treatment, *old*, and the cost and medical effectiveness of each treatment are C_{new}, C_{old} and E_{new}, E_{old}, respectively. In this case:

$$\text{(3–12)} \qquad\qquad \text{ICER} = \frac{C_{new} - C_{old}}{E_{new} - E_{old}}.$$

If the new treatment is less costly than the old ($C_{new} < C_{old}$) and more effective ($E_{new} > E_{old}$), then the new treatment is said to dominate the old and should be adopted. On the other hand, if the new treatment is both more costly and less effective than the old, then the old is dominant. In this situation, the new treatment should not be adopted.

The most interesting case is when the new treatment is more effective than the old and at the same time more costly. CEA becomes an important tool of analysis under this circumstance because a decision has to be made regarding whether the new treatment is worth adopting or not. The basic question becomes: Is the gain in improved health brought about by the new treatment worth the additional cost in dollars? For example, assume that the new treatment costs $5,000 per additional life-year saved. This seems like a rather small price to pay for a life-year and most would conclude that the new treatment should be adopted. But what happens if the cost is $150,000 per additional life-year saved? Is the cost of the new treatment worth the benefits in terms of life-years saved? Or, put in other terms, what is the threshold point at which a particular medical treatment or technology is simply too costly to adopt? Clearly, there is no straightforward answer. However, many agree that if the cost of a new medical treatment is less than $50,000 per additional year of life saved it is generally viewed favorably. Others contend that this threshold is arbitrary and too low (Grosse, 2008). For example, Cutler (2004) places the threshold at double that amount, arguing that the value of a year of life is around $100,000.

Finally, we have the case where the new technology is less costly and less effective than the old. The relevant question becomes whether the decrease in health is worth the cost savings. CEA is needed to provide the relative cost savings per life-year. Given that the major emphasis in medical care is on improving or extending life, very little attention is paid in the literature regarding this possibility.

If a new medical treatment or technology is being examined where none previously existed, then Equation 3–12 becomes

$$\text{(3–12)} \qquad\qquad \text{ICER} = \frac{C_{new}}{E_{new}}$$

---

6. Other objectives, such as reducing cholesterol levels or blood pressure, may also be specified.

The only difference is that the ICER is measured simply as the ratio of costs to effectiveness. For example, if a new technology costs $20,000 per year and the number of lives saved equal 2 per year, then the ICER, or cost of a life year saved, equals $10,000.

Even cost-effectiveness analysis is not without its critics. Some argue that life-years are not homogenous. Sometimes a medical intervention is associated with a significant number of life-years saved but a reduced quality of life. Conversely, a medical intervention may result in few life-years saved but an enhanced quality of life. For example, some analysts claim that coronary bypass operations do more to enhance the quality of life than they do to extend life.

As a result, another technique, called **cost-utility analysis**, has been used frequently in recent years. Cost-utility analysis considers the number of life-years saved from a particular medical intervention along with the quality of life. As a result, it adjusts the number of life-years gained by some type of index that reflects health status, or quality of life. While a few different rating scales are in use, the most common is **quality-adjusted life-years (QALYs)**.[7]

In mathematical terms, a QALY equals the number of life-years saved times a measure reflecting the quality of those life-years. The latter is referred to a **health-utility index** and it is normally measured on a scale from 1 to 0, where 1 equals one year of full health and 0 represents death.[8] For example, consider an individual who will die within one year without a given medical procedure. Assume that this individual could expect to live an additional eight years with a quality of life equal to 0.75 if he were to receive a particular medical procedure. In this case, the medical procedure generates 6.0 QALYs, or 8 times 0.75. Notice that the number of QALYs depends on both the number of life-years saved by the medical procedure and the ensuing quality of those life-years.

Three survey techniques are generally used by researchers to develop a health-utility index (Drummond et al., 1997). The first is a **rating scale** where individuals are asked to rate the quality of various health situations such as being blind or losing a limb. The researcher then converts the responses to a scale from 0 to 1. The second is a **standard gamble** whereby an individual is given two hypothetical health conditions. The first condition is a health outcome that is less than perfect, such as being unable to walk or hear. The second condition is that the individual undergoes a medical procedure that has a probability of success equal to π. If the procedure is successful, the individual will be in perfect health. However, if the procedure is unsuccessful with probability $(1 - \pi)$, the individual dies. The individual is then asked to choose the probability of success π that generates an indifferent response between the two conditions; living with the disability or undergoing the procedure with π probability of success. In most cases, the probability provided in the standard gamble equals the value of the health-utility index for the quality of the health outcome under discussion.

The third method is referred to as the **time trade-off**. In its simplest terms, an individual is given a hypothetical choice: she can live for x years in perfect health followed by death, or she can live y years with a particular chronic condition such as the inability to walk, where $y > x$. The number of healthy years x is then varied until the person is indifferent between the two outcomes. The health-utility index in this simple example equals x/y. For example, suppose that an individual feels that 15 years of perfect health is worth 20 years of life with the inability to walk. Using the time trade-off approach, this individual is giving the inability to walk a health-utility index of 0.75 (Dranove, 2003).

---

7. For example, the World Health Organization uses disability-adjusted life-years (DALYs), which measures potential life lost due to premature death and the years of productive life lost due to disability.

8. It is conceivable that a score of less than one could be generated. For example, some may prefer death to living one year as a quadriplegic.

Equation 3–13 can be used to calculate the cost-utility ratio from a new medical treatment or technology:

$$(3-13) \qquad \frac{\text{Cost}_{new} - \text{Cost}_{old}}{\text{No. of QALYs}_{new} - \text{No. of QALYs}_{old}}.$$

Notice that Equation 3–13 is very similar to Equation 3–11. The only major difference is that the denominator now has the number of QALYs for each intervention rather than the number of life-years.

The cost-utility approach is not without its critics. Some question whether the survey techniques used to develop the health-utility indexes accurately reflect any changes in the quality of life. Others are concerned that certain segments of society may be discriminated against because they have a shorter life expect-ancy (the elderly) or a lower quality of life (the disabled) (Dranove, 2003). Finally, like cost-effectiveness analysis, cost-utility analysis does not tell us whether the overall well-being of society is increased, as with cost-benefit analysis. It can only tell us whether one medical treatment or technology is more cost effective than another.

Cost-utility analysis has emerged as an accepted and common form of analysis in recent years. As an example, Greenberg et al. (2010) examine the results of over 230 studies that employed cost-utility analysis to understand the efficiency of various oncology practices. They found that the median cost-effectiveness ratios for treatments (in 2008 dollars) were $27,000 for breast cancer, $22,000 for colorectal cancer, $34,500 for prostate cancer, $32,000 for lung cancer, and $48,000 for hematologic cancers. As Greenberg et al. note, the results illustrate the many efficient investments in cancer care that have taken place in recent years. In another study, Stone et al. (2000) reviewed the findings of 50 studies that used cost-utility analysis to examine the effec-tiveness of clinical preventive services. They found the median cost utility ratio to equal $14,000 per QALY.

Cost-utility analysis can also be used to assess the viability of new medical technol-ogies. One case concerns whether or not digital mammography screening for breast cancer should replace the more traditional film mammography screening method. A digital mammography takes an electronic image of the breast that can be stored in a computer, thus providing the radiologist with enhanced computer technology to detect cancer. The dilemma is that while the digital mammography may be superior in its ability to detect cancer for certain subpopulations, it is far more expensive than film mammography. Tosteson et al. (2008) estimate that the replacement of all-film mam-mography screening with all-digital mammography screening would cost $331,000 per QALY gained. Targeted-digital mammography screening, on the other hand, for certain subpopulations based on age (women 50 and younger) or age and breast density (women 50 and younger plus women older than 50 with dense breasts) is much more cost effective, generating estimates of $26,500 and $84,500 per QALY, respectively. These results lead Tosteson et al. to conclude that digital mammography screening for all women is too costly and unjustified. They further conclude that digital screening can only be justified if limited to women 50 years of age and younger and those women older than 50 but with dense breasts.

By the Numbers: Cost-Effectiveness and Cost-Utility Analysis

Table 3–2 provides a simple example of cost-effectiveness and cost-utility analysis. The current medical option costs $20,000 and generates 2 life-years and 1.4 QALYs (2×0.7), while the new medical option under consideration results in 8 life-years gained and 3.2 QALYS (8×0.4). If quality of life is ignored, the incremental cost-effectiveness ratio for the new medical procedure equals $15,000 per life-year gained, or ($110,000 − $20,000) divided by (8 years − 2 years). Given the relatively low

TABLE 3–2
An Example of Cost-Effectiveness and Cost-Utility Analysis

Treatment Option	Cost	Life-Years Gained	Health-Utility Index	QALY
Current procedure	$20,000	2 years	0.7	1.4
New procedure	$110,000	8 years	0.4	3.2

© Cengage Learning 2013

ICER, it would appear that the new medical option should be adopted. When the quality of life is factored into the analysis, the cost-utility ratio equals $50,000 per QALY gained, or ($110,000 − $20,000) divided by (3.2 QALYs − 1.4 QALYs). In this case, the cost per QALY is much higher than the cost per life-year because the new procedure results in a decrease in the quality of life. For example, the new procedure may leave the patient with moderate pain or discomfort or decreased mobility. Now the decision to adopt the new treatment deserves further reflection because the cost per QALY is considerably higher.

The opposite would occur if the quality of life is significantly enhanced by the new technology. Assume for argument's sake that the new medical procedure improves health and the health-utility index equals 0.95. In this case, there are 7.6 QALYs (8 × 0.95) generated by the new medical option and the cost-utility ratio equals $14,516.

Before we move on, two points are worth stressing. First, notice that the cost of any medical procedure or technology is the same regardless of whether it is judged on a cost-effectiveness or cost-utility basis. Second, the quality of life associated with any medical option plays a critical role in determining its relative worth.

An Application of Cost-Effectiveness Analysis: Autologous Blood Donations—Are They Cost Effective?

Since the rise in the number of cases of acquired immunodeficiency syndrome (AIDS), there has been a growing concern about the safety of the U.S. blood supply. Many are worried that they may receive tainted blood through a transfusion and contract an infectious disease, such as HIV or hepatitis C. This has led to an increase in the number of autologous blood donations.[9] Although more costly than traditional community blood donations, autologous donations are safer because the risk of receiving any contaminated blood is zero. Unfortunately, autologous blood donations are also more costly because they involve more administrative and collection expenses and have higher discarding costs than allogeneic donations. The question now becomes whether the increase in safety brought about by using autologous blood donations is worth the additional costs.

Using CEA, Etchason et al. (1995) estimate the cost per QALY saved through autologous blood donations for four different surgical procedures: total hip replacement, coronary-artery bypass grafting, abdominal hysterectomy, and transurethral prostatectomy. The added, or marginal, costs of using autologous blood donations are provided in the first row of Table 3–3. As you can see, the marginal cost of autologous blood donations varies from $68 to $4,783 per unit. The difference results mostly from the disposal cost of discarded units of blood. The second row of Table 3–3 provides the QALYs gained from using autologous donated blood for each of the four procedures.

---

9. An autologous blood donation is one in which the donor and the recipient of the blood are the same person. An allogeneic donation is one in which the donor and the recipient are different people.

Etchason et al. arrived at these figures by first estimating the probabilities of acquiring a number of infections, such as hepatitis C and HIV, through transfusions of allogeneic blood and then estimating the number of disease outcomes that would result from those infections. These figures were used to determine changes in life expectancy for each of the four surgical procedures. Finally, Etchason et al. consulted the medical literature and adjusted their life expectancy figures to arrive at estimates for QALYs. For example, using autologous blood donations for a hip replacement would result in .00029 QALYs saved, or approximately 2.5 hours of perfect health.

The cost effectiveness per unit of autologous blood for each procedure can be arrived at by dividing the marginal cost of using autologous blood by the QALY saved per unit. For example, according to Table 3–3, the cost effectiveness for using autologous blood for a hip replacement equals $235,000 per QALY, or $68/.00029.

As you can see, the cost effectiveness per unit of autologous blood runs from $235,000 per QALY saved for a total hip replacement to more than $23 million for a transurethral prostatectomy. Although there is no rule concerning what constitutes a cost-effective expenditure for a medical intervention, the estimates generated by Etchason et al. (1995) seem to be high and suggest that the use of autologous blood donations represent a costly way of saving a life.

Implications of the Patient Protection and Affordable Care Act (PPACA) of 2010 Regarding Cost and Benefit Evaluation Methods

Much has been written over the last few years regarding the unevenness in the quality of care delivered in the United States and the possibility that some care may generate only marginal health benefits. If only health care providers, patients, and health insurers had a "better way to identify what works for which patient and under what circumstances," the result might be improved health at a potentially lower cost (Institute of Medicine, 2009, p. 1).

The PPACA of 2010 attempts to address this possibility with the creation of a not-for-profit Patient-Centered Outcomes Research Institute to provide people with the knowledge needed to make educated decisions regarding medical care (check out their web site: www.pcori.org). The goal is to help the public make informed choices as they navigate through a myriad of treatment options when faced with the prospect

TABLE 3–3
Estimated Cost Effectiveness of Autologous Blood Donations

	Abdominal Hysterectomy	Coronary-Artery Bypass Grafting	Transurethral Prostatectomy	Total Hip Replacement
Additional cost per unit of autologous blood transfused	$594	$107	$4,783	$68
QALY per unit transfused	0.00044	0.00022	0.00020	0.00029
Cost effectiveness (row one/row two)	$1,358,000	$494,000	$23,643,000	$235,000

SOURCE: Based on Jeff Etchason et al. "The Cost Effectiveness of Preoperative Autologous Blood Donations." New England Journal of Medicine 332 (March 16, 1995), Table 4.

of making an important health care decision. At the center of this initiative is creation of an infrastructure to spur the development and dissemination of comparative effectiveness research (CER). According to the Institute of Medicine (2009, p. 1), CER is defined as:

> the generation and synthesis of evidence that compares the benefits and harms of alternative methods to prevent, diagnose, treat, and monitor a clinical condition or to improve the delivery of care. The purpose of CER is to assist consumers, clinicians, purchasers, and policy makers to make informed decisions that will improve health care at both the individual and population levels.

At this point, the astute reader is likely asking: How does CER compare with CEA? Put in the clearest terms, while CEA specifically focuses on the costs relative to the effectiveness of alternative medical interventions, CER compares the efficacy of alternative diagnostic tests, treatments, or delivery methods without any explicit consideration of costs (Chandra et al., 2011).

Another way to look at the value of CER is to think in terms of the health production function introduced in Figure 2–3 of Chapter 2. As you recall, the health production function indicates the maximum amount of health generated from a fixed set of medical inputs given the state of technology. Each point along the TP curve plots the most efficient levels of clinical care needed to generate various levels of health. As such, the TP curve plots the most comparatively effective mix of health inputs for each level of health output. Put in more practical terms, "simply knowing what works and what doesn't will improve productive efficiency by shedding" medical practices that are less efficient and possibly even harmful (Chandra et al. 2011, p. 29).

One of the more interesting debates taking place in the context of health care reform is whether the widespread application of CER will result in lower health care costs at a macro level. As you might expect the answer to this question is not as straightforward as some in the media would suggest. Two examples illustrate the complexity of this issue. First, take the case of a CER study that determines a particular medical treatment option is ineffective. Under these circumstances the discontinued use of that medical treatment option will clearly result in lower medical costs. In fact, the discontinuation of the medical treatment may even improve the overall quality of care provided if the treatment is found to be harmful.

Second, assume that two distinct treatments have been developed simultaneously where none previously existed to address a particular medical problem. Treatment Alpha costs $20,000 per patient and results in two additional QALYs saved while Treatment Beta costs $500,000 per patient and results in four QALYs saved. Applying the criteria of CER, Treatment Beta would be chosen over Treatment Alpha and the result would be improved health care and higher health care costs. It is interesting to note, however, that if we apply the principle of CEA we get an entirely different outcome. Notice that the ICER for the Treatment Alpha, where none previously existed, is $10,000 per life-year saved ($20,000/2), while the ICER for Treatment Beta, where none previously existed, is $125,000 per life-year saved ($500,000/4). Not only is Treatment Alpha superior to Treatment Beta according to CEA but Treatment Beta also surpasses the threshold of $100,000, which is a commonly-used annual value of a human life.

While the question of whether CER will result in higher medical care costs is not likely to be resolved for some time, economists generally agree that the widespread development and dissemination of CER will likely provide patients and health care providers with the information necessary to make more informed choices.

Finally, one important feature of CER is that it can be considered a **public good**. As such, the information it provides can be consumed simultaneously by more than one individual and it is costly to exclude nonpayers from using the information (more on this in Chapter 9). Consequently, the good is usually underprovided by the market. Under this circumstance, funding for the Patient-Centered Outcomes Research Institute to encourage CER by the PPACA may be a proper role for government.

Summary

Because resources are limited, allocation decisions must be made based on cost-benefit analysis. If the benefits resulting from a health care decision exceed the costs, it is in the economic agent's best interests to pursue that decision. One problem that frequently arises when utilizing formal cost-benefit analysis is that of determining the monetary worth of a human life. The human capital approach is the most common method used to translate the value of a life into dollars. It involves estimating the discounted value of earnings gained through an extension of life. The willingness-to-pay approach is an alternative method that has been gaining wider acceptance in recent years. With the willingness-to-pay approach, the monetary value of a life is based on the amount people are willing to pay for small reductions in the probability of dying. The advantage of this approach is that it captures the total value of a life rather than simply the market value, as is the case with the human capital approach. Unfortunately, data limitations preclude the widespread use of the willingness-to-pay approach.

CEA is another method commonly used to determine the merits of health care policy options. Because the benefits of improved health are difficult to quantify, many analysts elect to use CEA. The analysis involves estimating the cost of achieving a given health care objective, usually a life-year saved. Another more sophisticated method analysis called cost-utility analysis takes into consideration both the quality and quantity of life-years saved. The most common rating scale is QALYs, which equals the product of life expectancy and an index reflecting the quality of remaining life-years.

The various techniques discussed in this chapter represent a sampling of the tools health care economists have at their disposal for analyzing the economic aspects of resource allocation. These tools provide policy makers with the information they need to make informed decisions concerning the allocation of scarce health care resources across competing ends.

Review Questions and Problems

1. We have learned that production efficiency is achieved when society is receiving the maximum amount of output from its limited resources. Explain how cost-benefit analysis can be used to achieve that outcome.

2. You have just been hired by your city's department of health. Your first task is to use cost-benefit analysis to evaluate a smoking awareness program that the department has been promoting for two years. Under the smoking awareness program, the department of health sends a team of health care professionals to various private firms free of charge to lecture to employees about the risks of smoking. The lecture takes one hour and is given during the workday. Describe the costs and benefits you should consider in your analysis.

3. In your own words, describe the difference between cost-benefit and cost-effectiveness analysis.

4. The Cost-Effectiveness Analysis Registry provides detailed information on more than 2500 cost-effectiveness analyses covering a variety diseases and intervention types. Consult the Registry at https://research.tufts-nemc.org/cear4/, find a current study published within the last year, and answer the following questions:
   A. What is the medical intervention the study is addressing?

B. What are the data sources for the study?

C. What costs were included in the study?

D. How did the study measure the health benefits derived from the medical intervention.

E. What were the results? Based on the findings, should the medical intervention be adopted?

5. According to Lee et al. (2009), the incremental cost-effectiveness ratio comparing the current dialysis treatment to the next least cost dialysis treatment is $61,294 per life year and $129,090 per QALY. Can you account for the different estimates?

6. According to estimates, between 60 and 70 percent of smokers who enter a hospital for an acute myocardial infarction (a heart attack) continue to smoke after being discharged from the hospital. Needless to say, those individuals are at high risk for a recurrent heart attack, stroke, and even death after they leave the hospital. Ladapo et al. (2011) study whether it is economically viable to implement a smoking cessation counseling program with follow-up contact after discharge for those individuals who continue to smoke. According to their estimates the cost effectiveness of a smoking cessation counseling program is $5,050 per QALY. Should per the program be implemented? Why?

7. The commissioner of health is concerned about the increasing number of reported cases of preventable childhood diseases, such as polio and rubella. It appears that a growing number of young children are not being vaccinated against childhood diseases as they should be. Two proposals to address the problem are sitting on the commissioner's desk. The programs have equal costs, but the commissioner has funding for only one. The first proposal involves providing free vaccinations at clinics around the country. The benefits from a free vaccination program are likely to be experienced immediately in terms of a drop in the number of reported cases of illness. The second program calls for educating young married couples about the benefits of vaccination. The benefits in this instance will not be felt for some years. The commissioner wants to use cost-benefit analysis to determine which proposal should be implemented. Explain to the commissioner the critical role the discount rate plays in determining which program is chosen. In particular, which program is more likely to be chosen if a relatively low discount rate is selected? Why?

8. Distinguish between the human capital and willingness-to-pay approaches for determining the value of a life. Why does the willingness-to-pay approach generally estimate the value of a life to be higher than the human capital approach does?

9. Read the following passage from an article in the *Wall Street Journal* (October 3, 1995, p. B1) and answer the following questions.

> *Diabetic Toby Warbet quit her secretarial job last year because of physical problems, including blurred vision and a general loss of sensation. Such was her desperation that when she heard about an unproven treatment that might help her, she decided to borrow $20,000 from relatives to pay for it.... "Even if the chances are one in a million, I was hoping I would be the one," says the Livingston, NJ resident.*

A. Use the human capital approach to provide a monetary estimate of the value of Toby Warbet's life as of October 3, 1995. Explain.

B. Use the willingness-to-pay approach to estimate the value of Toby Warbet's life. Explain.

C. Provide a reason for the discrepancy between the two approaches.

D. How might you measure the value of Toby Warbet's life using the human capital approach and attain a figure close to the willingness-to-pay approach?

10. According to Russell (1992), $1 million spent on two medical interventions yields the following life-years for elderly persons:

    Pneumococcal pneumonia vaccine   100 life-years
    Influenza vaccine   11,000 life-years

    Given this information, what is the opportunity cost of $1 million spent on the pneumococcal pneumonia vaccine? What is the opportunity cost of $1 million worth of influenza vaccine? If $1 million were available to spend on medical care for elderly people, how would it be spent based on the data provided if the goal is to save the greatest number of life-years?

11. Use the information below to answer the following questions.

	Cost	Effectiveness
Current treatment	$100,000	4 life-years gained
New treatment	$250,000	10 life-years gained

    A. Calculate the ICER for the new treatment, assuming that the new treatment would replace the old one.
    B. How does your answer change if the cost of the new treatment equals $75,000?

12. Given the information for question 11, calculate the number of QALYs for the current and new treatment, assuming that the health-utility index is 0.5 for the current treatment and 0.8 for the new treatment. Also, calculate the cost-utility index for new treatment. Should the new treatment be adopted? Why?

13. Cutler (2007) uses CEA to measure the value of revascularization (bypass surgery or angioplasty) after a heart attack. According to his estimates, the cost effectiveness for this medical technology is $33,246 per life-year saved. Is this procedure cost effective? Why or why not? Would your answer change if the cost per life-year saved was double that amount?

Online Resources

To access Internet links related to the topics in this chapter, please visit our website at **www.cengage.com/economics/santerre**.

References

Alberini, Anna, Maureen Cropper, Alan Krupnick, and Nathalia B. Simon. *Does the Value of a Statistical Life Vary with Age and Health Status? Evidence from the United States and Canada.* Washington, D.C.: Resources of the Future, April 2002.

American Heart Association. "Heart Disease and Stroke Statistics 2011 Update." *Circulation* 123 (2011), pp. e18–e209.

Behan, Donald F., and Samuel H. Cox. "Obesity and its Relation to Mortality and Morbidity Costs." *Society of Actuaries* (2010).

Chandra, Anitabh, Anupam B. Jena, and Jonathan S. Skinner. "The Pragmatist's Guide to Comparative Effectiveness Research." *Journal of Economic Perspectives* 25 (spring, 2011), pp. 27–46.

Cutler, David. "The Lifetime Costs and Benefits of Medical Technology." *Journal of Health Economics* 26 (2007), pp. 1081–1100.

Cutler, David. *Your Money or Your Life.* New York: Oxford University Press, 2004.

Cutler, David M., and Mark McClellan. "Is Technological Change in Medicine Worth It?"

Health Affairs 20 (September/October 2001), pp. 11–29.

Dall, Timothy, et al. "The Economic Burden of Diabetes." *Health Affairs* 29 (February, 2010), pp. 297–303.

Dranove, David. *What's Your Life Worth?* Upper Saddle River, N.J.: Prentice Hall, 2003.

Drummond, Michael F., Bernie J. O'Brien, Greg L. Stoddart, and George W. Torrance. *Methods for the Economic Evaluation of Health Care Programmes,* 2nd ed. Oxford: Oxford University Press, 1997.

Etchason, Jeff, et al. "The Cost Effectiveness of Pre-operative Autologous Blood Donations." *New England Journal of Medicine* 332 (March 16, 1995), pp. 719–24.

Greenberg, Dan, et al. "When is Cancer Care Cost-Effective? A Systematic Overview of Cost-Utility Analysis in Oncology." *Journal of the National Cancer Institute* 102 (January 20, 2010), pp. 82–88.

Grosse, Scott D. "Assessing Cost-Effectiveness in Healthcare: History of the $50,000 per QALY Threshold." *Pharmacoeconomic Outcomes Research* 8 (2008), pp. 165–178.

Institute of Medicine. "Initial National Priorities for Comparative Effectiveness Research." Report Brief (June, 2009).

Jackson, Lisa A., et al. "Should College Students Be Vaccinated against Meningococcal Disease? A Cost-Benefit Analysis." *American Journal of Public Health* 85 (June, 1995), pp. 843–46.

Keeler, Emmett B. "The Value of Remaining Lifetime Is Close to Estimated Values of Life." *Journal of Health Economics* (January, 2001), pp. 141–43.

Ladapo, Joseph A., et al. "Projected Cost-Effectives of Smoking Cessation Interventions in Patients Hospitalized With Myocardial Infarction." *Archives of Internal Medicine* 171 (January 10, 2011), pp. 39–46.

Lee, Chris P., Glenn Chertow, and Stefanos Zenios. "An Empiric Estimate of the Value of Life: Updating the Renal Dialysis Cost Effectiveness Standard. *Value in Health* 12 (November 2009), pp. 80–87.

McGuigan, James R., and R. Charles Moyer. *Managerial Economics,* 4th ed. St. Paul, Minn.: West, 1986.

Mrozek, Janusz R., and Laura O. Taylor. "What Determines the Value of Life? A Meta-Analysis." *Journal of Policy Analysis and Management* 21 (2002), pp. 253–70.

Rubenstein, Joel L. "The High Cost of Marginal Benefits." *Boston Globe,* May 12, 1994, p.70.

Russell, Louise B. "Opportunity Costs in Modern Medicine." *Health Affairs* 11 (summer 1992), pp. 162–69.

Stone, Patricia W., Steven Teutsch, Richard H. Chapman, Chaim Bell, Sue J. Goldie, and Peter J. Neumann. "Cost-Utility Analysis of Clinical Preventive Services." *American Journal of Preventive Medicine* 19 (2000), pp. 15–23.

Tosteson, Anna N. A., et al. "Cost Effectiveness of Digital Mammography Breast Cancer Screening." *Annals of Internal Medicine* 148 (January, 2008), pp. 1–10.

Viscusi, W. Kip, and Joseph E. Aldy. "The Value of a Statistical Life: A Critical Review of the Market Estimates Throughout the World." *The Journal of Risk and Uncertainty* 27 (2003), pp. 5–76.

CHAPTER 4

Health Care Systems and Institutions

ACOs, PPOs, HMOs, and DRGs are just a few of the many health care acronyms bandied around in the popular press. To the uninformed, they are simply the ingredients in an alphabet soup. Those familiar with them know that they stand for accountable care organizations, preferred provider organizations, health maintenance organizations, and diagnosis-related groups. They, like many other health care institutions, have evolved over the last several decades and have greatly contributed to the ongoing and wide-sweeping transformation of the U.S. health care system.

This chapter introduces and explains the structure and purpose behind various institutions and payment systems that typically compose a health care system. The knowledge gained will help you better understand how the different parts of a health care system are interrelated. In addition, the material will provide you with a greater appreciation for the remaining chapters of the book and help make you a more informed consumer or producer of health care services. Specifically, this chapter:

- *constructs a general model of a health care system*
- *discusses the reasoning for and responsibilities of third-party payers*
- *introduces and explains some of the different reimbursement methods used by third-party payers*
- *identifies some structural features associated with the production of medical services and the role of health care provider choice*
- *uses the general model to describe the health care systems in Canada, Germany, Switzerland, and the United Kingdom*
- *provides an overview of the U.S. health care system.*

Elements of a Health Care System

A **health care system** consists of the organizational arrangements and processes through which a society makes choices concerning the production, consumption, and distribution of health care services. How a health care system is structured is important because it determines who actually makes the choices concerning the basic questions, such as what medical goods to produce, how medical goods and services should be produced, and who should receive medical care. At one extreme, the health care system might be structured such that choices are decided by a centralized government, or authority, through a single individual or an appointed or elected committee. At the other extreme, the health care system might be decentralized. For example, individual consumers and health care providers, through their interaction in the marketplace, may decide the answers to the basic questions.

From a societal point of view, it is difficult to determine whether a centralized or decentralized health care system is superior. A normative statement of that kind entails value judgments, and trade-offs are inevitably involved. On the one hand, a centralized authority with complete and coordinated control over the entire health care system may be more capable of distributing output more uniformly and have a greater ability to exploit any large-sized economies. At the same time, a single centralized authority may lack the competitive incentive to innovate or respond to varied consumer-voter demands. A central authority may also face high costs of collecting information about consumer needs.

On the other hand, a health care system with a decentralized decision-making process, such as the marketplace (or a system of local governments), may provide more alternatives and innovation but may result in high costs in the presence of economies of size, nonuniformity, or lack of coordination. Determining the best structure for a health care system involves quantifying the value society places on a number of alternative and sometimes competing outcomes, such as choice, innovation, uniformity, and production efficiency, among other things. A study of that kind is difficult at best because it involves so many value judgments. Indeed, alternative health care systems exist throughout the world because people place different values on each of the various outcomes (Reinhardt, 1996). Reflecting the trade-offs involved, most health care systems today are neither purely centralized nor decentralized but rather take on elements of both systems of decision making. In any case, as we discuss the elements of various health care systems, it is important to keep in mind that understanding how and at what level decisions are made is critical to grasping how any health care system works.

Health care systems are huge, complex, and constantly changing as they respond to economic, technological, social, and historical forces. For example, the structure of the U.S. health care system involves a seemingly endless list of participants, some of which were foreign to us only a decade ago, such as preferred provider organizations. The list includes more than 900,000 physicians and dentists, about two million nurses, nearly 6,000 hospitals, and more than 80,000 nursing homes and mental retardation facilities, not to mention the millions of people who purchase medical care, the thousands of health insurers, and the multitude of government agencies involved in health care issues.

Because of the vastness and complexity of health care systems, many people have trouble understanding how they function. With that problem in mind, Figure 4–1 presents a general model of a health care system. Notice the diagram possesses a triangular shape, reflecting the three major players in any health care system: patients or consumers, health care providers or producers, and insurers or third-party payers. Sponsors, such as employers or the government, are also included in the general model because they act as intermediaries or brokers. As brokers, sponsors structure coverage, manage

FIGURE 4–1

A Model of a Health Care System

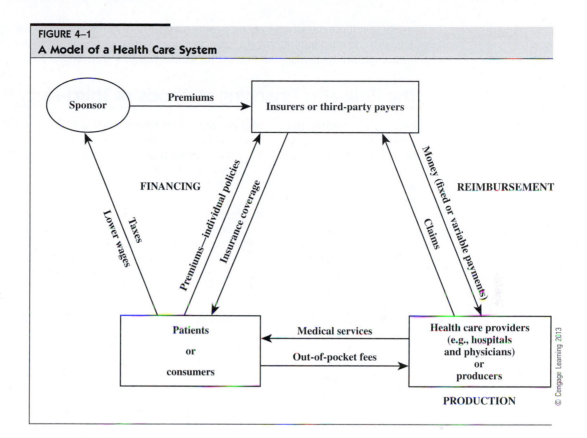

enrollment, contract and negotiate risk-sharing arrangements, and collect and submit the contributions of the insured (Van de Ven and Ellis, 2000). Contributions show up as forgone wage income resulting from either taxes or premium payments. The figure also illustrates the three elements common to all health care systems: financing, reimbursement, and production or delivery of medical care.

For a typical market transaction, the individual consumer and producer are the only ones involved in the exchange as shown in the bottom flow of the diagram. In that instance, the consumer's out-of-pocket price equals the full cost of the service provided. Buyer and seller are equally well informed, and the buyer pays the seller directly for the good or service. For example, the purchase of a loaf of bread at a local convenience store involves a normal market transaction. Both consumer and seller have the same information regarding the price and quality of the bread, and the transaction is anticipated and planned by the consumer. An unexpected outcome is not likely to occur, and, if it did, it could be easily rectified (e.g., stale bread can be easily returned).

In a medical market, the corresponding situation is a prespecified patient fee paid directly to a doctor or a hospital for some predetermined and expected quantity and quality of medical services. In the case of medical services, however, the transaction is often not anticipated, and the price, quantity, and quality of medical services are unknown until after the medical event occurs. The transaction is unanticipated because medical illnesses occur irregularly and unexpectedly (Arrow, 1963). The price, quality, and quantity of medical services are not known initially because much uncertainty surrounds the diagnosis and proper treatment of a medical problem. In addition, health care providers possess a greater amount of information relative to patients regarding the provision of medical services, giving rise to an asymmetry of information. Because no simple relation exists between diagnosis and treatment, and much is left to the discretion of health care providers, possibilities for opportunistic behavior arise. That is, health care providers may produce more treatments or a higher-quality treatment than economic considerations warrant.[1]

The Role and Financing Methods of Third-Party Payers

Because the timing and amount of medical treatment costs are uncertain from an individual consumer's perspective, third-party payers, such as private health insurance companies or the government, play a major role in medical care markets. Third-party payers often serve as intermediaries between the consumer and the health care producer and monitor the behavior of health care providers as a means of controlling medical costs.

Also, third-party payers are responsible for managing the financial risk associated with the purchase of medical services. A third-party payer faces a much lower level of risk than an individual consumer because it can pool its risk among various subscribers by operating on a large scale. The law of large numbers implies that whereas single events may be random and largely unpredictable, the average outcome of many similar events across a large population can be predicted fairly accurately. For example, it is difficult for one individual to predict whether he or she will experience a heart attack. An insurance company, on the other hand, can make a prediction of the heart attack rate with reasonable accuracy by evaluating past data from a large number of individuals. Third-party payers can use indicators such as occupational and demographic averages to forecast expected medical claims for a large group of individuals. A risk-averse consumer is better off by making a certain preset payment to an insurer for coverage against an unforeseen medical event rather than facing the possibility of paying some unknown medical costs. Essentially, consumers receive a net benefit from the financial security that third-party payers supply.[2]

Third parties make the health care system much more complex because the source of third-party financing and the method of reimbursement must be worked into the model. If the third-party payer is a private health insurance company, the consumer pays a premium in exchange for some agreed-upon amount of medical insurance coverage which may include a deductible, copayment, and/or coinsurance. The deductible provision requires the consumer to pay the first $X of medical costs, after which the health insurance company is responsible for reimbursement. With a coinsurance provision, the consumer pays a fixed percentage of the cost each time he or she receives a medical service. A copayment refers to a fixed amount per service that is paid by the consumer.

When a government agency (or a public health insurance company) acts as a third-party payer, the financing of medical care insurance usually comes from taxes. Premiums and taxes differ in the way risk is treated and the voluntary nature of the payment.[3] Premiums are paid voluntarily and often depend on the risk category of the buyer of health insurance. Tax payments are mandatory and represent a single fee without reference to risk category.

Some alternative ways to finance health care can be gleaned by examining the different methods used in Canada, Germany, Switzerland, and the United Kingdom.[4] We chose these particular countries because their health care systems possess unique features and they all possess some kind of universal or near-universal health insurance

---

1. Supplier-induced demand theory is explained in great detail in Chapter 12.

2. Health insurance principles are developed more fully in Chapters 5 and 6.

3. See Bodenheimer and Grumbach (1992) for an in-depth comparison of taxes and premiums for financing universal health insurance.

4. See Raffel (1997) for discussion on the health care systems in various industrialized countries. For manageability, we confine the discussion to the insurance, physician, and hospital services industries. No mention is made of the existing systems in the pharmaceutical and long-term care markets, for example.

program. In addition, most proposals for health care reform in the United States are based to some extent on the health care systems of these four countries.

Canada has a compulsory **national health insurance (NHI)** program administered (somewhat differently) by each of its 10 provinces and 3 territories. The NHI program provides first-dollar coverage, and no limit is imposed on the level of medical benefits an individual can receive during his or her lifetime. **First-dollar coverage** means complete health insurance coverage; the health insurer reimburses for the first and every dollar spent on medical services (i.e., there is no deductible or copayment amount). For all practical purposes, taxes finance the NHI program in each province.[5] In addition, the Canadian government provides up to 40 percent in direct cost sharing and makes hospital construction grants available to provinces. Private insurance is available for some forms of health care in Canada, although private coverage is prohibited for services covered by the NHI plan (although in 2005, the Supreme Court overturned this provision in Quebec). Because the public sector (rather than the private sector) insures against medical costs, there are no marketing expenses, no administrative costs of estimating risk status or determining whom to cover, and no allocation for profits.

The **socialized health insurance (SI)** program in Germany is based on government-mandated financing by employers and employees. The premiums of unemployed individuals and their dependents are paid by former employers or come from various public sources (the Federal Labor Administration and public pension funds). Private not-for-profit insurance companies, called **Sickness Funds,** are responsible for collecting funds from employers and employees and reimbursing physicians and hospitals. The statutory medical benefits are comprehensive, with a small copayment share for some services. Affluent and self-employed individuals are allowed to go outside the system and purchase private health insurance coverage. The Federal Ministry of Health sets premiums for the Sickness Funds.

The federal government in Switzerland began requiring all individuals to have health insurance coverage in 1996, which is referred to as a health insurance mandate (Reinhardt, 2004). For the most part, the Swiss health care system relies upon **managed competition** to deliver health insurance coverage. Managed competition leaves the provision of health insurance and health care largely to the private sector but the government creates a regulated framework within which the various health care industries operate. In Switzerland, consumers can choose among 70 standardized insurance benefits which are administered by private nonprofit insurers and offered on a regional basis in the various cantons (similar to states). The insurance plans are not sponsored by employers. In fact, employers rarely contribute to health insurance premiums. Low-income individuals receive subsidies from the government to purchase health insurance.

Consumers have the option of enrolling in expensive policies with low out-of-pocket payments or inexpensive policies with high out-of-pocket payments. Swiss citizens typically choose the inexpensive policies and therefore incur one of the highest out-of-pocket costs among industrialized countries. Health insurance premiums are determined by competition among health insurers and are community rated but subject to the approval of the federal government. A portion of all premium revenues are redistributed among insurers by the Swiss government to compensate for selecting individuals at greater medical risk. Some consumers purchase supplemental insurance which pays for private rooms and other items not covered by the basic plan. Insurers cannot profit from the basic plan but can make a profit on the supplemental insurance plans which are experience rated.

Mechanic (1995) and others refer to the health care system in the United Kingdom as a **public contracting** model because the government contracts with various

---

5. These premiums are not compulsory for coverage and will be paid by the province if individuals are unable to pay. Because these premiums are not adjusted for risk, they are essentially taxes.

providers of health care services on behalf of the people. The U.K. health care system, under the auspices of the **National Health Service (NHS),** offers universal health insurance coverage financed through taxation. The NHS provides global budgets to district health authorities (DHAs). Each DHA is responsible for assessing and prioritizing the health care needs of about 300,000 people and then purchasing the necessary health care services from public and private health care providers. Hospital services are provided by nongovernmental trusts, which compete among themselves and with private hospitals for DHA contracts. Community-based primary care givers also contract with the DHAs. In addition, general practitioner (GP) fundholders apply for budgets from the DHAs, and, with the budgets, service a minimum group of 5,000 patients by providing primary care and purchasing elective surgery, outpatient therapy, and specialty nursing services on their behalf. There is some limited competition among GP fundholders for patients.

Risk Management, Reimbursement, and Consumer Cost Sharing

Another important element of a health care system concerns the manner in which health care providers are reimbursed and the share of medical costs paid by consumers. Reimbursement is important because some payment methods shift much more financial risk onto health care providers than others. As Figure 4–1 indicates, insurers may reimburse health care providers with either a fixed or variable payment, although in practice the payment methods are sometimes combined. A fixed payment is set independent of the amount or cost of medical services actually provided to patients for a given and defined treatment episode. If the actual costs of delivering services to patients are less than the level of the fixed payment, health care providers are normally allowed to keep the surplus. However, health care providers also face the possibility that actual costs are greater than the fixed payment. Thus, some financial risk is shifted to health care providers when reimbursement takes place on a fixed-payment basis. A prospectively set fixed annual budget to a hospital or nursing home, or a fixed annual salary for an employee, are examples of fixed-payment systems. Regardless of how many resources a hospital or nursing home employs, or the number of hours an employee works during a given period, the payment remains the same.

Under a variable-payment system, the reimbursement amount varies with the quantity or cost of services actually delivered to patients. Retrospective reimbursement, in which the health care provider bills for actual costs incurred, and fee-for-service, in which a price is paid for each unit of a medical service, are two common examples of a variable-payment system. A few state governments still reimburse nursing homes on a retrospective basis for caring for Medicaid patients. The price paid for each physician office visit is an example of a fee-for-service payment. When reimbursement takes place on a variable-payment basis, health care providers face much less risk from cost overruns.

Similarly, the share of medical costs paid by consumers is important because a greater amount of cost sharing puts more financial risk on them. For example, take the extreme cases. The typical consumer faces very little financial incentive, if any, to care about the costs associated with his or her medical treatment if fully insured with no out-of-pocket expenses. Even if the medical costs equal $100, $1,000, or $10,000, the consumer pays a zero out-of-pocket price if fully insured. Conversely, that same consumer faces much more financial incentive to be concerned with the cost if required to pay the entire bill (that is, 100 percent out-of-pocket price) associated with the medical treatment. No one disagrees that opportunity cost is greater when paying $200 instead of $100 for an office visit.

FIGURE 4–2		Type of reimbursement scheme	
The Likelihood of a Large Volume of Medical Services for Different Reimbursement and Consumer Copayment Schemes		Fixed payment	Variable payment

		Fixed payment	Variable payment
Out-of-pocket price to consumer	Low	Low likelihood (1)	High likelihood (2)
	High	Very low likelihood (3)	Moderate likelihood (4)

© Cengage Learning 2013

The matrix in Figure 4–2 helps illustrate the importance of risk sharing. The matrix shows how the two reimbursement schemes previously discussed and the consumer's out-of-pocket price interact and affect the likelihood that a large volume of medical services will be supplied and demanded. The probability of a high volume of medical services is given inside each cell of the matrix for each combination of reimbursement method and consumer out-of-pocket price.

We can identify the opportunity for a large volume of medical services per patient by considering how the different provider reimbursement schemes and consumer payment plans affect the incentives of health care providers and consumers. For example, a health care provider that is reimbursed on a fixed-payment basis is very unlikely to supply a large volume of medical services to a patient unnecessarily. The cost of additional medical services immediately subtracts from the fixed payment and puts the health care provider at risk for cost overruns. In contrast, for the variable-payment schemes, health care providers do not absorb the financial risk of the higher costs associated with additional services.

We can conduct a similar analysis for the consumer. Consumers who face a low out-of-pocket price of obtaining medical services are more likely to seek out additional medical services (this is referred to as the moral hazard problem in Chapter 5). On the other hand, consumers who face a high out-of-pocket price are less inclined to seek out medical services given the greater opportunity cost of their money.

Combining the reimbursement and out-of-pocket payment schemes, the likelihood of a large volume of medical services per patient is the greatest in cell 2, where a variable-payment scheme interacts with a low consumer out-of-pocket price. Neither party loses much financially in the exchange of dollars for medical services. Conversely, a large volume of medical services is least likely in cell 3, where a fixed-payment plan coexists with a large consumer out-of-pocket scheme. Both parties in the exchange lose financially. Cell 4 offers a moderate likelihood of a large volume of medical services because the provider is not made financially worse off by providing additional services. For this to happen, however, either the consumer's out-of-pocket price must not be too high or the consumer must be relatively insensitive to price (i.e., highly inelastic demand). Finally, in cell 1, the health care provider is made worse off while the consumer is relatively unaffected by additional medical services, so the probability of a large volume of medical services is low.

A major current concern of health care policy makers is that a variable reimbursement system, when combined with a modest consumer out-of-pocket price, results in excessive medical services that provide low marginal benefits to patients but come at a high marginal cost to society. For example, medical care providers may offer expensive diagnostic tests to low-risk patients. The tests come at a high marginal cost to society but yield only small marginal benefits to patients given their low-risk classification. Small marginal medical benefits coincide with the "flat-of-the-curve" medicine observed in several empirical studies, as discussed in Chapter 2.

As a result, many health policy analysts believe that fee-for-service or retrospective payments and small consumer out-of-pocket payments are responsible for high-cost, low-benefit medicine. Policy makers typically argue that some cost sharing is needed on the supply and/or demand side of the market to reduce the potential for excess medical services (Ellis and McGuire, 1993). That is, they believe that fixed-payment reimbursement plans and nontrivial consumer payments are required to control unnecessary medical services.

We can appreciate the importance of the reimbursement method by examining and contrasting the countrywide reimbursement schemes practiced in Canada, Germany, Switzerland, and the United Kingdom. In Canada, everyone is eligible for the same medical benefits, and there are no copayments for most medical services. Patients essentially drop out of the reimbursement picture, and reimbursement exclusively takes place between the public insurer (the government) and the health care provider. In terms of Figure 4–1, this means that the monetary exchange is virtually nonexistent between patient and health care provider. The ministry of health in each province is responsible for controlling medical costs. Cost control is attempted primarily through fixed global budgets for hospitals and predetermined fees for physicians. Specifically, the operating budgets of hospitals are approved and funded entirely by the ministry in each province, and an annual global budget is negotiated between the ministry and each individual hospital. Capital expenditures must also be approved by the ministry, which funds the bulk of the spending.

Physician fees are determined by periodic negotiations between the ministry and provincial medical associations (the Canadian version of the American Medical Association). With the passage of the Canada Health Act of 1984, the right to **extra billing** was removed in all provinces. Extra billing or balance billing refers to a situation in which the physician bills the patient some dollar amount above the predetermined fee set by the third-party payer. For the profession as a whole, negotiated fee increases are implemented in steps, conditional on the rate of increase in the volume of services. If volume per physician rises faster than a predetermined percentage, subsequent fee increases are scaled down or eliminated to cap gross billings—the product of the fee and the volume of each service—at some predetermined target. The possible scaling down of fee increases is supposed to create an incentive for a more judicious use of resources. Physicians enjoy nearly complete autonomy in treating patients (e.g., there is no mandatory second opinion for surgery) because policy makers believe there is no need for intrusive types of controls given that the hospital global budgets and physician expenditure targets tend to curb unnecessary services.

The Sickness Funds in Germany, which collect employer and employee insurance premiums, pay negotiated lump-sum funds equal to the product of a capitation (per-patient) payment and the number of insured individuals by regional associations of ambulatory care physicians. These regional associations, in turn, reimburse individual physicians for services on the basis of a fee schedule. The fee schedule is determined through negotiation between the regional associations of Sickness Funds and physicians. To determine the fee schedule, each physician service is assigned a number of points based on relative worth. The price per point is established by dividing the lump-sum total budget by the actual number of points billed within a quarter by all physicians. The income to an individual physician equals the number of points billed times the price per point.

The Sickness Funds that operate in a given state also negotiate fixed prices for various procedures (based on the diagnosis-related group, or DRG) with local hospitals. Because hospitals can make profits or incur losses because of the fixed prices, there is an incentive for hospitals to save resources and specialize in certain procedures. For some procedures, hospital accommodations are reimbursed on a per diem basis but funds are limited by an overall budget. Hospital-based physicians are paid on a salary basis. Most of the hospital funds for capital acquisitions come from state and local governments and are reviewed and approved through a state planning process.

Medical fees are negotiated collectively between a "cartel" of insurers and representatives of health care providers, including physicians and private hospitals, in each canton of Switzerland. Providers must accept the negotiated payment and balance billing is not allowed. Health insurers are required by the government to contract with any physician and are allowed to enter into managed care arrangements. Hospitals, however, are excluded from managed care contracts. The 23 cantons in Switzerland provide half of the financing for public hospitals so the Canton governments set the prices for services delivered by public hospitals.

In the United Kingdom, the district health authorities (DHA) are allocated funds by the NHS on a weighted capitation basis, which considers age, sex, and health-risk factors as well as geographical cost differences. Independent community-based family practitioners contract with the NHS and are uniformly paid throughout the United Kingdom, primarily on a capitation basis. The DHAs prospectively reimburse individual hospital trusts based on the actual cost of providing the services. All hospital-based physicians and consultants are paid on a fixed salary basis by the trusts. Trusts are required to earn a 6 percent return on assets and the residual is returned to the DHA. Capital funding for the trusts is determined by the DHA and is based on its regional allocation.

Any funds allocated to GP fundholders are deducted from the DHA's allocation. GP fundholders annually negotiate funds to purchase elective and nonemergency services for their subscribers. About 41 percent of the population in England is served by GP fundholders. Any savings made by a fundholder may be reinvested in the practice or new services but cannot directly increase the GP's personal income. GP fundholders are not at personal financial risk as they are protected against any legitimate cost overruns by the DHAs.

In sum, these four countries have shied away from relying on an uncontrolled fee-for-service reimbursement scheme because of the concern that it creates incentives for high-cost, low-benefit medicine. The payment is on either a per diem, per-person, or negotiated fee-for-service basis. In addition, the payment for medical services is determined by a single payer—the government in Canada and the United Kingdom and representatives of the Sickness Funds in Germany and a cartel of insurers and representatives of health care providers in Switzerland. Policy makers in these countries believe that a single-payer, controlled-payment system can reduce the incentive to provide high-cost, low-benefit medicine and better contain health care costs.

The Production of Medical Services

The mode of production also differs across health care systems. Several distinguishing features of production are worth mentioning. We normally think of health care services as being produced on an inpatient care basis in hospitals or nursing homes or on an outpatient (ambulatory) care basis at physician clinics or in the outpatient department of a hospital. However, health care services are also produced in the home. Preventive care (such as exercise, dieting, and flossing) and first aid are two prime examples of home-produced health care services. In addition, long-term or chronic care services are often produced in the home rather than in an institution, such as a nursing home. Although acute care services can also be produced in the home, the cost of producing these services is usually prohibitive for the individual consumer because of the high per-person labor and capital expenses.[6] As a result, it is almost always cheaper for the individual consumer to purchase acute care services at a hospital because such an organization can exploit various large-size economies.

Outside the home, health care providers may be organized in a number of ways. For example, a hospital may be a freestanding, independent institution or part of a multi-hospital chain. Similarly, a physician may operate in a solo practice or belong to a group practice. Usually the size and scope of the medical organization depend on whether any economies exist from operating on a small or large scale. In addition, some physicians, such as radiologists and anesthesiologists, may be employees of the hospital. In contrast, some physicians on the medical staff may not be employees of the hospital but instead are granted admitting privileges.

Health care services may be produced in the private or public sector by health care providers in the medical services industry. If produced in the private sector, the health care provider may offer medical services on a not-for-profit or a for-profit basis. A not-for-profit organization is required by law to use any profits exclusively for the charitable, educational, or scientific purpose for which it was formed. For example, a hospital may use profits to lower patient prices, or finance medical equipment or hospital expansion.

Institutional Differences between For-Profit and Not-For-Profit Health Care Providers

Because not-for-profit institutions are so prevalent in the health care sector, it is important that we examine the institutional differences between for-profit and not-for-profit firms. There are five basic institutional differences between these two classes of organizations.

First, when for-profit firms are established, they acquire initial capital by exchanging funds for ownership with private individuals. Ownership gives those in the private sector a claim on future profits. Not-for-profit firms must rely on donations for their initial capital because they are not privately owned. In a broad sense, they are owned by the community at large. Second, for-profit providers are capable of earning accounting profits and distributing cash dividends to their owners, whereas not-for-profit firms face a **nondistribution constraint** and are prohibited from distributing profits to employees, managers, or company directors (Hansmann, 1996). A nondistribution constraint means that not-for-profit firms cannot legally distribute any revenues in excess of costs to individuals without regard to the charitable purpose for which the organization was formed. Third, for-profit organizations can easily be sold or liquidated for compensation by their owners, whereas it is very difficult to sell a not-for-profit organization. Fourth, not-for-profit providers are exempt from certain types of taxes and are eligible to receive subsidies from the government. In fact, it has been argued that the tax exemption and subsidies give not-for-profit firms an unfair advantage over for-profit firms. Finally, not-for-profit providers are restricted by law in the types of goods and services they can provide.

---

6. According to the *Mosby Medical Encyclopedia* (1992), long-term care is "the provision of medical care on a repeated or continuous basis to persons with chronic physical or mental disorders" (p. 471). Acute care is "treatment for a serious illness, for an accident, or after surgery…. This kind of care is usually for only a short time" (p. 11).

Why Are Not-For-Profit Health Care Providers So Prevalent?

Now that we understand the differences between for-profit and not-for-profit providers, the next item to address is why not-for-profit providers are so prevalent in the health care sector. Weisbrod (1988) discusses the issue in general terms but his analysis can easily be applied to the health care sector. According to Weisbrod, not-for-profit firms exist primarily as a result of market failure in the private sector. The market failure results from three factors.

First, the private sector works best when all market participants are perfectly informed. However, given the complexity of medical technology and the difficulty of assessing the appropriateness of medical care, consumers typically possess imperfect information about the health care sector. As a result, many consumers believe they are in a vulnerable situation and can easily be exploited by medical providers for the sake of profits through quality reductions. For that reason, they prefer to deal with not-for-profit providers, which presumably are driven by a "softer" incentive to compromise quality because of their nondistribution constraint.

The second reason for market failure concerns equity. Society as a whole believes that each citizen has a right to some minimum level of medical care that would not be provided if health care resources were allocated by the for-profit sector. The profit motive ensures that health care is allocated based on the ability to pay and not on need. As a result, some argue that not-for-profit providers are necessary to meet the needs of those who cannot pay for medical care.

The third reason for market failure involves the presence of externalities as discussed further in Chapter 9. When externalities exist, resources are not efficiently allocated because the for-profit sector does not consider all the costs and benefits associated with production. Thus, for these three reasons, the for-profit sector may fail to address the collective need for health care.

The next question that comes to mind is why the public sector does not simply take over the allocation of health care resources in the presence of market failure. The answer, Weisbrod contends, is that consumer needs are heterogeneous. When needs are widely diverse, the government has difficulty developing an appropriate overall policy that meets the desires of all consumers in a cost-effective manner. For example, "one-size-fits-all" medicine most likely would not appeal to everyone. Hence, a multitude of not-for-profit health care providers, such as hospitals and nursing homes, are required to satisfy heterogeneous demands. Each institution can be tailored to fit the individual demands of its constituents. For example, the Shriners run not-for-profit hospitals aimed at orthopedic pediatric care, while some religious organizations operate nursing homes specifically for elderly members of their own religion.

One last question deserves some discussion. If these market failures are substantial, why is the for-profit sector allowed to operate at all in the health care field? Consumer knowledge and preferences provide the answer to this question. Although some consumers lack the information they need to make informed decisions, others are much more informed. Informed consumers may "have no institutional preferences" and "prefer to deal with any organization, regardless of ownership form, that provides the wanted outputs at the lowest price" (Weisbrod, 1988, p. 124). Thus, the for-profit sector exists in the health care market primarily to satisfy the demands of these types of consumers.

Production of Health Care in the Four Systems

The organization of production in the four health care systems we have been discussing has some slight differences. In Canada, medical services are produced in the private sector. Most hospitals in the private sector are organized on a not-for-profit basis and are owned by either charitable or religious organizations. In Germany, medical services are produced primarily in the private sector because most physicians operate in private practices. Public hospitals control about 51 percent of all hospital beds in Germany. The remaining beds are managed by not-for-profit (35 percent) and for-profit hospitals (13 percent). In Germany, office-based physicians are normally prohibited from treating patients in hospitals, and most hospital-based physicians are not allowed to provide ambulatory care services.

The structure of production in the United Kingdom now largely takes place in the private, although mostly not-for-profit, sector. The present situation in the United Kingdom is in stark contrast to the method of production that prevailed before the passage of the National Health Service and Community Act of 1990. Up to 1990, almost all hospitals were publicly owned and operated and most doctors were employees of the NHS. Even before 1990, however, family practitioners were community-based in solo or small group practices and simply contracted with the NHS. The Swiss health care system relies upon a combination of private and public providers.

Physician Choice and Referral Practices

Important differences in the availability and utilization of medical services can also result from the degree of physician choice the health care consumer possesses and the types of referral practices used within the health care system. More choice typically provides consumers with increased satisfaction (Schmittdiel et al., 1997). However, greater choice may come at a cost if it leads to a large number of fragmented health care providers that are unable to sufficiently coordinate care or exploit any economies that come with large size (Halm et al., 1997).

In some health care systems, patients have unlimited choice of and full access to any physician or health care provider within any type of setting (such as a clinic or hospital). For example, at one time in the United States, insured individuals could directly seek out any general practitioner or specialist without financial penalty. Moreover, at one time in the United States, it was not unusual for a general practitioner to review the care of a patient referred for hospital services. We see later that conditions regarding physician choice and referral practices have changed a great deal in the United States.

Other countries have adopted different referral practices. Although the Canadian, German, and Swiss health care systems allow free choice of provider, general practitioners in the United Kingdom act as "gatekeepers" and must refer patients to a specialist or a hospital. Once the patient is referred to a hospital, the patient–general practitioner relationship is severed for any particular illness in both the United Kingdom and Germany. Unlike in Germany, however, patients are allowed to go directly to a family practitioner or a hospital for primary care in the United Kingdom, unless they are registered with a GP fundholder.

The Four National Health Care Systems Summarized

Based on our generalized model of a health care system, Table 4–1 provides a capsulized summary of the current structure of the national health care systems in the four countries we have been discussing. We take up a more formal discussion of performance differences in Chapter 16. Each national health care system is differentiated according to the degree of health insurance coverage, type of financing, reimbursement scheme, consumer out-of-pocket price, mode of production, and degree of physician choice. The essential features of the Canadian health care system are national health insurance, free choice of health care provider, private production of medical services, and regulated global budgets and fees for health care providers. The dominating features of the German health care system include socialized health insurance

TABLE 4–1
A Comparison of Health Care Systems

	Country (Type of System)				
Feature	Canada (NHI)*	Germany (SI)†	Switzerland (MC)‡	United Kingdom (PC)§	United States (Pluralistic)
Health insurance coverage	Universal	Near universal	Near universal	Near universal	84 percent
Financing	General taxes	Payroll and general taxes	Premiums	General taxes	Voluntary premiums and general taxes
Type of payer	Single-payer system	Single-payer system§	Single-payer system‖	Single-payer system	Multi-payer system
Reimbursement to hospitals	Global budgets to hospitals	Fixed payments to hospitals	Negotiated payments	Global budgets to hospitals	Mostly fixed payments to hospitals
Reimbursement to physicians	Negotiated fee-for-service to physicians	Negotiated point-fee-for-service to physicians	Negotiated fees	Salaries and capitation payments to physicians	Mostly fee-for-service to physicians
Consumer out-of-pocket price	Negligible	Negligible	High	Negligible	Positive, but generally small
Production	Private	Private	Public and private	Private but public contract	Private
Physician choice	Unlimited	Unlimited	Unlimited	Limited	Relatively limited

*NHI = national health insurance program

†SI = socialized insurance

‡MC = managed competition

§PC = public contracting

‖Multiple third-party payers are responsible for paying representatives of the health care providers, but the universal fees are collectively negotiated by the third-party payers.

financed through Sickness Funds, negotiated payments to health care providers, free choice of provider, and private production of health care services. In the case of Great Britain, the distinguishing characteristics include restrictions on choice of provider, public contracting of medical services, global budgets for hospitals, fixed salaries for hospital-based physicians, and capitation payments to family practitioners. Finally, reliance on managed competition is a unique characteristic of the Swiss health care system.

The U.S. health care system is discussed in detail in the next section, and the last column in Table 4–1 gives a quick preview. The pluralistic U.S. health care system contains some structural elements found in most of the other four systems (such as private production) but relies more heavily on a fee-for-service reimbursement scheme. In addition, health care providers are reimbursed through multiple payers, including the government and thousands of private insurance companies, in contrast to the single-payer system in Canada (government), Germany (Sickness Funds), and the United Kingdom (government).

An Overview of the U.S. Health Care System

Some analysts argue that the multifaceted nature of the health care system accounts for the relatively high expenditures devoted to medical care in the United States. Although this may be true and is a topic of discussion throughout this book, it most certainly is true that this diversity makes it very difficult to describe the U.S. health care system in sufficient detail. This section presents a brief overview of the current system in the United States based on the generalized model of a health care system. The remainder of the book discusses the operation and performance of the U.S. health care system in much greater detail, albeit on a piecemeal basis.

Financing of Health Care in the United States

The United States has no single nationwide system of health insurance. Health insurance is purchased in the private marketplace or provided by the government to certain groups. Private health insurance can be purchased from various for-profit commercial insurance companies or from nonprofit insurers, such as Blue Cross/Blue Shield. About 84 percent of the population is covered by either public (31 percent) or private (64 percent) health insurance.[7]

Approximately 55 percent of health insurance coverage is employment related, largely due to the cost savings associated with group plans that can be purchased through an employer. Employers voluntarily sponsor the health insurance plans. Nearly all privately-insured individuals belong to some type of managed care plan. As we discuss in Chapter 6, managed care plans are designed to practice cost-effective medicine and place varying degrees of restrictions on consumer choices.

In addition to private health insurance, some portion of the U.S. population is covered by public health insurance. The two major types of public health insurance, both of which began in 1966, are **Medicare** and **Medicaid**.[8] Medicare is a uniform, national public health insurance program for aged and disabled individuals (such as those with kidney failure). Administered by the federal government, Medicare is the largest health insurer in the country, covering about 15 percent of the population, and is primarily financed through taxes. The Medicare plan consists of two parts. Part A is compulsory and provides health insurance coverage for inpatient hospital care, very limited nursing home services, and some home health services. Part B, the voluntary or supplemental plan, provides benefits for physician services, outpatient hospital services, outpatient laboratory and radiology services, and home health services.[9]

The second type of public health insurance program, Medicaid, provides coverage for certain economically disadvantaged groups. Medicaid is jointly financed by the federal and state governments and is administered by each state. The federal government provides state governments with a certain percentage of matching funds ranging from 50 to 83 percent, depending on the per capita income in the state. Individuals who are elderly, blind, disabled, or members of families with dependent children must be covered by Medicaid for states to receive federal funds. In addition, although the federal government stipulates a certain basic package of health care benefits (hospital, physician, and nursing home services), some states are more generous than others. Consequently, in some states individuals receive a more generous benefit package under Medicaid than in others. Medicaid is the only public program that finances long-term

---

7. DeNavas-Walt, Proctor, and Smith (2011). The figures for private and public insurance coverage do not sum to 84 percent because of double-counting. For example, some people receiving public insurance coverage also purchase private health insurance.

8. See Chapter 10 for a more detailed discussion on the Medicare and Medicaid programs. The federal government is also responsible for providing health insurance to individuals in the military and to federal employees.

9. Part D, the Medicare coverage of prescription drugs is discussed in Chapter 10. It is voluntary but subsidized and requires premiums and cost-sharing.

nursing home care. Approximately 16 percent of the population is covered by Medicaid.

In summary, the financing of health care falls into three broad categories: private health insurance, Medicare, and Medicaid. However, another category of individuals exists: those who are uninsured. Approximately 16 percent of the U.S. population is estimated to lack health insurance coverage at any point in time. This does not mean these individuals are without access to health care services. Many uninsured people receive health care services through public clinics and hospitals, state and local health programs, or private providers that finance the care through charity and by shifting costs to other payers. Nevertheless, the lack of health insurance can cause uninsured households to face considerable financial hardship and insecurity. Furthermore, the uninsured often find themselves in the emergency room of a hospital, sometimes after it is too late for proper medical treatment. We take up this discussion in later chapters.

Reimbursement for Health Care in the United States

Unlike in Canada and Europe, where a single-payer system is the norm, the United States possesses a multipayer system in which a variety of third-party payers, including the federal and state governments, commercial health insurance companies, and Blue Cross/Blue Shield, are responsible for reimbursing health care providers. Naturally, reimbursement takes on various forms in the United States, depending on the nature of the third-party payer. The most common form of reimbursement is fee-for-service, although most health care providers accept discounted fees from private health insurance plans.

Physician services under Medicare (and most state Medicaid plans) are also reimbursed on a fee-for-service basis, but the fee is set by the government based on the time and effort involved in providing the care. Since 1983, the federal government has reimbursed hospitals on a prospective basis for services provided to Medicare patients. This Medicare reimbursement scheme, called the **diagnosis-related group (DRG)** system, contains 999 different payment categories based on diagnoses, procedures, age, gender, discharge status, and the presence of complications or comorbidities. A prospective payment is established for each DRG. The prospective payment is claimed to provide hospitals with an incentive to contain costs (cells 1 and 3 of Figure 4–2).

Beginning in the early 1980s, many states, such as California, instituted **selective contracting,** in which various health care providers competitively bid for the right to treat Medicaid patients. In fact, much of the favorable experience with selective contracting in the United States led to the adoption of the public contracting model in the United Kingdom (Mechanic, 1995). Under selective contracting, recipients of Medicaid are limited in the choice of health care provider. In addition, to better contain health care costs and coordinate care, the federal government and various state governments have attempted to shift Medicare and Medicaid beneficiaries into managed care organizations (MCOs). About 71 percent of all Medicaid recipients and roughly 23 percent of all Medicare beneficiaries were enrolled in MCOs.

Production of Health Services and Provider Choice in the United States

Like the financing and reimbursement schemes, the U.S. health care system is very diversified in terms of production methods. Government, not-for-profit, and for-profit institutions all play an important role in health care markets. For the most part, primary care physicians in the United States function in the private for-profit sector and operate in group practices, although some physicians work for not-for-profit clinics or in public organizations. In the hospital industry, the not-for-profit is the dominant form of ownership. Specifically, not-for-profit hospitals control about 70 percent of all hospital beds. The ownership structure is the reverse in the nursing home industry, however. More than 70 percent of all nursing homes are organized on a for-profit basis. One should also keep in mind that mental retardation facilities, dialysis facilities, and even insurance companies possess different ownership forms. The variety of ownership forms helps make health care a very difficult, but challenging and interesting, industry to analyze.

We previously mentioned that provider choice matters. Consumers typically receive greater satisfaction from facing more choices. We also discussed, however, that more choices may come at greater costs if small, differentiated providers are unable to fully exploit any economies associated with size. Hence, it is important to know how much choice consumers have over health care providers in the United States.

Up to the early 1980s, most insured individuals had full choice of health care providers in the United States. Consumers could choose to visit a primary caregiver or the outpatient clinic of a hospital, or see a specialist if they chose to. The introduction of restrictive health insurance plans and new government policies such as selective contracting have limited the degree to which consumers can choose their own health care provider. For example, some health care plans require that patients receive their care exclusively from a particular network; otherwise they are fully responsible for the ensuing financial burden. Furthermore, the primary caregiver acts as a gatekeeper and must refer the patient for additional care. Of course, the lower premiums of a restrictive plan compensate consumers at least to some degree for the restriction of choice. There are arguments for and against free choice of provider, and once again trade-offs are involved. This issue will be discussed throughout the text in more depth. For now let us just say that these trade-offs must be given serious thought when determining what degree of consumer choice is best from a societal point of view.

Summary

Every health care system must answer the four basic questions concerning the allocation of medical resources and the distribution of medical services. Some systems rely on centralized decision making whereas others answer the basic questions through a decentralized process. Health care systems are complex largely because third-party payers are involved. Third-party payers help reduce the financial risk associated with the irregularity and uncertainty of many medical transactions. Third-party payers also help monitor the behavior of health care providers.

The financing, reimbursement, and production methods and the degree of choice over the health care provider are important elements that make up a health care system. Medical care is financed by out-of-pocket payments, premiums, and/or taxes. Medical care providers are reimbursed on a fixed or variable basis. The production of medical care may take place in a for-profit, a not-for-profit, or a public setting, and medical care providers may operate in independent or large group practices. Choice of provider may be limited. All these features are important because they affect incentives and thereby often influence the operation and performance of a health care system. For example, many economists predict that fee-for-service insurance plans provide an incentive for medical care providers to produce a large volume of services.

The U.S. health care system is very pluralistic. For instance, considerable variation exists in the financing, reimbursement, and production of medical care. The remainder of this book provides a better understanding about how each of these elements affects the functioning of the U.S. health care system.

Review Questions and Problems

1. Answer the following questions pertaining to health care systems.
   A. Why isn't the market for health care services organized according to a typical consumer (patient) and producer (health provider) relationship?
   B. What are the basic differences between insurance premiums and taxes as sources of medical care financing?
   C. How might the reimbursement method differ among health care providers? Why might the reimbursement method make a difference?
   D. Identify the four basic kinds of health care systems discussed in this chapter.
   E. Point out some unique institutions (compared to the United States) associated with the health care systems of the various countries discussed in this chapter.

2. Suppose you had the opportunity to organize the perfect health care system. Explain how you would organize the financing method, reimbursement scheme, mode of production, and physician referral procedure.

3. Which of the following reimbursement and consumer copayment schemes would have the greatest and lowest likelihood of producing high-cost, low-benefit medicine? Explain your answers.
   A. Fee-for-service plan with 40 percent consumer copayment.
   B. Prepaid health plan with 40 percent consumer copayment.
   C. Fee-for-service plan with no consumer-cost sharing.
   D. Fixed-salary plan with no consumer-cost sharing.
   E. Prepaid health plan with no consumer-cost sharing.
   F. Fixed-salary plan with 40 percent consumer-cost sharing.

4. Answer the following questions regarding the U.S. health care system.
   A. What are the basic differences between conventional health insurance and managed care health insurance in terms of type of insurance offered and reimbursement practice?
   B. What is the difference between Medicare and Medicaid? How is Medicare financed? How is Medicaid financed?
   C. What is the DRG system? How are physicians currently reimbursed under the Medicare system?

Online Resources

To access Internet links related to the topics in this chapter, please visit our website at **www.cengage.com/economics/santerre**.

References

Arrow, Kenneth J. "Uncertainty and the Welfare Economics of Medical Care." *American Economic Review* 53 (December 1963), pp. 941–73.

Bodenheimer, Thomas, and Kevin Grumbach. "Financing Universal Health Insurance: Taxes, Premiums and the Lessons of Social Insurance." *Journal of Health Politics, Policy and Law* 17 (fall 1992), pp. 439–62.

DeNavas-Walt, Carmen, Bernadette D. Proctor, and Jessica C. Smith. "Income, Poverty, and Health Insurance Coverage in the United States: 2010."

U.S. Census Bureau, *Current Population Reports*, pp. 60–239, U.S. Government Printing Office, Washington, DC, 2011.

Ellis, Randall P., and Thomas G. McGuire. "Supply-Side and Demand-Side Cost Sharing in Health Care." *Journal of Economic Perspectives* 7 (fall 1993), pp. 135–51.

Halm, Ethan A., Nancyanne Causino, and David Blumenthal. "Is Gatekeeping Better Than Traditional Care?" *Journal of the American Medical Association* 278 (November 1997), pp. 1677–81.

Hansmann, Henry A. *The Ownership of Enterprise.* Cambridge, Mass.: The Bellnap Press of Harvard University Press, 1996.

Mechanic, David. "Americanization of the British NHS." *Health Affairs* 14 (summer 1995), pp. 51–67.

Mosby Medical Encyclopedia. New York: C. V. Mosby, 1992.

Raffel, Marshall W., ed. *Health Care and Reform in Industrial Countries.* University Park: Pennsylvania State University Press, 1997.

Reinhardt, Uwe. "Economics." *Journal of the American Medical Association* 275 (June 1996), pp. 23–25.

Reinhardt, Uwe. "The Swiss Health Care System: Regulated Competition Without Managed Care." *Journal of the American Medical Association* 292 (September 2004), pp. 1227–1241.

Schmittdiel, Julie, Joe V. Selby, Kevin Grumbach, and Charles P. Quesenberry. "Choice of Personal Physician and Patient Satisfaction in a Health Maintenance Organization." *Journal of the American Medical Association* 278 (November 1997), pp. 1596–99.

Van de Ven, Wynand, P. M. M., and Randall P. Ellis. "Risk Adjustment in Competitive Health Plan Markets." In *Handbook in Health Economics*, eds. A. J. Calger and J. P. Newhouse. Amsterdam: North-Holland, 2000, chap. 14, pp. 755–845.

Weisbrod, Burton A. The *Nonprofit Economy.* Cambridge, Mass.: Harvard University Press, 1988.

CHAPTER 5

The Demand for Medical Care

Many people have the misconception that economic theory has little relevance to the demand for medical care because economic factors are not important when someone needs urgent medical attention. Recall Joe in Chapter 1, who awoke one night with a pain in his chest and realized he was having a heart attack. It is highly unlikely that he and his wife considered the price of medical care as Joe was being rushed to the hospital.

However, most visits to a physician's office and the majority of visits to a hospital emergency room are not of a life-threatening nature. Thus, for many medical care transactions, there is sufficient time to make conscious choices, and price often plays an important role in the determination of choices. A recent survey of working adults with private insurance coverage substantiates the critical role price plays in determining the demand for medical care. According to the survey, over 40 percent of the respondents inquired about the price of the medical services prior to receiving care. Moreover, that percent increased with the size of the annual deductible, topping off at almost 70 percent for individuals with an annual deductible of $10,000 (Lynch and Smith, 2011).

This chapter explores the demand side of the medical care market. This chapter highlights:

- the theoretical derivation of the demand curve for medical services
- economic and noneconomic variables that influence the demand for medical services
- the impact of health insurance on the demand for medical services
- the concept of elasticity of demand
- a review of the empirical literature concerning the factors that determine the demand for medical care
- how various provisions of the Patient Protection and Affordable Care Act (PPACA) of 2010 may influence the demand for medical care.

The Demand for Medical Care and the Law of Demand

To derive the demand curve for medical care, we must first establish the relation between the quantity of medical care and utility. Recall from Chapter 2 that the stock of health can be treated as a durable good that generates utility and is subject to the law of diminishing marginal utility.[1] This means that each incremental improvement in health generates successively smaller additions to total utility. We also know that medical services represent an input in the production of health. As such, people consume medical care services for the express purpose of maintaining, restoring, or improving their health. However, the law of diminishing marginal productivity tells us the marginal improvement to health brought about by each additional unit decreases at some amount of medical care.

From this discussion, it follows that medical care indirectly provides utility in the sense that medical care helps to produce health, which in turn generates utility. Consequently, utility can be conceptualized as a function of the quantity of medical care consumed, albeit through an indirect process. Figure 5–1 depicts this hypothesized relation between the level of medical care consumed and utility. Utility is specified on the vertical axis, and the quantity of medical care (q) is measured on the horizontal axis. The shape of the total utility curve indicates that utility increases at a decreasing rate with respect to medical care, or that medical care services are subject to diminishing marginal utility. Marginal utility decreases because (1) each successive unit of medical care generates a smaller improvement in health than the previous

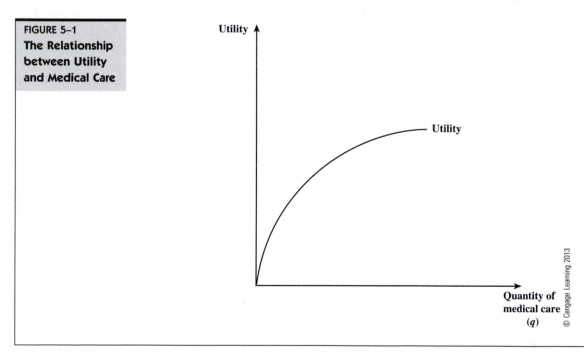

FIGURE 5–1
The Relationship between Utility and Medical Care

© Cengage Learning 2013

The shape of the utility curve illustrates that total utility increases at a decreasing rate with respect to the level of medical care consumed. The curve has a bow shape for two reasons. First, each additional unit of medical care consumed results in a smaller increase in health than the previous unit because of the law of diminishing marginal productivity. Second, each additional improvement in health generates a smaller increase in utility because of the law of diminishing marginal utility.

---

1. As a reminder, note that we continue to ignore the intermediate step between the stock of health, the services it provides, and utility.

unit (due to the law of diminishing marginal productivity) and (2) each increase in health, in turn, generates a smaller increase in utility (due to the law of diminishing marginal utility).

The Utility-Maximizing Rule

Given market prices at a particular point in time, consumers must decide which combination of goods and services, including medical care, to purchase with their fixed incomes. According to microeconomic theory, each consumer chooses the bundle of goods and services that maximizes utility. Without working through the mathematics underlying the process, logic dictates that consumer utility is maximized when the marginal utility gained from the last dollar spent on each product is equal across all goods and services purchased.[2] This condition is known as the **utility-maximizing rule**, and basically states that total utility reaches its peak when the consumer receives the maximum "bang for the buck" in terms of marginal utility per dollar of income from each and every good consumed. In mathematical terms, the rule states that utility is maximized when

(5–1) $$MU_q/P_q = MU_z/P_z,$$

where MU_q represents the marginal utility received from the last unit of medical care purchased, q, and MU_z equals the marginal utility derived from the last unit of all other goods, z. The latter good is often referred to as a *composite good* in economics. To illustrate why the utility-maximizing rule must hold theoretically, suppose that

(5–2) $$MU_q/P_q > MU_z/P_z.$$

In this case, the last dollar spent on medical care generates more additional utility than the last dollar spent on all other goods. It follows that the consumer can increase total utility by reallocating expenditures and purchasing more units of medical care and fewer units of all other goods. But remember, as the consumer purchases more medical services at the expense of all other goods (and recalling the consumer's income and the composite good's price are fixed), the marginal utility of medical care falls and the marginal utility of other goods increases. These spending adjustments, in turn, cause the value of MU_q/P_q to fall and the value of MU_z/P_z to increase. In fact, according to economic theory, the consumer continues to purchase additional units of medical services until the equality in Equation 5–1 again holds such that the last dollar spent on each medical care and all other goods generates the same amount of additional satisfaction. At this point, total utility is maximized and any further changes in spending patterns will negatively affect total utility.

The Law of Demand

The equilibrium condition specified in Equation 5–1 can be used to trace out the demand curve for a particular medical service, such as physician services. For simplicity, assume the prices of all other goods and income remain constant and initially the consumer is purchasing the optimal mix of physician services and all other goods. Now assume the price of physician services increases. As a result, the ratio MU_q/P_q declines relative to the ratio MU_z/P_z (where MU_q and P_q represent the marginal utility and price of physician services, respectively). Consequently, the consumer receives more satisfaction per dollar from consuming all other goods. Moreover, in reaction to the relative price increase, the consumer purchases fewer units of physician services and more units of all other goods. This reallocation continues until both MU_q/P_q and MU_z/P_z

---

2. That is, assuming all prices are known, income is spent over the period in question, and all products are subject to the law of diminishing marginal utility.

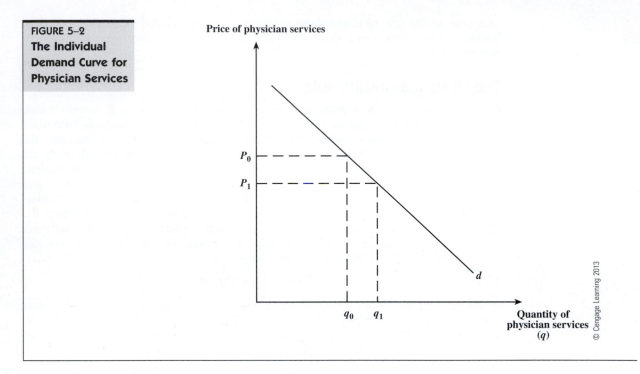

FIGURE 5–2
The Individual
Demand Curve for
Physician Services

The individual demand curve for physician services is downward sloping, illustrating that quantity demanded increases as the price of physician services drops. Utility analysis, or the income and substitution effects, can be used to derive this inverse relationship, which is called the *law of demand*.

adjust so that the equilibrium condition of Equation 5–1 is again in force such that the last dollar spent on each good generates an equal amount of utility. Thus, economic theory predicts an inverse relation exists between the price and the quantity demanded of physician services.

If the price of physician services continually changes, we can determine a number of points representing the relation between the price and the quantity demanded of physician services. Using this information, we can map out a demand curve like the one depicted in Figure 5–2, where the horizontal axis indicates the amount of physician services consumed (e.g., as measured by the number of office visits) and the vertical axis equals the price of physician services per visit. The curve is downward sloping and reflects the inverse relation between the price and the quantity demanded of physician services, *ceteris paribus*. For example, if the price of physician services equals P_0, the consumer is willing and able to purchase q_0. Notice that if the price falls to P_1, the consumer purchases q_1 amount of physician services.

In the case of medical care we should note that price represents the per-unit out-of-pocket expense the consumer incurs when purchasing medical services from a physician. As such, it equals the amount the consumer pays after the impact of third-party payments has been taken into account. Naturally, if the visit to the physician is not covered by a third party, the actual or market price of the visit equals the out-of-pocket expense.

Some noneconomists are bothered by the fact that marginal utility cannot be directly measured and, thus, are reluctant to agree with the previous analysis. In response, economists also point to the substitution and income effects normally associated with a relative price change as another theoretical justification for this inverse relation between price and quantity demanded. In the case of medical care, both of these effects predict that a higher price leads to a smaller quantity demanded and, conversely, a lower price results in a greater quantity demanded. According to the substitution effect, a decrease in the price of physician services causes the consumer to substitute away from relatively higher-priced medical goods, such as hospital outpatient services, and purchase more physician services. That is, lower-priced services are substituted for higher-priced ones. As a result, the quantity demanded of physician services increases as price decreases according to the substitution effect.

In terms of the income effect, a lower price also increases the real purchasing power of the consumer. As long as medical care represents a normal good (which we discuss later), the quantity demanded of physician services increases with the rise in purchasing power. This purchasing power effect also generates an inverse relation between price and quantity demanded because as price falls, real income increases and quantity demanded rises. Taken together, the substitution and income effects indicate that the quantity demanded of physician services decreases as price increases.

In summary, Figure 5–2 captures the inverse relationship between the price the consumer pays for medical care (in this instance, physician services) and quantity demanded. The curve represents the amount of medical care the consumer is willing and able to purchase at every out-of-pocket price. Utility analysis, or the income and substitution effects, can be used to generate this theoretical relationship which is often referred to as the **law of demand**. Note that the demand for medical care is a *derived* demand because it depends on the demand for good health. A visit to a dentist illustrates this point because an individual typically receives no utility directly from having a cavity filled. Rather, utility is generated from an improvement in dental health.

Of course, besides out-of-pocket price, other economic and noneconomic variables also influence how much health care services people actually buy. Unlike out-of-pocket price, which causes a movement along the demand curve, we will see that these other factors influence quantity demanded by altering the position of the demand curve. These other economic and noneconomic determinants of demand are the topic of the next section.

Other Economic Demand-Side Factors

It's probably not surprising to you but income is another important economic variable affecting the demand for medical services. How changes in income influence demand depend on whether specific types of medical care represent normal or inferior goods. Normal goods exhibit a direct relation between changes in income and demand whereas the demand for inferior goods shares an inverse relation with changes in income.[3] Figure 5–3 illustrates what happens to the demand for physician services when income increases, assuming physician services represent a normal good. The increase in income causes the demand curve to shift to the right from d_0 to d_1, because at each price the consumer is willing and able to purchase more physician services. Similarly, for each quantity of medical services, the consumer is willing to pay a higher price. This is attributable to the fact that at least some portion of the increase in income is spent on physician services. Conversely, a decrease in income causes the demand curve to shift to the left.

The demand for a specific type of medical service is also likely to depend on the prices of other goods, particularly other types of related medical services. For example, if two or more goods are jointly used for consumption purposes, economists say that they are **complements** in consumption: Because the goods are consumed together, an increase in the price of one good inversely influences the demand for

---

3. A classic nonmedical example of an inferior good is hamburger. As real income increases, the consumer may prefer to buy more expensive cuts of meat and purchase fewer hamburgers. Research has shown that tooth extractions represent inferior goods. That is, higher income individuals, when facing dental problems, pay for expensive procedures such as crowns and fillings rather than have their teeth extracted.

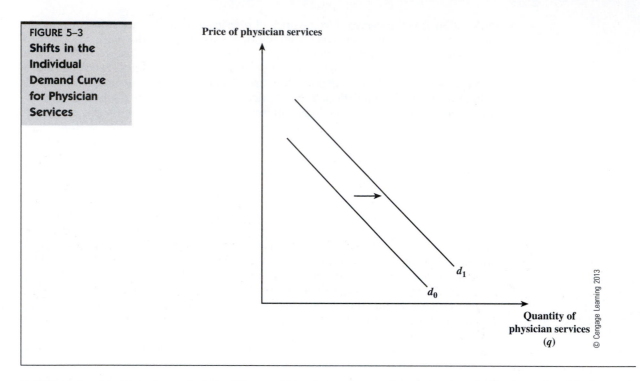

FIGURE 5-3
Shifts in the Individual Demand Curve for Physician Services

Price of physician services

d_1

d_0

Quantity of physician services (q)

© Cengage Learning 2013

Medical care is assumed to be a normal good, which means that as income increases the consumer spends at least a portion of the increase in purchasing power on additional physician services. As a result, the individual demand curve for physician services shifts to the right, from d_0 to d_1, when income increases. At each price, the consumer is now willing and able to purchase more physician services.

the other. For example, the demand for eyewear (i.e., glasses or contact lenses) and the services of an optometrist are likely to be highly complementary. Normally, an individual has an eye examination before purchasing eyewear. If these two goods are complements in consumption, the demand for optometric services should increase in response to a drop in the price of eyewear. In graphical terms, the demand curve for optometric services shifts to the right. A complementary relation may also exist between obstetric and pediatric services. If so, an increase in the price of pediatric services should inversely influence the demand for obstetric services. For example, a woman may postpone pregnancy and reduce her demand for obstetric services because of a high cost associated with pediatric services. Graphically, the demand curve for obstetric services shifts to the left in response to the higher price of pediatric services.

It is also possible for two or more goods to satisfy the same wants or provide the same characteristics. If that is the case, economists say that the goods are **substitutes** in consumption: The demand for one good is directly related to a change in the price of a substitute good. For example, suppose physician services and hospital outpatient services are substitutes in consumption. As the price of outpatient services increases, the consumer is likely to alter consumption patterns and purchase more physician services because the price of a visit to the doctor is cheaper in relative terms. That causes the demand curve for physician services to shift to the right. Generic and brand-name drugs provide another example of two substitute goods. The demand for brand-name drugs should decrease with a decline in the price of generic drugs. If so, graphically the demand curve for brand-name drugs shifts to the left. Finally, eyeglasses and contact lenses are likely to be substitutes in consumption.

Time costs may also influence the quantity demanded of medical services. Time costs include the monetary cost of travel, such as bus fare or gasoline, plus the opportunity cost of time. The opportunity cost of an individual's time represents the dollar value of the activities the person forgoes when acquiring medical services. For example, if a plumber who earns $50 an hour takes two hours off from work to visit a dentist, the opportunity cost of the time equals $100. The implication is that the opportunity cost of time is directly related to a person's wage rate. Given time costs, it is not surprising that children and elderly people often fill doctors' waiting rooms. Time costs can accrue while traveling to and from a medical provider, waiting to see the provider, and experiencing delays in securing an appointment. In other words, time costs increase the further an individual has to travel to see a physician, the longer the wait at the doctor's office, and the longer the delay in getting an appointment. It stands to reason that the demand for medical care falls as time costs increase (i.e., as the demand curve shifts to the left graphically).

The Relationship between Health Insurance and the Demand for Medical Care

Increasing medical insurance coverage in the United States is one of the most significant developments in the health care field since the 1960s. In particular, health insurance has had a profound influence on the allocation of resources within the medical care market, primarily through its impact on the out-of-pocket price that people pay for medical care services. In fact, out-of-pocket payments for health care dropped from almost half of total expenditures in 1960 to approximately one-eighth in 2010. Even more striking, out-of-pocket payments for hospital care fell from nearly 21 percent in 1960 to a mere 3 percent in 2010. Given that various features are associated with health insurance policies, it is impossible to discuss the economic implications of each one. Here we focus on three of the more common features of health insurance policies: coinsurance, copayments, and deductibles.

Coinsurance and Copayments. Many health insurance plans, particularly private plans, have a **coinsurance** component. Under a coinsurance plan, the consumer pays some fixed percentage of the cost of health care and the insurance carrier picks up the other portion. For example, under a plan with a coinsurance rate of 20 percent (a common arrangement), the consumer pays 20 cents out of every dollar spent on health care and the carrier picks up the remaining 80 cents. As you can imagine, an insurance plan like this one has a significant impact on the demand for health care because it effectively lowers the out-of-pocket price of health care by 80 percent.

Let's begin our discussion of coinsurance coverage by looking at the demand curve for medical care from an alternative perspective. We normally think of the demand curve as revealing the amount of a good that a consumer is willing and able to buy at various prices. However, a demand curve also shows the consumer's willingness to pay (or marginal benefit) for each unit of a good. The negative slope of the curve indicates that the willingness to pay falls as more of the good is consumed due to the law of diminishing marginal utility.

For example, the demand curve d_{WO} (WO = without insurance) in Figure 5–4 represents the consumer's demand or willingness to pay for office visits in the absence of health insurance coverage. This "effective" demand curve reveals that the consumer is willing to pay $50 for the fifth office visit. If $50 is the market price paid by the consumer, she visits the physician five times during the year in the process of maximizing utility because any additional office visits do not yield benefits that compensate for their higher out-of-pocket costs. Notice that the consumer's willingness to pay for the first four visits, as revealed by the effective demand curve, exceeds the market price of $50. The difference between the willingness to pay and the market price paid

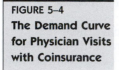

FIGURE 5–4
The Demand Curve for Physician Visits with Coinsurance

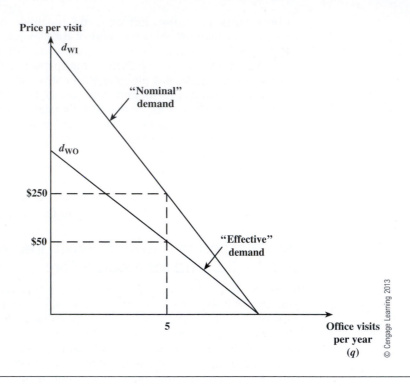

© Cengage Learning 2013

The graph illustrates how a coinsurance health plan impacts the individual demand curve for physician visits. The demand curve labeled d_{WO} is the individual's effective demand without insurance while the demand curve labeled d_{WI} is with insurance. The nominal demand curve d_{WI} traces out the total price for various physician visits and captures that portion paid by consumers as out-of-pocket payments as well as that portion paid by the insurance carrier. If you draw a vertical line from any point on the nominal demand curve to the horizontal axis, you can break down the amount paid by consumers (from the horizontal axis to the d_{WO} curve) and the amount paid by the insurance carrier (the wedge between the d_{WI} and d_{WO} curves). As the coinsurance rate falls, d_{WI} rotates upward and pivots off the point where the two curves cross the horizontal axis.

is referred to as a customer surplus and, in this example, reflects the net benefits received from visiting the doctor for the first four times.[4]

Now suppose the consumer acquires a health insurance plan that requires her to pay a certain fraction, C_0, of the actual price, P. In this case, the insurance coverage drives a wedge between the willingness to pay, or effective demand, and the actual price, or "nominal" demand, for the office visits. Because the utility-maximizing consumer determines the optimal number of times to visit the physician by equating her willingness to pay (or marginal benefit) to the out-of-pocket price (marginal cost), the relationship between the actual and out-of-pocket price can be specified by the following equation:

(5–3) $$P_W = C_0 P.$$

Here P_W stands for the consumer's willingness to pay for the last visit, and C_0 represents the coinsurance amount. If we solve Equation 5–3 for the actual price, we get

(5–4) $$P = P_W / C_0.$$

Because the coinsurance, C_0, is less than 1, it follows that the actual price paid, or nominal demand, for office visits is greater than the out-of-pocket price the consumer

---

4. As discussed in Chapter 8, market price considers both supply and demand conditions. The demand curves in Figure 5–4 represent the effective and nominal demands of an individual. Individual demands must be horizontally summed to arrive at a market demand and then interacted with supply to determine the market price.

pays. For example, if she is willing to pay $50 for five visits to a doctor and the coinsurance is 20 percent of the full price, the actual price equals $250 per visit, or $50/0.2.

The nominal demand curve labeled d_{WI} (WI = with insurance) in Figure 5–4 reflects the total price paid for medical services that takes into account a particular coinsurance rate paid by the insured. The vertical distance between d_{WI} and the horizontal axis represents the total price for office visits, which can be broken down into the amount the consumer pays and the amount the insurance carrier pays. The portion of the total price the consumer pays as an out-of-pocket payment equals the distance between the horizontal axis and the d_{WO} demand curve. The remaining distance between the two curves represents the amount the insurance carrier pays. It represents the wedge that coinsurance drives between the consumer's willingness to pay, or effective demand, and the total price paid, or nominal demand.

It is easy to see from this analysis that reductions in the coinsurance rate cause the nominal demand curve d_{WI} to rotate clockwise and pivot off the point where d_{WO} crosses the horizontal axis. At a zero willingness-to-pay price, insurance has no bearing on quantity demanded because medical care is a free good to the individual. In addition, the nominal demand curve d_{WI} becomes steeper as the coinsurance, C_0, decreases in value as indicated by Equation 5–4. That makes intuitive sense, because we expect the consumer to become less sensitive to changes in the total price as the coinsurance declines and less is paid out-of-pocket.

In the case where the consumer has full coverage ($C_0 = 0$), the nominal demand curve d_{WI} rotates out to its fullest extent and becomes completely vertical. This is shown in Figure 5–5. Because the consumer faces a zero price, she consumes medical care as though it were a free good, when in reality it has a nonzero price. Equation 5–4 can be used to illustrate that point. As C_0 approaches zero, the total price is potentially infinity for nonzero values of P_w.

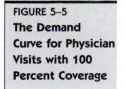

FIGURE 5–5

The Demand Curve for Physician Visits with 100 Percent Coverage

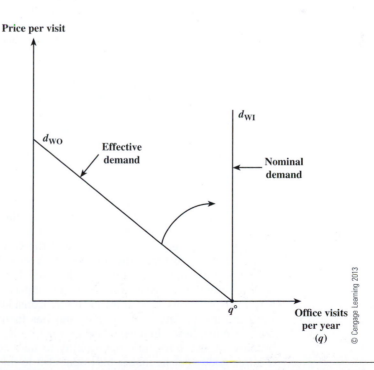

The graph illustrates the situation in which the individual has complete medical coverage and the coinsurance rate is zero. Notice that the nominal demand curve is vertical because the individual faces a zero out-of-pocket price and visits the physician without regard to the actual price.

Coinsurance should not be confused with a copayment. A **copayment** represents a fixed amount paid by the consumer that is independent of the market price or actual costs of medical care. For example, a person may be required to pay $10 for each office visit regardless of the actual fee negotiated by the health insurer with the physician. Like a lower coinsurance rate, a reduced copayment results in a movement down the effective demand curve and typically leads to greater quantity of care demanded. But unlike a change in the coinsurance rate, a change in the copayment does not cause a rotation of the nominal demand because the consumer's portion of the bill is independent rather than proportional to nominal demand (i.e., the actual price paid).

Also unlike coinsurance, a copayment does not automatically change with an adjustment in the costs of providing medical care. For example, suppose, in response to higher production costs, a physician negotiates a higher price with the insurer for each office visit so that the market price increases from $100 to $150. An insured individual who is responsible for paying 20 percent of the cost now faces a $10 increase in his coinsurance from $20 to $30 per office visit. However, an insured individual who is required to pay a copayment of $10 per office visit is unaffected by the higher negotiated price for an office visit (at least until the insurance policy is renegotiated). Thus, compared to a copayment, coinsurance makes consumers more sensitive to a change in the actual market price of medical care.

Deductibles. Many insurance policies have a deductible whereby the consumer must pay out of pocket a fixed amount of health care costs per calendar year before coverage begins. For example, the plan may call for the individual to pay the initial $200 of health care expenses with a limit of $500 per family per year. Once the deductible is met, the insurance carrier pays all or some portion of the remaining medical bills, depending on how the plan is specified. From the insurance carrier's perspective, the purpose of a deductible is to lower costs. This is accomplished in two ways.

First, the deductible is likely to lower administrative costs because fewer small claims will be filed over the course of a year. Second, the deductible is likely to have a negative impact on the demand for health care. The extent to which this is true, however, is difficult to determine and depends on such factors as the cost of the medical episode, the point in time when the medical care is demanded, and the probability of needing additional medical care for the remainder of the period. To illustrate, assume a new deductible is put in place at the beginning of each calendar year. Once the deductible is met, the consumer has full medical coverage. It is easy to see that the extent to which a deductible influences the demand for medical services for any one medical episode is likely to be inversely related to the cost of the medical services involved. For example, if the consumer faces a potentially large medical bill for an operation, the existence of a deductible is likely to have little impact on demand. This is because, in relative terms, the deductible represents very little money. On the other hand, a deductible may play a crucial role in the decision to purchase medical care if the cost of such care is relatively inexpensive. In this case, the out-of-pocket cost is substantial relative to the total cost, and the consumer may elect not to purchase the medical care or postpone the purchase to a later date.

It is slightly more difficult to understand how the health of the individual, along with the time of the year, influences the impact of a deductible on demand. The best way to explain this is with an example. Consider a normally healthy individual who contracts the flu late in November and has incurred no medical expenses up to this point. Under these circumstances, he may be less inclined to visit the doctor. This is because he will have little opportunity to take advantage of the fact that health care is a free good after he makes his initial visit to the physician and fulfills the deductible. On the other hand, this same individual is much more likely to visit the physician if he catches the flu early in February and his overall health is such that he can expect to visit the physician three or four more times over the remainder of the year. By visiting the doctor and meeting the deductible, he lowers the cost of any future visits to zero for the rest of the year. Therefore, a deductible is likely to have the greatest negative impact on the demand for medical care when the cost of the medical episode is low, the need for care is late in the calendar year, and the probability of needing future care is slight because the person is in good health.

Moral Hazard

Before we leave the subject of the impact of insurance on the demand for medical care, we need to introduce the concept of moral hazard. **Moral hazard** refers to the situation in which consumers alter their behavior when provided with health insurance. For example, health insurance may induce consumers to take fewer precautions to prevent illnesses or to shop very little for the best medical prices. In addition, insured consumers may purchase more medical care than they otherwise would have without insurance coverage. Let's illustrate this point by referring to Figure 5–4. According to the graph, a consumer without insurance purchases five units of medical services at a price of $50 per unit. If that consumer acquires full medical coverage such that the insurer's coinsurance rate, C_0, equals zero, the quantity demanded of medical care increases to the point where the demand curve crosses the horizontal axis. At this point, the consumer buys medical care as though it was a free good because she faces a zero price. Thus, any extension of medical insurance coverage has the potential to increase the consumption of medical care because consumers no longer pay the full price. The availability and extensiveness of health insurance may have a profound effect on medical care expenditures. Chapters 6 and 11 examine the implications of moral hazard in more detail.

Noneconomic Determinants of the Demand for Medical Care

Four general noneconomic factors influence the demand for medical services: tastes and preferences, physical and mental profile, state of health, and quality of care.

Taste and preference factors include personal characteristics such as marital status, education, and lifestyle, which might affect how people value their healthy time (i.e., their marginal utility of health), or might lead to a greater preference for certain types of medical services. Marital status is likely to impact the demand for health care in the marketplace primarily through its effect on the production of health care in the home. A married individual is likely to demand less medical care, particularly hospital care, because of the availability of a spouse to care for him at home, such as when recuperating from an illness.

The impact of education on the demand for medical care is difficult to predict. On the one hand, a consumer with additional education may be more willing to seek medical care to slow down the rate of health depreciation because that consumer may have a better understanding of the potential impact of medical care on health. As an example, an individual with a high level of education may be more inclined to visit a dentist for periodic examinations. Thus, we should observe a direct relation between educational attainment and demand.

On the other hand, an individual with a high level of education may make more efficient use of home-produced health care services to slow down the rate of health depreciation and, as a result, demand fewer medical care services. For example, such an individual may be more likely to understand the value of preventive medicine (such as proper diet and exercise). In addition, the individual may be more likely to recognize the early warning signs of illness and be more apt to visit a health care provider when symptoms first occur. As a result, health care problems are addressed early when treatment has a greater probability of success and is less costly. That means that we should observe an inverse relation between the level of education and the demand for medical care, particularly acute care.

Finally, lifestyle variables, such as whether the individual smokes cigarettes or drinks alcohol in excessive amounts, affect health status and consequently the amount of health care demanded. For example, a person may try to compensate for the detrimental health impact of smoking by consuming more health care services. That translates into an increased demand for medical care.

The *profile* variable considers the impact of such factors as gender, race/ethnicity, and age on the demand for medical services. For example, females generally demand more health care services than males primarily because of childbearing. In addition, certain diseases, such as cardiovascular disease, osteoporosis, immunologic diseases (such as thyroid disease and rheumatoid arthritis), mental disorders, and Alzheimer's disease, are more prevalent in women than men (Miller, 1994). Age also plays a vital role in determining the demand for medical care. As we stated in Chapter 2, as an individual ages, the overall stock of health depreciates more rapidly. To compensate for this loss in health, the demand for medical care is likely to increase with age, at least beyond the middle years (the demand curve shifts to the right). Thus, we should observe a direct relation between age and the demand for medical care.

State of health controls for the fact that sicker people demand more medical services, everything else held constant. As you might expect, health status and the demand for health care are also likely to be directly related to the severity of the illness. For example, a person who is born with a medical problem, such as hemophilia, is likely to have a much higher than average demand for medical care. In economics jargon, an individual who is endowed with less health is likely to demand more medical care in an attempt to augment the overall stock of health. As another example, Fuchs and Frank (2002) find an increased use of medical care, both inpatient and outpatient care, among Medicare recipients living in highly polluted metropolitan areas of the United States. The relationship holds even after controlling for population, education, income, racial composition, and cigarette use.

Finally, although nebulous and impossible to quantify, the *quality of care* is also likely to impact the demand for medical care. Because quality cannot be measured directly, it is usually assumed to be positively related to the amount and types of inputs used to produce medical care. Feldstein (1967, pp. 158–62) defines the quality of care as "a catch-all term to denote the general level of amenities to patients as well as additional expenditures on professional staff and equipment." For example, a consumer may feel that larger hospitals provide better-quality care than smaller ones because they have more specialists on staff along with more sophisticated equipment. Or, that same individual may think that physicians who have graduated from prestigious medical schools provide a higher quality of care than those who have not. It matters little whether the difference in the quality of medical care provided is real or illusory. What matters is that the consumer perceives that differences in quality actually exist.

With regard to the previous example, it is certainly not the case that larger hospitals provide better care for all types of hospital services. However, if the consumer generally feels that larger hospitals provide better services, the demand for medical services at larger hospitals will be greater than at smaller ones. As Feldstein's definition indicates, quality can also depend on things that have little to do with the actual production of effective medical care. For example, the consumer may prefer a physician who has a pleasant office with a comfortable waiting room along with a courteous support staff. Thus, any increase in the quality of care provided is likely to increase that consumer's demand for medical care regardless of whether it affects the actual production of health care.

Before we move on, we must distinguish between a movement along the demand curve and a shift of the curve. A change in the price of medical services generates a change in the quantity demanded, and this is represented by a movement along the demand curve. If any of the other factors change, such as income or time costs, the demand curve for medical services shifts. This shift is referred to as a change in demand. Thus, a change in the quantity demanded is illustrated by a movement along the demand curve, while a change in demand is illustrated by a shift of the curve.

In summary, let's review the variables we expect to influence an individual's demand for medical care. Economic theory indicates that the demand equation should look something like the following:

(5–5)   Quantity demanded $= f($out-of-pocket price, income, time costs, prices of

substitutes and complements, tastes and preferences,

profile, state of health, and quality of care$)$

Equation 5–5 states that the quantity demanded of medical services is a function of, or depends on, the general factors listed. Note that a change in the first factor results in a movement along a given demand curve, whereas adjustments in the other factors produce a shift of the demand curve. A rightward shift indicates a greater demand and a leftward shift reveals a lower demand.

The Market Demand for Medical Care

Up to now, we have been discussing an individual's demand for medical care services. The market demand for medical care, such as physician services, equals the total demand by all consumers in a given market. In graphical terms, we can construct the market demand curve for medical care services by horizontally summing the individual demand curves. This curve represents the amount of medical services that the entire market is willing and able to purchase at various prices. For example, if the average price of a visit to a doctor is $50 and at this price consumer A is willing to see a physician three times over the course of a year while consumer B is willing to make four visits, the total, or market, demand for physician services is seven visits per year at $50 per visit. The market demand curve is downward sloping for the same reasons the individual demand curves are downward sloping. In addition, the factors that shift the individual demand curves also shift the overall market demand curve, provided the changes take place on a marketwide basis. The market demand curve also shifts if the overall number of consumers in the market increases or decreases. For example, the demand for medical care in a particular community may increase if it experiences an influx of new residents. This causes the market demand curve to shift to the right.

The development of a market demand curve allows us to distinguish between the intensive and extensive margins. The **intensive margin** refers to how much more or less of a product consumers buy when its price changes. The **extensive margin** captures how many more or fewer people buy a product when its price changes. Obviously, this is an important distinction to make for a product like medical care. Many medical purchases such as surgeries happen only once for a particular individual. As another example, an individual can have a particular tooth pulled only once. This is also a one-shot purchase that either happens or does not happen. If the price of tooth extraction falls, however, we may still observe an inverse relationship between the price and number of teeth extracted. That is because at the extensive margin, more consumers elect to purchase this onetime form of dental services as price falls. Consequently, quantity demanded may increase with a reduction in price because of changes that occur at the intensive and extensive margins.

The Fuzzy Demand Curve

Up to this point, we have assumed the market demand curve for medical care is a well-defined line, implying a precise relation between price and quantity demanded. In reality this is usually not the case, and we need to refer to the derivation of the demand curve for medical care to see why. Recall that the demand for medical care is a derived demand and depends on the demand for health and the extent to which medical care influences the production of health. The relation between medical care and health, however, is far from exact. That is because there is a considerable lack of medical knowledge concerning the efficacy of certain types of medical interventions. As a result, health care providers disagree about the treatment of some types of medical problems, and the demand for medical services becomes fuzzy. For example, there is debate among physicians concerning when surgery is necessary for elderly males with prostate cancer.

In addition, in some instances consumers may lack the information or medical knowledge they need to make informed choices. Consequently, consumers tend to rely heavily on the advice of their physicians when making such decisions—as when a particular medical test or surgery is necessary. The implication is that physicians, rather than consumers, choose medical services, which makes the demand curve fuzzier. Further complicating matters is the inability to accurately measure medical care, an issue we touched on earlier. For example, how do we measure the quantity of medical care produced during a one-hour therapy session with a psychiatrist?

All these factors combined make it extremely difficult to accurately delineate the relation between the price and the quantity demanded of medical care. In other words, the relation between price and quantity demanded is rather fuzzy (Aaron, 1991). A more accurate depiction of the relation between price and quantity may not be a well-defined line but a gray band similar to the one depicted in Figure 5–6.

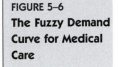

FIGURE 5–6
The Fuzzy Demand Curve for Medical Care

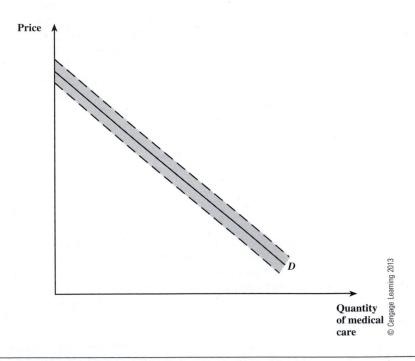

The gray band represents the possible fuzziness of the demand for medical care, given uncertainty and the role of the physician.

Two implications are associated with the fuzzy demand curve. First, for a given price, we may observe some variation in the quantity or types of medical services rendered. Indeed, researchers have documented variations in physician practice styles across geographical areas (see, for example, Phelps, 1992); we take up that discussion in Chapter 12. Second, for a given quantity or type of medical service, we are likely to witness price differences. For example, Feldstein (1988) reported a substantial variation in physician fees for similar procedures in the same geographical area. We must stress, however, that the existence of the band is unlikely to detract from the inverse relation between the price and the quantity demanded of medical care, as suggested by the empirical evidence that follows.

Elasticities

Economic theory gives us insights into the factors that influence the demand for medical care along with the direction of their influence. For example, we know that if the price of physician services increases by 15 percent, the quantity demanded falls. But by how much does it fall? Is there any way to determine whether the decrease is substantial or negligible? The answer is yes, with the help of a measure economists call an *elasticity*. Elasticity measures the responsiveness of quantity demanded to a change in an independent factor.

Own-Price Elasticity of Demand

The most common elasticity is the **own-price elasticity of demand.** This measure gauges the extent to which consumers alter their consumption of a good or service when its own price changes. The formula looks like this:

(5–6) $$E_D = \%\Delta Q_D / \%\Delta P,$$

where E_D denotes the price elasticity of demand, $\%\Delta Q_D$ represents the percentage change in quantity demanded, and $\%\Delta P$ is the percentage change in price. As you can see from the formula, E_D is a simple ratio that equals the percentage change in quantity demanded divided by the percentage change in price. Because elasticity is specified as a ratio of two percentage changes, it is scale free. This makes it much easier to compare elasticities across different goods. For example, we can compare the price elasticity of demand for physician services with that for nursing home care and not concern ourselves with the fact that the demand for physician services is usually measured in terms of the number of visits while the demand for nursing home care is measured in terms of the number of inpatient days.[5]

The value of E_D is negative and reflects the inverse relationship between price and quantity demanded. In economics, the normal practice is to take the absolute value of the price elasticity of demand measure, or $|E_D|$, and eliminate the minus sign. If the price elasticity of demand is greater than 1 in absolute terms ($|E_D| > 1$), the demand for the product is referred to as price elastic. In arithmetic terms, $|E_D| > 1$ if the absolute value of the percentage change in price is smaller than the absolute value of the change in the quantity demanded, or $|\%\Delta P| < |\%\Delta Q_D|$. For example, if the price elasticity of demand for dental services equals 1.2, this means the quantity consumed falls by 12 percent if the price of dental care increases by 10 percent, *ceteris paribus*.

The price elasticity of demand is referred to as **inelastic** if $|E_D| < 1$ but greater than zero. In this case, $|\%\Delta P| > |\%\Delta Q_D|$, or the percentage change in price is greater than the percentage in quantity demanded in absolute value terms. For example, if the elasticity of demand for physician services equals 0.6, a 10 percent decrease in price

---

5. The *point elasticity* formula can be used to calculate the elasticity of demand if the changes in the variables are small. The formula equals $(\Delta Q_D/Q_D)/(\Delta P/P)$. For readers with a background in calculus, it equals $(dQ_D/Q_D)/(dP/P)$ if the changes are infinitesimally small.

leads to a 6 percent increase in quantity demanded. If $|E_D|$ happens to equal 1 because $|\%\Delta P|$ equals $|\%\Delta Q_D|$, the price elasticity of demand is **unit elastic.** This implies that a 10 percent decrease in the price of the product leads to a 10 percent increase in the quantity demanded.

A demand curve that is vertical is said to be **perfectly inelastic** because no change occurs in the quantity demanded when the price changes. In mathematical terms, E_D equals zero because $\%\Delta Q_D$ equals zero. At the other extreme, if the demand curve is horizontal, it is referred to as being **perfectly elastic** and $|E_D|$ equals infinity (∞). Any change in price leads to an infinite change in the quantity demanded.

It stands to reason that the more elastic the demand for the product, the greater the response of quantity to a given change in price. Compare the effects of a 10 percent decrease in price on two goods—one with a price elasticity of −0.1 and another with a price elasticity of −2.6. In the first case, the quantity demanded increases by only 1 percent, while in the second case, it increases by 26 percent. We can also use the elasticity of demand to make inferences regarding the slope of the demand curve. Generally, a more elastic demand, translates into a flatter demand curve at any given price. This also means the curve is relatively steep at any given point for an inelastic demand. Consider the two linear demand curves that intersect at point P_0, Q_0 in Figure 5–7. If the price of the product increases to P_1, the quantity demanded decreases to Q_a off the flat curve (D_a) and to Q_b off the steep curve (D_b). Therefore, the same percentage increase in price generates a smaller percentage decrease in the quantity demanded for the steeper curve D_b than for the flatter curve D_a at a similar price of P_0. This means demand must be more price elastic for curve D_a than for

FIGURE 5–7
The Elasticity of Demand and the Slope of the Demand Curve

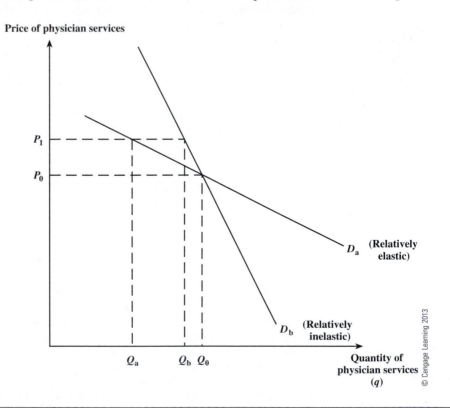

© Cengage Learning 2013

The steep demand curve, D_b, is relatively inelastic and illustrates that an increase in price from P_0 to P_1 generates only a modest decrease in quantity demanded from Q_0 to Q_b. The flatter demand curve, D_a, is relatively elastic and, in this case, the same increase in price from P_0 to P_1 generates a much larger decrease in quantity demanded from Q_0 to Q_a.

TABLE 5–1

A Summary of the Own-Price Elasticity of Demand

Perfectly Inelastic	Inelastic	Unit Elastic	Elastic	Perfectly Elastic
$\lvert E_D \rvert = 0$	$0 < \lvert E_D \rvert < 1$	$\lvert E_D \rvert = 1$	$1 < \lvert E_D \rvert < \infty$	$\lvert E_D \rvert = \infty$
$\%\Delta Q_D = 0$	$\lvert \%\Delta Q_D \rvert < \lvert \%\Delta P \rvert$	$\lvert \%\Delta Q_D \rvert = \lvert \%\Delta P \rvert$	$\lvert \%\Delta Q_D \rvert > \lvert \%\Delta P \rvert$	$\%\Delta Q_D = \infty$

curve D_b over the range P_0 to P_1. Table 5–1 summarizes our discussion thus far on price elasticity of demand.

The own-price elasticity of demand varies greatly across products, and economists point to several factors that determine its value. Among the factors most often mentioned are the portion of the consumer's budget allocated to the good, the amount of time involved in the purchasing decision, the extent to which the good is a necessity, and the availability of substitutes. Briefly, as the portion of a consumer's budget allocated to a good increases, the consumer is likely to become much more sensitive to price changes. Demand should therefore become more elastic. An increase in the decision-making time frame is also likely to make demand more elastic. If the consumer has more time to make informed choices, he or she is likely to react more strongly to price changes. Because the consumer typically pays a small portion of the cost of medical services because of insurance, and because medical services are sometimes of an urgent nature, these two considerations suggest that in many cases, the demand for medical services is inelastic with respect to price.

If a good is a necessity, such as a basic foodstuff, the own-price elasticity should be relatively inelastic. The product is purchased with little regard for price because it is needed. Basic cell phone service might be considered another example of a necessity because it is difficult to imagine a household functioning effectively without at least one cell phone. Naturally, basic health care falls into the same category. If an individual needs a particular medical service, such as an operation or a drug, and if not having it greatly affects the quality of life, we can expect that person's demand to be inelastic with respect to price. In addition, when a person needs a particular medical service in a life-or-death situation, demand is likely to be perfectly inelastic because the medical service must be purchased regardless of price if the person has sufficient income.

Given that many medical services are necessities, we expect the overall demand for medical services to be somewhat inelastic. A word of caution, however: this does not mean the amount of health care demanded does not react to changes in price. Rather, it means a given percentage change in price generates a small percentage change in the quantity demanded of medical services. For some types of medical care, however, demand may be more elastic. Elective medical care, such as cosmetic surgery, may fall into this category, because in most instances it is considered a luxury rather than a necessity. As a result, price may play an important role in the decision to have the surgery. To a lesser degree, dentist services and eyewear might fall into this category. In fact, any medical service that can be postponed is likely to display some degree of price elasticity.

The availability of substitutes is another determinant of price elasticity. As we saw earlier, various types of medical services may serve as substitutes for one another. The larger the number of substitutes, the greater the opportunity to do some comparison shopping. As a result, the quantity demanded of any medical service is likely to be more sensitive to price changes when alternative means of acquiring medical care are available. The own-price elasticity of demand for any given product should be directly related to the number of substitutes available. Stated another way, demand should become more price elastic as the number of substitutes expands. One implication is that the demand for an individual medical service or an individual medical care provider is likely to be more elastic than the market demand for medical care.

One more point concerning the elasticity of demand needs to be discussed before we leave this subject. The own-price elasticity of demand can be used to predict what happens to total health expenditures if price increases or decreases. Total revenues (or total expenditures, from the consumer's perspective) equal price times quantity. In mathematical notation,

(5–7) $$\text{TR} = PQ_\text{D},$$

where TR represents total revenue. Demand theory tells us that as the price of a product increases, the quantity demanded decreases, or that P and Q_D move in opposite directions. Whether total revenue increases or decreases when the price changes is dictated by the relative rates at which both variables change, or the elasticity of demand. Consider an increase in the price of physician services where demand is inelastic. This means that $|\%\Delta Q_\text{D}| < |\%\Delta P|$, or that the percentage increase in price is larger than the percentage decrease in quantity demanded in absolute value terms. In terms of Equation 5–7, P increases faster than Q_D falls. This means total revenue must increase with a higher price when demand is price inelastic. If demand happens to be elastic, the opposite occurs: quantity demanded falls faster than price increases, and, as a result, total revenue decreases. No change occurs in total revenue when demand is unit elastic because the increase in price is matched by the same percentage decrease in quantity demanded. We leave it to you to work out the implications of a price decrease on total revenue when demand is elastic, inelastic, and unit elastic.

Other Types of Elasticity

The concept of elasticity can be used to measure the sensitivity of quantity demanded to other demand-side factors as well. The **income elasticity of demand** represents the percentage change in quantity demanded divided by the percentage change in income, or $E_\text{Y} = \%\Delta Q_\text{D}/\%\Delta Y$, where $\%\Delta Y$ equals the percentage change in income. It quantifies the extent to which the demand for a product changes when real income changes. If E_Y is positive, the good is referred to as a *normal good* because any increase in income leads to an increase in quantity demanded. For example, if E_Y equals 0.78, this means a 10 percent increase in income causes the quantity consumed to increase by 7.8 percent. An *inferior good* is one for which E_Y is negative and an increase in income leads to a decrease in the amount consumed. For most types of medical care, the income elasticity of demand should be larger than zero.

The **cross-price elasticity** (E_C) measures the extent to which the demand for a product changes when the price of another good is altered. In mathematical terms, $E_\text{C} = \%\Delta Q_\text{X}/\%\Delta P_\text{Z}$, where the numerator represents the percentage change in the demand for good X and the denominator equals the percentage change in the price of good Z. If E_C is negative, we can infer that the two goods are complements in consumption. Returning to our earlier example, the cross-price elasticity between the demand for optometric services and the price of eyewear should be negative. If the price of eyewear increases, the demand for optometric services should drop. Two goods are substitutes in consumption when the cross-price elasticity is positive. For example, the cross-price elasticity of the demand for physician services with respect to the price of hospital outpatient services may turn out to be positive. Naturally, if E_C equals zero, the demand for the product is independent of the price of the other product.

Empirical Estimation

Numerous studies have attempted to empirically quantify how various factors influence the demand for medical care. Although the studies varied widely in terms of methodology and scope of analysis, certain broad conclusions emerged. Generally, some form of Equation 5–5 is estimated with the use of multiple regression analysis (see Appendix 1). Unfortunately, the dependent variable representing the amount of medical services consumed is very difficult to measure. Ideally, quantity demanded should capture both the utilization and the intensity of medical services. Data of these kinds are unavailable, so usually only some utilization measure, such as number of physician visits or hospital patient-days, is used to measure the quantity demanded of medical services. Proxy variables are then included as independent variables to control for variations in quality. A failure to properly control for quality biases the results. That is because changes in demand may be attributed to changes in other variables when in fact they are the result of differences in the quality of care provided.

The measurement of the out-of-pocket price of medical care also presents a problem for economists. This problem has become more severe in recent years given the increasing role of third-party payers. In a perfect world, the out-of-pocket price of medical services should equal the amount the consumer pays after the impact of insurance has been considered. Unfortunately, such data are rarely available, and economists often have to resort to using such variables as the average price of medical services rendered. An additional variable is then included in the equation to control for the presence of health insurance. The price variable should negatively affect the demand for medical care, while the presence of insurance should positively influence quantity demanded.

An income variable is included to capture the impact of purchasing power on demand, while time cost variables control for the effects of travel and waiting costs on demand. We expect the income variable to have a direct effect on demand and the time cost variables to have an inverse impact. The prices of various substitutes and complements in consumption should also be included in the regression equation. This has become even more important in recent years as medical markets have become more interrelated. For example, if we are trying to assess the quantity demanded of inpatient services at a hospital, we should control for the prices of hospital outpatient services (potentially a substitute service) and physician services (potentially a complementary service). The remaining factors (tastes and preferences, state of health, and quality of care) are referred to as *control variables* and capture the impact that various noneconomic factors may have on the demand for health care services.

Own-Price, Income, Cross-Price, and Time-Cost Elasticity Estimates

Overall, the empirical literature on the elasticity of demand for primary health care is rich and spans the globe. Table 5–2 provides just a sample of the studies on the topic. Although the range of price elasticity estimates is broad, studies tend to find the demand for primary health care to be relatively inelastic. For example, studies using medical expenditures as the dependent variable find the own-price elasticity of demand to vary from −0.04 to −0.7. Other studies that look at the demand for hospital and physician services find similar results. Taken as a whole, the estimates suggest that the own-price elasticity of demand for primary health care hovers from −0.1 to −0.7, which means that a 10 percent increase in the out-of-pocket price of medical services leads to a 1 to 7 percent decrease in the quantity demanded. The inelastic estimates also imply that total expenditures on hospital and physician services increase with a greater out-of-pocket price, *ceteris paribus*.

In general, the research indicates that the demand for other types of medical care is slightly more price elastic than the demand for primary care. That is not at all surprising given that the percentage of out-of-pocket payments tend to be the lowest for hospital and physician services. Everything else held constant, consumers should become more price sensitive as the portion of the bill paid out of pocket increases.

TABLE 5–2
The Price Elasticity of Demand for Health Care: Selected Studies

Dependent Variable	Study	Elasticity	Country
Medical Expenditures	Eichner (1998)	−0.62 to −0.75	United States
	Newhouse and the Insurance Experiment Group (1993)	−0.17 to −0.22	United States
	Phelps and Newhouse (1974)	−0.04 to −0.12	United States
	Rosett and Huang (1973)	−0.35 to −1.5	United States
	Van Vliet (2001)	−0.079	Netherlands
Hospital Care			
Admissions	Manning et al. (1987)	−0.1 to −0.2	United States
Hospital Inpatient	Davis and Russell (1972)	−0.32 to −0.46	United States
Hospital Outpatient	Davis and Russell (1972)	−1.0	United States
	Bhattacharya et al. (1996)	−0.12 to −0.54	Japan
Patient-Days	Feldman and Dowd (1986)	−0.74 to −0.80	United States
Physician Visits	Cockx and Brasseur (2003)	−0.13 to −0.03	Belgium
Mental Health Services			
No. of Mental Health Visits	Meyerhoefer and Zuvekas (2010)	−0.05	United States
No. of Mental Health Drugs	Meyerhoefer and Zuvekas (2010)	−0.61	United States
Nursing Home Care			
Probability of Entering a Nursing Home	Headen (1993)	−0.7	United States
Number of Patients	Nyman (1989)	−1.7	United States
Patient-Days	Mukamel and Spector (2002)	−3.46 to −3.85	United States
Number of Patients	Chiswick (1976)	−2.3	United States
Dental Services	Manning and Phelps (1979)	−0.5 to −0.7	United States
	Mueller and Monheit (1988)	−0.18	United States
Prescription Drugs			
Number	Smith (1993)	−0.10	United States
Expenditures	Contoyannis et al. (2005)	−0.12 to −0.16	Canada

For example, Manning and Phelps (1979) find the demand for dental services to be slightly more price elastic and to vary by type of service provided and the sex and age of the patient. The price elasticity of demand for dental services by adult females appears to vary between −0.5 and −0.7, and the demand for dental services by adult males and children seems to be slightly more price elastic. The demand for nursing home services also appears to be more price elastic than primary medical services. Chiswick (1976) finds the own-price elasticity for nursing home services to equal −2.3, and Mukamel and Spector (2002) estimate it to vary from −3.46 to −3.85.

The empirical estimates for the income elasticity of demand vary and merit discussion. One of the more interesting questions concerning this research has to do with whether health care is a luxury good. Economists define a luxury good as one that has an income elasticity above 1.0. In this case, an increase in income leads to an even larger increase in the quantity consumed of the good. For example, assume that the income elasticity of a good equals 1.2. In this case, a 10 percent increase in income leads to a 12 percent increase in the consumption of the good.

Studies have used international, national, regional, and state data sets and a vast array of very sophisticated estimating techniques to estimate the income elasticity of demand for medical care. The seminal work by Newhouse (1977) finds the income elasticity to range between 1.13 and 1.31 while Parkin et al. (1987) estimate the rate to be slightly below 1. Leu (1986), Gerdtham et al. (1992), and Murray et al. (1994) agree with Newhouse and find the aggregate income elasticity to be above 1. The empirical debate continues. Utilizing state data, Wang and Rettenmaier (2007) find that 32 states have income elasticities above 1 while 16 have income elasticities between 0 and 1. These results are contradicted by Moscone and Tosetti (2010) who find the majority of the states have income elasticities less than 1.

If the aggregate income elasticity of health care is above 1, this may provide a demand-side explanation as to why health care expenditures in the United States as a portion of national income have increased over the past few decades. As the U.S. economy grew over the past few decades and income per capita expanded, the nation allocated a greater portion of its income to health care because it is a luxury good. Consequently, the health care sector received a larger slice of the economic pie.

Time costs also appear to have a significant impact on the demand for medical services. In fact, research indicates that the travel time elasticity of demand is approximately equal to the own-price elasticity of demand. Using a data set generated in the United Kingdom, Gravelle et al. (2002) find elasticity of admissions with respect to distance to equal −0.35. Thus, a 10 percent increase in travel time reduces the quantity demanded for medical services by roughly 3 percent. It also appears that consumers place a value on the time spent waiting for medical services. McCarthy (1985) finds the wait time elasticity to range from −0.36 to −1.14, while Gravelle et al. (2002) estimate the elasticity of admissions with respect to waiting time to equal −0.25. Time costs also influence the decision to acquire medical care; Frank et al. (1995) determine the elasticity of travel time costs on the probability of a timely completion of childhood immunization to equal roughly −0.08.

The extent to which various types of medical services serve as substitutes or complements in consumption is not clear at this time. For example, there appears to be little consensus as to whether inpatient and outpatient hospital services are substitutes or complements. Davis and Russell (1972) found the cross-price elasticity between the price of inpatient services and number of outpatient visits to vary between 0.85 and 1.46, indicating that they are substitutes. These results were later qualitatively confirmed by Gold (1984). Thus, as the price of inpatient services at a hospital increases, consumers rely more on outpatient services to save money. Freiberg and Scutchfield (1976), on the other hand, found that no substitution occurs between these two types of hospital services. At the other extreme, Manning et al. (1987) suggested that they are complements in consumption. A similar debate in the literature concerns whether physician and hospital inpatient or outpatient services are substitutes or complements.

The Impact of Insurance on the Demand for Medical Care

Some economists have also investigated empirically how the transition from uninsured to insured status, or the reverse, and how different amounts of health insurance coverage affect the quantity demanded of medical care. For example, two recent studies, sponsored by the National Bureau of Economic Research, examine how health insurance status affects medical care demand. Anderson et al. (2010) study empirically what impact the loss of health insurance coverage had on the medical care demands of young adults who were "aged out" of their parents' insurance plans. These researchers show young adults are less likely to go to emergency rooms or be admitted to hospitals for inpatient services when they lose health insurance coverage by the family plan. Another study by Finkelstein et al (2011) looks at how random assignment into Oregon Medicaid plans impacted health care utilization. They demonstrate empirically that one year after enrollment, insurance coverage was associated with substantial increases in health care utilization including primary and preventive care as well as hospitalizations.

Without a doubt, the RAND Health Insurance Study (HIS) (Manning et al., 1987) is the most comprehensive research to date, specifically addressing the impact of health insurance coverage on the demand for medical care.[6] This study does not examine how transitioning from uninsured to insured status affects medical care utilization. Rather, in this study, families were randomly assigned to 14 different fee-for-service plans. The plans varied in terms of consumer coinsurance rates and the upper limit on annual out-of-pocket expenses. Every plan had a *maximum* limit of $1,000 in out-of-pocket expenses per year. Table 5–3 presents selected results for five of the plans: free (zero coinsurance rate), 25 percent coinsurance rate, 50 percent coinsurance rate, 95 percent coinsurance rate, and individual deductible. The individual deductible plan had a 95 percent coinsurance rate for outpatient services, subject to a limit of $150 per person or $450 per family, and free inpatient care. Essentially, an individual or a family with this plan receives free medical care after meeting the deductible for outpatient expenditures. In Table 5–3, face-to-face visits equal the number of visits per year to a medical provider, such as a physician. This category excludes visits for radiology, anesthesiology, or pathology services. The third, fourth, and fifth columns list, respectively, total expenditures per person for outpatient, inpatient, and all medical services, excluding dental care and psychotherapy. The sixth column indicates the probability of using any medical services over the course of the year.

The results largely confirm economic theory's prediction concerning the impact of coinsurance on the demand for health care. As the coinsurance rate rises, or the out-of-pocket price of medical care increases, consumers demand less medical care. The number of face-to-face visits decreased from 4.55 per year when health care was a free good to 2.73 when the consumer paid 95 percent of the bill. The largest drop in visits took place between the free plan and the 25 percent coinsurance plan. This overall decrease in visits was matched by an identical drop in outpatient expenses from $340 to $203 per year. According to Manning et al. (1987), this indicates that as the out-of-pocket price of medical care increases, consumers reduce medical expenditures largely by cutting back on the number of visits to health care providers and not on the amount spent on each visit. It is interesting to note that the authors reported no significant differences in the amount spent on inpatient services across plans. This, they concluded, was the result of the $1,000 cap put on out-of-pocket expenditures. In 70 percent of the cases where people were admitted for inpatient services, the cost exceeded the $1,000 limit.

The last two columns in Table 5–3 also largely support economic theory regarding the impact of insurance on the demand for medical services. In every case, as the level of coinsurance increased, the probability of using any medical services, along with total medical expenditures, diminished. The only exception occurred between the 25 and 50 percent coinsurance rates for total medical expenditures.

---

6. The present discussion focuses on the results published by Manning et al. (1987). However, a number of other articles analyze the data from the RAND HIS study. Among them are Newhouse et al. (1981), Keeler and Rolph (1983), O'Grady et al. (1985), Manning et al. (1985), Leibowitz et al. (1985b), Leibowitz et al. (1985a), and Manning et al. (1986). For a summary of the entire RAND HIS study, consult Newhouse and the Insurance Experiment Group (1993).

TABLE 5–3
Sample Means for Annual Use of Medical Care per Capita

Plan*	Face-to-Face Visits	Outpatient Expenses (1984 $)	Inpatient Dollars (1984 $)	Total Expenses (1984 $)	Probability of Using Any Medical Services
Free	4.55	$340	$409	$749	86.8
25%	3.33	260	373	634	78.8
50%	3.03	224	450	674	77.2
95%	2.73	203	315	518	67.7
Individual deductible	3.02	235	373	608	72.3

*The *chi*-square test was used to test the null hypothesis of no difference among the five plan means. In each instance, the *chi*-square statistic was significant to at least the 5 percent level. The only exception was for inpatient dollars.

SOURCE: Willard G. Manning et al. "Health Insurance and the Demand for Medical Care: Evidence from a Randomized Experiment." *American Economic Review* 77 (June 1987), Table 2.

Finally, the results from the individual deductible plan illustrate the inverse impact of deductibles on the consumption of medical care. In every instance, less medical care was consumed with the deductibles than would have been the case if medical care had been a free good. It seems that individuals with this plan consumed medical services at a rate somewhere between the 25 and 95 percent coinsurance rate.

The results also indicate that the own-price elasticity of demand is sensitive to the amount of insurance coverage. When the coinsurance rate ranged from 25 to 95 percent, the elasticities of demand for all care and outpatient care were calculated as -0.14 and -0.21. These numbers decreased to -0.10 and -0.13 when the coinsurance rate ranged from 0 to 25 percent. This makes economic sense. As the coinsurance rate drops, consumers become less sensitive to price changes due to lower out-of-pocket payments.

In conclusion, the results from these studies point to the significant impact of health insurance on the demand for medical care. It is apparent that if either the coinsurance rate or the deductible falls, the amount of health care consumed increases.

The Impact of Noneconomic Factors on the Demand for Medical Services

Empirical research also indicates that a host of other factors, such as tastes and preferences or the stock of health, affect the demand for medical care. Researchers generally agree that age and severity of illness directly influence the demand for medical care, while the overall health of the individual inversely affects the demand for care. There does not, however, appear to be a consensus concerning the impact of education on the demand for health care. This may indicate that the direct impact of education on the demand for medical care (a greater willingness to seek care) is offset by the inverse effect (a greater ability to produce health care at home) or that more research needs to be done in this area.

It is interesting to note that a few researchers have focused specifically on the effect of medical knowledge on the demand for medical care. Unlike the results for general education, a direct relationship appears to exist between consumers' medical knowledge and the demand for medical care. This means that consumers with a more extensive background in medicine tend to consume more medical services. For example, Kenkel (1990) found that consumers' medical knowledge directly relates to the probability of visiting a physician for medical care, while Hsieh and Lin (1997) uncovered that those elderly who had a better understanding of health were more likely to acquire preventive medical care. Both studies suggest that consumers with a lack of medical knowledge tend to underestimate the impact of medical care on overall health and, as a result, fail to consume an appropriate amount. It may also be the case that more medical information enhances the ability of individuals to effectively consume medical care, causing the marginal product of medical care to increase (consult Chapter 2). As a result, the demand for various types of medical care increases with consumer information.

Provisions of the Patient Protection and Affordable Care Act (PPACA) of 2010 Relating to the Demand for Health Care

One of the major objectives of the PPACA is to extend health insurance coverage to millions of uninsured Americans. Given both the theoretical and empirical relation between health insurance coverage and the demand for health care, it is easy to understand why this legislation should have a sizeable impact on the overall demand for health care in the United States.

The health reform package takes a two-pronged approach to reducing the number of uninsured through the expansion of public programs and changes in private insurance coverage. In terms of public programs, the Medicaid program will be expanded to cover all non-Medicaid recipients under the age of 65 with incomes up to 133 percent of the federal poverty level.

Four significant changes are slated to take place in the private insurance market aimed at decreasing the number of uninsured: individual mandates, health insurance exchanges, employer requirements, and new insurance regulations. According to provisions in the legislation, all individuals are mandated to have health insurance coverage by 2014. Those who elect not to acquire insurance will face a penalty equal to $695 per person (up to a maximum of $2,085 per family) or 2 percent of household income, whichever figure is greater. These penalties are to be phased in from 2014 through 2016. States are required to design and create American Health Benefit Exchanges to provide individuals and small businesses access to affordable health insurance. Each exchange is required to offer health plans that offer an established set of minimum benefits, and subsidies will be provided to individuals who cannot afford the premium payments based on sliding income scale.

While the legislation does not require an employer mandate, any employer with 50 or more employees that does not offer health insurance coverage is required to pay a $2,000 fee per full-time employee in excess of 30 employees, providing the employer has at least one employee who receives the maximum subsidy through the purchase of health insurance through an exchange. In addition, any employer with 50 or more employees that does offer health insurance and has at least one employee receiving the maximum subsidy through the purchase of health insurance via an exchange will also be assessed a fee. The intent of these provisions is to provide large employers the incentive to offer health insurance to their employees as part of their benefits package.

Finally, there are a number of insurance market regulations in the legislation aimed at making it easier for individuals to acquire and retain health insurance. For example, children will have the opportunity to stay on their parent's health insurance plan up to age 26. Many of these changes are discussed in greater detail in Chapter 6.

Estimates vary regarding the number of individuals who will obtain insurance coverage as a result of the health care reform legislation. Recent estimates by Buettgens and Carroll (2012) put the number of individuals at 26 million, of which almost 70 percent gain insurance through the Medicaid expansion and the remaining 30 percent through private insurance.

Summary

Economic theory suggests that the demand for medical care represents a derived demand because it is but one input in the production of health. As a result, the utility received from consuming medical care comes in the form of the satisfaction that accrues from improvements in the stock of health. Utility analysis also indicates that the quantity demanded of health care is inversely related to price because improvements in health are subject to diminishing returns. The demand for medical care, like the demand for many other services, depends on the out-of-pocket price, income, the prices of substitutes and complements, and time costs, along with a host of noneconomic factors, such as tastes and preferences, quality of care, and the state of health.

Economists use the concept of elasticity to measure the extent to which one variable changes in response to a change in another variable. Own-price elasticity of demand measures the extent to which consumers react to a change in the price of a good or service. In mathematical terms, it equals the percentage change in quantity demanded divided by the percentage change in price. If the demand for a product is elastic, the consumer's willingness to purchase the product is very sensitive to a price change. On the other hand, if the demand for the product is inelastic, price changes play a less significant role in determining overall demand. From a graphical perspective, the more elastic the demand for a product, the flatter the demand curve. Additional types of elasticities, such as the income elasticity of demand, have also been employed to assess how demand reacts to changes in variables other than own price.

The empirical evidence indicates that the demand for medical care is inelastic with respect to price. Medical care also appears to be a normal good in that the demand for medical care increases with real income. In addition, time costs along with many non-economic variables, such as age, gender, severity of illness, education, and consumer knowledge, influence demand. The evidence from the RAND HIS study and other research verifies that health insurance plays a major role in determining the demand for medical care. As economic theory suggests, when the amount of health insurance coverage rises, the amount of medical care demanded increases while the price elasticity of demand becomes more inelastic.

Review Questions and Problems

1. In your own words, use utility analysis and production theory to explain why the demand curve for medical care is downward sloping.
2. After reading the chapter on demand theory, a classmate turns to you and says, "I'm rather confused. According to economic theory, people demand a good or service because it yields utility. This obviously does not apply to medical services. Just last week I went to the dentist and had a root canal, and you can't tell me I received any utility or satisfaction from that!" Explain to your classmate how utility analysis can be used to explain why he went to the dentist.
3. Use a graph to illustrate how the following changes would affect the demand curve for inpatient services at a hospital in a large city.

    A. Average real income in the community increases.

    B. In an attempt to cut costs, the largest employer in the area increases the coinsurance rate for employee health care coverage from 10 percent to 20 percent.

    C. The hospital relocates from the center of the city, where a majority of the people live, to a suburb.

    D. A number of physicians in the area join together and open up a discount-price walk-in clinic; the price elasticity of demand between physician services and inpatient hospital services is −0.50.

4. Many elderly people have purchased medigap insurance policies to cover a growing Medicare copayment. These policies cover some or all of the medical costs not covered by Medicare. Use economic theory to explain how these policies likely influence the demand for health care by elderly people.

5. If you are covered by a private or a public insurance plan, obtain a pamphlet outlining the benefits provided and the cost of the plan. Are there any copayments or deductibles? If so, use economic theory to explain how they may influence your demand for medical care.

6. In your own words, explain what a fuzzy demand curve is. Why does it exist? What are its implications?

7. In reaction to higher input costs, a physician decides to increase the average price of a visit by 5 percent. Will total revenues increase or decrease as a result of this action? Use the concept of price elasticity to substantiate your answer.

8. You have just been put in charge of estimating the demand for hospital services in a major U.S. city. What economic and noneconomic variables would you include in your analysis? Justify why each variable should be included in the study, and explain how a change in each variable would likely affect the overall demand for hospital services.

9. Define *own-price elasticity of demand*, and explain how it is related to the demand curve. Provide four reasons why the demand for medical services is likely to be inelastic with respect to its price.

10. You are employed as an economic consultant to the regional planning office of a large metropolitan area, and your task is to estimate the demand for hospital services in the area. Your estimates indicate that the own-price elasticity of demand equals −0.25, the income elasticity of demand equals 0.45, the cross-price elasticity of demand for hospital services with respect to the price of nursing home services equals −0.1, and the elasticity of travel time equals −0.37. Use this information to project the impact of the following changes on the demand for hospital services.

    A. Average travel time to the hospital diminishes by 5 percent due to overall improvements in the public transportation system.

    B. The price of nursing home care decreases by 10 percent.

    C. Average real income decreases by 10 percent.

    D. The hospital is forced to increase its price for services by 2 percent.

11. According to Whitney et al. (1997), the price of dental services "decreased by $4.86 per day wait for a new-patient appointment and by $5.20 per minute wait in the reception room" (p. 783). Based on these findings, what would happen to the position of the demand curve for dental services if patients had to wait even longer for an appointment with a dentist?

12. Some have asked whether pharmacotherapies (the use of drugs to treat diseases) and outpatient services are substitutes or complements. Meyerhoefer and Zuvekas (2010) find the cross-price elasticity between physician health visits and the price of drugs to be −0.09. Based upon that estimate, what is the answer to that question?

13. A study estimates the demand for over-the-counter cough and cold medicines to be:

$$\text{Log } Q = 0.885 - 0.744 \log(P) - 0.50 \log(\text{INC}) + 0.253 \log(\text{ADV}) - 0.30 \log(\text{PHYSP})$$
$$\quad\quad (5.52)\quad (4.92)\quad\quad\quad (1.40)\quad\quad\quad\quad (6.64)\quad\quad\quad\quad\quad (0.99)$$

Adj. $R^2 = 0.30$

$N = 243$

where Q = Annual dosages demanded of cough and cold medicines
$\quad\quad P$ = Price per dosage of cough and cold medicines
$\quad\quad$ INC = Average income of buyers
$\quad\quad$ ADV = Advertising expenditures on cough and cold medicines
$\quad\quad$ PHYSP = Market price of a physician visit
$\quad\quad$ t-statistics shown in parentheses below the estimated coefficient

All variables expressed in logarithms so the coefficient estimates can be interpreted as elasticities.

A. Which of the estimated coefficients have signs contrary to theoretical expectations? Explain. Be specific in your explanation.
B. Which coefficient estimates are statistically significant from zero at the 5 percent level or better? Explain.
C. What percentage of the variation in dosages demanded remains unexplained? Explain.
D. Suppose the price per dosage increased by 10 percent. By how much would dosages demanded change? Explain. Would total revenues to cold medicine producers increase or decrease? Explain.

References

Aaron, Henry J. *Serious and Unstable Condition: Financing America's Health Care*. Washington, D.C.: The Brookings Institution, 1991.

Anderson, Michael, et al. "The Effect of Health Insurance Coverage on Use of Medical Care." National Bureau of Economic Research (NBER) Working Paper No. 15823. Cambridge, Mass.: NBER, March 2010.

Bhattacharya, Jayanta, William B. Vogt, Aki Yoshikawa, and Toshitak Nakahara. "The Utilization of Outpatient Medical Services in Japan." *Journal of Human Resources* 31 (1996), pp. 450–76.

Buettgens, Matthew and Caitlin Carroll. "Timely Analysis of Immediate Health Policy Issues." *The Urban Institute* (January 2012).

Chiswick, Barry. "The Demand for Nursing Home Care." *Journal of Human Resources* 11 (summer 1976), pp. 295–316.

Cockx, Bart, and Carine Brasseur. "The Demand for Physician Services: Evidence from a Natural Experiment." *Journal of Health Economics* 22 (2003), pp. 881–913.

Contoyannis, Paul, Jeremiah Hurley, Paul Grooten-dorst, Sung-Hee Jeon, and Robyn Tamblyn. "Estimating the Price Elasticity of Expenditure for Prescription Drugs in the Presence of Non-Linear Price Schedules: An Illustration from Quebec, Canada." *Health Economics* 14 (2005), pp. 909–23.

Davis, Karen, and Louise B. Russell. "The Substitution of Hospital Outpatient Care for Inpatient Care." *Review of Economics and Statistics* 54 (May 1972), pp. 109–20.

Eichner, Matthew J. "The Demand for Medical Care: What People Pay Does Matter." *American Economic Review Papers and Proceedings* 88 (May 1998), pp. 117–21.

Feldman, Roger, and Bryan Dowd. "Is There a Competitive Market for Hospital Services?" *Journal of Health Economics* 5 (1986), pp. 272–92.

Feldstein, Martin S. *Economic Analysis for Health Services Efficiency*. Amsterdam: North-Holland, 1967.

Feldstein, Paul. *Health Care Economics*. New York: Wiley, 1988.

Finkelstein, Amy, et al. "The Oregon Health Insurance Experiment: Evidence from the First Year." NBER Working Paper No. 17190. Cambridge, Mass.: July 2011.

Frank, Richard G., et al. "The Demand for Childhood Immunizations: Results from the Baltimore Immunization Study." *Inquiry* 32 (summer 1995), pp. 164–73.

Freiberg, Lewis, Jr., and F. Douglas Scutchfield. "Insurance and the Demand for Hospital Care: An Examination of the Moral Hazard." *Inquiry* 13 (March 1976), pp. 54–60.

Fuchs, Victor R., and Sarah Rosen Frank. "Air Pollution and Medical Care Use by Older Americans: A Cross Areas Analysis." *Health Affairs* 21 (November/December 2002), pp. 207–14.

Gerdtham, Ulf-G, et al. "An Econometric Analysis of Health Care Expenditure: A Cross-Section Study of the OECD Countries." *Journal of Health Economics* 1, no. 1 (1992), pp. 63–84.

Gold, Marsha. "The Demand for Hospital Outpatient Services." *Health Services Research* 19 (August 1984), pp. 384–412.

Gravelle, Hugh, Mark Dusheiko, and Matthew Sutton. "The Demand for Elective Surgery in a Public System: Time and Money Prices in the UK National Health Service." *Journal of Health Economics* 21 (May 2002), pp. 423–49.

Headen, Alvin E. "Economic Disability and Health Determinants of the Hazard of Nursing Home Entry." *Journal of Human Resources* 28 (1993), pp. 80–110.

Hsieh, Chee-ruey and Shin-jong Lin. "Health Information and the Demand for Preventive Care among the Elderly in Taiwan." *Journal of Human Resources* 32 (1997), pp. 308–33

Keeler, Emmett B., and John E. Rolph. "How Cost Sharing Reduced Medical Spending of Participants in the Health Insurance Experiment." *Journal of the American Medical Association* 249 (April 22–29, 1983), pp. 2220–22.

Kenkel, Don. "Consumer Health Information and the Demand for Medical Care." *Review of Economics and Statistics* 72 (1990), pp. 587–95.

Leibowitz, Arleen, et al. "Effects of Cost-Sharing on the Use of Medical Services by Children: Interim Results from a Randomized Controlled Trial." *Pediatrics* 75 (May 1985a), pp. 942–50.

Leibowitz, Arleen, Willard G. Manning, and Joseph P. Newhouse. "The Demand for Prescription Drugs as a Function of Cost-Sharing." *Social Science and Medicine* 21 (1985b), pp. 1063–69.

Leu, Robert E. "The Public-Private Mix and International Health Care Costs." In *Public and Private Health Services*, eds. A. J. Culyer and B. Jonsson. Oxford: Basil Blackwell, 1986.

Lynch, Wendy, and Bard Smith. "Altarum Institute Survey of Consumer Health Care Opinions." *Altarum Institute* (fall 2011).

Manning, Willard, et al. "How Cost Sharing Affects the Use of Ambulatory Mental Health Services." *Journal of the American Medical Association* 256 (October 10, 1986), pp. 1930–34.

Manning, Willard G., et al. "Health Insurance and the Demand for Medical Care: Evidence from a Randomized Experiment." *American Economic Review* 77 (June 1987), pp. 251–77.

Manning, Willard G., Howard L. Bailit, Bernadette Benjamin, and Joseph P. Newhouse. "The Demand for Dental Care: Evidence from a Randomized Trial in Health Insurance." *Journal of the American Dental Association* 110 (June 1985), pp. 895–902.

Manning, Willard G., and Charles E. Phelps. "The Demand for Dental Care." *Bell Journal of Economics* 10 (autumn 1979), pp. 503–25.

McCarthy, Thomas. "The Competitive Nature of the Primary-Care Physicians Service Market." *Journal of Health Economics* 4 (1985), pp. 93–118.

Meyerhoefer, Chad D., and Samuel H. Zuvekas. "New Estimates of the Demand for Physical and Mental Health Treatment." *Health Economics* 19 (2010), pp. 297–315.

Miller, Lisa. "Medical Schools Put Women in Curricula." *Wall Street Journal*, May 24, 1994, p. B1.

Moscone, F and E. Tosetti. "Health Expenditures and Income in the United States," *Health Economics* 19 (2010), pp. 1385–1403.

Mueller, Curt D., and Alan C. Monheit. "Insurance Coverage and the Demand for Dental Care." *Journal of Health Economics* 7 (1988), pp. 59–72.

Mukamel, Dana B., and William D. Spector. "The Competitive Nature of the Nursing

Industry: Price Mark Ups and Demand Elasticities." *Applied Economics* 34 (2002), pp. 413–20.

Murray, C. J. L., R. Govindaraj, and P. Musgrove. "National Health Expenditures: A Global Analysis." *Bulletin of the World Health Organization* 74 (1994), pp. 623–37.

Newhouse, Joseph P. "Medical-Care Expenditures: A Cross-National Survey." *Journal of Human Resources* 12 (winter 1977), pp. 115–24.

Newhouse, Joseph P., et al. "Some Interim Results from a Controlled Trial of Cost Sharing in Health Insurance." *New England Journal of Medicine* 305 (December 17, 1981), pp. 1501–7.

Newhouse, Joseph P., and the Insurance Experiment Group. *Free for All? Lessons from the RAND Health Insurance Experiment*. Cambridge, Mass.: Harvard University Press, 1993.

Nyman, John A. "The Private Demand for Nursing Home Care." *Journal of Health Economics* 8 (1989), pp. 209–31.

O'Grady, Kevin F., Willard G. Manning, Joseph P. Newhouse, and Robert H. Brook. "Impact of Cost Sharing on Emergency Department Use." *New England Journal of Medicine* 313 (August 22, 1985), pp. 484–90.

Parkin, David, Alistair McGuire, and Brian Yule. "Aggregate Health Care Expenditures and National Income: Is Health a Luxury Good?" *Journal of Health Economics* 6 (1987), pp. 109–27.

Phelps, Charles E. "Diffusion of Information in Medical Care." *Journal of Economic Perspectives* 6 (summer 1992), pp. 23–42.

Phelps, Charles E., and Joseph P. Newhouse. "Coinsurance, the Price of Time, and the Demand for Medical Service." *Review of Economics and Statistics* 56 (August 1974), pp. 334–42.

Rosett, Richard N., and Lien-fu Huang. "The Effect of Health Insurance on the Demand for Medical Care." *Journal of Political Economy* 81 (April 1973), pp. 281–305.

Smith, Dean G., "The Effects of Copayments and Generic Substitution on the Use and Costs of Prescription Drugs." *Inquiry* 30 (summer 1993), pp. 189–98.

Van Vliet, Rene C. J. A. "Effects of Price and Deductibles on Medical Care Demand, Estimated from Survey Data." *Applied Economics* 33 (October 10, 2001), pp. 1515–24.

Wang, Zijun, and Andrew Rettenmaier. "A Note on Cointegration of Health and Incomes." *Health Economics* 16 (2007). pp. 559–78.

Whitney, Coralyn W., et al. "The Relationship between Price of Services, Quality of Care, and Patient Time Costs for General Dental Practice." *Health Services Research* 31 (February 1997), pp. 773–90.

CHAPTER 6

The Demand for Medical Insurance: Traditional and Managed Care Coverage

Remember Joe, who suffered a heart attack at the beginning of Chapter 1? Things turned out quite well, both medically and financially, for our friend Joe. You see, Joe's medical bills were covered by a Blue Cross PPO insurance plan he had obtained through his employer. Joe could thus afford the best hospital care money could buy, and the triple bypass surgery he received at the prestigious private teaching hospital was highly successful. Angela, his wife, and their two children are tickled pink now that Joe is back to his former self.

But how might events have differed if Joe had not been covered by medical insurance, or if Joe was enrolled in an HMO plan? Moreover, what are some of the reasons why Joe and his family were covered by health insurance? Also, why was Joe covered by a PPO rather than an HMO plan? What are the differences between the two types of plans? These are among the questions for which we search for answers in this chapter.

Specifically, this chapter:

- presents and compares the conventional and Nyman models of the demand for health insurance
- examines empirical estimates of the price and income elasticities of the demand for health insurance
- discusses the health insurance product, contrasting traditional, managed care, and consumer-directed insurance coverage
- addresses the regulation of managed care organizations
- points out how the Patient Protection and Affordable Care Act (PPACA) of 2010 may impact the demand for health insurance in the United States.

Introduction

As pointed out briefly in Chapter 4 and further discussed in Chapter 11, employment-related insurance is the dominant type of private health insurance coverage in the United States. Only a small percentage of the population purchases health insurance directly from insurance companies. Because most private health insurance is purchased through employers, many people believe that employers pay for their health insurance coverage. But economic theory suggests that nothing could be further from the truth because employees pay for their health insurance coverage in the form of reduced or forgone wages.

Economic theory implies that a trade-off exists between insurance premiums and wages because, during a particular time period, workers tends to generate a certain value or marginal revenue product (MRP) for a company. The MRP that workers generate depends on their marginal productivity and the price of the good or service in the marketplace that they help produce (assuming that output is produced in a competitive market). More precisely, economic theory posits that MRP equals the price of the product times the marginal productivity of the worker. It follows that a higher price and greater productivity both increase a worker's MRP or worth to a company.

Employers are typically pressured by competition in the goods and labor markets to compensate workers based on their market-determined MRP. That is, if an employer compensated its employees at a rate in excess of their MRP, that company would be forced to raise product prices and thereby lose business and profits to competitors in the goods market. At the same time, if the employer did not compensate its employees at a rate that at least matched the market-determined MRP, the company would lose productive employees to competitors in the labor market and thereby also lose business and profits. Consequently, economic theory predicts that workers are compensated for their MRP as long as markets are reasonably competitive. However, compensation comes in the form of both wages and fringe benefits such as life insurance, health insurance, and paid vacations. If you think in terms of total compensation, it follows that more expensive health insurance coverage leads to lower wages or reductions in other fringe benefits for a given level of the MRP. Thus, this trade-off can also be interpreted to mean that employees actually pay for their health insurance coverage through a reduction in other types of compensation.

Of course, markets are not as frictionless as economic theory sometimes seems to suggest. For example, because of mobility costs, some workers find themselves with more or less health insurance coverage than they truly desire. Also market imperfections, such as wage discrimination, sometimes occur in the real world such that specific workers receive compensation that falls below the competitive rate. However, market forces tend to support long-run outcomes consistent with workers being paid their MRPs, as frictions such as mobility costs become less inhibiting and competition for the best workers intensifies.

Representative of several studies, Miller (2004) empirically examines the wage and health insurance trade-off using data for a sample of male workers between ages 25 and 55 during the period of 1988–1990. As one might imagine, a wage–health insurance tradeoff is difficult to discern statistically because more productive workers tend to receive both higher wages and increased health insurance coverage (as well as greater amounts of other benefits). Thus, it is important that both observable (such as education and experience) and unobservable (such as motivation, dependability, and intelligence) indicators of productivity are held constant in the empirical analysis to isolate the hypothesized inverse relation between wages and the presence of employer-sponsored health insurance. Controlling for observable and unobservable measures of productivity and other factors, Miller finds empirically that health insurance coverage results in 10 to 11 percent less wages. However, Miller warns that his estimate of the trade-off between wages and health insurance may also reflect the presence of other types of fringe benefits such as paid vacations and sick leave, which he was unable to control for because of data limitations. But when health insurance is valued at 11 percent of average wages, the resulting figure of $2,000 compares very closely to the average annual cost of employer-sponsored insurance plans at that time. Thus, Miller's study lends empirical support for the wage and health insurance trade-off and the idea that employees pay for their own health insurance benefits in terms of forgone wages.

The notion that employers do not pay for the health insurance benefits of their employees and therefore only sponsor the insurance is important for the discussion that follows. Both models of the demand for health insurance presented assume workers pay for and choose their own coverage. The first model, the conventional theory or standard gamble model, assumes people purchase health insurance to avoid or transfer risk. In this case, insurance serves as a pooling arrangement to replace the high risk or variability of individual losses with the reduced risk or variability associated with aggregated losses. The second model, the Nyman model, views people as desiring financial access to medical care that health insurance offers. In this case, a pooling arrangement allows individuals, in the event they become ill, to receive a transfer of income from those who remain healthy. The transfer helps solve an affordability constraint that people face when their net worth falls below the cost of medical treatments. Both of these models offer important insights into the reasons why people demand health insurance and valuable lessons regarding the proper role of public policy with respect to health insurance markets.

The Conventional Theory of the Demand for Private Health Insurance

Because of imperfect information, many of the choices individuals make as health care consumers or providers involve a substantial amount of uncertainty. For example, for an individual consumer, many medical illnesses occur randomly, and therefore the timing and amount of medical expenditures are uncertain. Likewise, from the health care provider's perspective, patient load and types of treatment are unknown before they actually occur. Because these events are difficult to predict on an individual basis, they involve a substantial degree of risk. Because most people generally dislike risk, they are willing to pay some amount of money to avoid it.

Consumers actually purchase a pooling arrangement when they buy a policy from an insurance company. Pooling arrangements help mitigate some of the risk associated with potential losses. We will illustrate this point through an example. Suppose, two individuals, named Joe and Leo, face the same distribution of losses. We can think of a loss distribution as showing the probability of a number of different occurring outcomes, with the sum of the probabilities equaling 1 or 100 percent. More specifically, assume that both Joe and Leo each face a 20 percent probability of losing $20 and an 80 percent probability of losing nothing.[1] Also assume that the losses of Joe and Leo are perfectly uncorrelated, or independent of one another. That is, Leo does not incur a loss just because Joe incurs a loss, and vice versa.

Standard statistics theory suggests that the expected value, μ, of a distribution of outcomes such as losses can be computed as the sum of the weighted values of the outcomes, L_i, with the probabilities, π, serving as the weights. The expected value

---

1. Most individual loss distributions are characterized by a low probability of losing a large sum of money and a high probability of losing very little. The dollar losses are kept to a minimum to ease the calculations that follow. The ensuing discussion may be more meaningful if you think in terms of thousands or millions of dollars.

serves as a summary measure of the distribution of outcomes. For our example, the expected loss equals:

(6–1) $$\mu = \pi_1 L_1 + \pi_2 L_2 = 0.2 \times \$20 + 0.8 \times \$0 = \$4.$$

Equation 6–1 can be interpreted as meaning Joe and Leo can each expect to lose $4 on average.

But people are also concerned about the variability of the expected loss. It stands to reason that a distribution of likely outcomes involves greater risk when more variability exists around the expected value. For example, Joe and Leo are likely to feel financially more secure knowing they can expect to lose somewhere between $3 and $5 than between $1 and $7. Statistics theory suggests we can measure the variability or variance of a distribution of outcomes such as losses using the following formula:

(6–2) $$\text{Variance} = \sum \pi_i (L_i - \mu)^2 = 0.2(\$20 - \$4)^2 + 0.8(\$0 - \$4)^2$$
$$= 51.20 + 12.80 = 64$$

Along with the expected value, the variance also serves as a summary measure of a distribution. Notice that the variance increases when the actual outcomes, L_i, are further away from the expected outcome, μ. It can also be shown that the variance increases when the probability of extreme outcomes increases. That is, the variance increases when extreme outcomes are more likely to occur than the intermediate outcomes along a distribution. Typically, the variability of a distribution of outcomes is represented by its standard deviation rather than its variance. The standard deviation, which is found mathematically by taking the square root of the variance, equals $8 in this case.

Both the expected loss of $4 and its standard deviation of $8, in this example, can be thought of as measures of risk. Generally speaking, more risk is associated with a higher expected loss and when the distribution of the expected loss, or standard deviation, exhibits wider variability. If both Joe and Leo are risk averse to some degree, we can show that they might be better off by pooling their losses. Risk aversion occurs when people receive disutility from taking on additional risk and are willing to pay to avoid it or must be paid to accept it.

Let's now explore how Joe and Leo might mutually gain from entering into a pooling-of-losses arrangement. The idea is that both Joe and Leo will share in covering the losses of the other if a loss occurs. If Joe and Leo enter into a pooling arrangement, four possible outcomes are likely. One likely outcome is that both Joe and Leo lose no money at all. The joint probability of both Joe and Leo facing zero losses is found by multiplying the individual probabilities of zero losses occurring, or $0.8 \times 0.8 = 0.64$. Notice that the probability of an extreme outcome is lowered by the pooling arrangement from 0.80 on an individual basis to 0.64 on a group basis.[2] This result already provides a favorable sign that Joe and Leo may be better off by entering into a pooling arrangement.

The second likely outcome is that Joe loses $20 but Leo suffers no losses, and the third likely outcome is that Leo loses $20 but Joe does not. Each of these separate outcomes must be weighted by their respective probabilities of occurring, 0.2 and 0.8, respectively. The final likely outcome is that both Joe and Leo simultaneously suffer a loss of $20. The joint probability of this outcome occurring is found by multiplying the individual probabilities of occurrence, 0.2×0.2, which amounts to 0.04. Notice once again that the probability of an extreme outcome occurring is reduced by the pooling arrangement. Table 6–1 summarizes the four likely outcomes and their probable values. Notice that the probabilities of the four outcomes sum to 1 or 100 percent, as they should.

---

2. This is similar to the joint probability of flipping a coin and obtaining two consecutive heads. The probability of a head toss equals 0.50, so the probability of two consecutive head tosses equals 0.25.

TABLE 6–1

The Expected Loss from Entering into a Pooling Arrangement

Outcome	(1) Combined Probability	(2) Combined Loss	(1) × (2) Probable Loss from That Outcome	(2) ÷ 2 One Person's Share of Loss
Both Joe and Leo face zero losses	0.8 × 0.8 = 0.64	$0	$0	$0
Joe loses $20 but Leo does not	0.2 × 0.8 = 0.16	$20	$3.20	$10
Leo loses $20 but Joe does not	0.2 × 0.8 = 0.16	$20	$3.20	$10
Both Joe and Leo lose $20	0.2 × 0.2 = 0.04	$40	$1.60	$20
		Expected total loss	$8.00	
		Joe's and Leo's share of the expected loss	$4.00	

© Cengage Learning 2013

The calculations in Table 6–1 suggest that the pooling arrangement does not make either Joe or Leo better off in terms of the expected loss. Each person faces an expected loss of $4 with or without the pooling arrangement. But when people face the same distribution of outcomes, a pooling arrangement is not about reducing the expected loss; the pooling arrangement is all about reducing the standard deviation or variability of the loss. If we apply the formula for the variance in Equation 6–2, we can obtain the variability of the share of the losses faced by either Joe or Leo as

$$(6–3) \qquad \text{Variance} = 0.64(0-4)^2 + 0.16(10-4)^2 + 0.16(10-4)^2 + 0.04(20-4)^2$$
$$= 32$$

It follows that the standard deviation associated with the expected loss equals the square root of the variance, or $5.66.

Notice that the standard deviation of the loss distribution declines from $8 without the pooling arrangement to $5.66 with the pooling arrangement. Both Joe and Leo clearly gain from the reduced variability associated with their expected losses of $4. What may be unclear at this point, however, is the intuition behind the reduction in the variability of the losses that each individual faces because of the pooling arrangement. Entering into a pooling arrangement essentially replaces each person's individual loss distribution with the average loss distribution of the group. The average loss distribution of the group involves a lower probability of extreme outcomes occurring because it is much less likely that both Joe and Leo will simultaneously lose nothing or lose $20. In other words, what happens to one individual will typically be offset because the other individual does not simultaneously experience that same occurrence.

In addition, the variability of the expected loss decreases as more individuals with similar individual loss distributions join a pooling arrangement. Assuming losses are not perfectly correlated, more individuals joining the pooling arrangement help reduce the probability of the extreme outcomes occurring and thereby make the expected loss less variable and more predictable. It also can be shown that the group loss distribution becomes more symmetrical and bell-shaped, unlike an individual loss distribution, which is heavily skewed toward the right.[3] A loss distribution heavily skewed toward the right means small dollar losses occur more frequently than large dollar losses.

---

3. See Harrington and Niehaus (2004) for an excellent treatment of basic insurance principles.

The preceding discussion suggests that consumers typically gain from entering into pooling arrangements because the pooling helps reduce the variability of the expected losses. Certainly, consumers benefit when they enter into a medical expense pool. The individual loss function associated with medical expenses is heavily skewed toward the right, indicating that only a very few people will actually incur large medical expenses in the absence of insurance. Indeed for the United States as a whole, a mere 5 percent of all patients accounted for more than half of all health care spending in 1996 (Berk and Monheit, 2001). From an individual consumer's perspective, a pooling arrangement can reduce the variability associated with medical expenses to some degree.

We have not yet established why insurance companies become involved in pooling arrangements. Certainly, people enter into simple forms of pooling arrangements on their own. For example, large families often provide informal sharing of losses, and businesses with a large number of employees sometimes self-insure. However, in cases involving people with no informal or formal relationships, personal pooling arrangements involve an unnecessarily large number of contracts written.[4] In contrast, when the pooling arrangement is developed by an insurance company, only one contract is written between each policyholder and the insurer. Also, if those in the personal pooling arrangement decide to increase the size of the group, they must engage in marketing and underwriting (i.e., determining whom and on what terms to cover) activities, among others. Most people lack expertise in these areas, but insurance companies can hire the necessary personnel and monitor their activities. Hence, insurance companies often serve as intermediaries and develop and sell pooling arrangements to individuals.

Thus, consumers pay an insurer a certain amount of income (i.e., a premium), and the insurer covers some or all of the medical costs in the event an illness actually occurs. During any given period the actual benefits paid out by an insurer to any single consumer may be higher or lower than the premiums received from that consumer. By operating on a large scale, an insurer pools or spreads the risk among many subscribers so that, on average, the total premiums received *at least* compensate for the total cost of paying for medical services, particularly in the long run. In addition, given some amount of competition in the health insurance market, the difference between total premiums and total benefits paid out to all subscribers (or the loading fee) should approximate a "normal" amount.

Consumers differ in terms of the amounts and types of health insurance coverage they buy, and these differences are reflected in such items as the deductible amount, the coinsurance rate, and the number and types of events covered. (We examine the health insurance product more closely later on in the chapter.) In general, a high deductible and a high coinsurance rate reflect less extensive or less complete health insurance coverage. For example, some consumers purchase health insurance plans that offer first-dollar coverage for all types of medical services, including routine care. Others purchase health insurance plans with large deductibles and copayments that cover only catastrophic illnesses. Differences in health care coverage can be explained by a host of factors, including the price of obtaining health insurance, the individual's degree of risk aversion, the perceived magnitude of the loss relative to income, and information concerning the likelihood that an illness will actually occur. The following section offers a model to address how each of these factors individually affects the demand for health insurance.

Deriving the Demand for Private Health Insurance

We can better understand how these factors influence the quantity demanded of health insurance by focusing on Figure 6–1, where the actual utility, U, associated with

---

4. The number of contracts would equal $[n(n - 1)]/2$, where n equals the number of individuals in the pool.

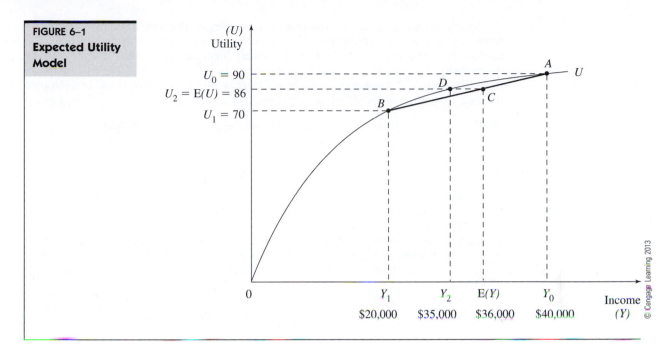

FIGURE 6–1

Expected Utility Model

The curve shows the actual utility associated with different levels of income (not drawn to scale). The concavity of the curve illustrates risk aversion. Suppose a person has $40,000 of income and a medical illness costs $20,000. Assuming no health insurance, chord *AB* represents the expected utility associated with different probability values (π) between 0 and 1 of an illness occurring. Points A and B represent two extreme outcomes for which the illness is not expected to occur ($\pi = 0$) and the illness is perfectly certain ($\pi = 1$). Point *C* reflects an example of an intermediate position where there is a 20 percent chance ($\pi = 0.20$) of an illness occurring such that expected income after the loss equals $36,000 and expected utility equals 86. Notice that a risk-averse person is indifferent in terms of utility levels between losing a known amount of $5,000 at point *D* and an expected amount of $4,000 at point *C*. Thus, the expected utility model suggests that a risk-averse person can be made better off by paying an insurer some amount above the expected loss to be relieved of the associated risk.

different levels of income, Y, is shown for a representative consumer (ignore the chord AB for now). The slope of this utility function at any point is $\Delta U/\Delta Y$ and represents the marginal utility of income. The declining slope, or marginal utility of income, is based on the premise that the individual is risk averse. This means the risk-averse person is opposed to a fair gamble where there is a 50–50 chance of losing or gaining $1 because a dollar loss is valued more highly than a dollar gain. That is, for any given level of income, the pain of losing an incremental dollar exceeds the pleasure associated with gaining an additional dollar.

Suppose a person has an income of Y_0 equaling $40,000. As indicated in Figure 6–1, this income level yields actual utility of U_0, which amounts to 90 utils.[5] Further, suppose the person faces a choice concerning whether to purchase health insurance. The decision is based partly on a belief that if an illness occurs, the medical services will cost $20,000. Consequently, if the illness occurs and the consumer pays the entire medical bill, income declines to $20,000 and the level of actual utility falls to U_1, or 70 utils.

The two outcomes that can occur if the consumer does not purchase health insurance are represented by points A and B. At point A, no illness occurs and income remains at $40,000 such that actual utility equals U_0. At point B, an illness occurs and (net) income falls to $20,000 such that actual utility equals U_1. Because the

5. For expository purposes, we assume utility can be measured directly in units called *utils*.

resulting outcome is unknown before it actually occurs, the individual forms expectations concerning the probability of each outcome occurring. With these subjective probabilities, the expected (rather than actual) levels of utility and income can be determined. Specifically, the individual's expected level of utility, $E(U)$, can be determined by weighing the actual utility levels associated with the two possible outcomes by their subjective probabilities of occurrence, π_0 and π_1.

(6–4)
$$E(U) = \pi_0 \times U_0(Y_0 = \$40{,}000) + \pi_1 \times U_1(Y_1 = \$20{,}000),$$

or

(6–5)
$$E(U) = \pi_0 \times 90 + \pi_1 \times 70,$$

where π_0 and π_1 sum to 1. Based on Equation 6–5, the chord AB in Figure 6–1 shows the level of expected utility for various probabilities that the illness will occur. As the probability of getting ill increases, expected utility declines, and this outcome is associated with a point closer to B on the chord. The precise probability value the individual attaches to the illness occurring is based on his best personal estimate. It is likely to depend on such factors as the individual's stock of health, age, and lifestyle.

Suppose the consumer attaches a subjective probability of 20 percent to an illness actually occurring. Following Equation 6–5, the expected utility is

(6–6)
$$E(U) = 0.8 \times 90 + 0.2 \times 70 = 86$$

and the expected level of income, $E(Y)$, is

(6–7)
$$E(Y) = \pi_0 \times Y_0 + \pi_1 \times Y_1 = 0.8 \times 40{,}000 + 0.2 \times 20{,}000 = 36{,}000.$$

Equation 6–7 represents the weighted sum of the two income levels with the probability values as the weights. Thus, expected income equals $36,000 and the expected level of utility is 86 utils if insurance is not purchased (and full risk is assumed), given that the perceived probability of illness equals 0.2 and the magnitude of the loss equals $20,000. The levels of expected income and expected utility are also shown in Figure 6–1.

Notice in the figure (not drawn to scale) that the person is just as well off in terms of actual utility by paying a third party a "certain" amount of $5,000 to insure against the expected loss of $4,000. The certain loss of $5,000 reduces net income to $35,000 and provides the consumer with an actual utility level of 86 utils, which equals the expected utility level without insurance. To the consumer, the $1,000 discrepancy, or distance CD, represents the maximum amount she is willing to pay for health insurance above the expected loss. It reflects the notion that a risk-averse consumer always prefers a known amount of income rather than an expected amount of equal value. This preference reflects the value the consumer places on financial security. It is for this reason that the typical person faces an incentive to purchase health insurance.

It is easy to see from this analysis why an insurance company is willing to insure against the risk. Assuming this person is the average subscriber in the insured group and the probability of an illness occurring is correct from an objective statistical perspective, the insurance company could potentially receive premium revenues of $5,000 to pay the expected medical benefits of $4,000 with enough left over to cover administrative expenses, taxes, and profits. The expected medical benefits can also be referred to as the actuarial fair value or "pure premium." To the insurer, the difference between the total premium and medical benefits paid out, or pure premium, is referred to as the **loading fee**. In the economics of insurance literature, the loading fee is also typically referred to as the *price of insurance*.

Factors Affecting the Quantity Demanded of Health Insurance

The model in Figure 6–1 can be used to explain how the price of insurance affects the quantity demanded of health insurance. Under normal circumstances, the consumer purchases health insurance if the actual utility with health insurance exceeds the expected utility without it.[6] In Figure 6–1, that happens whenever the loading fee leads to an income level associated with a point between D and C on the actual utility curve for the given set of circumstances (i.e., probability values, degree of risk aversion, and magnitude of loss). In terms of the present example, the consumer demands health insurance if the loading fee is less than $1,000 because actual utility exceeds expected utility at that dollar amount. If expected utility exceeds actual utility, the consumer does not purchase health insurance coverage because the price is too high (a loading fee producing actual utility between points D and B). This happens if the loading fee exceeds $1,000 in our example. Finally, if actual and expected utility are equal due to the loading fee, the individual is indifferent between buying and not buying health insurance (point D or a loading fee of $1,000). Both options make the consumer equally well off. Therefore, it follows that the loading fee, or the price of health insurance, helps establish the completeness of insurance coverage and the number of people who insure against medical illnesses. Specifically, as the price of insurance declines, actual utility increases relative to expected utility and the quantity demanded of health insurance increases—*ceteris paribus.*

At this point, it is useful to note that employment-related health insurance premiums, unlike cash income, are presently exempt from federal and state income taxes even though they are a form of in-kind income. For example, if an employer pays cash wages of $800 and provides health insurance benefits equal to $200 per month to an employee, only the $800 is subject to taxes even though total compensation equals $1,000. Assuming a 20 percent marginal tax rate, the individual pays $160 in taxes on $800 of cash income rather than $200 on $1,000 of total compensation.

Thus, relative to cash income (or all other goods purchased out of cash income), health insurance is effectively subsidized by the government because of its tax-exempt status. We can view this tax subsidy on health insurance benefits in another way. Each time the employer raises the employee's wage by $1, the employee receives only $(100 - t)$ percent of that $1 as after-tax income, where t is the marginal tax rate. However, if employer health insurance contributions increase by $1, the employee receives the entire dollar as benefits. In effect, the government picks up t percent of the price of the health insurance in forgone taxes and the employee pays the remaining $(100 - t)$ percent in forgone wage income (since both wages and in-kind benefits are substitute forms of compensation). Given $t = 20$, the government implicitly pays 20 cents and the employee pays 80 cents of the marginal dollar spent on health insurance. If we allow for the possibility that not all health insurance premiums are tax exempt (such as the health insurance premiums of some individuals who purchase individual policies), the user price of health insurance can be written as $(1 - et/100)P$, where e is the fraction of health insurance premiums exempted from taxes and P is the price of health insurance (the loading fee). The user price of health insurance obviously decreases with a higher marginal income tax rate and tax-exempt fraction.

Figure 6–2 provides a graphical illustration explaining how the tax exemption of insurance premiums influences the quantity demanded of health insurance. In the figure, the vertical axis captures the loading fee or price, P, and the horizontal axis indicates the amount of insurance coverage demanded, q. A rightward movement along the horizontal axis indicates policies with lower deductibles and copayments or more

---

6. The theoretically correct comparison is between the expected utility with health insurance and the expected utility without health insurance. However, because the amount of the premium payment is perfectly certain with a probability of occurrence equal to 1, the expected and actual utility with health insurance are equal. We use actual utility here to avoid confusion.

FIGURE 6–2
The Effect of the Tax Exemption on Insurance Coverage

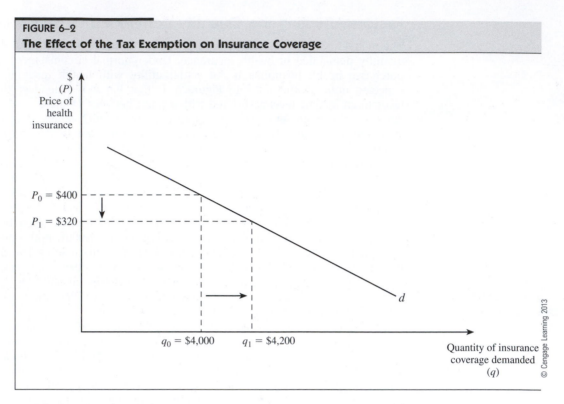

Given the 20 percent tax rate, the tax exemption on health insurance premiums lowers the opportunity cost of purchasing health insurance from $400 to $320 and thereby leads to more insurance coverage purchased as long as demand is not perfectly inelastic with respect to price.

risky events covered by the plan, and consequently, a higher premium payment. An individual's demand for insurance coverage is drawn as a downward-sloping curve to reflect the law of diminishing marginal utility. In addition, a downward-sloping demand for insurance might signify that people typically face relatively few high-risk situations but many more low-risk events. As price declines, people are therefore more willing to have more of these less-risky events covered by insurance.

Let's simplify the discussion by taking the employer out of the picture. Suppose the demand in Figure 6–2 represents a self-employed worker's demand for health insurance. Before 1996, self-employed workers were allowed to exempt only 25 percent of their premiums from taxable earnings. However, for discussion purposes, let's suppose that initially the self-employed worker is not allowed a tax exemption on any type of spending and that her income is taxed at 20 percent. Let's also assume that the self-employed worker earns $60,000 of annual income and the loading fee for an insurance policy is set in the marketplace at $400. The government therefore collects $12,000 in taxes ($60,000 times 0.2) from this self-employed worker.

Thus, price P_0 in Figure 6–2 equals $400. The individual matches up market price with marginal benefit, as indicated by demand, and purchases q_0 amount of insurance in the process of maximizing utility. We assume that q_0 equals $4,000 worth of insurance coverage. Notice in this case that an additional dollar spent on health insurance comes at the same cost of an additional dollar spent on any other type of good or service because taxes are applied equally to all types of spending out of income. That is, an additional dollar of pretax income purchases only 80 cents of insurance and any other good or service the individual might buy because of the 20 percent tax rate on wage income. Alternatively stated, the opportunity cost of $1 of additional insurance coverage is $1 spent on all other goods and services.

Now suppose the government exempts all insurance premiums of the self-employed from income taxation, which reflects what actually occurred beginning in 2003. Now, because of the differential tax treatment, an additional dollar out of pretax income purchases $1 of insurance but only 80 cents of all other goods and services. Thus, the opportunity cost of an additional dollar spent on insurance declines from $1 to 80 cents. In terms of our example, this means that the opportunity cost of purchasing health insurance is no longer $400 but now equals $320 or $(1 - t)P_0$.

Figure 6–2 shows the impact of the lower after-tax price of health insurance on the quantity demanded of health insurance. As long as demand is not perfectly inelastic, the self-employed worker responds to the lower after-tax price by purchasing more health insurance, which for discussion purposes is set at $4,200. The government now collects $11,160 of taxes from the self-employed worker.

Thus, economic theory suggests people purchase more health insurance because of the preferential tax treatment of health insurance premiums. The tax exemption effectively serves as a subsidy for the purchase of health insurance coverage. As we saw in our example, the government effectively pays 20 percent of the loading fee and thereby reduces the individual's out-of-pocket price when purchasing health insurance. Also, note that the government gives up tax revenues because of the preferential tax treatment of health insurance premiums. These lost tax revenues could have been used to finance various public goods and services. In this example, the government lost $840 of tax revenues. In the aggregate, estimates suggest the government lost roughly $150 billion of tax revenues in 2004 because of the tax exemption (Sheils and Haught, 2004).

The expected utility model in Figure 6–1 can also help explain other factors affecting the demand for health insurance. First, the subjective probability of an illness occurring affects the amount of health insurance demanded. In terms of the figure, as the probability of an illness increases from 0 to 1, the relevant point on chord AB moves from A toward B. Given the shapes of the two curves, the horizontal distance between the actual utility curve and the expected utility line, which measures the willingness to pay for health insurance beyond the expected level of medical benefits, at first gets larger, reaches a maximum, and then approaches 0 with a movement from A to B. Therefore, all else held constant, including the loading fee, the quantity demanded of health insurance first increases, reaches a maximum amount, and then decreases with respect to a higher probability of an illness occurring. The implication is that individuals insure less against medical events that are either highly unlikely (closer to A) or most probable (closer to B). In the latter case, it is cheaper for the individual to self-insure (that is, save money for a "rainy day") and avoid paying the loading fee. For example, assume the probability of illness is 1. In this case, the expected and actual levels of utility are equal at point B in Figure 6–1. In this situation, it is cheaper for the individual to self-insure than to pay a loading fee above the medical benefits actually paid out. Alternatively stated, there is no need for insurance since the outcome is certain. The uncertainty of an illness occurring is one reason more people insure against random medical events than against routine medical events, such as periodic physical and dental exams, which are expected.

Another factor affecting the amount of insurance coverage is the magnitude of the loss relative to income. Assuming the same probabilities as before, the expected utility line (chord AB) in Figure 6–1 rotates down and pivots off point A if the magnitude of the loss increases. In this case, the new expected utility line meets the actual utility curve somewhere below point B. For the same probability values as before, the horizontal distance between the expected and actual utility curves increases. Thus, the willingness to purchase health insurance increases with greater magnitude of a loss. This implies that a greater number of people insure against illnesses associated with a large loss, at least relative to income. Insurance coverage is also more complete.

The potential for a greater loss is one reason more people have hospital insurance than dental or eye care insurance coverage.

The final factor affecting the amount of health insurance demanded is the degree of risk aversion. Obviously, people who are more risk averse have more insurance coverage than otherwise identical people who are less risk averse. Greater risk aversion makes the utility curve more concave. In fact, if the person is risk neutral, the marginal pain of a dollar loss equals the marginal pleasure of a dollar gain and the slope of the utility curve is constant (a straight line through the origin). In this case, a person would be indifferent with respect to purchasing or not purchasing insurance because the expected and actual utilities are equal at different levels of income. For a risk lover, the pleasure of an additional dollar gained exceeds the pain of an incremental dollar loss and the slope of the utility curve increases in value. In the case of a risk lover, no insurance is purchased because expected utility is greater than actual utility at any level of income.

In sum, according to conventional theory, we can specify the quantity demanded of health insurance, Q, as a function of the following factors:

$$(6\text{–}8) \qquad Q = f[(1 - et/100) \times P, \text{Degree of risk aversion, Probability}$$
$$\text{of an illness occurring, Magnitude of loss, Income}].$$

Note that a change in the first explanatory factor results in a movement along a given demand curve, whereas an adjustment in any of the other four factors results in a shifting of the curve.

With suitable data, Equation 6–8 can be estimated to determine the user price and income elasticities of the demand for health insurance. In practice, however, it is very difficult to measure the user price and quantity demanded of health insurance. Therefore, various proxies are used depending on data availability. For example, the price of health insurance, P, is sometimes proxied by the size of the insured group. The expectation is that the loading fee, or the price of health insurance, falls with a larger group size due to administrative and risk-spreading economies. Some studies assume that the price of health insurance is the same for all individuals and allow only marginal tax rates, t, and the tax-exempt fraction, e, to vary.

Proxy measures for the quantity of health insurance must also be employed. The quantity of health insurance is usually measured by either total insurance premiums, some measure of insurance coverage completeness, or a coverage option (e.g., less versus more restrictive health insurance plans). Table 6–2 displays some of the estimated price and income elasticities of the demand for health insurance reported in various studies. The studies reveal that individuals possess a price-inelastic demand for health insurance. Furthermore, while health insurance is considered a normal good (that is, it

TABLE 6–2
Price and Income Elasticities of the Demand for Health Insurance

Study	Price Elasticity	Income Elasticity
Taylor and Wilensky (1983)	−0.21	0.02
Farley and Wilensky (1984)	−0.41	0.04
Holmer (1984)	−0.16	0.01
Short and Taylor (1989)	−0.32	0.13
Manning and Marquis (1989)	−0.54	0.07
Marquis and Long (1995)	−0.03	0.15
Liu and Christianson (1998)	−0.33	0.12
Santerre (2008)	−0.19	0.27

has an income elasticity greater than zero), the studies found a relatively small income effect. Even the demand for long-term care insurance is found to be inelastic, with price and income elasticities of about -0.39 and 0.18, respectively (Kumar et al., 1995).

However, these studies generally assume the individual is able to make marginal changes in the insurance policy. But employer-sponsored group insurance policies are largely beyond the control of the single individual employee. Typically, the employer or union representatives make decisions concerning the insurance package by considering the welfare of the overall group rather than that of any one individual employee.[7] See Goldstein and Pauly (1976) or Pauly (1986) for further discussion on this point. When employees can select from multiple similar plans offered by the employer and must pay more out-of-pocket for more expensive plans, demand is found to be much more responsive to price. For example, Dowd and Feldman (1994/95) find that when multiple similar plans are offered, the demand for a health plan (with respect to price) is highly elastic, at about 27.9. Strombom et al. (2002) estimate elasticities ranging from 22.0 to 28.4 depending on the cost of switching plans as measured by age, job tenure, and medical risk category.

Nyman's Access Theory of the Demand for Private Health Insurance

As we discussed previously, standard insurance theory suggests that risk-averse individuals purchase health insurance as a way of transferring or avoiding some of the risk associated with the variability of medical care expenses. They avoid or transfer some of the risk by entering into a pooling arrangement to replace their individual loss distributions with the average loss distribution of the group. Compared to the individual loss distributions, the average loss distribution involves less variability around the expected loss and thereby results in less risk faced by an individual when engaged in a pooling arrangement.

John Nyman (2003) advanced an alternative reason why people desire medical insurance coverage. Nyman begins by pointing out that many medical interventions, such as a liver transplant or coronary artery bypass surgery, cost more than most people hold in terms of their net worth (value of assets less the value of liabilities). For example, a liver transplant can cost around $300,000, yet most households hold as little as $50,000 in net worth. In addition, banks are reluctant to loan out money for a potentially lifesaving medical intervention when they are unsure whether the ill person will be able to repay the loan. Thus, in the absence of medical insurance coverage, many people might be denied access to lifesaving medical interventions because they lack the financial means to pay for them.

Because many people lack the wherewithal to purchase the medical care required by a major medical intervention, Nyman argues that people value medical insurance because they desire an income transfer from those who remain healthy in the event they become seriously ill. Notice that, unlike in the standard model, income rather than risk is being transferred in the Nyman model. As an illustration, suppose actuarial data indicate that 1 out of 75,000 people will require a liver transplant in a given year. Also suppose 75,000 people join an insurance pool and the liver transplant costs $300,000. Thus, for an actuarial fair premium of $4 ($300,000/75,000), a person with a relatively low net worth has access to a potentially lifesaving medical intervention because she will receive an income transfer of $299,996 from the other 74,999 individuals in the pool if she requires a liver transplant. Insurance offers a solution to an affordability problem brought about by the need for a major medical intervention. According to Nyman, medical insurance creates value by providing financial access to medical care that people could not otherwise afford.

---

7. Nevertheless, most studies find that the demand for individual health insurance is also inelastic with respect to price. For example, see Marquis et al. (2004) or Auerbach and Ohri (2006).

Conventional Insurance Theory according to Nyman

Most economists agree that a model should be judged by the plausibility of its assumptions and its ability to accurately predict behavior in the real world. For example, students typically learn in principles of macroeconomics that John Maynard Keynes (1936) refuted classical theory by showing that several of its key assumptions, such as perfect wage and price flexibility, do not always hold in practice. Keynes also pointed out that classical theory predicts full employment, yet 25 percent of the workforce was unemployed at one point during the Great Depression of the 1930s. Hence classical theory was not a useful model at that period of time, according to Keynes, because of its weak assumptions and failure to predict correctly.

In a similar vein, Nyman points to several inconsistencies associated with the assumptions and predictions of the conventional insurance model as a way of judging its usefulness as a theory of the demand for health insurance. Most of these inconsistencies are fairly technical in nature so we highlight only a few of the more crucial ones, especially those whose scrutiny offers direct insights into the Nyman model.

Moral Hazard Is Always Welfare Decreasing.   Conventional theory treats medical insurance coverage as reducing the representative consumer's out-of-pocket price of medical care. The lower out-of-pocket price, in turn, creates a movement down along the demand curve and leads to additional units of medical care demanded for which their marginal costs exceed marginal benefits. In Chapter 5, we referred to this situation as the moral hazard problem. Figure 6–3 helps to describe the economic reasoning behind the conventional treatment of moral hazard.

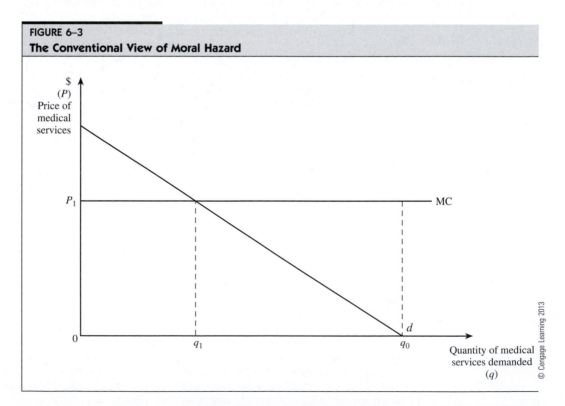

FIGURE 6–3
The Conventional View of Moral Hazard

Complete coverage causes the consumer's out-of-pocket price to fall from P_1 to 0. As a result, quantity increases from q_1 to q_0. The additional units are treated as creating a welfare loss because MC exceeds willingness to pay.

In the figure, the horizontal axis represents the quantity of medical services demanded by a representative consumer. The typical consumer's demand for medical care, d, is shown as being downward sloping and MC, the marginal cost of delivering of medical care, is assumed to be constant with respect to the amount of medical care produced. Consumer equilibrium, for the uninsured individual, occurs where MC and demand intersect at a price of P_1 and quantity of q_1. The amount of medical care consumed is considered efficient because for every unit between the origin and q_1, willingness to pay or marginal benefit, as revealed by demand, never falls below MC.

Now suppose that the representative consumer purchases full insurance coverage. According to conventional theory, complete insurance coverage can be treated as simply lowering the fully-insured consumer's out-of-pocket price down along the demand curve from P_1 to 0. At the new fully-insured consumer equilibrium, the amount of medical care now increases to q_0 and a welfare loss occurs because each additional unit of medical care between q_1 and q_0 generates more costs than benefits at the margin. These additional units may reflect spending on discretionary items such as prescription sunglasses and cosmetic surgery—things people purchase with insurance coverage they would not have otherwise purchased if they had to pay the full price. These additional units of medical care may also reflect extra visits to doctors or longer stays in hospitals than medically necessary. Thus, conventional theory treats the transition from uninsured to insured status as resulting in the consumption of frivolous or unnecessary medical care.

Nyman believes that this prediction of the conventional model offers an inconsistency because several empirical studies have found the transition from uninsured to insured status results in vast improvements in people's health, especially among vulnerable populations such as infants and the elderly (see Chapter 2). Nyman also refers to empirical studies indicating the uninsured often fail to receive standard care and delay or defer seeking medically needed care. Given that health improves when people transition from uninsured to insured status, Nyman argues that the additional medical care consumed cannot be as frivolous or clinically unnecessary as conventional theory tends to suggest it is.

Nyman claims that conventional theory makes this false prediction because it treats the medical insurance payoff as resulting solely in a lower out-of-pocket price and not producing a corresponding income transfer. If the insurance payoff is treated as an income transfer at time of sickness, as Nyman proposes, then the demand for medical care effectively shifts to the right and results in much less inefficiency. Figure 6–4 shows what happens when the insurance payoff is treated as an income payoff.[8]

Assuming the consumer purchases full insurance coverage, the demand for medical care shifts from D_U, the uninsured demand, to D_I, the insured demand. The greater demand represents the income transfer that the consumer receives at the time of illness from those who remain healthy. Obviously, the consumer possesses a greater willingness to pay for medical care when sick and has the income to pay for it. Consequently, an important distinction between the two models is that conventional theory assumes that willingness to pay is determined before the payout takes place, whereas Nyman treats willingness to pay as being determined at the time the payout is made.

If the insurance payoff were accomplished through a lump-sum transfer and price remained at P_1, the new equilibrium quantity of medical care would be represented by q_N. Notice that this equilibrium is characterized by additional units of

8. In Figure 6–4, q_0 exceeds q_2 because the premium payment reduces the amount of income available to purchase additional medical care. Our purpose here is to compare the Nyman model to the conventional model for a situation in which the consumer possesses complete insurance coverage. It should be pointed out, however, that a different demand curve exists for each coinsurance rate. The demand curve shown in Figure 6–4 is the one for a zero coinsurance rate. If the coinsurance rate is 0.5, for example, the demand curve shifts half of the distance to the right from D_U and point q_2 moves half of the distance closer to q_0 because the premium payment is now proportionally lower. The total amount of medical care demanded, in the case, is determined at the point on the demand curve where the coinsurance rate equals $0.5P_1$.

FIGURE 6–4

Nyman's View of Moral Hazard

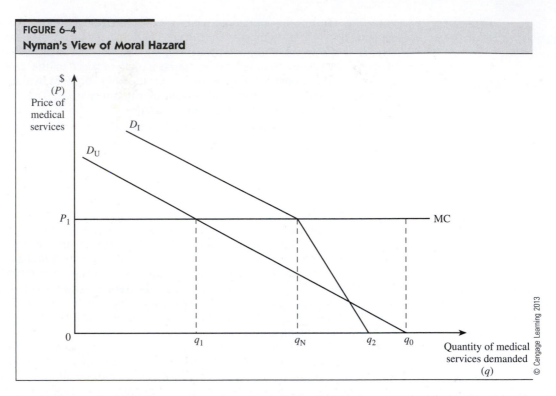

Complete insurance leads to both an income transfer and a substitution effect. The income transfer shifts the demand from D_U to D_I and quantity demanded increases from q_1 to q_N as a result. The insurance, because it is designed as a price-payoff contract, also results in a substitution effect from q_N to q_2. The range between q_1 and q_N represents efficient moral hazard, whereas the range between q_N and q_2 represents inefficient moral hazard.

medical care for which willingness to pay or marginal benefit exceeds MC. However, the new equilibrium actually occurs at q_2, with a **price-payoff contract** accounting for the additional units of medical care demanded between q_N and q_2. A price-payoff contract pays out by reducing price rather than offering a lump-sum reimbursement. For example, a medical expense contract may specify that the insured will be reimbursed for the actual cost of physician services less any stipulated coinsurance each time she makes an office visit. In our hypothetical case, as depicted in Figure 6–4, we assume that the price-payoff contract reduces price to zero. In both cases, the price reduction feature of the price-payoff contract potentially triggers a substitution effect (as well as the income effect discussed previously).

Recall that a substitution effect occurs when people switch away from higher- to lower-priced goods. In this specific case, people may switch away from other goods and purchase more medical care than they otherwise would have because of the substitution effect brought on by the insurance coverage. As a result, the price-payoff contract is associated with some inefficient moral hazard similar to what we learned from the conventional analysis of moral hazard. This inefficient moral hazard represents the cost of using a price reduction to pay off the insurance contract. The benefit of a price-payoff contract is that health care providers monitor and verify illnesses on behalf of the insurance companies and thereby prevent consumer fraud. That is, if the insurance company paid their insured a lump sum amount for an illness, rather than a reduced price when seeking treatment through health care providers, many people might falsely claim to be ill to receive a payout.

Thus, another significant distinction between the two models is that both efficient and inefficient moral hazard may occur in the Nyman model. That is, insurance coverage causes people's behavior to change but some behavioral changes result in efficiencies whereas others do not. The conventional theory considers only inefficient moral hazard. In Figure 6–4, the efficient moral hazard is represented by the quantity of medical care between q_1 and q_N because marginal benefit exceeds MC and the inefficient medical care falls between q_N and q_2.

Voluntary Purchasing of Health Insurance Makes People Worse Off.   Conventional theory assumes that people purchase health insurance to avoid risk. Thus, health insurance offers the benefits of risk reduction. As we just saw, conventional theory also argues that health insurance creates corresponding costs by resulting in excessive spending levels associated with (inefficient) moral hazard. Interestingly, conventional theory suggests that the benefits of risk reduction and moral hazard costs tend to move in opposite directions with changes in the coinsurance rate. For example, raising the coinsurance rate increases the consumer's risk exposure but lowers the moral hazard costs.

Within this perspective, people make trade-offs between risk exposure and moral hazard costs when they purchase health insurance just as they make trade-offs when choosing among cars with different gas mileages, styles, and other characteristics. For instance, highly risk-averse individuals who are drawn to plans with less exposure to risk (that is, a lower coinsurance rate) must accept potentially greater moral hazard costs and pay a greater premium. Consequently, one would think that the characteristics of real-world insurance contracts reflect what consumers personally find ideal or utility maximizing given the trade-offs they face. In particular, the coinsurance rate selected by individuals should reflect their rational choice between risk reduction benefits and moral hazard costs.

Based upon conventional theory, several researchers have calculated estimates of the optimal coinsurance rate and compared them to the coinsurance rates specified in real-world insurance policies. Feldstein (1973) shows that the optimal coinsurance rate depends on values for the price elasticity of demand for medical services and the consumer's degree of risk aversion. He finds that raising the coinsurance rate to 66 percent would improve consumer welfare. More recently, Manning and Marquis (1996) estimate the demand for health insurance to measure the degree of risk aversion and the demand for health care services to measure the price elasticity of demand. They use data from the RAND health insurance study of the 1970s (discussed in Chapter 5) and find an optimal coinsurance rate of 40 to 50 percent.

Nyman points out that these estimates of the optimal coinsurance rate are much higher than the ones specified in actual health insurance policies (typically well below 30 percent). This discrepancy leads Nyman to wonder why people would voluntarily purchase a policy that made them worse off. In other words, why would the typical consumer pay a higher premium and receive more coverage than she truly finds optimal? As we discussed in Chapter 3, rational economic behavior predicts that people never purposely and knowingly make themselves worse off. As a result, this inconsistency led Nyman to conclude that something must be wrong with conventional theory if it predicts irrational behavior. It also provided him with the motivation to develop an alternative theory of the demand for health insurance—one that is not driven by risk avoidance.

A Simple Exposition of the Nyman Model

Similar to the conventional model, the Nyman model is based on a comparison of the expected utility from being insured (EU_I) with the expected utility from remaining uninsured (EU_U). Insurance is purchased if $EU_I > EU_U$. However, the Nyman model does not depend on consumers being risk averse. The basic idea behind the Nyman model is that purchasing insurance reduces one's income when healthy by the amount of the premium (opportunity cost) but potentially raises one's income through a transfer when sick (the benefit). This means that one factor affecting the purchasing of medical expense insurance is a person's preference regarding when she would rather

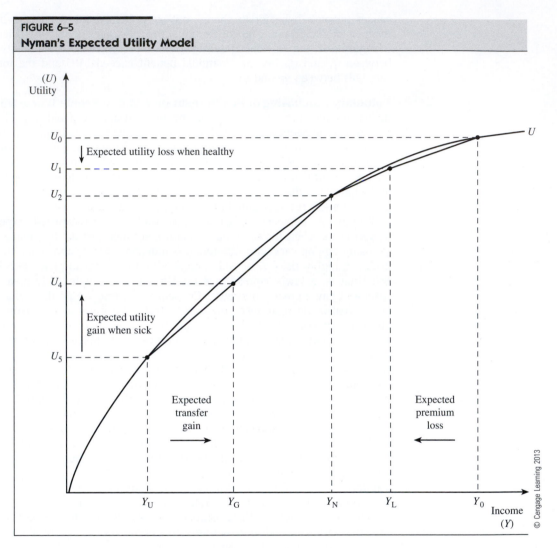

FIGURE 6–5
Nyman's Expected Utility Model

The expected premium payment results in an expected dollar loss of $Y_0 - Y_L$. The insurance payoff results in an expected dollar gain of $Y_G - Y_U$. Since the expected utility gain of $U_4 - U_5$ exceeds the expected utility loss of $U_1 - U_0$, insurance will be purchased. In this case the expected gain from the income transfer when ill exceeds the expected cost of the insurance policy when remaining healthy.

have more income. Would a person prefer a gain of income when sick or a similar gain of income when well? Most people are willing to give up some income when well to receive an income transfer when sick. In effect, the payment of the premium when well reduces utility less than an equal expected income transfer raises utility when sick. The main reason is that additional income is more valuable to an individual when she has less of it, and the cost of medical care causes uninsured people, when sick, to have less income to spend on other goods and services.

Figure 6–5 shows a simplified graphical model offered by Nyman.[9] We suppose that the consumer initially possesses Y_0 amount of income. If she remains healthy, she

9. This simplified approach assumes that the utility function for income is independent of health status, the quantity of medical care does not enter the utility function, and insurance is not associated with any substitution or income effects. Basically we want to compare this approach with the conventional approach under fairly similar circumstances to illustrate their differences.

stays at this level of income and enjoys U_0 amount of utility. However, if she is without medical insurance, becomes sick, and spends M dollars on medical care, only $Y_0 - M$ dollars would be left over to spend on other things, so income falls to $Y_U = (Y_0 - M)$ and utility falls to U_5.

Now suppose the person purchases insurance, remains healthy, and pays no coinsurance. In that case she has to pay an actuarially fair insurance premium of πM, reflecting the probability of an illness occurring, π, and medical costs, M. Income net of the premium falls to Y_N. However, if the individual pays the premium only when healthy, the expected cost of paying the premium equals the probability of remaining healthy, $(1 - \pi)$ times the actuarial fair premium such that the expected loss of income when healthy and insured corresponds to the horizontal distance between Y_0 and Y_L. Income less the expected loss of income when healthy and insured is associated with an expected utility of U_1. Hence, the expected utility loss of purchasing health insurance is represented by the vertical distance $U_0 - U_1$.

Now, if the individual purchases insurance and becomes ill, she potentially receives a net income transfer equal to $(1 - \pi)M$ from those who remain healthy. When this income transfer is added to the amount of income left over to spend on all other goods when uninsured, Y_U, it results in an income level of Y_N and utility level of U_2. Y_N and U_2 reflect the level of income and utility that actually result if she becomes sick and receives the stipulated medical insurance coverage. Given the probability of becoming sick, she can expect to receive π times the income transfer, or $\pi(1 - \pi)M$, which, when added to Y_U, corresponds to the level of expected income represented by point Y_G and expected utility of U_4 in Figure 6–5. Thus, the expected utility gain from purchasing medical insurance is represented by the vertical distance $U_4 - U_5$, the difference between the uninsured utility level and the expected utility level with insurance coverage.

Notice that the expected cost of paying the premium when healthy, as measured by the horizontal distance $Y_0 - Y_L$, equals the expected gain when sick, as measured by the horizontal distance $Y_G - Y_U$, as it should, given that an actuarial fair premium was assumed. Also notice that the expected utility gain from the transfer when sick, $U_4 - U_5$ exceeds the expected utility loss from paying the premium when healthy, $U_1 - U_0$. As Nyman (2003) notes (p. 52), "With this specification of the expected utility model, it is simply necessary that the income transfer gain be evaluated on a steeper portion of the utility function than the premium loss, for insurance to be purchased." It is important to recognize that the law of diminishing marginal utility with respect to income, and not risk aversion, is all that is necessary to draw this implication from the Nyman model. It is because of the law of diminishing marginal utility that the expected utility gain from health insurance is typically valued more highly than its expected utility loss.

In sum, Nyman offers a model of the demand for health insurance that is not based on risk aversion. When deciding whether to purchase health insurance, a person compares the expected utility forgone by paying a premium and remaining healthy to the expected utility received from an income transfer in the event that she becomes ill. For most people the expected loss in utility of paying a premium when healthy is less than the expected gain in utility from receiving the income transfer when sick because uninsured medical expenses would seriously reduce their wealth or income. Hence the expected utility from the income transfer is evaluated at a steeper point on the utility curve than the expected utility loss from the premium payment.

Insights and Policy Implications of the Nyman Model

The Nyman model appears to offer an exciting and internally consistent alternative to the conventional model and provides a number of important insights. First, people demand medical expense insurance because they desire an income transfer if they become ill and purchase insurance when the expected utility gain from receiving the income transfer when sick exceeds the expected utility loss of paying the premium when healthy.[10] Second, insurance that pays off by paying medical expenses generates both efficient and inefficient moral hazard. Previously, economists focused exclusively on the inefficiencies associated with medical insurance. Third, inefficient moral hazard results from the price-payoff feature of health insurance contracts, which is necessary for transaction cost reasons. Fourth, the demand for medical insurance essentially represents a derived demand because its value derives from the ability of medical care to restore, maintain, and improve the quality and quantity of lives. As such, medical insurance offers value to consumers by improving their access to medical care.

The policy implications associated with the Nyman model are equally significant and worth mentioning. For one, Nyman points out that rising health care costs since the mid-1960s reflect, in part, the increasing number of people covered over the years by medical insurance. As income has been redistributed from the healthy to the sick because of insurance coverage, the sick have been able to exercise their greater willingness to pay for medical care, causing medical expenditures to rise over time. Consequently, rising health care costs and insurance premiums capture the growing social benefits of medical care, and public policies designed to contain health care costs may come at a sizable trade-off in terms of the quality and quantity of lives lost.

Two, many economists have advocated greater consumer cost sharing as a means to prevent (inefficient) moral hazard. But increased consumer cost sharing may also squeeze out efficient moral hazard. As Nyman asks, who would regard as optimal an insurance policy that requires a $150,000 out-of-pocket payment on a $300,000 liver transplant? Third, subsidizing insurance premiums may be efficient. Nyman stresses that people value the additional income they receive from insurance when they become ill more than they value the income they lose when they pay a premium and remain healthy. Because everyone has an equal chance of becoming ill, the redistribution of income from the healthy to the ill is efficient because it increases the welfare of society.

Fourth, some health care analysts have considered that high medical prices might encourage efficiency by discouraging consumption of medical care and preventing (inefficient) moral hazard. For example, within that perspective, an efficiency justification might be made for allowing a horizontal merger between two local hospitals that would knowingly lead to high hospital prices. Nyman points out, however, that policies should promote low medical prices to increase access to medical care and encourage more efficient moral hazard. Finally, Nyman warns that managed care organizations may be socially beneficial if they help prevent inefficient moral hazard but may be harmful if they reduce access to needed medical care through restrictive policies.

The Health Insurance Product: Traditional versus Managed Care Insurance

Before the 1980s, the health insurance product was fairly easy to define because the consumer, insurer, and health care provider relationship was much less complicated. Most consumers, through their employers, purchased conventional insurance that allowed for free choice of health care provider. Insurance premiums were largely determined by **community rating**, in which the premium is based on the risk characteristics of the entire membership. In contrast, when premiums are determined using

---

10. Recall that conventional theory treats the loading fee as the price of health insurance. In contrast, the premium payment reflects the price of health insurance in the Nyman model because it represents the opportunity cost of purchasing health insurance (that is, the additional goods and services that might have been consumed when healthy).

experience rating, insurers place individuals, or groups of individuals, into different risk categories based on various identifiable personal characteristics, such as age, gender, industrial occupation, and prior illnesses. The main difference among health insurance plans before the 1980s was simply the amount of the deductible and copayment, if any, that the subscriber had to pay for medical services and the specific benefits covered under the plan.

Because physicians typically operated in solo practices, enrollees dealt directly with individual physicians or local hospitals for care rather than with a network of providers before the 1980s. Health care providers had full autonomy and practiced medicine as they deemed appropriate. The main function of the insurer was to manage the financial risk associated with medical care and to pay the usual, customary, or reasonable (UCR) charge for any medical services rendered by physicians. UCR means that the fee is limited to the lowest of three charges: the actual charge of the physician, the customary charge of the physician, or the prevailing charge in the local area.

Since 1980, however, managed care organizations (MCOs) have exploded on the health care scene. The phrase *managed care* has been assigned to these organizations because, by design, they are supposed to emphasize cost-effective methods of providing comprehensive services to enrollees. MCOs integrate the financing and delivery of medical care. The integration often involves such practices as a network of providers, reimbursement methods other than UCR charges, and various review mechanisms. MCOs also rely to a greater degree on experience rating of enrollees because of the resulting price competition.

The main types of MCOs are the health maintenance organization, the preferred provider organization, and the point of service plan. A **health maintenance organization (HMO)** combines the financing and delivery of care into one organization. A distinguishing feature of an HMO is that the assigned or chosen primary care provider acts as a gatekeeper and refers the patient for specialty and inpatient care. Four distinct types of HMOs are generally recognized:

> *Staff model:* In this type of HMO, physicians are directly employed by the organization on a salary basis. In terms of Figure 4–1, a staff HMO completely merges the insurer and provider functions. Because medical care is not reimbursed on a fee-for-service basis, physicians have little if any personal financial incentive to overutilize medical services.
>
> *Group model:* This type of HMO provides physician services by contracting with a group practice. Normally the group is compensated on a capitation basis. As a result, physicians in the group face a strong disincentive to overutilize medical services.
>
> *Network model:* The only difference between the group model and the network model is that in the latter case, the HMO contracts with more than one group practice for physician services. As is the case with the group model, compensation is generally on a capitation basis.
>
> *Individual Practice Association (IPA) model:* This form of HMO contracts with a number of independent physicians from various types of practice settings for medical services. In this situation, physicians generally provide care in a traditional office setting and are normally compensated on a fee-for-service basis, but at a discounted rate. In return, the HMO promises a large and continuous volume of patients.

A **preferred provider organization (PPO)** is a different type of insurer and health care provider arrangement. A PPO exists when a third-party payer provides financial incentives to enrollees to acquire health care from a predetermined network of physicians and hospitals. The incentive can be in terms of a higher coinsurance or a higher deductible when someone acquires medical care outside the network of health care providers. To participate in a PPO network, physicians agree to accept a lower fee for services rendered. In return for a lower fee, physicians are promised a steady supply of patients. Normally, patients can directly seek out specialty or inpatient care if they belong to a PPO. Because of their less restrictive policies, Robinson (2002) labels PPOs as managed-care-lite organizations.

Like PPOs, **point-of-service (POS) plans** provide generous coverage when enrollees use in-network services and cover out-of-network services at reduced reimbursement rates. Unlike PPOs but similar to HMOs, POS plans assign each enrollee a primary caregiver who acts as a gatekeeper and authorizes specialty and inpatient care.

Estimates indicate that 99 percent of all privately insured workers in 2011 were covered by MCOs, reflecting a continual decline in conventional insurance coverage which stood at 73 percent as recently as 1988. Most of the enrollment increase has taken place in the least restrictive managed care plans over the last decade. HMOs witnessed a decline in market share from a high of 31 percent in 1996 to 17 percent in 2011. PPOs, the least restrictive of the MCOs, enjoyed the largest surge in enrollment, from 11 percent in 1988 to 55 percent by 2011. Enrollments in POS plans also witnessed a decline in market share, from a height of 24 percent in 1999 to 10 percent in 2011 (KFF/HRET, 2011).

Landon et al. (1998), among others, argue that the traditional distinction among health insurance products, such as conventional insurance and MCOs, or even the distinction among MCOs, has become blurred in practice. For example, even conventional insurance plans now involve some type of utilization review program. Given that the traditional taxonomy of insurance plans may no longer adequately describe the differences among organizations, it is better to differentiate among health insurance products based on the types and restrictiveness of the financial incentives and management strategies facing patients and health care providers. Let us elaborate.

Financial Incentives and Management Strategies Facing Consumers/Patients

Depending on the precise nature of the health insurance product, consumers/patients face different financial incentives to use medical care. As examined theoretically in Chapter 5, the consumer's out-of-pocket price, as captured by the size of the deductible and coinsurance, inversely affects the quantity demanded of medical care. Some health insurance plans contain high deductibles and coinsurance as a way of containing medical prices. In addition, some plans set their premiums on an experience-rated basis as an incentive for subscribers to adopt more healthy lifestyles.

In addition to indirect financial incentives, insurers may also adopt various management strategies to directly affect the consumer's utilization of medical care. First, the insurer may require prior medical screening to avoid insuring high-risk patients or exclude coverage for preexisting conditions. Insurers may also restrict the choice of provider by building provider networks in which the consumer must participate. In addition, the insurer may employ a primary care gatekeeper to determine whether further services are medically warranted. Pre-authorization of medical services, a type of utilization review practice, is another management strategy affecting the consumer's direct use of medical care.

By combining the financial incentives and management strategies facing patients, we can get a better understanding of the underlying health insurance product. For example, a health insurance plan with a high deductible and coinsurance and experience-rated premiums, combined with limits on choice of physician and pre-authorization, offers much less insurance than one with no out-of-pocket costs or pre-authorization, community-rated premiums, and full choice of provider. The latter situation aptly describes the conventional insurance offered by Blue Cross plans back in the 1970s.

A POS plan comes close to an example of the former situation as far as management strategies facing consumers are concerned.

Financial Incentives and Management Strategies Facing Health Care Providers

The health insurance product may also contain financial incentives and/or management strategies to affect the delivery of medical care by health care providers. As a result, the health insurance product can also be differentiated based on the types and restrictiveness of the financial incentives and management strategies facing health care providers. In terms of financial incentives, the health insurance product may adopt different provider reimbursement practices, such as fee-for-service, capitation, bonuses, and/or withholds. Withholds occur when the insurer withholds part of the health care provider's reimbursement until after a stipulated period at which the appropriate use of medical care has been evaluated. Inappropriate use of medical care results in the physician not receiving all or part of the withheld money. The prospect of incomplete reimbursement payments presumably acts as an incentive for health care providers to offer truly medically necessary care.

As we saw in Chapter 4, fixed payment systems, such as capitation, can discourage the delivery of high-cost, low-benefit medicine. Capitation places health care providers financially at risk for any cost overruns. When properly designed, performance-based measures, such as bonuses and withholds, can accomplish that same goal.

Insurers can also directly influence the delivery of medical care through various management strategies. Selective contracting, deselection of providers, physician profiling, utilization review, practice guidelines, and formularies are among the more common management strategies facing health care providers. Selective contracting occurs when managed care plans contract solely with an exclusive set of providers. The selection and **deselection** of providers involves the establishment of the criteria and process by which health care providers will be included in or terminated from the network. For example, insurers may include physicians in their network who are of high quality and/or utilize cost-effective practice patterns. **Physician profiling** may be used to monitor performance in the selection or deselection process. The profiling may include information, for example, on the primary care physician's track record regarding referrals to specialty and inpatient care as a way to identify high-cost providers, or it may include information on quality of care or patient satisfaction.

Utilization review programs "seek to determine whether specific services are medically necessary and whether they are delivered at an appropriate level of intensity and cost" (Ermann, 1988, p. 683). **Practice guidelines** provide information to health care providers about the appropriate medical practice in certain situations. A **formulary** contains a list of pharmaceutical products that physicians must prescribe whenever necessary. All these management strategies are designed to directly affect how a physician behaves in a specific clinical circumstance.

Consequently, the health insurance product also differs based on the type of provider reimbursement method and the existence and restrictiveness of various management strategies. For example, a capitation reimbursement scheme in conjunction with utilization review and practice guidelines means a much different insurance product than one with a fee-for-service payment system in which the health care provider has full autonomy over patient care. The former situation resembles the staff HMO whereas the latter reflects the traditional Blue Cross/Blue Shield (BC/BS) or commercial insurance of the 1970s.

The first column in Table 6–3 provides a summary of the four basic features of any health insurance product: patient financial incentives, consumer management strategies, provider financial incentives, and provider management strategies. Below each

TABLE 6–3
Spectrum of Health Insurance Products

Basic Features (Examples)	Unrestricted or Complete Insurance Plan	Restrictive Insurance Plan
Patient Financial Incentives	No or low deductible with no coinsurance	Significant deductible with a high coinsurance
Deductibles		
Coinsurance	Community rated	Experience rated
Premiums		
Consumer Management Strategies	No restrictions	Consumers must receive care exclusively from the network of providers
Prior medical screening		
Restrictions on choice		
Gatekeeper		
Pre-authorization		
Provider Financial Incentives	None—UCR charges	Capitation with bonuses or withholds
Risk-sharing and/or bonus arrangements		
Provider Management Strategies	None	An array of management strategies are employed to control costs
Selective contracting		
Deselection		
Physician profiling		
Utilization review		
Practice guidelines		
Formularies		

© Cengage Learning 2013

feature is a list of specific policies aimed at altering the behavior of either consumers or health care providers. As you can see, health insurance is a complex and multidimensional product. At one extreme lies the perfectly unrestricted health insurance plan, the basic characteristics of which are provided in the second column of Table 6–3. With this type of insurance, consumers pay no out-of-pocket prices; health care providers are reimbursed based on the usual, customary, and reasonable fee for service; and there are no consumer or provider management strategies. At the other extreme, the basic characteristics of a perfectly restrictive insurance plan are shown in the third column of Table 6–3. In this case, significant financial incentives and management strategies face both consumers and health care providers. In terms of examples, the traditional Blue Cross/Blue Shield insurance plan of the 1970s compares quite closely to the unrestricted plan described in Table 6–3, while the staff HMO, except for the significant out-of-pocket price, fits the insurance plan described in the last column of Table 6–3.

Although Table 6–3 provides a good framework for defining and conceptualizing the health insurance product, some caveats are in order. It is important to realize that any one health insurer may offer multiple health insurance products. For example, a health insurer may offer both a staff HMO and a traditional indemnity plan. Of course, the prices of the two plans should differ significantly. It is also important to realize that any one health care provider may deal with various health insurance products. A large physician practice may treat some patients who belong to a PPO plan and others who subscribe to HMO plans, for example. An additional complexity is that a group physician practice may be reimbursed on a capitation basis by the insurer whereas the individual physician within the practice is compensated on a salary basis. It is also important to mention that financial incentives and management strategies may serve as complementary or substitute methods of controlling the behavior of consumers and providers. As Gold et al. (1995, p. 315) point out:

> For example, plans that capitate primary care physicians and place them at risk for specialty referrals and inpatient care through a withholding account may be expected to place particular emphasis on monitoring physicians to ensure that the financial incentives do not result in underservice. On the other hand, plans operating in areas where physicians are resistant to accepting much financial risk may rely particularly heavily on nonfinancial mechanisms such as utilization management to influence practice patterns.

Consumer-Directed Health Care Plans

After reading this book it should become apparent, if it isn't already, that the U.S. health care system, particularly its insurance side, has undergone tremendous structural change with respect to the products offered. Prior to the 1980s, competition among health care providers, such as hospitals, was driven largely by the quality concerns of patients who faced very low out-of-pocket prices because of the way conventional plans were designed. In fact, many health economists argue that this **patient-driven health care** helped fuel rising health care prices and expenditures in earlier years (see Chapter 13).

In response to growing health care costs after the 1980s, **payer-driven** replaced patient-driven health care. Managed care insurers, as payers, took on the duty of more intensely negotiating prices with health care providers. Although some success was achieved with respect to controlling health care costs in the late 1990s, many of the insured turned away from more restrictive plans such as HMOs to PPOs with looser networks, less risk sharing for health care providers, and fewer utilization reviews. Not surprisingly, health care costs began to increase more rapidly with the backlash against restrictive plans.

As a result, insurers and policy makers have, in more recent years, turned their attention to **consumer-driven** health care as a way of controlling health care costs. Consumer-driven health care takes form in various consumer-directed health care plans (CDHPs), which include a high deductible of $1,000 per person or $2,000 per family or more. The relatively high deductible provides a financial incentive for consumers to become more involved in purchasing decisions regarding their health care. The idea is that consumers will use medical care more wisely and shop for high value medical care. The large deductibles are often combined with either a health savings account (HSA) or health reimbursement account (HRA). Both of these accounts are tax-advantaged savings accounts that may be used to pay for qualified medical expenditures. However, HSAs are owned by the employee, whereas HRAs are owned by the employer. By combining the high deductible with the health savings accounts, consumers are made more cost-sensitive without being subjected to the financial risk of catastrophic illnesses. As of 2011, about 13 percent of the workforce was covered by CDHPs in the United States (KFF/HRET, 2011).

While the potential benefits are well understood, many question the value of CDHPs on several grounds. First, will favorable selection into CDHPs burden the sick and poor? Because the plans are tax-exempt and the premiums are lower, the concern is that high income and healthy individuals will choose CDHPs over more traditional types of health insurance. If so, the poor and unhealthy may find themselves in health insurance plans without any cross-subsidizations from higher income and healthier individuals. Premiums for these plans will increase as a result, putting the poor and unhealthy at a financial disadvantage.

Second, it is unclear if CDHPs will spur people to make prudent health care choices or lead to cutbacks in appropriate and necessary care. There is a concern that people may not possess the necessary information to make wise choices, especially with respect to medical care which is complicated for many individuals. Supporters, however, argue that consumer financial responsibility will produce greater demand for better information such as comprehensive and electronic medical records. Also, an additional concern is that people may forgo preventive medical care because of high out-of-pocket costs.

Finally, it is uncertain if CDHPs will constrain the growth of overall health care costs or be able to drive needed improvements in medical care quality. As previously noted, a majority of all health care costs is spent on a minority of individuals—the chronically ill. As a result, some analysts point out that little clinically unnecessary medicine may exist in the system for CDHPs to squeeze out. Yet, others point out that increased financial incentives may influence lifestyle choices that people make over time. Better lifestyle choices will help constrain health care costs.

Buntin et al. (2006) reviewed the literature and summarized the evidence about these three concerns. With respect to the first issue, they report some evidence of favorable selection. That is, higher-income individuals and those in better health are more likely to choose CDHPs over other types of insurance policies. Although the favorable selection makes cost comparisons difficult, they find that CDHPs are likely to produce a one-time reduction in medical care usage and costs between 4 to 15 percent. In addition, they point out that many CDHPs include financial incentives for preventive care and/or provide information on the importance of preventive care but report mixed results regarding the impact of CDHPs on quality of care. They note that better information about prices, quality, and treatment choices are critical for CDHPs to effectively function.

It is not known if consumer-directed health care will expand in the future and engage market forces to control health care spending and improve quality for all health care consumers. Many policy experts predict that enrollments in CDHPs will grow in the future if tax incentives are granted to all consumers, and not just employees, or if insurance coverage is mandated on an individual basis in the United States as discussed later in Chapter 16. It will be interesting to watch and track the development of CDHPs as conditions in the health economy continue to change. If CDHPs make no progress with respect to cost containment and quality improvements, **government-driven** health care, similar to the health insurance system in Canada, may be the only other remaining option.

The Regulation of MCOs

There has been considerable debate in the academic literature and the popular press concerning the effect of managed care plans on the cost and quality of medical care. By design, MCOs are supposed to employ cost-effective methods of delivering a comprehensive set of services to enrollees. The original proponents of managed care thought that MCOs would encourage preventive and coordinated primary care as a way of reducing the need for more expensive specialty and inpatient care. Also, advocates thought that MCOs would eliminate the high-cost, low-benefit medicine associated with traditional fee-for-service indemnity insurance (i.e., the moral hazard problem). As a result, high quality of care and low operating costs were expected from MCOs.

Because lower quality of care translates into lower costs and higher profits, critics claim that MCOs face an incentive to reduce the quality of care, perhaps by denying or skimping on costly but necessary medical treatments. Health care providers have no recourse but to follow the wishes of the MCOs given the restrictive financial incentives and management strategies they face, according to the critics.

Given this controversy, which we discuss more fully in later chapters, many states and the federal government have introduced or enacted various regulations to influence the behavior of MCOs. Miller (1997, p. 1102) notes that the regulatory actions taken to control managed care practices have been "referred to as 'patient protection' or 'patient bill of rights' acts by proponents and as 'anti-managed' bills by those opposed." The legislation has attempted to extend the rights of patients and physicians and also improve the patient/physician relationship under managed care. According to Miller, in just six months from January to July 1996, more than four hundred bills were introduced in the various states to control managed care practices. Most of the laws concern such issues as anti-gag rules, limits on financial incentives, continuity of care, and expanding the rights of health care professionals. Let's examine each of these issues more closely.

Gag rules prohibit doctors in a managed care plan from discussing treatment options not covered under the plan, from providing information on plan limitations, or from commenting unfavorably on the plan. Opponents of managed care argue that gag rules cause physicians to deny care by suppressing useful information on alternative treatments the managed care plan may not find cost effective to provide. Managed care representatives claim the gag rules are designed to prevent physicians from disparaging the plan or releasing proprietary information concerning compensation and similar issues.

Critics further argue that managed care payment systems, such as capitation or performance-based systems like bonuses or withholds, create a financial incentive for physicians to deny medically appropriate or useful treatments. Indeed, much mention has been made in the popular press of "drive-through medicine," involving short maternity stays in hospitals or mastectomies taking place in outpatient rather than inpatient facilities because of managed care financial arrangements. Laws limiting financial incentives are designed to prevent denial of care from taking place. Managed care representatives, on the other hand, argue that the financial incentives of MCOs are necessary to control the moral hazard problem.

Miller (1997) notes that state policies offer little concrete guidance about how the general prohibition against financial incentives applies to the myriad financial arrangements set by MCOs. As a result, she claims that without additional clarification, regulatory actions against managed care financial arrangements will have to be argued on a case-by-case basis, creating much uncertainty for the various parties involved.

Medical experts argue that continuity of care is an important consideration for the patient/physician relationship and for patient well-being, especially for certain groups, such as pregnant women or the severely ill. Critics of MCOs claim that continuity of care is at stake because some employers subscribe to only one managed care plan, and the managed care plan may change its networks of physicians, or deselect physicians from its plan. In all these cases, consumers have to pay more to visit a physician of their own choice and the continuity of care may be compromised. Although proponents argue that MCOs can only provide the desired health care cost savings for society by directing patients to selected physicians, laws have been introduced in many states to extend the option of continued care from primary caregivers.

In addition, numerous laws have been introduced across states that aim to expand the rights of health care professionals. With the growth of MCOs, many health care professionals feel the pressure from market demands and also the loss of autonomy brought on by contracts with managed care plans. For example, some physicians find themselves unable to participate in or deselected from managed care plans without being provided with the rationale.

The first laws introduced concerned any willing provider (AWP) or freedom of choice (FOC) laws. According to Hellinger (1995, p. 297), "AWP laws require managed care plans to accept any qualified provider who is willing to accept the terms and conditions of a managed care plan." According to the law, MCOs do not have to contract with all providers but must explicitly state evaluation criteria and ensure "due process" for providers wishing to contract with the plan. Due process rights provide professionals with access to information regarding MCO standards, termination decisions, and physician profiling. FOC laws allow a patient to be reimbursed for medical services received from qualified physicians from outside the network. FOC laws do not guarantee that the patient will incur the same out-of-pocket cost, however. Proponents of AWP and FOC laws argue that they increase the continuity of care by offering a fuller choice of providers. Opponents argue that without selective contracting, managed care plans are unable to obtain volume discounts because they are powerless to channel patients to selected providers. In addition, it is alleged that these laws lead to a diminished quality of care because of the higher monitoring costs brought on by a greater number of health care providers.

In sum, anti-gag laws, laws restricting the financial incentives of MCOs, laws promoting continuity of care, and laws extending the rights of health care professionals are among the various regulations advanced by various states to control the practices of MCOs. The basic hypothesis is that MCOs face an incentive to restrict the quality of care because increased profits can be made. Critics claim that various financial incentives and management strategies help MCOs achieve their objective of maximum profits. Interestingly, all these laws essentially attempt to transform MCOs into indemnity plans. The superiority of indemnity and managed care plans remains a controversial issue and is the subject of ongoing theoretical and empirical debates.

Provisions of the Patient Protection and Affordable Care Act of 2010 Relating to the Demand for Health Insurance

Besides the requirement that health insurers extend health insurance coverage to all dependent children under 26 years of age (at a higher premium of course), the single most important provision of the PPACA that will undoubtedly and fundamentally shape the demand for private health insurance is the health insurance mandate which begins in 2014. This mandate will require all but those with an **affordability exception** to obtain acceptable health insurance coverage or pay a penalty. An affordability exemption is given to people who would have to pay more than 8 percent of their annual income for the cheapest health insurance plan.

It stands to reason that the health insurance mandate will not be binding on those individuals with sufficient incomes who have already voluntarily chosen to purchase insurance either individually or through their employers. Most unfavorably impacted will be those individuals, with sufficient ability to pay, who have chosen not to purchase health insurance because, from their perspective, the expected utility with health insurance had been less than the expected utility without health insurance. These individuals may have felt that way about health insurance coverage because they expected to remain in fairly good health throughout the year as a result of their relatively young age or generally good health status. Or, they may have figured that they could avoid paying the insurance loading fee by showing up in the emergency room of a hospital at the point they become ill. Unless the penalty, which will amount to as much as 2.5 percent of taxable income, is perceived as being relatively small, the mandate should lead to an increased demand for private health insurance coverage by individuals in this group.

Another group more favorably affected by the mandate will be those individuals who may have been willing, but financially unable, to purchase health insurance coverage before the law was effective. The Act makes tax credits available through **insurance exchanges** to ensure people can obtain affordable coverage as long as their incomes are above the Medicaid-eligible level but below 400 percent of poverty income. An insurance exchange is a government-created marketplace in which consumers purchase health insurance with a stipulated minimum benefit package and other plan characteristics as determined by the government. Tax credits are available for both premiums and cost-sharing to ensure that no family faces bankruptcy because of medical expenses. Workers who qualify for an affordability exemption to the health insurance mandate, but do not qualify for tax credits, can take their employer contribution and join an insurance exchange plan.

The Act also contains small business tax credits for qualified small employers to purchase health insurance for their employees. Initially, the credit is up to 35 percent of the employer's premium contribution. Later when exchanges are operational, tax credits will be up to 50 percent of premium contributions. Also large firms (with more than 50 workers) will be encouraged to offer insurance coverage by a sizable annual penalty of $2000 for each full-time worker not offered health insurance coverage after an exemption for the first 30 workers. Taken together, the insurance mandate, the employer penalty, and the tax credit should lead to a dramatic increase in the demand for private health insurance coverage by low-income workers.

The PPACA also imposes an excise tax of 40 percent on insurance companies and plan administrators for any health insurance plan that is above the threshold premium of $10,200 for self-only coverage and $27,500 for family plans beginning in 2018. The tax would apply to the amount of the premium in excess of the threshold. The threshold would be indexed by the consumer price index in future years. An additional threshold amount of $1,650 for singles and $3,450 for families is available for retired individuals over the age of 55 and for plans that cover employees engaged in high risk professions. Employers, with higher costs on account of the age or gender demographics of their employees when compared to the age and gender demographics nationally, may adjust their thresholds even higher.

The objective is to effectively take away the tax subsidy that high-end private health care insurance plans currently receive under the tax code. In terms of Equation 6–8, this provision is aimed at reducing the amount of insurance premiums exempted from taxation, e, and therefore increasing the user price for those purchasing these gold-plated plans. Presumably, to avoid the tax, employers and employees will shift to less generous health insurance plans with more cost-sharing, making patients more responsible for health care costs. In the long run, employers may shift the cost savings to employees in terms of higher wages.

Another provision of the PPACA that should significantly impact the demand for private health insurance relates to the medical loss ratio (MLR), or the percent of premiums paid out in medical claims cost. The MLR makes up part of the loading fee which was discussed in this chapter. The PPACA requires that health insurers offering group policies pay out at least 85 percent of their premiums as medical claim costs. The minimum MLR is set at 80 percent for individual policies. Insurers, who spend less than the MLR, must rebate the difference to consumers. The intent behind the MLR is to reduce the loading fee so that consumers pay lower premiums. However, one concern is that health insurers may negotiate less aggressively with health care providers because they will not be able to appropriate any cost-savings below the MLR.

The last provision of the PPACA that may affect the demand for private health insurance is the anticipated expansion in the Medicaid program. Specifically, in 2014, everyone, including individuals and couples without children, become eligible for Medicaid coverage if their income falls below 133 percent of the federal poverty line. If Medicaid crowding out occurs, as some studies seem to suggest (see Chapters 10 and 11), then this provision may lower the demand for private health insurance, assuming all other factors remain the same.[11]

Summary

To someone schooled in economics, it should be quite obvious that people demand private health insurance, just as they voluntarily demand any other consumer good or service, because it provides utility or satisfaction for them. Less obvious is the exact mechanism by which insurance coverage translates into utility gains. To clear up some of the ambiguity, two models of private health insurance demand are introduced in this chapter to more carefully explore the linkage between insurance coverage and utility.

The first model, conventional theory, argues that risk-averse people gain from the risk reduction offered by insurance coverage. More precisely, people can reduce the variability of their financial losses, potentially resulting from irregular and unpredictable medical expenditures, by joining a sharing-of-losses arrangement. The reduced variability of losses or risk avoidance provides utility to risk-averse individuals, according to conventional theory. Within an expected utility maximization model, the conventional demand for medical expense insurance is a function of the user price of health insurance, degree of risk aversion, probability of a loss, magnitude of the expected loss, and income. In general, empirical studies based on conventional theory suggest that the demand for private health insurance is relatively inelastic with respect to both user price and income.

The second model, Nyman's access theory, treats insurance coverage as offering people an income transfer from those who remain healthy to themselves in the event they become ill. Given that most uninsured people lack sufficient funds, insurance coverage helps provide financial access to medical care at time of illness. The income transfer at time of illness or access value provides utility, according to Nyman. Within an expected utility framework, people purchase health insurance when the expected utility gain from the income transfer when ill exceeds the expected utility loss of paying the premium and remaining healthy.

A comparison of the conventional and Nyman models yields a number of insights. One insight of particular importance to economists concerns the interpretation of moral hazard. Conventional theory treats insurance as simply lowering the out-of-pocket price the insured consumer pays for medical care. Accordingly, the lowered price triggers a substitution effect that results in an increased quantity of medical care demanded for which marginal costs exceed marginal benefits. Thus, the additional units of medical care reflect a welfare loss and suggest that all moral hazard is inefficient.

In contrast, the Nyman model points out that the insurance payout also possesses an income effect. The income effect leads to a greater demand for medical care at time of illness and leads to efficient moral hazard. Consequently, not all moral hazard is inefficient, according to the Nyman model.

Finally we discussed the health insurance product. We learned that the health insurance product is multidimensional and complex because many attributes, such as benefits covered, out-of-pocket expenses, choice of provider, and the provider payment scheme, must be considered. Nearly all of the privately insured in the United States are covered by some type of managed care plan. Managed care plans differ with respect to the restrictiveness of the financial incentives and management strategies facing both consumers and health care providers. In addition, we discussed the reason behind

---

11. In addition, health insurers will no longer be able to deny health insurance coverage based upon preexisting conditions in 2014. Of course, everyone will likely pay higher premiums as a result.

and the success to date of CDHPs. Lastly, we learned that many states have enacted various regulations to control the restrictiveness of the financial incentives and management strategies adopted by managed care plans. The efficiency properties of these regulations continue to be explored and debated by economists and policy makers.

Review Questions and Problems

1. Suppose Joe and Leo both face the following individual loss distribution:

Probability of Loss	Amount of Loss
0.7	$0
0.2	$40
0.1	$60

   A. Determine the expected loss and standard deviation of the expected loss faced by Joe and Leo on an individual basis.
   B. Suppose that Joe and Leo enter into a pooling-of-losses arrangement. Show what happens to the expected loss and variability of the expected loss as a result of the pooling arrangement.
2. Given their benefits, why don't most people simply form their own pooling-of-losses arrangements rather than involve insurance companies?
3. Joe is currently unemployed and without health insurance coverage. He derives utility (U) from his interest income on his savings (Y) according to the following function:

$$U = 5Y^{1/2}.$$

   Joe presently makes about $40,000 of interest income per year. He realizes that there is about a 5 percent probability that he may suffer a heart attack. The cost of treatment will be about $20,000 if a heart attack occurs.
   A. Calculate Joe's expected utility level without any health insurance coverage.
   B. Calculate Joe's expected income without any health insurance coverage.
   C. Suppose Joe must pay a premium of $1,500 for health insurance coverage with ACME insurance. Would he buy the health insurance? Why or why not?
   D. Suppose now that the government passes a law that allows all people—not just the self-employed or employed—to have their entire insurance premium exempted from taxes. Joe is in the 33 percent tax bracket. Would he buy the health insurance at a premium cost of $1,500? Why or why not? What implication can be drawn from the analysis?
   E. Suppose Joe purchases the health insurance coverage and represents the average subscriber, and his expectations are correct. Calculate the loading fee the insurance company will receive.
4. During the Reagan administration, the marginal tax rate on wage income fell dramatically. For example, the top rate was sliced from 70 to 33 percent. Use the demand theory of health insurance to predict the effect of this change on the quantity demanded of employer-sponsored health insurance.
5. Explain the effect of the following changes on the quantity demanded of health insurance.
   A. A reduction in the tax-exempt fraction of health insurance premiums
   B. An increase in buyer income
   C. An increase in per capita medical expenditures
   D. New technologies that enable medical illnesses to be predicted more accurately
   E. A tendency among buyers to become less risk averse, on average

6. What are the primary differences between the HMO, PPO, and POS plans?

7. Explain the following terms:
   A. Community rating
   B. Experience rating
   C. Selective contracting
   D. Utilization review
   E. Physician profiling
   F. Practice guidelines
   G. Formulary
   H. Gatekeeper
   I. Gag rules
   J. Any willing provider law
   K. Freedom of choice law

8. Suppose that an individual's demand for the number of physician visits per year, Q, can be represented by the following equation: $Q = 5 - 0.04P$, where P, the market price of an office visit, equals the marginal cost of $100. Determine the efficient number of office visits according to conventional theory. Now assume that the person purchases complete health insurance coverage and the demand for (but not quantity demanded of) physician care remains unchanged. How many times would this fully insured person visit the physician? Calculate the welfare loss or moral hazard cost associated with the insurance coverage.

9. Graphically and in words, explain how the analysis in Question 8 might change if we adopt the conceptual framework provided by Nyman.

10. Use all of the information in Questions 1 and 3 to calculate the expected utility loss of paying the premium and remaining healthy and compare it to the expected utility gain of the income transfer if ill (ignore the tax exemption feature of premium payments). Would Joe purchase health insurance according to the Nyman model? How does that prediction compare to the prediction of the conventional model under similar circumstances?

11. According to Nyman, conventional theory predicts that people behave irrationally. How does he justify this criticism? Explain.

12. Briefly summarize the two ways that managed care might affect the cost and quality of medical care.

13. If you had a choice between a traditional unrestricted indemnity plan with a 10 percent copayment and a staff HMO with no copayment, at what percentage difference in premiums (that is, 10 percent, 20 percent, 30 percent) would you be indifferent between the plans? Do you think your choice of the percentage difference is a function of your age and/or health status? If you were elderly and/or sickly, which plan would you prefer if they cost you the same amount? Why?

Online Resources

To access Internet links related to the topics in this chapter, please visit our website at **www.cengage.com/economics/santerre**.

References

Auerbach, David I. and Sabrina Ohri. "Price and the Demand for Nongroup Health Insurance." *Inquiry* 43 (June 2006), pp. 122–34.

Berk, Marc L., and Alan C. Monheit. "The Concentration of Health Care Expenditures, Revisited." *Health Affairs* 20 (March/April 2001), pp. 9–18.

Buntin, MeLinda B., et al. "Consumer-Directed Health Care: Early Evidence About Effects on Cost and Quality." *Health Affairs* Web Exclusive (October 24, 2006), pp. 516–30.

Dowd, Bryan, and Roger Feldman. "Premium Elasticities of Health Plan Choice." *Inquiry* 31 (winter 1994/95), pp. 438–44.

Ermann, Dan. "Hospital Utilization Review. Past Experience, Future Directions." *Journal of Health Politics, Policy, and Law* 13 (winter 1988), pp. 683–704.

Farley, Pamela J., and Gail Wilensky. "Household Wealth and Health Insurance as Protection against Medical Risks." *In Horizontal Equity, Uncertainty, and Economic Well-Being*, eds. David Martin and Timothy Smeeding. Chicago: University of Chicago Press for the NBER, 1984, pp. 323–54.

Feldstein, Martin S. "The Welfare Loss of Excess Health Insurance" *Journal of Political Economy* (March–April 1973), pp. 257–80.

Gold, Marsha, Lyle Nelson, Timothy Lake, Robert Hurley, and Robert Berenson. "Behind the Curve: A Critical Assessment of How Little Is Known about Arrangements between Managed Care Plans and Physicians." *Medical Care Research and Review* 52 (September 1995), pp. 307–41.

Goldstein, Gerald S., and Mark V. Pauly. "Group Health Insurance as a Local Public Good." In *The Role of Health Insurance in the Health Services Sector*, ed. Richard Rossett. New York: NBER, 1976, pp. 73–110.

Harrington, Scott E., and Gregory R. Niehaus. *Risk Management and Insurance*. Boston: McGraw-Hill/ Irwin, 2004.

Hellinger, Fred J. "Update: Any-Willing-Provider and Freedom-of-Choice Laws: An Economic Assessment." *Health Affairs* 14 (winter 1995), pp. 297–302.

Holmer, Martin. "Tax Policy and the Demand for Health Insurance." *Journal of Health Economics* 3, no. 3 (1984), pp. 203–21.

The Kaiser Family Foundation and Health Research and Education Trust (KFF/HRET). *Employer Health Benefits: 2011 Annual Survey*, http://ehbs.kff.org/pdf/2011/8225.pdf, accessed September 28, 2012.

Keynes, John Maynard. *The General Theory of Employment Interest and Money*. New York: Harcourt Brace and Company, 1936.

Kumar, Nanda, Marc A. Cohen, Christine E. Bishop, and Stanley S. Wallack. "Understanding the Factors behind the Decision to Purchase Varying Coverage Amounts of Long-Term Care Insurance." *Health Services Research* 29 (February 1995), pp. 653–78.

Landon, Bruce E., Ira B. Wilson, and Paul D. Cleary. "A Conceptual Model of the Effects of Health Care Organizations on the Quality of Medical Care." *Journal of the American Medical Association* 279 (May 6, 1998), pp. 1377–82.

Liu, Chuan-Fen, and Jon B. Christianson. "The Demand for Health Insurance by Employees in a Voluntary Small Group Insurance Program." *Medical Care* 36 (1998), pp. 437–43.

Manning, Willard, and M. Susan Marquis. "Health Insurance: The Trade Off Between Risk Pooling and Moral Hazard." *Journal of Health Economics* 15 (1996), pp. 609–59.

Manning, Willard G., and M. Susan Marquis. "Health Insurance: The Trade-Off between Risk Pooling and Moral Hazard." (R-3729–NCHSR) Santa Monica, Calif.: RAND, 1989.

Marquis, M. Susan, Melinda B. Bunting, Jose J. Escarce, Kanika Kapur, and Jill M. Yegian. "Subsidies and the Demand for Individual Health Insurance in California." *Health Services Research* 39 (October, 2004), pp. 1547–70.

Marquis, M. Susan, and Stephen H. Long. "Worker Demand for Health Insurance in the Non-Group Market." *Journal of Health Economics* 14 (1995), pp. 47–63.

Miller, Richard D. "Estimating the Compensating Differential for Employer-Provided Health Insurance." *International Journal of Health Care Finance and Economics* 4 (2004), pp. 27–41.

Miller, Tracy E. "Managed Care Regulation: In the Laboratory of the States." *Journal of the American Medical Association* 278 (October 1, 1997), pp. 1102–9.

Nyman, John A. *The Theory of Demand for Health Insurance*. Stanford University Press, 2003.

Pauly, Mark V. "Taxation, Health Insurance, and Market Failure in the Medical Economy." *Journal of Economic Literature* 24 (June 1986), pp. 629–75.

Robinson, James C. "Renewed Emphasis on Consumer Cost Sharing in Health Insurance Benefit Design." *Health Affairs* Web Exclusive (March 2002), pp. 139–54.

Santerre, Rexford E. "Which Price is Right: Load or Premium?" *Geneva Risk and Insurance Review* 33 (December 2008), pp. 90–105.

Sheils, John, and Randall Haught. "The Cost of Tax-Exempt Health Benefits in 2004." *Health Affairs*, http://www.healthaffairs.org, accessed February 25, 2004.

Short, Pamela F., and Amy K. Taylor. "Premiums, Benefits, and Employee Choice of Health Insurance Options." *Journal of Health Economics* 8 (1989), pp. 293–311.

Strombom, Bruce A., Thomas C. Buchmueller, and Paul J. Feldstein. "Switching Costs, Price Sensitivity and Health Plan Choice." *Journal of Health Economics* 21 (2002), pp. 89–116.

Taylor, Amy K., and Gail R. Wilensky. "The Effect of Tax Policies on Expenditures for Private Health Insurance." In *Market Reforms in Health Care*, ed. Jack Meyer. Washington, D.C.: American Enterprise Institute, 1983.

U.S. Government Accountability Office (GAO), *Consumer Directed Health Plans*. GAO Report # GAO-06-514, April 2006.

CHAPTER 7

Medical Care Production and Costs

In December 2000, it was announced that Northeast Georgia Health System, a 338-bed not-for-profit hospital in Gainesville, Georgia, proposed to buy Lanier Park Hospital, a 119-bed for-profit hospital also in Gainesville, for $40 million. The acquisition would result in only one hospital in Gainesville. Executives at the hospitals claim the acquisition would save $2 million annually (Kirchheimer, 2000). Similarly, in July 2005, it was announced that United Health Group, the nation's second-largest health insurer, planned to join with Pacifi-Care Health Systems, the second-largest private administrator of Medicare health plans. The combination would create one of the nation's largest private health plan providers with about 26 million subscribers. A spokesperson for the two insurers claimed that the merger would cut operating costs by an estimated $100 million in the first year alone (Jablon, 2005).

Even more recently, Merck and Schering-Plough finalized their merger in November of 2009, marking a major consolidation of two highly visible and respected New Jersey drug makers (Schmidt, 2009). The deal amounted to $41.1 billion and purportedly gave the new Merck a pair of prospective blockbuster products within a few years and strengthened Merck's ability to make new cancer drugs and potent biologic medicines in the future. This merger follows the $68 billion acquisition of Wyeth by the pharmaceutical giant Pfizer the previous month. Representatives of Merck predicted the merger would result in annual savings of $3.5 billion beginning in 2011.

These are just four examples of the many mergers that typically take place in the health care sector. Recent combinations among firms in other health care markets, such as the physician, medical devices, and nursing home industries, also testify to the assertion that larger firm size confers significant cost advantages. But are there any plausible economic reasons to support the claim that cost savings are associated with larger organizational size? If so, sound economic reasoning can justify a merger among two or more firms in the same industry. On the other hand, might operating costs actually increase as a firm gets too large? If that is the case, a merger among firms is not desirable if cost savings are the overriding concern.

This chapter introduces various microeconomic principles and concepts that can be used to analyze the cost structure of medical firms and thereby determine the true relation between firm size and costs of production. In addition, this chapter:

- discusses various production characteristics, including marginal and average productivity and the elasticity of substitution among inputs
- uses the resulting production theory to derive short-run and long-run costs of production
- examines economies and diseconomies of scale and scope and learning-by-doing
- studies the economic rationale behind vertically integrated health care systems
- points out how the Patient Protection and Affordable Care Act (PPACA) of 2010 may impact the delivery of medical care in the United States.

The Short-Run Production Function of the Representative Medical Firm

All medical firms, including hospitals, physician clinics, nursing homes, and pharmaceutical companies, earn revenues from producing and selling some type of medical output. Production and retailing activities occur regardless of the form of ownership (i.e., for-profit, public, or not-for-profit). Because these activities take place in a world of scarce resources, microeconomics can provide valuable insights into the operation and planning processes of medical firms. In this chapter, we focus on various economic principles that guide the production behavior of all types of firms, including medical firms. We begin by analyzing the short-run production process of a hypothetical medical firm.

To simplify our discussion of short-run production, we make five assumptions. First, we assume the medical firm produces a single output of medical services, q. Second, we initially assume only two medical inputs exist: nurse-hours, n, and a composite capital good, k. We can think of the composite capital good as an amalgamation of all types of capital, including any medical equipment and the physical space in the medical establishment. Third, since the short run is defined as a period of time over which the level of *at least* one input cannot be changed, we assume the quantity of capital is fixed at some amount. This assumption makes intuitive sense, because it is usually more difficult to change the stock of capital than the number of nurse-hours in the short run. Fourth, we assume for now that the medical firm faces an incentive to produce as efficiently as possible. Finally, we assume the medical firm possesses perfect information regarding the demands for its product. We relax the last two assumptions at the end of the chapter.

As we know from Chapter 2, a production function identifies how various inputs can be combined and transformed into a final output. Here, the production function identifies the different ways nurse-hours and capital can be combined to produce various levels of medical services. The production function allows for the possibility that each level of output may be produced by several different combinations of the nurse and capital inputs. Each combination is assumed to be **technically efficient,** since it results in the maximum amount of output that is feasible given the state of technology. Later we will see that both technical and economic considerations determine a unique least-cost, or economically efficient, method of production.

In the present example, the short-run production function for medical services can be mathematically generalized as

(7–1)
$$q = f(n, \overline{k}).$$

The short-run production function for medical services in Equation 7–1 indicates that the level of medical services is a function of a variable nurse input and a fixed (denoted with a bar) capital input. We begin our analysis by examining how the level of medical services, q, relates to a greater quantity of the variable nurse input, n, given that the capital input, $\overline{k}$, is assumed to be fixed. Various microeconomic principles and concepts relating to production theory are used to determine the precise relation between the employment of the variable input and the level of total output. As mentioned in Chapter 2, one important microeconomic principle from production theory is the law of diminishing marginal productivity. This is not really a law; rather, it is a generalization about production behavior and states that total output at first increases at an *increasing* rate, but after some point increases at a *decreasing* rate, with respect to a greater quantity of a variable input, holding all other inputs constant.[1]

---

1. In Chapter 2, we assumed for simplicity that the law of diminishing marginal returns sets in immediately; that is, the marginal product of medical services was always declining. In this chapter, we take a less restrictive approach to allow for the theoretical possibility that the marginal product of the variable input may increase initially. The fundamental idea remains the same, however. Eventually a point is reached where additional units of an input generate smaller marginal returns.

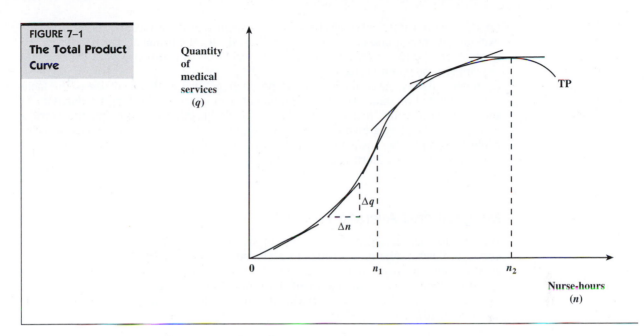

FIGURE 7–1

The Total Product Curve

The total product curve shows that output initially increases at an increasing rate from 0 to n_1 nurse-hours, then increases at a decreasing rate from n_1 to n_2 nurse-hours, and finally declines after n_2 nurse-hours as the medical firm employs more nurse-hours. Diminishing marginal productivity provides the reason why output fails to expand at an increasing rate after n_1 nurse-hours.

Figure 7–1 applies the law of diminishing productivity. It shows a graphical relation between the quantity of medical services on the vertical axis and the number of nurse-hours on the horizontal axis. The curve is referred to as the *total product* (TP) curve because it depicts the total output produced by different levels of the variable input, holding all other inputs constant. Notice that the quantity of services first increases at an increasing rate over the range of nurse-hours from 0 to n_1. The rate of increase is identified by the slope of the curve at each point. As you can see, the slope of the TP curve increases in value as the tangent lines become steeper over this range of nurse-hours.

Beyond point n_1, however, further increases in nurse-hours cause medical services to increase, but at a decreasing rate. That is the point at which diminishing productivity sets in. Notice that the slope of the TP curve gets smaller as output increases in the range from n_1 to n_2 (as indicated by the flatter tangent lines). At n_2, the slope of the TP curve is zero, as reflected in the horizontal tangent line. Finally, beyond n_2, we allow for the possibility that too many nurse-hours will lead to a reduction in the quantity of medical services. The slope of TP curve is negative beyond n_2.

In terms of the production decision at the firm level, we have not yet accounted for the specific reasoning underlying the law of diminishing marginal productivity. Economists point to the fixed short-run inputs as the basis for diminishing productivity. For example, when nurse-hours are increased at first, there is initially a considerable amount of capital, the fixed input, with which to produce medical services. The abundance of capital enables increasingly greater amounts of medical services to be generated from the employment of additional nurses. In addition, a synergy effect may dominate initially. The synergy effect means that nurses, working cooperatively as a team, are able to produce more output collectively than separately because of labor specialization, for example.

At some point, however, the fixed capital becomes limited relative to the variable input (e.g., too little medical equipment and not enough medical space), and additional nurse-hours generate successively fewer incremental units of medical services. In the extreme, as more nurses are crowded into a medical establishment of a fixed size, the quantity of services may actually begin to decline as congestion sets in and creates unwanted production problems.

In general, any physical constraint in production, such as the fixed size of the facility or a limited amount of medical equipment, can cause diminishing productivity to set in at some point. In fact, if it weren't for diminishing productivity, the world's food supply could be grown in a single flowerpot and the demand for medical services could be completely satisfied by a single large medical organization. What a wonderful world it would be! Unfortunately, however, diminishing productivity is the rule rather than the exception.

Marginal and Average Products

We can also use marginal and average product curves rather than the total product curve to illustrate the fundamental characteristics associated with the production process. In general, the marginal product is the change in total output associated with a one-unit change in the variable input. In terms of our example, the marginal product or quantity of medical services associated with an additional nurse-hour, MP_n, can be stated as follows:

(7–2) $$MP_n = \Delta q / \Delta n.$$

The magnitude of the marginal product of a nurse-hour reveals the additional quantity of medical services produced by each additional nurse-hour. It is a measure of the marginal contribution of a nurse-hour in the production of medical services.

In Figure 7–1, the slope of the total product curve at every point represents the marginal product of a nurse-hour, since it measures the rise (vertical distance) over the run (horizontal distance), or $\Delta q / \Delta n$. Consequently, we can determine the marginal product of an additional nurse-hour by examining the slope of the TP curve at each level of nurse-hours. Figure 7–2 graphically illustrates the marginal product of a nurse-hour. Initially, MP_n is positive and increases over the range from 0 to n_1 due to increasing marginal productivity. In the range from n_1 to n_2, the marginal product is positive but decreasing because diminishing marginal productivity has set in. At n_2, the marginal product of a nurse-hour is zero and becomes negative thereafter. The marginal product curve suggests that each additional nurse-hour cannot be expected to generate the same marginal contribution to total output as the previous one. The law of diminishing marginal productivity dictates that in the short run, a level of output is eventually reached where an incremental increase in the number of nurse-hours leads to successively fewer additions to total output (because some other inputs are fixed).

In addition to MP_n, the average product of a nurse-hour can provide insight into the production process. In general, the average product equals the total quantity of output divided by the level of the variable input. In terms of the present example, the average product of a nurse-hour, AP_n, is calculated by dividing the total quantity of medical services by the total number of nurse-hours:

(7–3) $$AP_n = q / n.$$

The average product of a nurse-hour measures the average quantity of medical services produced within an hour. For example, suppose we (crudely) measure total medical services by the number of daily patient-hours at a medical facility. In addition, suppose 200 nurse-hours are employed to service 300 daily patient-hours. In this example, the average product of a nurse-hour equals 300/200 or 1½ patients per hour.

We can also derive the average product of a nurse-hour from the total product curve, as shown in Figure 7–3(a). To derive AP_n, a ray from the origin is extended to

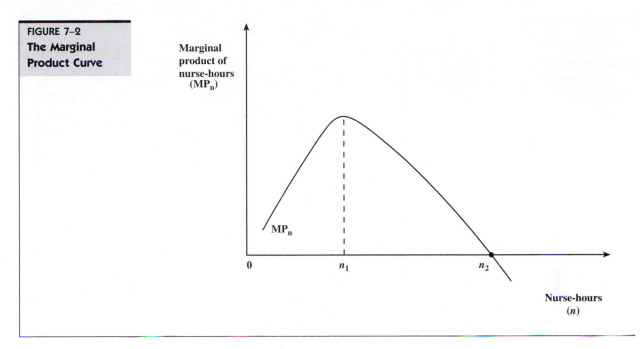

FIGURE 7–2
The Marginal Product Curve

Marginal product of nurse-hours (MP$_n$)

MP$_n$

0   n_1 n_2

Nurse-hours (n)

The marginal product of an additional nurse-hour is found by dividing the change in output by the change in the number of nurse-hours and is measured by the slope of the total product curve. Marginal productivity first increases with the number of nurse-hours because of synergy and labor specialization and then falls because of the fixed input that exists in the short run.

each point on the TP curve. The slope of the ray measures AP$_n$ for any given level of nurse-hours, since it equals the rise over the run, or q/n. In Figure 7–3(a), three rays, labeled 0A, 0B, and 0C, emanate from the origin to the TP curve. The slope of ray 0A is flatter than that of 0B and therefore is of a lower magnitude. In fact, as it is drawn, ray 0B has a greater slope than any other ray emanating from the origin. At this level of nurse-hours, the average product is maximized. The slope of ray 0C is flatter and of a lower magnitude than that of 0B. The implication is that average product initially increases over the range from 0 to n_3, reaches a maximum at n_3, and then decreases, as shown in Figure 7–3(b). It is the law of diminishing marginal productivity that accounts for the shape of AP$_n$.

In Figure 7–4, the marginal and average product curves are superimposed to illustrate how they are related. Some characteristics of the relation between these two curves are worth mentioning. First, the marginal product curve cuts the average product curve at its maximum point. In fact, it is a common mathematical principle that the marginal equals the average when the average is at its extreme value.[2] Second, MP$_n$ lies above AP$_n$ whenever AP$_n$ is increasing. This too reflects a common mathematical principle and should come as little surprise to the reader. For example, if your average grade in a course is a B+ until the final and you receive an A on the final exam, this incremental higher grade pulls up your final average grade. Third, MP$_n$ lies below AP$_n$ whenever AP$_n$ is declining. This relation between marginal and average values also

2. *Proof:* For simplicity, suppose the production function relates the quantity of output, q, to a single input of nurse-hours, n, such that $q = f(n)$. The average product of nurse-hours, AP$_n$, can be written as $f(n)/n$. To determine where AP$_n$ reaches a maximum point, we can take the first derivative of AP$_n$ and set it equal to zero. Following the rule for taking the derivative of a quotient of two functions (see Chiang, 1984), it follows that

(7–1a) $$f'(n) = \frac{f(n)}{n}$$

since $f'(n)$ equals MP$_n$ and $f(n)/n$ equals AP$_n$, MP$_n$ = AP$_n$ when AP$_n$ is maximized.

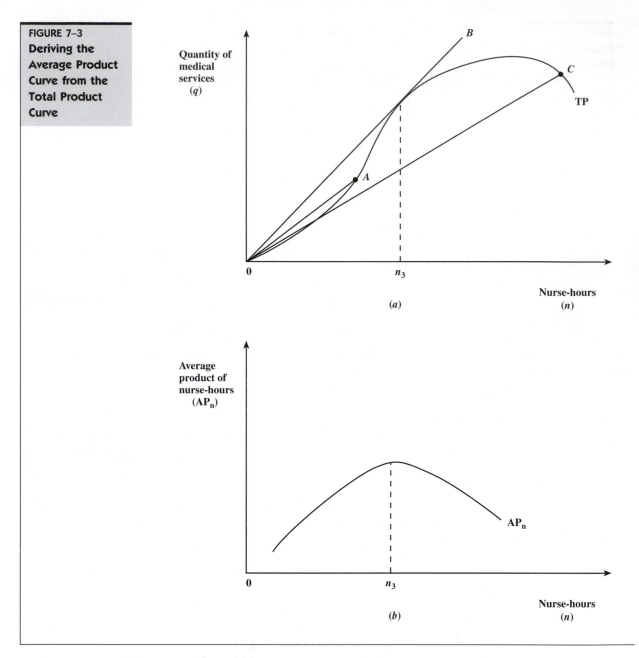

FIGURE 7–3
Deriving the Average Product Curve from the Total Product Curve

The average product of a nurse-hour is found by dividing total output by the total number of nurse-hours and can be derived by measuring the slope of a ray emanating from the origin to each point on the total product curve. Average productivity first increases with the number of nurse-hours and then declines because of increasing and then diminishing marginal productivity.

should not be surprising. As you know, your course grade slips if you receive a lower grade on the final exam relative to your previous course average.

Putting the grades aside (because learning is more important than grades—right?), we can discuss the relation between the marginal and average product curves in terms of our example concerning nurse-hours and the production of medical services. For this discussion, it helps to think of the marginal product curve as the amount of

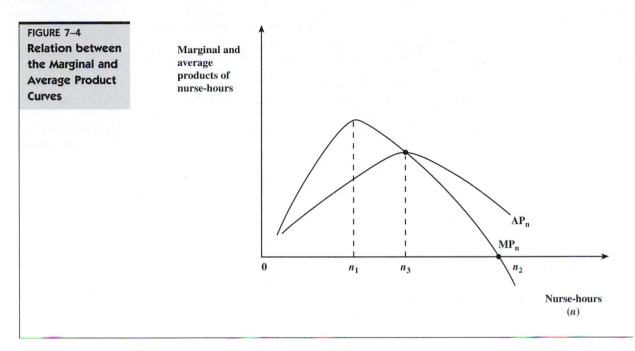

Average productivity rises when marginal productivity exceeds average productivity. Average productivity falls when marginal productivity lies below average productivity. Marginal productivity equals average productivity when average productivity is maximized.

medical services generated hourly by the next nurse hired. Also, we can think of the average product curve as the average quantity of medical services generated by the existing team of nurses within an hour—that is, the "team" average.

Looking at Figure 7–4, notice that the next nurse hired always generates more services per hour than the team average up to point n_3. Consequently, up to this point, each additional nurse helps pull up the team's average level of output. Beyond n_3, however, the incremental nurse hired generates less services per hour than the team average; as a result, the team average falls. It is important to realize that any increase or decrease in the marginal product has nothing to do with the individual talents of each additional nurse employed. Rather, it involves the law of diminishing marginal productivity. At some point in the production process, the incremental nurse becomes less productive due to the constraint imposed by the fixed input. The marginal productivity, in turn, influences the average productivity of the team of nurses.

At first glance, it seems logical to assume that a medical firm desires to produce at a point like n_1 or n_3 in Figure 7–4. After all, they represent the points at which either the marginal or the average product is maximized. In most cases, however, a medical firm finds it more desirable to achieve some financial target, such as a maximum or break-even level of profits. As a result, we need more information concerning the revenue and cost structures the medical firm faces before we can pinpoint the desired level of production. In later chapters we will see that under normal conditions, the relevant range of production in Figure 7–4 is somewhere between n_3 and n_2.

Elasticity of Input Substitution

Up to now, we have assumed only one variable input. Realistically, however, the medical firm operates with more than one variable input in the short run. Thus, there may be some possibilities for substitution between any two variable inputs. For example, licensed practical nurses often substitute for registered nurses in the production of inpatient services, and physician assistants sometimes substitute for physicians in the production of ambulatory services. The actual degree of substitutability between any two inputs depends on technical and legal considerations. For example, physician assistants are limited by law from prescribing medicines in most states. In addition, licensed practical nurses normally lack the technical knowledge needed to perform all the duties of registered nurses.

In general terms, the elasticity of substitution between any two inputs equals the percentage change in the input ratio divided by the percentage change in the ratio of the inputs' marginal productivities, holding constant the level of output, or

$$\textbf{(7--4)} \qquad \sigma = \frac{\Delta(I_1/I_2)}{I_1/I_2} \div \frac{\Delta(MP_2/MP_1)}{MP_2/MP_1},$$

where I_i $(i = 1,2)$ stands for the quantity employed of each input. The ratio of marginal productivities, MP_2/MP_1, referred to as the *marginal rate of technical substitution*, illustrates the rate at which one input substitutes for the other in the production process, at the margin. For example, suppose the marginal product of a registered nurse-hour is four patients and the marginal product of a licensed practical nurse-hour is two patients. It follows that two licensed practical nurse-hours are needed to substitute completely for one registered nurse-hour.

Theoretically, σ (Greek letter sigma) takes on values between 0 and $+\infty$ and identifies the percentage change in the input ratio that results from a 1 percent change in the marginal rate of technical substitution. The magnitude of σ identifies the degree of substitution between the two inputs. For example, if $\sigma = 0$, the variable inputs cannot be substituted in production. In contrast, when $\sigma = \infty$, the two variable inputs are perfect substitutes in production. In practice, it is more common for σ to take on values between these two extremes, implying that limited substitution possibilities exist.

A Production Function for Hospital Admissions

Jensen and Morrisey (1986) provide one of the more interesting empirical studies on the production characteristics of hospital services. In keeping with Equation 7–1, Jensen and Morrisey estimated a production function for admissions at 3,540 nonteaching hospitals in the United States as of 1983 in the following general form[3]:

(7--5)   Case-mix-adjusted hospital admissions $= f$(Physicians, nurses, other
nonphysician staff, hospital beds, X).

Notice that hospital admissions serve as the measure of output. Given the heterogeneous nature of hospital services, however, this output measure was adjusted for case-mix differences across hospitals by multiplying it by the Medicare patient index. This index is the weighted sum of the proportions of the hospital's Medicare patients in different diagnostic categories where the weights reflect the average costs per case in each diagnostic group. The number of physicians, nurses (full-time equivalent [FTE] units), and other nonphysician staff (FTE) represented the labor inputs; the number of beds constituted the capital input; and X stood for a number of other production factors not central to the discussion.

To put Equation 7–5 in a form that can be estimated with a multiple regression technique, Jensen and Morrisey specified a translog production function. The form and properties of this particular mathematical function are too complex to describe briefly;

---

3. For the sake of brevity, we do not discuss their results for the sample of teaching hospitals.

it suffices to note that the translog is a flexible functional form that imposes very few restrictions on the estimated parameters.[4]

From the empirical estimation, Jensen and Morrisey were able to derive estimates of each input's marginal product. As expected, the marginal products were all positive. Jensen and Morrisey noted that the marginal product of each input declined in magnitude with greater usage, as the law of diminishing marginal product suggests. The estimated marginal product of a physician implied that an additional doctor generated 6.05 additional case-mix-adjusted annual admissions. The nurse input was by far the most productive input. In particular, the marginal nurse was responsible for producing about 20.3 additional case-mix-adjusted annual admissions. The marginal products of other nonphysician staff and beds were found to be 6.97 and 3.04 case-mix-adjusted annual admissions, respectively.

The estimation procedure also generated sufficient information to enable Jensen and Morrisey to measure the input substitution possibilities available to hospitals. Each input was found to be a substitute for the others in production. In particular, the substitution elasticities between physicians and nurses, physicians and beds, and nurses and beds were reported to be 0.547, 0.175, and 0.124, respectively. The relatively large elasticity of 0.547 between physicians and nurses tells us the average hospital can more easily substitute between these two inputs. This particular input elasticity estimate can be interpreted to mean that a 10 percent increase in the marginal productivity of a doctor causes a 5.47 percent increase in the ratio of nurses to doctors, *ceteris paribus*. These positive substitution elasticities suggest that hospital policy makers can avoid some of the price (wage) increase in any one input by substituting with the others. For example, to maintain a given level of admissions, a wage increase for nurses might be partially absorbed by increasing the number of hospital beds.

Short-Run Cost Theory of the Representative Medical Firm

Before we begin our discussion of the medical firm's cost curves, we need to address the difference between the ways economists and accountants refer to costs. In particular, accountants consider only the *explicit costs* of doing business when determining the accounting profits of a medical firm. Explicit costs are easily quantified because a recent market transaction is available to provide an accurate measure of cost. Wage payments to the hourly medical staff, electric utility bills, and medical supply expenses are all examples of the explicit costs medical firms incur because disbursement records can be consulted to determine the magnitudes of these expenditures.

Economists, unlike accountants, consider both the explicit and implicit costs of production. *Implicit costs* reflect the opportunity costs of using any resources the medical firm owns. For example, a general practitioner (GP) may own the physical assets (such as the clinic and medical equipment) used in producing physician services. In this case, a recent market transaction is unavailable to determine the cost of using these assets. Yet an opportunity cost is incurred when using them because the physical assets could have been rented out for an alternative use. For example, the clinic could be remodeled and rented as a beauty salon, and the medical equipment could be

---

4. In a translog function, (the natural log of) each independent variable enters the equation in both linear and quadratic form. In addition, a cross-product linear term is created between any two independent variables and specified in the function. Similar cross-product terms are eliminated from the specification. To ensure a well-behaved function, restrictions are normally imposed on the parameter estimates.

rented out to another physician. Thus, the forgone rental payments reflect the opportunity cost of using the physical assets owned by the GP.[5]

Consequently, when determining the economic (rather than accounting) profits of a firm, economists consider the total costs of doing business, including both the explicit and implicit costs. Economists believe it is important to determine whether sufficient revenues are available to cover the cost of using all inputs, including those rented and owned. For example, if the rental return on the physical assets is greater than the return on use, the GP might do better by renting out the assets rather than retaining them for personal use.

The Short-Run Cost Curves of the Representative Medical Firm

Cost theory is based on the production theory of the medical firm previously outlined and relates the quantity of output to the cost of production. As such, it identifies how (total and marginal) costs respond to changes in output. If we continue to assume the two inputs of nurse-hours, n, and capital, $\overline{k}$, the short-run total cost, STC, of producing a given level of medical output, q, can be written as

(7–6) $$STC(q) = w \times n + r \times \overline{k},$$

where w and r represent the hourly wage for a nurse and the rental or opportunity cost of capital, respectively. Input prices are assumed to be fixed, which means the single medical firm can purchase these inputs without affecting their market prices. This is a valid assumption as long as the firm is a small buyer of inputs relative to the total number of buyers in the marketplace.[6]

Equation 7–6 implies that the short-run total costs of production are dependent on the quantities and prices of inputs employed. The wage rate times the number of nurse-hours equals the total wage bill and represents the total variable costs of production. Variable costs respond to changes in the level of output.[7] The product of the rental price and the quantity of capital represent the total fixed costs of production. Obviously, this cost component does not respond to changes in output, since the quantity of capital is fixed in the short run.

The TP curve not only identifies the quantity of medical output produced by a particular number of nurse-hours but also shows, reciprocally, the number of nurse-hours necessary to produce a given level of medical output. With this information, we can determine the short-run total cost of producing different levels of medical output by following a three-step procedure. First, we identify, through the production function, the necessary number of nurse-hours, n, for each level of medical output. Second, we multiply the quantity of nurse-hours by the hourly wage, w, to determine the short-run total variable costs, STVC, of production, or $w \times n$. Third, we add the short-run total fixed costs, STFC, or $r \times \overline{k}$, to STVC to derive the short-run total costs, STC, of production. If we conduct this three-step procedure for each level of medical output, we can derive a short-run total cost curve like the one depicted in Figure 7–5.

Notice the reciprocal relation between the short-run total cost function in Figure 7–5 and the short-run total product curve in Figure 7–1. For example, when total product is increasing at an *increasing* rate up to point n_1 in Figure 7–1, short-run total costs are increasing at a *decreasing* rate up to point q_1 in Figure 7–5. This is because the increasing productivity in this range causes the total costs of production to rise slowly. Output

---

5. The GP's labor time should also be treated as an implicit cost of doing business if he independently owns the clinic. As an entrepreneur, the GP does not receive an explicit payment but instead receives any residual profits that are left over after all other costs are paid. If the physician does not receive an appropriate rate of return, he may leave the area or the profession to get a better rate of return.

6. If the single firm were a large or an influential buyer, it might possess some "monopsony" power and could affect the market prices of the inputs.

7. For simplicity, we assume the wage rate represents total hourly compensation, including any fringe benefits.

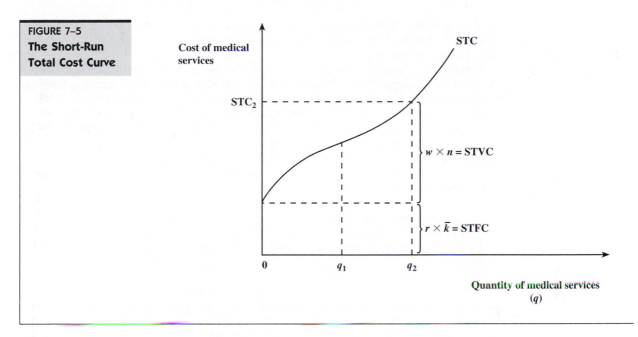

FIGURE 7–5

The Short-Run Total Cost Curve

The short-run total cost, STC, of producing medical services equals the sum of the total variable, STVC, and fixed costs, STFC. STC first increases at a decreasing rate up to point q_1 and then increases at an increasing rate with respect to producing more output. STC increases at an increasing rate after q_1 because of diminishing marginal productivity.

increases at a *decreasing* rate immediately beyond point n_1 in Figure 7–1 (as shown by the slope of the TP curve), and, as a result, short-run total costs increase at an *increasing* rate beyond q_1 in Figure 7–5. Also notice that total costs increase solely because additional nurses are employed as output expands. Figure 7–5 also shows how short-run total cost can be decomposed into its variable and fixed components for the level of output q_2.

In practice, distinguishing between fixed and variable costs can be particularly challenging. Recall that variable costs change proportionately, whereas fixed costs do not change, in response to any adjustment in the quantity of output actually produced. Fixed costs occur in the short run, during the so-called *operating period,* when the levels of some inputs are fixed. In contrast, all inputs are variable during the long run or *planning period*, when, for instance, future budgets are being designed. The physical size of a production facility is often treated as a fixed input because a significant amount of time is needed to construct or relocate to a larger building. Hourly workers are typically treated as a variable input because they can be promptly hired or laid off, depending on the desired adjustment in output. As you can see, time plays a crucial role in determining the fixity of inputs and costs. It follows that long-term contracts, although potentially providing offsetting benefits, impose more fixed costs into a firm's budget.

In an article in the *Journal of the American Medical Association,* Roberts et al. (1999) were interested in distinguishing between the fixed and variable costs at a hospital because they wanted to know whether a significant amount of hospital costs could be saved by discouraging unnecessary hospital services. Reductions in hospital services can result in more cost savings when variable costs comprise a greater percentage of overall costs. But as Roberts et al. note: "A computed tomographic (CT) scan is thought of as an expensive test and a source of significant cost savings if it is not performed. However, the scanner and space have already been rented or paid for, and the technician receives a salary that must be paid whether any individual receives a CT scan or not. If the radiologist who interprets the test is also receiving a salary, the additional cost to the hospital of doing the test is minimal—the price of radiographic film, paper and contrast."

Roberts et al. examine the distribution of variable and fixed costs at Cook County Hospital in Chicago, Illinois, which was an 886-bed urban-public-teaching hospital when the study was done in 1993. The authors included capital, employee salaries, benefits, building maintenance, and utilities in the fixed-cost category. Note that employee salaries were included in the fixed-cost category, with the assumption being that Cook County was contractually obligated to pay these salaries during the budget period. Variable costs were specified to include health care worker supplies, such as gloves, patient care supplies, paper, food, radiographic film, laboratory reagents, glassware, and medications with their delivery systems such as intravenous catheters or bottles.

The authors find that the fixed costs comprised 84 percent of Cook County's total budget at that time. However, they caution that their results may not be applicable to cases in which hospitals hire more hourly or fee-for-service workers. At Cook County Hospital, most employees were salaried. But even in the case of nonsalaried personnel, Roberts et al. note that the intense employee specialization may make it more difficult for hospitals to downsize than traditional firms. For example, pediatric nurses may not be able to promptly adapt to adult cardiac care units. Given that a majority of costs were fixed, their study implies that a reduction in hospital services would have very little impact on Cook County's costs in the short run.

Short-Run Per-Unit Costs of Production

Another way to look at the reciprocal relation between production and costs is to focus on the short-run marginal and average variable costs of production. The short-run marginal costs, SMC, of production are equal to the change in total costs associated with a one-unit change in output, or

$$(7\text{–}7) \qquad\qquad \mathrm{SMC} = \Delta \mathrm{STC}/\Delta q.$$

In terms of Equations 7–6 and 7–7, the SMC look like the following:

$$(7\text{–}8) \qquad\qquad \mathrm{SMC} = \Delta(w \times n + r \times \overline{k})/\Delta q.$$

Because the wage rate and STFC are constant with respect to output, Equation 7–8 can be rewritten in the following manner:

$$(7\text{–}9) \qquad\qquad \mathrm{SMC} = w \times (\Delta n/\Delta q) = w \times (1/\mathrm{MP_n}) = w/\mathrm{MP_n}.$$

Notice on the right-hand side of Equation 7–9 that short-run marginal costs equal the wage rate divided by the marginal product of nurse-hours.

The short-run average variable costs, SAVC, of production equal the STVC, divided by the quantity of medical output. Because STVC is the total wage bill (that is, $w \times n$),

$$(7\text{–}10) \qquad\qquad \mathrm{SAVC} = \mathrm{STVC}/q = (w \times n)/q = w \times (1/\mathrm{AP_n}) = w/\mathrm{AP_n}$$

such that SAVC equals the wage rate divided by the average product of a nurse-hour. Notice that the short-run marginal and average variable costs are inversely related to the marginal and average products of labor, respectively. Thus, marginal and average variable costs increase as the marginal and average products fall, and vice versa. Figure 7–6 shows the graphical relation between the per-unit product and cost curves.

The two graphs in Figure 7–6 clearly point out the reciprocal relation between production and costs. For example, after point n_1 in Figure 7–6(a), diminishing productivity sets in and the marginal product begins to decline. As a result, the short-run marginal costs ($= w/\mathrm{MP_n}$) increase beyond output level q_1 given a fixed wage.

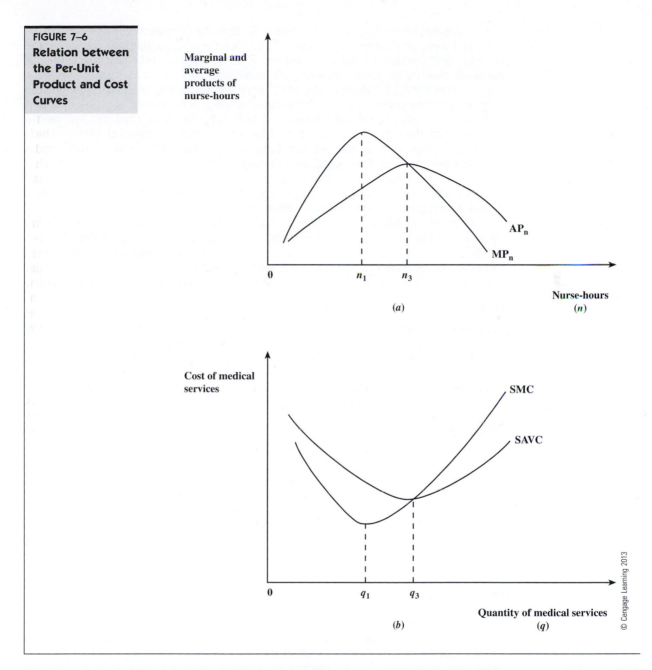

FIGURE 7–6
Relation between the Per-Unit Product and Cost Curves

Short-run marginal cost, SMC, equals the change in total costs brought on by a one-unit change in output. Short-run average variable cost, SAVC, equals short-run total variable cost divided by total output. SMC and SAVC are inversely related to marginal and average productivity. For example, marginal costs decline as marginal productivity increases.

Similarly, the average product of a nurse-hour declines beyond n_3, so the average variable costs of production increase beyond q_3. Obviously, the shapes of the marginal cost and average variable cost curves reflect the law of diminishing marginal productivity. Because of this reciprocal relation, production and costs represent dual ways of observing various characteristics associated with the production process.

It is apparent from Equations 7–9 and 7–10 that the maximum points on the marginal and average product curves correspond directly to the minimum points on the marginal and average variable cost curves. Note in Figure 7–6(b) that the short-run marginal cost curve passes through the minimum point of the short-run average variable cost curve. In addition, the SMC curve lies below the SAVC curve when the latter is decreasing and above the SAVC curve when it is increasing.

In simple terms, the graph in Figure 7–6(b) identifies how costs behave as the medical firm alters output in the short run. Initially, as the medical firm expands output and employs more nurse-hours, both the marginal and average variable costs of production decline. Eventually, diminishing productivity sets in due to the fixed inputs, and both marginal and average variable costs increase. It follows that the marginal and average variable costs of production depend in part on the amount of output a medical firm produces in the short run.

Besides the marginal and average variable costs of production, decision makers are interested in the short-run average total costs of operating the medical firm. Following Equation 7–6, we can find the short-run average total costs of production by summing the average variable costs and average fixed costs.[8] Short-run average fixed costs (SAFC) are simply total fixed costs (STFC) divided by the level of output, or

(7–11)
$$SAFC = STFC/q.$$

Because by definition the numerator in Equation 7–11 is fixed in the short run, the SAFC declines as the denominator, medical services, increases in value. Consequently, the average fixed costs of production decline with greater amounts of output because total fixed costs (or overhead costs) are spread out over more and more units.

Figure 7–7 shows the graphical relation among SMC, SAVC, and, short-run average total cost, SATC. Note that the marginal cost curve cuts the average total cost curve at its minimum point. (The minimum SATC lies to the right of the minimum SAVC. Why?) Also, note that the vertical distance between the average total and variable cost curves at each level of output represents the average fixed costs of production. This should not be surprising, since total costs include both variable and fixed costs. The vertical distance between the two curves gets smaller as output increases because the SAFC approaches zero with increases in output. One implication of the model is that average total costs increase at some level of output because eventually the cost-enhancing impact of diminishing productivity outweighs the cost-reducing tendency of the average fixed costs.

The unwitting reader may think that the medical firm should choose to produce at the minimum point on the SATC curve because average costs are minimized. As mentioned earlier, however, the level of output the medical firm chooses depends on the firm's objective (e.g., to achieve maximum or break-even level of profits). Hence, a proper analysis requires some knowledge of the revenue structure in addition to the cost structure. In later chapters, we entertain some alternative objectives that may motivate the production behavior of medical firms. For now, however, assume for pedagogical purposes that the firm has chosen to produce the level of medical output, q_0, in Figure 7–7. Let's identify the various costs associated with producing q_0 units of medical output.

---

8. Equation 7–6 can be rewritten as

(7–6a)
$$STC = STVC + STFC.$$

Dividing both sides of Equation 7–6a by the level of output gives

(7–6b)
$$STC/q = STVC/q + STFC/q.$$

Thus, by definition,

(7–6c)
$$SATC = SAVC + SAFC.$$

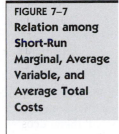

FIGURE 7–7

Relation among Short-Run Marginal, Average Variable, and Average Total Costs

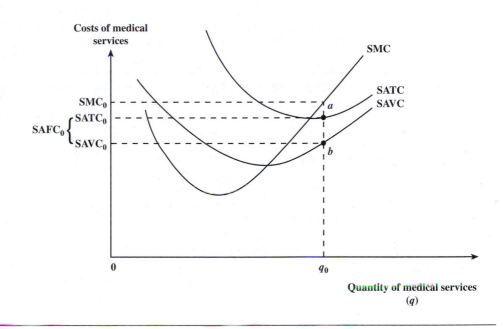

Short-run average total cost, SATC, equals the sum of short-run average variable cost, SAVC, and short-run average fixed cost, SAFC. Hence, SAFC is reflected in the vertical distance between the SATC and SAVC curves at each level of output. SMC cuts both of the average cost curves at their minimum points. SMC lies above the SAVC and SATC curves when they are rising and below them when they are falling.

The identification of the per-unit cost of producing a given level of output is a fairly easy matter. We can determine the per-unit cost by extending a vertical line from the appropriate level of output until it crosses the cost curves. For example, the average total cost of producing q_0 units of output is $SATC_0$, while the average variable cost is $SAVC_0$. The average fixed cost of producing q_0 units of output is represented by the vertical distance between $SATC_0$ and $SAVC_0$, or distance ab. In addition, SMC_0 identifies the marginal cost of producing one more unit assuming the medical firm is already producing q_0 units of medical services.

Now suppose that instead of the per-unit costs, we want to identify the various total costs (that is, STC, STVC, and STFC) associated with producing q_0 units of output. We can do this by multiplying the level of output by the per-unit costs of production. For example, the rectangle $SAVC_0 - b - q_0 - 0$ in Figure 7–7 measures the total variable costs of producing q_0 units of output, since it corresponds to the area found by multiplying the base of $0 - q_0$ by the height of $0 - SAVC_0$. Following similar logic, the total fixed costs are represented by rectangle $SATC_0 - a - b - SAVC_0$, and total costs can be measured by area $SATC_0 - a - q_0 - 0$. The ability to interpret and read these cost curves is useful for the discussion that follows.

Factors Affecting the Position of the Short-Run Cost Curves

A variety of short-run circumstances affect the positions of the per-unit and total cost curves.[9] Among them are the prices of the variable inputs, the quality of care, the patient case-mix, and the amounts of the fixed inputs. Whenever any one of these variables changes, the positions of the cost curves change through either an upward or a downward shift depending on whether costs increase or decrease. For example,

---

9. The position of the average and total fixed cost curves is influenced by the price of the fixed input. Fixed costs do not affect the typical marginal decision in the short run. Therefore, we do not discuss the factors affecting the position of the fixed cost curves.

if input prices increase in the short run, the cost curves shift upward to reflect the higher costs of production (especially since $SAVC = w/AP_n$ and $SMC = w/MP_n$). If input prices fall in the short run, the cost curves shift downward to indicate the lower production costs. Thus, if two otherwise similar medical care organizations were compared, we would expect the one paying higher wages to also face higher per-unit costs.

Furthermore, suppose two medical firms are otherwise comparable but then one adopts a more severe patient case-mix. For example, suppose initially that two hospitals only perform vaginal deliveries of babies and then one of them decides to also deliver babies by cesarean section (C-section). Assuming that C-sections are more risky (and therefore more costly) than vaginal deliveries, the per-unit cost curves respond by shifting upward for the hospital now adopting that procedure. Each labor hour is unable to produce as much output (treat as many mothers and their babies) when conditions are more complicated. In terms of our formal analysis, a more severe patient case-mix reduces the average and marginal productivity of the labor input and thereby raises the costs of production. Conversely, a switch to a less severe patient case-mix is associated with lower per-unit cost curves.

The level of quality may also influence the position of the per-unit cost curves. Recall from Chapter 2 that Donabedian believes quality differences show up in the structure, process, or outcomes of a medical facility. In fact, consider the following general production function: $q = f(n, k)$, previously shown as Equation 7–1. Within this framework, we can think of the level of structural quality as influencing the quality of the inputs used by the organization, such as n or k. For example, nurses might be better trained and the medical equipment may be newer and more clinically precise. Moreover, we can consider process quality as affecting the functional operator, f, which reflects the transformation process of turning inputs into outputs. For example, think of the transformation process that takes place when doctors and nurses, along with their supplies and medical equipment, deliver babies. Generally, more time, patience, and diligence devoted to the process (deliveries in our example) mean better quality. Finally, outcome quality shows up in q, reflecting, in our running example, the success rate of delivering live, healthy babies.

It stands to reason that higher levels of structural or process quality typically increase the per-unit costs of providing medical care. In particular, higher levels of structural quality usually mean more-educated and better-trained employees, newer medical equipment, or nicer facility amenities. These higher-quality inputs cost more to purchase on a per-unit basis and overall. Thus, if not matched by commensurate increases in productivity, the higher-quality inputs result in greater per-unit costs of production. Similarly, better process quality means more time spent with any one patient. Once again, it can be expected that higher levels of process quality translate into higher per-unit costs of production.

In contrast, the level of outcome quality may have the opposite impact on per-unit costs. Specifically, if the treatment or procedure is correctly performed the first time, then the patient does not have to revisit the medical organization for that same purpose. For example, being readmitted to a hospital for the same illness means hospital resources must be drawn away from alternative purposes. These resources therefore have an opportunity cost. Consequently, higher levels of outcome quality might actually result in lower per-unit costs of production.

Finally, a change in the amount of the fixed inputs can alter the costs of production. For example, it can be shown that excessive amounts of the fixed inputs lead to higher short-run costs (Cowing and Holtmann, 1983). We discuss the specific reasoning underlying the relation between fixed inputs and short-run costs when we examine the long-run costs of production later in this chapter.

In sum, a properly specified short-run total variable cost function for medical services should include the following variables:

(7–12) $STVC = f(\text{output level, input prices, quality of care, patient case-mix,}$
$\text{quantity of the fixed inputs}).$

We suspect that these factors can explain cost differentials among medical firms in the same industry. Specifically, output influences short-run variable costs by determining where the medical firm operates along the cost curve, whereas the other factors affect the location of the curve. Most likely, high-cost medical firms are associated with more output, higher wages, increased quality, more severe patient case-mixes, and/or an excessive quantity of fixed inputs.

Estimating a Short-Run Cost Function for Hospital Services

Cowing and Holtmann (1983) empirically estimated a short-run total variable cost function for a sample of 138 short-term general care hospitals in New York using 1975 data. Along the lines of Equation 7–12, they specified the short-run total variable cost, STVC, function in the following general form:

(7–13) $STVC = f(q_1, q_2, q_3, q_4, q_5, w_1, w_2, w_3, w_4, w_5, w_6, K, A).$

Each q_i ($i = 1,5$) represents the quantity of one of five different patient services—emergency room care, medical-surgical care, pediatric care, maternity care, and other inpatient care—measured in total patient days; each w_j ($j = 1,6$) stands for one of six different variable input prices for nursing labor, auxiliary labor, professional labor, administrative labor, general labor, and material and supplies; K is a single measure of the capital stock (measured by the market value of a hospital); and A is the fixed number of admitting physicians in the hospital.[10]

Compared to Equation 7–12, Cowing and Holtmann's specification of the cost function is more complex and introduces a greater degree of realism into the empirical analysis. First, the hospital is realistically treated as a multiproduct firm, simultaneously producing and selling five different types of patient services. Second, instead of our single variable input price (i.e., hourly nurse wage), six different variable input prices are specified. Finally, Cowing and Holtmann include the number of admitting physicians in the model because they play such a key role in the hospital services production process.

The authors assumed a multiproduct translog cost function for Equation 7–13. We do not discuss the properties associated with this specific functional form; it suffices to note that this flexible form enables us to assess a large number of real-world characteristics associated with the production process.

First, this functional form allows for an interaction among the various outputs so that economies of scope can be examined. **Economies of scope** result from the joint sharing of resources, such as nurses, auxiliary workers, and administrative labor among related outputs. Scope economies exist if the cost of producing two outputs jointly is less than the sum of the costs of producing the two outputs separately. For example, many colleges and universities produce both an undergraduate and a graduate education jointly due to perceived cost savings from economies of scope. The same professors, library personnel, and buildings can be used in producing both educational outputs simultaneously.

---

10. Cowing and Holtmann also specify two dummy variables reflecting for-profit versus not-for-profit ownership status and teaching versus nonteaching institution as a way to control for differences in quality and case-mix severity across hospitals. The inadequate control for quality and severity of case-mix is one of the few faults we can find with this paper.

Cowing and Holtmann found some very intriguing results. First, their study reveals evidence of **short-run economies of scale**, meaning that an increase in output results in a less than proportionate increase in short-run total variable costs. Evidence of short-run economies indicates that the representative hospital operates to the left of the minimum point on the short-run average variable cost curve and implies that larger hospitals produce at a lower cost than smaller ones in the short run. They point out that this result is consistent with the view that aggregate hospital costs could be reduced by closing some small hospitals and merging the services among the remaining ones.

Second, in contrast to scale economies, Cowing and Holtmann discovered only limited evidence for economies of scope with respect to pediatric care and other services. They also found evidence to support diseconomies of scope with respect to emergency services and other services. In fact, they argued that the results for both scope and scale economies indicate that larger but more specialized hospitals may be more effective given the significance of the scale effects and the general lack of any substantial economies of scope.

Third, Cowing and Holtmann also noted that the short-run marginal cost of each output, $\Delta STVC/\Delta q_i$, declined and then became constant over the levels of output observed in their study. For example, the marginal cost of an emergency room visit was found to be approximately $32 for 54,000 visits per year and about $20 for 100,000 visits per year. For medical-surgical care, marginal cost was found to fall from $255 per patient day for 6,000 annual patient days to around $100 for 300,000 annual total patient days. For maternity care, the evidence suggests that the marginal costs of $540 per patient day for hospitals with 1,500 total annual patient days declined to $75 for hospitals with 20,000 total annual patient days. Eventually each of the marginal costs leveled off.

Finally, Cowing and Holtmann estimated the short-run elasticities of input substitution between all pairs of variable inputs. They reported that the results indicate a substantial degree of substitutability between nursing and professional workers, nursing and general workers, nursing and administrative workers, and professional and administrative labor.

The Cost-Minimizing Input Choice

A medical firm makes choices concerning which variable inputs to employ. Recognizing that there is usually more than one way to produce a specific output, medical firms typically desire to produce with the least-cost or cost-minimizing input mix. For example, suppose administrators desire to produce some given amount of medical services, q_0, at minimum total cost, TC, using two variable inputs: registered nurses, RN, and licensed practical nurses, LPN. (For ease of exposition, we ignore the capital input in this example.) These two inputs are paid hourly wages of w_R and w_L, respectively. The medical firm wants to minimize

(7–14) $$TC(q_0) = w_R \times RN + w_L \times LPN$$

subject to

(7–15) $$q_0 = f(RN, LPN)$$

by choosing the proper mix of registered nurses and licensed practical nurses.

Taken together, Equations 7–14 and 7–15 mean that administrators want to minimize the total cost of producing q_0 units of medical services by choosing the "right," or efficient, mix of RNs and LPNs so that $TC(q_0)$ is as low as possible but yet sufficient amounts of the two inputs are available to produce q_0. The efficient combination depends on the marginal products and relative prices of the two inputs. By using a mathematical technique called *constrained optimization*, we can show that the efficient mix of RNs and LPNs is chosen when the following condition holds[11]:

(7–16) $$MP_{RN}/w_R = MP_{LPN}/w_L.$$

Equation 7–16 means that the marginal product to price ratio is equal for both registered nurses and licensed practical nurses in equilibrium. The equality implies that the last dollar spent on registered nurses generates the same increment to output as the last dollar spent on licensed practical nurses. As a result, a rearranging of expenditures on the two inputs cannot generate any increase in medical services, since both inputs generate the same output per dollar at the margin.[12]

To more fully appreciate this point, suppose this condition does not hold such that

(7–17) $$MP_{RN}/w_R < MP_{LPN}/w_L.$$

In that case, the last dollar spent on a licensed practical nurse generates more output than the last dollar spent on a registered nurse. A licensed practical nurse is more profitable for the hospital at the margin because the medical organization receives a "bigger bang for the buck." But as the organization hires more LPNs and fewer RNs, the marginal productivities adjust until the equilibrium condition in Equation 7–16 results. Specifically, the marginal productivity of the LPNs decreases, while the marginal productivity of the RNs increases due to diminishing marginal productivity.

For example, suppose a newly hired RN can service six patients per hour and a newly hired LPN can service only four patients per hour. At first blush, with no consideration of the price of each input, the RN might appear to be the "better buy" because productivity is 50 percent higher. But suppose further that the market wage for an RN is $20 per hour, while an LPN requires only $10 per hour to work at the medical facility. Given relative input prices, the 50 percent higher productivity of the RN costs the medical facility 100 percent more. Obviously, the LPN is the better buy. That is, the last dollar spent on an LPN results in the servicing of 0.4 additional patients per hour, while a dollar spent on an RN allows the servicing of only 0.3 more patients per hour.

As another example, most physicians are not hospital employees and are not paid explicit salaries by the hospitals; instead they are granted admitting privileges by the hospitals. The granting of admitting privileges comes at a cost to the hospital, however. For example, the hospital incurs costs when it reviews and processes the physician's application, monitors the physician's performance to ensure quality control, and allows the physician to use its resources. Based on their empirical procedure discussed earlier, Jensen and Morrisey (1986) were able to estimate the shadow price, or implicit cost, of a physician with admitting privileges at a representative hospital. They imputed the shadow price of a physician by using the condition for optimal input use. Following the format of Equation 7–16, the optimal combination of doctors, doc, and nurses, n, is chosen when

(7–18) $$MP_{doc}/w_{doc} = MP_n/w_n.$$

By substituting in the estimated marginal products for doctors (6.05) and nurses (20.3) from their study, and the sample average for the annual nurses' salary ($23,526), Jensen and Morrisey solved for the shadow price of a doctor, w_{doc}. The resulting figure implies that the typical hospital in the sample incurred implicit costs of approximately $7,012 per year from granting admitting privileges to the marginal physician.

11. The interested reader can consult Chiang (1984).

12. The astute reader most likely recognizes that Equation 7–16 is similar to the utility-maximizing condition noted in Chapter 5.

Long-Run Costs of Production

Up to now, we have focused on the short-run costs of operation and assumed that one input is fixed. The fixed input leads to diminishing returns in production and to U-shaped average variable and total cost curves. In the long run, however, when the medical firm is planning for future resource requirements, all inputs, including capital, can be changed. Therefore, it is also important to analyze the relation between output and costs when all inputs are changed simultaneously in the long run.

Long-Run Cost Curves

The long-run average total cost curve can be derived from a series of short-run cost curves, as shown in Figure 7–8. The three short-run average total cost curves in the figure reflect different amounts of capital. For example, each curve might reflect the short-run average total costs of producing units of medical services in physically larger facilities of sizes k_1, k_2, and k_3. If decision makers know the relation among different-size facilities and the short-run average total costs, they can easily choose the SATC or size that minimizes the average cost of producing each level of medical services in the long run.

For example, over the range 0 to q_a, facility size k_1 results in lower costs of production than either size k_2 or k_3. Specifically, notice that at output level q_1, SATC$_2$ exceeds SATC$_1$ by a significant amount. Therefore, the administrators choose size k_1 if they desire to produce q_1 units of medical services at least cost in the long run. Similarly, from q_a to q_b, facility size k_2, associated with SATC$_2$, results in lower costs than either size k_1 or k_3. Beyond q_b units of medical services (say, q_2), a size of k_3 enables lower costs of production in the long run.

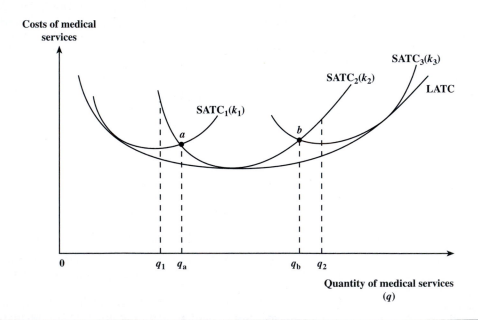

FIGURE 7–8

The Short-Run Average Cost Curves and the Long-Run Planning Curve

All inputs are variable in the long run. SATC$_1$, SATC$_2$, and SATC$_3$ represent the cost curves for small, medium, and large facilities, respectively. If decision makers choose the efficiently sized firm for producing output in the long run, a long-run average total cost, LATC, can be derived from a series of short-run average total cost curves brought on by an increase in the stock of capital. The U shape of the LATC reflects economies and diseconomies of scale.

The three short-run cost curves in Figure 7–8 paint a simplistic picture, since conceptually each unit of medical services can be linked to a uniquely sized cost-minimizing facility (assuming capital is divisible). If we assume a large number of possible sizes, we can draw a curve that connects all the cost-minimizing points on the various short-run average total cost curves. Each point indicates the least costly way to produce the corresponding level of medical services in the long run when all inputs can be altered. Every short-run cost curve is tangent to the connecting or envelope curve, which is referred to as the long-run average total cost (LATC) curve. The curve drawn below the short-run average cost curves in Figure 7–8 represents a long-run average total cost curve.

Notice that the U-shaped long-run average cost curve initially declines, reaches a minimum, and eventually increases. Interestingly, both the short-run and long-run average cost curves have the same shape, but for different reasons. The shape of the short-run average total cost curve is based on the law of diminishing productivity setting in at some point. In the long run, however, all inputs are variable, so by definition a fixed input cannot account for the U-shaped long-run average cost curve. Instead, the reason for the U-shaped LATC curve is based on the concepts of *long-run economies* and *diseconomies of scale*.

Long-run economies of scale refer to the notion that average costs fall as a medical firm gets physically larger due to specialization of labor and capital. Larger medical firms are able to utilize larger and more specialized equipment and to more fully specialize the various labor tasks involved in the production process. For example, people generally get very proficient at a specific task when they perform it repeatedly. Therefore, specialization allows larger firms to produce increased amounts of output at lower per-unit costs. The downward-sloping portion of the LATC curve in Figure 7–8 reflects economies of scale.

Another way to conceptualize long-run economies of scale is through the direct relation between inputs and output, or returns to scale, rather than output and costs. Consistent with long-run economies of scale is increasing returns to scale. **Increasing returns to scale** result when an increase in all inputs results in a more than proportionate increase in output. For example, a doubling of all inputs that results in three times as much output is a sign of increasing returns to scale. Similarly, if a doubling of output can be achieved without a doubling of all inputs, the production process exhibits long-run increasing returns, or economies of scale.

Most economists believe that economies of scale are exhausted at some point and diseconomies of scale set in. **Diseconomies of scale** result when the medical firm becomes too large. Bureaucratic red tape becomes common, and top-to-bottom communication flows break down. The breakdown in communication flows means management at the top of the hierarchy has lost sight of what is taking place at the floor level. As a result, poor decisions are sometimes made when the firm is too large. Consequently, as the firm gets too large, long-run average costs increase. Diseconomies of scale are reflected in the upward-sloping segment of the LATC curve in Figure 7–8.

Diseconomies of scale can also be interpreted as meaning that an increase in all inputs results in a less than proportionate increase in output, or **decreasing returns to scale**. For example, if the number of patient-hours doubles at a dental office and the decision maker is forced to triple the size of each input (staff, office space, equipment, and so on), the production process at the dental office is characterized by decreasing returns, or diseconomies of scale.

Another possibility, not shown in Figure 7–8, is that the production process exhibits constant returns to scale. **Constant returns to scale** occur when, for example, a doubling of inputs results in a doubling of output. In terms of long-run costs, constant returns imply a horizontal LATC curve, in turn implying that long-run average total cost is independent of output.

Shifts in the Long-Run Average Cost Curve

The position of the long-run average cost curve is determined by a set of long-run circumstances that includes the prices of all inputs (remember, capital is a variable input in the long run), quality (including technological change), and patient case-mix. When these circumstances change on a long-run basis, the long-run average cost curve shifts up or down depending on whether the change involves higher or lower long-run costs of production. For example, an increase in the long-run price of medical inputs leads to an upward shift in the long-run average cost curve. A cost-saving technology tends to shift the long-run average cost curve downward. Conversely, a cost-enhancing technology increases the average costs of production in the long run and shifts the LATC curve upward. Higher quality of care and more severe patient case-mixes also shift the LATC curve upward.

Long-Run Cost Minimization and the Indivisibility of Fixed Inputs

Long-run cost minimization assumes that all inputs can be costlessly adjusted upward or downward. For an input such as an hourly laborer, employment adjustments are fairly simple because hours worked or the number of workers can be changed relatively easily. Capital inputs cannot always be as easily changed, however, because they are less divisible. As a result, a medical firm facing a sharp decline in demand may be unable to reduce the physical size of its facility. For example, Salkever (1972) found that hospitals realize less than 10 percent of the desired cost savings per year.[13] Therefore, medical firms may adjust slowly to external changes, not produce in long-run equilibrium, and operate with excess capital relative to a long-run equilibrium point.

Figure 7–9 clarifies this point. Suppose that initially a dental clinic produces q_0 amount of output (say, dental patient-hours) with a facility size of 1,200 square feet, as represented by the curve $SATC_2$. This represents a long-run equilibrium point because the efficient plant size is chosen such that $SATC_2$ is tangent to the LATC curve at q_0; that is, q_0 is produced at the lowest possible long-run cost and 1,200 square feet is the efficiently sized facility. Now suppose output sharply falls to q_1 due to a decline in demand. Long-run cost minimization suggests that the dental firm will reduce the size of its facility to that represented by $SATC_1$ and operate at point a on the LATC curve. It might do this by selling the old facility and moving into a smaller one. Because it may take time to adjust to the decline in demand, the dental clinic may not operate on the long-run curve at q_1 (point a) but instead continue to operate with the larger facility as represented by point b on $SATC_2$. The dental clinic incurs higher costs of production as indicated by the vertical distance between points b and a in the figure.

Cowing and Holtmann (1983) derived a test to determine whether firms are operating in long-run equilibrium. Using a simplified version of Equation 7–12, we can write a long-run total cost (LTC) function as

(7–19) $$LTC = STVC(q, w, k) + r \times k,$$

where all variables are as defined earlier. According to Equation 7–19, long-run total costs equal the sum of (minimum) short-run total variable costs and capital costs. The level of short-run total variable costs is a function of, or depends on, the quantity of output, the wage rate, and the quantity of capital (and other things excluded from the equation for simplification).

---

13. As cited in Cowing et al. (1983, p. 265).

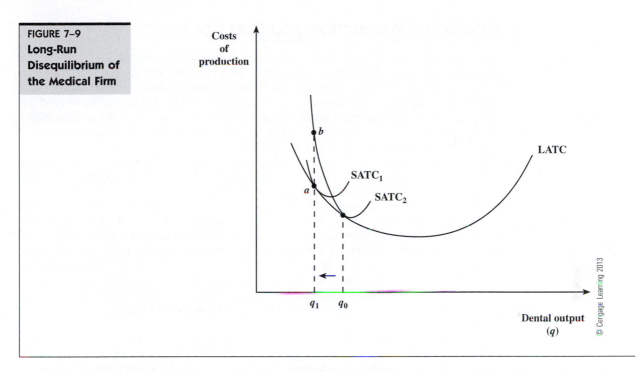

FIGURE 7–9
Long-Run Disequilibrium of the Medical Firm

A firm may not operate in long-run equilibrium because of the sizeable costs of adjusting to a sharp change in demand. For example, assuming that the dental clinic is initially producing in long-run equilibrium at q_0 and output sharply falls to q_1, it may take time for the dental clinic to downsize its capital facility. As a result, the dental clinic may operate with costs, point b, that are higher than that predicted by long-run equilibrium, point a.

According to Cowing and Holtmann, a necessary condition for long-run cost minimization is that $\Delta STVC/\Delta k = -r$.[14] The equality implies that the variable cost savings realized from substituting one more unit of capital must equal the rental price of capital in long-run equilibrium. That is, the marginal benefits and costs of capital substitution should be equal when the firm is minimizing the long-run costs of production. A nonnegative estimate for $\Delta STVC/\Delta k$ is a sufficient condition for medical firms to be overemploying capital. A nonnegative estimate implies that the cost of capital substitution outweighs its benefit in terms of short-run variable cost savings.

In their study, Cowing and Holtmann specified two fixed inputs: capital and the number of admitting physicians. As with capital, hospitals may operate with an excessive number of admitting physicians relative to a long-run equilibrium position. That is because the loss of one admitting physician can mean the loss of many more patients in the future. Cowing and Holtmann estimated the change in short-run total variable costs resulting from a one-unit change in capital and number of admitting physicians. Both estimates were found to be positive rather than negative. Thus, Cowing and Holtmann found that the "average" hospital in their New York sample operated with too much capital and too many physicians. Their empirical results suggest that hospitals could reduce their costs by limiting the amount of capital and controlling the number of physicians.

---

14. This equality can be derived by taking the first derivative of Equation 7–19 with respect to k and setting the resulting expression equal to zero.

Additional Production and Cost Concepts

A number of other factors can affect the costs of production and, therefore, the way a medical organization behaves in the short or long run. We already mentioned one of them, economies of scope, when we discussed the hospital cost study by Cowing and Holtmann (1983). Recall that economies of scope occur when it is less costly to produce two or more products jointly instead of producing them separately. Cost-savings might result from economies of scope if similar inputs, such as labor or capital, are used simultaneously in the production of the multiple products.

For example, suppose we are comparing two otherwise comparable medical device companies. The difference is that one company produces only one type of pacemaker, whereas the other, as a multiproduct medical device company, manufactures several types of pacemakers. If economies of scope hold in practice, then we can view the per-unit cost curves for producing that one type of pacemaker as being lower for the multiproduct company than the single-product medical device company. It is the cost-savings associated with the joint production that accounts for the lower per-unit costs for the multiproduct medical device company. However, in practice, diseconomies of scope may hold. For example, an organization could lose its focus when producing a number of related but still distinctly different products. If so, the loss of focus results in a lessening of productivity and a shifting upward of the per-unit cost curves of the multiproduct firm.

Learning-by-doing (or "practice makes perfect") is another factor that might affect observed cost differences among firms in the same industry. Learning-by-doing occurs when greater cumulative production over time results in lower per-unit costs of production or better quality for the same amount of costs. Note that "cumulative output" deals with more production over time, whereas scale economies relate to more output produced at a particular point in time such as a year. For example, a more experienced firm, which, say, has been in the industry for 10 years or more, may have a unit-cost advantage over a new startup company because it has more fully exploited the learning curve. The learning curve tends to be downward sloping at least over some range of cumulative output or years of practice. Perhaps, the more experienced firm has already fully learned the technical aspects of providing the service or producing the good, which has enabled the more experienced firm to raise its overall productivity. If that is the case, then the more experienced firm faces lower per-unit costs of producing the same product as the startup company at a particular point in time. Thus, the more experienced firm faces lower per-unit cost curves than the startup company.

However, it is important to remember that although "experience is a good teacher" (but sometimes rather harshly so), the learning curve likely flattens out at some point in time or after a certain amount of experience. That is, at some point, additional years or additional experience may matter little. Also, in some medical care industries, learning-by-doing may matter more than in others. For example, learning-by-doing may matter much more in the hospital than in the nursing home industry given the more complicated patient case-mix in the former than in the latter. Finally, it is also important to remember that markets are very dynamic. The experience learned today can easily become a disadvantage when new products and/or technologies enter the market.

Finally, the amount of **sunk costs** is another factor that potentially influences the behavior of medical care organizations. Sunk costs are past or historical costs that have already been incurred and cannot be avoided or recovered. For example, if a medical organization pays to construct a very specialized building that only suits its own purpose with little, if any, resale value, then the entire costs of that building, once constructed, represent sunk costs. Sunk costs generally do not affect marginal decisions regarding how much of a good or service to produce (or buy) because that type of decision is more prospective and looks at anticipated revenues and costs. For example, research and development (R&D) expenditures represent a sizeable sunk cost for pharmaceutical companies and likely do not affect how much of a drug that a drug company produces and sells once patented and commercialized. Later on in this book, however, we will learn that the prospect of sunk costs can affect the decision to enter a particular industry. Or, in the case of a drug firm, the prospect of R&D costs, may affect the decision to pursue innovation on a particular drug.

Neoclassical Cost Theory and the Production of Medical Services

The cost theory introduced in this chapter, typically referred to as *neoclassical cost theory* under conditions of perfect certainty, assumes firms produce as efficiently as possible and possess perfect information regarding the demands for their services. Based on the underlying theory, the short-run or long-run costs of producing a given level of output can be determined by observing the relevant point on the appropriate cost curve. However, when applied to medical firms, this kind of cost analysis may be misleading for two reasons.

First, some medical firms, such as hospitals or nursing homes, are not-for-profit entities or are reimbursed on a cost-plus basis or both. Therefore, they may not face the appropriate incentives to produce as cheaply as possible and, consequently, may operate above rather than on a given cost curve. Second, medical firms may face an uncertain demand for their services. Medical illnesses occur irregularly and unpredictably, and therefore, medical firms such as hospitals may never truly know the demand for their services until the actual events take place. Accordingly, medical firms may produce with some amount of reserve capacity just in case an unexpected large increase in demand occurs.

Although these two considerations may pose problems when conducting a cost analysis of medical firms, do not be misled into thinking that the material in this chapter is without value. That is clearly not the case. These two considerations are modifications that can and should be incorporated into the cost analysis when possible. Indeed, a strong grounding in neoclassical cost analysis under conditions of perfect certainty is necessary before any sophisticated analyses or model extensions can be properly conducted and understood.

Integrated Delivery Systems

As will be mentioned in Chapter 12, the autonomous, solo-physician clinic, once the mainstay organization in the physician industry, is being gradually replaced by the multiphysician group practice. Interestingly, the hospital industry is undergoing a similar transformation as many formerly independent hospitals are now becoming part of multihospital chains or systems. These horizontal mergers among individual physician practices and among individual hospitals take place largely because increased market power is being pursued (see Chapter 8) or because of economies of scale, economies of scope, and the other cost advantages associated with larger health care systems, as previously discussed.

Another organizational arrangement that takes place in the health care sector that involves both the hospital and physician industries is the integration of physician practices with hospitals. According to Robinson (1997, p. 6), "The **integrated delivery system (IDS)** combines physicians and hospitals into a vertically integrated organization with a single ownership and structure, a single chain of authority, and a single bottom line." There are basically four types of IDSs: the physician-hospital organization, the management service organization, the foundation model, and the integrated health organization, although other hybrid organizational forms also exist. These alternative physician-hospital arrangements differ in the degree to which risk, governance, revenue and capital, planning, and management are shared (Burns and Thorpe, 1993). An IDS may include nursing homes, home health care units, and an insurance component in addition to physicians and hospitals.

IDSs have developed in large part due to the financial pressure from MCOs, which in recent years have exercised their growing power to control costs. A movement by the government toward fixed payment systems, such as the prospective payment system for hospitals and the resource-based relative value scale system for physicians, also served as an impetus for change (Burns and Thorpe, 1993; Morrisey et al., 1996).

Why vertically integrated systems are formed is a question that interests economists, among others. Economists generally analyze organizational arrangements through the "conceptual lens" of agency theory and transaction cost economics (Robinson, 1997; Shortell, 1997). **Agency theory** considers the contractual relationships among parties. According to agency theory, the principal, or owner(s), of the firm enters into a multitude of contracts, either implicitly or formally, with other firms or agents who are the suppliers of inputs. Each contract stipulates the input or product that will be provided, the price that will be paid, and other terms of the agreement, such as product quality and time of delivery. Consequently, agency theory regards the firm as a nexus of many contracts. Within the agency model, the firm essentially serves as a facilitator and coordinator of the many contracts and is responsible for transforming the resulting inputs into an output or multiple outputs. The contractual relationships provide the firm with considerable flexibility to switch among input suppliers when better terms of exchange, such as a lower price or better product quality, become available.

But if agency theory perfectly describes the firm, why do we observe some firms producing inputs internally rather than contracting out for them? For example, why do some hospitals possess their own maintenance staffs, MRI facilities, or nursing home units while others contract out for these same services?

Transaction costs economics provides a reason why firms choose to produce inputs or services internally rather than contracting out. Transaction costs refer to the costs associated with the negotiating, writing, and enforcing of contracts and includes the costs of searching out the best price and quality. Transaction cost theory considers that many contracts are incomplete because not all possible contingencies can be written into a contract. Bounded rationality, especially in the face of uncertainty, is one reason for incomplete contracts. Bounded rationality refers to the limited capacity of the human mind to formulate and solve problems (Williamson, 1985). When contracts are incomplete, some stipulations require renegotiation. During the renegotiation process, one of the parties may have an advantage and the advantage can lead to **opportunistic behavior.** Opportunistic behavior involves self-interest seeking with guile and allows for strategic behavior or deception. The potential for opportunistic behavior increases the cost of contractual relationships.

As an example, suppose a hospital contracts with a company to repair the masonry around the bricks on the exterior of its buildings for $17,000. The company rents and installs the necessary scaffolding and begins the repairs. Upon closer inspection, however, the repair crew realizes that a good proportion of the repair is unnecessary and informs the hospital administrator. Naturally, the hospital administrator asks how much of the $17,000 will be returned. The contractor relates that the scaffolding must be rented for a minimum of one month. The contractor also mentions that transporting, installing, and disassembling the scaffolding is very costly. As you can see, the contractor is in a good position to practice opportunistic behavior by inflating the cost figures. Who would have thought to stipulate a contingency of that kind in the contract?

Transaction cost theory suggests that firms sometimes find internal production more efficient than outsourcing due to the relatively high cost of contracting. The theory by itself, however, suggests that firms should continually find it optimal to vertically integrate through greater internal production or by merging with suppliers. Obviously there must be some limiting factors; otherwise, only one firm would exist in every industry.

The same agency relationship discussed earlier places a limiting factor on the size of firms. Like outside contractors, employees and management are bound to the firm through implicit or formal contracts. For example, employees are expected to show up for work on time and perform well; otherwise, their jobs may be in jeopardy. While ownership of the nonhuman assets gives the firm more control over internal negotiations than external ones (Hart, 1995), greater firm size may lead to higher production costs at some point. As a firm grows physically larger, it becomes increasingly more complex and costly for the owners to monitor the behavior of management and employees. Inefficient behavior may arise as a result of the high monitoring costs.

For example, consider a large corporation in which the principal is represented by the stockholders, and the chief executive officer (CEO) serves as the primary agent. Stockholders, desiring high dividends and stock value appreciation, want the CEO to maximize profits. The CEO, however, may attempt to pursue goals other than maximum profits, especially when he is paid a fixed salary. For example, the CEO may use some of the firm's profit to pay for plush office accommodations, a limousine, or various other expensive perquisites. Alternatively, the CEO may be more interested in empire building and, therefore, may acquire several other less profitable companies rather than maximize profits. As a result, the corporation may perform poorly because of the CEO's actions. The CEO, however, may blame general economic conditions, and therefore, the unknowing stockholders may not punish the CEO for the unprofitable behavior.

As another example, salaried employees, particularly when they work as a team, may shirk their responsibilities, engage in on-the-job leisure time, and free-ride on the productive efforts of others. If a sufficient number of those on the team behave similarly, team output suffers and profits decline. The larger the organization, the greater the cost of monitoring the efforts of management and employees because of the proportionately greater interactions among workers (Carlton and Perloff, 1994).

To prevent internal agents, such as CEOs or employees, from operating in an unproductive manner, agency theory suggests that compensation might be tied to performance or profits so as to align the interests of the principal and agents. For example, the CEO's pay may be linked to the profits or stock value of the company. CEOs often receive bonus pay and stock options as part of their total compensation for that reason. The contracts help align the interests of the principal and agents so the interests of the principal are better served. It is important to note, however, that employment contracts are not always complete, so inefficient behavior may result as the firm continues to produce increasingly more services internally rather than purchasing them in the marketplace. Organizational independence, in contrast to internal production, preserves the risk and rewards for efficient performance (Robinson, 1997).

As another limit on firm size, managerial diseconomies may set in as the firm gets too large because of bounded rationality. Managers at the top may lose sight of the production process taking place at the floor level. Communication flows from top to bottom may break down. Bureaucratic inertia may also set in as regimentation replaces innovation and risk taking is not properly rewarded. The loss of control, breakdowns in communication, and loss of innovativeness may all place limits on the size of the firm.

As long as decision makers act rationally, each firm can be expected to choose the size where marginal benefit equals marginal cost. A greater amount of internal production creates benefits because of reduced transaction costs but also may come at a cost as larger firms become more costly and complex to monitor and innovation suffers. The costs of contracting and monitoring differ from firm to firm and from industry to industry. Some firms find market exchange more efficient than internal production at the margin. Transaction costs depend on various factors, such as the degree of market uncertainty, the number of suppliers in the market, and how often the service or input must be obtained. In general, when market conditions are more uncertain, the number of suppliers is fewer and frequency of use is greater, transaction costs are greater, and internal production becomes more efficient than contracting out.

You are probably asking yourself how the discussion of agency theory and transaction cost economics relates to physician-hospital integration. Hospitals and physician practices vertically integrate or fail to vertically integrate for the same reasons as other organizations do. Vertical integration leads to lower transaction costs but can impose incentive problems in large organizations. Robinson (1997) expands on this theme by noting that a contractual relationship between a hospital and physicians can be thought of as **virtual integration.** The term *virtual integration* is just a convenient way of stating that a combination of two or more organizations takes place through contractual relationships rather than through unified ownership. Robinson goes on to compare the relative advantages of vertical and virtual integration with regard to coordination, governance, and clinical innovation, three key activities in a hospital-physician relationship.

Coordination deals with how the individual parts are woven into an overall productive unit. For example, are the various services that combine to form medical care, such as lab tests, imaging, physician care, and inpatient hospital services, all coordinated through one large, unified structure or through two or perhaps more contractual relationships? At the extreme, authority and induced loyalty and commitment might be used to coordinate care in a unified model, while negotiation may be relied on in a purely contractual network (Robinson, 1997; Shortell, 1997). For example, a hospital may offer to process the bills of a physician or to purchase and then rent a medical facility to a physician as a way of achieving better coordination through contracting. As another example, hospital and physician services might be better coordinated by allowing more physicians to serve on the hospital's board of trustees.

Governance considers who controls the firm's policies and how much flexibility the firm has to adapt and modify its policies when confronted with changing external events. An important aspect of governance is whether the decision-making process is centralized or decentralized and whether it is dependent on for-profit or not-for-profit objectives. Decentralized governance tends to provide more flexibility, but vertical arrangements between decentralized for-profit and not-for-profit organizations may not last because of a clash of missions (e.g., the virtual integration of a Catholic hospital with a physician practice providing abortion services).

Clinical innovation is a function of the entrepreneurial, risk-taking spirit. At the one extreme, virtual integration involves arm's-length agreements with little sharing of financial risks. At the other extreme, vertical integration, hospitals and physician groups might jointly share in the financial risks of the organization through an ownership stake. One issue here is how the resulting organizational arrangement affects the incentive of the firm to minimize costs and undertake innovative activities. For example, Robinson (1997) notes that when "physicians sell their practices and merge into larger systems, they risk losing the entrepreneurial, risk-taking spirit and developing the civil service mentality of the hospital employee" (p. 17). The incentive attenuation might be overcome, however, by providing the physician with an ownership stake in the larger system or by paying performance-based compensation.

Shortell (1997) points out that vertical and virtual arrangements can be thought of as a continuum with respect to the essential activities of coordination, governance, and clinical innovation. In the real world, integration is rarely at either extreme but instead is somewhere along the virtual-vertical continuum. Along the coordination continuum, for example, a corporate joint venture falls somewhere in the middle of contracts and unified ownership. Under a joint venture, a hospital and physician group might remain legally separated but agree to jointly coordinate some single type of patient care, for example. A joint task force or committee represents an intermediate governance structure. A Physician Hospital Organization, in which a hospital and physicians jointly own and operate ambulatory care projects or jointly act as an agent for managed care contracts, provides an example of an organizational structure that falls halfway along the clinical innovation continuum.

Shortell further notes that organizations position themselves along the various continuums depending on the demands of the local marketplace for a coordinated health care system, the organization's own capabilities, and the historical context of the organization. For example, if the local market demands a perfectly seamless, coordinated health care system, the unified ownership of vertical integration will be favored over the contractual relationship.

Many analysts initially anticipated that IDSs would lead to improved financial performance for hospitals as well as encourage greater quality of care through coordinated delivery systems. But only about 23 percent of all hospitals participated in some kind of physician-hospital arrangement in 1993 and much vertical disintegration has occurred since that date (Morrisey et al. 1996; Burns and Pauly, 2002). Vertical disintegration most likely occurred because studies failed to find any systematic evidence linking IDSs with greater financial performance (Goes and Zhan, 1995). Burns and Pauly (2002) argue that hospitals and physicians entered into vertical arrangements for reasons that conflict with economic logic.

Provisions of the Patient Protection and Affordable Care Act (PPACA) of 2010 Relating to Medical Care Production and Costs

It stands to reason that nearly every provision in the PPACA influences medical care costs in some way or another. Here we are only interested in those provisions that directly influence the way in which medical care is delivered or medical care production is organized. Encouraging the creation of **accountable care organizations** (ACOs) is one of the most significant provisions of the PPACA affecting the delivery of medical care. In fact, Gold (2011) writes that: "Accountable Care Organizations take up only seven pages of the massive new health law yet have become one of the most talked about provisions."

Like an integrated delivery system, an ACO comprises a network of physicians and hospitals that share responsibility for treating patients. These ACOs may be paid on a fee-for-service or capitation basis. While the former reimbursement method is more likely, in both cases an ACO would receive bonuses under the Medicare program for providing cost savings while achieving predetermined quality benchmarks. The bonuses are expected to create an incentive for all health care providers to cooperate and perform less unnecessary tests and procedures. ACOs are expected to improve upon the largely fragmented health care system in the United States by providing patients with continuity of care and by emphasizing prevention and the managing of chronic diseases. Some ACO-like institutions already exist in the United States, but many more are expected to be launched after January 2012.

One major concern is that these ACOs may not only involve the vertical integration of various health care providers such as physician clinics, hospitals, and rehabilitation facilities, but also result in the horizontal integration of competitors (Berenson et al., 2010; Richman and Schulman, 2011). If the latter occurs, ACOs may achieve some market power and, therefore, the ability to raise their prices. We consider the issue of market power in Chapter 8. For now, let us point out that the limited empirical evidence on the vertical integration of physicians and hospitals does not point to market power effects (Ciliberto and Dranove, 2006). Also, recall from our previous discussion on IDSs that studies have not found any statistical evidence suggesting that integrated health care delivery systems actually "deliver" on their promised cost savings.

Summary

In this chapter, we focused on characteristics and concepts pertaining to the costs of producing medical services. First, we examined the underlying production behavior of a single medical firm. The short-run production function that resulted from this examination relates productivity to input usage. Among the more important principles we examined was the law of diminishing marginal productivity, the notion that the marginal and average productivities of a variable input first increase but eventually fall with greater input usage because a fixed input places a constraint on production.

Second, we discussed the inverse relation between productivity and costs. Simply stated, increasing marginal and average productivities translate into decreasing marginal and average variable costs. Conversely, declining productivities imply higher per-unit costs of production. As a result, the average variable cost curve is U shaped, implying that the average variable cost of production first decreases with greater production but at some point begins to increase as output expands. Taking the property of fixed costs into consideration, we also derived a U-shaped short-run average cost curve, which relates average operating costs to the amount of medical services produced.

Finally, we examined some concepts relating to long-run costs of production, including economies and diseconomies of scale. We also discussed the determinants of the optimal input mix, learning-by-doing, economies of scope, and sunk costs.

Review Questions and Problems

1. Suppose you are to specify a short-run production function for dental services. What inputs might you include in the production function? Which would be the variable inputs and which the fixed inputs?
2. In your own words, explain the law of diminishing marginal productivity. Be sure to mention the reason this law tends to hold in the short run.
3. Explain the difference between technical efficiency and economic efficiency.
4. Discuss the relation between the marginal and average productivity curves and the marginal and average variable cost curves.
5. What does the elasticity of substitution illustrate? How is it expressed mathematically? What two factors affect its magnitude?
6. Explain the difference between the explicit and implicit costs of production. Cite an example of each.
7. Suppose that with 400 patients per year, the SAFC, SATC, and SMC of operating a physician clinic are $10, $35, and $30 per patient, respectively. Furthermore, suppose the physician decides to increase the annual patient load by one more patient. Using short-run cost theory, explain the impact of this additional patient on the SAVC and SATC. Do they increase or decrease? Why?
8. What factors shift the SAVC and SATC curves? Explain why these curves would shift up or down in response to changes in these factors.
9. Suppose you are to specify a STVC function for a nursing home. Explain the variables you would include in the function. What is the expected relation between a change in each of these variables and STVCs?

10. What does *economies of scope* mean? Provide an example.
11. Explain the reasoning behind the U shape of the long-run average total cost curve. Why might this cost curve shift upward?
12. You are responsible for hiring one of two hygienists for a dental office. The first dental hygienist has 25 years of experience. Given her record, he is likely to satisfactorily service 16 patients per day. Her hourly wage would be approximately $16 per hour. The other hygienist is new to the industry. He is expected to satisfactorily service 10 patients per day at an hourly wage of $8. Which dental hygienist would be the better hire? Why?
13. Santerre and Bennett (1992) estimated the STVC function for a sample of 55 for-profit hospitals in Texas (*t*-statistics are in parentheses below the estimated coefficients).

$$\ln \text{STVC} = 1.31 + 0.47\ln q + 0.80\ln w + 0.73\ln \text{QUALITY} + 0.11\ln \text{CASEMIX}$$
$$\quad (0.69) \quad (3.31) \qquad (4.42) \qquad (2.58) \qquad\qquad (1.48)$$

$$+\ 0.29\ln k + 0.07\ln \text{DOC} + \text{Other factors}$$
$$\quad (3.16) \qquad (0.88)$$

Adj. $R^2 = 0.95$
$N = 55$

where STVC = short-run total variable cost, q = a measure of output (total inpatient days), w = average wage rate or price of labor, QUALITY = a measure of quality (number of accreditations), CASEMIX = an indicator of patient case-mix (number of services), k = a measure of capital (beds), and DOC = number of admitting physicians. All variables are expressed as natural logarithms (ln), so the estimated coefficients can be interpreted as elasticities.
   A. How much of the variation in STVC is explained by the explanatory variables? How do you know that?
   B. Which of the estimated coefficients are not statistically significant? Explain.
   C. Does the estimated coefficient on output represent short-run economies or diseconomies of scale? Explain.
   D. What are the expected signs of the coefficient estimates on w, QUALITY, and CASEMIX? Explain.
   E. Provide an economic interpretation of the magnitude of the estimated coefficient on w.
   F. What do the estimated coefficients on k and DOC suggest about the amount of capital and physicians at the representative hospital?
14. Draw a U-shaped LATC curve. Then draw the related long-run marginal cost (LMC) curve, keeping in mind the geometric relation between marginal cost and average cost (see the discussion on short-run cost curves). What is the relation between LATC and LMC when increasing returns to scale are present? Between LATC and LMC when the production process exhibits decreasing returns to scale? What type of returns to scale holds when LMC equals LATC?
15. Describe the two limitations associated with the cost theory provided in this chapter when it is applied to explain the behavior of medical firms.
16. Suppose that you are interested in comparing the costs of producing inpatient services at Saving Grace Hospital with those at ACME Hospital. Further suppose that the two hospitals annually admit about 24,000 and 32,000 patients, respectively, at average STCs per admission of roughly $11,000 and $12,000.

A. Why may these average STC figures not represent the economic cost of providing inpatient services at these two hospitals? Explain fully.

B. Suppose that these cost figures accurately reflect the economic costs of providing inpatient services at these two hospitals and that the two hospitals face the same average total cost curve. Draw a graphical representation of the average total cost curve (only) and graphically show and verbally explain why ACME Hospital produces at a higher cost than Saving Grace Hospital.

C. Using cost theory as presented in the text, identify and fully discuss four other factors that might explain why ACME Hospital has higher average costs of production than Saving Grace Hospital.

D. Fully explain how the comparative analysis becomes muddled if one considers that one (or both) of the two hospitals is not organized on a for-profit basis.

17. Why may vertically integrated delivery systems lead to lower production costs? Why may these systems lead to higher costs? Use agency theory and transaction cost economics in your explanation.

Online Resources

To access Internet links related to the topics in this chapter, please visit our website at **www.cengage.com/economics/santerre**.

References

Berenson, Robert A., Paul H. Ginsburg, and Nicole Kemper. "Unchecked Provider Clout in California Foreshadows Challenges to Health Reform." *Health Affairs* 29 (April 2010), pp. 699–705.

Burns, Lawton R., and Mark V. Pauly. "Integrated Delivery Networks: A Detour on the Road to Integrated Health Care?" *Health Affairs* 21 (July/August 2002), pp. 128–43.

Burns, Lawton R., and Darrell P. Thorpe. "Trends and Models in Physician-Hospital Organization." *Health Care Management Review* 18 (fall 1993), pp. 7–20.

Carlton, Dennis W., and Jeffrey M. Perloff. *Modern Industrial Organization*. Reading, Mass.: Addison-Wesley, 1994.

Chiang, Alpha C. *Fundamental Methods of Mathematical Economics*. New York: McGraw-Hill, 1984.

Ciliberto, Federico and David Dranove. "The Effect of Physician-Hospital Affiliations on Hospital Prices in California." *Journal of Health Economics* 25 (2006), pp. 29–38.

Cowing, Thomas G., and Alphonse G. Holtmann. "Multiproduct Short-Run Hospital Cost Functions: Empirical Evidence and Policy Implications from Cross-Section Data." *Southern Economics Journal* 49 (January 1983), pp. 637–53.

Cowing, Thomas G., Alphonse G. Holtmann, and S. Powers. "Hospital Cost Analysis: A Survey and Evaluation of Recent Studies." In *Advances in Health Economics and Health Services Research*, Vol. 4, eds. Richard M. Schefflier and Louis F. Rossiter. Greenwich, Conn.: JAI Press, 1983, pp. 257–303.

Goes, James B., and Chun Liu Zhan. "The Effects of Hospital-Physician Integration Strategies on Hospital Financial Performance." *Health Services Research* 30 (October 1995), pp. 507–30.

Gold, Jenny. "ACO is the Hottest Three-Letter Word in Health Care." *Kaiser Health News*, March 31, 2011, http://www.kaiserhealthnews.org/Stories/2011/January/13/ACO-accountable-care-organization-FAQ.aspx, accessed October 19, 2011.

Hart, Oliver. *Firms, Contracts, and Financial Structure*. Oxford: Clarendon Press, 1995.

Jablon, Robert. "Health Merger Worries Consumer, Doctor Groups." *The Providence Journal*, July 9, 2005, p. B3.

Jensen, Gail A., and Michael A. Morrisey. "The Role of Physicians in Hospital Production." *Review of Economics and Statistics* 68 (1986), pp. 432–42.

Kirchheimer, Barbara. "Ga. Hospitals to Combine." *Modern Healthcare*, December 11, 2000.

Morrisey, Michael A., Jeffrey Alexander, Lawton R. Burns, and Victoria Johnson. "Managed Care and Physician/Hospital Integration." *Health Affairs* 15 (winter 1996), pp. 62–73.

Richman, Barak D. and Kevin A. Schulman. "A Cautious Path Forward on Accountable Care Organizations." *Journal of the American Medical Association* 305 (February 2011), pp. 602–603.

Roberts, Rebecca R., et al. "Distribution of Variable vs. Fixed Costs of Hospital Care." *Journal of the American Medical Association* 281 (February 17, 1999), pp. 644–49.

Robinson, James C. "Physician-Hospital Integration and the Economic Theory of the Firm." *Medical Care Research and Review* 54 (March 1997), pp. 3–24.

Salkever, David. "A Microeconomic Study of Hospital Cost Inflation." *Journal of Political Economy* 80 (November 1972), pp. 1144–66.

Santerre, Rexford E., and Dana C. Bennett. "Hospital Market Structure and Cost Performance: A Case Study." *Eastern Economic Journal* 18 (spring 1992), pp. 209–19.

Schmidt, Julie. "Merck Bids $41.1B for Schering-Plough." *USA Today*, March 9, 2009.

Shortell, Stephen M. "Physician-Hospital Integration and the Economic Theory of the Firm: Comment." *Medical Care Research and Review* 54 (March 1997), pp. 25–31.

Williamson, Oliver E. *The Economic Institutions of Capitalism*. New York: Free Press, 1985.

CHAPTER 8

Structure, Conduct, Performance, and Market Analysis

"Genentech's Activase Faces Competition from New Set of Blood-Clot Dissolvers" (*Wall Street Journal*)

"Market Forces Are Starting to Produce Significant Cuts in Health-Care Costs" (*Wall Street Journal*)

"Price Competition Hits Hospitals" (*Hartford Courant*)

"Yes, the Market Can Curb Health Costs" (*Fortune*)

In Chapter 3, we discussed the efficient allocation of resources in the context of a benevolent surgeon general in a hypothetical economy. We learned, from a theoretical perspective, that an efficient allocation of resources occurs when each good and service is produced at the point where marginal social cost equals marginal social benefit. Taking the discussion a step further, Chapter 4 pointed out that actual decisions in the real world concerning resource allocation may be conducted at a centralized or decentralized level.

Continuing with this line of reasoning, this chapter develops a theoretical framework to examine how resource allocation takes place in a decentralized medical marketplace. That is, instead of a benevolent dictator, the decisions of individual consumers and producers allocate society's scarce resources among various goods and services. The analysis allows the marketplace to take on varying degrees of competition.

At the top of this page are a number of headlines from the popular press extolling the existence and virtues of competitive markets for medical services. The belief many people hold in the ability of competitive markets to efficiently allocate resources should not surprise anyone schooled in economics. According to traditional microeconomic theory, perfect competition creates a "survival of the fittest" market mentality and thereby forces firms to satisfy consumer wants and produce with least-cost methods of production. If competition has the power to weave this same magic in medical markets, incentives exist for medical firms to offer high-quality, cost-effective medical products at the lowest possible prices. With health care costs comprising such a significant percentage of national income, competitive behavior among medical firms might be a welcome sight in today's health economy.

But are the various features normally associated with perfect competition applicable to medical care industries? Do the characteristics necessary for a perfectly competitive framework hold in medical markets? If some particular medical industries closely resemble the perfectly competitive model, how are markets expected to behave according to economic theory? What happens to market outcomes if markets are not perfectly competitive? This chapter answers these questions.

Specifically, this chapter:

- introduces the structure, conduct, and performance paradigm of industrial organization
- discusses the structural characteristics of perfect competition, monopolistic competition, oligopoly, and monopoly

- shows how a perfectly competitive market determines the price and quantity of a good or service, allocates resources, and corrects for shortages and surpluses
- examines the characteristics of pure monopoly
- compares and contrasts perfect competition and pure monopoly with respect to resource allocation
- discusses intermediate market outcomes between the polar extremes of perfect competition and pure monopoly
- provides a conceptual and empirical framework for defining the relevant market, measuring market concentration, and identifying market power.

Structure, Conduct, and Performance Paradigm

When conducting an industry study, many economists rely on the structure, conduct, and performance (SCP) paradigm developed in industrial organization (IO), a field of economics interested in the behavior of firms and markets. Figure 8–1 illustrates the major elements that constitute the SCP paradigm. The first of the three important elements in the IO triad, **market structure**, establishes the overall environment or playing field within which each firm operates. Essential market structure characteristics include the number and size distribution of the sellers and buyers, the type of product offered for sale, barriers to entry, and whether any asymmetry of information exists between buyers and sellers. Entry barriers reflect any increased costs that new firms must incur relative to existing firms when entering a particular market. As we will see in this chapter, high costs may deter entry. Product type considers whether firms in the same industry produce standardized or differentiated products. As we will learn, differentiated products are less substitutable and may thereby reduce the level of actual competition observed in an industry. Also notice in Figure 8–1 that market structure often differs across industries because of variations in basic conditions, including the underlying technological base, the legal environment, demand conditions, and economies of scale and scope. All of these basic conditions tend to affect the number and size distribution of firms in an industry.

Market conduct, the second element, shows up in pricing, promotion, and research and development activities. Whether a firm decides its policies independently or in conjunction with other firms in the market has a crucial impact on the conduct of the industry. The third element, **market performance**, feeds off conduct and is reflected in the degree of production and allocative efficiencies, equity, and technological progress.

Overall, the IO triad predicts that the structure of an industry, in conjunction with the objectives of firms (see Figure 8–1), determines the conduct of the firms, which in turn influences market performance. While significant feedback effects exist among the three elements, the overriding implication of the model is that the structure of the market indirectly affects industrial performance through its impact on the market conduct of individual firms. An underlying belief of the SCP analysis is that society values greater efficiency and technological progress, and fairness in the distribution of income. If unfettered markets do not produce desired levels of performance, the general idea is that public policies should be aimed at correcting this failure of the market. For example, public policies may involve restructuring or regulating an industry. For this reason, public policies also show up in the SCP paradigm of Figure 8–1.

Microeconomic theory offers the theoretical connection between market structure and performance as discussed more fully in this chapter. The theory argues that profit-seeking firms are usually driven by competitive market forces to serve the interests of society by efficiently allocating scarce resources—the well-known invisible hand of Adam Smith. When competitive market forces are absent or weak because firms acquire **market power**, profit seeking may lead to a misallocation of society's

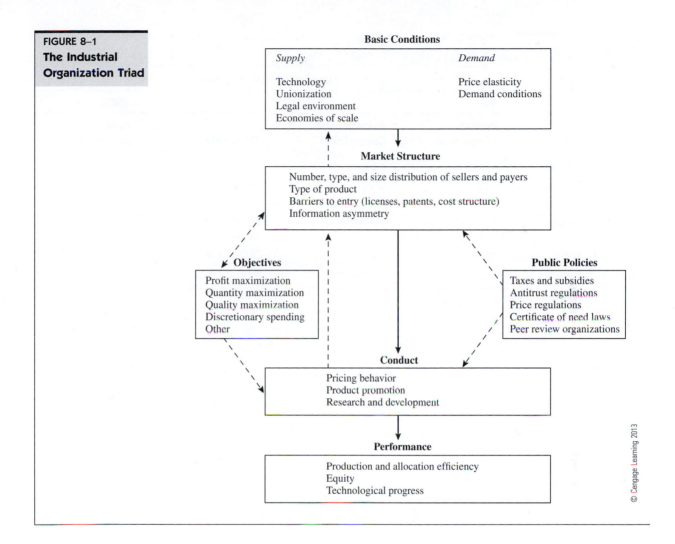

FIGURE 8–1
The Industrial Organization Triad

Basic Conditions

Supply	*Demand*
Technology	Price elasticity
Unionization	Demand conditions
Legal environment	
Economies of scale	

Market Structure

Number, type, and size distribution of sellers and payers
Type of product
Barriers to entry (licenses, patents, cost structure)
Information asymmetry

Objectives

Profit maximization
Quantity maximization
Quality maximization
Discretionary spending
Other

Public Policies

Taxes and subsidies
Antitrust regulations
Price regulations
Certificate of need laws
Peer review organizations

Conduct

Pricing behavior
Product promotion
Research and development

Performance

Production and allocation efficiency
Equity
Technological progress

© Cengage Learning 2013

resources. Market power refers to the firm's ability to restrict output (or quality) and thereby raise price. The amount of market power held by an individual firm or a collection of firms is a matter of degree and is dictated by the various characteristics that make up market structure. Table 8–1 presents the various structural characteristics that interact to affect the degree of market power possessed by firms. Across the top of the table, the degree of market power is measured from 0 to 100 percent. The next row gives four market structure classifications commonly identified by economists, from the most (perfect competition) to the least (pure monopoly) competitive. The body of the table lists the major characteristics of each type of market structure.

According to Table 8–1, the characteristics of **perfect competition** are many sellers possessing tiny market shares, a homogeneous product, no barriers to entry, and perfect buyer information. The characteristics of many sellers with tiny market shares and homogeneous products, taken together, mean that a considerable amount of **actual competition** exists in the industry because many substitute firms offer identical products. No barriers to entry suggest that the threat of **potential competition** is high because nothing prevents new firms from entering the industry. For example, a single supplier of frozen pizzas may be reluctant to increase prices if the resulting higher

TABLE 8–1
Market Structure and Market Power

	Degree of Market Power			
	0%	...		100%
Characteristics	Perfect Competition	Monopolistic Competition	Oligopoly	Pure Monopoly
Number of sellers	Many	Many	Few, dominant	One
Individual firm's market shares	Tiny	Small	Large	100%
Type of product	Homogeneous	Differentiated	Homogeneous or differentiated	Homogeneous by definition
Barriers to entry	None	None	Substantial	Complete
Buyer information	Perfect	Slightly imperfect	Perfect or imperfect	Perfect or imperfect

© Cengage Learning 2013

profits entice new firms offering frozen pizzas to enter the market. The high degree of both actual and potential competition in a perfectly competitive market indicates that a single firm lacks any market power.

Monopolistic competition refers to a market that has many sellers possessing relatively small market shares, a product that is somewhat differentiated across firms, no barriers to entry, and some slight imperfections concerning consumer information. Numerous sellers and no entry barriers imply that a single monopolistically competitive firm may also lack market power. However, a monopolistically competitive firm may gain some power over output and price in a niche market because of its differentiated product.

A few dominant firms and substantial barriers to entry characterize an **oligopoly**. Given the relatively large size of each firm and protection from new firms because of high barriers to entry, oligopolistic firms either individually or collectively may be able to exercise market power. However, competition among the few dominant firms, provided collusion does not take place, has the potential of harnessing each firm's behavior. Finally, the least competitive market structure is a **pure monopoly**, in which one firm is the sole provider of a product in a well-defined market with complete or perfect barriers to entry. These circumstances offer the greatest potential for a single firm to exploit its market power in a socially undesirable manner.

To gain a better appreciation of the differences among these four market classifications and their impact on performance, we next examine the polar cases of perfect competition and monopoly. After this discussion, we'll study the intermediate cases of monopolistic competition and oligopoly.

Is a Perfectly Competitive Market Relevant to Medical Care?

People who have had little exposure to the study of economics tend to have different ideas about what perfect competition entails. To some, perfect competition means that each firm in the marketplace strives to attain the greatest market share by charging low, cutthroat prices. Others believe that perfectly competitive firms compete for customers through advertisements or preferred locations. Perfect competition, however, is an abstract concept—a model—and therefore involves the five conditions specified in Table 8–1. It also involves the assumptions of utility and profit maximization that underlie conventional microeconomic analysis. That is, standard or neoclassical microeconomics assumes buyers maximize utility, pay the market price for the good, and firms maximize profits. If any one of these characteristics or assumptions is violated, firms and markets are unlikely to behave as the perfectly competitive model predicts.

When applied to medical care industries, many of the assumptions behind conventional microeconomic analysis and characteristics of perfect competition often do not fit well. Several examples highlight this point. First, the not-for-profit status of many medical enterprises means that health care providers may not pursue maximum economic profits. Second, physician licensure creates an occupational barrier to entry and may shield highly salaried physicians from new competition. Third, consumers do not pay the full-market price for the good because of insurance coverage. Finally, consumers typically lack perfect information about the prices and technical aspects of many medical services. Lack of information places health care providers in a strong position to practice opportunistic behavior.

While deviations from the assumptions of microeconomics and characteristics of perfect competition occur in practice, we believe the model serves a number of important functions. First, the supply and demand model, which is based on perfect competition, often provides a useful framework for explaining or predicting changes in the price and quantity of some good or service at the market level, particularly when the markets are "reasonably" competitive. In fact, we will see that rising health care costs over time in the United States (and elsewhere) can be explained quite well by a supply and demand model of medical care. Second, the perfectly competitive market outcome serves as a valuable benchmark with which to compare market outcomes under noncompetitive conditions. For example, in this chapter we compare the monopoly outcome to the perfectly competitive outcome in terms of the price charged and quantity of output produced. In later chapters, we relax other assumptions associated with the perfectly competitive model, even the profit maximization assumption, and compare that outcome to the perfectly competitive one.

A Model of Supply and Demand

As mentioned previously, perfect competition is based on a model in which a large number of buyers maximize their personal utilities and many producers individually maximize their economic profits. The massive number of buyers and sellers results in each individual buyer and seller acting as a **price taker**. By definition, a price taker can buy or sell as much quantity as it wants without affecting market price. To maximize (personal) utility, the typical buyer continues to buy units of a good or service up to the point where marginal private benefit, MPB, as revealed by demand, equals market price. Similarly, the representative profit-maximizing firm continues to produce and sell units of a good or service up to the point where market price equals marginal private cost, MPC. Consequently, a perfectly competitive market clears at the level of output where the marginal private benefit to buyers equals the marginal private costs to producers, with market price serving as a coordinating device. We can use a graphical version of a supply and demand model to illustrate the market-clearing process.

Suppose the supply and demand model in Figure 8–2 represents the market for generic aspirin. The per-unit price of generic aspirin, P, is specified on the vertical axis, and the quantity of generic aspirin, Q, is shown on the horizontal axis. The market demand curve, D, is downward sloping, reflecting the substitution and income effects normally associated with a lower relative price for a product, as discussed in Chapter 5. The demand curve also shows the diminishing marginal private

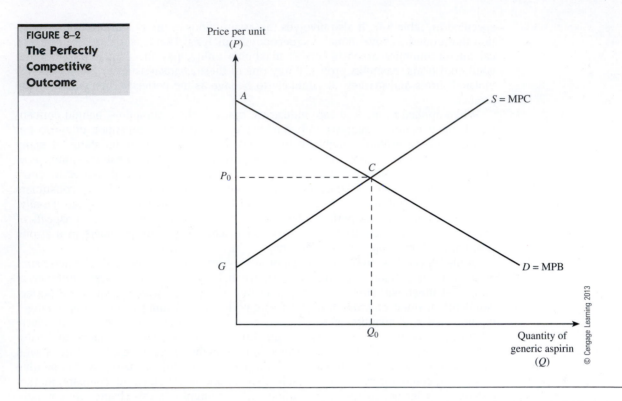

**FIGURE 8–2
The Perfectly
Competitive
Outcome**

Market demand, D, represents the marginal private benefit, MPB, associated with the consumption of various units of a good. MPB is downward sloping to reflect the law of diminishing marginal utility. Market supply, S, reflects the marginal private cost, MPC, of production and is upward sloping to reflect the law of diminishing marginal productivity. Equilibrium in a perfectly competitive market occurs at the intersection of supply and demand. The triangular area P_0AC represents consumer surplus and the triangular area P_0CG captures producer surplus. Total social surplus equals the triangle ACG and shows that both buyers and sellers mutually gain from free trade.

benefit that consumers receive from additional tablets of aspirin. The supply curve, S, is upward sloping, indicating that marginal private cost increases with respect to the production of additional tablets of aspirin. Marginal private cost reflects the variable costs of production that individual firms incur from hiring labor and purchasing materials. As noted in Chapter 7, marginal private cost typically increases in the short run because of a capacity constraint caused by a fixed input (such as the size of the production facility or amount of equipment). Because of the rising marginal cost, a higher price is necessary to encourage producers to produce and sell more aspirin.[1]

The equilibrium, or market-clearing, price and output of aspirin are at the point where demand intersects with supply or where quantity demanded equals quantity supplied. By definition, equilibrium occurs when there is no tendency for further change. At the equilibrium price of P_0, consumers are willing and able to purchase Q_0 tablets of aspirin because that represents the utility-maximizing amount. In addition, manufacturers of aspirin wish to provide Q_0 tablets on the market at this price because that represents the profit-maximizing amount. Thus, both consumers and producers are perfectly satisfied with the exchange because both can purchase or sell their desired quantities at a price of P_0. The area under the demand curve but above price (triangle P_0AC) measures **consumer surplus**, reflecting the net benefit to

1. Recall from Economics 101 that each perfectly competitive firm, as a price taker, faces an infinitely elastic or horizontal demand for its product. Also recall that market supply is derived by horizontally summing across all firms the portion of the marginal cost curve that lies above the minimum point on the average variable cost curve.

consumers from engaging in free exchange. Consumer surplus shows the difference between what the consumer would be willing to pay and what the consumer actually has to pay over the relevant range of output. Similarly, the area below market price but above the supply curve (triangle P_0CG) represents **producer surplus**, signaling the net benefit to producers from participating in free trade. Producer surplus measures the difference between the actual price received by the seller and the required price as reflected in the marginal costs of production. The sum of consumer and producer surplus captures the total net gains from trade to both consumers and producers (triangle ACG).

Notice the similarity between the market supply and demand curves in Figure 8–2 and the marginal social benefit (MSB) and marginal social cost (MSC) curves of Figure 3–2, where we learned that an efficient allocation of resources occurs in an economy when MSB equals MSC for each and every good. The similarity between the two figures should not be surprising because consumers and producers constitute an important part of society in a market economy. If demand and supply represent the full marginal social benefit and cost of the exchange, that is, if MPB = MSB and MPC = MSC, a perfectly competitive market results in allocative efficiency in the process of individual consumers maximizing their private utilities and individual producers maximizing economic profits. Under these conditions, decentralized decision making in the marketplace automatically results in allocative efficiency when markets are perfectly competitive.

However, an inefficient allocation of resources may result in a perfectly competitive market when others, in addition to market participants, are affected either beneficially or adversely by a market exchange. Inefficiency results because utility-maximizing consumers and profit-maximizing producers consider only their marginal private benefits and costs and not the full social impact of their choices. It is likely that allocative efficiency results for our generic aspirin example because others besides the consumers and producers of aspirin are normally unaffected by that exchange. We take up externalities and public goods, two situations where a perfectly competitive market may fail to allocate resources efficiently, in Chapter 9. We also learn later in this chapter that a monopoly fails to efficiently allocate resources.

Comparative Static Analysis

The supply and demand model can be used to examine how surpluses and shortages of goods temporarily develop, as well as to study changes in the price and quantity of goods and services in the marketplace. Using the model to study changes in price and quantity is referred to as **comparative static analysis**. Comparative static analysis examines how changes in market conditions influence the positions of the demand and supply curves and cause the equilibrium levels of price and output to adjust. As the demand and supply curves shift, we can trace out price and output effects by comparing the different equilibrium points. Comparative static analysis can be used to explain the effects of market changes in the past or to forecast future market outcomes.

As discussed in Chapter 5, several factors, such as the number of buyers, consumer tastes, income, and the prices of substitutes and complements, affect the position of the market demand curve. Similarly, various factors, including input prices and technology, determine the position of the supply curve by affecting the costs of production (see Chapter 7). A change in any one of these factors shifts the corresponding curve and alters the price and output of goods and services in the marketplace.

For example, suppose buyer income increases by a significant amount. Assuming aspirin represents a normal good, the higher income causes the demand curve to shift to the right. In Figure 8–3, notice that as the demand curve shifts to the right, a temporary shortage of EF is created in the market for aspirin if price remains constant.

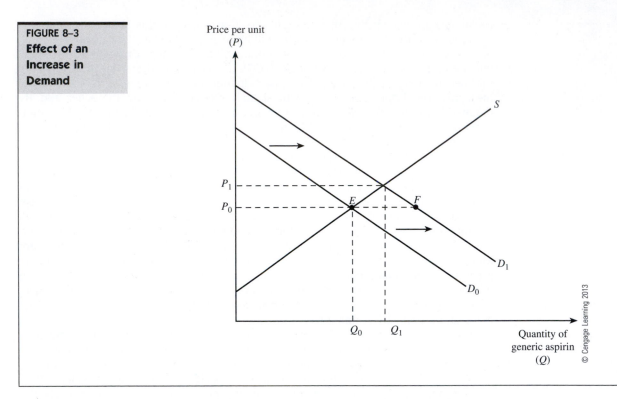

FIGURE 8–3
Effect of an Increase in Demand

© Cengage Learning 2013

A change in demand causes a change in the equilibrium price and quantity of a good. Here the demand increases from D_0 to D_1 because of an increase in buyer income, assuming that generic aspirin is a normal good. As a result, a temporary shortage equal to the horizontal distance EF is created in the market at the existing price of P_0. Eventually price increases in the market from P_0 to P_1 in response to the increase in demand. Quantity also increases from Q_0 to Q_1.

A shortage develops because at the initial price, the quantity demanded on the new demand curve, D_1, exceeds the quantity supplied of aspirin. However, price does not remain constant in a competitive market and is eventually bid up from P_0 to P_1. The higher price creates an incentive for manufacturers to offer more aspirin in the marketplace, and quantity supplied increases from Q_0 to Q_1. The higher prices also create an incentive for buyers to purchase less aspirin than originally planned at point F, perhaps by switching to alternative painkillers, consuming only half of a tablet per use, or postponing their consumption. Thus, under normal conditions, supply and demand analysis predicts that a higher price and quantity of aspirin are associated with greater buyer income, *ceteris paribus.*

As another example, suppose aspirin manufacturers adopt a cost-saving technology that increases supply. Therefore, the supply of aspirin shifts to the right, as shown in Figure 8–4. If the price of aspirin remains at P_0, a surplus of AB results because quantity supplied exceeds quantity demanded. In a competitive market, however, the surplus creates an incentive for the price of aspirin to decline from P_0 to P_1. Consequently, the quantity demanded of aspirin increases from Q_0 to Q_1 as price declines and buyers face an incentive to purchase more aspirin. At the same time, the quantity that producers are willing to supply falls when price declines toward equilibrium. These actions result in a new equilibrium and market-clearing price and quantity. Thus, supply and demand analysis predicts that the adoption of a cost-saving technology causes price to decline and quantity to increase, assuming all else remains constant.

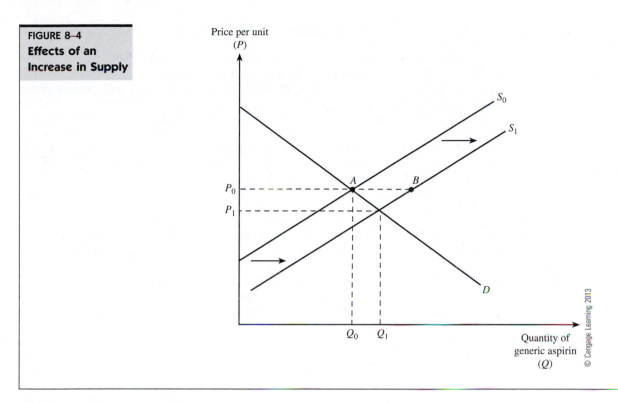

FIGURE 8–4

Effects of an Increase in Supply

A change in supply causes a change in the equilibrium price and quantity of a good. Here the supply increases from S_0 to S_1 because of the introduction of a cost-saving technology. As a result, a temporary surplus of horizontal distance AB is created in the market at the existing price of P_0. Eventually price decreases in the market from P_0 to P_1 in response to the increase in demand. Quantity increases from Q_0 to Q_1.

Notice in the previous discussion that price serves several important functions. First, price provides useful information to both buyers and sellers regarding the relative availability and value of a good or service in the marketplace. Second, price serves as a coordination device, bringing the actions of buyers and sellers into harmony and helping to clear markets. Third, price serves as a rationing device, distributing the goods or services to the buyers who value them the most. Fourth, price acts as an incentive mechanism, encouraging more resources to markets with shortages and less resources to markets with surpluses of goods.

A Note on Long-Run Entry and Exit in a Perfectly Competitive Market

The analyses thus far have concerned short-run adjustments because the number of firms in the market has remained unchanged. But entry and exit of firms may take place in the long run as sellers take advantage of changing profit opportunities in various markets. For example, since there are no barriers to entry in a perfectly competitive marketplace, excess profits create an incentive for new firms to enter an industry as they strive to make a higher than normal rate of return. Conversely, economic losses create an incentive for firms to leave an industry as they try to avoid an unusually low rate of return on their investment. Finally, when normal profits exist in a perfectly competitive industry, the market is in long-run equilibrium and firms have no incentive to either enter or exit the industry. **Normal profits** result when there are just enough revenues to cover the opportunity cost of each and every input, including a normal return to capital.

Long-run entry in response to excess profits can be treated as shifting the short-run market supply curve to the right. Similarly, long-run exit causes the short-run market supply curve to shift to the left. Given a stable demand curve, these adjustments in the short-run supply curve create a change in the price of the good and eventually restore a normal profit situation. In particular, long-run entry lowers price and eliminates excess profits, whereas exit leads to higher prices and eliminates the economic losses of the firms that remain in the industry. Because of entry and exit, we can expect that the typical perfectly competitive firm earns a normal profit in the long run.

The importance of long-run adjustments in a market can be illustrated by the following example. In the mid-1980s, physicians, dentists, and other health care providers became concerned about contracting the AIDS and hepatitis B viruses in the work environment. This concern caused a considerable increase in the demand for form-fitting disposable latex gloves, which are preferred over vinyl gloves because they allow flexibility for detail work and are impermeable to blood and body fluids. From 1986 to 1990, annual sales of latex gloves increased by approximately 58 percent (Borzo, 1991). Initially, as the demand for latex gloves increased, a tremendous shortage of latex gloves developed. As the shortage gave way to higher prices in the short run, medical supply manufacturers operated their plants around the clock in an attempt to make higher profits. Consequently, the shortage declined as price increased and created an incentive for increased production. Greater profit opportunities in this market created incentives for medical suppliers to construct new manufacturing plants to produce more disposable latex gloves. According to the popular press, at one point in 1988, 116 permits were pending in Malaysia for the construction of disposable latex glove factories (Zikos, 1988). These new plants provided for new entry and an increased supply of latex gloves in the long run.

This example helps highlight the importance of entry and exit in a marketplace. Entry of new firms leads to a greater allocation of resources in response to favorable profit opportunities. Likewise, exiting of firms helps eliminate relatively inefficient resources and producers from a market. Profit, in both cases, serves as an important incentive mechanism and brings about an efficient allocation of resources in the long run. Of course, entry and exit of firms can take place in perfectly competitive markets because entry and exit barriers are nonexistent. In the following discussion of monopoly, we will see that barriers prevent new firms from entering markets, resulting in an inefficient allocation of resources.

Using Supply and Demand to Explain Rising Health Care Costs

Supply and demand analysis offers many reasons why national health care expenditures in the United States exploded from 5.1 percent in 1960 to more than 16 percent of the nation's income during more recent times. Specifically, the demand for medical care increased because of rising income, an aging population, and a falling out-of-pocket price since 1960. In terms of the supply and demand model, all of these factors simultaneously created a shift in the demand curve to the right, causing a higher price and quantity of medical care over time. Expenditures on medical care, the product of price and quantity, also increased as a result.

On the supply side, Baumol (1967) points out that wages in service industries, like medical care, tend to increase with higher wages in the manufacturing sector. Higher wages in the manufacturing sector result from increased worker productivity caused by technological advances. Because wage increases in various medical care industries are directly tied to the growing manufacturing wage but are not necessarily matched with commensurate increases in productivity, per-unit costs of medical care are driven upward. In terms of supply and demand analysis, the supply curve for medical care has shifted to the left over time because of wages outpacing productivity. As a result, the price of medical care increased. And because the demand for medical care tends to be price inelastic, the increase in price caused health care expenditures to increase [see Hartwig (2008) for empirical evidence supporting this Baumol cost disease model].

Cost-enhancing technologies provide another explanation for rising health care costs on both the supply and demand sides of the market. Over the years, a number of new medical technologies, such as computer tomography (CAT) scans, magnetic resonance imaging (MRI), and organ transplant technology, have raised the quality and costs of providing health care services. New technologies tend to supplement rather than supplant old technologies in the medical field. The widespread adoption of these cost-enhancing (rather than cost-saving) technologies shifted the supply curve to the left, causing health care expenditures to rise given the price-inelastic demand curve. In addition, since these technologies often simultaneously create a demand for new treatments because they can help extend lives and are less risky, the demand curve also shifted to the right. Consequently, medical care expenditures increased due to the lower supply and greater demand caused by cost-enhancing technology.

In conclusion, rising income, an aging population, a declining out-of-pocket price, and the demand for new treatments helped fuel higher health care costs from the demand side of the market for medical care. From the supply side, the adoption of new technologies and higher wages also may have contributed to rising medical costs. Thus, supply and demand analysis can serve as a useful tool for explaining market changes even though the underlying assumptions do not perfectly conform to market realities.

The Monopoly Model of Market Behavior and Performance

If a firm has some market power, the competitive model is an inappropriate tool of analysis and a noncompetitive model should be employed. The difference between the two models concerns how the individual firm treats market price. In a perfectly competitive market, the individual firm is a price taker. That is, price is beyond the control of a single firm, so each time a perfectly competitive firm sells an additional unit of output, market price measures the additional revenues received. Economists refer to **marginal revenue** (MR) as the additional revenues received from selling one more unit of a good. Thus $P = MR$ for a price taker. A noncompetitive firm with some degree of market power, in contrast, faces a downward-sloping demand curve and thereby has some ability to influence the market price by reducing or restricting the quantity produced. To illustrate how a noncompetitive model can be used to examine firm behavior, we first consider a pure monopoly in which there is only one producer of a good or service in the entire market. A pure monopoly is the logical opposite of a perfectly competitive market. We will compare the equilibrium outcome for a monopoly to that of a perfectly competitive market.

Monopoly versus Perfect Competition

In precise terms, a monopoly is the sole provider of a product in a well-defined market with no close substitutes. Because it is the only firm in the market, a monopolist faces the market demand curve, which is always downward sloping because of the substitution and income effects associated with a price change. Given the downward-sloping demand, the only way the monopolist can increase quantity sold is to lower the price of the product. Assuming price is the same for all units sold at a point in time, price must be lowered not only for the additional unit but for the previous units as well.

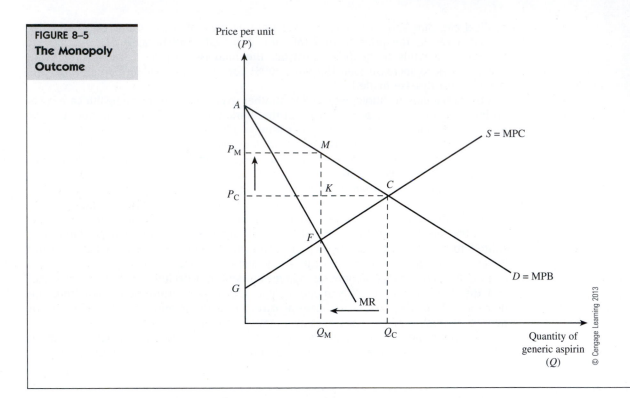

FIGURE 8–5
The Monopoly Outcome

© Cengage Learning 2013

This illustration compares the perfectly competitive and monopoly outcomes. The perfectly competitive outcome is represented by point *C*. A monopoly produces at Q_M where MR = MC and charges price P_M. Because a monopoly exists in the market, consumer surplus shrinks to the triangle $P_M AM$ and the producer surplus increases to the area outlined by $P_M MFG$. Reflecting that society's scarce resources are misallocated, a deadweight loss of area *MCF* is created by the monopolist.

As a result, marginal revenue will be less than price at each level of output. In fact, it can be shown for a linear demand that marginal revenue has the same intercept but twice the slope.[2]

Figure 8–5 can be used to show how the equilibrium price and quantity for a monopolist compare to the market price and quantity in an otherwise equivalent perfectly competitive market. As before, our example is the market for generic aspirin. The market demand for aspirin is labeled *AD*. The supply curve is labeled *GS* and reflects the marginal private cost of producing aspirin. (Ignore the curve AMR for now.) Point *C* represents equilibrium in a perfectly competitive market where the supply and demand curves intersect. The market price and output of aspirin equal P_C and Q_C, respectively. Consumer surplus equals the triangular area $P_C AC$ and producer surplus equals the triangular area $P_C CG$. The entire triangular area *ACG* reflects the net gain from trade in a perfectly competitive market.

Now suppose only one firm produces and sells aspirin in that same market. Perhaps the award of a government franchise provides the aspirin manufacturer with the monopoly position. Further suppose that an entry barrier, such as the government franchise, prevents other firms from entering the market. Relevant to the monopolist's choice of price and quantity is the marginal revenue curve labeled MR. Notice that

---

2. Suppose the (inverse) demand is captured by the equation $P = a - bQ$. Total revenues equal P times Q or $(a - bQ)Q = aQ - bQ^2$. Taking the first derivative of this revenue function with respect to Q to get dTR/dQ gives $MR = a - 2bQ$. Notice that MR has the same intercept but twice the slope of the demand.

marginal revenue shares the same intercept as the linear demand but has twice its slope. The monopolist chooses market price and quantity such that profits are maximized. Profit maximization occurs at the level of output, Q_M, where MR = MC because producing and selling additional tablets of aspirin always add more to revenues than costs up to that point. Beyond the Q_M level of output, additional production does not add to total profits because marginal cost exceeds marginal revenue. Consequently, the monopoly outcome is represented by point M and the price charged equals P_M.

Notice that a monopoly charges a higher price and produces less aspirin than a perfectly competitive market. Also notice that the monopolist receives some of the surplus that consumers receive in a perfectly competitive market. More precisely, consumer surplus shrinks from triangular area $P_C AC$ in a perfectly competitive market to triangular area $P_M AM$ in a market dominated by a monopoly. Producer surplus increases from area $P_C CG$ to area $P_M MFG$. The rectangular area $P_M MKP_C$ reflects the surplus transferred from consumers to producers in a market controlled by a monopoly. In addition to this redistribution of income is the deadweight loss created by a monopoly. Notice that the net gain from trade is much smaller in a monopoly market than in a perfectly competitive market. The difference is the triangular area MCF that reflects the deadweight loss created by a monopoly. The deadweight loss shows that the value of the units no longer produced is greater than the opportunity costs of the resources used to produce them. It follows that a monopoly underproduces output and thereby misallocates society's scarce resources. The societal cost of a monopoly shows up in the size of the deadweight loss.

Barriers to Entry

For a firm to maintain its market power for an extended period of time, some type of barrier to entry must exist to prevent other firms from entering the industry. As Haas-Wilson (2003, pp. 127–28) explains, "entry of new competitors will most likely occur in at least one of three ways: (1) Established firms in the local market, not currently selling X (for example, a physician organization of internists in the local market) may begin to sell X even though they had not done so in the past; (2) established firms currently selling X, but not in the local market (for example, a physician organization of pediatricians located in a distant city) may open a local office and begin to sell X in the local market; and (3) new business may start (for example, pediatricians establishing their first practices after completing their medical education). This entry of additional competitors and the associated increase in the availability of product X defeats the incumbent's attempt to exercise market power."

Barriers to entry make it costly for new firms to enter markets in a timely manner and may exist for technical or legal reasons. Exclusive control over a necessary input, sunk costs, an absolute cost advantage, and scale economies represent some technical reasons to suspect that entry barriers may exist in some market environments. If a firm has exclusive control over a necessary input, competitors are without the required resources to produce substitute products. Exclusive control over bauxite, a necessary input in the production of aluminum, provided Alcoa with a monopoly position in the 1940s. After losing its antitrust suit, Alcoa was required to sell some of its bauxite to two new competitors, Reynolds and Kaiser Aluminum, created by the government. Likewise, incumbent health insurers may have already developed exclusive contracts with various health care provider networks in an area. The difficulty of establishing a network of health care providers may make it difficult for a new insurer to sell its health plans in an area.

Sunk or irretrievable costs can result in a barrier to entry into an industry. Recall from Chapter 7 that sunk costs may take the form of specialized buildings and equipment, advertising, or the establishment of a reputation or brand name. Contestability theory suggests that markets are more contestable or potentially competitive when sunk costs are low because new entrants realize they can leave an industry relatively costlessly if economic circumstances do not turn out as initially suspected. Conversely, if sunk costs are significant, firms may be reluctant to enter new markets, *ceteris paribus*. Hence, the prospect of high exit costs can discourage firms from entering an industry. All other factors held constant, incumbent firms have less market power in "hit and run" industries in which sunk costs are low.

An absolute cost advantage arises when the incumbent firm can produce at a lower cost than potential competitors. Incumbents may be able to produce at a lower cost because suppliers offer them a price discount for materials as a result of the favorable reputation they have built up over the years. Incumbents can also benefit from learning-by-doing. As Chapter 7 points out, the greater cumulative output and experience translates into lower average costs of production for a given level of quality or a higher level of quality for a given level of costs. Absolute cost advantages can make it difficult or more costly for new firms to enter the market and effectively compete against incumbent firms.

Scale economies may also serve as an entry barrier. When production exhibits economies of scale, a firm operates on the downward-sloping portion of the long-run average total cost curve, ATC, and the average cost of production decreases as output expands, as shown in Figure 8–6. An existing firm in that situation has a cost advantage that results from the scale of production. Potential competitors could not effectively compete with the established firm on a cost basis. In fact, the larger existing firm with average costs of C_X could set its price slightly below the average cost of the potential entrant, C_E; earn profits; and discourage the potential entry from actually

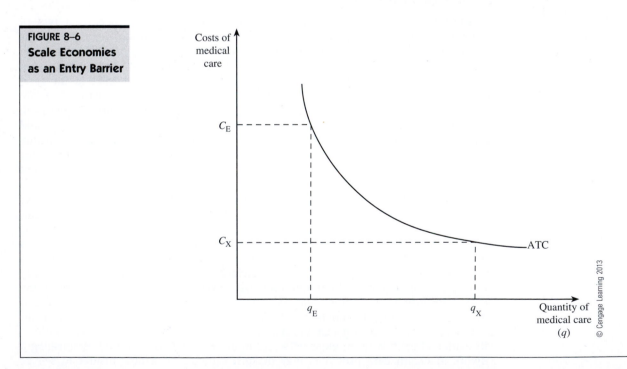

FIGURE 8–6
Scale Economies as an Entry Barrier

The declining average total cost curve, ATC, reflects scale economies in production. An existing firm producing a large volume of output at q_X produces at a cost of C_X. An entrant with a relatively small volume of output of q_E produces at a cost of C_E. Because of the scale economies, an existing firm can charge a price slightly below C_E and discourage a potential entrant from actually entering the market. This practice is referred to as limit pricing.

entering the market. Pricing to deter entry is called **limit pricing**. Thus, economies of scale can serve as a barrier to entry that insulates an existing firm from potential competitors. Price regulations are often necessary when a firm holds a monopoly position of this kind (e.g., TV cable service).[3]

Legal restrictions that prevent other firms from entering markets and providing services similar to those of existing firms can also serve as a barrier to entry. Legal patent protection provides a firm with a 20-year monopoly right to a product. As another example, prior to the late 1970s, the U.S. government purposely limited the number of firms in many industries, such as air transportation and long distance telephone services. However, deregulation took place in the late 1970s because many people were dissatisfied with the performance of these industries.

Drug patents, occupational licenses, and certificate of need (CON) laws are sometimes treated as examples of legal entry barriers into medical care markets. A CON law requires health care providers to obtain government approval before constructing new buildings or purchasing expensive capital equipment. Some feel that CON laws are necessary to prevent health care organizations from unnecessarily duplicating resources within an area. For example, a number of hospitals may simultaneously purchase and offer the same new, expensive piece of capital equipment to treat patients in an area. Because each of the various hospitals may be unable to sufficiently spread the large, fixed costs, given a limited number of patients in the area, the average cost per patient of using the expensive equipment is higher than if only one hospital purchased and offered services from the capital item.

Others argue, however, that CON laws unduly inhibit entry into medical care markets. Because of the restricted entry in a market area, health insurance plans are less able to negotiate competitive prices from the limited number of health care providers. The higher prices paid by health insurers reflect in part that incumbent firms can exploit their market power by reducing output and driving up medical prices because they feel less threatened by the prospect of potential competitors.

Not too many studies have empirically examined the impact of CON laws on the entry of medical firms into industries other than hospital services (see Chapter 13 for some of those). Among the few, Ford and Kaserman (1993) analyzed the impact of CON laws on the entry of new firms into the dialysis industry. Specifically, the authors used multiple regression analysis to explain entry into the dialysis industry across the 50 states of the United States over the period from 1982 to 1989. As independent variables, they specified a 0/1 dummy variable indicating whether a particular state possessed CON regulations regarding dialysis clinics in a particular year, along with a number of control variables. The control variables essentially captured the potential profitability of firms entering the dialysis industry in the 50 states and included various costs and demand-side factors. Recall that economic theory suggests increased entry takes place when profits are higher and entry barriers are lower. Among their results, Ford and Kaserman found empirically that the presence of CON laws significantly reduced the entry and expansion of dialysis firms. This finding led them to conclude that "CON regulation of the dialysis industry has sustained the monopoly power of incumbent clinics and thereby provided the wherewithal to increase profits by reducing service quality" (p. 790).

The Buyer Side of the Market

Up to now the buyer side has been treated as being highly fragmented because numerous price-taking buyers or consumers are assumed to operate in the market. Indeed,

---

3. Not all economists agree that scale economies serve as an entry barrier. Bain (1956) defines an entry barrier as any factor that allows sellers to elevate price above marginal costs. Stigler (1968) defines an entry barrier as costs that new entrants, but not incumbents, face. Therefore Bain treats scale economies as an entry barrier but Stigler does not.

this same situation continues to be assumed for the following discussion of intermediate market structures. However, in the real world, buyers can possess varying degrees of market power. If so, the competitive and monopoly market equilibriums may differ from those depicted in Figure 8–5. The exact outcome depends upon the relative bargaining power of the buyers and sellers in both of those markets.

We mention this possibility because most medical care is purchased or bought by institutional buyers, such as health insurers or the government, rather than by individual consumers. As a result, buyers may possess a great deal of bargaining power in some health care markets.

For example, the federal government certainly wields considerable buying power in the Medicare program. Moreover, state governments may have some influence on price when purchasing various types of medical care under the Medicaid program. Finally, some health insurers may be dominant in their local market areas. In fact, in Chapter 11, we will discuss the possibility of health insurers possessing "monopsony" power. Monopsony occurs when only one buyer exists in a particular market.

The possibility of the buyer side of the market being noncompetitive does not mean the previous discussion of market outcomes is without merit. All it means is that we must also examine the buyer side of the market when considering market outcomes in the real world. For instance, a powerful buyer or group of buyers may be able to offset or countervail the monopoly power of a seller and bring about a more competitive outcome in the marketplace. Thus, like the structural aspects of the seller side, we cannot ignore the structural aspects of the buyer side of the market.

Monopolistic Competition and Product Differentiation

Now that we have discussed the models of perfect competition and monopoly, we need to turn our attention to the other two models listed in Table 8–1. In a monopolistically competitive market structure, there are many firms and low or no barriers to entry. The distinguishing characteristic of monopolistic competition is that firms within the same industry sell a slightly differentiated product. The product differentiation may result from a preferred location, different levels of quality (either real or perceived), or advertising and other promotional strategies. Because of product differentiation, each firm faces a downward-sloping demand curve that is highly but not perfectly elastic. Since the demand curve is downward sloping, the monopolistically competitive firm has some limited ability to raise price without losing all of its sales. Product differentiation leads to a certain degree of brand loyalty, which is why the individual firm can raise price and continue to sell output. Everything held equal, a more differentiated product translates into a less elastic demand curve facing the monopolistically competitive firm.

Figure 8–7 illustrates a model of a profit-maximizing, monopolistically competitive firm. Notice the highly elastic demand curve facing the individual firm, reflecting the relatively large number but imperfect substitutes for its product. Bayer Aspirin may be a good example of a branded product that faces a downward-sloping demand. Bayer competes against many generic producers of aspirin but has a brand name that allows it to charge a higher price. Given the linear demand, the marginal revenue is drawn with the same intercept but has twice the slope. The long-run average total cost, ATC, and marginal cost, MC, curves allow economies and then diseconomies of scale.

Given the downward-sloping demand, the individual firm may earn an economic profit in the short run if the price charged is greater than average total cost at the level of output where marginal cost equals marginal revenue. However, the absence of any barriers to entry prevents excess profits from continuing in the long run in a monopolistically competitive industry. Over time other firms are attracted to the industry by the possibility of earning economic profits. As more firms enter the market,

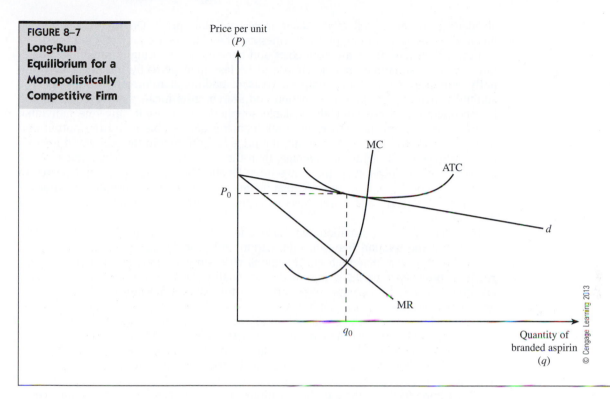

FIGURE 8–7

Long-Run Equilibrium for a Monopolistically Competitive Firm

A monopolistically competitive firm faces a downward-sloping demand curve because of product differentiation. Because there are no meaningful entry barriers, firms continue to enter the market until the representative firm earns only a normal profit. Hence, in the long run, the representative monopolistically competitive firm produces at q_0 where MR = MC and charges a price equal to average total costs.

each firm sees its market share slowly diminish, which translates into a decrease in the demand for its product. The demand curve faced by each firm continues to shift to the left as firms enter the market until the market price for the product is driven down to the point where economic profits are zero, or price equals average total cost. Demand becomes more elastic as well. At that point firms are no longer attracted to the industry and the market settles into a long-run equilibrium situation where economic profits are zero.

Figure 8–7 shows long-run equilibrium in a monopolistically competitive industry. Notice that the demand curve is tangent to the average total cost at the level of output where MR = MC. The monopolistically competitive firm earns zero profits in the long run because price or average revenue equals average total costs. Notice that the monopolistically competitive firm does not produce at the point where price equals marginal cost as does a perfectly competitive firm. As a result, one might argue that this type of industry inefficiently allocates resources. But before that conclusion can be drawn, we must first consider the costs and benefits of production differentiation and whether such things as advertising and brand names impede or enhance competition among firms.

Procompetitive and Anticompetitive Aspects of Product Differentiation

In the perfectly competitive model, buyers are treated as being perfectly informed about the prices and quality of all goods and services in the marketplace. The assumption that all buyers possess perfect information about prices implies that all identical products sell at the same lowest possible price. Otherwise, high-priced businesses lose sales to low-priced businesses when buyers are perfectly informed.

But, realistically, there are both costs and benefits to acquiring information. Therefore, in many situations, people choose to be less than perfectly informed, or **rationally ignorant**, because the marginal costs of additional information outweigh the additional benefits. Positive information and search costs mean that buyers may find it uneconomical to seek out all available suppliers. As a result, any one individual supplier faces a less than perfectly elastic demand and is able to restrict output and raise price to some degree. As a result, the price of a product in the real world is likely to be dispersed and higher, on average, than the competitive ideal (since theoretically prices cannot be lower than the competitive level). The average price and degree of price dispersion depend on the marginal benefits and costs of acquiring price information. Higher benefits and lower costs of acquiring information imply lower and less dispersed prices.

Imperfect buyer information may also affect the level of quality observed in a market, but the relation between information and product quality is more involved. It stands to reason that high-quality goods cost more to produce than low-quality goods. If buyers are perfectly informed, high-quality goods sell at a higher price than low-quality goods in a competitive market. In the real world with imperfect information, however, buyers are not fully knowledgeable about product quality. Consequently, if buyers base their willingness to pay on the average quality in the market and pay the average price, low-quality products drive out high-quality products, and the process continues until only low-quality products remain. The implication is that the level of product quality is higher when buyer information is more readily available.

Given imperfect information about various products in the real world, some economists argue that various features of production differentiation, such as advertising, trademarks, and brand names, convey important information regarding the value of a good or service. For example, they argue that advertising provides relatively cheap information to buyers about the price and quality of a good and thereby promotes lower prices and higher quality. In fact, studies by Benham (1972), Cady (1976), and Kwoka (1984) found that the prices of eyeglasses and prescription drugs were higher, on average, in areas where price advertising was prohibited. Even when price and quality information is not directly conveyed, a large advertisement in the local newspaper or on the internet, for example, may signal consumers that the firm is willing to incur a sizeable expense because it is confident that it is offering a quality product at a reasonable price. Through repeat buying, the firm hopes to get a sufficient return on its advertising investment. In this case, the mere presence of an expensive advertising message generates information about the value of a product.

Other economists such as Klein and Leffler (1981) argue that brand names and trademarks serve a similar purpose for promoting competition. Because the quality of many products cannot be properly evaluated until after purchase (or repeat purchase), brand names and trademarks help identify businesses that have enough confidence in the quality of their products to invest in establishing a reputation. Given the sunk-cost nature of the investment, the argument is that a business will not sacrifice its established reputation by offering shoddy products on the market and take the chance of losing repeat buyers. A firm that expends considerable sums of money to polish its image and establish a brand name can lose a valuable investment by selling inferior products and tarnishing that image.

However, not all economists agree that advertising, trademarks, and brand names are always procompetitive. Some economists are concerned that promotional activities are used to establish brand loyalty, mislead consumers, and thereby cause "habit buying" rather than "informed buying." In this view, promotional activities are anticompetitive and advertising is treated as being persuasive rather than informative.

Persuasive advertising attempts to convince consumers that the attributes of product A are better than those of product B. Sometimes the advertising message points out real differences, but often the advertising is used to create imaginary or perceived differences across goods or services. For example, both Bayer and generic brands contain the same aspirin ingredient, yet many people are willing to pay a higher price for the Bayer product. Some argue that people pay a premium for branded products because past advertising successfully convinced people that Bayer aspirin, for example, is a superior product. Instead of creating a new market demand, persuasive advertising attempts to attract consumers from competitor firms. Considering advertising, trademarks, and brand names as quality signals, Robinson (1988) points out "a signal can be heard as long as it stands out over and against the background level of noise. As each seller amplifies his or her signal, the background noise level rises, necessitating further amplification on the part of individual sellers. This is clearly undesirable from a social perspective because the signaling mechanism imposes costs" (p. 469).

According to the anticompetitive view, product differentiation manipulates the demand for a product. For example, a successful advertising campaign can influence consumer tastes and preferences and thereby affect the position of the demand curve for the product. Advertising may affect the position of the demand curve in two ways. First, the demand curve may shift upward as a result of successful advertising because consumers are now willing to pay a higher price for the firm's product. Second, advertising may cause the demand curve to become less elastic with respect to price and, as a result, give the firm some ability to reduce output and raise the price of the good or service.

Existing firms may also use advertising or other types of product differentiation to create barriers to entry. If existing firms can control consumers through advertising, for example, new firms have a difficult time entering a market because they are unable to sell a sufficient amount of output to break even financially. It follows that product differentiation directed toward creating artificial wants, habit buying, or barriers to entry results in a misallocation of society's scarce resources. Resources are misused if they are employed to create illusory rather than real value.

When evaluating the social desirability of product differentiation, it is useful to remember that all products are homogeneous within the abstract model of the competitive industry and that most people agree that variety is the spice of life. People like diversity and enjoy choosing among a wide assortment of services selling at different money and time prices. People also receive utility when buying goods of different colors, shapes, and sizes. In this vein, the higher-than-competitive price that is paid for product differentiation may simply reflect the premium consumers place on variety. Nevertheless, economic theory suggests that firms may use product differentiation as a way to increase demand in some situations. If supply creates demand in this manner, some of society's scarce resources may be wasted.

Oligopoly

Oligopoly involves a market structure with a few large or dominant firms and relatively high barriers to entry. While there may be a large number of firms in the industry, those other than the few dominant firms have relatively small market shares and act as price takers. The important aspect of oligopoly is that the dominant firms must be sufficiently sized and limited so the behavior of any one firm influences the pricing and output decisions of the other major firms in the market. It is this **mutual interdependence** among firms that distinguishes oligopoly from the other market structures. Because the nature of the interdependence varies, economists have been unable to develop a single model of oligopoly behavior. As a result, many formal and informal models of oligopoly have been developed that depict firm behavior under a variety of different scenarios. It is beyond the scope of this text to delve into all of these models, so we have limited the discussion to two broad models of firm behavior: the collusive and competitive models of oligopoly.

Collusive Oligopoly

According to the **collusive oligopoly** model, all the firms in the industry cooperate rather than compete on price and output and jointly maximize profits by collectively acting as a monopolist. To illustrate, assume that there are only three identical firms in a given market with similar demand curves and that these firms have decided to collude and jointly maximize profits. Under these circumstances, the firms collectively act like a monopolist and jointly set the price and output indicated by point *M* on the market demand curve in Figure 8–5. It follows that a deadweight loss and a misallocation of society's scarce resources results from the collusive oligopoly.

The collusion among the oligopolistic firms may be of an overt or a tacit nature. Overt collusion refers to a situation in which representatives of the firms formally meet, perhaps in a clandestine location such as a smoke-filled room, and coordinate prices and divide up markets. Tacit collusion occurs when firms informally coordinate their prices. The price leadership model represents an example of tacit collusion in which the firms in an industry agree that one firm will serve as a price leader. The rest of the firms in the industry simply match or parallel the price of the leader. The resulting conscious parallelism can theoretically produce the same monopoly outcome as overt collusion, and deadweight losses result (point *M* in Figure 8–5).

While it appears that firms in an oligopoly have a strong incentive to collude and form a cartel, a number of factors make collusion difficult. First and foremost are legal and practical considerations. The Sherman Antitrust Act prohibits overt collusion. Firms found in violation of overt price fixing can be subjected to severe financial penalties and the CEOs of these companies can be imprisoned.

However, antitrust officials, largely because of the difficulty of establishing proof, do not pursue cases involving tacit collusion. Firms in an industry may parallel their actions simply because they react to the same swings of demand and costs in the marketplace. But a tacit collusive arrangement has its practical difficulties. The informality of a tacit price-fixing arrangement can lead to problems because other firms in the industry may have a difficult time interpreting why the industry leader adjusts price. For example, suppose that the price leader decreases its price. Other firms in the industry can interpret this either as a simple reaction to an overall decrease in market demand or as an aggressive attempt on the part of the price leader to improve market share. In the first case, the other firms would simply lower prices and go about their business. In the second case, however, they may aggressively counteract this move by decreasing their prices even further in an attempt to initiate a price war.

Second, cost differences make it more difficult for firms to cooperate and agree on a common price. High-cost firms will desire a higher price than low-cost firms. But the success of a cartel depends on all of the firms adhering to a common price. Third, collusion is less successful when entry barriers are low. New firms offering lower prices will seize market share away from the cartel members when entry barriers are low. Fourth, for several reasons, collusion is more likely when few firms exist in an industry. One reason is that the ability to collude becomes more difficult as more firms enter into collusive agreement. Low negotiation costs make it much easier for two firms to collude than a dozen. Another reason is that more firms increase the probability that any one firm will act as a maverick and act independently by charging a lower price than others. Finally, more firms increase the probability that one firm may cheat or chisel on the agreement. For example, one firm may grant a secret price concession to a large buyer to improve sales. Naturally, when the other firms in the industry learn of this behavior they will abandon the collusive agreement and strike out on their own. The potential for cheating behavior is greater when more firms exist in the industry because of high monitoring and detection costs. For these four reasons, collusive agreements are more difficult to negotiate and maintain than most people imagine.

Competitive Oligopoly

Competitive oligopoly lies at the opposite extreme of collusive oligopoly. **Competitive oligopoly** considers that rivals in an oligopolistic industry may not coordinate their behavior but instead aggressively seek to individually maximize their own profits. If the firms in an oligopolistic market sell relatively homogeneous products, and thus one firm's product is a strong substitute for the others', each firm may realize that buyers will choose to purchase the product offering the lowest price. If so, each firm faces an incentive to lower its price to marginal cost because at that level it will at least share part of the market with the others and not be undersold. If oligopolistic firms act in a competitive manner like this, market output is produced at the point where price equals marginal cost and resources are efficiently allocated (point C in Figure 8–5), even though a few dominant firms exist in the industry.

Collusive or Competitive Oligopoly?

Whether firms act as a collusive or competitive oligopoly, or somewhere in between, depends on how each firm forms its beliefs or **conjectural variations** about how its rivals will react to its own price and output decisions. Conjectural variations consider how, say, firm A believes its rivals will react to its output decision. For example, firm A might believe that rivals will offset its behavior by producing more if it reduces output. Firm A has no incentive to restrict output given that market output and price remain the same because of offsetting behavior. On the other hand, firm A might believe that its rivals will react by matching its behavior and producing less. The matching behavior results in less market output and a higher price for the product. Thus, if firms form similar conjectural variations and each expects matching behavior, a point closer to point M in Figure 8–5 and the associated deadweight losses result. In contrast, if firms form similar conjectural variations and each expects offsetting behavior, a point closer to point C in Figure 8–5 and the related efficiency gains occur.

Economic theory indicates that firm characteristics and market conditions influence the conjectural variations held by oligopolistic rivals. Many involve the same characteristics and conditions mentioned earlier that affect the success of a collusive oligopoly. First, firms are more likely to expect matching behavior when fewer firms exist and entry barriers are high because each firm realizes the greater profit potential from engaging in matching behavior. For example, each firm receives 50 percent of the monopoly profits when only two firms exist in the industry, so greater expectations can be attached to matching behavior.

Rivals are more likely to expect matching behavior when they share social and historical ties. Social and historical ties consider such things as industry trade associations, maturity and growth of an industry, and the proximity of firms in an industry. Specifically, rivals are more likely to anticipate matching behavior in industries in which trade associations play an important role. Trade associations foster cooperative behavior by establishing common bonds and the sharing of information among firms. Anticipation of matching behavior is greater among rivals in older industries that are growing slowly. Less entry takes place and fewer new owners exist in older, slow-growing industries. New owners are more likely to act as independent mavericks and reduce the likelihood of matching behavior.

The proximity of firms in an industry considers how close firms are on a number of dimensions including location, products, technologies, and sources of capital. Rivals in closer proximity more likely share similar expectations. The organizational structure of the firms in an industry may also affect conjectural variations. More centralized firms respond slowly to market changes and thus may be biased toward cooperation and expecting matching behavior. Also, prices tend to be determined at the top of the hierarchy while output decisions are made at the lower levels in more centralized organizations. If firms within an industry possess similar centralized organizational structures, the hierarchical arrangement may lead to price rigidity but output flexibility. Lastly, bounded rationality may favor expectations of matching behavior among rivals. **Bounded rationality** refers to the limited ability of human behavior to solve complex problems. Bounded rationality may lead to rules of thumb for pricing in an industry and act as a facilitating device for firms to match or coordinate their behavior.

Oligopolistic Behavior in Medical Care Markets

The two different models just discussed indicate that oligopolistic firms are more likely to compete among themselves, rather than tacitly or overtly coordinate their policies, when firms are more numerous and entry barriers are lower, among other factors. Consequently we may witness only two firms in an industry and yet aggressive price competition because entry barriers are low, for instance. In contrast, another industry may be characterized by five firms that coordinate their policies because entry barriers are high and the firms share similar histories and common bonds. Sorting out the behavior of real-world oligopolistic firms typically requires a careful study that simultaneously controls for a host of conditions that impact how firms may react to each other's decisions.

With that caveat in mind, we illustrate a couple of real-world situations that portray two different medical care industries as reflecting the behavior of a competitive oligopoly. That is, the existence of rivals resulted in lower prices. The first example relates to the $2 billion blood banking industry during the late twentieth century. Interestingly, this case involves two dominant not-for-profit firms.

In the mid-1990s, American Red Cross held a 46 percent share of the nation's blood banking business. Its closest national rival, America's Blood Centers (ABC), an affiliation of local independent blood banks, controlled another 47 percent. Individual hospital blood banks across the nation collectively held the remaining 7 percent of the market. Despite their relatively equivalent national market shares, either American Red Cross or a local member of ABC enjoyed a monopoly position in many regional markets at that time because federal policy since the 1970s had sanctioned local blood monopolies.

However, in 1998, American Red Cross made a bold move to increase its national market share to 65 percent by entering various regional markets such as Kansas City, Dallas, and Phoenix, originally monopolized by one of the local members of ABC. Based on this aggressive behavior, a competitive oligopoly model appears to do a better job of predicting the behavior of these two dominant firms than does a collusive oligopoly model. Evidence indicates that a lower price of blood resulted in local markets where a member of ABC coexisted with American Red Cross than in markets where an independent operated alone. For example, the price of a unit of blood cells was about $60 in Florida, one of the nation's most cutthroat markets, and $105 in upstate New York, where competition was minimal (Hensley, 1998).

Our other example pertains to Johnson & Johnson (J&J), the well-known drug and medical device manufacturer. The relevant product in this case is a stent.[4] At the beginning of 1997, J&J was a dominant firm controlling 95 percent of the $600 million

---

4. A stent resembles a small metal mesh tube, no thicker than a pencil lead, which is squeezed onto a tiny balloon and threaded into the heart's arteries. At the blockage site, the balloon is inflated to expand and deposit the stent, creating a scaffolding device resembling a ballpoint pen spring that remains in place to keep the vessel open after the balloon is withdrawn. Blood can then flow through the previously blocked artery.

stent market through its patent protection. By the middle of 1998, the stent market had grown to yearly sales of $1 billion but J&J only held a meager 8 percent market share at that time! How could a company lose nearly 90 percent of its market share with a patented product over an 18-month span? It appears that J&J made a major blunder by failing to consider potential competition.

To be more specific, J&J angered key customers with rigid pricing for its $1,600 stent, refusing discounts even for hospitals that purchased more than $1 million worth of stents per year. With no comparable stent options, the buyers of stents had little alternative but to pay the high price. The high prices eventually caused cardiologists to pressure the Food and Drug Administration to approve new stents as quickly as possible. Physicians helped quicken the approval process by willingly testing the stents offered by new firms. Guidant Corporation took advantage of this new approval process and, 45 days after its patent was approved, controlled 70 percent of sales in the stent industry.[5]

The situations in the blood bank and stent industries, just discussed, reflect instances where general market conditions fostered price competition despite an oligopolistic environment in which only a few dominant sellers operate and substantial entry barriers likely exist. Perhaps, in the first case, it was difficult or costly for American Red Cross to establish communication or some type of bond with the various local affiliates of ABC, given their independent nature in different areas of the United States. In the second case, maybe J&J's maverick attitude prevented any formal or informal ties from developing with other stent companies.

While both of these examples provide evidence to support the competitive oligopoly model, it is important to note that a collusive oligopoly may be more relevant in other situations. For example, in May of 2010, several parties, including the Idaho Orthopaedic Society (IOS), Idaho Sports Medicine Institute (ISMI), and five orthopedists, as principal actors and IOS members, were accused of conspiring to gain more favorable fees by agreeing to coordinate their actions. At the time of the conspiracy (2006 to 2008), IOS consisted of approximately 75 orthopedists, each operating in a solo or group practice. At that same time, ISMI was an orthopedic practice group of which most of the doctors were members of IOS.

The suit against these defendants involved two conspiracies. For the first conspiracy, the defendants agreed, through a series of meetings and other communications that took place over a year-long period, not to treat patients covered by workers' compensation insurance. The conspirators agreed that their boycotting of the services would cause the Idaho Industrial Commission to raise their rates for orthopedic services (which would effectively increase the conversion factors for their resource-based relative value-system-determined fees). According to the suit *U.S. v. Idaho Orthopaedic Society, et al.* (2010, p. 4), "orthopedists and practice administrators regularly monitored adherence with the group boycott and pressured doctors to maintain a disciplined front." The agreed-upon group boycott eventually forced the Idaho Industrial Commission to increase the rates at which orthopedists are reimbursed for treating injured workers by 61 percent. Shortly after the rate increase, the doctors resumed participation in the workers' compensation program.

With respect to the second conspiracy, the accused parties agreed, again through a series of meetings and other communications, to threaten termination of their Blue Cross of Idaho (BCI) contracts for orthopedic services. In fact, between April and June 2008, 12 practice groups, representing 31 of 67 orthopedists in the Boise area and containing many IOS practices and the ISMI, gave BCI their termination notices. In response to the group boycott, BCI offered an additional contracting option. The new option allowed orthopedists to choose between continuing to participate in BCI's network at current rates for one year with the possibility of higher rates the next year or to lock in existing rates for a three-year period.

---

5. In fact, J&J announced its exit from the stent industry in June of 2011.

Unfortunately for the conspiring doctors, the new offer from BCI split apart the orthopedists in the Boise area. Even more damaging for them, the conspirators were unable to convince a large Boise practice to join the boycott against BCI. Thus, BCI was able to contract with a reasonable number of orthopedists and maintain a viable physician network. Realizing no further concessions from BCI would be made available, nearly all practice groups rescinded their termination notices within a month or so.

This example of a colluding oligopoly is interesting and relevant for a variety of reasons. First, we typically think of oligopolists as influencing private prices but here we see that colluding parties may also be able to influence government-set prices. Second, the example shows the importance of facilitating devices for the success of a cartel. Facilitating devices are commercial practices or institutions that a group of conspirators may use to make it easier to attain or stabilize an anticompetitive arrangement of some type. In particular, notice how IOS membership may have helped to facilitate the collusive arrangement because most of the orthopedists in the areas shared this common bond. Third, a collusive arrangement often fails at some point because members cheat or chisel on their agreement. Notice how the orthopedists' boycott against the workers' compensation insurance required regular monitoring to be successful. Fortunately for the conspirators, it didn't take the Idaho Industrial Commission very long to raise rates. Finally, economic theory suggests that a collusive arrangement will be less successful when more firms are involved. Recall how the disagreement over the new offer by BCI and the relatively large number of orthopedists in the area eventually led to the demise of the boycott in the second conspiracy case.

Defining the Relevant Market, Measuring Concentration, and Identifying Market Power

This chapter has focused on the theoretical relationship between market structure, conduct, and performance. We learned that the structural characteristics of a market influence how firms conduct themselves with respect to pricing and other business practices, which in turn affects the performance of the industry. Little regard, however, has been given to delineating the precise boundaries of a market. Hypothetically, we know that a market reflects a place where the buyers and sellers of a product, through their collective negotiations, determine the price and quantity of a good or service that is bought and sold. While a hypothetical definition may be fine for theoretically studying the welfare implications of various market structures such as monopoly, a more practical definition of the market is necessary when conducting real-world analysis for private and public policy purposes. If a market is defined too broadly (narrowly) in practice, firms will appear to possess less (more) market power than they actually hold.

Consequently, if we intend to apply the SCP model to better understand and predict market behavior and performance, determining the precise boundaries of a market becomes an important exercise. To begin with, we have to determine the precise product being bought and sold. We also have to figure out how many sellers of that particular product are located in the market area. We discuss next some of the theoretical issues and practical limitations involved when defining markets. We also consider how market concentration and market power are often measured in practice.

The Relevant Product and Geographical Markets

While hypothetically easy to imagine, a market is very hard to define in practice. Economists note that a market has two dimensions. The first dimension, the **relevant product market (RPM)** considers all of the various goods and services that a set of buyers might switch to if the price of any one good or service is raised by a nontrivial amount for more than a brief amount of time. Obviously, these goods and services must share some similarity or substitutability in terms of satisfying demand. For instance, general and family practitioners are likely to substitute for one another, whereas urologists and pediatricians are not because the latter two types of physicians fulfill different demands. As another example, suppose clinic-based physicians raise their fees by 5 percent or more and hold them at that level for at least a year. If a reasonable number of insurers, as the buyers of physician services, respond to this nontrivial and nontransient price increase by adding the outpatient facilities of hospitals to their network of ambulatory care providers, then services of clinic-based and hospital-based doctors can be considered as offering goods and services in the same RPM. If insurers do not switch, then hospital outpatient facilities most likely cannot be considered to be in the same RPM as clinic-based services.

The **relevant geographical market (RGM)** represents the second dimension of the market. The RGM establishes the spatial boundaries in which a set of buyers purchase their products. A RGM may be local (physician, nursing home care, acute hospital care, and dialysis services), regional (tertiary care hospitals, health insurance), national (prestigious medical academic centers) or international (pharmaceuticals, medical devices) in scope. For example, a hospital in Utica, New York, is unlikely to compete with a hospital in Hartford, Connecticut (about 205 miles away) for the same patients or insurers, but it may compete with a hospital in Rome, New York (about 16 miles away). Similar to determining the RPM, the conceptual exercise is to imagine all of the sellers of the same good or service that a set of buyers might switch to as a result of a nontrivial, nontransient price increase (or quality decrease). The RGM is then defined to include all of the seller locations to which buyers might switch. For example, suppose dental practices in Ivy Towers raise their prices by 5 percent or more and the price increase is expected to last indefinitely. If consumers and insurers are observed switching to dental practices in communities other than Ivy Towers, then all of the dental practices in all of those communities to which the buyers switch should be included in the RGM.

Although its practical relevance is limited, this conceptual exercise of a nontrivial, nontransient price increase is helpful because it tells us that we cannot necessarily rely on current purchasing practices when defining the relevant market for different types of medical care. For example, suppose several health insurers have contracts for all of their ambulatory care needs with three independent group physician practices in an area. Now suppose that these three independent group practices announce that they plan to merge their organizations in the upcoming year. If only current purchasing arrangements are relied on, we might be led into believing that the consolidated physician practice would result in monopoly pricing. However, that may not be the case if the insurers can switch to other providers of ambulatory care in that same immediate area or switch to providers outside the immediate area. The availability of substitutes can be expected to inhibit the newly consolidated practice from raising price. In fact, it is conceivable that the consolidation of the three physician clinics might actually benefit the community if scale economies exist and lower, rather than higher, prices result.

In any case, it should be evident that determining the scope of the RGM and the RPM remains more of an art than a science. Typically, analysts refer to current purchasing practices and expert opinion when determining the current willingness of buyers to substitute among products and among sellers at different locations. They also must consider that other substitute products and sellers at different locations may be available but are not yet economical at existing prices. Their mere existence, however, prevents current sellers from raising price. We must also remember that new suppliers help maintain reasonable prices when entry barriers are low and they can easily and quickly enter markets.

Measuring Market Concentration

Suppose we are reasonably comfortable with our definition of the relevant market for a good or service after considering both its product and geographical dimensions. Further suppose that we want to measure the degree of **market concentration** as reflected in the number and size distribution of the firms within an industry. For instance, we learned that perfectly competitive markets are characterized by a large number of firms with tiny market shares, whereas a few dominant firms characterize an oligopolistic industry. We want to capture the structural aspect of an industry with a relatively simple statistic, with the general idea that a market can be viewed as being more highly concentrated when fewer firms produce a larger share of industry output.

Economists typically offer the concentration ratio and the Herfindahl-Hirschman index (HHI) as measures of market concentration. The concentration ratio identifies the percentage of industry output produced by the largest firms in an industry. The four-firm concentration ratio, CR_4, which is the most common, equals the sum of the market shares of the four largest firms. Industry output is often measured in terms of sales, volume of output, or employment. The CR_4 ranges between 0 and 100 percent, with a higher value reflecting that the largest four firms account for a larger share of industry output or, alternatively stated, that the industry is more highly concentrated. For example, a CR_4 of 60 percent indicates that the four largest firms account for 60 percent of all industry output.

Over the years, economists have assigned labels to industries depending on their four-firm concentration ratios. An industry with a CR_4 of 60 percent or more is considered to be tightly oligopolistic, whereas an industry with a CR_4 between 40 and 60 percent is labeled as a loose oligopoly. Industries with a CR_4 of 40 percent or less are treated as being reasonably competitive. However, some words of caution: these industry classifications consider only the number and size distribution of firms. As we learned earlier, other market conditions, such as the height of any entry barriers, should also be considered when evaluating the relative structural competitiveness of an industry.

When data are available only for total industry output and the output produced by the few largest firms but not for the rest of the firms in an industry, a concentration ratio must be used to gauge the degree of industrial concentration. But concentration ratios possess a shortcoming because they do not identify the distribution of industry output among the largest firms. For example, if the CR_4 in some market equals 60 percent, it is unclear whether the largest four firms each produce 15 percent of industry output, or the largest firm produces 57 percent and the others each produce 1 percent. The distribution of output among the largest firms can make a difference in terms of the market conduct of firms. Economists tend to agree that firms are more likely to engage in active price competition when they are more similarly sized compared to a market environment where one firm dominates the industry and the others are much smaller. In the latter case, the smaller firms are likely to act as followers and simply mirror the pricing behavior of the dominant firm. We talked earlier about this type of tacit collusion in the context of the price leadership model.

Because a concentration ratio fails to reveal the distribution of industry output among the largest firms, most economists prefer to use the HHI, when the necessary data are available, to measure the degree of industry concentration.[6] The HHI is derived by summing the squared market shares of all the firms in the relevant market, or

(8–1)
$$\text{HHI} = \sum_{i=1}^{N} S_i^2 = S_1^2 + \cdots + S_N^2,$$

---

6. The disadvantage of the HHI is that market share data are needed for all of the firms in the industry with shares of more than 1 percent. The four-firm concentration ratio requires only market share data for the largest four companies.

where S_i stands for the percentage market share or percentage of industry output produced by the ith firm and $0 < \text{HHI} \leq 10,000$.

When a market is dominated by one firm, the HHI equals its maximum value of 10,000 or 100^2. The HHI takes on a value closer to zero when a greater number of firms, N, exist in the market and/or when the existing firms are more equally sized. As the value of the HHI approaches zero, an industry is considered to be less concentrated or more structurally competitive.

For example, in 2003 the five largest manufacturers of soft contact lenses were Vistakon (J&J), Ciba Vision, Bausch & Lomb, Cooper Vision, and Occular Sciences, with market share, based on total patient visits when dispensed, of 36.2%, 23.1%, 14.0%, 13.1%, and 12.4%, respectively.[7] Supposing that soft contact lenses represent the RPM, the CR_4 can be calculated by summing the four largest market shares. The resulting figure of 86.4 percent suggests that the four major producers of soft contact lenses in the United States account for slightly more than 86 percent of all soft contact lenses dispensed. In terms of market concentration, the soft contact lens industry clearly resembles a tight oligopoly, given that the CR_4 greatly exceeds 60 percent. But notice that the CR_4, by itself, does not reveal the distribution of output among the four largest firms. For example, the CR_4 would also equal 86.4 percent if Vistakon's market share were 80 percent and the three other firms accounted for the remaining amount of industry output.

The distribution of market shares among the largest firms in the soft contact lens industry can be considered by applying Equation 8–1 and computing the HHI as 2,370. To gain some insight into the meaning of this figure, suppose that the two smallest contact lens suppliers, Occular Sciences and Cooper Vision, decide to consolidate their companies. The postmerger HHI would be $(36.2^2 + 23.1^2 + 14^2 + 25.5^2)$ or 2,690. Notice that a smaller number of firms leads to a higher value for the HHI and reflects the greater concentration of output among a smaller number of firms in the industry. Now suppose the market shares of the four remaining soft contact lens suppliers become equal over time. If so, the HHI declines to 2,500 ($25^2 \times 4$). In general, it can be shown that the HHI takes on a lower value when a larger number of equally sized firms exist in an industry.

Although the SCP model predicts that firms are more likely to unilaterally or collectively exploit their market power by restricting output and raising price (and reducing quality) when firms are fewer in number, that same theory is unable to predict the precise value of the HHI at which behavior of this kind takes place. The HHI reflects only the structural competitiveness of the market; it reveals nothing explicit about the behavioral intensity of competition among firms. Consequently, economic theory alone is unable to identify a specific competition-monopoly cutoff level for the HHI.

However, the Department of Justice (DOJ) and Federal Trade Commission (FTC) have jointly established some guidelines concerning the level of the HHI that the agencies believe triggers a concern about the potential exploitation of market power (DOJ/FTC, 2010). In fact, these guidelines are used by the DOJ and FTC when deciding to challenge a merger among firms in the same industry. In particular, the DOJ and FTC believe that reasonably competitive conditions hold when the HHI is less than 1,500. In this case, horizontal mergers resulting in unconcentrated markets are generally treated as having no adverse competitive effects and ordinarily are not given any further analysis by the agencies.

In addition, an industry is treated by the DOJ and FTC as being mildly concentrated when the HHI falls between 1,500 and 2,500. Mergers that result in moderately concentrated markets and involve an increase in the HHI of more than 100 points potentially raise significant competitive concerns and often warrant scrutiny by the FTC and

7. See http://www.ftc.gov/reports/contactlens/050214contactlensrpt.pdf (accessed October 18, 2005). The figures sum to 98.8 percent because the smallest firms have been omitted.

DOJ. Finally, the DOJ and FTC regard an industry as being highly concentrated when the HHI exceeds 2,500. Mergers that result in highly concentrated markets and involve an increase in the HHI of between 100 points and 200 points potentially raise significant competitive concerns and often warrant scrutiny by the two agencies. Mergers that result in highly concentrated markets and involve an increase in the HHI of more than 200 points are presumed most probable to enhance market power by the DOJ and FTC.[8]

Identifying Market Power

As mentioned throughout this text, resources are scarce at a point in time so any economic system must seriously address how these scarce resources should be allocated to different purposes. In a market system, resources are allocated to alternative uses based on supply and demand forces. In long-run equilibrium, if the market is perfectly competitive, price reflects the marginal benefit associated with consuming, and also the marginal cost of producing, the last unit of output. In the absence of any externalities, the market outcome represents efficiency because price or marginal social benefit equals marginal social costs. Also, if the market is perfectly competitive, and therefore entry barriers are nonexistent, the representative firm earns no more than a normal economic profit because competition among firms drives price down to equal average total costs.

It follows that the efficiency of an industry can be judged, to some degree, by the excessiveness of its economic profits. That is, if long-run economic profits are greater than the normal level, it may indicate that firms in the industry exploit their market power by restricting output and raising price above the marginal costs of production. If so, consumer welfare is harmed and resources are misallocated from a societal point of view.

Lerner (1934) provides an alternative but related way of thinking about market power. In the context of a monopoly, Lerner argues that market power can be measured by how high price, P, can be elevated above the marginal costs, MC, of production. He shows mathematically that the ability to elevate price above costs depends on the price elasticity of market demand, E_M, facing the monopolist. Specifically, the Lerner index of monopoly power, L, can be written as

$$(8\text{–}2) \qquad L = \frac{(P - MC)}{P} = \frac{1}{|E_M|}.$$

The Lerner index implies that the markup of price above marginal cost as a percentage of price is inversely proportional to the price elasticity of market demand (in absolute terms). That is, the ability to elevate price above marginal cost is limited by the responsiveness of buyers to a price increase. For example, supposing that price elasticity of market demand equals −2.0, the Lerner index suggests that the markup of price above cost equals 50 percent of the price. If, instead, the price elasticity of market demand was more elastic and equaled −10.0, the index indicates that the markup falls to only 10 percent of price. It stands to reason that a firm, facing many substitute products, is unable to elevate price high above the marginal given a more elastic demand. In fact, the Lerner index for a perfectly competitive firm equals zero because it faces a perfectly elastic demand. Thus, the Lerner index is often treated as a measure of market power.

---

8. There is also a measure referred to as the *numbers equivalent HHI*, which is found by dividing 10,000, the maximum value of the HHI, by the actual HHI for an industry. This measure provides a picture of an industry regarding the number of equally sized firms potentially represented by a given HHI. For example, an HHI of 2,000 reflects a market environment where roughly 5 (10,000/2,000) similarly sized firms exist in an industry.

If we assume that marginal costs equal average total costs (i.e., a horizontal per unit cost curve), the Lerner index can be rewritten as

(8–3)
$$L = \frac{(P - ATC)}{P}.$$

By multiplying both the numerator and the denominator of the right-hand term by Q/Q, the following expression can be obtained:

(8–4)
$$L = \frac{Q(P - ATC)}{QP} = \frac{(TR - TC)}{TR} = \frac{\pi}{TR}.$$

Equation 8–4 indicates that the Lerner index can be approximated by the ratio of economic profits to total revenues or sales. A higher value for the ratio of economic profits to sales indicates that the firm or industry possesses greater market power.

Given the strong theoretical underpinnings, it should not be surprising that economists often use profit rates to draw inferences about the market power of real-world firms and industries. In practice, other measures of profitability, such as profits as a fraction of stockholder equity or total assets, are examined in addition to the profit return on sales when the necessary data are available. Using several bases to measure profit rates represents a sound practice because profits sometimes differ across firms and industries simply because of variations in production methods (labor versus capital intensive) or reliance on debt versus equity financing, for example.

However, economists realize that several conditions must be considered when drawing inferences about market power from profit data. First, economists consider that the reported rates represent accounting and not economic profits. Recall from Chapter 7 that economic profits reflect the opportunity cost of all resources and not just resources purchased by companies. Alternatively stated, accounting profits do not reflect adequately the opportunity cost of resources owned by businesses such as buildings, land, and equipment. Hence, accounting profits generally overstate economic profits and can complicate comparisons across companies.

Second, we must also consider that even perfectly competitive firms earn a normal, economic profit rate. Profit-maximizing firms must receive at least a normal return on their capital or they will exit the industry to earn a higher return elsewhere. Thus, we must allow for some economy-wide competitive rate of return. For example, industries in the general economy may normally earn a 6 percent return on their capital. Any economic profits received after allowing a 6 percent return on capital might then be considered as being excessive or above the normal amount.

Third, investments in some industries are riskier than others. Economic theory suggests that risk-adverse investors require a risk premium to invest in more risky industries, *ceteris paribus*. Thus observed differences in profit rates across industries must be adjusted for risk before inferences about relative profitability can be made. For example, an industry rate of return on capital of 8 percent may reflect a 6 percent normal return and a 2 percent risk premium.

Finally, economic theory suggests that a perfectly competitive industry earns a normal rate of return in the long run. However, favorable or unfavorable industry or economy-wide shocks may cause actual (and risk-adjusted) economic profits to deviate from the long-run normal rate in the short run. Also, short-run above normal profits and economic losses should not persist in the long run because firms eventually enter and exit markets. Hence, we must be careful not to draw any strong conclusions about excessive profitability from a simple snapshot of industry performance that does not capture market dynamics. That is, we must determine whether the excessive profits persist over time because of entry barriers before drawing any conclusions about market power.

In sum, economic theory indicates that economic profits should persistently be greater than zero when firms possess and exploit their market power. As a result, profit rates can sometimes be used to draw inferences about the market power and efficiency of real-world firms and industries. However, from an economic perspective, it is important to consider the long-run risk-adjusted economy-wide competitive rates of return before the presence of market power can be properly assessed.

Summary

In this chapter, the SCP paradigm was offered as a way of conceptualizing how market structure affects both industry conduct and market performance. We saw that markets range from being perfectly competitive to pure monopoly depending on factors such as the number and size distribution of firms, height of any barriers to entry, and the type of product offered for sale by firms in an industry. In general, a greater degree of both actual and potential competition leads to greater efficiency because individual firms have less market power.

Perfect competition was the first market structure that we analyzed in some detail. Perfect competition means that individual firms are price takers and maximize profits, buyers maximize utility or economize, no barriers to entry exist, and buyers possess perfect information. Based on these characteristics, it was shown that perfectly competitive markets allocate resources efficiently when all social benefits and costs are internalized by those engaged in the market exchange. Perfect competition also results in the maximum sum of consumer and producer surplus, another sign of allocative efficiency.

The model of pure monopoly was then offered as a logical extreme to the perfectly competitive model. One seller of a good or service and perfect barriers to entry characterize monopoly. Because a monopoly has market power and faces a downward-sloping demand, it was shown theoretically that a monopoly results in a restriction of output and a misallocation of society's resources. A deadweight loss and redistribution of income also occur when a monopolist exists in a market.

Monopolistic competition was introduced as an intermediate market structure. The distinguishing feature of monopolistic competition is a differentiated product. A differentiated product means that the individual firm possesses some slight market power because it can raise price without losing all sales. Because entry barriers are nonexistent in the long run, the typical monopolistically competitive firm makes normal profits in the long run. Given that variety is highly valued by consumers, the only legitimate criticism against a monopolistically competitive firm may be its use of product differentiation. While elements of product differentiation such as advertising, trademarks, and brand names may provide cheap information and promote competition, it was also argued that these same features might impede competition through habit buying and creating entry barriers.

Oligopoly, another intermediate market structure, was examined next. A few large dominant firms and, thus, mutual interdependence among firms distinguish oligopoly from the other market structures. The efficiency of an oligopolistic industry depends on whether the individual firms in the industry compete or cooperate with one another. Cooperation or collusion leads to monopoly-like behavior and a restriction of output and a misallocation of society's scarce resources. It was pointed out that the conjectural variations formed by firms influence their behavior if they expect offsetting or matching behavior by rivals in the industry. Expecting offsetting (matching) behavior leads to the competitive (monopoly) outcome. It was further discussed that matching behavior is more likely to be expected when the number of firms is fewer, entry barriers are higher, trade associations exist, the industry is mature and slow growing, organizational structures are more centralized, and firm decision makers possess bounded rationality.

Finally, the chapter ended with a discussion concerning how to define the relevant market, measure the degree of market concentration, and identify market power. We learned that the relevant market possesses both a product and spatial dimension. In particular, when addressing the relevant market in which a firm operates, one must consider all of the other products and companies that buyers might turn to if one firm raised price or lowered the quality of a specific product by a nontrivial amount for a nontemporary period of time. All of the other products and companies that buyers switch to would be considered as being in the same relevant market as the firm and product for which the price has increased or quality has declined.

To measure the degree of market concentration, the four-firm concentration ratio (CR_4) and Herfindahl-Hirschman index (HHI) are typically calculated. The CR_4 is calculated by adding up the market shares of the four largest firms in a market. As the CR_4 increases in value, the market is treated as being more highly concentrated. The HHI is found by squaring and summing the market shares of all firms in the same relevant market. The HHI varies between 0 to 10,000 with higher values indicating a more highly concentrated industry and takes on a greater value when fewer, dissimilarly sized firms exist in an industry. The HHI is typically preferred over the CR_4 because it captures the distribution of output among the largest firms in an industry. An industry is considered to be highly concentrated when the HHI is greater than 2,500. Finally, we discuss the measuring of market power. We learned that the Lerner index indicates that once properly adjusted, profit rate can serve as a reflection of market power and efficiency.

Before concluding this chapter, it should be pointed out that the SCP analysis might become muddled when applied to medical markets for two reasons. First, conventional microeconomic theory is based on a profit maximization assumption, whereas many medical organizations are organized on a not-for-profit basis. Second, the industrial organization triad may not be appropriate for the medical care industry because quality usually matters more than price to consumers and government takes a more active role in the production, regulation, and distribution of output. These considerations diminish the role that profits and price play in the allocation of health resources and rationing of medical goods and services.

Despite these considerations, we believe that the SCP paradigm remains a useful tool for analyzing health care markets. Even the conduct of not-for-profit organizations is influenced by market structure to some degree. For example, market structure places a restraint on the maximum price not-for-profit firms can charge, and even not-for-profit organizations are subject to a financial solvency constraint. Also, for-profit firms are strongly represented in the health care sector. Many community hospitals, home health and hospice care agencies, mental health facilities, and nursing homes are organized on a for-profit basis. All pharmaceutical and commercial health insurance companies and nearly all physician, dental, and optometric clinics are also organized on a for-profit basis. Thus, while the quest for profits may have a smaller impact on the behavior of firms in the health care sector than on that of firms in other industries, profits still play an important role. Certainly, the investigator should conduct the industry analysis very carefully and be cognizant of the peculiarities of health care industries when drawing any inferences from the SCP paradigm.

Review Questions and Problems

1. Suppose the supply curve of medical services is perfectly inelastic. Analyze the impact of an increase in consumer income on the market price and quantity of medical services. Next, assume the demand for medical services is perfectly

inelastic while the supply curve is upward sloping. Explain the impact of an increase in input prices on the market price and quantity of medical services.

2. In the country of Drazah Larom (moral hazard spelled backward), health insurance is nonexistent and all medical markets are perfectly competitive. Use supply and demand analysis to explain the impact of the following changes on the price and output of physician services.
   A. A decrease in the wage of clinic-based nurses
   B. The adoption of cost-enhancing medical technologies
   C. An aging population and a correspondingly more severe patient case-mix
   D. Declining consumer income
   E. A lower market price for physician services (be careful here!)

3. In the 1980s, a shortage of registered nurses in the United States led to an increase of almost 21 percent in the real average hourly earnings of RNs from 1981 to 1989 (Pope and Menke, 1990). This increase was the highest of any occupational group. Use supply and demand theory to show the shortage and explain why a dramatic rise in the wage rate occurred.

4. Using supply and demand analysis, show graphically and explain verbally some of the factors that may have led to rising health care costs in the United States from 1960 to the present day.

5. In the mid-1980s, female nurses became increasingly aware that a relatively large number of attractive job opportunities existed outside the medical services industry. In fact, a large number of colleges offered life and transfer credits for nurses so that they could change careers at less cost. Using an equilibrium model of the market for nurses, show what impact this market change had on the wage rate and employment of nurses. Work through the comparative static analysis and explain whether a temporary shortage or surplus occurred and the various market adjustments that took place as a result of the temporary imbalance.

6. Assume the sale of human organs is legalized and a free market develops. Furthermore, assume the market is in equilibrium. Trace through the price and output effects of the following:
   A. An increase in the incomes of potential buyers of human kidneys
   B. A decrease in the price of kidney dialysis
   C. The development of a new drug that leaves the immune system intact while preventing transplant rejection (Waldholz, 1992)
   D. A greater willingness by individuals to supply human kidneys

7. A June 10, 1996, *Wall Street Journal* article titled "Americans Eat Up Vitamin E Supplies" discusses the shortage that existed for vitamin E at that time. According to the article, the shortage was created by two changes in the marketplace. First, the supply of soybeans, from which vitamin E is extracted, declined sharply. Second, a stream of scientific research from mainstream institutions shows that vitamin E helps to ward off such ailments as heart disease and cancer and some symptoms of aging.
   A. Using two separate supply and demand graphs, graphically show and verbally explain how a shortage is created by each of the two changes.
   B. Explain what eventually happens to price because of a shortage in a free market.
   C. Explain how suppliers and buyers adjust their behavior as the shortage is eliminated in each of the two cases.
   D. Explain what adjustment may occur in the long run because of these changes.

8. Show graphically and explain verbally how a monopoly results in a deadweight loss. Also, point out the redistribution that takes place in society because of monopoly.

9. Explain why economic profits are zero under monopolistic competition in the long run.

10. Explain the difference between the collusive and competitive oligopoly models and explain the role that the number of firms and barriers to entry play in determining how real-world oligopolistic industries behave.
11. Use the four market structures provided in the chapter to explain the critical role played by barriers to entry in determining the level of competition in any given market.
12. Critically evaluate the following statement made by a marketing executive: "Advertising is good because it always promotes competition."
13. What beneficial role do trademarks and brand names serve when information imperfections otherwise exist?
14. Explain the economic reasoning underlying the following statement: "People often fail to acquire information about the price they pay for medical services because of health insurance."
15. Discuss the two ways product differentiation affects the demand for a product.
16. Explain how lack of information affects the price and quality of a medical good relative to a perfectly competitive situation.
17. Suppose XER Inc. is a monopoly and produces a drug that cures the common cold. The weekly (inverse) market demand for its product takes the form $P = 660 - 4Q$, where Q is measured as number of tablets. The marginal costs and average total costs are equal at $100 per tablet (i.e., a horizontal marginal cost curve).
    A. Given this information, solve for the level of output that will be produced by XER Inc. if it maximizes profits (you may need to consult Footnote 2 in this chapter).
    B. Solve for the price charged and amount of profits earned by XER Inc.
    C. From a societal point of view, does the profit-maximizing level of output represent an efficient level of output? Why or why not? Calculate the social damages created by XER Inc. (*Hint:* You will have to know how to calculate the area of a triangle.)
    D. Suppose the source of the entry barrier was removed so XER Inc. is no longer a monopoly. How would equilibrium change? Explain fully.
18. Suppose that the annual number of admissions can be used as a measure of output for a group of hospitals operating in the same RGM. Categorize the type of market based on the degree of structural competition as measured by the four-firm concentration ratio and the HHI.

Hospital	Number of Admissions (in thousands)
Saving Grace Hospital	4,000
Mercy Me Hospital	3,000
Price Plus Hospital	1,500
HealthMart Hospital	750
Health Depot Hospital	1,000
Health R Us Hospital	1,500

19. Explain why it is also important to analyze the structural aspects of the buyer-side of the market.
20. Identify the theoretical underpinnings associated with using profit rate as a measure of market power. What adjustments must be made to reported profit rates for economic reasons?

Online Resources

To access Internet links related to the topics in this chapter, please visit our website at **www.cengage.com/economics/santerre**.

References

Bain, Joe S. *Barriers to New Competition.* Cambridge, Mass.: Harvard University Press, 1956.

Baumol, William J. "Macroeconomics of Unbalanced Growth: The Anatomy of Urban Crisis." *American Economic Review* 57 (June 1967), pp. 415–26.

Benham, Lee. "The Effect of Advertising on the Price of Eyeglasses." *Journal of Law and Economics* 15 (October 1972), pp. 337–52.

Borzo, Greg. "Glove Shortage Creates Anxiety." *Health Industry Today* 54 (November 1991), p. 1.

Cady, John F. "An Estimate of the Price Effects of Restrictions on Drug Price Advertising." *Economic Inquiry* 14 (December 1976), pp. 493–510.

Department of Justice and Federal Trade Commission (DOJ/FTC). *Horizontal Merger Guidelines*, August, 2010, http://www.ftc.gov/os/1010/08/100819hmg.pdf, accessed October 24, 2011.

Ford, Jon M., and David L. Kaserman. "Certificate-of-Need Regulation and Entry: Evidence from the Dialysis Industry." *Southern Economics Journal* 59 (April 1993), pp. 783–91.

Haas-Wilson, Deborah. *Managed Care and Monopoly Power: The Antitrust Challenge.* Cambridge, Mass.: Harvard University Press, 2003.

Hartwig, Jochen. "What Drives Health Care Expenditure? Baumol's Model of Unbalanced Growth Revisited." *Journal of Health Economics* 27 (2008), pp. 603–23.

Hensley, Scott. "Out for Blood." *Modern Healthcare,* June 22, 1998, pp. 26–32.

Klein, Benjamin, and Keith B. Leffler. "The Role of Market Forces in Assuring Contractual Performance." *Journal of Political Economy* 89 (August 1981), pp. 615–41.

Kwoka, John E. "Advertising and the Price and Quality of Optometric Services." *American Economic Review* (March 1984), pp. 211–16.

Lerner, Abba P. "The Concept of Monopoly and the Measurement of Monopoly Power." *Review of Economic Studies* 1 (1934), pp. 157–75.

Pope, Gregory C., and Terri Menke. "Data-Watch: Hospital Labor Markets in the 1980s." *Health Affairs* 9 (winter 1990), pp. 127–37.

Robinson, James C. "Hospital Quality Competition and the Economics of Imperfect Information." *Milbank Memorial Quarterly* 66 (1988), pp. 465–81.

Stigler, George. *The Organization of Industry.* Homewood, Ill.: Richard D. Irwin, 1968.

U.S. v. Idaho Orthopaedic Society, et al. Competitive Impact Statement. 75 Fed. Reg. 32,210 (2010).

Waldholz, Michael. "New Drug Leaves Immune System Intact While Preventing Transplant Rejection." *Wall Street Journal,* August 7, 1992, p. B8.

Zikos, Joanna. "It's Tough to Get Grip on Rubber Gloves." *Worcester Evening Gazette,* August 10, 1988, p. 1.

The Role of Government

PART TWO

CHAPTER 9

Government, Health, and Medical Care

"Needham, Mass., Biotech Company Executive Criticizes FDA" (*Knight Ridder Tribune Business News*)

"FTC Soon to Clear $6B Bayer-Aventis Merger" (*The Daily Deal*)

"State Looks at Tax on Hospitals" (*Crain's Detroit Business*)

"Doctors Resolve Antitrust Charges" (*USA Today*)

"Unwanted HMOs, Hundreds of Massachusetts Doctors, Citing Low Fees, Refuse Medicare Plans" (*Boston Globe*)

Up to this point, we have given little attention to the role and effects of government intervention in the U.S. health care system. Yet, as the preceding headlines suggest,[1] government plays an important role in the various medical markets and either directly or indirectly influences the health of the population in a number of ways. For example, regulatory and taxing policies affect the production and/or consumption of certain products (such as prescription drugs, narcotics, alcohol, and tobacco) and thereby beneficially or adversely affect the population's health. Regulations also have the potential to alter the price, quantity, or quality of medical services and can thereby inhibit or promote efficiency in the allocation of resources. The degree of government intervention varies considerably across the country. Some state governments choose to actively regulate the production and reimbursement of nursing home, hospital, and psychotherapy services. Other state governments take more of a laissez-faire attitude toward the health care industry.

We have already seen several examples of government intervention in the health care sector. For example, earlier chapters pointed out that government-created legal barriers to entry, such as professional licensure requirements and certificate of need (CON) laws, often confer monopoly status on the established health care providers in a market. In addition, we know that the Medicare and Medicaid programs provide public health insurance to elderly people, people with disabilities, and selected economically disadvantaged groups. These are just a few of an immeasurable number of government policies that affect the conduct and performance of medical care markets and the health status of American consumers.

This chapter provides an overview of the impact of public sector policies on the allocation of medical resources and the distribution of medical output. Although the design, complexity, and nature of health care policies differ across states, and federal health care policies are multidimensional in scope, a common body of economic theory is drawn upon to analyze such policies.

---

1. FDA and FTC stand for the Food and Drug Administration and the Federal Trade Commission, respectively.

Specifically, this chapter:

- examines the economic reasons for government intervention in a market-based health care system
- discusses the implications of various types of public sector involvement, such as price and quality regulations and antitrust laws
- explores the methods used by government to redistribute income in society and the reason for such redistribution
- points out how the Patient Protection and Affordable Care Act (PPACA) of 2010 may impact government's economic role in U.S. health affairs.

Economic Reasons for Government Intervention

Two general alternative economic views or models describe why government intervenes in a market-based health care system. These are the public interest and special interest group theories of government behavior. According to the **public interest theory**, government promotes the general interests of society as a whole and chooses policies that enhance efficiency and equity. Recall from Chapter 3 that an efficient allocation of resources is achieved when, for a given distribution of income, each good and service is produced at the point where marginal social benefit (MSB) equals marginal social cost (MSC). In the presence of market imperfections, such as imperfect consumer information or monopoly, markets fail to allocate resources efficiently. We will see shortly that market failure also occurs when public goods such as national defense or externalities such as air pollution are involved, or when distributive justice is a concern.

The public interest is served when government corrects instances where the market fails to allocate resources efficiently or to distribute income equitably. When the market fails, government attempts to restore efficiency and promote equity by encouraging competition, providing consumer information, reducing harmful externalities, or redistributing income in society. Consequently, the public interest model of government behavior predicts that the laws, regulations, and other actions of government enhance efficiency and equity.

According to the **special interest group theory** (Stigler, 1971; Peltzman, 1976; and Becker, 1983), the political forum can be treated like any private market for goods and services; that is, the amounts and types of legislation are determined by the forces of supply and demand. Vote-maximizing politicians represent the suppliers of legislation, while wealth-maximizing special interest groups are the buyers of legislation. In this model, incumbent politicians attempt to increase their probability of being reelected by supplying legislation that promises to redistribute wealth away from the general public and toward various special interest groups. In return, politicians expect votes, political support, and campaign contributions. Professional lobbies representing the special interest groups negotiate with politicians and arrive at the market-clearing prices and quantities of different kinds of legislation. Special interest group legislation changes over time when relative power shifts among different interest groups. Power or political pressure is determined by the amount of resources the group controls, the size of the group, and the efficiency with which the group transforms resources into pressure.

The successful politician stays in office by combining the legislative programs of various special interest groups into an overall fiscal package to be advanced in the political arena. The beneficiaries are the special interest groups, while the costs fall disproportionately on the general public. For example, individual pieces of legislation that provide protection from imported automobiles, milk price supports, and a larger education budget individually benefit those associated with the Automobile Workers Union, the American Dairy Association, and the National Education Association, respectively. The same politician can offer wealth transfers to each of these three groups and in return receive their combined votes, political support, and contributions. Naturally, special interest groups and politicians are made better off by the political exchanges; otherwise, these exchanges would not occur. Politicians retain or acquire elected positions, while the special interest groups receive wealth-enhancing legislation.

The general public, however, is unknowingly made worse off by the political exchanges. Individuals are typically rationally ignorant about the wealth implications of government activities because the personal cost of acquiring information about the true effect of legislation is high, whereas the corresponding private benefit is low. For example, suppose a certain piece of legislation redistributes $300 million a year away from the general public to a special interest group. Although this wealth transfer is a large amount of money in absolute terms, it is insignificant when expressed in per capita terms. In the United States, the cost of this wealth transfer is only about $1 per person. Raising the per capita cost of special interest group legislation to $100 increases the total wealth transfer to $30 billion. Yet even at a potential per-person savings of $100, few people are likely to become involved due to the money and time costs associated with political activity. To challenge special interest group legislation, a group or an individual must organize a legitimate counter political movement, inform others, circulate a petition, and engage in lobbying. All these activities entail sizeable personal time and money costs.

Ross Perot's grassroots bid for the presidency in 1992 exemplifies this point on a grandiose scale. Perot attempted to challenge the political establishment by running for president as a third-party candidate. After spending millions of his own money, he garnered a respectable 19 percent of the overall vote, but not enough to win the presidential election. Imagine all the other potential "Perots" who never get involved in the political process at even the local or state level because of the staggering costs involved.

The special interest group model of government behavior implies that the typical individual consumer is "nickeled and dimed" by wealth-transferring legislation. Even worse, the wealth transfer is not simply a dollar-for-dollar transfer from the general public to the special interest groups. The political negotiations leading to the wealth transfer involve scarce resources such as the politicians' time and professional lobbies. As more resources are diverted to political negotiations, fewer are available for productive purposes. In addition, any additional taxes imposed on the general public, to support the wealth-transfers, create a disincentive for individuals to commit resources to production. Consequently, inefficiencies are normally associated with special interest group legislation.

Therefore, according to the special interest group theory of government behavior, public regulations and laws exist because some special interest group benefits at the expense of the general public. Individuals in a special interest group are collectively powerful because they share a common concentrated interest. Consumers as a group, however, are generally diverse, fragmented, and powerless. Organization costs typically prohibit general consumers from taking action even when wealth transfers are known.

As an example, Ohsfeldt and Gohmann (1992) analyze whether various state regulations concerning AIDS-related health insurance underwriting practices are influenced by the pressure of special interest groups. They focus on state regulations prohibiting (1) questions during the insurance application process about past HIV testing, (2) insurers from requiring insurance applicants to submit to HIV antibody tests,

(3) questions on the application regarding sexual orientation, and (4) the exclusion of any AIDS-related costs from the services covered by the health insurance contract.

Ohsfeldt and Gohmann argue that the losers from these insurance regulations are private health insurance companies (due to lower profits) and private insurance holders with a low average risk for AIDS (higher premium costs). Individuals who gain include those at high risk for AIDS (lower premium costs) and private providers of health care services (higher profits from more generous private insurance coverage). In general, the empirical findings of their regression analysis support the hypothesis that the presence of state regulations restricting AIDS-related health insurance underwriting practices is related to special interest group pressure. Specifically, Ohsfeldt and Gohmann find that underwriting regulations are more likely in states where the AIDS prevalence rate (as a proxy for the AIDS group) is high and insurance industry strength is low.

The public interest and special interest group models are two contrasting theories regarding the economic reasons government intervenes in a market-based system. In the real world, government most likely intervenes for both reasons. In some instances, government actions correct for market failure and thereby promote efficiency. In other situations, government policies enhance the well being of specific groups at an overall cost to society and thereby cause an inefficient allocation of resources and/or an inequitable distribution of income. Indeed, a careful cost-benefit analysis would have to be conducted before the winners and losers could be identified and the efficiency and equity implications determined for each piece of legislation. It is important to remember that both the government and the marketplace are imperfect institutions and, as a result, both fail to some extent; that is, government failure and market failure can coexist. Our job as policy makers or informed consumers is to determine which institution can accomplish which objective in the more efficient and equitable manner.

Types of Government Intervention

Government can alter the performance of markets in terms of efficiency and equity by providing public goods, levying taxes, correcting for externalities, imposing regulations, enforcing antitrust laws, operating public enterprises, and sponsoring redistribution programs. As an example of a public good, a government health officer inspects the sanitary conditions at local restaurants to protect the public's health. To correct for an externality, the government taxes the emissions of firms to reduce the level of air or water pollution in an area. A certificate of need (CON) law is essentially a health care regulation that restricts entry into hospital and nursing home markets, whereas the Sherman Antitrust Act of 1890 prohibits independent physicians from discussing their pricing policies to prevent monopolistic practices, such as price fixing. A hospital operated by the Veterans Administration provides an example of a government medical enterprise. Finally, the Medicare and Medicaid programs are examples of public medical care redistribution programs. Each of these government policies either directly or indirectly influences the allocation of medical resources and the distribution of medical care in the U.S. health economy. The following sections discuss the effects of these types of government intervention in more detail.

Public Goods

One legitimate function of government is to provide public goods. A public good must satisfy two criteria. First, unlike a private good, more than one individual can simultaneously receive benefits from a public good. That is, a public good exhibits nonrivalry in consumption, thus allowing one person to increase the consumption of a good without diminishing the quantity available for others. Second, it is costly to exclude nonpaying individuals from receiving the benefits of a public good.

National defense is a good example of a public good. Everyone simultaneously benefits, and it is impossible to exclude nonpayers from receiving the benefits of national defense. The preservation of water quality in public swimming areas by the local public health department is another example of a public good. A large number of people can simultaneously enjoy the benefits of improved water quality (at least until the beaches become overcrowded). In addition, it is costly to exclude nonpayers from receiving the benefits of improved water quality at the local pond (unless the entire pond can be fenced off). Because of the high cost of excluding nonpaying individuals, private firms are unwilling to produce and sell public goods; thus, the private sector fails to provide public goods, and government intervention is necessary. Government ensures that public goods are produced in either the private or public sector and collects the necessary funding through taxation.[2]

Some people incorrectly consider medical services to be public goods because they are so essential for life. From a theoretical standpoint, however, the benefits of medical services are almost completely internalized by the individual buyer, and the cost of excluding nonpayers from receiving medical care is very low. Simply put, prospective patients can be required to pay the necessary fee at the door of the medical facility or be denied access to medical services. Thus, medical care services are not public goods.[3]

Externalities

Ordinarily, all costs and benefits are fully internalized by the parties directly involved in a market transaction, and others not involved in the exchange are unaffected. For example, consider an individual who wakes up one morning with a bad toothache and decides to visit the dentist. After some probing, the dentist informs the patient that a wisdom tooth is causing the problem and recommends that the tooth be extracted immediately. The (uninsured) patient consents, the task is expertly performed, and the $100 fee is paid at the desk. In a competitive market, the $100 fee reflects the marginal benefit the individual receives from being relieved of pain and the dentist's marginal cost of providing the service. Notice that in this example, only the individual consumer and dentist internalize the benefits and costs of the market transaction. This transaction is efficient because both parties are made better off; otherwise, the transaction would not have taken place.

Sometimes, however, a market transaction affects parties other than the buyers and sellers. In this situation, an externality occurs. An **externality** is an unpriced by-product of production or consumption that adversely or beneficially affects another party not directly involved in the market transaction. When an externality occurs, the buyers and sellers do not fully internalize all the costs and benefits of the transaction. As a result, external costs or benefits are generated, and the product is usually under- or overproduced from a societal perspective. In the following discussion, we examine the impact and implications of some demand-side and supply-side externalities relating to health and medical care.

---

2. The aggregate demand for a public good is derived through a vertical summation of individual demands. See Chapter 6 in Rosen (1995).

3. Closely related to a public good is the notion of a *merit good.* Musgrave and Musgrave (1989) point out that people are often bound by similar historical experiences or cultural traditions. The common bond gives rise to common interests, values, and wants—"wants which individuals feel obliged to support as members of the community" (p. 57). For example, people in the community may believe that everyone needs at least some minimal amount of food, housing, or medical services and therefore may be willing to support the provision of those merit goods through redistribution of income.

Demand-Side Externalities. A demand-side externality occurs when the marginal social benefit diverges from the marginal private benefit associated with a good or service. A **positive demand-side externality** means that marginal social benefit is greater than marginal private benefit; a **negative demand-side externality** implies that marginal social benefit is less than marginal private benefit. Cigarette smoking provides a contemporary example of a negative demand-side externality.

According to Manning et al. (1989), external costs are associated with cigarette smoking, meaning smokers impose costs on nonsmokers. The external costs are generated in three ways. First, collectively financed programs, such as health insurance, pensions, sick leave, disability insurance, and group life insurance, are financed by taxes or group premiums and sometimes do not differentiate between smokers and nonsmokers. Because smokers have shorter life expectancies, they pay less taxes and premiums into the system. Second, smokers may incur higher health care costs than nonsmokers. Third, external costs arise when nonsmokers die prematurely from both passive smoking and smoking-related fires. The implication is that nonsmokers subsidize smokers and incur costs for which they are not compensated in the private marketplace.

Figure 9–1 shows the effect of cigarette smoking on resource allocation. The supply curve, S, corresponds to both marginal private and social costs and represents the marginal costs of using various inputs to manufacture and retail cigarettes. Thus, it is assumed that all resource costs of production are internalized on the supply side of the market. On the demand side, we must allow for the fact that the marginal private benefit is likely to be greater than the marginal social benefit of cigarette consumption. The MPB curve in the figure represents the marginal private benefit received from smoking, or the private demand curve for cigarettes. The MSB curve considers the additional costs inflicted on society and therefore lies below the MPB curve. The external costs underlie the difference between the two benefit curves.

For discussion purposes, we assume external costs per pack are the same at each level of cigarette consumption so that the two benefit curves are parallel to each other. We also assume the marginal social benefit is positive at every level, although it might be negative if the external costs exceed the marginal private benefits of cigarette consumption. As an illustration, Sloan et al. (2004) estimate the pure external

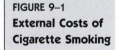

FIGURE 9–1
External Costs of Cigarette Smoking

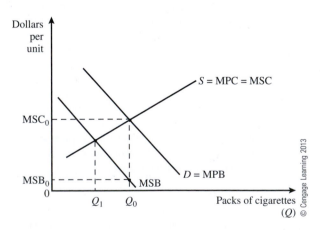

The graph captures the market for cigarettes. In the process of consumers maximizing utility and producers maximizing profits, market equilibrium results in the outcome at Q_0 where marginal private benefit, MPB, equals marginal private cost, MPC. However, the market outcome is inefficient because at that point, marginal social cost, MSC, exceeds marginal social benefit, MSB, because of the external damages caused by cigarette smoking. An efficient allocation of resources occurs at Q_1 because MSB = MSC. Left alone, the market tends to overproduce goods that generate negative externalities in consumption.

costs of cigarette smoking at approximately $1.50 per pack. However, if damages to family members of smokers are treated as quasi-external costs, the total external costs rise to $7.00 per pack.

Consumers compare their marginal private benefit only to price (i.e., their internal costs) when deciding how many packs of cigarettes to purchase. Thus, in the process of maximizing personal utilities, consumers purchase Q_0 packs of cigarettes. This amount of cigarette consumption is inefficient from a societal perspective because at Q_0, the marginal social cost, MSC_0, exceeds the marginal social benefit, MSB_0, of cigarettes; that is, some nonsmokers are adversely affected by the consumption of cigarettes, and these external costs are not considered by smokers in the private marketplace. Since consumers and producers do not fully internalize all the costs and benefits of their actions, the quantity of cigarettes is overproduced and overconsumed. An efficient quantity of cigarettes exists at Q_1, where MSB equals MSC. Because consumers and producers are unlikely to voluntarily alter their consumption and production behavior, some type of government intervention, such as a tax on cigarettes, may be necessary to curb this harmful type of consumption activity.

This example represents a negative consumption externality because others not directly involved are made worse off by the exchange. A positive consumption externality can also occur when a consumption activity generates external benefits such that others not involved are made better off by the exchange. A vaccination to prevent an infectious disease, such as rabies, is an example of a positive consumption externality. Figure 9–2 illustrates the logic underlying this example.

In the figure, the number of dogs receiving a rabies vaccine is shown on the horizontal axis. The MPB curve reflects the value dog owners place on the rabies vaccination. The MSB curve reflects the MPB plus all external benefits. The external benefits include the dollar benefit others receive when a dog gets the rabies vaccine and prevents the spread of the infection to humans or other animals. The supply curve, S, reflects the resource cost of providing the rabies vaccine.

In a free market, consumers compare their marginal private benefit to price when deciding whether to get the rabies vaccine for their dogs. As a result, Q_0 represents the total number of vaccinations in a free market where demand and supply intersect. But notice that at Q_0, the marginal social benefit, MSB_0, is greater than the marginal

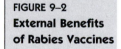

FIGURE 9–2
External Benefits of Rabies Vaccines

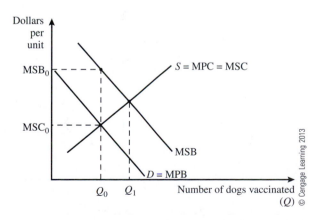

The graph captures the market for rabies vaccinations. In the process of consumers maximizing utility and producers maximizing profits, market equilibrium results in the outcome at Q_0 where marginal private benefit, MPB, equals marginal private cost, MPC. However, the market outcome is inefficient because at that point, marginal social benefit, MSB, exceeds marginal social cost, MSC, because of the external benefits caused by rabies vaccinations. An efficient allocation of resources occurs at Q_1 because MSB = MSC. Left alone, the market tends to underproduce goods that generate positive externalities in consumption.

social cost, MSC$_0$, of providing the rabies vaccine. An inefficient outcome occurs because some individuals place very little value on the rabies vaccination (when maximizing personal utility) since they do not consider its external benefits. From a societal perspective, therefore, there are too few rabies vaccinations in a free market. An efficient number of vaccinations occurs at Q_1. This implies that government intervention of some kind, such as a mandatory requirement and a fine, may be needed to ensure the efficient number of rabies vaccinations. (For example, many states require a rabies vaccination to obtain a dog license, and failure to get a dog license results in a fine.)

In sum, externalities can arise on the demand side of a market if the social costs and benefits of a consumption activity are not fully internalized by the participants directly involved in the exchange. If the consumption activity generates either external benefits or costs, the good or service is likely to be under- or overproduced from a societal perspective. Consequently, government intervention may be necessary to correct the market's failure to allocate society's resources efficiently.

Supply-Side Externalities.   As you now know, an externality creates an inefficient allocation of resources when the actions of one market participant affect another and no compensation is forthcoming. As in the case of a demand-side externality, the presence of an externality on the supply side usually distorts the allocation of resources in a market economy. While both positive and negative supply-side externalities are possible, here we only discuss a negative externality because that type is more relevant to health and medical care.

A **negative supply-side externality** exists if, for example, firms inflict an uncompensated cost on others during their production processes. Our example in this discussion relates to industrial pollution. In this case, a deviation arises between the marginal social cost and the marginal private cost of production. Because firms normally base their output decisions on the private cost of production and not on the social cost, the good is usually overproduced from a social perspective. Figure 9–3 depicts this situation for a competitive market.

The demand curve, or MSB curve, is labeled $D = $ MSB; the supply curve, or MPC curve, is labeled $S = $ MPC. The latter curve represents the amount it costs private

| **FIGURE 9–3**
Negative
Supply-Side
Externality | 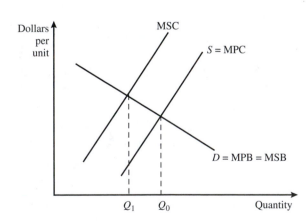 |

The graph captures a market where firms emit pollution as a by-product of production. Because of the external costs from pollution, marginal social cost, MSC, exceeds the marginal private cost, MPC, of production. In the process of consumers maximizing utility and producers maximizing profits, market equilibrium results in the outcome at Q_0 where marginal private benefit, MPB, equals marginal private cost, MPC. However, the market outcome is inefficient because at the point, marginal social cost, MSC, exceeds marginal social benefit, MSB, because of the external damages caused by the pollution. An efficient allocation of resources occurs at Q_1 because MSB = MSC. Left alone, the market tends to overproduce goods that generate negative externalities in production.

industry to produce each additional unit of output in terms of labor, materials, and capital costs. The MSC curve stands for the marginal social cost of production, and it lies above the MPC curve because it equals not only the marginal private cost of production but also the additional per-unit cost that industrial pollution inflicts on others. For example, several studies cited in Chapter 2 show that infant health may be adversely affected by various types of industrial pollution. The marginal external cost, the difference between the MSC and MPC, reflects the value of the reductions in infant health and any associated medical costs resulting from the industrial pollution.

Profit and utility maximization dictates that the good be produced up to point Q_0, where the MPC equals the MPB. At Q_0, however, the marginal social cost of production exceeds the marginal social benefit of the product. From a societal perspective, resources are efficiently allocated at Q_1 because the marginal social cost of production equals the marginal social benefit and the total social surplus is maximized. Because the market fails to assign the total social cost of production to firms, in the case of negative supply-side externalities, the good is overproduced and resources are inefficiently allocated.

Taxes and Subsidies as Corrective Instruments. By using taxes and subsidies, government can alter economic incentives and correct the unconstrained tendency of the market to misallocate society's resources when externalities are present. Specifically, taxes and subsidies can be used to alter the price of a good and discourage either overconsumption or underconsumption. Market participants are forced to consider the true net social benefit of their actions. For example, government can encourage an efficient amount of cigarette consumption by imposing a per-unit tax, T, on cigarette manufacturers equal to the vertical distance between MPB and MSB at Q_1 in Figure 9–4. Because of the per-unit tax, the market price of cigarettes increases to P_1 and cigarette consumption falls to the socially efficient level (MSB = MSC). Cigarette producers receive P_2, the difference between the market price of P_1 and the per-unit tax (or vertical distance between the MPB and MSB) as after-tax revenues per unit.

Notice in this example that both sellers and consumers share the burden from the cigarette tax. The consumers pay the portion $P_1 - P_0$, and the sellers pay the portion $P_0 - P_2$. The sellers' portion of the tax burden typically results in a smaller profit

FIGURE 9–4

A Tax as a Corrective Instrument

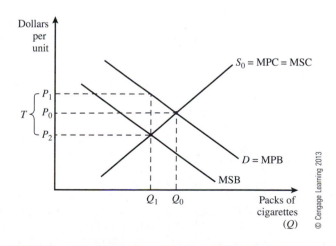

The graph captures the market for cigarettes. As before, an unfettered market results in the outcome where MPB = MPC at Q_0. Efficiency, however, exists at the point where MSB = MSC at Q_1. Government, in this case, can bring about a more efficient allocation of resources by setting a tax equal to the external damages caused by cigarette smoking at the efficient level. In this example, both consumers and producers share the tax burden. Consumers pay the portion $P_1 - P_0$ and producers pay $P_0 - P_2$. In general, the incidence of a tax depends on the relative demand and supply elasticities.

margin or is shifted backward to input suppliers. In our example, the cigarette tax may force producers to pay lower wages to their employees or lower the prices they pay to tobacco farmers. Whether consumers or producers pay a greater share of the cigarette tax depends on the relative magnitudes of the price elasticities of supply and demand. In general, when the price elasticity of demand (in absolute terms) exceeds the price elasticity of supply, the producer pays a greater fraction of the tax burden. The consumer incurs a relatively greater portion of the tax burden when the price elasticity of supply exceeds the price elasticity of demand.[4]

Governments face an incentive to tax goods for which demand is price inelastic. That is because the quantity demanded declines by a smaller percentage than the percentage increase in the per-unit tax or tax rate when demand is price inelastic. Thus, the total tax revenue to government, the product of the per-unit tax and quantity, increases when demand is price inelastic. In fact, one reason "sin taxes" on cigarettes and alcohol products are so politically popular is that the demand for these two products is price inelastic, thus providing a fruitful source of revenues for government.

The point is that taxes or a threat of fines can be used to discourage socially harmful activities. In contrast, subsidies can be used to encourage socially beneficial activities that are otherwise undervalued in the marketplace. Recall that underproduction and underconsumption occur when marginal social benefit exceeds marginal private benefit. A subsidy that reduces price creates an incentive for more buyers to engage in a socially beneficial activity.

Regulations

A government regulation that attempts to control either the price, quantity, or quality of a product or the entry of new firms into the marketplace represents another kind of government intervention. According to the public interest theory, the regulation is justified because a market imperfection exists that would otherwise cause a misallocation of society's resources. For example, insufficient consumer information often justifies government-imposed quality requirements. As another example, government might grant monopoly status to a firm and regulate its price because one large firm can produce output more cheaply than a large number of small firms (i.e., a natural monopoly, such as an electric utility or a local telephone company). The effect of government regulations in medical markets is hard to predict. Whether government impedes or promotes efficiency depends on a host of factors, such as the competitiveness of the market, the cost structure faced by the individual medical firm, objectives motivating medical decision makers, and whether the exclusion principle holds (i.e., externalities, third-party payers, and public goods are not important considerations). In the next section, we examine the impact of a price ceiling within both a competitive and monopoly market assuming that consumers possess health insurance coverage—the most common situation in medical markets.

The Effects of a Price Ceiling in a Competitive Market.   The price paid for a good or service is one item the government might regulate. Government might regulate the price by establishing a maximum price or reimbursement level. In that case, the government sets a **price ceiling** for a product, and sellers are prohibited by law from charging a higher price to buyers covered under the ceiling. Figure 9–5 shows the effect of a price ceiling within a supply and demand model of a market for physician services.

The market demand, D, in Figure 9–5, represents the demand for physician services by many different health insurers on behalf of their consumer/subscribers. Recall that

---

4. The answers to several questions at the end of the chapter provide the logic behind this statement. In general, it can be shown that the consumers' portion of the tax revenues equals ES/(ED + ES), where ES and ED stand for the price elasticities of supply and demand.

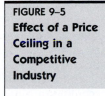

FIGURE 9–5

Effect of a Price Ceiling in a Competitive Industry

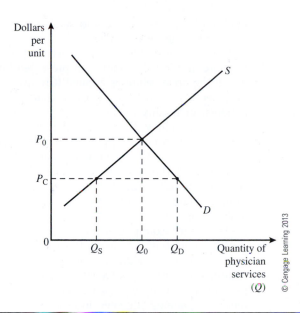

The graph represents a competitive market for physician services in which a large number of insurers negotiate with physicians and determine the market price and output of P_0 and Q_0, respectively. A price ceiling of P_C results in a shortage in the short run equal to the distance $Q_D - Q_S$.

market demand is derived theoretically by horizontally summing the individual consumer demands considering insurance features such as deductibles, copayments, and coinsurance paid by consumers. Essentially, D represents the nominal demand for medical services at the market level and represents the total price that health insurance companies are willing to pay for different quantities of physician services. As we know, supply represents the different quantities of services that physicians are willing to make available for sale at various prices. The competitive market equilibrium occurs at a price of P_0 and quantity of Q_0.

Now suppose that, for cost containment reasons, the government sets a cap or price ceiling at P_C. Because of the positively sloped supply curve, the lower price creates an incentive for physicians to reduce the quantity supplied to Q_S. Similarly, the price ceiling creates an incentive for health insurers to want to buy more of the now lower-priced service and the quantity demanded of physician services increases to Q_D. The difference between Q_D and Q_S represents a shortage of physician services that develops in the market because of the price ceiling.

In a price ceiling situation where a shortage ensues and the price mechanism is not employed as a rationing device, some unintended outcomes may occur. For one, physicians may treat patients on a first-come, first-served basis even if some patients require more urgent attention than others. Physicians may also reduce the quality of visits in an attempt to lower costs. The quality reduction may mean a longer waiting time for a visit or shorter time spent with physicians during the actual visit. In addition, some unethical physicians may accept illegal side payments from wealthy people who want to jump to the front of the waiting line. Political concerns may also dictate how scarce medical services are rationed when a shortage exists. Perhaps politicians decide that medical services should be rationed on the basis of age, illness, or the amount of political influence the individual can exert.

The point is that medical cost containment is typically not a free lunch. According to the preceding model, cost containment under plausible circumstances can result in shortages, longer waiting lines, nonprice methods of rationing, and reductions in the quality of care. Society has to seriously consider the likely trade-offs before adopting cost containment strategies.

It should be mentioned that the exact behavioral response of the medical firm may be more multidimensional than presented thus far and depends largely on the base to which the price ceiling is applied (Cromwell, 1976). Specifically, health care providers, in general, may react to a lower charge by adjusting the length of stay, number of patients, or quality of services. For example, if hospitals are paid according to a per diem price ceiling (i.e., average revenue per patient-day), they may respond to a lower per diem charge by increasing the number of patient-days to obtain additional revenues and also by lowering quality. The number of patient-days can be increased by increasing the number of new admissions and/or increasing the average length of stay. By increasing the patient's length of stay, hospitals can use the profits received from the later days to subsidize the more costly, service-intensive earlier days and make greater profits.

As another example, hospitals (or nursing homes) that are reimbursed on a per-case or per-patient basis are likely to respond to a lower per-case charge by admitting more patients to obtain additional revenues and lowering quality and length of stay. In this regard, some observers have argued that harmfully low diagnosis related group (DRG) payments, which are per-case reimbursements, have caused hospitals to release their Medicare patients "quicker and sicker."

In addition, some critics have argued that the DRG per-patient payment has created an incentive for patient dumping by hospitals. Although illegal in certain cases under the Federal Emergency Medical Treatment and Active Labor Act, **patient dumping** refers to the practice whereby private hospitals fail to admit severely sick patients and instead dump them on public hospitals. In practice, this may happen because the DRG payment is based on the historical cost of providing services to patients with an average level of sickness and does not necessarily cover the cost of providing hospital services to patients with severe illnesses.

The Effect of a Price Ceiling in a Monopoly Market. We just learned that a price ceiling can create a shortage of medical care within a perfectly competitive market. But would the outcome change if the price ceiling was applied within a pure monopoly market setting? To that we now turn our attention.

Figure 9–6 shows a hypothetical situation where a monopolist controls the market for physician services. We continue to maintain our assumption of a large number of health insurers/buyers in the market. According to economic theory, a monopolist/ physician group produces at Q_0 to maximize profits, because MR = MC at that point, and charges a price of P_0. Quantity falls below, and price rises above, the competitive levels because of the monopoly restriction of physician services in the marketplace.

Now suppose that the government sets a price ceiling of P_C for physician services. The price ceiling effectively removes the incentive of the monopolist to restrict output by prohibiting prices above the price ceiling of P_C. Stated alternatively, the price ceiling becomes the new fixed marginal revenue curve facing the monopolist-provider over that range of the demand curve. To maximize profits, the physician organization delivers the amount of services demanded by the buyers at the controlled price as long as the price ceiling lies above the marginal cost of production. In Figure 9–6, the price ceiling results in Q_C amount of physician services provided by the monopolist. In fact, if the price ceiling was set at the point where S intersects with D, then the monopolist supplies the competitive level of physician services. If the price ceiling is set below the competitive level by the government, however, then a shortage develops just like in a competitive setting. The other negative effects such as discrimination, waiting lines, and quality reductions may also develop because of the price ceiling. The exact response also depends on the base to which the price ceiling is applied (e.g., fee-for-service as assumed, per diem, or per person).

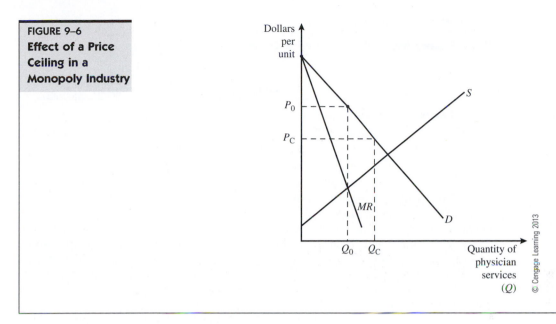

FIGURE 9–6

Effect of a Price Ceiling in a Monopoly Industry

© Cengage Learning 2013

The graph represents a monopoly market for physician services in which a large number of insurers negotiate with one large physician group and determine a market price and output of P_0 and Q_0, respectively. A price ceiling of P_C results in a greater quantity of Q_C.

The Efficiency Implication of a Price Ceiling. The earlier discussion suggests that the effect of a price ceiling on the amount of services supplied depends on the competitive nature of the market environment. A price ceiling in a competitive market results in a shortage of goods and services. In contrast, a well-designed price ceiling in a monopoly market can actually result in more output supplied in the marketplace because a monopolist's profit incentive to restrict output is removed.

A more complex question concerns the efficiency implication of a price ceiling. Recall that efficiency requires a good or service to be produced at the point where MSB equals MSC. In nonmedical markets under normal conditions, such as no externalities, utility-maximization, profit-maximization, and reasonably-informed consumers paying the full price of the good, a perfectly competitive market results in the efficient level of output while a monopoly market does not, as we learned in Chapter 8.

But, looking back at Figures 9–5 and 9–6, we must realize that the market demand for physician services represents the nominal but not necessarily the effective demand since some amount of moral hazard factors into it because of health insurance coverage. We must also recall from the discussion of the Nyman model in Chapter 6 that both efficient and inefficient moral hazard can result from health insurance. The relationship between the nominal demand and marginal social benefit depends on the nature of the moral hazard. Let's take the extreme cases to make the point.

On the one hand, suppose that all moral hazard is inefficient such that people use the insurance payoff to purchase designer prescription sunglasses, extra days in the hospital, or too many visits to the doctor. If so, the nominal demand overstates the marginal social benefit. On the other hand, assume complete efficient moral hazard as defined by Nyman. In that case, the nominal demand is identical to the marginal social benefit because the insurance provides access to life-improving medical care that people could not otherwise afford.

Table 9–1 provides a summary of the way in which the efficiency of a price ceiling depends on the interaction between the competitiveness of the market environment and whether efficient or inefficient moral hazard results from health insurance

TABLE 9–1

The Efficiency Implications of a Price Ceiling for Two Interacting Conditions

		Type of Market Structure	
		Competitive	Monopoly
Type of Moral Hazard	Efficient	Welfare-Reducing (1)	Welfare-Improving (2)
	Inefficient	Welfare-Improving (3)	Welfare-Reducing (4)

coverage. Let's first discuss cell 1 where a competitive market structure interacts with efficient moral hazard resulting from health insurance. We can predict that a price ceiling reduces social welfare in this case for the following reason. When insurance generates mostly efficient moral hazard, the market demand for medical care more closely represents marginal social benefit. That is, the health insurance helps people buy valuable medical care they could not otherwise afford. Since a competitive market normally matches up market demand with supply or marginal social cost, an efficient allocation of resources results. But a price ceiling causes a shortage when applied in a competitive market setting; therefore the price ceiling is welfare-reducing because quantity supplied will be at a level where marginal social benefit exceeds marginal social cost.

In contrast, a price ceiling can be welfare-improving when applied in a setting where a monopoly market environment interacts with efficient moral hazard, as in cell 2. Once again, market demand more closely reflects marginal social benefit when efficient moral hazard results from health insurance coverage. An unconstrained monopolist naturally restricts output such that marginal social benefit is likely to exceed marginal social cost so the price ceiling, by encouraging more output supplied, can be welfare-enhancing.

Let's now consider the case in cell 3, where a competitive market structure interacts with inefficient moral hazard. Inefficient moral hazard occurs when people stay too long in the hospital or visit the doctor more often than the socially efficient level. In this case, because of the inefficient moral hazard, (nominal) market demand overstates marginal social benefit and too much output is produced from a societal perspective by a competitive market. The price ceiling, by producing a shortage and bringing about a better alignment of marginal social benefit with marginal social cost, can be welfare improving. We leave the reader to provide the reasoning behind the welfare-reducing tendency of a price ceiling in cell 4 where a monopoly market interacts with inefficient moral hazard.

Of course, the analysis concerning efficiency can become more complicated because real-world markets are never perfectly competitive or monopolistic and insurance is likely to produce varying degrees of efficient and inefficient moral hazard. In fact, Koc (2011) finds that moral hazard effects vary considerably across disease-specific physician services. Specialist visits not associated with any medical conditions resulted in the highest moral hazard effects whereas chronic-condition related specialist care was associated with the least moral hazard effects. Certainly, the type of medical care (e.g., hospital, physician, or pharmaceuticals) also plays a role in determining the nature of the moral hazard and competition. For example, physician services markets tend to be more competitive than hospital services markets. As another example, one might expect a price ceiling on coronary bypass surgeries would be welfare-reducing in a highly competitive hospital services market because not much inefficient moral hazard or frivolous medicine is likely involved. In contrast, a price ceiling on coronary bypass surgeries might be welfare-improving if only one dominant hospital and high entry barriers exist in the market area.

Price Regulations: A Summary.   The impact of a price ceiling on the performance of a health care industry is difficult to predict. Its precise impact depends on a host of factors including the extensiveness of third party involvement, the type of moral hazard produced by health insurance, the competitiveness of the market, and the base to which the price ceiling is applied. Experience in other markets, such as natural gas and housing, has taught economists that price controls often create unwanted shortages of goods and can cause other unintended effects such as reductions in quality, longer waiting lines, and discrimination against selected groups, for instance. Sometimes price controls are implemented as a means to contain costs. If so, policy makers should be aware that cost containment may come with a considerable trade-off. However, sometimes a price ceiling is adopted so more individuals can afford a particular good. The irony is that the price ceiling may lead to a shortage, such that the good or service becomes more affordable, perhaps, but less available. This situation should not be interpreted as suggesting that we should ignore individuals who are unable to pay for life's necessities. Rather it may be that more efficient ways of providing equity are available. We consider some of these redistribution methods later in this chapter.

The Effects of Quality Regulations.   Government may also attempt to regulate the quality of medical services when consumers are rationally ignorant. As mentioned earlier, quality differences show up in the structure, process, and outcomes of production. Because procedural and outcome guidelines are more difficult to set and enforce, quality regulations are typically directed at the structure of operation. For example, a public agency may require that medical workers be professionally licensed or may mandate a minimum staff-to-patient ratio. In both cases, the assumption is that a higher level of structural quality promotes increased quality at the process and outcome stages.

Regulations aimed at the quality of the employees typically mean higher costs of production and thereby reduce the supply of medical services in the medical marketplace. The reduction of supply occurs because the acquisition of a professional license requires a greater human capital investment by the medical employee and raises the cost of providing the medical service. Figure 9–7 shows the implications of a quality

FIGURE 9–7
Effect of Professional Licensure

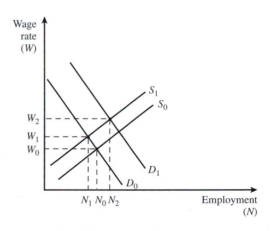

The graph represents a market for professional labor. Without occupational licensing, market equilibrium occurs at employment N_0 where D_0 intersects S_0. Occupational licensing potentially has two effects. First, the licensing requirement increases the human capital investment necessary to enter the occupation and thereby reduces supply from S_0 to S_1. Second, the higher wage of W_1 brought on by the supply reduction creates an incentive for professionals to improve their job performance. The quality assurance of occupational licensing, brought on by the improved job performance, leads to a greater demand for the output of the professional labor. As a result, demand increases from D_0 to D_1. If the demand shift exceeds the supply shift such that N_2 exceeds N_0, the occupational licensing reflects an efficient policy serving the public interest.

regulation, such as professional licensing. The original supply and demand curves for medical employees are S_0 and D_0 and the corresponding market wage and employment levels are W_0 and N_0, respectively. Professional licensing, which raises the cost of entering an occupation due to the increased human capital investment, reduces supply to S_1, and thereby raises the wage rate to W_1. The difference between W_1 and W_0 captures the **compensating wage differential** necessary to attract the marginal worker with the appropriate professional license to the labor market.

Two questions follow from the analysis. First, is professional licensing truly associated with increased procedural and outcome quality? If not, the result may not justify the method of controlling quality. Second, was a professional group behind the implementation of the professional licensing requirement? This question follows because those individuals already in the labor group (particularly those who lack the required license but are grandfathered into their positions) obviously gain from the higher wage rate.

Svorny (1987) provides an interesting way to analyze the second question by comparing a professional license to a trademark or brand name. All three of these devices may signal quality assurance to consumers. Specifically, Svorny argues that the higher wage resulting from the professional license creates a financial incentive for the typical medical worker to perform efficiently, satisfy patient wants, and provide a desirable amount and quality of output. This is because opportunistic behavior, when discovered, results in job termination and causes the medical worker to receive a low or negative return on the original human capital investment. The quality assurance generated by the higher wage, in turn, raises the marginal value of the employee's services to the consumer. The higher quality assurance can be represented by a shift to the right of the demand curve from D_0 to D_1 in Figure 9–7.

Due to the greater demand arising from the increased quality assurance, the wage rate increases further to W_2 and employment rises from N_1 to N_2. Svorny goes on to note that the model provides a useful test of whether professional licensure requirements (and other quality regulations) serve the public interest or some special interest group, such as the entrenched medical employees. If the quality regulation provides benefits (quality assurance) that exceed its cost (human capital investment), the shift of the demand curve to the right should be greater in magnitude than the shift of the supply curve to the left. Thus, employment should increase overall if society is made better off and the public interest is served by the quality regulation (i.e., N_2 should exceed N_0). However, if the opposite occurs—the supply curve shifts to the left by more than the demand curve shifts to the right—the quality regulation favors special interests.

Svorny uses the analysis to test whether basic science certification and citizen requirements for medical licensure made any difference in the number of physicians per capita across the 48 contiguous states of the United States in 1965. She notes that both requirements potentially involve some degree of human capital investment that increases wages and establishes a future return to discourage opportunistic behavior. Using multiple regression analysis, Svorny finds an inverse relation between the presence of both requirements and the number of physicians. The theory suggests that an inverse relation is evidence for the special interest model of the regulatory process.

The implication is that these quality regulations result in lower rather than higher consumption of physician services. A lower consumption of physician services results because the licensure restrictions increased entry costs by more than they increased the consumer benefits from quality assurance. Overall, the study found evidence supporting the special interest group theory of the regulatory process.

Two interesting studies on the relationship between regulatory barriers and health care outcomes also deserve mentioning. Anderson et al. (2000) find empirically that physician income is higher in states with regulations restricting the practice of homeopathy, a type of alternative medicine. Kleiner and Kudrle (2000) find that tougher dental licensing does not improve dental health but does raise the price for consumers and the earnings of dental practitioners. Consequently, these studies also support the special interest theory of regulation.

Antitrust Laws

Government also intervenes in a market economy by enacting and enforcing antitrust laws. Antitrust laws are concerned primarily with promoting competition among the firms within an industry and prohibiting firms from engaging in certain types of market practices that may inhibit efficiency. The Sherman Antitrust Act, passed in 1890, is the cornerstone of all antitrust laws. Other antitrust laws, such as the Clayton Act of 1914, the Federal Trade Commission Act of 1914, and the Celler-Kefauver Amendment of 1950, either clarify, reinforce, or extend the Sherman Act. The Sherman Act stipulates two important provisions:

> *Section 1:* Every contract, combination in the form of trust or otherwise, or conspiracy, in restraint of trade or commerce among the several states or with foreign nations, is hereby declared illegal.
>
> *Section 2:* Every person who shall monopolize, or conspire with any other person or persons to monopolize any part of the trade or commerce among the several states, or with foreign nations, shall be guilty of a misdemeanor.

Price Fixing, Boycotting, and Market Allocation.   The Sherman Antitrust Act has been interpreted as prohibiting anticompetitive business practices, such as price fixing, boycotting, market allocations, and mergers, that promote inefficiencies in the marketplace. **Price fixing** occurs when business rivals in an industry abide to a collusive agreement, refrain from price competition, and fix the price of a good or service. Essentially, firms collectively act as a monopolist, maximize joint profits, and, according to monopoly theory, create a higher price and a lower level of output. An agreement among a number of large hospitals to establish the price of various hospital services is an example of price fixing. Physicians who have been denied staff privileges frequently allege that the existing hospital physicians violated Section 1 of the Sherman Act by unlawfully conspiring to exclude them from the hospital (Jacobsen and Wiggins, 1992).[5]

A **boycott** is an agreement among competitors not to deal with a supplier or a customer. For example, suppose that in response to a Blue Shield ban on balance billing, the physicians in an area collectively agree not to offer services to Blue Shield patients.[6] While it is legal for any one physician to unilaterally refrain from dealing with Blue Shield, the combination is in violation of the Sherman Antitrust Act. In this case, the rival physicians are essentially trying to fix the price of medical services charged to Blue Shield subscribers.

Market allocation occurs when competitors agree not to compete with one another in specific market areas. This business practice can ultimately produce the same undesirable outcome that price fixing does, since each firm within the area is free to set a monopoly price and restrict output with no concern about competitive entry. Price fixing, boycotting, and market allocations are *illegal per se;* that is, they are unreasonable by their very nature and therefore illegal. To be found in violation of the Sherman Act, the plaintiff must only prove that those practices took place.

An antitrust action involving a number of health care providers in Alamogordo, New Mexico, provides a good example of a price-fixing and boycotting agreement.

---

5. See Felsenthal (1992) for an insightful discussion of how physicians and hospitals have attempted to fend off low-cost competitors such as nurse-midwives, chiropractors, and optometrists.

6. A physician boycott of this kind occurred in *Kartell v. Blue Shield of Massachusetts,* 749 F.2d 922 (1984). See Frech (1988) for an economic assessment of this antitrust suit.

In this case, the Federal Trade Commission (FTC) charged that a number of independent physicians and nurse anesthetists refused to deal individually with health plans and instead engaged in collective negotiations with them. Eighty-four percent of all physicians independently operating in the area and all nurse anesthetists participated in this arrangement. The collective price negotiations took place through a private agency that provided consulting and contracting services to a physician/hospital organization in the area. Through this private agency the health care providers orchestrated collective refusals to deal with payers that resisted their terms. The FTC argued that the joint negotiations did not enhance efficiency or consumer welfare. Those participating in the price-fixing and boycotting arrangement eventually settled by accepting the consent order of the FTC to discontinue their practice of collectively negotiating prices.[7]

Horizontal Mergers. The Sherman Act (in conjunction with Section 7 of the Clayton Act) has also been cited as a basis for preventing horizontal mergers among firms. A **horizontal merger** takes place when two or more firms in the same industry combine together. The economic concern is that a merger may harm consumers by making it easier for the remaining firms in the market to collude, expressly or tacitly (e.g., by following the leader), and thereby force price above the competitive level.

Although a combination of two or more competitor firms can result in higher prices to the consumer, the merger may also benefit the consumer if economies exist with respect to large-scale production. Larger firms may not only produce with economies of scale and organizational economies but also may have better access to technological innovations. Any cost or resource savings means society can produce more output from a given amount of inputs. For example, according to hospital officials, a proposed merger of the 710-bed Iowa Methodist Medical Center and the 319-bed Iowa Lutheran Hospital in Des Moines "could save as much as $12 million annually during the first three years of the merger" (Burda, 1993, p. 24). Similarly, officials at St. Joseph Mercy and North Iowa Medical in Mason City claimed their proposed merger "would reduce their operating expenses by $2 million to $3 million per year." Thus, potential anticompetitive and procompetitive effects must be properly weighed when determining the social desirability of a merger. Assessing the net social benefits of a business practice such as a merger is referred to as the **rule of reason** doctrine.

The Williamson (1969) merger trade-off model in Figure 9–8 provides an insightful way to conceptualize the net social benefit of a horizontal merger. Suppose the market in some geographical area is competitive before the merger and the industry is characterized by constant costs. As a result, the market price and quantity of hospital services are P_0 and Q_0, respectively, where the demand curve intersects the original supply curve S_0. Now suppose a merger of two hospitals in the area makes it easier for the remaining firms to collude and reduce output to Q_1 and raise price to P_1. Relative to the original competitive equilibrium, a deadweight loss of area *bad* occurs. The deadweight loss reflects the social cost, C, associated with the merger.

Suppose that due to the horizontal merger and the associated greater production efficiency, the per-unit cost of producing hospital services declines from AC_0 to AC_1. Cost savings might accrue from economies of scale at the firm level, improved access to capital markets, purchasing discounts, or managerial economies. This reflects some important resource cost savings to society. Resources are saved and can be used for other purposes if a larger firm is more efficient in production. Compared to the costs in a competitive market, the total resource cost savings is measured by area P_0akh. The area reflects the social benefit, B, that arises from the merger. The net benefit of the merger is found by subtracting the deadweight loss of area C from the resource

7. See http://www.ftc.gov/opa/2004/09/whitesands.htm (accessed January 22, 2012). Also, see Chapter 8 for another example involving collusion among orthopedists.

FIGURE 9–8
Williamson's Merger Trade-Off

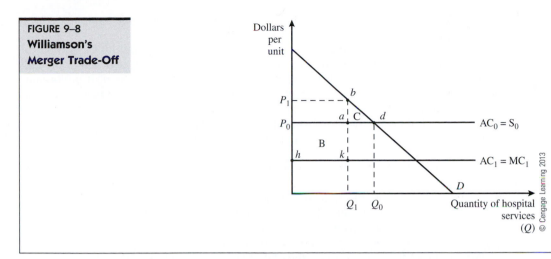

The graph represents the market for hospital services supposing a constant-cost industry. Suppose the hospital market is initially in equilibrium at Q_0 where D intersects S_0. Now suppose two relatively large firms merge and the resulting collusion among the firms in the market causes output to fall to Q_1 and price to rise to P_1. The deadweight loss of area bad represents the cost, C, of the merger. But suppose the merger also results in cost savings such that average costs falls to AC_1. The cost savings, represented by the area P_0akh, reflect the benefits of the merger. To determine whether if the merger provides net social benefits, the benefits of the merger must be compared to the costs of the merger.

cost savings of area B. As drawn, the merger provides positive net benefits to society. Of course, actual mergers may cause net benefits or losses depending on the relative magnitudes of the cost savings and deadweight losses. The bottom line is that a proposed horizontal merger should be given careful scrutiny using cost-benefit analysis.

Exclusive Dealing Contracts. An **exclusive dealing contract** is another business practice that may impede efficiency and therefore violate antitrust laws. An exclusive dealing occurs, for example, when a manufacturer allows only one distributor to sell its product or products in a market area. Economists consider an exclusive dealing arrangement as one of several types of vertical restrictions that often take place between manufacturers and distributors. Vertical restrictions are viewed as an alternative to a vertical merger, where firms at different stages of production, such as a manufacturer and distributor, merge their operations. Other types of vertical restrictions include exclusive territories, resale price agreements, tying contracts (explained shortly), and franchise arrangements.

In general, vertical restrictions can have anticompetitive or procompetitive impacts and thereby potentially harm or benefit consumers. In terms of exclusive dealings, consumers may be harmed if rival manufacturers are foreclosed from offering their products through the distributor in a market area. The foreclosure limits competition and raises product prices.

However, exclusive dealing contracts can also reduce the free-rider problem that sometimes accompanies exchanges between manufacturers and distributors. For example, suppose that two manufacturers in the same industry, A and B, want to sell their reasonably similar products through a distributor in a market area. Further suppose that manufacturer A invests a considerable sum of money training the staff of the area distributor about the intricate details behind its product. Or, suppose that manufacturer A advertises the general availability of its product and provides a list of potential consumers to the distributor. Obviously, consumers gain from the advertising message and when they purchase quality products from an informed distributor. It also follows that manufacturer A may have to charge a higher price for its product to cover the training and advertising costs and the establishment and updating of the customer list.

However, the rival manufacturer, manufacturer B, may free-ride the investment of manufacturer A by selling its products to the same distributor at a lower price, and receiving the benefits of a well-trained staff and the advertising at the distribution outlet. In fact, if no exclusive dealing contract existed, such that each manufacturer faced an incentive to free-ride the first-mover investment of the other, much less training and advertising would take place and consumers would be potentially harmed. Exclusive dealings represent a solution to the underinvestment caused by this free-rider problem.

The courts have generally embraced a rule of reason approach to cases involving exclusive dealing arrangements. First, the manufacturer involved in the dealing must be shown to possess a critical degree of market power in the relevant market. Second, the exclusive arrangement must be shown to inhibit competition and harm consumers. The ultimate proof of inhibited competition is to show that consumers pay higher prices and receive fewer services because of the exclusive dealing contract.

For example, in January 1999, the Department of Justice (DOJ) filed an antitrust lawsuit against Dentsply International, Inc., a dental supply company in York, Pennsylvania. The lawsuit alleged that Dentsply, which controlled more than 70 percent of the U.S. market for prefabricating artificial teeth over the previous ten-year period, illegally entered into exclusive dealing arrangements with its dealers. The DOJ claimed that the exclusive dealing contracts prevented independent dealers from selling other brands of false teeth, resulting in reduced competition and higher prices for false teeth. The DOJ (1999, p. 14) argued, "Dentsply's exclusion of its rivals has resulted in higher prices, loss of choice, less market information, and lower quality of artificial teeth."

The U.S. District Court for the District of Delaware ruled in 2003 that Dentsply International, Inc. did not violate federal antitrust laws. While the market power of Dentsply was recognized, the court ruled that the DOJ failed to prove that Dentsply's policy prevented competition in the market. The court pointed out that competing manufacturers could sell to their customers—the dental laboratories—directly or through new dealers. Moreover, Dentsply's dealers were free to leave Dentsply whenever they chose. Hence the court maintained that Dentsply had not used its market power in the artificial teeth market to create a market with artificially high prices and thus did not violate the Sherman Act under a rule of reason analysis.

Interestingly, the court was not convinced that Dentsply's exclusive dealing arrangement was necessary to protect its investment in the promotion of artificial teeth. Instead, the court found that Dentsply was motivated by anticompetitive intent when it adopted the policy in February 1993. But bad intent is not sufficient to find a firm in violation of antitrust laws when the conduct cannot harm competition, the court observed.

However, on appeal in 2005, the United States Court of Appeals for the Third Circuit reversed this earlier decision in the Dentsply case. The Appeals Court ruled that the ultimate consumer of artificial teeth was both the dealers and the dental laboratories. In many cases, this court pointed out, dental laboratories may prefer on economic grounds to purchase from dealers rather than directly from manufacturers of artificial teeth. Moreover, the choices of many dental laboratories may have been limited by Dentsply's exclusionary practice because they were unable to purchase artificial teeth from Dentsply's rivals through dealers. Considering that Dentsply had a high market share in the relevant market which had been maintained for more than 10 years, the Court argued that Dentsply maintained its monopoly position by acting with predatory intent to foreclose both actual and potential rivals from distributing through established dealers. In addition, the Court pointed out that Dentsply never provided a sound procompetitive argument for its exclusionary dealings with its distributors. As a result, Dentsply was found in violation of Section 2 of the Sherman Act and ordered to end its exclusionary contracts with distributors of artificial teeth.

Tying Contract.   Tying occurs when the seller of product A will sell A (the tying product) only if the buyer also purchases product B (the tied product). Similar to an exclusive dealing contract, both procompetitive and anticompetitive explanations can be offered for the use of a tying contract. Promoting high quality and reducing transaction costs are two of the several procompetitive explanations often offered for tying contracts. For instance, a vacuum cleaner may operate well only if a specific vacuum cleaner bag is used. Or, it may be logistically more costly for a seller to sell two products separately rather than together as a bundle. For example, a car typically comes with some type of radio already installed, and a computer typically comes with various software programs already installed.

In terms of its potential anticompetitive effects, a tying contract theoretically can enable a seller to practice **price discrimination**. Price discrimination occurs when different customers are charged different prices for the same good. When practiced successfully, price discrimination allows a seller to transform some portion of what would have been consumer surplus with uniform pricing into additional profits. However, price discrimination works only when the firm possesses some degree of market power, can distinguish among buyers based on willingness to pay, and can prevent the product from being resold. In the case of a tying contract, the seller charges all consumers the same fixed price for the tying product (say, a vacuum cleaner) but then uses the tied product (vacuum cleaner bags) to reveal intensity of use and charges a higher per-unit price to buyers with greater intensity. In essence, the tying contract serves as a two-part tariff with a fixed charge for the tying product and a variable charge for the tied product.

Leveraging provides another anticompetitive explanation for tying contracts. Leverage theory suggests that a monopolist in one market may attempt to extend its market power into another market with the use of a tying contract. If buyers can purchase the tying product only if they buy the tied product, and if the tying product dominates its market, the logic is that the tied product will also dominate its market. The dominance results in greater profits for the company in the tied market and overall.

While potentially resulting in either procompetitive or anticompetitive effects, the courts have tended to apply a "modified" per se ruling, rather than a rule of reason, to cases involving tying contracts (Viscusi et al., 2000). Under a modified per se ruling, the plaintiff must show both that the seller possessed market power and that the practice took place such that buyers were forced into a tying contract. Recall that for a per se violation, the plaintiff must show only that the practice took place (e.g., price-fixing, boycotting, market-sharing arrangements) and that demonstration of market power is unnecessary.

Jefferson Parish Hospital v. Hyde provides an example of an antitrust case involving a tying contract in a medical care setting (Lynk, 1994). In 1977, Dr. Hyde, a board-certified anesthesiologist, wanted to practice his services at East Jefferson Hospital and applied for privileges. The board of directors at the hospital, however, denied his application, citing that a contract had already been secured for all of the hospital's anesthesia requirements with Rioux & Associates. In response to the denial of admission, Dr. Hyde claimed that East Jefferson Hospital was in violation of the Sherman Antitrust Act. He argued that the hospital unnecessarily bundled operating and anesthesiology services as a type of tying contract and that the hospital had acquired market power for operating services in its area. Therefore, consumers were forced into purchasing anesthesiology services through the hospital if they desired surgical services.

However, in 1984, a majority of justices on the Supreme Court ruled in favor of Eastern Jefferson Hospital, citing that the hospital had little market power. Therefore, the hospital had little to gain financially from any tying contract because, without market power, the hospital was unable to profitably practice price discrimination or use any leverage.[8] This case is interesting because a minority of justices expressed the opinion that no sound reason existed for treating operating and anesthesia services as separate services because patients are interested in purchasing anesthesia only when they receive surgical services. Therefore, purposely tying the two together cannot result in greater profits because that's the way consumers desire the two services. Also, the minority opinion expressed the view that it might be desirable in the future to replace the modified per se approach to tying contracts with a rule of reason.

Most-Favored Nation Clause. A most-favored nation (MFN) clause reflects a situation where a contract specifies that the seller charges the buyer the lowest price that is charged to any other comparable buyer. Alternatively, a MFN may specify that the seller promises the buyer that the price paid will not be any higher than the price charged to any other comparable buyer (Doherty and Ras, 2006). Contracts between health insurers and health care providers, such as hospitals and physician groups, sometime specify "floor" or "ceiling" MFN clauses such as those, but typically the health insurer must have the necessary market power to receive MFN status.

According to economic theory, MFN clauses can have procompetitive or anticompetitive effects on the marketplace. With respect to the former, consumers may benefit from the lower insurance premiums that result when a health insurer faces less risk of losing market share to rivals who would otherwise be able to negotiate relatively lower prices from health care providers. In the extreme, the health insurer without the MFN clause could be priced out of the market. Also, consumers may pay lower premiums because of the lower-negotiated health care prices due to the MFN.

Anticompetitive impacts may result from MFN clauses for a number of reasons. First, new insurers may be discouraged from actually entering the market because they will be unable to compete on price by obtaining low prices similar to those charged to the entrenched, dominant insurers. This is particularly true when the new insurers are smaller sized, and therefore unable to offer enough business to offset the health care provider's loss of patient volume caused by the termination of the MFN clauses with more dominant insurers.

Second, a health care provider may be unwilling to give a discount to smaller-sized insurers simply because it would be obligated to also provide that same discount to the dominant insurers in the area. This price rigidity means that prices, on average, will not be lower than they would otherwise have been in the absence of the MFN clause. In fact, the price established by the dominant health insurer can become the price charged to all of the competitors in the market area that deal with the same providers. The MFN clause thereby suppresses competition.

In terms of enforcement, the courts seemed to have applied a rule of reason when deciding cases involving MFN clauses (Doherty and Ras, 2006). The key factor focused on is the market share that the health insurance company controls. If the insurer possesses sufficient market power, then the impact on competition, consumer choice, and prices are examined.

For example, in one antitrust case involving RxCare's pharmacy network, the FTC raised concern that a "MFN clause imposed by a dominant group of competing sellers

---

8. The hospital also couldn't gain financially because Rioux & Associates, the anesthesiology group, was reimbursed directly by payers.

can establish a price floor and restrict competition that otherwise would allow price to go below that floor" (FTC, 1996). At that time, RxCare's pharmacy network included more than 95 percent of all chain and independent pharmacies in Tennessee according to the FTC. The FTC alleged in its complaint that RxCare required pharmacies to agree to the MFN clause to participate in its network, that RxCare enforced the clause, and that RxCare urged pharmacies to refrain from participating in networks that offer lower reimbursement rates.

One very recent case involving a MFN clause deserves some discussion. In October of 2010, the DOJ filed an antitrust lawsuit against Blue Cross Blue Shield of Michigan (BCBSM) alleging that provisions of BCBSM's MFN agreements with hospitals in Michigan raised hospital prices, prevented other insurers from entering the marketplace, and discouraged discounts. According to the DOJ, BCBSM used MFNs or similar clauses in its contracts with at least 70 of Michigan's 131 general acute care hospitals, including many major hospitals in the state. These MFN agreements, the DOJ argued, resulted in Michigan consumers paying higher prices for their health care services and health insurance. At the time of the antitrust allegations, BCBSM insured more than nine times as many Michigan residents as its next largest commercial health insurance competitor, covering more than 60 percent of Michigan's three million commercially insured residents (Pear, 2010).

More specifically, BCBSM's negotiated MFN clauses require a hospital either to charge BCBSM no more than it charges its competitors or to charge the competitors a specified percentage more than it charges BCBSM, which amounted to, in some cases, between 30 to 40 percent more (DOJ, 2010). The DOJ's complaint alleged that BCBSM's use of MFN provisions reduced competition in the sale of health insurance in Michigan by raising hospital costs to BCBSM's competitors. The MFN clauses also discouraged other health insurers from entering into or expanding within markets throughout Michigan, according to the DOJ. The complaint further alleged that BCBSM agreed to raise the prices that it paid certain hospitals to obtain the MFNs, thus buying protection from rivals by increasing its own costs. At the time of this writing, the case was at the pretrial stage. It will be interesting to learn how BCBSM defends its MFN contracts on a procompetitive basis.

History of Antitrust Enforcement.   Although the Sherman Act was enacted in 1890, the health care field escaped its purview until the mid-1970s. Up to that time, it was believed that members of the medical profession, like other professionals, such as lawyers and engineers, were exempt from antitrust laws. In the *Goldfarb v. Virginia State Bar* case of 1975, the Supreme Court unanimously rejected any claim to a professional exemption and stated,

> *The nature of an occupation, standing alone, does not provide sanctuary from the Sherman Act ... nor is the public service aspect of professional practice controlling in determining whether section 1 includes professions.*

Some early signs appeared to indicate that the courts would aggressively enforce antitrust laws in health care markets. For example, in *Arizona v. Maricopa County Medical Society* in 1982, the Supreme Court condemned as price fixing the attempt by a professionally sponsored foundation to set a maximum price on the fees charged to member physicians for services underwritten by insurers that had agreed to abide by the foundation's fee schedule. Typically, when firms collude and pursue their joint interests, they agree to a price floor rather than a price ceiling. The foundation claimed that the maximum price was fixed for the benefit of the consumer. In this particular case, the Supreme Court invoked the per se illegality of price fixing, but opened the door to a possible rule of reason ruling in the future. The Court explained that the public service aspect and other features of the medical profession may require that a particular practice that could be properly viewed as a violation of the Sherman Act in another context be treated differently. The Court went on to explain that in *Maricopa*, the price-fixing arrangement was not premised on public service, ethical norms, or quality of care considerations.

Two merger cases prior to the mid-1990s, *Hospital Corporation of America v. FTC* (807 F.2d 1381 [7th Cir. 1986]) and *U.S. v. Rockford Memorial Corporation* (898 F.2d 1278 [7th Cir. 1990]) also demonstrated the Court's willingness to enforce antitrust laws aggressively and disallow horizontal mergers in the hospital services industry if they substantially lessen competition or tend to create a monopoly. In the *Rockford* case, for example, the U.S. government brought suit to prevent the horizontal merger of Rockford Memorial Corporation and Swedish American Corporation, both of which are not-for-profit institutions. Citing a high postmerger market share and, consequently, the potential for monopoly pricing, the Court ruled against the merger.

However, not all health policy analysts believe that antitrust laws should be stringently enforced in the health services industries. Some argue that various institutions, such as third-party payments, not-for-profit organizations, and excessive government regulations, mean that antitrust laws are less applicable and necessary in health care markets than in other markets. With health care costs continually increasing, many analysts claim that the enforcement of antitrust laws could actually worsen the situation as cost-minimizing joint ventures and mergers are discouraged. Indeed, legislation in Maine, Minnesota, Ohio, Wisconsin, and Washington allows hospitals to cooperate if the benefits of the proposed venture substantially outweigh the disadvantages of any reduction in competition (Felsenthal, 1993). In 1993, the DOJ and the FTC issued a joint statement of antitrust enforcement in health care markets, basically echoing the notion that the procompetitive and anticompetitive effects of various business activities, such as mergers, joint ventures, joint purchasing, and provider networks, will be weighed when making an antitrust determination.

Greaney (2002) argues that anti–managed care sentiment has reduced the enthusiasm for applying competitive principles in health care markets since the mid-1990s. With respect to the hospital industry, for example, Greaney points out that the FTC and DOJ won five of six cases challenging hospital mergers between 1984 and 1994. Many other mergers were settled or abandoned after government investigation spotlighted potential antitrust concerns. However, Greaney explains that federal and state antitrust enforcement agencies failed to successfully challenge a hospital merger case, losing all seven cases brought before the federal court after 1995. This losing record lasted for more than a decade. Reasons for the government's lack of success in the antitrust arena during this period include the Court's willingness to accept the merging hospital's efficiency defenses, differential treatment of nonprofit hospitals, tendency to broadly define the relevant geographical market for hospital services, and inclination to treat the relevant buyer as patients rather than health plans (Rice, 2010).

But after 2007, signs suggest that the antitrust pendulum may have swung back in the favor of the government, at least in terms of antitrust merger enforcement. As one example, in 2007, the FTC won its challenge with respect to the Evanston merger case. The Evanston case is particularly noteworthy because the FTC challenged the merger between two hospitals four years after it had taken place. The retrospective nature of the challenge allowed the FTC to show the actual price effects of the merger. Evidence suggested that the newly merged hospitals were able to raise their prices about 11 to 18 percent higher than other hospitals as a result of the merger. An administrative law justice, who deliberated on the Evanston case, ordered a divestiture of the two hospitals. Upon appeal, however, the full commission waived the structural remedy and settled on a conduct remedy which required the hospitals to establish separate and independent teams to negotiate reimbursement rates with health plans (Rice, 2010).[9]

As another example, in 2009, the FTC issued an administrative complaint against Carilion Clinic, a large hospital system in Virginia, alleging that its 2008 purchase of two outpatient clinics in Roanoke, Virginia, was anticompetitive. Coincidentally, this complaint against Carilion Clinic represented another post-acquisition challenge to a merger by the FTC. According to the complaint, the acquisition of the two outpatient clinics left Carilion facing competition for outpatient imaging and surgical services from only one remaining provider, Hospital Corporation of America, the other major hospital system in the Roanoke area. According to the FTC, the acquisition would increase out-of-pocket expenses for some procedures by more than 800 percent. Carilion settled with the FTC by agreeing to sell the two independent clinics (Rice, 2010; FTC, 2009).

Public Enterprise

Instead of indirectly influencing the structure, conduct, or performance of private industry, government may take a more direct role in health care provision by producing and distributing a specific health care service. For example, many local governments are responsible for providing county and city hospital services to local residents. In addition, some nursing homes and mental health facilities are operated by local or state government agencies. Moreover, the federal government runs and operates Veterans Administration and military hospitals. Despite the fact that the government may operate health care facilities, economic analysis is still useful for analyzing the many production decisions that take place. Valuable resources are used in production, and some type of economizing behavior occurs.

The primary difference between public enterprise and private, for-profit enterprise is the lack of a profit motive. Like not-for-profit entities, public health care providers may pursue goals other than profit maximization. The upshot is that public health care providers may not minimize the cost of producing a given quantity of medical care services or attempt to satisfy consumer wants. Of course, even public agencies are subject to least-cost constraints of various kinds. For example, bureaucrats and politicians are either directly or indirectly influenced by the consumer/voters' response to excessive taxation. The potential loss of job tenure may create a sufficient incentive for cost minimization even in public facilities.

Many analysts argue that public medical facilities are more likely to provide services to more severely ill patients. Unlike their for-profit (and even not-for-profit) counterparts, public medical facilities do not have to worry about the profit consequence of servicing high-cost patients. Therefore, public provision of medical services is often argued to be more equitable because all individuals, rich and poor, are provided with equal access to public facilities.

Lindsay (1976) develops a useful model of government enterprise that may explain why public hospitals tend to operate with lower per-unit costs of production than proprietary hospitals. The author assumes that politicians tie managerial compensation to the level of net social income that public organizations generate. Net social income, an analogue to profits in the private sector, is the difference between the social value of

---

9. It does not appear likely that this conduct remedy will be particularly effective at promoting competition. Even though the two hospitals cannot collectively negotiate rates, if one hospital was to significantly raise its prices, health plans would simply switch to the other hospital. Over time, the other hospital can also raise its prices in response to the greater demand. Since the hospitals belong to the same system, prices will be higher on average yet quantity will remain roughly the same for the system of hospitals (assuming health plans do not switch to hospitals outside the system. Both the administrative law justice and full commission agreed that few rivals existed in the relevant market area).

the output and the total cost of production. Higher managerial pay results from a higher level of net social income.

To estimate the value of the output provided by the public agency, politicians monitor the levels of various attributes associated with the product. Some attributes are observable and measurable; others are not. Bureau managers, in pursuit of higher pay, face an incentive to divert resources away from the production of attributes that are not easily measurable to those that are, and thus increase the perceived social value of their output. Therefore, a financial incentive exists to make the output of public institutions contain too few "invisible" attributes, such as quality (as reflected in the number of staff visits to a hospital ward, words of encouragement, number of smiles, etc.), and too many visible attributes, such as quantity (e.g., number of patients). In contrast, managers of private organizations are disciplined to a greater degree by the marketplace and forced by consumer demand to provide the desired level of quality. Price falls if private firms fail to satisfy the quality demands of customers, unlike in a public agency, where price is essentially fixed by politicians.

Lindsay's model of government enterprise predicts that the average cost of government enterprise—that is, total cost divided by visible output—will be lower than the comparable average cost of proprietary enterprise. The author offers some empirical evidence to support his view of government enterprise.

The Redistribution Function of Government

In addition to providing public goods, correcting for externalities, enforcing regulations and antitrust laws, and operating public enterprises, another function of government is to redistribute income more equitably because a pure market system cannot guarantee that everyone receives an adequate level of income. Some people own very little labor, capital, and land resources, and hence are often unable to generate a subsistence level of income in the marketplace. Redistribution involves taxing one group and using the resulting tax revenues to provide subsidies to another group. One may question why people in a free democratic society, such as that of the United States, support redistribution and rely on government to administer various programs. One justification for redistribution advanced by economists is the existence of interdependent utility functions such that donors get utility from increasing the welfare of recipients.

More formally, when utility functions are interdependent, person A derives greater utility when person B's welfare improves upon receiving a transfer of income from her. The income transfer may take the form of cash or in-kind benefits such as food or clothing. However, just like for any other good, diminishing marginal utility sets in at some point with respect to the amount of redistribution as person A gives up an increasing amount of income and forgoes other goods and services in the process of raising person B's utility. As a result, the redistribution of income ceases once the marginal benefit of the redistribution no longer exceeds its marginal cost.

Consequently, redistribution takes place in a free society because it provides utility to both recipient and donor groups. Government must administer and require people by law to contribute to the redistribution scheme through taxation because some people in the donor group might otherwise attempt to free-ride the voluntary contributions of others. For example, person C may also derive utility if person B is made better off, but may attempt to free-ride by relying on the sole contributions of person A to finance the redistribution program. Person A, in turn, may decide not to voluntarily contribute to the redistribution scheme given that others, such as person C, will indirectly benefit but will not share in the overall costs. Given the likelihood of a free-rider problem on a large scale, redistribution tends to be underprovided in a free market. So, in effect, government acts as an intermediary or fiscal agent by legally stipulating and collecting the necessary taxes from the donor group and redistributing the income to the recipient group.

But how do we know if the government's chosen redistribution scheme is equitable from a societal perspective? When judging the fairness of a redistribution scheme, economists point to the two principles of vertical and horizontal equity. To determine whether these principles are being met in a society, a basis for comparisons must first be selected. In terms of financial equity, income is normally selected as the proper basis for comparisons.

Vertical equity, which means "unequals are treated unequally," is considered as being achieved when those with higher incomes, or with greater ability to pay, incur more taxes and receive fewer benefits from government than those with lower incomes. Notice that both the tax and benefit incidence associated with government programs are considered. While taxes reduce the economic well-being of individuals, government expenditures typically raise economic well-being. Thus, both the incidence of taxes and government benefits should be considered when judging overall fiscal incidence or the overall fairness of any redistribution scheme. For example, high-income individuals may pay greater taxes but they may also greatly benefit from many of the services and subsidies offered by the public sector. Thus, net tax incidence tends to be a better measure of the overall tax burden or fairness of government policies.

However, from an equity standpoint, it is unclear how much more net taxes higher-income people should pay. For example, suppose a household with $10,000 of income pays $2,000 in net taxes and another household with $100,000 pays $4,000 in net taxes. In absolute terms, the richer household pays more taxes. When taxes are expressed as a fraction of income, however, taxes comprise only 4 percent of the rich household's income compared to 20 percent of the poor household's income.

In practice, many consider vertical equity to be achieved when the net tax system is sufficiently progressive. A redistribution scheme is considered to be **progressive** if net taxes, as a fraction of income, rise with income. The underlying belief is that higher-income individuals should pay more net taxes in both absolute and relative terms. The federal income tax system comes closest to being a progressive tax scheme because its average tax rate rises with income.

In comparison, net taxes as a fraction of income must remain constant with respect to income for a redistribution scheme to be considered as being **proportional**. The Medicare tax is a proportional tax because all payroll income is subject to a fixed percentage rate. Finally, net taxes as a fraction of income fall with income if the redistribution scheme is **regressive**. A sales tax is generally considered to be a regressive tax because although everyone pays the same tax rate, consumption expenditures as a fraction of income tend to decrease with income and consumption expenditures are the base to which the sales tax is applied.

Notice in the earlier examples we are only able to comment on the relative progressivity of various taxes. There was no mention of the progressivity of the benefits received by different income groups from various types of government programs. This is largely due to the fact that the expenditure incidence of various public programs is more complex to evaluate. For example, are more government funds disproportionately spent on goods and services consumed by higher-income or lower-income families? That's a tough question to answer empirically.

Even if we could identify how much government funds are spent on various publicly-provided services consumed by different income groups, it still would be difficult to assign monetary benefits to those services. For example, how much value would a person assign to a fully government-subsidized influenza vaccination program that costs the government $40 per dose? The actual dollar benefits people place on the vaccination would likely depend on their health status, age, and how much they value their healthy time, among other factors. Some people may have been willing to pay $40 but others may have been willing to pay much less. We don't know because these people are not spending their own money and therefore do not reveal their true willingness to pay for the vaccination. So although net taxes as a percentage of income is a preferred measure of the overall tax burden or economic incidence of a redistribution scheme, net tax burdens are often difficult to measure in practice.

With vertical equity in mind, Ketsche et al. (2011) analyze the distribution of the health care financing burden associated with the U.S. health care system. Specifically, Ketsche et al. determine the health care financing burden on families with different incomes using national data for 2004 and consider premium contributions, out-of-pocket expenses, tax savings resulting from the exemption of employer-paid health benefits, and the taxes paid to finance Medicaid, Medicare, and the health benefit tax exclusion. Their results showed that lower-income families devote a much larger share of their incomes toward health care than do higher-income families. In fact, the lowest-income families spent nearly 23 percent on their income on health care, whereas the wealthiest families spent only about 15 percent.

Overall, they point out that the burden of financing health care in the United States is regressive, mainly because only federally funded health care spending relies on progressive taxation. Missing from their analysis, however, is that low-income individuals are likely to gain disproportionately from some of the public programs that the various state and federal taxes fund. For example, low-income families are also more likely than higher-income families to receive Medicaid benefits and uncompensated care. But as mentioned earlier, the net tax burden, while a better measure of the overall tax burden of a health care system, is also much more difficult to evaluate in practice.

Horizontal equity means that "equals should be treated equally." Using income as the standard of comparison, horizontal equity implies that individuals with the same income should pay the same amount of net taxes. If not, the resulting outcome is not fair according to the principle of horizontal equity. For example, Santerre (2002) argues that the U.S. Medicaid program imposes horizontal inequities among low-income individuals. Horizontal inequities result because considerable nonuniformity exists within the Medicaid program since each of the 50 states, the District of Columbia, and the 5 territories is individually responsible, within broad federal guidelines, for its administration. The nonuniformity shows up in different eligibility requirements, benefits (e.g., package of services, number of reimbursable visits, prescription coverage), and health care provider reimbursement rates. Low physician reimbursement rates, for instance, have been shown to create severe access problems for Medicaid recipients (see Chapter 10 for more detail). As a result of these differences across states, a Medicaid-eligible family with $35,000 of income in Massachusetts may be treated much differently than a family with a similar amount of income in Alabama, causing inequities.

With these principles of horizontal and vertical equity in mind, we now examine supply-side and demand-side subsidies as different ways to redistribute medical services.

Supply-Side Subsidies. A **supply-side subsidy** is essentially a grant of money from the government aimed at reducing the internal costs of producing some consumer-oriented good or service. As an example, the subsidy may be awarded to an institution such as a public hospital, or used to finance the education of an important labor input such as a nurse or physician. A supply-side subsidy typically expands the production of a good in the marketplace by lowering the marginal private cost of production. Given a downward-sloping market demand curve, the price of the good to the consumer declines and quantity demanded increases.

In the absence of any positive externalities, economists generally argue that a supply-side subsidy leads to a misallocation of resources in a market economy. The subsidy distorts market prices and provides a false signal that production is cheaper than it really is. Output in the subsidized sector expands and resources are drawn from nonsubsidized sectors. Hence, too much output is produced in the subsidized sector and not enough resources are allocated to the nonsubsidized sectors. Some economists also argue that supply-side subsidies are an inequitable way of redistributing income. Because the subsidies are directed at the supply side of the market, individuals with different levels of income similarly benefit from the lower prices at the subsidized firms. Rich and poor alike end up paying the same price when redistribution takes place with a supply-side subsidy. Therefore, the principle of vertical equity is sometimes compromised with a supply-side subsidy.

Demand-Side Subsidies. Because a supply-side subsidy is often viewed as inefficient because it distorts resource allocation and is inequitable because it benefits all rather than only poor consumers, many economists favor **demand-side subsidies**. Often (but not always, as in the case of Medicare or the tax exemption on health care benefits), people must qualify for demand-side aid by passing a means test. A means test requires that a household of a certain size has a combined income below some stipulated level to be eligible for the aid. Tying eligibility to household income is one way to satisfy the principles of vertical and horizontal equity.

One type of demand-side aid is an **in-kind** subsidy that provides needy individuals with specific goods or vouchers for such items as food, housing, medical services, or transportation. The food stamp program, Medicare, and Medicaid are examples of in-kind subsidies. A second type of demand-side aid is a cash subsidy. People are granted a certain amount of income that they can use to purchase various goods and services of their own choice. Temporary Assistance for Needy Families (TANF) and the Supplemental Security Income (SSI) programs provide recipients with cash subsidies. The in-kind subsidy attempts to increase the quantity demanded of a specific good, whereas the cash subsidy is designed to increase the demand for various goods based on the recipient's preferences. Both programs are typically funded by taxes and do not directly affect the prices of the goods and services in the marketplace as long as the subsidized individuals are relatively few in number. A cash subsidy is preferred over in-kind aid if the goal of the donor group is to raise the utility of the recipients to the highest possible level for a given amount of transfer payments. The cash subsidy provides more utility per dollar because recipients are free to choose how they spend the money. If the donor group's goal is to ensure that the recipients consume at least a minimal amount of some specific goods, it can more easily target specific purchases with in-kind aid, given the difficulty associated with enforcing spending restrictions on cash subsidies.

Welfare Loss of Taxation. So far we have been discussing the transfer side of the redistribution program. But we cannot overlook the fact that redistribution also involves taxation. That is, some group must be taxed to finance the transfer payments made to the recipient group. According to economic theory, a tax on a resource involved in production may cause a deadweight loss by creating a disincentive for individuals to commit those resources into production. In practice, the tax may fall on the income generated by a number of different resources including labor (such as personal income tax), business capital (corporate business tax), and land (property tax). In the following discussion we consider the impact of a tax on the employment of labor because the personal income tax generates most of the revenues received by both state and federal governments. The same analytical framework can be applied to taxes on other resources and revenue bases (such as sales) as well.

Figure 9–9 shows the supply of labor, S, in some hypothetical market.[10] Notice that market supply is drawn as being upward sloping to suggest that laborers are willing to work more hours at a higher hourly wage rate. A higher hourly wage is

---

10. A demand for labor is not specified because we are interested in showing only the excess burden of the tax and not the incidence of the tax.

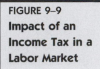

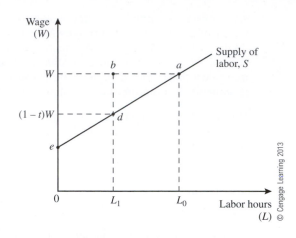

A tax on a productive resource such as labor tends to create an excess burden. Before the tax, laborers devote L_0 hours to production and receive labor surplus of Wae at an hourly wage of W. When the after tax wage falls to $(1 - t)W$, workers commit only L_1 hours to production. Labor surplus fall to the area $[(1 - t)W]de$ and tax revenues equal the area $Wbd[(1 - t)W]$. Excess burden is measured by the area bad that is lost because of the tax.

necessary to induce more labor hours into production because workers are giving up leisure time. As leisure time diminishes and becomes scarcer with a movement up the labor supply curve, the increased work hours come at a higher opportunity cost. Hence, increased wages are necessary to induce workers to commit more labor time into production.

We suppose that the hourly wage equals W before the tax is implemented such that laborers are willing to work L_0 hours. Total labor income equals the area formed by the rectangle WaL_00 and laborer (similar to producer) surplus equals the triangle formed by the area Wae. Laborer surplus equals the difference between labor income and the opportunity cost of leisure time, as measured by the area under the labor supply curve. Laborer surplus reflects the net benefit to the laborers from committing their time to production rather than leisure.

Now suppose the government imposes a proportional tax on labor income of rate t. As a result, the after tax wage rate falls to $(1 - t)W$. For example, the tax rate may equal 20 percent such that workers keep 80 percent of the income they earn per hour. Given the supply of labor, at that lower after-tax wage rate, the hours supplied by workers falls to L_1 in the market. With the tax, notice that worker surplus now falls to the triangular area formed by $[(1 - t)W]de$. Also notice that the tax revenue to the government equals the area $Wbd[(1 - t)W]$. This income tax revenue might be used to finance the transfer payment programs we discussed earlier.

The negative aspect of the tax is reflected in the area bad, the laborer surplus or net benefit that is lost because of the tax. This area is referred to as the *excess burden* of the tax. An excess burden results because worker choices between labor and leisure have been distorted such that less labor is committed to production and therefore fewer goods and services are produced in society. Alternatively stated, if the labor supply curve captures the true marginal social cost of labor and W reflects the marginal social benefit of labor, then the amount of labor is not supplied at the point where MSC equals MSB. In short, an inefficient allocation of labor takes place because of the tax and this is reflected in excess burden.

The amount of excess burden created by the tax depends on the elasticity of the supply curve with respect to the wage rate. A more elastic (flatter) supply suggests that a tax imposes a larger excess burden. In fact, a perfectly inelastic supply indicates that a tax on labor income imposes no distortion on the choice between labor and leisure. However, empirical evidence typically lends little support for a perfectly inelastic supply of labor in various markets. The upshot is that taxes can create distortions in input markets and can cause inefficiencies. Thus decision makers must carefully weigh the benefits (equity) and costs (inefficiencies) associated with redistribution programs.

Provisions of the Patient Protection and Affordable Care Act (PPACA) of 2010 Relating to Government, Health and Medical Care

The PPACA, because it is a creation of the government and will have considerable impact on the national deficit, health, and medical care, clearly relates to just about every concept and issue we discussed in this chapter. For instance, we can only wonder which provisions of PPACA reflect genuine attempts at promoting the public interests and which indicate politicians trying to satisfy various special interest groups as a way to get reelected to their offices. For example, was the individual health insurance mandate, which begins in 2014, motivated by a desire to fill the pockets of health insurance companies with more profits or an interest in eliminating a negative externality? In this particular case, a negative externality could result from uninsured individuals showing up in the emergency rooms of hospitals and not paying their bills. If left unchecked, free-riding behavior of this kind can cause negative spillovers by causing insured individuals to pay higher taxes and premiums to cover the uncompensated care of the uninsured.

Five more provisions of PPACA are discussed here that relate directly to government's role in the health economy. Two of them relate to government subsidy programs and three represent examples of some new tax initiatives contained in the new health care reform package. The first subsidy deals with public health services. In sharp contrast to medical care, which deals with personal health issues, public health services reflect the actions taken by society to advance the general health of the population as a whole. Although population-based health services take on myriad forms, most public health spending funds the surveillance and prevention of communicable diseases, testing and preservation of water quality, maintenance of sanitary conditions (e.g., approval of septic systems), ensuring of food protection (restaurant inspections), and provision of health information. Nearly 3,000 local public health departments deliver public health services in almost every area of the United States (NACCHO, 2006).

The PPACA authorized the largest expansion in federal support for public health activities in decades—a projected $15 billion over 10 years through the Prevention and Public Health Fund. Public health spending has comprised about 3 percent of all health care spending in the United States since the 1970s and pales in comparison to the vast amount of money and resources devoted to medical care. Thus, these funds represent a significant amount of additional spending on public health services in the United States. Given that Mays and Smith (2011) empirically find that local public health spending is associated with sizeable reductions in preventable deaths, these additional public health dollars, authorized by PPACA, may be well spent in terms of cost-effectiveness.

A second subsidy, offered by the PPACA, is directed toward community health centers (CHCs). CHCs are not-for-profit, community-directed providers located in high-need areas and mainly service financially indigent and vulnerable population segments. In 2008, over 1200 CHCs offered community-based medicine at 8,000 delivery sites to about 20 million people in the United States (Avalere Health LLC, 2009). CHCs treat a disproportionate share of Medicaid recipients and uninsured individuals.

In 2008, 36 percent of health center patients were covered by Medicaid and 38 percent were uninsured.

Several empirical studies have shown that CHCs are associated with lower costs and help patients, especially those with chronic conditions, to avoid unnecessary complications and acute care treatment despite the more severe patient case-mix that they tend to treat (Avalere Health LLC, 2009). PPACA provides $11 billion to create, expand, and renovate community health centers over the next 5 years effective fiscal year 2011 (on top of $155 million already authorized by the American Recovery and Reinvestment Act of 2009 to support 126 new health centers). Given the expansion in the Medicaid program, also authorized by PPACA, the additional money directed toward CHCs may also be well spent, particularly if empirical studies on the cost-effectiveness of CHCs are correct.

The PPACA also authorizes a 2.3 percent tax on the first sale or use of a medical device. Exempted from the excise tax are eyeglasses, contact lenses, hearing aids, and any device of a type that is generally purchased by the public at retail for individual use. The purpose of this tax is to help finance various public initiatives which expand health insurance coverage to the currently uninsured. As discussed in this chapter, the incidence of this tax depends on the relative elasticities of the supply and demand for medical devices.

In a recent paper, Schmutz and Santerre (2012) question how the excise tax may affect the research and development (R&D) activities of medical device companies. Previous studies on the pharmaceutical industry have shown that R&D spending is strongly and directly related to the amount of cash firms hold internally and also the market value of the companies (see Chapter 14). Internal cash flow is important for R&D because the external costs of borrowing tend to be much greater due to transaction costs and other reasons. Thus, R&D spending tends to be greater when firms have larger cash flows. The current market value of a company is important for R&D because it reflects the present value of expected profits over the near future (see Chapter 3 if you have forgotten about the concept of present value). As you might suspect, investors are typically drawn to companies with higher market values, *ceteris paribus*, because of their greater expected profitability.

Schmutz and Santerre assembled a panel data set of medical device companies over the years 1962 to 2008 to test if the R&D spending of medical device companies is sensitive to their cash flows and market values. These researchers find empirically that the elasticities of R&D spending with respect to cash flow and market value are approximately 0.58 and 0.31, respectively. The first elasticity means that medical device R&D spending increases by 5.8 percent when cash flow increases by 10 percent. Similarly, the second elasticity means that medical device R&D increases by 3.1 percent when market values increases by 10 percent.

However, a 2.3 percent excise tax reduces both cash flow and market value. Assuming the market demand for medical devices is not perfectly inelastic so medical device companies cannot completely avoid the tax, cash flow declines because taxes must be paid out of those funds. Market value is lowered because future net profits (gross profits less tax) decline as a result of the excise tax. Through a simulation based on these R&D elasticities, Schmutz and Santerre determine that roughly $4 billion of medical device R&D will be lost because of the excise tax over the first 10 years of its enactment. Moreover, based on previous quality-adjusted life year (QALY) studies relating to medical devices and a $200,000 value for a life year, the authors conclude that the medical device excise tax will result in a minimum loss of $20 billion of human lives over those same 10 years.

The indoor tanning services tax, which is likely less socially painful than the previous tax (pun intended), is also authorized by PPACA. This tax was effective for services rendered after July 1, 2010, and is applied to services that use an electronic product with one or more ultraviolet lights to induce tanning. The intent of this tax is to also help with financing of the extension of health insurance coverage to the previously uninsured. Its economic incidence depends on the relative elasticities of the supply and demand for indoor tanning services and is a function of whether sellers or buyers of tanning services can more easily avoid the tax by shifting to substitute, non-taxable activities. The questions are these: given this tax on indoor tanning, to what other activities can sellers of tanning services switch their resources toward producing, versus, to what other methods can consumers turn to for a tan? Given that consumers have the alternatives of no tanning and outdoor tanning, and because of the specialized nature of the tanning equipment, it may be the case that sellers eventually wind up paying a larger portion of the indoor tanning tax, particularly during the summer.

The last tax authorized by PPACA, which we discuss in this section, is the additional Medicare tax on high-wage workers. Under the current Medicare tax, employees and employers each pay a flat 1.45 percent of a worker's wage and salary income. Beginning in 2013, the Medicare tax rate is raised for single filers with incomes over $200,000 and married filers with incomes over $250,000 by 0.9 percentage points on the portion of household earnings that exceed those thresholds. In addition, a Medicare tax of 3.8 percent (employer's share of 1.45 plus employee's share of 1.45 plus the surcharge of 0.9) is applied to any nonlabor or unearned income that affluent households receive, such as income from capital gains, dividends, and royalties, above the $200,000 (or $250,000) threshold. These additional tax revenues are intended to help finance the expansion of health coverage to the currently uninsured, would affect only U.S. households at the very top of the income scale, and could improve tax equity by introducing more progressivity into the tax structure.

Summary

Government intervention is often necessary to correct situations where the market fails to allocate resources efficiently or distribute income fairly. In this context, government has been assigned the task of providing public goods, correcting externalities, redistributing income, and regulating the marketplace. We should keep in mind, however, that market failure is a necessary but not a sufficient condition for government intervention. Although markets may fail and impose costs on society, the costs of government intervention may be much greater. For example, it may cost the government $10 million in labor and capital costs to correct a problem in the marketplace that is imposing $8 million of damages on society. If so, it is efficient to leave the problem uncorrected. Also, both markets and governments fail in certain circumstances. One objective of economics is to determine which institution can provide which particular services in the most efficient and equitable manner.

Review Questions and Problems

1. Discuss the two views of government intervention in a market-based health care system. What role does the politician play in both of these views?
2. Health officials have suggested that the spread of AIDS can be partly contained if more males use condoms while engaging in sexual intercourse. Use the concept of a demand-side externality to explain why the number of condoms sold in the United States is likely to be lower than the optimal number. Explain some ways the government might promote a more optimal use of condoms.
3. The discussion on price ceilings supposed that the medical industry faces increasing marginal costs of production. Suppose a for-profit, monopolistic hospital is experiencing economies of scale (i.e., downward-sloping average and marginal cost curves) in the relevant range. Show graphically and discuss in writing the problems associated with a price ceiling set where the demand curve intersects the

marginal cost curve and a price ceiling set where the demand curve intersects the average cost curve. Think in terms of allocative efficiency and financial solvency.

4. Allied health professionals (e.g., social workers) are required by law to possess a professional certificate in some states; in others, they are not. Assuming sufficient data exist, discuss how you might test empirically whether this law exists to protect the public interest or to provide benefits to special interests.

5. Minnesota and Tennessee, among other states, have recently begun to tax the sales of health care providers, such as hospitals and physicians. Analyze the incidence of this sales tax for three different scenarios: (a) the demand for medical services is completely inelastic, while the supply curve is positively sloped to the right; (b) the demand curve is downward sloping and supply is completely inelastic (for this case, it is best to shift the demand curve downward by the amount of the per-unit tax); and (c) the demand curve is downward sloping and the supply curve is positively sloped. When does the consumer or the health care provider pay a larger portion of the tax? Why?

6. Do you think subsidies should be provided to lower the cost of a medical education? Why or why not? Use a graphical model in your explanation, if possible.

7. Answer the following questions regarding redistribution.
   A. Why must the government perform the redistribution function?
   B. What are horizontal and vertical equity?
   C. What are the differences among proportional, progressive, and regressive taxation?
   D. What are the three ways subsidies can be provided in practice?
   E. Comment on the relative efficiency and equity of these three methods.

8. Define *price fixing*, *boycotting*, *exclusive dealing contracts*, *tying contracts*, and *market allocations*. How have these business practices been viewed by the courts? Explain.

9. Discuss why the courts use a rule of reason when determining whether to allow a horizontal merger.

10. According to Lindsay (1976), why are the average costs of production likely to be lower for a public hospital than for an otherwise identical private hospital?

11. Suppose that the supply of labor is perfectly inelastic with respect to the wage rate in some labor market. Show graphically that no excess burden results from a tax on labor income. What does a perfectly inelastic supply of labor suggest about the opportunity cost of leisure time?

12. Suppose the laborers in a particular market are currently working 20 hours per week at a wage of $40 per hour. Further suppose that the government implements a 25 percent tax on labor income and that these same laborers are willing to work 18 hours at $30 per hour. Calculate the size of the excess burden resulting from this tax (you must know how to calculate the area of a triangle). Using this information, also calculate the elasticity of labor supply with respect to the wage rate. Average the two observations for hours worked and the wage rate when determining the base to calculate each percentage change. Now suppose that the laborers are willing to work 10 hours at $30 per hour. Recalculate the excess burden from a 25 percent tax on labor income and the wage elasticity of labor supply. What does this exercise suggest about the relation between excess burden and the supply of labor?

13. Explain the logic behind the welfare-reducing tendency of a price ceiling in cell 4 of Table 9–1.

Online Resources

To access Internet links related to the topics in this chapter, please visit our website at **www.cengage.com/economics/santerre**.

References

Anderson, Gary M., Dennis Halcoussis, Linda Johnston, and Anton D. Lowenberg. "Regulatory Barriers to Entry in the Healthcare Industry: The Case of Alternative Medicine." *Quarterly Review of Economics and Business* 40 (2000), pp. 485–502.

Avalere Health LLC. *The Effect of Community Health Centers on Healthcare Spending & Utilization*, 2009, National Association of Community Health Centers, www.nachc.com/client/Avalere_NACHC_Report_Final_10.2.09.pdf, accessed December 1, 2011.

Becker, Gary S. "A Theory of Competition among Pressure Groups for Political Influence." *Quarterly Journal of Economics* 93 (August 1983), pp. 371–400.

Burda, David. "Flurry of Merger Plans Has Eyes Focused on Iowa." *Modern Healthcare*, April 12, 1993, p. 24.

Cromwell, Jerry. "Hospital Productivity Trends in Short-Term General Nonteaching Hospitals." *Inquiry* 11, no. 2 (1976), pp. 181–87.

Department of Justice (DOJ). *Justice Department Files Antitrust Lawsuit Against Blue Cross Blue Shield of Michigan*, October 18, 2010, http://www.justice.gov/opa/pr/2010/October/10-at-1160.html, accessed November 9, 2010.

Department of Justice (DOJ). *United States of America vs. Dentsply International*, Civil Action No. 99-005, 1999, http://www.usdoj.gov/atr/cases/f2100/2164.htm, accessed June 18, 2002.

Doherty, James F. and Monique Ras. Most Favored Nation Clauses in Payor/Provider Agreements." *HMOs and Health Plans* 9 (winter 2006), pp. 1–7.

Federal Trade Commission (FTC). *Commission Order Restores Competition Eliminated by Carilion Clinic's Acquisition of Two Outpatient Clinics*, October 7, 2009, http://www.ftc.gov/opa/2009/10/carilion.shtm, accessed November 28, 2011.

Federal Trade Commission (FTC). *FTC Challenges "Most Favored Nation" Clause in Tennessee Pharmacy Network Contract*, January 19, 1996, http://www.ftc.gov/opa/1996/01/rxcare.htm, accessed November 9, 2011.

Felsenthal, Edward. "Antitrust Suits Are on the Rise in Health Field." *Wall Street Journal*, October 29, 1992, p. B1.

Felsenthal, Edward. "New Rules Let Hospitals Start Joint Ventures." *Wall Street Journal*, May 14, 1993, p. B1.

Frech, H. E. "Monopoly in Health Insurance: The Economics of *Kartell v. Blue Shield of Massachusetts*." In *Health Care in America*, ed. H. E. Frech. San Francisco: Pacific Research Institute for Public Policy, 1988, pp. 293–322.

Greaney, Thomas L. "Whither Antitrust? The Uncertain Future of Competition Law in Health Care." *Health Affairs* 21 (March/April 2002), pp. 185–96.

Havighurst, Clark C. "The Contributions of Antitrust Law to a Procompetitive Health Policy." In *Market Reforms in Health Care*, ed. Jack A. Meyer. Washington, D.C.: American Enterprise Institute, 1983, pp. 295–322.

Jacobsen, Raymond A., Jr., and Robert B. Wiggins. "Denials of Staff Privileges Face Increased Antitrust Scrutiny." *Health Care Management Review* 17 (fall 1992), pp. 7–15.

Ketsche, Patricia, E. Kathleen Adams, Sally Wallace, Viji Diane Kannan, and Harini Kannan. "Lower-Income Families Pay a Higher Share of Income Toward National Health Care Spending than Higher-Income Families." *Health Affairs* 30 (September 2011), pp. 1637–1646.

Kleiner, Morris M., and Robert T. Kudrle. "Does Regulation Affect Economic Outcomes? The Case of Dentistry." *Journal of Law and Economics* 43 (October 2000), pp. 547–82.

Koc, Cagatay. "Disease-Specific Moral Hazard and Optimal Health Insurance Design for Physician Services." *The Journal of Risk and Insurance* 78 (2011), pp. 413–46.

Lindsay, Cotton M. "A Theory of Government Enterprise." *Journal of Political Economy* 84 (October 1976), pp. 1061–77.

Lynk, William J. "Tying and Exclusive Dealing: *Jefferson Parish Hospital v. Hyde*." In *The Antitrust Revolution*, 2nd ed., eds. J. E. Kwoka, Jr., and L. J. White. New York: HarperCollins, 1994.

Manning, Willard G., et al. "The Taxes of Sin: Do Smokers and Drinkers Pay Their Way?" *Journal of the American Medical Association* (March 17, 1989), pp. 1604–9.

Mays, Glen. P. and Sharla. A. Smith. "Evidence Links Increases in Public Health Spending to Declines in Preventable Deaths." *Health Affairs* 30 (2011), pp. 1585–1593.

Musgrave, Richard A., and Peggy B. Musgrave. *Public Finance in Theory and Practice.* New York: McGraw-Hill, 1989.

National Association of County and City Health Officers (NACCHO). *2005 National Profile of Local Health Departments.* Washington, D.C.: NACCHO, 2006.

Ohsfeldt, Robert L., and Stephan F. Gohmann. "The Economics of AIDS-Related Health Insurance Regulations: Interest Group Influence and Ideology." *Public Choice* 74 (July 1992), pp. 105–26.

Pear, Robert. "U.S. Sues Michigan Blue Cross over Pricing" *New York Times*, October 18, 2010, http://www.nytimes.com/2010/10/19/business/19insure.html, accessed November 9, 2010.

Peltzman, Sam. "Toward a More General Theory of Regulation." *Journal of Law and Economics* 19 (August 1976), pp. 211–40.

Rice, Erica L. "Evanston's Legacy: A Prescription for Addressing Two-Stage Competition in Hospital Merger Antitrust Analysis." *Boston University Law Review* 90 (2010), pp. 431–463.

Rosen, Harvey S. *Public Finance.* Homewood, Ill.: Richard D. Irwin, Inc., 1995.

Santerre, Rexford E. "The Inequity of Medicaid Reimbursement in the United States" *Applied Health Economics and Health Policy* 1 (2002), pp. 25–32.

Schmutz, Bryan P. and Rexford E. Santerre. "Examining the Link Between Cash Flow, Market Value, and Research and Development Investment Spending in the Medical Device Industry." *Health Economics* (forthcoming 2012). Early view: http://onlinelibrary.wiley.com/doi/10.1002/hec.1825/abstract.

Sloan, Frank A., Jan Ostermann, Gabriel Picone, Christopher Conover, Donald H. Taylor, Jr. *The Price of Smoking.* Cambridge, Mass.: MIT Press, 2004.

Stigler, George J. "The Theory of Economic Regulation." *Bell Journal of Economics and Management Sciences* 2 (1971), pp. 137–46.

Svorny, Shirley V. "Physician Licensure: A New Approach to Examining the Role of Professional Interests." *Economic Inquiry* 25 (July 1987), pp. 497–509.

Viscusi, E. Kip, John M. Vernon, and Joseph E. Harrington. *Economics of Regulation and Antitrust*, 3rd ed. Cambridge, Mass.: MIT Press, 2000.

Williamson, Oliver E. "Economies as an Antitrust Defense: Reply." *American Economic Review* 59 (December 1969), pp. 954–59.

Government as Health Insurer

"No longer will older Americans be denied the healing miracle of modern medicine. No longer will illness crush and destroy the savings they have so carefully put away over a lifetime so they might enjoy dignity in their later years. No longer will young families see their own income, and their own hopes eaten away simply because they are carrying out their deep moral obligations to their parents, and to their uncles, and to their aunts. . . . No longer will this Nation refuse the hand of justice to those who have given a lifetime of service and wisdom and labor to the progress of this progressive country." (Speech by President Lyndon Johnson on July 30, 1965, at the Truman Library in Independence, Missouri, upon signing into law the Medicare and Medicaid programs, as quoted in DeParle [2000].)

And thus began the Medicare and Medicaid programs, the most important domestic legislation of the post–World War II era. The legislation was the political brainchild of Congressman Wilbur Mills and was referred to as a "three-layer cake." The first layer was the Johnson administration's proposed Medicare plan, a mandatory program to cover the hospital costs of the elderly and referred to as Part A. The second layer, called Medicare Part B, which was initially proposed by the AMA and Republicans who were opposed to the mandatory program, was designed to provide voluntary coverage to the elderly for physician costs. The third layer, Medicaid, expanded federal assistance to states for public insurance coverage of the poor elderly and disabled, and parents and their dependent children (DeParle, 2000).

These two public health insurance programs have continued to evolve and expand over the years. The combined cost of Medicare, Medicaid, and now State Children's Health Insurance Program (SCHIP) totaled more than $937 billion in 2010, or approximately one-third of all national health care expenditures. All indications show that this figure is going to increase in the future. The Centers for Medicare and Medicaid Services (CMS) recently estimated that the programs' total price tag would increase to a staggering $2 trillion by 2020. This represents an increase of more than 100 percent in a decade! Needless to say, elected officials are going to have their hands full over the next few years as they try to balance the desire to provide high-quality health care against competing needs and the want to hold the line on any major tax increases.

Given the importance of these public health insurance programs, this chapter:

- Describes the structure and operation of the Medicaid and Medicare programs
- Describes the State Children's Health Insurance Program (SCHIP)
- Discusses recent changes that have taken place in these programs
- Analyzes the implications of the Patient Protection and Affordable Care Act (PPACA) of 2010 with respect to Medicare, Medicaid, and SCHIP.

The information presented should be useful to you in your role as a concerned citizen, a health care policy maker, a health care provider, or a future recipient of Medicare services.

Why Does the Government Produce Health Insurance?

In the case of the Medicare and Medicaid programs, which are the focus of this chapter, government acts as a *producer* of health insurance for certain segments of U.S. society (elderly people, some disadvantaged groups, and people with certain disabilities). As a producer, government collects the tax and/or premium revenues, bears some residual risk, and establishes the reimbursement paid to health care providers.[1] Economists normally argue that government should intervene when a market fails to allocate resources efficiently or distribute income equitably. As we saw in earlier chapters, an inefficient allocation of resources occurs when a small number of powerful sellers dominate the industry, barriers to entry are substantial, consumers lack perfect information, or the exclusion principle does not hold (as for externality or public good considerations). An inequitable distribution of income results when some people lack the production characteristics needed to generate a sufficient level of income in the private marketplace.

Usually, when markets fail, government intervenes by either subsidizing the prices of goods and services when inequities are present (e.g., through food stamps and housing allowances) or regulating the production of goods and services when inefficiencies otherwise exist in an unregulated environment (such as electric utilities). That is, government typically subsidizes or regulates private production instead of directly producing the good or service. Consequently, the current system of public production of health insurance for certain population segments raises the question: Why does the government act as a producer of health insurance for certain population segments?

Imperfect information appears to provide the primary economic rationale for government intervention in the health insurance industry. In particular, consider that public health insurance presently coexists with private for-profit and private not-for-profit health insurance in the United States. As we saw in Chapter 4, different forms of ownership may coexist in markets where imperfect information exists and demands for services are heterogeneous. The imperfect information exists because some consumers lack the information they need to understand the technical terms and conditions contained in health insurance policies. Think about it. The description and explanation of health insurance nomenclature, such as deductibles, copayments, benefit coverage, and maximum liability can be mind-boggling for even the most educated individuals (Garnick et al., 1993).

Individual consumers who are uninformed may feel vulnerable to noncompetitive behavior on the part of for-profit insurers and therefore may prefer to deal with not-for-profit insurance providers that they perceive as being less likely to profit from consumer ignorance. However, not all people are uninformed. Some people are fairly knowledgeable or belong to group policies represented by informed individuals. Informed consumers may be willing to deal with for-profit health insurance providers, especially when offered quality coverage at a low price.

As a result, it is likely that government acts as a producer of health insurance in the United States as a result of informational problems and an associated demand for government-produced health insurance by certain population segments. It should be noted that the Medicare and Medicaid programs were originally structured to provide health insurance to the "medically needy"—elderly, disabled, and poor individuals—a unique group in society. As a producer, the government not only subsidizes the health insurance to promote equity but also helps to avoid the inefficiencies normally associated with information imperfections in the private health insurance market.[2]

---

1. The government often pays private health insurance companies to "administer" public health insurance. Private health insurers process the claims and pay the stipulated amounts to health care providers.

2. Due to imperfect information, adverse selection problems are also associated with the private provision of health insurance. See Chapter 11.

The Medicaid Program

The Medicaid program is designed to provide medical insurance coverage to certain individuals with low incomes. Federal and state governments jointly share the cost of the program, but states administer the program and have wide latitude in determining eligibility and the medical benefits provided. As a result, it is difficult to describe the program except in the broadest of terms.

Eligibility under the Medicaid program is determined at the state level and varies extensively across states. At a minimum, states must provide medical coverage to most individuals covered under other federal income maintenance programs, such as the Temporary Assistance for Needy Families (TANF) and Supplemental Security Income (SSI) programs, to receive matching federal funds. Among other requirements, states must provide coverage to children under age 6 and to pregnant women whose family incomes are below 133 percent of the federal poverty level, and to all children who are under age 19 and are in families with incomes at or below the federal poverty level. The federal government also requires that certain basic medical benefits be provided, such as (but not limited to) inpatient and outpatient hospital services, physician services, prenatal care, and vaccines for children.

As you can see from Table 10-1, the total number of Medicaid recipients hovered between 21 and 25 million throughout most of the 1980s. At the close of the 1990s, however, things changed dramatically as economic growth stagnated throughout the country and changes in the Medicaid program expanded eligibility. From 1990 to 2009, the number of Medicaid recipients more than doubled to 62.5 million individuals. A breakdown of recipients in 2009 shows that the single largest group was dependent children under age 21, accounting for 45.8 percent of the recipients. The next largest group, with 22.2 percent of the recipients, was adults in families with dependent children. Individuals with permanent and total disabilities (14.4 percent) and individuals age 65 and older (6.7 percent) constituted the next two largest groups of Medicaid recipients.

A look at total vendor payments by group tells a slightly different story. The lion's share of vendor payments went to individuals with permanent and total disabilities (43.4 percent). The next largest group was elderly people, with 19.8 percent of total

TABLE 10–1

Total Number of Medicaid Recipients and Total Vendor Payments for Medicaid, Selected Years 1980–2009

Year	Total Number of Recipients (millions)	Total Vendor Payments (millions)
1980	21.6	$ 23,311
1985	21.8	37,508
1990	25.3	64,859
1995	36.3	120,141
2000	42.9	168,442
2005	57.6	275,569
2009	62.5	320,752

SOURCE: U.S. Department of Health and Human Services, Social Security Administration. *Annual Statistical Supplement,* 2011, Table 8.E.

payments, followed by dependent children with 17.9 percent. Finally, adults in families with dependent children accounted for 13.5 percent of the Medicaid payments. The change in order between the two groupings based on total recipients and total costs reflects the high cost of caring for elderly and disabled individuals. For example, in 2009 the average Medicaid payment for elderly and disabled people was $15,169 and $15,454, respectively. For dependent children the average payment was only $2,004; for adults it was $3,111. Much of the difference is explained by the high cost of nursing home care for elderly and disabled Medicaid recipients.

The Financing and Cost of Medicaid

Medicaid is financed jointly by the federal and state governments, with the federal portion varying between a low of 50 percent and a potential high of 82 percent. States with the lowest per capita income receive the largest federal subsidy. In 2012, 13 states were reimbursed at the minimum level. Mississippi received the largest subsidy (74.18 percent), followed by West Virginia (72.62 percent). The average share subsidized by the federal government stands at around 60 percent.

The cost of the Medicaid program has increased substantially over time. As Table 10–1 indicates, the Medicaid program cost a little more than $23 billion in 1980 and that figure ballooned to more than $320 billion by 2009. A number of reasons account for this large increase in cost. First and foremost was a significant rise in the number of enrollees, especially between 1990 and 2002, when the number of enrollees nearly doubled. The increase primarily resulted from a number of changes in the Medicaid program that extended coverage to children and pregnant women. For example, federal mandates dictated that by 1990 Medicaid coverage was to be extended to children under age 6 and pregnant women in families with incomes below 133 percent of the federal poverty line.

Another reason for the increase in cost was a significant increase in medical prices, which forced states to increase reimbursement rates to medical care providers. High rates of medical price inflation and technological advances largely accounted for the increase in medical prices. Another factor was the increase in the number of elderly and disabled individuals in need of long-term care.

Efforts on the part of states to increase federal funding of Medicaid also contributed to rising Medicaid costs. As you can imagine, these efforts were met with some resistance from the federal government, which has had its own budgetary difficulties. Some of these efforts have been dubbed "Medicaid maximization" and involve shifting state-run health programs into the Medicaid program so that they will qualify for matching federal funds. Mental health and mental retardation services were the most common services shifted into state Medicaid programs (Coughlin et al., 1994).

Finally, **disproportionate share hospital payments** contributed to the rise in Medicaid expenditures. This was a way for states to acquire federal funds and help defer the expenses of hospitals that cared for a disproportionately high number of low-income individuals.

Do Differences in the Medicaid Program Make a Difference?

To receive federal funds to support the Medicaid program, the federal government mandates that certain population segments receive medical care coverage and that certain basic medical services be included in the coverage. After these minimum requirements are met, states are free to change the program to meet their individual needs. As a result, Medicaid programs vary widely across the country in terms of eligibility requirements, medical services covered, beneficiary contributions, and payments to providers. In addition, the program has gone through a number of changes at the federal level that have involved relaxing eligibility requirements to provide health care coverage to needy populations, specifically children and pregnant mothers. The basic question arises as to whether differences in the program over time and across states have any impact on the health of Medicaid-eligible populations.

Not surprisingly, Long and Coughlin (2001/2002) find that significant differences exist across states in terms of access to and use of health care by children with Medicaid coverage even after controlling for demographic, socioeconomic, and health factors. Kronebusch (2001) examines the impact of policy changes across states and finds that recent federal policy changes have increased Medicaid enrollment of children nation-wide and at the same time have decreased state-level variations in enrollment patterns over time. However, significant state-level policy differences still existed, particularly with regards to fee structures.

If the rates are set too low by state authorities, access problems are created for individuals covered under Medicaid. If rates are too low, profit-maximizing health care providers may find it in their best interest not to participate in the Medicaid program at all. That's because their time may be better spent servicing the medical needs of more lucrative private-pay or Medicare patients. Low Medicaid fees may also impact the quality of the care provided to Medicaid patients. Take the case of the physician who finds the Medicaid fee for a well-child office visit to be below some acceptable level. To make up the difference, the physician may spend less time with the child than otherwise would be the case and at the same time minimize the level of beneficial services provided.[3] In either case, the overall quality of care provided to children on Medicaid is adversely impacted because the physician is being compensated at a level below the comparable private-pay or Medicare rate.

Curious about the precise extent to which Medicaid fees vary across states, Zuckerman et al. (2009) report on changes in Medicaid physician fees from 2003 through 2008. Zuckerman et al. find that the average Medicaid fee varied widely across the country. Developing an index that equaled 1.00 for the national average, they find that fees ranged from a low of 0.58 for New Jersey to a high of 2.05 for Alaska. Sixteen states had Medicaid fees that were at least 25 percent greater than the national weighted average; two states had fees that were at least 25 percent lower than the national weighted average. The survey also uncovered that Medicaid fees lag behind comparable Medicare fees, as the average Medicaid-to-Medicare ratio for the entire country equaled 0.72 in 2008, up from 0.69 in 2003.

The evidence appears to suggest that Medicaid fees have a direct impact on the level of medical care provided to Medicaid recipients. Shen and Zuckerman (2005) find that higher Medicaid payments increase the probability of beneficiaries having a usual source of care and the probability of having at least one visit with a health care professional. Higher fees, however, did not improve access to all forms of care such as use of preventive care. Decker (2009) finds that cuts in Medicaid physician fees result in a reduction in the number of physician visits by beneficiaries relative to privately insured patients. Taking the discussion one step further, Gray (2001) establishes a connection between Medicaid fees and health care outcomes by uncovering a relationship between Medicaid physician fees and birth outcomes. According to the study, a 10 percent increase in the average relative Medicaid fee decreased the risk of low birthweight for a newborn by 0.074 percent and the risk of a very low birthweight by 0.035 percent.[4]

Medicaid programs across states also differ in terms of beneficiary contributions. These contributions can take the form of modest premium payments, deductibles, copayments and/or coinsurance. The federal government, however, prohibits any type of cost sharing for certain populations and medical services, and places limits on

---

3. The economics of price differentials resulting from the Medicaid program are discussed in more detail in Chapter 15. The interested reader is urged to jump to the section on the dual market model and apply the model to the current pricing problem.

4. A low birthweight is less than 2.5 kg., a very low birthweight is less than 1.5 kg.

the maximum amounts those covered by public health programs can be required to pay. Even with these restrictions, however, a vast majority of states have implemented some type of cost-sharing requirement. While it is difficult to generalize given the wide variety of programs, in most cases the cost-sharing requirements are income sensitive and do not come into play until the individual or family in question has an income in excess of some threshold, generally specified as a percent of the poverty level (i.e., 150 percent of the poverty level).

The purpose of these cost-sharing measures is rather controversial. Some argue that the cost-sharing measures give states the ability to address issues of equity by expanding health insurance coverage to include higher income groups, while at the same time limiting the cost impact on state budgets. Others contend that such policies give states the ability to partially offset the rising cost of health care on those populations who can least afford to pay. Still others argue that such cost-saving measures help contain health care costs in the long run by making people more responsible for their health care and lifestyle choices.

Regardless of the motive behind these cost-sharing policies, the empirical evidence indicates that any increase in premiums or out-of-pocket payments impacts access to medical care. After reviewing the findings from 13 different studies covering seven different states, Artiga and O'Malley (2005) conclude that recent increases in premiums have caused some to drop public health care coverage altogether and become uninsured, while increases in out-of-pocket payments have caused others to curtail the consumption of needed medical care. As you can imagine, the magnitude of the impact varies significantly across states. Kenney et al. (2006/2007) and Livermore et al. (2007/2008) also find that increases in public health insurance premiums reduced enrollment, although in the later study the reduction is rather modest.

This body of literature is extremely helpful to policy analysts because it suggests that any meaningful policy initiative aimed at improving health outcomes among needy populations by expanding Medicaid coverage must involve not only a careful look at eligibility requirements but also Medicaid fees and beneficiary cost-sharing arrangements. Better health outcomes are likely related to less restrictive eligibility requirements, higher Medicaid fees, and reduced beneficiary cost sharing. Naturally, this information is not likely to be greeted kindly by politicians and taxpayers because it implies an increase in both the number of enrollees in the Medicaid program and the cost per enrollee.

The State Children's Health Insurance Program (SCHIP)

In 1996, approximately 42 million people in the United States were without health insurance coverage and almost a quarter of that group were children under age 18. Feeling the political pressure to address what some felt was a national disgrace, Congress enacted the SCHIP as part of the Balanced Budget Act of 1997. The ultimate objective of SCHIP is to decrease the number of uninsured children by providing federal funds to states that initiate plans to expand insurance coverage to low-income, uninsured children. The federal government committed approximately $40 billion to the program over a 10-year period from 1998 through 2007. After much debate, the Medicaid, Medicare, and SCHIP Extension Act of 2007 was signed into law extending federal funding for SCHIP through March of 2009. Pretty much the same debate over the future of the program took place two years later, and after much political wrangling, legislation saving the program was passed by Congress and signed into law in 2009 extending the program through 2013.

State participation in SCHIP is voluntary. To participate, each state must submit a plan for approval that articulates how it intends to utilize the funds. States have the option of expanding insurance coverage through their existing Medicaid programs, developing separate child health insurance programs, or using a combination of the two. At the moment, combination programs are the most prevalent with nearly half of the states having developed such programs. The remaining states, in roughly equal numbers, have opted to implement a separate SCHIP or expand coverage under their current Medicaid programs.

While funding for SCHIP is similar to the Medicaid program, in that they are both jointly financed by the federal and state governments, there are a few important differences. Unlike the Medicaid program, where funding levels are unlimited, SCHIP is a block-grant program with funding caps set nationally and at the state levels. In addition, states are permitted to establish waiting lists or cap enrollments if funding limits are met. Such is not the case with the Medicaid program.

SCHIP currently provides insurance coverage to millions of children. Enrollment in the program increased sharply upon its inception and has continued to increase in recent years, albeit at a lower rate. More than 5.2 million children were enrolled in SCHIP during 2010, up from more than 660,000 children in 1998. With the expanded coverage, improved access to medical care is a definite benefit. Based on a survey of new enrollees in three states (Florida, Kansas, and New York), Dick et al. (2004) find that new enrollees have greater access to medical care along with enhanced satisfaction. This is just one of many studies that document the positive impact of SCHIP on access to health care.

Despite these achievements, there are still a large number of children without health insurance coverage. Kenney et al. (2010) estimate that in 2008, 7.3 million children were uninsured and of that number 65 percent were eligible for either Medicaid or SCHIP but not enrolled. They also find that participation rates vary significantly across states from a low of 55 percent to a high of 95 percent. In fact, slightly more than 39 percent of children eligible for insurance coverage but uninsured resided in California, Texas, or Florida.

Are the Medicaid and State Children's Health Insurance Programs "Crowding Out" Private Health Insurance?

The recent enrollment expansion in Medicaid and SCHIP has led some to question the extent to which private health insurance is being substituted for public insurance. This phenomenon, referred to in the literature as "crowding out," occurs when an individual elects to enroll in a public health insurance program when private health insurance is available. Crowding out occurs for a variety of reasons. For example, an uninsured individual who becomes eligible for Medicaid might otherwise not purchase private insurance. Or, an individual or family may elect to drop private health insurance coverage and enroll in a public plan. Finally, an employer may decide not to offer health insurance as a benefit to its employees because of the availability of public health insurance (Blewett and Call, 2007).

A recent study by Gruber and Simon (2008) finds significant levels of crowding out. In particular, the authors discover that as much as 60 percent of any expansion in public health insurance coverage results in a decrease in private insurance coverage. Other studies have estimated more modest levels of crowding out. For example, Yazici and Kaestner (2000) estimate that almost 19 percent of the increase in Medicaid enrollment resulted in crowding out of private insurance. Blumberg et al. (2000) estimate the displacement impact to be a very modest 4 percent. Finally, a study by Long et al. (2006) finds substantial variation in the amount of crowding out across four states. According to Long et al., the variability may be explained by a host of factors such as differences in the private insurance markets, eligibility standards, and other public program requirements across states. Collectively, these studies suggest that while there appears to be a certain amount of crowding out, the majority of the increase in Medicaid and SCHIP enrollment in recent years comes from the ranks of the uninsured. After reviewing the literature, Blewett and Call (2007) place the overall level of crowding out at between 25 and 50 percent.

The Medicare Program

The primary objective of the Medicare program is to improve access to medical care for elderly people by underwriting a portion of their medical expenditures. Anyone of age 65 or older and individuals with end stage renal disease are eligible for the program. The program is made up of four distinct components. Part A, the hospital insurance portion of the program primarily covers (1) inpatient hospital services, (2) some types of posthospital care, and (3) hospice care. The number of people age 65 and older covered under Part A has increased rapidly over the years and reflects the growing elderly population. In 1966, when the program first began, slightly more than 19 million elderly individuals were enrolled, and by 2009 the number of Medicare enrollees had grown to more than 46 million.

Part B, the supplementary medical insurance (SMI) program, provides benefits for (1) physician services, (2) outpatient medical services, (3) emergency room services, and (4) a variety of other medical services. Although Part B of Medicare is voluntary and requires a monthly premium to participate, a large number of elderly people have elected to purchase the insurance. During the initial year of the program, slightly more than 17 million elderly people participated and by 2009 the number had increased to nearly 43 million, almost matching the number of enrollees in the compulsory portion of Medicare. This trend reflects the fact that the federal government heavily subsidizes the cost of the SMI program.

Part C, the Medicare Advantage (MA) program, formally known as the Medicare + Choice program, provides Medicare beneficiaries the choice to join private insurance plans in an attempt to improve the efficiency and quality of health care services. Finally, Part D is voluntary for most individuals (for dually eligible Medicaid/Medicare individuals it is mandatory) and offers Medicare beneficiaries prescription drug benefits for a heavily subsidized monthly premium.

The Financing and Cost of Medicare

Since its inception, total expenditures on the Medicare program have increased at a brisk pace. In 1966 the federal government spent $7.7 billion on the Medicare program; by 1980 this figure had increased almost fivefold to $37.8 billion. As of 2010, total expenditures exceeded $524 billion. The rise in Medicare expenses through the years is explained by an increase in both the number of enrollees and reimbursement per enrollee, with the latter accounting for the majority of the increase.

Figure 10–1 displays the major funding sources for the hospital insurance program or Part A. The main source of funding has been a payroll tax of 2.9 percent, which employees and employers share equally. The payroll tax accounted for approximately 84 percent of total revenues in 2010. The second-largest revenue source has been interest income emanating from the Federal Hospital Insurance Trust Fund, which was established at the inception of the program and has built up over the years. Interest income topped $16.1 billion in 2010 and accounted for 7.5 percent of total receipts. Income from the taxation of Medicare benefits accounted for another 6.4 percent of total receipts. The remaining receipts, "Other" in Figure 10–1, made up 1.7 percent of total receipts and included transfers from the railroad retirement account, reimbursements from general revenues for uninsured people and military wage credits, and premiums of voluntary enrollees.

Medicare beneficiaries face a number of financial incentives similar to those of the privately insured to curb expenses. As we learned in Chapter 5, the out-of-pocket price, as captured by the size of the deductible and coinsurance, inversely affects the quantity demanded of medical care. The first three columns in Table 10–2 supply deductible and coinsurance information for Part A of Medicare. In 1966 the deductible was $40. It

FIGURE 10–1
Receipts for the Hospital Insurance Program, 2010

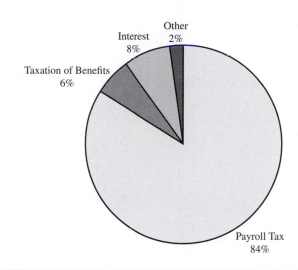

SOURCE: U.S. Department of Health and Human Services, Social Security Administration. *Annual Statistical Supplement*, 2011.

TABLE 10–2
The Cost Sharing for Medicare, Selected Years 1966–2012

| | Hospital Insurance | | | | SMI | | |
| | Deductible Daily Coinsurance | | | | Payment | | |
	1-60 days	61-90 days	After 90 days		Annual	Insurance	Monthly
1966	$ 40	$ 10	-		$ 50	20%	$ 3.00
1970	52	13	26		50	20	5.30
1980	180	45	90		60	20	9.60
1990	592	148	296		75	20	28.60
2000	776	194	388		100	20	45.50
2012	1,156	289	578		140	20	99.90

SOURCE: U.S. Department of Health and Human Services, Social Security Administration. *Annual Statistical Supplement*, 2011; and Medicare website (http://www.medicare.gov).

increased steadily through the years and by 2012 it equaled $1,156. Once the deductible is met, Medicare covers all inpatient hospital expenses for the first 60 days. For days 61–90, the enrollee is required to pay a daily coinsurance payment equal to 25 percent of the inpatient hospital deductible, or $289. After day 90, Medicare no longer covers hospital inpatient expenses. However, each enrollee is provided with an additional 60-day lifetime reserve. The reserve can be used only once and has a daily coinsurance rate of 50 percent for inpatient hospital deductible, which equaled $578 a day in 2012. Notice that once the deductible is met, the coinsurance rate is initially zero and then increases with the number of hospital inpatient days. Clearly, the intent of Medicare Part A is to provide insurance coverage for short-term hospital stays.

The SMI program, or Part B of Medicare, is financed partly through premium payments for enrollees. In 2010, total revenues exceeded $270 billion, with premium

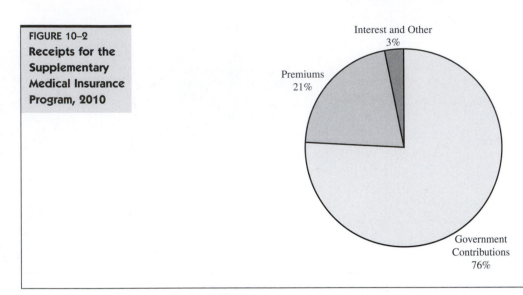

FIGURE 10–2
Receipts for the Supplementary Medical Insurance Program, 2010

Interest and Other
3%

Premiums
21%

Government
Contributions
76%

SOURCE: U.S. Department of Health and Human Services, Social Secruity Administration. *Annual Statistical Supplement,* 2011.

payments contributing 21.6 percent of the total. According to Figure 10–2, the largest source of revenues has been contributions by the government and represents the extent to which the federal government subsidies premiums. Over the years, the government has consistently provided approximately 75 percent of total revenues for the SMI program. The final source has been interest income from a trust fund and other sources, which has provided only a small fraction of revenues over the years (2.7 percent in 2010).

Despite the rapid growth in enrollees over the years, SMI premiums had to increase to provide the necessary revenues. As noted earlier, this is largely because expenditures per enrollees grew at a much faster pace than the number of new enrollees. According to Table 10–2, the monthly premium was $99.90 in 2012, up from $3 a month in 1966. In addition, the enrollee is obligated to pay an annual deductible equal to $140 and a coinsurance rate equal to 20 percent on most charges.

Given that the monthly premium is set below the expected benefits to be paid out because of the rather generous government subsidy, Medicare-eligible recipients have a strong incentive to enroll in the SMI program. The heavily subsidized premium, coupled with a modest annual deductible and a 20 percent coinsurance rate, explains why the national enrollment figures for Part B of Medicare, which is voluntary, nearly match those of Part A, which is compulsory.

The new Medicare Part D drug benefit, which began January 1, 2006, provides Medicare beneficiaries the opportunity to purchase private insurance plans that offers coverage for prescription drugs. Part D is set up such that the federal government funds approximately 75 percent of the basic prescription drug coverage, while the remaining 25 percent is funded from premiums collected from enrollees. Part D spending equaled $59 billion in 2010 and that is up from $43 billion in 2006. In 2011, more than 35 million elderly were enrolled in Part D and the average monthly premium rate for a stand-alone prescription drug plan was about $40 in 2012.

Medicare Program Reforms

In response to rising health care costs and concerns about clinical effectiveness, the Medicare program has changed dramatically since its inception. Instead of examining each of the many policy changes over the years, we focus on Medicare policies that are relevant for today's health economy. These policies are the diagnosis-related groups system, the resource-based relative value system of reimbursing physicians, Medicare volume performance standard for controlling physician expenditures, the Medicare Advantage (MA) program, and Part D of Medicare.

Diagnosis-Related Groups (DRG) System. The DRG system, first introduced in 1983, reimburses hospitals for providing care to Medicare beneficiaries based on a prospective payment system (PPS). As discussed in Chapter 4, the general idea is that a PPS creates an incentive for health care providers to more efficiently provide medical services because they are at risk for any cost overruns. Under the PPS, Medicare patients are classified based on their principal diagnosis into one of approximately 1,000 or so DRGs on entering a hospital. The prospective payment received by the hospital is a fixed dollar amount per discharge and largely depends on the DRG classification with adjustments made for factors that contribute to cost differences across hospitals.

In particular, Medicare sets a separate operating and capital payment rate for every discharge. These rates "are intended to cover the operating and capital costs that efficient facilities would be expected to incur in furnishing covered inpatient services" (MedPAC, 2002, p. 12). In most cases, the payment is established by multiplying a base payment by the relative weight for each DRG. Adjustments are made to account for variations in input prices across the country and a number of hospital- and case-specific attributes.

Each DRG weight reflects the average cost of medical care for that particular medical problem relative to the average Medicare case. The DRG weight is an index number, based on the total medical charges, that reflects the relative costs across all hospitals of providing care to the average patient in a particular DRG. The higher the DRG weight, the greater is the prospective payment.

Starting in 2008 CMS began replacing the DRG payment system with a new MS-DRG system that considers the severity of illness. This change is part of an overall strategy to improve the payment system by basing payments on costs rather than charges. The new MS-DRG payment structure consolidates the number of groups and splits others into subgroups to reflect severity of illness based on major complications or co-morbidities (MCC), complications or co-morbidities (CC), or no complications (Non-CC). Payment weights have been adjusted to reflect the differences in cost. For example, in 2012 the relative weight for an allergic reaction for someone under the age 18 was 0.275 (DRG 270) while the relative weight for a heart transplant or implant of a heart assist system with major complications and co-morbidities was 23.8227 (DRG 1). Overall the new payment system is projected to remain near budget neutral. However, hospitals treating more severely ill and costlier patients should experience an increase in Medicare payments, while hospitals treating patients with fewer complications should experience a decline in Medicare payments.

Even though the DRG system has been part of the health economy for nearly 30 years, health economists still debate its merits. Some like the idea that hospitals face a PPS and therefore carefully consider the economic costs of their actions. Others liken the DRG system to a price control where the quantity and quality of care may suffer. Recall our earlier reference in Chapter 9 to hospitals potentially releasing Medicare patients "quicker and sicker" because of the federal price control. After reviewing the literature on this topic, however, Feinglass and Holloway (1991) conclude that there "is little direct, generalizable evidence that PPS has reduced the quality of care of Medicare patients" (p. 107).

Resource-Based Relative Value Scale (RBRVS) System. Since 1992, Medicare has been reimbursing physicians based on the RBRVS system. The RBRVS system of fees considers the time and effort of physician work, or physician resources, necessary to produce physician services. The relative work values are based on the research of

William Hsiao and colleagues at Harvard University (Hsiao et al., 1988) and make up approximately half of the total value of physician services under the new fee schedule. Currently, the fee schedule is based on three weights: physician work, practice expense, and professional liability insurance. These weights are adjusted for geographic differences and multiplied by a conversion factor to determine payment. The conversion factor is updated yearly to reflect cost changes (MedPAC, 2008). Similar to the DRG system, it is expected that the prospective nature of the payment creates an incentive for physicians to produce services provided to Medicare beneficiaries more efficiently.

The RBRVS fee schedule is not without its critics. According to Hadley (1991), the entire approach is inconsistent with the theory of cost. A resource-based method determines the value of a service primarily by physician work effort and fails to consider input prices. Thus, contrary to the theory of costs presented earlier, input prices play no role in determining the marginal and average costs of production or the supply and prices of physician services. An example similar to the one developed by Hadley proves this point. In 1993, slightly more than 38,000 general surgeons were practicing in the United States. What would have happened had this number doubled by 1994, *ceteris paribus*? Supply and demand theory suggests that the average fee for surgical services would have dropped as the supply of general surgeons increased, or the supply curve would have shifted to the right. With a resource-based payment scheme, however, lower surgical fees do not result from a greater supply of surgeons because fees are based on work effort. Input prices play no role in determining market price.

Also, one might criticize the resource-based fee schedule on the grounds that it constitutes a price control. If relative fee schedules are set incorrectly, shortages or surpluses of different physician services may result. For example, more generous relative fees for specialty care services may encourage an oversupply of those services and an undersupply of primary care services in the future. Consequently, considerable care must be taken when establishing the appropriate fees for the different services.

Medicare Volume Performance Standards. While the RBRVS system controls the price of physician services to some degree under the Medicare program, it does not control for the quantity or volume of services that physicians provide. Thus, in an attempt to gain more control over the growth of Medicare expenditures, the product of price and quantity, Congress adopted a Medicare volume performance standards (VPS) system in the early 1990s that establishes expenditure limits. Each year Congress establishes a target rate of growth for physician expenditures under Medicare, or a VPS. The target considers such items as inflation, the number and ages of enrollees, barriers to access, the level of inappropriate care given, changes in technology, and any legislative changes in the program. Whether the target was met in a given year is used as a basis for determining the extent to which fees are updated the following year through the conversion factor. In other words, if the actual rate of growth in physician expenditures exceeds the VPS in a given year, the increase in physician fees for the following year may be set lower than planned through updates in the conversion factor. If, on the other hand, the actual rate of increase is below the target, the increase in fees may move upward (Physician Payment Review Commission, 1993).

The benefits from a VPS system are twofold. First, the VPS gives Congress a mechanism with which to control the rate of growth of physician expenditures. Second, the VPS gives physicians, as a group, the incentive to provide appropriate care. If excessive amounts of inappropriate care are provided, overall expenditures are driven upward, and this dampens the extent to which fees are increased in the future. Critics, however, point out that the system provides inappropriate incentives to physicians because it fails to take physician practice style into account. Given the wide variation in practice styles, a uniform payment system provides inequitable payments for medical services.

In addition, a free-rider problem may exist because such a large number of physicians participate in the system. No one physician has the incentive to eliminate inappropriate care because there is no direct relationship between individual physician behavior and future fee increases (Holahan and Zuckerman, 1993; Miller and Welch, 1993). Ginsburg (1993) responds to the latter criticism by pointing out that the intent was to directly influence the behavior of physician organizations rather than that of individual physicians. The system was later modified and the conversion factor is now tied to a Sustainable Growth Rate (SRG) that considers growth in the overall economy.

The MMA of 2003 and Medicare Advantage Plans.   The Medicare Prescription Drug Improvement and Modernization Act (MMA) of 2003 was a momentous piece of legislation because it called for major structural changes to expand the role of private insurance plans in Medicare (Davis et al., 2005). The goal of the MMA was to allow Medicare beneficiaries to enroll in a number of different managed care plans such as health maintenance organization (HMOs) and preferred provider organizations (PPOs) rather than the traditional Medicare program. The MMA also instituted a new method for calculating payment rates in an attempt to stabilize the number of private firms taking part in the Medicare program. The objective is to set the rate high enough to attract private firms and low enough to contain costs.[5] Since 2006, the CMS has established a benchmark against which private plans bid. The benchmark for each plan is based primarily on the average spending for beneficiaries enrolled in the traditional Medicare program at the county level. If the plan covers enrollees from multiple counties, then the benchmark is a weighted average of Medicare expenditures per enrollee across counties. If the submitted bid is above the benchmark, the benchmark becomes the level of payment. Finally, if the submitted bid is below the benchmark, then Medicare shares 75 percent of the difference with the private plan, provided that the funds are used by the private insurance company to enhance benefits, reduce cost sharing, or cut premiums. The remaining 25 percent of the difference is retained by the government (MedPAC, 2005).

The MMA of 2003 also established Part D of Medicare, which provides prescription drug coverage to Medicare enrollees as of January 1, 2006. This piece of legislation was significant for two reasons. First, it called for the largest onetime increase in benefits in the history of the Medicare program. Second, the legislation called for significant structural changes in the Medicare program. Specifically, it is the first time in the history of the program that a major benefit is offered that is not available through the traditional Medicare program (Davis et al., 2005).

Under Part D, Medicare beneficiaries have two options to obtain prescription drug coverage. They can remain in the traditional Medicare program under Part A and purchase a private stand-alone prescription drug plan, or they can join an MA plan that offers medical and prescription drug coverage. Under the standard benefit package, the beneficiary pays a monthly premium to a private insurer, estimated to be around $39 for 2012. The premium payment is intended to cover approximately 25 percent of the total cost of the drug benefit across beneficiaries. The remaining 75 percent of the cost is subsidized by the federal government.

The standard benefit package for 2012 includes an annual deductible of $320 and a 25 percent copayment for the next $2,610 in prescription drug expenses. Thus if a beneficiary has drug expenses of $2,930 for the year, the insurance plan covers $1,957.50 and the beneficiary has an out-of-pocket expense of $972.50 (the deductible of $320 plus 25 percent of $2,610). For drug expenses between $2,930 and $4,700 per year, the coinsurance rate is 100 percent and the beneficiary is responsible for any additional amount up to $2,610. This gap in coverage has been referred to in the popular press as

---

5. For a review of the literature, consult Coulan and Gaumer (1991), Feinglass and Holloway (1991), or Chapter 13 in this text.

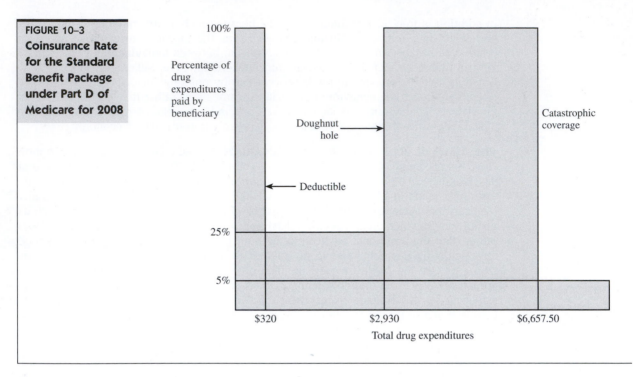

FIGURE 10–3
Coinsurance Rate for the Standard Benefit Package under Part D of Medicare for 2008

SOURCE: Rexford E. Santerre and Stephen P. Neun.

the **doughnut hole** because it represents a gap in insurance coverage. For all drug expenses beyond $4,700 per year, the beneficiary receives catastrophic insurance coverage and the coinsurance rate drops from 100 to 5 percent. In other words, the catastrophic benefit comes into play only after the beneficiary pays a total out-of-pocket drug expense of $4,700 for the year.

Figure 10–3 provides an illustration of the doughnut hole in which drug expenditures are measured on the horizontal axis and the coinsurance rate is measured on the vertical axis. The shaded area represents the percentage of each dollar spent on drugs that is the responsibility of the beneficiary. Notice that the out-of-pocket price is 100 percent for the first $320 in drug expenditures. Once the deductible has been fulfilled, the coinsurance rate drops to 25 percent and remains there up to the point where the total drug costs reach $2,930. After that point, the beneficiary is in the "doughnut hole" and the coinsurance rate increases to 100 percent. Catastrophic coverage takes hold for any drug expenses beyond $6,657.50 and the coinsurance rate drops to 5 percent.

Three points of clarification need to be discussed before we move on. First, premium and cost-sharing subsidies are provided by the federal government to beneficiaries with limited incomes. Second, the premium payments and coverage may vary across plans to reflect geographical differences in the cost of drugs and more generous benefit packages. Third, premiums, deductibles, and other out-of-pocket thresholds are indexed to increase in the future to reflect increases in per capita drug spending over time.

While it is difficult to discuss the implications of the new Medicare drug benefit, some published analysis gives us a glimpse of the program's impact. Enrollment figures supplied by CMS (www.cms.gov.) indicate that as of 2010, more than 86 percent of the more than 46 million eligible for the Medicare drug benefit have enrolled in the program in one form or another. Of those who have enrolled, approximately 44 percent have enrolled in stand-alone prescription drug plans (PDPs), while slightly more than

25 percent have enrolled in MA plans. Approximately 16 percent qualified for the low-income subsidy, and the remaining 15 percent acquired drug coverage through other means (i.e., a retirement benefit plan).

The private market for PDPs seems to be reasonably competitive, suggesting that the elderly are not victims of economic profits. In 2011, seven firms offering the top ten most popular plans controlled 77 percent of the market—four of largest firms include United-Health, CVS Caremark, Humana, and Coventry Health Care (Mark Farrah Associates, 2011). A quick calculation of the Herfindahl-Hirschman Index (HHI) suggests a mildly competitive industry with an HHI of 1,271 for the seven largest firms.

Medicare Part D has increased prescription drug use as economic theory would predict. According to Lichtenberg and Sun (2007), Medicare Part D increased prescription drug use among the elderly by 12.8 percent and increased total use in the United States by 4.5 percent in 2006. This is to be expected, given that the program reduced the out-of-pocket price of prescription drugs among the elderly by 18.4 percent in 2006. What is interesting is that Lichtenberg and Sun estimate the crowd-out rate at 72 percent. Yin et al. (2008) also find that the Medicare Part D prescription benefit resulted in an increase in drug use and a decrease in out-of-pocket expenditures.

One intriguing question deals with the impact that Part D will have on spending for hospital and physician services. The answer, in part, hinges on demand theory and whether prescription drugs and hospital or physician services are complements or substitutes in consumption. Recall from Chapter 3 that when two goods are complements in consumption, a decrease in the out-of-pocket price of one good (prescription drugs) should cause the demand for other good (hospital/physician services) to increase. If, on the other hand, the two goods are substitutes in consumption, then a drop in the out-of-pocket price of prescription drugs should cause the demand for hospital/physician services to decrease.

From a theoretical perspective, one could argue that prescription drugs and hospital/physician services are complements. For example, it may be possible that the use of prescription drugs might require frequent visits to a physician. As a result, any increase in the demand for prescription drugs will bring about an increase in the demand for physician visits. Prescription drugs can also be substitutes in consumption of other medical services. For instance, an increase in consumption of prescription drugs may prevent the use of hospital inpatient or outpatient services in the future.

Stuart et al. (2007) find no consistent pattern in the relationship between prescription drug coverage and spending for hospital or physician services for the Medicare population. The evidence suggests a complex relationship between the demand for prescription drugs and other medical services with neither effect dominating the relationship. The upshot is that the Medicare Part D benefit is unlikely to provide cost savings for Medicare spending on hospital or physician services over time.[6]

Competitive and Market Power Elements in Medicare[7]

As mentioned previously, Medicare benefits were originally provided only one way, through a government program that paid health care providers on a fee-for-service (FFS) basis. However now, in addition to this traditional or FFS Medicare program, the federal government also allows Medicare beneficiaries to choose among various taxpayer-subsidized health insurance plans offered by private insurers. While FFS Medicare is still the most popular means by which beneficiaries receive Medicare

6. But see the discussion on the new drug cost offset effect in Chapter 14 which argues that "new" drugs may save overall costs by keeping patients from receiving expensive inpatient services.

7. We thank Austin Frakt of the Veterans Administration and Boston University for contributing this section of the text. Austin blogs about health economics and health policy at the Incidental Economist (http://TheIncidental Economist.com).

coverage (currently about three-quarters of all enrollees) some beneficiaries are covered by private health insurance plans under the MA program.

MA enrollment has grown in recent years, averaging about 15 percent of all Medicare beneficiaries during the 1999 to 2005 period and then rising from 16 percent in 2006 to its current rate of 25 percent (Gold et al., 2011). Enrollment in MA generally follows how generously the government subsidizes private health insurance plans (Frakt et al., 2009). Though MA plans may offer prescription drug coverage, Medicare beneficiaries may also receive prescription drug coverage from stand-alone, taxpayer-subsidized PDPs offered by private insurers. About 60 percent of beneficiaries are enrolled in a Medicare drug plan, either through an MA plan or from a PDP (Kaiser Family Foundation, 2011). Of these, about 70 percent are enrolled in a PDP (Frakt et al., 2011). (Only beneficiaries enrolled in FFS Medicare or in MA plans known as private fee-for-service [PFFS] plans may elect to enroll in a PDP.)

The following subsections describe the MA program and PDPs in more detail and the nature of the competition between and among FFS Medicare, MA, and PDPs. We will see that the practices of these private plans are influenced to varying degrees by market concentration and their competition for beneficiaries with the traditional Medicare program.

Medicare Advantage (MA). As mentioned previously, MA plans are qualifying private health insurance plans that offer Medicare Parts A (hospital insurance), B (physician and outpatient coverage) and, optionally, D (outpatient prescription drug coverage, to be covered later) services. MA plans may elect in which geographical areas to offer coverage. Some MA plans offer coverage on a county-by-county basis whereas others provide insurance to Medicare beneficiaries in multistate regions. In many urban areas, beneficiaries can choose between MA and FFS Medicare coverage. Like FFS Medicare, MA plans are heavily subsidized by the government (taxpayers). For its non-drug coverage, each plan's payment from the government is determined by a formula that involves a benchmark, as explained previously in this chapter.

Since MA (per enrollee) payment rates are driven by rules established by Congress and play a large role in the overall subsidy cost of the MA program to taxpayers, much of the politics of Medicare hinges on the appropriate levels of these rates. Before 1997, plans were paid 95% of their estimated costs. Since then, plan payments have been only indirectly related to costs, and, in recent years, plans have been paid far above what it would cost to cover a beneficiary in FFS Medicare (Frakt et al., 2009). By law, plans must use a portion of the amount by which they are paid above their estimated costs to provide additional benefits, reduced cost sharing, or lower premiums. However, it appears that the consumer surplus associated with the additional generosity provided to MA subscribers is relatively low. For example, the value to beneficiaries of each taxpayer dollar spent on additional benefits above those provided in 2003 was only about 15 cents in 2006 (Pizer et al., 2009).

Though there are many types of MA plans, the two principal variants are coordinated care plans (CCPs), mostly HMOs and PPOs, and PFFS plans. The principal difference, as far as market competition is concerned, is that PFFS plans do not establish provider networks whereas CCPs do. At each visit, a physician may accept or decline to see a PFFS patient. CCPs, in contrast, enter into a network arrangement with individual providers, which may afford them some degree of bargaining power. In particular, to the extent CCPs can direct patients to providers in their networks, they have more leverage to negotiate lower reimbursement rates from health care providers. The lower health care provider reimbursement rates allow CCPs to provide Medicare benefits at a lower cost than PFFS plans.

In fact, in urban areas where many providers are present, some CCPs are able to provide the Medicare benefit at a cost below that of traditional FFS Medicare. In other areas, CCP costs are above those of FFS Medicare. In those areas, health care providers participate in FFS Medicare because they can expect a relatively large volume of patients to compensate for the lower rates. It stands to reason that CCPs don't participate equally in all geographical areas because not all areas are similarly profitable due to the health care provider reimbursement rates that they can negotiate (Pizer et al., 2005; Pizer et al., 2008).

MA plans compete with each other based on the price charged to Medicare subscribers (premium and cost sharing) and the amount of any additional medical benefits offered such as dental, vision, or hearing coverage. The degree of market concentration among MA plans varies geographically but is generally very high. In 2011, the market share of the top three firms or affiliates was over 90% in 15 states and DC and below 75% in 17 states and only below 50% in one state (Gold et al., 2011). The effects of competition among MA plans are comparable in importance to those of the payment rates from the government. Increased competition (lower HHI), like higher government payment rates, lowers premiums and raises the generosity of benefits (Pizer and Frakt, 2002). Lower competition (higher HHI) has been shown to be associated with greater copays for generic and brand-name drugs and lower drug caps or limits on drug coverage (Pizer et al., 2003). Higher market concentration in the MA market, has also been associated with lower entry into the MA market (fewer plans). Frakt et al. (2011) argue that this is consistent with the presence of barriers to entry. Plans that capture more of the market may obtain preferential terms with providers, effectively or explicitly foreclosing the market to potential entrants.

MA plans also compete with FFS Medicare for enrollees, though rates of enrollment in MA versus FFS tracks generosity of government subsidies as pointed out previously. This raises an important question: What would be an appropriate, market-based payment rate provided to MA plans? One way to address that question would be for plans, both MA plans and FFS Medicare, to compete for the subsidy rate, essentially submitting bids in a type of auction. Such a "competitive bidding" or "competitive pricing" concept has been studied by economists and policy analysts. According to one estimate by Coulam et al. (2009) such a system could reduce Medicare program spending by 8 percent by setting the government payment rate at the lowest submitted bid. Beneficiaries wishing to enroll in costlier plans (e.g., those that provided additional benefits or have a higher cost structure) would have to pay more out of pocket.

The Part D Drug Program.   Medicare Part D is the most recent major expansion of Medicare (implemented in 2006), offering voluntary, universal access to subsidized prescription drug coverage through private plans. MA plans can offer drug benefits (those that do are termed MA-PD plans), and for beneficiaries not enrolled in a CCP, there are stand-alone PDP options. In fact, there are a lot of them, about 30 available to every beneficiary. One of the concerns about Part D is that, with so many options, beneficiaries have a hard time making the best choice (Abaluck and Gruber, 2011).[8]

The large number of plans suggests a vigorous amount of competition exists among Part D plans. One finding consistent with that notion is that beneficiaries are relatively price sensitive in the PDP market, more so than for MA plans. Frakt and Pizer (2010) estimate the premium elasticity of demand to be −1.45, meaning a 10 percent increase in a plan's premium would lead to a reduction in enrollment of 14.5 percent. However, despite the large number of plans available, two organizations—United Healthcare and Humana—account for about half of PDP enrollment (Frakt and Pizer, 2010).

The Part D market differs from the MA market in its competitive design. In contrast to the administered pricing system of MA, all plans offering Part D (PDPs and MA-PDs) participate in a competitive bidding (auction) process that sets the rate at which they are subsidized by the government. About 75 percent of the national average bid establishes the subsidy rate and beneficiaries pay more in terms of an out-of-pocket premium for costlier plans. They pay a lower premium for cheaper ones.

---

8. The transaction costs associated with a large number of insurance choices is also discussed in Chapter 11 in the context of Medigap and non-elderly private health insurance.

One of the controversies that arose in debates over Part D legislation was how the prices paid by plans would be set. Some wanted prices set program-wide, using a government fee schedule available to other government health programs like Medicaid and the Veterans Health Administration (see Chapter 14). Others thought private plans should negotiate with drug manufacturers in the market place. Proponents of a market-based approach won, but the legislation included some constraints on the degree to which plans can leverage their negotiating power.

For example, formulary requirements constrain how vigorously plans can negotiate with manufacturers. Part D plans must include two drugs in every drug class and "all or substantially all" in six designated classes. The requirement to include a minimum number of drugs in all classes and the inability of plans to exclude drugs from six specific classes hampers their ability to extract lower prices from manufacturers (Frakt et al., 2008).

In contrast to Part D plans, the Veterans Administration (VA) offers veterans a formulary with substantially fewer drug options, though with no evidence of adverse health effects. Though the average Part D plan covers 85 percent of the most popular 200 drugs, the VA covers only 59 percent of them. In part due to its tighter formulary, the VA is able to purchase drugs from manufacturers at prices 40 percent below those of Part D plans. Frakt et al. (2011) estimated that if Part D plans could offer formularies as restrictive as the VA and pay the corresponding VA-like prices, Medicare would save $510 per beneficiary per year. However, the reduced access to drugs would come at a price, measured as a loss of consumer surplus of $405 per beneficiary per year. Notice, however, that the loss in consumer surplus is lower than the savings. So, in principle, beneficiaries could be more than compensated for their losses.

In conclusion, Medicare offers a blend of subsidized private and public coverage, within which plans are paid according to different schemes. Across parts of the program, plans (public and private) compete with each other to varying extent and have different degrees of negotiating leverage with respect to providers and suppliers. The ad hoc and hybrid public-private structure of the program reflects political compromises. Though economic analysis of aspects of Medicare offer considerable insight into the program, to fully understand how it is shaped and how it will evolve requires consideration of more than just economics. The political economy of Medicare is equally relevant to its structure and performance, if not more so (Oberlander, 2003).

Implications of the Patient Protection and Affordable Care Act (PPACA) of 2010 for Medicare, Medicaid and SCHIP

The following discussion summarizes the major provisions in the PPACA of 2010 impacting Medicare, Medicaid, and SCHIP. We begin with a discussion of the impact of the PPACA on the Medicare program.

A number of provisions in the health care reform act will impact both the cost and delivery of care in the Medicare program. While some of the Medicare provisions will increase the cost of Medicare, others will decrease the cost and according to a report by the Kaiser Foundation (Potetz, 2011), the net impact of these changes will be a reduction on Medicare spending of $424 billion through 2019. First and foremost, the PPACA calls for a reduction in the growth of Medicare payments to certain providers over time and ties future fee increases to the overall growth in productivity in the economy. Additional cost savings will be achieved by phasing out the payments for MA plans in excess of the FFS costs. These two changes alone account for more than one-half of the projected Medicare savings through the PPACA. Other cost savings provisions in the PPACA include requiring high-income beneficiaries to pay higher premiums for coverage under Parts B and D, the formation of an Independent Payment Advisory Board to recommend ways to reduce the per capita growth in Medicare expenditures, and the piloting of a number of alternative delivery system reforms.

The new law also calls for a 10 percent increase in Medicare fees for primary care services. The intent is to support the delivery of primary rather than specialty care by providing primary care physicians with additional revenue. The question is whether such a policy change will increase or decrease the cost of the Medicare program. On the one hand, raising the fees for primary care services will cause both the number and cost of primary care services to increase, thereby increasing the overall cost of the Medicare program. On the other hand, with a greater emphasis on primary care may come lower costs as Medicare beneficiaries substitute lower cost primary care for specialty care. There are other cost savings that may come with a greater use of primary care such as early detection of medical problems, greater continuity of care, and a reduction in the use of inpatient services. Using a simulation model, Reschovsky et al. (2012) estimate the impact of a 10 percent increase in Medicare fees for primary care ambulatory visits. They find that while the increase in fees causes primary care visits and the overall cost of primary care to increase, that increase is more than offset by a reduction in Medicare costs for other services. Much of the decrease in costs is attributed to lower predicted use of hospital and postacute care. The net result is that they predict Medicare spending would decrease by almost 2 percent with a 10 percent increase in the primary care fee. As a further stimulus to the use of primary and preventative care, the PPACA improves Medicare coverage to beneficiaries for certain preventive services and will provide 100 percent coverage for one annual comprehensive wellness visit.

A few provisions will likely increase the cost of the Medicare program. The main provision increasing the costs of the Medicare pertains to the gradual closing (by 2020) of the coverage gap, or doughnut hole, that currently exists in the Medicare prescription drug program. In the meantime, beneficiaries who fell into the coverage gap in 2010 received a $250 rebate, and in 2011 received a 50 percent discount on brand-name drugs. In addition, the act raises the low-income subsidy to Medicare-eligible individuals who wish to purchase but cannot afford drug coverage under Medicare Part D.

Finally, two provisions are aimed at enhancing Medicare revenue generation. First, the act calls for an increase in the Medicare tax for high-income households. Recall, that the main source of funding for Part A, the Hospital Insurance Program, has been a payroll tax of 2.9 percent, which employees and employers share equally. This rate will be increased by 0.9 percent for individuals earning over $200,000 and couples earning more than $250,000 beginning in 2013. Additional Medicare taxes will be levied on investment income received by high-income households. The health care reform act also generates additional revenue by increasing the Part B premium for high-income Medicare beneficiaries and by imposing an income-sensitive premium for Medicare beneficiaries in Part D. Finally, the act calls for a fee on drug manufacturers to be deposited in the trust fund for the SMI program (Part B).

We now turn to a review of implications of the PPACA for Medicaid and SCHIP. The "individual mandate" provision of the PPACA calls for most Americans to obtain health insurance coverage by 2014. To assist those who cannot financially afford insurance coverage the new law expands Medicaid coverage to all non-Medicare eligible individuals with incomes up to 133 percent of the federal poverty rate. In addition, states are required to maintain current eligibility standards for children in Medicaid and/or SCHIP through 2019. Estimates by the Congressional Budget Office (www.CBO.gov) indicate that these changes will expand Medicaid/SCHIP coverage by about 16 million individuals, which represents about one-half of the estimated 30 to 33 million individuals who gain insurance coverage through the health care reform law.

Recall that the Medicaid program is jointly financed by state and federal governments and that some states fund up to 50 percent of the expenditures for Medicaid. Needless to say in these economic times, the expansion of Medicaid coverage has the potential for placing an untenable financial burden on states. According to MedPAC (2012), current expenditures on the Medicaid/SCHIP programs account for 20 percent of all state spending and up to 25 percent in nine states. To ease the financial burden on state budgets, the PPACA provides additional matching federal funding to finance coverage for those who become newly eligible for Medicaid. The matching rate starts at 100 percent in 2014 and then slowly drops to 90 percent by 2020. In addition, the legislation provides funding for SCHIP through 2015 (two additional years).

The reform act also calls for an increase in Medicaid payments in FFS and managed care plans for services provided by primary care physicians to 100 percent of the Medicare rate. The hope is that higher payments for primary care will provide Medicaid beneficiaries with improved access to primary and preventive medical care.

On the cost saving side of the ledger, the reform act calls for a reduction of Medicaid disproportionate share hospital payments from 2014 through 2020 and an increase in the Medicaid drug rebate percentage to the government for brand-name drugs. Combined these changes are estimated to generate savings in excess of $50 billion through 2019.

This rather basic review of the PPACA of 2010 indicates that the Medicare and Medicaid programs along with SCHIP are going to continue to be the largest providers of health insurance in the United States for many years to come. At the moment, the three programs provide health insurance to a little more than 110 million individuals. If you factor in a modest growth in number of Medicare beneficiaries along with the growth in enrollment projected from the Medicaid expansion, the total number of individuals covered by these programs is likely to top 135 million by 2020, which will amount to slightly more than one-third of the population in the United States.

Summary

This chapter focuses on the Medicaid and Medicare programs, two public health insurance programs that account for a high and rising share of total health care costs in the United States. The Medicaid program has seen tremendous change in recent years and these changes have placed a number of states in rather precarious positions. States all across the country have been forced to control costs and at the same time meet federal mandates that call for the relaxation of eligibility requirements for certain segments of the poor. Most have turned to managed care as a way to contain Medicaid expenditures. Whether managed care offers the solution to Medicaid cost containment will most likely be a lively source of debate in the near future.

The Medicare program has also experienced significant change in the recent past. First and foremost the Medicare program over the last few decades has moved away from an FFS method of payment as its major method of payment to a prospective payment system in an attempt to contain costs. This movement started with the implementation of the diagnosis-related group payment program in the 1980s and was followed by the resource-based payment program for physician services in the 1990s. More recently, PPSs have been adopted for many other types of medical services covered by Medicare. The Medicare program has also turned to managed care with mixed results in the hopes of containing costs. Most recently, the passage of the MMA of 2003 calls for expanding the role of private insurance in Medicare and the extension of prescription drug coverage to the elderly.

Review Questions and Problems

1. Using economic theory, justify the need for the Medicaid and Medicare programs.
2. Discuss the methods states use to contain Medicaid costs.
3. Discuss the importance of Medicaid fees in determining the success of the Medicaid program in improving health outcomes of the poor.

4. What is the Medicaid crowding-out problem and why is it important?
5. In 1983, Congress adopted the prospective payment system (PPS) to compensate hospitals for medical services. Prior to that point, hospitals were paid on a retrospective basis. Provide the economic justification for such a move.
6. Explain some of the advantages and disadvantages of the resource-based method of payment for physician services under Medicare.
7. The muffler on your car suddenly needs repair, and there are only two automobile repair shops in town. You drive to the first shop, and the mechanic tells you to leave the car and he will repair it. Payment will be due when you pick it up. A mechanic at the second shop looks at your car and guarantees that she will charge you only $99.95 to repair the muffler, as advertised. Which repair shop is likely to provide costly needless repairs to your car, and why? Which one may underprovide quality? In your answers, discuss the concepts of prospective and retrospective payment for services.
8. How does the Medicare Advantage (MA) program differ from the traditional Medicare program?
9. What is the doughnut hole?
10. Why is Medicare Part D considered such a major change to the Medicare program?
11. According to Dorn et al. (2008) a one percentage point increase in the national unemployment rate would increase enrollments in the Medicaid and SCHIP programs by 1 million individuals and cause the number of uninsured to increase by 1.1 million. In light of these findings, explain the budgetary challenges state governments would face if the economy were to go into a recession and the unemployment rate were to increase.

Online Resources

To access Internet links related to the topics in this chapter, please visit our website at **www.cengage.com/economics/santerre**.

References

Abaluck J., and Gruber J. "Choice Inconsistencies among the Elderly: Evidence from Plan Choice in the Medicare Part D Program." *American Economic Review* 101 (June 2011), pp. 1180–210.

Artiga, Samantha, and Molly O'Malley. "Increasing Premiums and Cost Sharing in Medicaid and SCHIP: Recent State Experiences." *The Kaiser Commission on Medicaid and the Uninsured* (May 2005).

Blewett, Lynn A., and Kathleen T. Call. "Revisiting Crowd-Out." *The Synthesis Program Robert Wood Johnson Foundation*, September 2007, www.policysyntheses.org, accessed February 15, 2012.

Blumberg, Linda J., Lisa Dubay, and Stephen A. Norton. "Did the Medicaid Expansions for Children Displace Private Insurance? An Analysis Using the SIPP." *Journal of Health Economics* 19 (January 2000), pp. 33–66.

Coughlin, Teresa A., et al. "State Responses to the Medicaid Spending Crisis: 1988 to 1992." *Journal of Health Politics, Policy and Law* 19 (winter 1994), pp. 837–64.

Coulam R, et al. *Bring Market Prices to Medicare*. AEI Press: Washington DC, 2009.

Coulan, R. F., and G. L. Gaumer. "Medicare's Prospective Payment System: A Critical Appraisal." *Health Care Financing Review* (annual supplement, 1991), pp. 45–77.

Davis, Karen, Marilyn Moon, Barbara Cooper, and Cathy Schoen. "Medicare Extra: A Comprehensive Benefit Option for Medicare Beneficiaries." *Health Affairs* Web Exclusive, (October 4, 2005).

Decker, Sandra. "Changes in Medicaid Physician Fees and Patterns of Ambulatory Care." *Inquiry* 46 (fall 2009), pp. 291–304.

DeParle, Nancy Min. "Celebrating 35 Years of Medicare and Medicaid." *Health Care Financing Review* 22 (fall 2000), pp. 1–7.

Dick, Andrew W., et al. "SCHIP's Impact in Three States: How Do the Most Vulnerable Children Fare?" *Health Affairs* 23 (September/October 2004), pp. 63–75.

Dorn, Stan, Bowen Garrett, John Holahan, and Aimee Williams. "Medicaid, SCHIP and Economic Downturn: Policy Challenges and Policy Responses." *The Kaiser Commission on Medicaid and the Uninsured* (April 2008).

Feinglass, Joe, and James J. Holloway. "The Initial Impact of the Medicare Prospective Payment System on U.S. Health Care: A Review of the Literature." *Medical Care Review* 48 (spring 1991), pp. 91–115.

Frakt A, and Pizer S. "Beneficiary Price Sensitivity in the Medicare Prescription Drug Plan Market." *Health Economics* 19 (January 2010), pp. 88–100.

Frakt A, Pizer S, and Feldman R. 2009. "Payment Reduction and Medicare Private Fee for Service." *Health Care Financing Review* 30 (spring 2009), pp. 15–25.

Frakt A, Pizer S, and Feldman R. 2011. "Should Medicare Adopt the Veterans Health Administration Formulary?" *Health Economics*, April 2011, www.wileyonlibrary.com, accessed February 12, 2012.

Frakt A. B., Pizer S. D., and Feldman R. 2011. "The Effects of Market Structure and Payment Rates on Private Medicare Health Plan Entry." *Inquiry* 49 (spring 2012), pp. 15–36.

Frakt A, Pizer S, and Hendricks A. "Controlling Prescription Drug Costs: Regulation and the Role of Interest Groups in Medicare and the Veterans Health Administration." *Journal of Health Politics, Policy and Law* 33 (December 2008), pp. 1079–106.

Garnick, Deborah W., et al. "How Well Do Americans Understand Their Health Coverage?" *Health Affairs* 12 (fall 1993), pp. 204–12.

Ginsburg, Paul B. "Refining Medicare Volume Performance Standards: Commentary." *Inquiry* 30 (fall 1993), pp. 260–64.

Gold M., Jacobson G., Damico A., and T. Neuman. *Medicare Advantage Enrollment Market Update.* Kaiser Family Foundation, September 2011, http://www.kff.org/medicare/upload/8228.pdf.

Gray, Bradley. "Do Medicaid Physician Fees for Prenatal Services Affect Birth Outcomes?" *Journal of Health Economics* 20 (July 2001), pp. 571–90.

Gruber, Jonathan, and Kosali Simon. "Crowd-Out 10 Years Later: Have Recent Public Insurance Expansions Crowded Out Private Health Insurance." *Journal of Health Economics* 27 (2008), pp. 201–17.

Hadley, Jack. "Theoretical and Empirical Foundations of the Resource-Based Relative Value Scale." In *Regulating Doctors' Fees: Competition, Benefits and Control under Medicare*, ed. H. E. Frech III. Washington, D.C.: AEI Press, 1991.

Holahan, John, and Stephen Zuckerman. "The Future of Medicare Volume Performance Standards." *Inquiry* 30 (fall 1993), pp. 235–48.

Hsiao, William C., et al. "Results and Policy Implications of the Resource-Based Relative-Value Scale." *New England Journal of Medicine* 319 (September 29, 1988), pp. 881–88.

Kaiser Family Foundation. *The Medicare Prescription Drug Benefit: Fact Sheet*, November 2011, http://www.kff.org/medicare/upload/7044-12.pdf, February 12, 2012.

Kenney, Genevieve, et al. "Who and Where Are the Children Yet to Enroll in Medicaid and the Children's Health Insurance Program." *Health Affairs* 29 (October, 2010), pp. 1920–29.

Kenney, Genevieve, Jack Hadley, and Fredic Blavin. "Effects of Public Premiums on Children's Health Insurance Coverage: Evidence from 1999 to 2003." *Inquiry* 43 (winter 2006/2007), pp. 345–61.

Kronebusch, Karl. "Children's Medicaid Enrollment: The Impact of Mandates, Welfare Reform, and Policy Delinking." *Journal of Health Politics, Policy and Law* 26 (December 2001), pp. 1217–22.

Lichtenberg, Frank R., and Shawn X. Sun. "The Impact of Medicare Part D on Prescription Drug Use by the Elderly." *Health Affairs* 26 (November/December 2007), pp. 1735–46.

Livermore, Gina A. et al. "Premium Increases in State Health Insurance Programs: Lessons from a Case Study of the Massachusetts Medicaid Buy-In Program." *Inquiry* 44 (winter 2007/2008), pp. 428–42.

Long Sharon K., Stephen Zuckerman, and John A. Graves. "Are Adults Benefiting From State Coverage Expansions?" *Health Affairs* Web Exclusive (January 17, 2006).

Long, Sharon, K., and Teresa A. Coughlin. "Access and Use by Children on Medicaid: Does State Matter?" *Inquiry* 38 (winter 2001/2002), pp. 409–22.

Mark Farrah Associates, www.markfarrah.com/healthcarebs.asp, accessed January 15, 2012

_____. *Medicare Payment Policy Report to Congress*. Washington D.C., March 2002.

_____. *Report to the Congress: Medicare Payment Policy* Washington, D.C., March 2005.

_____. *Medicare Payment Policy Report to Congress*. Washington, D.C., June 2005.

_____. *Medicare Payment Policy Report to Congress*. Washington, D.C. March 2008.

_____. *Medicare Payment Policy Report to Congress*. Washington, D.C., March 2012.

Miller, Mark E., and W. Pete Welch. "Growth in Medicare Inpatient Physician Charges per Admission, 1986–1989." *Inquiry* 30 (fall 1993), pp. 249–59.

Oberlander J. *The Political Life of Medicare*. Chicago: The University of Chicago Press, 2003.

Physician Payment Review Commission. *Annual Report to Congress*. Washington, D.C.: PPRC, 1993.

Pizer S, Feldman R, and Frakt A. "Defective design: Regional Competition in Medicare." *Health Affairs Web Exclusive* (August, 2005), pp. w5-399-411.

Pizer S, and Frakt A. Payment Policy and Competition in the Medicare + Choice Program. *Health Care Financing Review* 24 (fall 2002), pp. 83–94.

Pizer S, Frakt A, and Feldman R. "Payment Policy and Inefficient Benefits in the Medicare + Choice Program." *International Journal of Health Care Finance and Economics* 3 (June 2003), pp. 79–93.

Pizer S, Frakt A, and Feldman R. "Predicting Risk Selection Following Major Changes in Medicare." *Heath Economics* 17 (April, 2008), pp. 453–68.

Pizer S, Frakt A, and Feldman R. "Nothing for Something? Estimating Cost and Value for Beneficiaries from Recent Medicare Spending Increases on HMO Payments and Drug Benefits." *International Journal of Healthcare Finance and Economics* 9 (March 2009), pp. 59–81.

Potetz, Lisa, et al. "Spending and Financing: A Primer." *The Henry J. Kaiser Family Foundation*. February, 2011.

Reschovsky, James, et al. "Paying More for Primary Care: Can it Help Bend the Medicare Cost Curve?" *The Commonwealth Fund Issue Brief* (March 2012).

Shen, Yu-Chu, and Stephen Zukerman. "The Effect of Medicaid Payment Generosity on Access and Use among Beneficiaries." *Health Services Research* 40 (June 2005), pp. 723–44.

Stuart, Bruce C. et al. "Will Part D Produce Savings in Part A or Part B? The Impact of Prescription Drug Coverage on Medicare Program Expenditures." *Inquiry* 44 (summer 2007), pp. 146–56.

U.S. Department of Health and Human Services, Social Security Administration. *Annual Statistical Supplement*, 2011. Washington, D.C., 2011.

Yazici, Esel Y., and Robert Kaestner. "Medicaid Expansions and the Crowding Out of Private Health Insurance among Children." *Inquiry* 37 (spring 2000), pp. 23–32.

Yin, Welsey et al. "The Effect of the Medicare Part Prescription Benefit on Drug Utilization and Expenditures." *Annals of Internal Medicine* 148 (February 2008), pp. 169–77.

Zuckerman, Stephen, Almee Williams, and Karen Stockley. "Trends in Medicaid Physician Fees, 2003–2008." *Health Affairs* 28 (2009), pp. w511–w520.

Industry Studies

PART THREE

The Private Health Insurance Industry

Our pal Joe was sort of lucky. Sure he suffered a heart attack. That in itself can be a medically frightening and painful experience. But as a federal employee, Joe and his family were covered by a sound and generous health insurance policy, so at least they did not have to bear the sharp psychological sting of the financial insecurity that can result from an unexpected medical occurrence.

However, Leo, Joe's brother, was not so fortunate. You see, Leo worked as a machinist in a specialty parts fabrication shop that employs five workers. Given the competitive nature of the market for specialty machined goods, Leo's employer was financially unable to sponsor any health insurance for the workers. But Leo and his wife, Sarah, really didn't care about the lack of health insurance anyway. They were both in their early fifties, which is relatively young by today's standards, and seemed to be in great health. They had built up a small nest egg of $100,000 and planned on using the money to support an early semi-retirement in which Leo would quit his job and open a machine shop in his garage. At age 65 both Leo and Sarah would be eligible for Medicare and then they were all set—or so they thought.

Then all hell broke loose. Sarah found a lump in her breast! A visit to a local doctor confirmed her most feared suspicion. She was diagnosed with a cancerous tumor. Since Sarah had not received annual mammograms due to what she considered an unnecessary out-of-pocket expense, the cancer was at an advanced stage. It was too late for a simple lumpectomy or chemotherapy; a radical mastectomy was deemed the necessary treatment. Not only were Leo and Sarah distraught over Sarah's physical and mental well-being, but also saddened that their hard-earned life savings would be completely wiped out.

This story raises a number of important questions:

1. Who exactly are the uninsured? That is, are specific groups or individuals, such as employees of small businesses, at a greater risk of being uninsured than others?
2. Suppose that Leo had participated in a group health insurance policy with his employer but decided to change jobs. Would he and Sarah be immediately eligible for health insurance with the new employer, especially with Sarah's condition already diagnosed?
3. If Leo did not have a group health insurance policy with his employer, would he face higher health insurance premiums or would Sarah be excluded from the policy?

This chapter deals with these questions, among others, and raises a host of other problems and issues pertaining to the private health insurance industry. The examination is couched in terms of the structure, conduct, and performance paradigm discussed in Chapter 8. Specifically, this chapter:

- provides a brief history of the private health insurance industry
- analyzes the structure of the private health insurance industry in terms of the number and types of sellers, buyer characteristics, barriers to entry, and other factors

- describes the conduct of firms in the private health insurance industry with respect to pricing methods, managed care effects, and risk selection
- assesses the performance of the private health insurance industry with regard to the number of insured and uninsured, pricing, and moral hazard
- points out how the Patient Protection and Affordable Care Act (PPACA) of 2010 may impact the health insurance industry in the United States.

A Brief History of the Private Health Insurance Industry

The modern private health insurance industry started around 1929 when Baylor University in Dallas began accepting insurance premiums from local schoolteachers to cover any medical services provided at the university hospital (Temin, 1988).[1] The idea quickly spread during the Great Depression of the 1930s as a number of hospitals adopted similar financing methods. Shortly thereafter, the American Hospital Association created and organized several insurance plans, named Blue Cross, which allowed subscribers free choice among the hospitals within a given city. Corresponding to the alleged public service nature of Blue Cross plans, premiums were determined by community rating. The Blue Cross plans enjoyed a virtual monopoly position in the hospital insurance market throughout the 1930s.

The hospital insurance market expanded and the level of competition intensified during World War II, when the federal government imposed wage and price controls. Because wage increases were restricted, the only way employers could attract additional laborers was to offer fringe benefits, such as private health insurance. Initially, employers did not report the value of the fringe benefits to the Internal Revenue Service, but eventually regulations were passed requiring employers to include the value of medical care as part of reported wage income. By that time, however, workers had become accustomed to the tax-exempt status of medical insurance and expressed considerable alarm. Congress responded, and health insurance has remained tax exempt ever since (Friedman, 1992).

Commercial insurance companies were slow to branch off into the health insurance market because they were uncertain about its profitability (Sapolsky, 1991) and doubted whether medical care was an insurable risk due to the difficulty in predicting losses accurately (Iglehart, 1992). The Blue Cross experience demonstrated the viability of health insurance to commercial insurers. By the time the commercials entered the industry in the late 1940s, Blue Cross plans were viewed as pro-union, having established a strong union allegiance. As employers looked to alternative sources for private health insurance, commercial plans searched for clients. The commercial insurance segment later grew as the rate of union membership declined among workers and experience rating became more common among employer groups. According to Temin (1988), "Blue Cross accounted for only two-thirds of hospital insurance by the war's close, and it had less than half of the market in the 1950s and 1960s" (p. 89).

Today, the private health insurance industry is the source of funds for 34 percent of all personal health care expenditures, providing coverage to nearly two-thirds of the population. The modern health insurance industry is pluralistic and composed of many different types of health plan providers that include health maintenance organizations, preferred provider organizations, self-insurers, third-party administrators, and traditional insurers with and without utilization review. Some of these insurers are not-for-profit entities, whereas others are for-profit organizations. Moreover, many of them rely on different methods of reimbursing health care

---

1. According to Sapolsky (1991), a few paternalistic employers, including General Motors and Procter & Gamble, established welfare programs with medical benefits for their employees prior to 1926.

providers for medical services rendered to their subscribers. The rest of this chapter examines the structure, conduct, and performance of the private health insurance industry.

The Structure of the Private Health Insurance Industry

As noted in Chapter 8, structure is an important feature of an industry because it influences the conduct and performance of the member firms. In the following discussion, we look closely at some of the structural characteristics associated with the private health insurance industry.

Number, Types, and Size Distribution of Health Insurers

Private health insurance in the United States involves many different health insurers, including commercial carriers, Blue Cross/Blue Shield (BCBS) plans, health maintenance organizations (HMOs), and other types of managed care plans. Several practices of private health insurers are worth noting. First, a private health insurer, such as a commercial company or BCBS, normally offers its subscribers a choice among traditional plans and various types of managed-care plans. Second, insurers may specialize in either group or individual health insurance, or may choose to offer both.

At the national level, data suggest that a large number of insurers with relatively small market shares offer private health insurance for sale in the United States. Specifically, Chollet et al. (2003) estimate that 2,151 insurers participated in the group health insurance industry and 643 insurers operated in the individual health insurance market in 2001. According to Modern Healthcare (2010), the 10 largest health insurers in terms of revenue (with approximate national market shares shown in parentheses) were United Health Group (12.3%), WellPoint (8.9%), Kaiser Foundation (7.8%), Aetna (4.5%), Humana (4.2%), Health Care Service Corp. (2.9%), Aflac (2.4%), Highmark (2.0%), Coventry Health Care (2.0%), and Healthnet (1.8%) in 2009.

However, Kopit (2004, p. 29) explains that "health insurance markets are local, because they are derivative of the provider networks used by the plan. In a state the size of Rhode Island, the geographic market could be the entire state, but in larger states such as Pennsylvania, the sale of health insurance products in Pittsburgh does nothing for local employers in Philadelphia or even Harrisburg." For this reason, the relevant geographical market for the health insurance industry is typically defined more narrowly for antitrust purposes as the metropolitan statistical area (MSA).

At the MSA level, the American Medical Association (AMA) offers one of the more comprehensive studies on the structural competitiveness of the private health insurance industry.[2] In 2009, the AMA study analyzed 368 MSAs in the United States and treated the relevant product market as being broadly defined (i.e., all health insurance products). Based on this broad product market definition, the AMA established that the Herfindahl-Hirschman index (HHI) exceeded 2,500 in 83 percent of the MSAs analyzed. Recall that an HHI in excess of 2,500 indicates a highly concentrated industry. Therefore, similar to the findings of more aggregated statewide studies (e.g., General Accounting Office, 2005 and Robinson, 2004), the AMA finds that high concentration characterizes the health insurance industry in most major MSAs of the United States.

Consequently, the contemporary private health insurance industry appears to be relatively concentrated in most market areas of the United States. However, for some large employers, self-insurance offers an alternative to purchased health insurance. Large employers with self-insured plans assume the financial risk associated with

---

2. See AMA, *Competition in Health Insurance: A Comprehensive Study of U.S. Markets, 2011* Update at http://www.ama-assn.org.

paying medical claims, although third-party administrators may administer the plan for a fee. Alternatively, large employers may self-fund their plans but purchase stop-loss insurance to cover the risk of large losses or severe adverse claims experiences. If a third-party does administer the self-funded plan or provides stop-loss insurance, then the degree of health insurer concentration may matter in terms of the fee or price that is charged for both of those services.

About 60 percent of all workers were covered by fully or partially self-funded plans in 2011, rising from 44 percent as recently as 1999.[3] Self-insured plans expanded over time because they are exempt from paying premium taxes, which can run as high as 2 percent. Self-funded plans also expanded because they are subject to the Employee Retirement Income Security Act (ERISA) of 1974, which exempts self-insured plans from providing state-mandated benefits.

State-mandated benefits require that an insurance company or a health plan cover specific benefits, health care providers, or patient populations. For example, mandates may include providers such as chiropractors, podiatrists, social workers, and massage therapists; benefits such as mammograms, well-child care, alcohol abuse treatment, acupuncture, and hair prostheses (wigs); and populations such as adopted and noncustodial children.

The Council for Affordable Health Insurance has identified more than 2,100 mandated benefits and providers as of 2010. Mandated benefits may apply only to certain types of coverage and typically vary from state to state. For example, a mandated benefit may exempt individual or small-group coverage or may apply to only insurance companies that are domiciled within a state. The most common mandated benefits are those for mammograms, maternity stays, breast reconstruction, diabetic supplies, emergency services, alcohol treatment, and mental health parity.[4]

The welfare implications of state health insurance mandates can be debated on both efficiency and equity grounds. In particular, inefficiencies may result if the costs of these state mandates are not justified by their benefits. That is, while these state mandates make health insurance coverage more comprehensive, they can also lead to higher premiums and, consequently, a reduction in the number of people covered by insurance if consumers perceive that the benefits of the additional coverage do not exceed the additional premium costs. In addition, horizontal and vertical inequities may be created because ERISA exempts self-funded plans but not purchased plans from state mandates. For example, workers in large firms, which are more likely to be covered by self-funded plans, may pay lower premiums than otherwise similar workers in small firms because of the ERISA exemption from state mandates. Given these efficiency and equity concerns, the desirability of state mandates continues to be debated by analysts and policy makers.

Barriers to Entry

Although the data portray the private health insurance industry as being relatively concentrated, theory tells us that health insurers may face an incentive to behave efficiently if they face a threat from potential competitors. Potential competition makes it more difficult for existing firms to collude and raise their prices because they encounter the likelihood that new entrants may break into the market by offering a better deal to their customers. The likelihood of potential competition depends on the height of any barriers to entry. When high enough, barriers deter the entry of new firms.

In the private health insurance industry, scale economies in administering health insurance may serve as a barrier to entry. Scale economies enable existing firms with

3. Employer Health Benefits 2011 Annual Survey, Https://ehbs.krr.org (accessed December 7, 2011).

4. Council for Affordable Health Insurance, http://www.cahi.org (accessed December 7, 2011).

large volumes of output to underprice new, low-volume competitors and discourage their entry. As discussed in Chapter 8, pricing to deter entry is referred to as limit pricing. Blair et al. (1975) examine the existence of economies of scale by using multiple regression analysis to investigate the relationship between administration expenses and the size of insurance output for a sample of 307 insurance companies in 1968. If per-unit administrative costs decline with output, that would be evidence that scale economies exist in the administration of health insurance.

Blair et al. find that per-unit administrative costs were inversely related to output, as measured by premiums, suggesting long-run economies of scale exist in the administration of health insurance. One policy implication of the empirical findings is that the administration of health insurance should be centralized among one or a few insurance companies if the goal is to minimize administrative costs. Another implication is that incumbent firms may face an advantage over new entrants because of scale economies.

However, in a follow-up study, Blair and Vogel (1978) use survivor analysis (Stigler, 1958) to examine the existence of economies of scale in the provision of health insurance. **Survivor theory** supposes that firm-size classes with expanding populations are more efficient than those with shrinking populations over time. Firms in expanding size classes have obviously met and survived the market test. The survivor test, unlike the econometric test discussed earlier, reflects overall economies in the provision of health insurance, not just scale economies associated with the administrative function.

Blair and Vogel find that the optimal size extends over quite a large range of output, except for the smallest size category, providing support for constant returns to scale over a relatively vast range of output. According to Blair and Vogel (p. 528), the econometric and survivor tests, taken together, indicate the administrative scale economies "must have been swamped by diseconomies elsewhere" in some other function(s), such as risk bearing, marketing, and so on. Hence, this study suggests that scale economies do not provide incumbent firms with a relative advantage over new entrants.

Wholey et al. (1996) examine whether HMOs experience scale economies by using a national sample of HMOs over the period 1988 to 1991. They recognized the multiproduct nature of HMO insurance by allowing for both non-Medicare and Medicare coverage. Like Blair and Vogel (1978), Wholey et al. find that small HMOs face scale economies associated with both non-Medicare and Medicare beneficiaries but the scale economies are exhausted relatively quickly. Thus, incumbent insurers do not benefit from scale economies.

In general, inter-industry entry barriers do not seem to seriously impede entry into the health insurance industry. About 40 health insurance companies operate within the typical state, although most of these insurers make up the competitive fringe (Chollet et al., 2003). Economists refer to the large number of firms with tiny market shares that coexist with dominant firms as the competitive fringe. Also, the sunk costs of entering the health insurance industry appear to be relatively low because health provider networks can sometimes be rented from incumbent sellers and many lines of the insurance business are fairly fungible. This latter point refers to the idea that it may not be that costly for existing insurance companies to switch among alternative lines of insurance business such as life, health, and disability, for example, in reaction to changes in expected profits. The threat of competitors switching among product lines may inhibit companies in any one line from setting price far above the marginal costs of production.

While inter-industry entry barriers are not particularly limiting, intra-industry entry barriers may exist. Intra-industry barriers prevent or slow sellers from moving from the competitive fringe into the concentrated core of an industry. In the case of health insurance, a few major players such as Aetna, Cigna, and WellPoint tend to dominate the industry, and the market shares of these dominant sellers tend to be fairly stable over time. It may be that some intra-industry mobility barriers are preventing small health insurers from gaining additional market share. Brand names and advertising are sometimes credited with creating intra-industry mobility barriers.

Relatively high consumer switching costs is perhaps one of the more significant intra-industry entry barriers into the health insurance industry. Samuelson and Zeckhauser (1988) show that status quo bias typically generates high insurance switching costs. This bias is amplified when most customers obtain health insurance through employer-sponsored group plans with limited provider networks. As employers manage their insurance costs by limiting changes to life events and open enrollment periods, customers have limited opportunity to change to a new plan. Although switching costs may be an important entry barrier, empirical evidence relating to health insurance is limited to a few studies (e.g., Strombom et al., 2002; or Atherly et al., 2005). Not surprisingly, both of these studies find switching between plans increases when benefits decline and premiums rise, but they also suggest that switching costs increase with age such that older people are less likely to change their health plans.

Consumer Information

One of the likely noncompetitive features of the private health insurance industry concerns consumer knowledge. Recall that when individuals possess imperfect information they may pay higher prices and/or receive lower quality when compared to a situation with perfect information. For people belonging to a group plan, this problem may not be as severe since specialists, such as human resource managers or union representatives, often provide individuals with the information to make more educated choices. However, people purchasing individual plans may lack the technical information needed to accurately assess the true value of a health insurance policy. For instance, an individual may be confronted with numerous plans, each offering slightly different benefits, exclusions, and out-of-pocket payments.

Prior to the Omnibus Budget Reconciliation Act (OBRA) of 1990, the market for medigap insurance provided a good example of the importance of consumer information when purchasing insurance. Medigap policies are purchased by individuals to cover any medical payments not reimbursed by Medicare, such as the monthly premium under Part B. Prior to the act, insurers were allowed to offer any number of medigap policies. Reinhardt (1992) pointed out that these policies had been so difficult to comprehend that "many of the elderly have been induced to buy multiple, duplicate policies—probably an intended byproduct of an intended confusion" (p. A5). Reinhardt goes on to note the low payout rate (percent of premiums paid out as benefits) and therefore higher price among commercial insurers for medigap policies (66 percent on average compared to 93.4 percent for traditional BCBS policies) and on small business insurance plans (as low as 77 percent for firms with fewer than 20 employees).

Included as part of OBRA of 1990, was a provision to reform the medigap market. The legislation attempted to provide more informed consumer choice and thereby promote competition in the medigap market. The law stipulated that after July 1992 only 10 standard insurance policies, based on increasing levels of comprehensiveness, could be sold as Medicare supplements to individuals. The basic belief was that 10 policies represented sufficient choice and that standardization would facilitate comparisons and promote informed buying of medigap policies.

According to McCormack et al. (1996), the legislation had the intended impact. After the law went into effect, consumer complaints declined considerably in various states because shopping for a policy became easier and more straightforward. Many of those interviewed believed that consumer confusion declined as a result of standardization and because consumers were able to make more informed decisions. In addition, the researchers found the price of medigap insurance had declined, as theory suggests when consumers make more informed decisions. Specifically, the price of an individual medigap policy fell from an average of $1.29 per benefit dollar during the period 1990 to 1992 to an average of $1.27 for the period 1993 to 1994.

However, other private health insurance policies are not as standardized as medigap policies are now. Those not covered by Medicare often face a choice among a multitude of plans with varying benefits, clauses, and exclusions. Although diversity of choices often provides utility, diversity can also be costly when it leads to confused choice. Cebul et al. (2011) point out that **search frictions** can arise from the imperfections in the process by which employer groups are matched to insurers. Search frictions make it difficult for employers to identify the available policy best suited for the needs and preferences of their workforce. This search problem is made even more difficult because frictions give insurers limited market power such that they adopt heterogeneous pricing policies, with some adopting high-price, low-volume strategies while others adopt low-price, high-volume strategies.

Cebul et al. show that search frictions lead to a premium distribution for which all premiums are in excess of marginal cost. Cebul et al. explain that the potential profits, due to search frictions, might cause health insurers to engage in a marketing arms race, which leads to excessive spending on promotion. These researchers find that search frictions increase insurance premiums enough to transfer 13.2 percent of consumer surplus from fully-insured employer groups (i.e., not self-insured employer plans) to insurers and increase insurance turnover by an average of 64 percent. So not only does the rent transfer harm consumers, but the heightened turnover reduces incentives for insurers to invest in the future health of their subscribers because they are unable to appropriate any of the resulting medical cost savings. They conclude that a publicly provided insurance option might improve the efficiency of private insurance markets by reducing search-friction-induced distortions in pricing and marketing efforts. Consequently, informational imperfections may result in some noncompetitive behavior in various segments of the private health insurance industry.[5]

From a structural perspective, the private health insurance industry appears to resemble an oligopoly with a relatively large competitive fringe. Although many health insurers sell group policies in the typical state, only a few insurers account for a relatively large proportion of earned premiums. Inter-industry entry barriers do not seem to seriously impede entry into the industry, which probably accounts for the relatively large competitive fringe. But this competitive fringe of firms likely faces high costs when attempting to enter the dominant core of the industry because of intra-industry entry barriers resulting from nontrivial buyer switching costs, brand names, and persuasive advertising. Also, buyer information imperfections may provide dominant health insurers with a source of market power. This insulation from competitive forces likely influences the behavior of dominant health insurers as the structure, conduct, and performance (SCP) paradigm suggests it should. Within this context, we now focus on several behavioral issues such as pricing, managed care effects, rate setting, cherry-picking behavior, and adverse selection.

The Conduct of the Private Health Insurance Industry

The Dominant Insurer Pricing Model

According to the data on the number and size distribution of health insurers in the United States, the health insurance industry in most market areas resembles a tight oligopoly with a relatively large competitive fringe. For various reasons, some

---

5. See Wroblewski (2007) for additional discussion on the social benefits of more uniform health insurance information.

health insurers have become quite dominant over time while others have remained fairly small in terms of market share. Business organizations typically become dominant in their market for various reasons including sheer luck, technical and pecuniary economies, superior performance, or mergers with other organizations. Let us elaborate.

Like individuals, some organizations are just luckier than others. Mere chance may mean several successive years of tremendous growth such that a relatively small organization can be quickly transformed into a much larger one. Once the firm is relatively large, it becomes difficult for smaller competitors to catch up.

Organizations may also become dominant as they strive for survival in the marketplace by attempting to exploit any economies from larger size. Technical economies refer to any economies of scale or scope that may be conferred to a larger organization. Pecuniary economies occur when large organizations purchase inputs and supplies at a lower price than similar but smaller organizations. If a very large size is necessary to fully exploit technical and pecuniary economies in a particular industry, firms in that industry will seek a large size over time to survive in a competitive market. Thus, a few dominant firms may evolve and be observed in industries characterized by vast technical and pecuniary economies.

Some analysts refer to the existence of a few dominant firms that result from seeking the gains from large size as the Rule of Three. The Rule of Three states, "In competitive, mature markets, there is room for only three major players along with several (in some markets, many) niche players" (Sheth and Sisodia, 1998, p. A22). The large dominant firms are volume-driven generalists who compete across a wide range of differentiated, name-brand products and services while the smaller organizations either are niche players or produce standardized versions of the name-brand products. According to Sheth and Sisodia, the Rule of Three can be observed in the beer, cereals, tires, insurance, aluminum, oil, chemicals, and airline industries, among others. Note the inclusion of the insurance industry among those affected by the Rule of Three.

Superior performance may also provide a business with a dominant market share. Superiority may result from an excellent product or a low-cost production process. Microsoft represents a good example of dominance resulting from a superior product. In fact, many analysts argue that a superior product tends to provide the best explanation for dominance, although various business tactics and strategies such as limit pricing or persuasive advertising must be employed to prevent dominant market shares from eventually receding (recall from Chapter 8 the success and then failure of Johnson & Johnson in the stent industry). Indeed, over the last several decades, several business practices of Microsoft were challenged by antitrust officials in the United States.

Finally, organizations may become dominant in a particular market through horizontal or vertical integration. Recall that horizontal integration takes place when firms producing similar products merge together. As discussed in the context of the Williamson model in Chapter 9, horizontal mergers benefit consumers if cost savings and lower prices result from the larger size. However, noncompetitive pricing may occur if the larger size confers market power onto the firm. We learned in Chapter 7 that vertical integration involves the combination of firms that produce at successive stages of production, or stated differently, among buyers and sellers. Let us just note here that vertical integration, like exclusive dealing contracts which represent a type of virtual integration, may also have procompetitive or anticompetitive impacts on consumers.

Now that we have some idea about how one or a few firms may grow to dominate an industry, an interesting question emerges concerning how a dominant firm may influence the price of a good or service in a market when a competitive fringe of sellers also exists. When a dominant firm operates in a market with a competitive fringe, economists often use the dominant firm pricing model to analyze how market price and quantity are determined. The dominant firm pricing model involves the following assumptions.

The first assumption is that only one dominant firm exists in the industry. While few markets, even health insurance markets, are characterized by a single dominant firm, this model still holds if the few dominant firms act in a concerted fashion by either overtly or tacitly coordinating their prices. Second, the dominant firm is assumed to be a low-cost producer relative to the rest of the firms in the competitive fringe. In fact, the dominant firm gains its dominance in this model because of its favorable position as a low-cost producer. Third, the model assumes that a fixed number of firms constitute the competitive fringe and that each firm can be treated as being a price taker. Fourth, the dominant firm is assumed to know industry demand and how much the competitive fringe firms will collectively supply at various prices. Finally, all firms, including the dominant firm and those in the competitive fringe, are assumed to produce a homogeneous product, which sells at an identical price.

Figure 11–1 provides a graphical depiction of the dominant firm pricing model in the context of a market for health insurance. The quantity of health insurance (perhaps the number of policies written) is shown on the horizontal axis, and dollar values are shown on the vertical axis. Market demand is represented by the downward-sloping demand curve labeled D and the supply of the fringe firms is captured by the upward-sloping curve S_F. To maximize profits, the dominant firm must determine how much health insurance to sell and what price to charge given the market demand for health insurance and the competitive fringe supply.

Let's suppose that ACME Insurance Company represents the dominant health insurer in some market area. To maximize profits, ACME must first determine its residual demand. Residual demand equals the amount of health insurance left over for ACME in the market after deducting the amount of health insurance offered for sale by the competitive fringe insurers. Mathematically, ACME's residual demand is

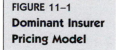

FIGURE 11–1

Dominant Insurer Pricing Model

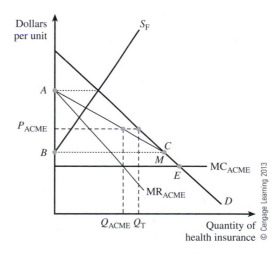

D represents the market demand curve for health insurance and the supply of the competitive fringe firms is labeled as S_F. ACME Insurance, the dominant firm in the market, derives its residual demand by subtracting the fringe supply from market demand at each and every price. At the price represented by point A, ACME offers no insurance on the market whereas ACME completely fills market orders for health insurance at a price indicated by point B. ACME's residual demand is thus found by the curve labeled as A-C-M-E. Following the usual procedure for a linear demand curve, ACME's marginal revenue curve, MR_{ACME}, is derived from its demand curve. ACME is assumed to be a lower-cost producer than the competitive fringe and assumed to produce with constant marginal costs so the marginal cost curve is drawn as MC_{ACME}. To maximize profits where $MR = MC$, ACME sells Q_{ACME} amount of health insurance and charges P_{ACME}. The fringe firms take the price set by ACME and produce the rest of the market output indicated by the horizontal distance between Q_{ACME} and Q_T.

found by subtracting the quantity supplied of the competitive fringe insurers from market demand at each and every price. Figure 11–1 reflects the graphical derivation of the residual demand curve facing ACME. At a price represented by point A, ACME's residual demand equals zero because the fringe supply insurers completely satisfy market demand at that price. Oppositely, at a price indicated by point B, market demand equals ACME's residual demand because at that price, the competitive fringe insurers do not produce and sell any health insurance. In fact, at any price below point B, market demand also represents ACME's residual demand.

ACME's residual demand curve can be derived by drawing a line from point A to point C, opposite B on the market demand curve, and connecting it to the segment of the market demand curve labeled as ME. Thus, A-C-M-E represents ACME's kinked residual demand curve. Let's assume that section AC of ACME's demand curve represents the relevant range for price, so the kink in its demand curve plays no role in the analysis. Given this assumption, ACME's marginal revenue curve can be derived from its demand curve. Recall from Chapter 8 that the marginal revenue curve shares the same intercept as a linear demand curve but has twice its slope (in absolute terms). Following this procedure, ACME's marginal revenue curve is graphically depicted and labeled as MR_{ACME}.

One of the assumptions behind this model is that the dominant firm is a low-cost producer. As a result, ACME's marginal cost curve is drawn below the fringe supply. Following the empirical studies previously discussed, it is further assumed that ACME produces health insurance with constant marginal costs, so a horizontal marginal cost curve is drawn.

To maximize profits, ACME sells the amount of health insurance indicated by Q_{ACME} because marginal revenue equals marginal costs at that point. ACME charges a price of P_{ACME} for its health insurance. As price takers, the competitive fringe accepts the price set by ACME and produces the rest of the market demand as indicated by the horizontal distance between Q_{ACME} and Q_T. Conceptually, that horizontal distance is the same as the one between the origin and the quantity read off the fringe supply curve at a price of P_{ACME}.

Several implications can be drawn from the dominant firm pricing model. First, market price is lower because of the dominant firm. In our example, market price would be determined by the intersection of market demand and fringe supply at point A in Figure 11–1 if ACME, with its lower costs, did not exist. However, if ACME acts competitively and charges a price corresponding to its marginal costs of production, market price is even lower. In fact, if ACME sets a price corresponding to its marginal costs at point E, the competitive fringe is driven from the market according to the graphical model in Figure 11–1.

Second, the model implies that a larger competitive fringe causes the price set by the dominant firm to fall. In Figure 11–1, a larger competitive fringe can be treated as a fringe supply located further to the right. If so, the residual demand facing ACME shifts downward to the left and thus market price falls. Third, a more elastic fringe supply also puts downward pressure on the market price set by the dominant firm according to the model. For example, if the fringe supply in Figure 11–1 becomes flatter (more elastic) but pivots off of the same vertical point, ACME's residual demand shifts downward to the left and price declines.

In sum, the dominant firm pricing model is a useful conceptual device when considering the pricing behavior of a market characterized by a single dominant firm or a few dominant firms, and containing a competitive fringe. The model suggests that even a dominant firm must consider the reaction of the smaller firms when setting prices. Moreover, the model predicts that the dominant firm faces more pressure to set a low price when the competitive fringe market share is greater and when the fringe supply is more responsive to a price change.

Do Health Insurers Possess Monopoly (or Market) Power?

As we have just learned, the dominant firm pricing model suggests that a dominant firm or a group of dominant firms may raise price above marginal costs and thereby exercise market power. Economic theory suggests that their ability to exercise market power depends on the height of any inter- and intra-industry barriers to entry. So the question then becomes, Does any empirical evidence suggest that health insurers possess market power?

One way to address this question is to examine the impact of actual competition, as measured by the number of firms or an HHI, on measures of economic profitability or price (see Chapter 8). When low entry barriers hold within an industry, the rate of economic profitability and level of price should remain fairly constant even if the actual number of competitors equals 1, 10, 100, or 1,000 because existing firms are unable to raise price above costs due to the high threat of potential entry. In this case, no relationship should be found empirically between the degree of actual competition and price or economic profits. However, if entry barriers exist in an industry, then an inverse (a direct) relationship should be found empirically between measures of market competition (market concentration, say the HHI) and price or profits.

One of the first studies addressing this question was a cross-sectional study conducted by Pauly et al. (2002). These researchers analyze the impact of competition among HMOs on their overall profitability using a sample of 262 U.S. metropolitan areas in 1994. Competition is measured by the number of HMOs and also by the relative size distribution of the various HMOs in each metropolitan area. Pauly et al. find that greater competition among HMOs tends to be associated with lower profit rates, as measured by metropolitan area-wide HMO profits divided by the comparable premium revenues. Their simulation showed that profits decline by about 12 to 30 percent if one new HMO enters the market with a 10 percent market share. However, Pauly et al. also found that high profitability did not persist over the period 1994 to 1997, suggesting that entry and expansion forced HMOs to actively compete in the longer run.

Wholey et al. (1995) also investigate the impact of market structure on the performance of HMOs but on the level of premiums rather than profits. Specifically, they investigate the impact of the number of HMOs on HMO premiums in 1,730 metropolitan areas during the period 1988 to 1991. They find that a greater number of HMOs is associated with lower HMO premiums.

Dafny (2010) takes an alternative approach to determining if health insurers possess market power. Specifically, she questions if health insurers are able to practice price discrimination by charging higher premiums to more profitable employers. According to economic theory, price discrimination is possible only when a firm possesses at least some degree of market power. In her study, Dafny makes use of a privately gathered national database of insurance contracts agreed upon by a sample of large, multisite employers enrolling over 10 million Americans annually between 1998 and 2006. Based upon that data set, she finds more profitable employers pay higher health insurance premiums, suggesting that health insurers do possess market power.

In a follow-up study, Dafny et al. (2009) use the same data set to examine the extent to which market concentration in the U.S. health insurance industry has led to higher overall employer-sponsored insurance premiums. They explore the relationship between premium growth and changes in market concentration driven by the 1999 merger of Aetna and Prudential Health Care. Dafny et al. find that the merger-induced change in concentration brought about a 7 percentage point increase in premiums during the study period. Consequently, similar to Dafny's price discrimination approach, this study finds that greater health-insurer market concentration leads to increased employer-sponsored health insurance premiums.

Finally, Bates et al. (2012) use a panel data set of the 50 states and the District of Columbia over the years from 2001 to 2007 to investigate how health-insurer market concentration, as measured by a statewide HHI, influences the percentage of people in each state with private health insurance. According to economic theory, market power results in both higher prices and lower output, so increased health-insurer market concentration may show up in fewer people covered by private health insurance. Their results indicated that greater health-insurer market concentration reduced the percentage of people covered by individually purchased insurance but not the percentage of people covered by employer-sponsored health insurance. Moreover, premium volume was found to be greater in states with increased health-insurer market concentration, suggesting that premium rates may also be higher in those states. Finally, their findings suggested that the effect of health-insurer market concentration was much more pronounced in states that do not regulate individually purchased health insurance premium rates.

Taking the evidence as a whole, it appears that health insurers do possess market power when it comes to pricing their products. In particular, empirical studies find variations in health-insurer market concentration across geographical areas with higher levels of market concentration associated with greater premiums and insurer profits, and fewer people covered by health insurance. Apparently, various intra-industry entry barriers make it difficult for the many firms on the competitive fringe to directly compete against the more dominant players in the health insurance industry.

Managed Care Organizations and Insurance Premiums

Managed care organizations (MCOs), which include HMOs and PPOs, integrate the delivery of health care with the insurance function to some extent. Advocates have claimed that MCOs are capable of reducing the level and growth of health insurance premiums. The reduction of health insurance premiums comes about in two ways. First, MCOs of various kinds, by design, are expected to moderate the scope of the moral hazard problem by adopting various financial incentives and management strategies aimed at both consumers and health care providers, as discussed in Chapter 6. Examples include utilization controls and negotiated price discounts from health care providers. Competition among MCOs pressures each managed care insurer to set premiums closer to the actual costs of servicing its own subscribers. Second, the competition from MCOs motivates traditional insurers to make similar improvements in utilization and costs, and to reduce their premiums or face the prospect of losing business.

In practice, a private health insurance company sets the premium equal to the expected benefits to be paid out (E[BEN]), plus any marketing and administrative expenses (ADMIN), federal, state, and local taxes (TAX), and profits (PROFIT), or

(11–1) $$\text{Premium} = \text{E[BEN]} + \text{ADMIN} + \text{TAX} + \text{PROFIT}.$$

The dollar benefits the insurance company expects to pay out are equal to the actual benefits, BEN, plus some forecast error, e; that is,

(11–2) $$\text{E[BEN]} = \text{BEN} + e.$$

Since people can expect to receive some of their premiums back in the form of reimbursed medical expenditures, health economists sometimes measure the price of insurance, or loading fee, using the ratio of premiums to actual benefits paid out, or Premium/BEN. The ratio can be obtained by substituting Equation 11–2 into Equation 11–1 and dividing by the actual dollar benefits paid out, or

$$(11\text{–}3) \qquad\qquad \text{Price} = 1 + \frac{\text{ADMIN} + \text{TAX} + \text{PROFIT} + e}{\text{BEN}}.$$

The price of health insurance reveals the average amount that must be spent in premiums to receive \$1 in benefits. For example, a price of \$1.25 means the representative individual pays \$1.25 to receive \$1 in benefits, on average. The remaining 25 cents is the loading fee. The magnitude of the loading fee depends on a host of factors, including the administrative technology, tax laws, any forecast errors, and the competitive nature of the market for private health insurance (Sindelar, 1988).

In a competitive market, the loading fee is driven to a normal level, that is, a level sufficient to pay for necessary administrative and marketing costs, taxes, and a normal profit rate (if a for-profit insurer). However, many health insurers compete not only on the basis of price (loading fee) but also on the ability to control health care costs—the actual health benefits paid out. Prior to the 1980s, the not-for-profit Blue Cross plans dominated many markets and were controlled by hospital interests. Lacking incentives, Blue Cross plans pursued a policy of encouraging complete health insurance coverage. The policy led to high hospital prices and medical costs and elevated health insurance premiums (Hay and Leahy, 1987). Now most insurers are forced by cost conscious buyers, such as employers, to control health benefits paid out by adopting managed care practices. Thus, competition has created an incentive for health insurers to hold down both the loading fee and actual medical benefits paid out.

In trying to contain both the loading fee and benefits paid, health insurers now face an interesting trade-off. Managed care contains health care costs (or benefits paid out) most effectively through various administrative functions such as utilization review. However, more spending on administrative functions leads to a higher loading fee (see Equation 11–3). Economic principles suggest that an insurer chooses the optimal amount of an input by equating its marginal benefit and marginal cost. Certainly a profit-maximizing insurer would never knowingly implement a policy or function for which its program costs exceed its benefits in terms of additional revenues or cost savings. For example, when the backlash mounted against the restrictive cost-control practices of MCOs in the 1990s, companies began to abolish "preauthorization," the practice of making doctors get permission for certain tests or treatments. Most companies realized they were spending millions of dollars each year assessing the practice decisions of physicians, yet ultimately denying only 2 percent of their requests.

Hence, any further push for cost containment means that managed care activities will continue to increase in scope and, consequently, larger loading fees are likely to result. The magnitude of the premium level, the sum of benefits paid out, and the loading fee reflects the overall success or failure of managed care activities. With that idea in mind, the following section discusses the role and effects of managed care organizations.

As discussed in Chapter 13, a host of studies (e.g., Manning et al., 1984; Rapoport et al., 1992; Miller and Luft, 1994) have found that MCOs, especially HMOs, attain medical cost savings of about 15 to 20 percent through a reduced hospital-intensive practice style.[6] The question we raise here is whether the reduced medical costs brought about by managed care translate into lower premiums systemwide. According to Morrisey (2001), the answer to this question depends on the degree to which employers change plans in response to lower premiums, the extent to which competition among managed care plans leads to lower managed care premiums, and how lower

---

6. See the various health care industry studies in the following chapters for detailed information about the relation between managed care and medical cost savings.

managed care premiums influence the premiums of traditional insurers. As discussed in Chapter 6, the few studies examining choice of plans from the perspective of the employer found relatively high premium elasticities ranging as high as 28 when multiple plans are offered, and employees must pay more for expensive plans. Consequently, available studies, for the most part, suggest that employers do respond to lower premiums.

In terms of whether managed care premiums decline, some economists point out that the greater administrative costs (loading fee) associated with MCOs may swamp any medical cost savings (benefits paid out). McLaughlin (1988) argues that the health insurance market initially responded to managed care insurance with cost-increasing rivalry, not price competition, as both traditional and managed care insurers have chosen to compete on service offering rather than on price. Feldman et al. (1993) note that "many companies accuse HMOs of 'shadow-pricing,' that is, setting their premiums just below that of commercial carriers. HMOs can profit from shadow pricing if they tend to enroll a disproportionate share of young, healthy workers in the firm" (p. 781). Feldman et al. compared the weighted average HMO and fee-for-service (FFS) premiums in firms that offer both HMOs and FFS plans to the premium of FFS-only firms. They found that offering an HMO plan raises rather than lowers the average premium of an insurance policy for family and single coverage. Insurance premiums rise if HMOs skim the healthiest patients and thereby drive up FFS costs and premiums (Baker and Corts, 1995).

Studies using data after the late 1980s, however, support the notion that increased HMO penetration reduces premiums. For example, Wickizer and Feldstein (1995) used multiple regression analysis to isolate and examine the impact of the HMO market penetration rate on the growth of indemnity premiums for 95 insured groups over the period 1985 to 1992. They found empirically that the HMO penetration rate had an inverse impact on the growth of indemnity premiums.

Baker et al. (2000) investigate the impact of HMO market penetration on the costs of employer-sponsored health insurance. Using data for more than 20,000 private employers in both 1993 and 1997, Baker et al. find that costs for employer health plans were about 8 to 10 percent lower in metropolitan areas with an HMO market penetration rate above 45 percent than ones with HMO market penetration rates below 25 percent. The result reflects both lower HMO premiums and lower premiums for non-HMO plans in markets where the HMO penetration rate exceeds 25 percent. This latter result refutes the notion that HMOs achieve savings by only selecting the healthiest and least expensive patients because, if so, non-HMO premiums would increase with greater HMO penetration.

In sum, MCOs, particularly HMOs, have achieved sizeable medical cost savings from various utilization and cost-control techniques. Recent studies have tended to find that these cost savings have translated into lower premiums provided that a sufficient degree of competition exists among HMOs. In addition, recent evidence suggests that systemwide premiums savings result from the increased penetration of HMOs.

Do Health Insurers Possess Monopsony Power?

One way that health insurers might reduce medical costs is by forcing health care provider reimbursement rates below the competitive level. Theoretically, an outcome like that can occur when one or a few health insurers enjoy a sizeable amount of buying power within a market. The lower reimbursement rates, in turn, may discourage providers from offering services on the market. This reduction of medical services may seriously compromise the quantity and quality of care received by the people in an area.

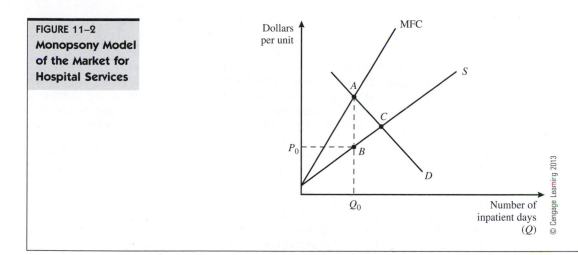

FIGURE 11–2

Monopsony Model of the Market for Hospital Services

Point C in the graph indicates the competitive outcome when all market participants are price takers. The MFC curve represents the incremental cost of purchasing an additional patient day when the insurer has monopsony power. In this case, the monopsonist purchases hospital inpatient days up to the point where the demand curve crosses the marginal factor cost curve, Q_0, and pays P_0. Notice that when the buyer has monopsony power both price and quantity are lower than the competitive level.

When payers possess enough buying power to drive price below the competitive level, market power is said to exist on the demand side of the market. The extreme case is that of a monopsony when only one buyer of a good or service exists in a market. Oligopsony is a situation involving a few dominant buyers of a product. When a monopsony exists in an otherwise competitive marketplace, economic theory suggests that both the price and quantity of the product are lower than the competitive model predicts. Figure 11–2 clarifies the economic logic behind this point by examining the impact of a hypothetical monopsonist in the market for hospital services. The price and quantity of inpatient days are shown on the vertical and horizontal axes, respectively. Market demand and supply are labeled D and S, respectively (ignore the MFC curve for now).

In a competitive market consisting of a large number of buyers and sellers, each individual buyer and seller acts as a price taker. For example, suppose we view the market for hospital services as containing a relatively large number of hospitals supplying services and a large number of health insurance companies negotiating hospital prices on behalf of subscribers. If each health insurer and each hospital represents only a tiny fraction of the total market, all market participants can be treated as price takers. In effect, each health insurer faces a horizontal individual supply curve (rather than market supply) of hospital services and, given its inconsequential market share, can purchase hospital services without influencing its market price. Each hospital, also as a price taker, faces a horizontal or perfectly elastic demand for its product and cannot influence the market price of hospital services. As all of the hospitals and health insurers each act as price takers, competitive equilibrium occurs at point C in Figure 11–2, as supply and demand theory suggests.

Now, instead of a large number of health insurers with tiny individual market shares, suppose only one health insurer, as a monopsonist, covers all of the people and represents the only purchaser of hospital services in an area. However, continue to suppose the existence of a large number of hospitals with relatively small market shares such that each hospital can be treated as a price taker. As a monopsonist, the health insurer faces the market supply curve for hospital services, which is positively sloped reflecting the higher costs for hospitals when supplying additional inpatient days. The positively sloped supply curve means the monopsonist must pay a higher price to negotiate a greater number of inpatient days at the beginning of the contract period. Assuming that a uniform price is set for each and every day, a monopsonistic health insurer must pay a higher price not only for any additional higher-cost inpatient days but also for the other lower-cost inpatient days, when negotiating for additional days. Since the monopsonist must pay a higher price for each and every day when purchasing an additional inpatient day, the total incremental cost to the insurer of purchasing an additional day exceeds the average cost per inpatient day as revealed by the supply curve. As a result, the marginal factor cost (MFC) associated with an additional inpatient day lies above market supply, as depicted by the MFC curve in Figure 11–2. The MFC reflects the additional costs of both the marginal and "inframarginal" days from the perspective of the monopsonist insurer. Inframarginal in this case, refers to the "previous" days.

To determine the profit-maximizing amount of inpatient days to purchase from the hospitals, the monopsonistic health insurer equates demand, which represents the marginal value of each inpatient day, to marginal factor cost. In the figure, the profit-maximizing number of inpatient days occurs at Q_0. The price necessary to attract this number of inpatient days from the various hospitals in this area can be read off the supply curve as P_0. Thus, monopsony theory suggests that a single buyer pays a lower price and purchases a lower quantity than the competitive level typically indicates. A deadweight loss equal to the triangular area ACB results from the monopsonistic distortion, reflecting an inefficient allocation of resources. Monopsony, like monopoly, is clearly undesirable from a societal point of view.

Feldman and Wholey (2001) investigate whether HMOs have monopsony power in the markets for ambulatory and inpatient hospital services. They use a data set containing all of the HMOs in the United States from 1985 through 1997. Feldman and Wholey use multiple regression analysis to investigate the importance of an HMO as a buyer on both the price paid and utilization. Feldman and Wholey rightfully argue that monopsony theory predicts that *both* price and quantity should decline with the importance of an HMO as a buyer. Finding that price declines is not enough to indicate monopsony power because HMOs, through their buying power, may simply "beat back" or countervail the monopoly power of medical suppliers rather than drive price below the competitive level.

Their empirical results show that HMO buying power over hospitals has a negative and significant effect on hospital price per day but no impact on the price of ambulatory visits. They also find that HMO buying power led to increased hospital use but had no statistically significant effect on ambulatory visits. Feldman and Wholey note that their results support the "monopoly busting" and not the monopsony view of HMO buying power. They also suggest that greater HMO buying power improves the efficiency of the hospital services industry. Consequently, their study finds that the typical HMO does not possess monopsony power.

Bates and Santerre (2008) take the analysis one step further by asking if private health insurers possess monopsony power. They use a panel-data set of 86 metropolitan areas for the years 2001 to 2004 and examine how HMO and PPO buying power, as measured by an HHI for each type of payer based on enrollments, separately affect the amount of various services offered by hospitals in the metropolitan area. Like the study of Feldman and Wholey, Bates and Santerre find no evidence of monopsony power and determine empirically that health insurers are able to bust the monopoly power of hospitals. That is, metropolitan hospitals offer more services when the buyer side of the market is more highly concentrated.[7]

---

7. Melnick et al. (2011) and Moriya et al. (2010) also find that increases in health-insurer market concentration are associated with decreases in hospital prices. However, neither study analyzed the impact of health-insurer market concentration on measures of hospital output, so we are unable to draw conclusions regarding whether health insurers possess monopsony or monopoly-busting power. The latter is more likely, however, because most hospital market areas are highly concentrated.

Whereas both Feldman and Wholey, and Bates and Santerre find evidence of health-insurer monopoly-busting power in hospital services markets, Dafny et al. (2009) determine that health insurers possess monopsony power in the market for physicians. These researchers find evidence that consolidation helped health insurers exercise monopsony power over physicians whose absolute employment and relative earnings declined as a result of the merger-induced increase in health-insurer market concentration. This finding by Dafny et al. that physicians are exploited by health insurers is certainly credible as the market for physician services is typically much less concentrated than the market for hospital services.

However, Schneider et al. (2008) reach a different conclusion regarding the monopsony power of health insurers in physician markets. While these researchers find that greater physician organization (PO) market concentration leads to higher physician prices as economic theory suggests, they do not find that greater commercial health plan market concentration leads to lower prices charged by physician organizations in California county-markets. Schneider et al.'s results may differ from those of Dafny et al. because of variations in the structural features of the market areas that were investigated by the two studies. Specifically, it appears that Schneider et al. examined market areas where large-sized physician organizations dominate. For example, about one half of the market-counties in Schneider et al.'s sample exhibited PO-HHIs in excess of 3,600. Yet only 24 percent of the health insurance plans had concentration levels in that range.

Considering the literature as a whole, health insurers likely possess monopoly-busting power in hospital services market areas where they possess the necessary market size, and hospitals are large sized and few in number. In contrast, health insurers may sometimes wield monopsony power in physician services markets because those markets are typically not that highly concentrated.

Rating of Premiums, Adverse Selection, and Risk Selection

As shown in Equation 11–1, health insurers consider the expected medical benefits to be paid out when establishing health insurance premiums. How closely the premiums paid by a particular person mirrors the expected medical benefits depends on whether the insurance company uses community or experience rating or some combination of the two rating methods when setting premiums. When an insurance company practices community rating, expected medical benefits are based on the risk characteristics of the entire plan membership and not the health history or risk status of a particular person. However, even pure community-rated premiums may differ across individuals because of geographical location due to cost-of-living considerations, type of contract (individual or family), and benefit design (level of copayments, coinsurance, deductibles, and benefits covered).

In contrast, when premiums are determined by experience rating, insurers place individuals, or a group of individuals, into different risk categories based on various identifiable personal characteristics, such as age, gender, occupation, and prior illnesses. Premiums are then based on geographical location, type of contract, and benefit design but also on the relation between risk category and expected health care costs as determined by using historical data. Under experience rating, individuals or groups of individuals pay a price closer to their expected medical benefits.

Analysts and policy makers continue to debate the relative merits of community and experience rating of premiums in terms of their efficiency and equity considerations. For example, some analysts point out that experience rating of premiums is more efficient because it creates an incentive for people to adopt favorable lifestyles. That is, if people are required to pay more for health insurance because they smoke cigarettes or drink excessively, for example, they will be more inclined to practice good health behaviors. Advocates of experience rating also note that if high-risk people are wealthier than low-risk people, community-rated premiums can end up redistributing income from the poor to the rich. For example, young low-income individuals may cross-subsidize wealthy elderly individuals when premiums are community rated.

Advocates also point out that experience rating can reduce the practice of adverse selection to some degree. **Adverse selection** occurs when high-risk consumers, who know more about their own health status than insurers do, subscribe to an insured group composed of lower-risk individuals. To secure low premiums, the high-risk consumers withhold information concerning their true health status. Once these consumers are insured, the insurer has no alternative but to increase premiums for all plan subscribers in the next period due to the higher utilization rates of high-risk consumers. As low-risk subscribers leave the higher-priced policies, "musical insurance plans" may develop as high-risk individuals follow low-risk individuals in pursuit of lower premiums. In addition, some insurers may find it difficult to earn a normal profit. Alternatively, some low-risk individuals may eventually find it cheaper to self-insure. If so, high-risk individuals end up in homogeneous pools paying high premiums or being excluded from health insurance coverage (Rothschild and Stiglitz, 1976). Insurers can prevent adverse selection to some degree by limiting people's ability to change plans or through prior screening and experience rating.

Figure 11–3 shows how community rating of premiums can lead to cross-subsidizing of insurance costs and inefficiencies, at least temporarily. In the figure, varying premium levels are shown on the vertical axis and the amount of insurance coverage is measured along the horizontal axis. We begin by assuming that two equally sized low-risk, D_L, and high-risk, D_H, groups are demanding insurance coverage but both groups belong to the same plan, at least initially. Notice that both demands are downward sloping to indicate that more coverage is purchased at a lower premium regardless of risk category. Also note that the high-risk group possesses a greater demand for insurance coverage at each premium level. The greater demand of the high-risk group reflects the greater expected medical benefits to be paid out on their behalf by the insurer at each level of coverage relative to the low-risk group.

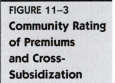

FIGURE 11–3
Community Rating of Premiums and Cross-Subsidization

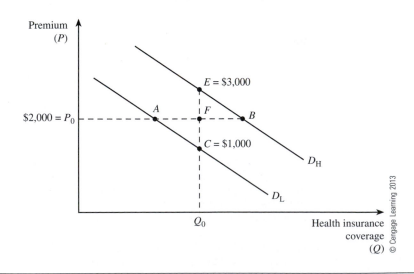

Suppose the employer offers Q_0 amount of coverage at a premium of $2,000 to all of its employees. If so, low-risk employees, as reflected in the demand curve, D_L, cross-subsidize high-risk employees, D_H. If low-risk employees have other choices, they opt out of the plan and the premium eventually rises to $3,000.

Further suppose that the administrator (e.g., the employer), by considering the welfare of the average person in the plan and the trade-off between premiums and wage income, chooses the level of coverage indicated by Q_0. Given that points C ($= \$1,000$) and E ($= \$3,000$) reflect the likely benefits paid out to the two groups at Q_0 amount of coverage, the insurance company charges a uniform community-rated premium of P_0 ($= \$2,000$) per enrollee that averages the risk status and medical costs of the two groups.

Notice at the premium of P_0 that the low-risk group prefers less insurance coverage as indicated by point A in Figure 11–3. Stated differently, low-risk individuals are required to purchase more insurance than they find optimal at a price of P_0. In addition, the figure shows that low-risk individuals cross-subsidize the costs of high-risk individuals. The size of the cross-subsidy paid by the low-risk group is measured by the vertical distance between their willingness to pay for Q_0 amount of coverage at point C ($= \$1,000$) and point F ($= \$2,000$), the actual premium they are required to pay.

Also note that high-risk individuals prefer more insurance coverage at a premium of P_0 as indicated by point B. Thus, the model suggests that both groups could be made better off in separate plans at the existing price of P_0. But the model suggests that high-risk individuals would end up paying a higher premium in the absence of the cross-subsidy from the low-risk individuals. The unsubsidized premium, in turn, prices some of the high-risk individuals out of the insurance market. That happens when high risk people become unwilling to pay anything more than their actual losses because those losses are almost certain. Health insurers would not receive enough revenues to cover their expenses as a result.

In the longer run, the community-rated premium situation in Figure 11–3 may not represent a stable equilibrium, particularly when individuals are free to choose among alternatives. For example, low-risk individuals may seek out other insurance plans in which a lower premium conforms more closely to their expected medical benefits paid out. Or if low-risk individuals are not free to select among policies, they may choose to self-insure if that is an option. Consequently, if health insurance is not mandatory, theory suggests that low-risk individuals will try to leave community-rated health plans such that high-risk individuals will find themselves in more homogenous pools and paying a higher premium for their coverage or excluded from coverage.

However, advocates of community rating of premiums view the situation differently and argue that experience rating of premiums is both inequitable and inefficient. Experience rating is deemed inequitable because some people are charged a higher price for health insurance simply because of their poor health status. The inequity of experience rating is particularly acute when poor health status is uncontrollable rather than a function of a chosen adverse lifestyle.

Advocates of community rating further claim that experience rating of premiums encourages insurers to engage in risk selection or cherry-picking behavior. The best cherries (the healthy ones) are picked off the tree, while the worst are left dangling. It has been pointed out that if insurers practiced community rating of premiums and accepted all applicants for coverage, they would be more interested in creating systemwide medical cost savings rather than choosing among individual low-risk subscribers. However, community rating often creates cherry-picking behavior. Because of community rating, insurers cannot raise premiums to reflect the higher medical costs of high-risk individuals. Consequently, insurance companies have little alternative but to select only low-risk individuals to maintain a more profitable portfolio of subscribers when community rating of premiums is required.

Individuals who belong to large, employment-based group policies, which are the predominant form of private health insurance in the United States, are relatively insulated from this cherry-picking problem. While premiums for experience-rated group policies are adjusted annually based on the actual claims experience of the group and changes in medical care prices, the total cost is distributed equally among all group members, thus minimizing the burden for any one individual.

In contrast, people who apply for insurance, either individually, as a family, or through small businesses, are usually subject to stringent insurance underwriting procedures because providing insurance to these individuals is much riskier. A health status questionnaire or physical exam is normally required. Assuming no community rating, the insurance company sets the premium based upon risk status and typically excludes coverage for any preexisting conditions for a period of one year or more. Preexisting conditions are serious illnesses that were diagnosed before the policy took effect and might include cancer, heart disease, AIDS, or care for low-birthweight babies. Conditions that trigger higher rates vary widely across insurance companies but routinely include such common conditions as hypertension, allergies, arthritis, and asthma. Thus, for individual purchasers of health insurance, especially those with chronic health problems or high-risk conditions, high premiums, rather than denial, may be an obstacle to obtaining coverage. Community rating of premiums, however, can lead to denial or cherry-picking because insurers are unable to set premiums in accordance with risk status.

Health insurers may practice cherry-picking (or equivalently, cream-skimming) behavior in a number of subtler ways depending on what information they possess (Van De Ven and Ellis, 2000). If unable to identify the health risks of individuals in the market and what the precise health risks are, insurers may structure their health insurance coverage so high-risk individuals reveal themselves. For example, the benefits package may not cover prescription drugs or may contain high out-of-pocket expenses. If insurers know the precise health risks for conditions such as AIDS but not the risk characteristics of specific individuals, they may not contract with physicians known to treat patients with high-cost illnesses. Finally, if insurers can predict unprofitable individuals, marketing strategies might be focused away from high-risk individuals and toward low-risk individuals.

While this view of cherry-picking behavior and access denial is generally accepted at face value, empirical studies on this topic have been relatively lacking. One of the few studies to date, by Beauregard (1991), used data from the 1987 National Medical Expenditure Survey to estimate the number of uninsured people who were denied private health insurance or could purchase only limited coverage because of poor health. Beauregard's study found that benefit denial is not as widespread as typically believed. In particular, only a very small proportion of the uninsured population, less than 1 percent, was found to have ever been denied private health insurance due to poor health. However, Beauregard cautions that the figure does not include currently insured individuals whose policies exclude coverage for preexisting conditions.

Pollitz et al. (2001) provide a very compelling study concerning access to coverage for those in less-than-perfect health in the individual health insurance market. The study involves seven "hypothetical" health insurance applicants, aged 12 to 62, of both genders, and with different preexisting conditions such as hay fever, depression, prior knee injury, and "HIV-positive status." Although the specific conditions are not representative of the general population, they are similar to those experienced by a large number of people. Sixty applications for each hypothetical person were submitted to nineteen insurance companies in eight market areas around the country, including six BCBS plans, six HMOs, and seven national or regional commercial carriers.

Each insurer was asked to underwrite the applications. Underwriting involves determining whether to cover someone and on what terms. The participating insurers responded to these hypothetical applications by accepting the applicant for standard coverage at a standard rate for a healthy person, rejecting the applicant, offering coverage with special restrictions on covered benefits, or offering coverage at a higher-than-standard premium. Carriers were asked for information about their most frequently sold policies in each individual market with a $500 annual deductible and a $20 office visit copayment. Carriers were also asked to provide the standard premium rate for policies with these features corresponding to the age and gender of the seven hypothetical applicants for the healthiest applicants.

The results from the experiment were insightful. Of the 420, only 43 (10%) applications resulted in standard coverage at the standard rate. The applications were rejected 154 times, with the HIV applicant accounting for 60 of the rejections. Of the accepted applications (63%), most imposed benefit restrictions (118 applications), premium surcharges (56), or both (49). The researchers found that the results varied somewhat across states, with different state rules regarding community rating and guaranteed access explaining some of the difference.

The results of their study imply that consumers who are in less-than-perfect health clearly face significant barriers to obtaining health insurance coverage in the individual health insurance market. Insurance companies often decline to cover people who have preexisting conditions, and when they offer coverage, they frequently impose limitations and/or raise premiums. Higher premiums can often price people with preexisting conditions out of the individual market.

Guaranteed Renewability in the Individual Health Insurance Market

Individual health insurance offers two advantages over group health insurance. First, unlike employer-sponsored plans, the consumer has considerable choice over the specifics of the health insurance policy. Second, an individual health insurance plan offers more portability in the sense that coverage can be retained even if a person changes jobs. However, we learned in the preceding discussion that individual health insurance also may have various disadvantages associated with it such as adverse selection, experience rating, and risk selection (that is, cream-skimming). But Patel and Pauly (2002) explain that individual health insurance contracts can be written with a guaranteed renewability clause such that adverse selection, experience rating, and cream-skimming present less of a problem for individuals and insurance companies.

Guaranteed renewability is a contractual feature in an insurance policy that requires the insurer to (1) sell another policy on the anniversary date of the current period and (2) charge a premium for that policy that is not affected by any individual loss experience or change in the insured person's circumstances during the current period. This feature means that the insurer cannot re-underwrite an insurance contract on renewal. However, the insurer has the right to increase premium rates for the underwriting class in which a policy is initially placed (e.g., based on age and gender).

It stands to reason that higher premiums are charged when an insurance contract offers the guaranteed renewability (GR) feature. In essence, the consumer is purchasing two policies for a single premium. The first policy pays for the claims experienced during the current term and the second policy covers the claims of individuals in the rating class who become above-average risks at some point.

Patel and Pauly explain that the GR feature helps solve some of the problems associated with the individual market when risk varies among individuals. Because of GR, people are individually protected against unexpected jumps in premiums relating to the onset of a chronic condition. That is, once a person becomes chronically ill, the GR provision means that he has locked into a premium that is independent of his individual health status, and therefore experience rating cannot be practiced on renewal. This feature does not protect people against age adjustments, which are predictable. Also, GR does not protect against rising health care costs because market-wide risks cannot be reduced through pooling.

The GR feature reduces the likelihood of adverse selection because people who start off expecting average risks and then learn of higher risk in the next period cannot capitalize on that information by purchasing more coverage at the GR rate. Also, people who remain a low risk are not priced out of the market because the initial premium includes the expected higher risks in future periods that they have already agreed to pay. In effect, premiums in the next period are unaffected by individuals who become chronically ill and remain in the plan, because premiums have been established with that likely transition in mind.

Cream-skimming also becomes less likely because of the GR feature. Individuals with higher risks have a legal right to stick with the policy; insurers cannot legally deny them coverage. In addition, those who remain average risks face a premium they should be willing to pay because it reflects the likelihood that they themselves may become chronically ill at some point.

Patel and Pauly point out some problems potentially associated with the GR feature. First, if buyers possess inside information about their health conditions when purchasing the initial policy, the GR feature will not stop adverse selection from taking place. Hence, people are encouraged to purchase individual health insurance early in their lives. In fact, the lock-in feature of GR provides an incentive for people to purchase health insurance coverage while still in good health rather than waiting to be diagnosed with a chronic condition.

Second, if consumers become high risk before seeking insurance, they will be charged high premiums. In this case, social transfers may be necessary for low-income, chronically ill individuals. This is another reason why people should be encouraged to seek out health insurance with the GR feature early in their lives. Third, insurers may not abide by the terms of the contract or may lower quality or service to discourage high risks from renewing. In addition, insurers may raise premiums for an insured class of individuals more than experience dictates, and then offer lower rates to lower risks once they threaten to leave the plan. Practices like these, however, are illegal and can tarnish the image of insurers and thereby lower the market value of their companies. In any case, some regulations and monitoring of health insurers may be necessary.

Patel and Pauly point out that the Health Insurance Portability and Accountability Act (HIPAA) of 1996 requires GR but is silent about limiting the rates charged at renewal. Specifically, HIPAA does not require that premiums be the same for all insured people in a rating class. However, based on their survey, Patel and Pauly find that almost all states require GR and that premiums are the same for all people within the same rating class. Furthermore, they find that re-underwriting would be challenged by most state governments.

Individual health insurance offers the benefits of more choice and increased portability. However, individual health insurance is characterized by the problems of adverse selection, risk selection, and experience rating. Guaranteed renewability is a contractual feature in individual health insurance plans that can deal with these three problems to some degree.

The Performance of the Private Health Insurance Industry

The structural characteristics of the private health insurance industry imply that individual health insurers may possess market power in some areas of the United States. These structural features include a few dominant insurers in most local markets and high intra-industry barriers to entry. In fact, some empirical evidence finds that health insurers are able to raise premiums and reduce health insurance coverage in geographical areas with high market concentration. In this section we examine evidence on the aggregate performance of the health insurance industry in the United

States. Specifically, we consider measures and issues relating to the price and quantity of health insurance and the profitability of health insurers.

The Price of Private Health Insurance in the United States

One indicator of the performance of an industry is the price of the product being sold. At a point in time, economic theory suggests that consumer surplus is maximized when prices are set equal to the marginal costs of production. In contrast, when prices are set above marginal cost, consumer welfare is reduced. Economic theory also implies that prices adjust over time in response to any changes in demand or the costs of production. In fact, these price variations serve an important purpose by allocating resources to their best uses, coordinating demand and supply, and rationing goods to the highest bidder.

We mentioned in Chapter 6, and previously in this chapter, that the price of health insurance is sometimes measured by the loading fee, the portion of the premium payment above expected medical benefits. However, once MCOs began to dominate the industry, health insurers were expected to compete among themselves not only on the basis of the loading fee but also by controlling moral hazard as represented by the size of the medical benefits paid out.

As discussed earlier, *moral hazard* refers to a situation in which individuals, once they are covered by health insurance, change their behavior because they are no longer financially responsible for the full cost of their actions (Pauly, 1968). In particular, people may choose to pursue activities that increase the probability and/or magnitude of the loss covered by health insurance. To the individual consumer, the current health insurance premium represents a sunk cost and is unaffected by her spending on medical care services. In addition, any one individual is likely to believe that her own medical spending in isolation does not affect the future premiums of the insured group. However, if a sufficient number of people act in a similar fashion and increase their spending on medical services due to the moral hazard situation, future insurance premiums increase to reflect the greater benefits paid out.

Seidman (1982) likens the moral hazard problem to restaurant-bill splitting. If two people have lunch together and decide to split the bill, each person may realize that he is paying only half of the cost of every additional dollar spent on the meal. Therefore, each individual might purchase the higher-priced imported beer rather than the lower-priced domestic beer or order the restaurant specialty rather than the less expensive special of the day. Of course, if both people behave similarly and overspend, the restaurant bill is higher than it would be if they paid separately for their own meals. Also, each person's share of the bill falls as the size of the sharing group increases (say, from two to six). As a result, the incentive to overspend increases with the size of the group, *ceteris paribus,* when the bill is split evenly.

In terms of the market for medical services, moral hazard results from five types of actions. First, at any point in time when an insured event takes place, the quantity demanded of medical services may exceed the amount the consumer would buy if she had to pay the full cost. Quantity demanded may be greater because the insured consumer faces a price that lies below the marginal cost of the medical service. We discussed this type of **ex post moral hazard** in Chapter 6 when we compared the conventional and Nyman models of the demand for health insurance. The extent to which quantity demanded increases depends on the price elasticity of demand. A more elastic demand results in greater quantity demanded as a result of the reduced out-of-pocket price, *ceteris paribus.*

Second, the moral hazard problem may show up over time as consumers have less incentive to guard against an insured event. Reductions in preventive activities such as exercise or dieting may raise the probability of an illness occurring. Raising the probability of an illness occurring is sometimes referred to as **ex ante moral hazard** because that action takes place before, unlike *ex post* moral hazard which happens after, the medical illness occurs. As discussed in Appendix 2, microeconomics theory generally views medical insurance as lowering the out-of-pocket price of curative inputs relative to the price of preventive inputs and thereby distorting the choice of inputs because preventive and curative services are typically substitutes in the production of health. As a consequence of its relatively higher out-of-pocket price, prevention declines, the probability of sickness rises, and an increased consumption of medical care occurs. The medical costs of maintaining a given level of health rises and production inefficiency develops as a result.

Because of "nine limiting conditions," however, some researchers note that medical insurance may not generate much *ex post* or *ex ante* moral hazard (Crew, 1969; Schlesinger and Venezian, 1986; Pauly and Held, 1990; Kenkel, 2000; Nyman, 2003; Dave and Kaestner, 2006). First, health care providers may possess market power. The resulting restriction of output negates the typical *ex post* moral hazard effect of medical insurance toward overconsumption. Second, the *ex ante* moral hazard effect may be small because medical insurance does not completely cover the utility loss associated with sickness (pain and suffering). Third, preventive inputs may remain attractive because the choice of health inputs actually involves completely preventing versus incompletely curing illness. The attractiveness of preventive inputs, however, is limited by the fact that prevention can never reduce the probability of illness to zero.

Fourth, medical insurance premiums may be risk-rated and thereby deter both *ex ante* and *ex post* moral hazard. While that might be true for individual medical insurance plans, it is not true for employer-sponsored and public medical insurance plans which cover most people in the United States. Fifth, health insurers may invest directly in prevention to reduce the probability of a loss. Sixth, employers may offer subsidized worksite health promotion activities such as smoking cessation programs. This subsidization of preventive activities may offset the distortionary effect of medical insurance on the price of curative care. Seventh, people may tend to transition frequently between insured and uninsured status so insurance matters little when the decision to purchase medical care is actually made. However, people may also game this transition by shifting expensive medical treatments into the insured period.

Eighth, a health promotion effect may result as people visit their primary care givers more frequently because of medical insurance and their primary care givers point out cost-effective ways of generating better health. Finally, as discussed in Chapter 6, medical insurance may promote efficient *ex post* moral hazard by providing low-income individuals with financial access to life-saving medical care they could not otherwise afford. While these nine limiting conditions suggest insurance may generate little inefficiency, the moral hazard effects of insurance can show up in three other ways.

Moral hazard may arise from a third type of behavior that deals with technological advances in medical care. Third-party payments may encourage the development and adoption of new technologies offering low-benefit, high-cost care (Weisbrod, 1991). The adoption and diffusion of these high-priced technologies, in turn, causes the demand for health insurance and the range of services covered by health insurance to increase. A vicious cycle encompassing health insurance, technology, and rising medical costs is set in motion.

Moral hazard may result from a fourth behavioral change as insurance coverage lowers the consumer's incentive to monitor the behavior of health care providers. Less monitoring gives the health care provider the ability to prescribe unnecessary tests or surgery when a financial incentive exists to engage in opportunistic behavior or supply inducement of this sort. Since the consumer's out-of-pocket costs are largely unaffected by the unnecessary services, the consumer has little incentive to seek a second opinion. Finally, a moral hazard effect occurs when insurance lowers the consumer's incentive to shop around and find the lowest price for medical services.

To effectively control claim costs, the managed care insurer must adopt and implement various consumer and health care provider financial incentives and management strategies to prevent these five types of moral hazard behavior. But recall from our discussion of the Nyman model in Chapter 6 that not all moral hazard may be inefficient. Therefore, health insurers want to discourage only those types of behavior that result in the marginal cost of medical care exceeding marginal benefit. Also recall that financial incentives and management strategies result in either higher administrative costs or lower premium rates because the health insurance product effectively offers less insurance coverage to consumers. The successful MCO competes by appropriately balancing the trade-off between premium revenues, the administrative expense load, and medical benefits paid out. Hence, the premium rate provides a better indication of the price of health insurance than the loading fee because it reflects both the size of the medical benefits paid out and the expense load, which must be properly balanced by the successful MCO. It is interesting to note that the premium captures the price of health insurance in the Nyman model because it reflects how much income (and all other goods) a person in good health must willingly give up to claim an income transfer if he becomes ill.

Figure 11–4 provides annual estimates of the average real premium and the average real premium as a percentage of real income per capita for the period from 1960 to 2010. The data in the figure suggest that the price of health insurance increased dramatically over the 51-year period both in real terms and as a fraction of income. Indeed, as a fraction of income, health insurance premiums increased from slightly less than 2 percent in 1960 to over 20 percent in 2010. However, some periods experienced much faster growth in the price of health insurance than others. The period from 1987 to 1993 stands out in the figure because real premiums grew at a significantly faster rate than during the previous periods both in real terms and as a fraction of income. During this period enrollment in managed care plans expanded, with the

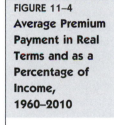

FIGURE 11–4
Average Premium Payment in Real Terms and as a Percentage of Income, 1960–2010

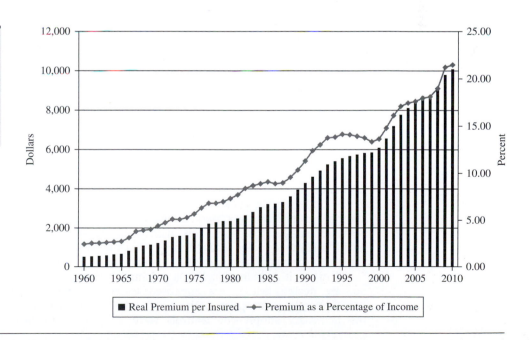

SOURCE: Authors' estimates based on data from the Research and Statistics section of the website at the Centers for Medicare and Medicaid Services, http://www.cms.gov (Accessed December 20, 2011).

percentage of workers in traditional plans declining from 73 to 46 percent.[8] Reflecting the shift to managed care plans, this period was characterized by intense innovation in new strategies to control moral hazard (Danzon, 1992). That is, MCOs adopted various financial incentives and management strategies, such as utilization review, case management, and selective contracting, with the intent of reining in medical claim costs. The costs of implementing these strategies appear as claims administration costs and can raise the premium payment, as discussed earlier, if not offset by commensurate reductions in medical benefits paid out. Apparently these earlier initiatives to control moral hazard were not very effective on an industry-wide basis, given that real premium increased rapidly during this period.

The next six years tell a different story concerning the effectiveness of MCOs at controlling medical claims costs. During the period from 1993 to 1999, real premium growth slowed both in real terms and as a fraction of income. In fact, the percentage of income devoted to health insurance premiums actually declined slightly during this period. The mid- to late 1990s is considered to represent the "heyday" of managed care because a relatively large percentage of insured individuals were enrolled in restrictive managed care plans, which relied heavily on supply-side strategies such as utilization controls. In fact, 52 percent of all workers were enrolled in HMOs or point-of-service plans in 1999. While these restrictive plans cost more to administer, the medical cost savings more than compensated for the rise in administration costs such that the health insurance premium rate tended to grow much less quickly during this period than in previous periods.

However, beginning in 1999, medical care consumers and providers felt adversely impacted by the restrictive supply-side policies adopted by MCOs. For instance, both consumer and provider groups complained that MCOs should not be allowed to preauthorize medical services, set the number of days that a patient can stay within a hospital, or determine which drugs to reimburse. This backlash resulted in a significant exodus of consumers from more restrictive to less restrictive managed care plans. For example, from 1999 to 2005, the percentage of insured workers in PPO plans increased sharply from 39 to 61 percent. As people voted with their feet and wallets, managed care organizations of all types, including HMOs, subsequently began changing their financial and management strategies away from tight supply-side controls (such as preauthorization and narrow networks of providers) and toward looser demand-side strategies such as higher copayments or coinsurance rates. This change in strategy by MCOs resulted in more choice for consumers and, not surprisingly, led to higher health insurance premiums.

In particular, notice in Figure 11–4 that health insurance premiums, both in real terms and as a percentage of income, rose with the switch to less-restrictive plans during the 2000 to 2003 period. Interestingly, this growth spurt in health insurance premiums was relatively short-lived with the next four years witnessing a slowing of health insurance premium growth. The specific reasoning for the slower health insurance premium growth during the 2004 to 2007 period is unclear but may be related to the underwriting cycle which we discuss in the next section. Beginning in 2007, another reversal can be observed; health insurance premiums rose quickly once again as a percentage of income. This increase in the share of income devoted to private health insurance likely resulted more from the loss of jobs and incomes, because of the recession which began in 2007, than higher health insurance premiums.

All in all, it appears that MCOs accomplished what they initially were expected to do. By design, MCOs are supposed to control moral hazard costs, something the indemnity plans prior to the 1980s were not designed to accomplish. However, the necessary supply-side controls were viewed by medical care consumers and

---

8. Kaiser Family Foundation, http://www.kff.org/insurance/7315/sections/upload/7375.pdf (accessed November 1, 2005).

providers as being unduly restrictive and the emphasis eventually changed toward demand-side controls. It is too early to speculate on the effectiveness of the demand-side controls such as medical savings accounts. The learning curve may be fairly flat and more time may have to pass before the effects of demand-side controls can be observed. After all, it did take some time for the effects of supply-side controls to show up in slower premium growth.

Before leaving this topic, it should be mentioned that rising health insurance premiums do not necessarily reflect inefficiencies in the private health insurance industry. Prices naturally rise in a competitive market when willingness to pay increases, as revealed by demand, and costs increase, as reflected in supply. For example, people have become insured for many more types of medical care and to a greater degree in terms of lower out-of-pocket costs over the years. In addition, new medical technologies have been very successful at saving, enhancing, and extending lives (Cutler and McClellan, 2001). Hence the demand for health insurance coverage may be rising over time because people wish to gain access to these expensive life-saving medical technologies (Nyman, 2003; Santerre, 2006). As such, a rising price of health insurance may signify success in both the medical and insurance markets and does not necessarily indicate failure. Moreover, any attempts at regulating the price of health insurance might mean less access to new medical innovations and, subsequently, a reduction in the quantity and quality of lives compared to what could have been otherwise.

The Underwriting Cycle of Health Insurance. Complicating the interpretation of any short-term changes in health insurance premiums is a phenomenon called the underwriting or profitability cycle. Private health insurers have generally experienced three consecutive years of underwriting gains, followed by three consecutive years of underwriting losses, in the group health insurance market. The underwriting cycle holds for both commercial insurers and not-for-profit BCBS plans.

Health insurance premium increases are shown to follow the underwriting cycle with a lag of about two years (Gabel et al., 1991). Rather than consistently and moderately rising, premiums appear to cycle over a six-year period with three consecutive years of rapid premium growth during the so-called hard market phase followed by three successive years of slowing premium growth during the soft market phase. Seeking to explain the root cause of the underwriting cycle, Gabel et al. point to three broad causes: supply and demand forces, industry pricing actions, and external factors. According to Gabel et al., supply and demand forces can affect the profitability of health insurers in two ways.

First, because of relatively free entry into health insurance markets, firms enter the market in times of excess profits. As a result, price falls and some firms experience losses and exit the market. Exit reduces supply, price increases, and profits return. The cycle begins once again. Second, Samuelson's (1939) "cobweb" model may explain the cycle. When the price of health insurance is relatively high in the present period, insurers act on the information by deciding to sell more insurance policies in the next period. The greater supply, in turn, leads to lower prices in the next period, especially because the demand for group health insurance is relatively price inelastic and modest supply changes lead to dramatic price changes. Hence, current prices affect future supply decisions, and this linkage results in a continual cycling of prices and profits.

Industry pricing actions consider that insurers may reduce prices to increase market share and raise them later to compensate for past losses. In addition, actuarial pricing techniques often extrapolate the recent past to the future from recent claims experience. If decision makers form "adaptive expectations" of this kind, they systematically overestimate true premiums in periods of falling claims and underestimate true premiums in periods of rising claims. According to Gabel et al., this type of pricing behavior, although irrational, has been shown to result in a cyclical profitability pattern.

Another industry pricing explanation supposes that all insurers tacitly collude at first and follow the pricing pattern of the leader firm(s). At some point, however, individual firms are tempted to reduce prices to gain greater market share, and the informal cartel breaks down. Eventually, the pattern repeats itself. Finally, external factors, including underlying claims events and general economic conditions, may cause the profitability cycle. That is, medical care costs and general factors ranging from the budget deficit, national unemployment, and interest rates may follow a business cycle pattern and generate the insurance profitability cycle.

As you can see, economists have offered a number of alternative theories for the underwriting cycle in the health insurance industry. Very few studies, however, have tried to empirically determine which of these competing theories provide a better explanation for the cycle. Born and Santerre (2008) use national data for the United States over the period from 1960 to 2004 to compare the predictive power of some of these theories. Among their empirical results, they find that fluctuations in medical claims costs primarily determine the cycling of insurance premiums.

Grossman and Ginsburg (2004) point out that, beginning in the 1990s, the traditional underwriting cycle seemed to break, with longer and more uneven periods of gains and losses and less extreme fluctuations in profitability. They argue that the traditional underwriting cycle broke down because of structural changes in the health insurance industry and because of a closer relationship between cost trends and premium adjustments. More specifically, they argue that consolidations among insurance companies have reduced the amount of price competition in the industry. They also point out that more experience with managed care products and electronic processing of provider claims have enabled insurance companies to better predict medical claims costs. Grossman and Ginsburg anticipate that health insurance premiums may be higher but less volatile if insurance companies continue to consolidate in the future. They also anticipate that the underwriting cycle will not disappear and will be characterized by more muted swings in the future.

An important lesson from this discussion is that premium increases must be properly interpreted in the context of the underwriting cycle. To say that premium increases are low this year does not mean that some trend of low premium increases has set in. Rather, the low premium increases of today may mean that tomorrow's premium increases will be larger if the profitability cycle continues to hold.

Output of Private Health Insurance in the United States

Private Health Insurance Coverage.   Another measure of the performance of an industry is the amount of output provided. Incentives should exist so suppliers produce the optimal amount of a product—neither too much nor too little. In the case of the private health insurance industry, optimal provision implies that the right number of people is covered by private health insurance. Theoretically, the efficient number of insured individuals occurs at the level where the marginal social benefit and marginal social cost of health insurance coverage are equal. Those pushing strongly for universal health insurance coverage in the United States apparently believe that marginal social benefit exceeds costs at all levels of the population.

Table 11–1 offers some data on the percentage of people with private health insurance coverage in the United States for selected years from 1940 to 2010. Private insurance plans are defined as all supplemental, comprehensive, and catastrophic insurance policies, including those individually purchased, both by the nonelderly and elderly (e.g., medigap) and group policies sponsored by employers or trade associations. A number of observations can be drawn from the data. For one, notice that the number of privately insured individuals increased overall from 9 percent to roughly 64 percent of the population from 1940 to 2010. The tremendous jump in private insurance coverage during the 1940s reflects the point made at the beginning

TABLE 11–1
People with Private Health Insurance Coverage, Selected Years, 1940–2010

Year	Number (millions)	Percentage of Population
1940	12.0	9.1%
1945	32.0	22.9
1950	76.6	50.3
1960	122.5	67.8
1970	154.3	75.3
1975	164.8	76.3
1980	169.7	74.7
1985	176.3	74.1
1990	182.1	73.2
1995	185.9	70.3
2000	205.6	73.5
2005	203.2	69.2
2010	195.9	64.0

SOURCE: Health Insurance Association of America (HIAA). *Source Book of Health Insurance Data 1999/2000.* Washington, D.C.: HIAA Insurance Association of America, 2001, Table 2–10; and DeNavas-Walt, Proctor, and Smith (2011)

of this chapter that employers offered health insurance as a tax-exempt fringe benefit during the wage and price control period of World War II.

The 1950s and 1960s witnessed further huge increases in private insurance enrollments. Enrollments in private insurance expanded, in part, because of the declining health insurance prices during that time as a result of experience-rated premiums. According to Morrisey (2001), "commercial insurers identified employer groups that had lower than average claims experience and offered them premiums lower than those charged by the then dominant carrier, Blue Cross" (p. 209).

Also, notice that the percentage of people covered by private health insurance reached a peak of more than 76 percent in the mid-1970s but declined thereafter. In fact, because of the decline, the percentage of the population covered by private health insurance decreased by 3.8 percentage points over the entire 50-year period from 1960 to 2010. Several factors account for the decline in the percentage of privately insured individuals after the mid-1970s.

One simple reason for the relative decline in private health insurance coverage is the growing percentage of the population aged 65 years and older in the United States. Recall that Medicare took effect in the late 1960s and that people become automatically eligible for Medicare on reaching age 65. Medicare recipients made up nearly 15 percent of the population in 2010 but only around 10 percent in 1975, for instance. It should be noted, however, that many people covered by Medicare also purchase medigap coverage from private insurance carriers. Those who purchase medigap coverage are included in the figures reported in Table 11–1 as also possessing private health insurance coverage, and most elderly people have some medigap coverage. Thus, Medicare coverage may not explain much of the decline in the percentage of the population covered by private health insurance since 1975.

Rising health insurance premiums provide the second and probably most significant reason for the decline in private health insurance coverage. As we saw previously, health insurance premiums rose rapidly from the mid-1980s to early 1993. This caused many employers, mostly small businesses, to either raise employee contributions or drop health insurance coverage altogether. Health insurance premiums also increased sharply after 2000 in response to the backlash against restrictive managed care plans, as shown in Table 11–1. This spike in health insurance premiums may account for part of the fall in the percentage of the population covered by private health insurance after 2000. Notice that enrollment in private health insurance increased as a percentage of population over the period from 1995 to 2000, when real premiums as a percentage of real income per capita marginally decreased.

A third explanation for declining private coverage deals with occupational shifts from traditionally higher-coverage manufacturing sector jobs to lower-coverage service sector jobs. However, Long and Rodgers (1995) find that employment shifts explain about only 15 percent of the decline in employer-provided private health insurance coverage. A fourth reason for declining coverage is the growing fraction of people covered by Medicaid. For example, less than 8 percent of the population was covered by Medicaid in 1980. Several expansions took place in the Medicaid program, and this percentage figure blossomed to almost 16 percent by 2010 (DeNavas-Walt et al., 2011). While many people became eligible for Medicaid coverage because they lost private health insurance coverage for the reasons previously mentioned, several studies find that Medicaid program expansions created a financial incentive for some families to drop their private health insurance coverage in favor of Medicaid. As discussed further in Chapter 10, public coverage tends to crowd out private coverage and may have caused some of the decline in health insurance coverage since the mid-1970s. Finally, empirical evidence suggests that the percentage of the population with private health insurance fell during the 2007 to 2010 period because of the Great Recession and its slow recovery (Holahan, 2011).

Who Are the Uninsured? The U.S. Census Bureau began collecting data on insurance coverage on a systematic basis beginning in 1987. Those interviewed by census officials are asked a series of questions regarding whether they were covered in the previous year by insurance and by what type of insurance. People are considered insured if they were covered by any type of health insurance for at least part of the previous year, and everyone else is considered uninsured. Research shows that health insurance coverage is underreported for a variety of reasons by the Census Bureau. Some people, for example, report their insurance coverage status at the time of their interview rather than their coverage status during the previous calendar year.

With this caveat in mind, data reported by the Census Bureau over the last 10 years suggest that between 14 and 16 percent of the U.S. population tends to be uninsured (DeNavas-Walt et al., 2011). Being uninsured is not without significant personal and social costs. The uninsured sometimes face the sharp psychological sting from the financial insecurity that can result from an unanticipated medical occurrence. Others may postpone necessary medical care for chronic conditions. In addition, uninsured individuals are more likely to find themselves in the emergency room of a hospital, sometimes after it is too late for proper medical treatment, with their resulting poorer health and shorter lives causing sizeable social costs. As an illustration, Miller et al. (2004) estimate a lower-bound dollar value of the health forgone (at $65 to $130 billion per year) because of uninsurance in the United States. Thus, reducing the uninsured population seems a legitimate social goal, and identifying why some people are without private health insurance coverage becomes a valuable endeavor for public policy purposes. Policy makers generally wish to know which groups and individuals are more at risk so that policies might be properly designed to reduce the number of people who are uninsured.

Logic suggests that people are without private health insurance for a variety of reasons. We learned in Chapter 6 that people alter their purchasing of health insurance in response to changing economic circumstances such as the price of insurance or their income just as they change their demands for other goods and services. That is, some people choose to be without private health insurance coverage or choose only minimal coverage. For example, an individual may decide to self-insure because she expects to gain little from market-provided health insurance as a result of its high price relative to expected medical benefits. Behavior of this kind may account, at least partly, for the 27 percent of the population between ages 18 and 24 that do not have health insurance coverage. Some in this age group normally expect to receive very little in terms of medical benefits reimbursed and may have to cross-subsidize the higher premium costs of more elderly individuals.

Others may be without private health insurance coverage for reasons other than its voluntary nature. By borrowing from the different classifications for unemployment offered by labor economists, three categories of uninsurance can be specified, although admittedly these classifications are not mutually exclusive in the context of uninsurance. First, some people may lack private health insurance coverage during a particular time period because they become frictionally uninsured. **Frictional uninsurance** occurs when a person leaves one job that offered health insurance and is searching for another job or waiting to become eligible for insurance at a new job. Seventy-three percent of employees covered by health insurance work for companies that require a waiting period averaging three months before extending medical insurance benefits to a new employee (Steinmetz, 1993).

In fact, the Consolidated Omnibus Budget Reconciliation Act (COBRA) of 1985 was developed expressly with frictional uninsurance in mind by requiring employers with more than 20 workers to allow former employees and their dependents the option to retain their health insurance coverage for up to 18 months after terminating employment. However, given that this act requires the frictionally uninsured to pay the full premiums and an administrative fee of 2 percent, only about 20 percent of those eligible extend their health insurance under COBRA while between jobs (Madrian, 1998).

Frictional uninsurance also occurs when people are temporarily without private health insurance because of a mismatch of information. Because of imperfect information, consumers take time to shop around for the right insurers while health insurers search for the right customers. It stands to reason that insurance agents and brokers can impact the number of individuals frictionally uninsured and the duration of frictional uninsurance by providing timely and reliable information (Conwell, 2002). Within the context of frictional uninsurance, Swartz et al. (1993) find that monthly family income, educational attainment, and industry of employment in the month prior to losing health insurance are the characteristics with the greatest impact on the duration of a spell without health insurance.

Second, structurally uninsured individuals constitute another category of those without private health insurance. Included in the **structurally uninsured** category are individuals who are without private health insurance on a long-run basis because of chronic illnesses, preexisting conditions, employment that does not offer health insurance coverage, and/or insufficient income. For example, noncoverage rates tend to fall as household income rises. Nearly 27 percent of households with annual incomes of $25,000 or less lacked health insurance coverage of any kind in 2010. The comparable figure for households with annual incomes of $75,000 or more was only 8 percent. In addition, 21 percent of all blacks and 31 percent of all Hispanics were uninsured in 2010 compared to a rate of only 12 percent for non-Hispanic whites. Blacks, and particularly Hispanics, are more likely to accept casual employment in small firms that are less likely to offer health insurance coverage to their employees.

Swartz (1994) stresses that the duration of the spell without health insurance coverage is another important consideration. She estimates that the median spell without health insurance coverage is about six months. A median uninsured spell of six months means that 50 percent of all spells without insurance are rather short and end before six months. However, another 50 percent of spells last longer than six months. At least 28 percent of uninsured spells last more than one year, and 15 to 18 percent last more than two years. Those with long uninsured spells are clearly among the structurally uninsured.

Finally, individuals who are cyclically uninsured make up the last category of those without private insurance. **Cyclical uninsurance** pertains to individuals (and their families) who change insurance status as they migrate in and out of jobs offering group health insurance benefits as the macroeconomy normally expands and contracts in the short term. Cyclically uninsured individuals tend to possess few skills and may fluctuate between working in small and large firms over the course of the business cycle. For example, part-time workers and those without a job are more likely to be uninsured compared to those who work full time. Specifically, about 28 percent of all part-time workers and the unemployed lacked health insurance coverage compared to a figure of 15 percent for full-time workers in 2010.

Job Lock. While employer-sponsored group health insurance offers several advantages over individual health insurance, such as lower premiums and informed purchasing, group insurance also offers some disadvantages. First, workers are typically unable to choose among a variety of health insurance products. Instead, they must choose among a few products already determined by their employer.

The second disadvantage is that workers cannot take their employer-sponsored insurance policy to their next place of employment. This nonportability of employer-sponsored health insurance could mean that the next employer does not offer any insurance at all. Or the employer at the next job may not offer the same plan, particularly a plan with the same out-of-pocket payments or network of health care providers. In addition, long waiting periods, preexisting conditions, and the potential for less extensive health coverage at the new job all increase the financial risk associated with extensive unanticipated medical events, making the move to a new job a costly endeavor. Thus, some workers may become locked into their current jobs because of variations in the insurance products sponsored by different employers. The resulting job lock disrupts the proper functioning of a macroeconomy because workers are discouraged from switching to jobs where they are more efficient producers. This immobility of labor resources can lead to a lower level of labor productivity and national income. Whether job lock severely inhibits job mobility is of interest to many health care policy makers.

As one might imagine, it is not easy to determine empirically whether, and how frequently, job lock occurs in practice. Researchers must carefully control for all other factors affecting job turnover decisions other than health insurance, such as initial wages and expected wage offers at new employment, job security, other fringe benefits, experience, education, and workers' and dependents' health status. In addition, employer-provided health insurance may be correlated with other unobservable job attributes also affecting job choice (such as workplace conditions and collegiality), which makes it difficult empirically to distinguish between association and causation.

Gruber and Madrian (2002) review 18 empirical papers on the topic that differ with respect to sample coverage, explanatory variables, methodology, and identification strategy (that is, distinguishing between association and causation). Overall they claim that the empirical literature on the relationship between health insurance and job choice is certainly not unanimous. About an equal percentage of studies find evidence supporting and not supporting the hypothesis that health insurance reduces job mobility. Of the papers uncovering a statistically significant relationship, Gruber and Madrian note a consistent finding that health insurance reduces job mobility by 25 to 50 percent. While Gruber and Madrian believe that job lock exists as a result of their extensive review (and their own research in this area), they stress that it is unclear whether these effects result in large welfare or efficiency losses.

Health Insurance Portability and Accountability Act of 1996. Concern over the nonportability of health insurance, lengthy waiting periods for preexisting conditions, and insurance benefit denial led to the passage of the Health Insurance Portability and Accountability Act (HIPAA) in 1996. The basic idea behind HIPAA was to make it more difficult for health insurers to segment insurance risk pools and deny or revoke access to specific individuals or groups on the basis of health status. At the time of its passage, the HIPAA was considered by many as the most significant federal health care reform legislation since the passage of the Medicare and Medicaid programs in 1965. HIPAA created the first national standards for the availability and portability of group and individual health insurance coverage.

Prior to HIPAA (or the Kassebaum-Kennedy Act), uniform standards were lacking in the health insurance industry for two reasons. First, states had been granted authority over health insurers within their jurisdictions by the McCarran-Ferguson Act of 1945 (Nichols and Blumberg, 1998). Some states chose to aggressively regulate and set standards in the health insurance industry; others did not. Second, the federal government has full responsibility for self-insured plans under the Employee Retirement Income Security Act (ERISA) of 1974. States are therefore unable to regulate the health insurance of a large percentage of U.S. workers. Furthermore, no federal regulations existed regarding the availability and portability of health insurance for self-insured plans.

HIPAA has wide-sweeping implications, as the law generally applies to all health plans, including large- and small-group plans, state-regulated plans, self-funded ERISA plans, indemnity and HMO plans, and individual plans. The major provisions as they relate to the health insurance industry are as follows:

Guaranteed Access and Renewability

1. With certain exceptions, insurers participating in the small-group market (2 through 50 employees) cannot exclude a small employer or any of the employer's eligible employees from coverage on the basis of health status.
2. Eligibility or continued eligibility of any individual to enroll in a group plan, regardless of size, cannot be conditioned on the following health-related factors: health status, medical condition (physical or mental), claims experience, receipt of health care, medical history, genetic information, or evidence of insurability or disability.
3. Individuals within a group plan cannot be charged a higher premium based on their health status. This requirement does not restrict the amount an employer may be charged for coverage under a group plan.
4. Except for certain specific exceptions (such as fraud, nonpayment, and discontinuance of market coverage), all group coverage in both the small- and large-group markets and individual coverage must be renewed.
5. Generally, individual insurers must provide coverage to individuals coming off group insurance if the individual had previous coverage for 18 months, was not eligible for other group coverage, was not terminated from the previous plan due to nonpayment, and was not eligible or had exhausted COBRA-type coverage.
6. Individual insurers must guarantee to provide at least two policies. These two policies may be the insurer's most popular plans, based on premium volume, or a package of lower-level and higher-level coverage plans based on actuarial averages. The latter plans must be covered under a risk-spreading mechanism. States may elect to institute an approved alternate mechanism to provide the transition from group to individual coverage.

Portability

1. Employees moving from one employer to another (and individuals coming off group coverage to individual coverage) are protected against a newly imposed preexisting condition limitation. In general, a plan may not impose a new preexisting condition if no more than 63 days have passed between covered jobs, not including any applicable employer waiting period for new hires. The plan must also give credit for the portion of the preexisting condition satisfied under a prior plan, which can include individual coverage, dependent coverage, and so on.
2. The maximum exclusion period for preexisting conditions is no more than 12 months, or 18 months for a late enrollee. The look-back period to determine a preexisting condition is no more than six months prior to the person's enrollment date.
3. Preexisting condition exclusions may not apply in the case of pregnancies, or for newborns and adopted children who are covered by insurance 30 days from the date of birth or adoption.

By setting national standards, proponents hope that HIPAA encourages health insurers to compete more on the basis of efficiency and quality than on risk selection. Moreover, by setting national standards for availability and portability, it is hoped that there are greater opportunities for risk pooling. Opponents fear that the reforms will raise the price of health insurance to individuals and thereby reduce the number of insured individuals. It should be pointed out that HIPAA does not change how health care is delivered or how it is financed. Moreover, HIPAA does not increase access to health insurance for the uninsured or regulate the rates that health plans can charge (Atchinson and Fox, 1997). While HIPAA represents a major step, advocates of health care reform believe that much more work remains to be done in health insurance markets.

Profitability in the Private Health Insurance Industry

We learned in Chapter 8 that, after various adjustments, profit rate can serve as an indicator of market power. In short, persistently excessive profits may reflect that the firms in an industry are able to exploit their market power by restricting output and thereby raising the price of the good or service. With that possibility in mind, Figure 11–5 reports figures for the operating profit margins of some major private health insurers during the 2000 to 2010 period. These five health insurers accounted for over 30 percent of all health-care-related revenues in 2009.

Notice, in the figure, that all of these health insurers, except Aetna, showed a continuously positive operating margin throughout the period. Aetna's low returns in the early 2000s reflect how it "crashed and almost burned as a result of excessive acquisition growth" (Robinson, 2004, p. 19). Over the entire 11 years, United Health Care earned the highest operating margin of 8.8 percent followed by Cigna (8.3%), WellPoint (7.8%), and Aetna (6.9%).

At first blush, one might conclude from the figures that these health insurers possess market power because their operating margins are much greater than zero on a fairly consistent basis. However, we must remember that various adjustments to the reported profit rate must be made before drawing conclusions about market power. First, these reported rates reflect accounting profits rather than economic profits. Second, we must allow for a normal rate of return on their invested capital. As an example, sizeable surplus funds must be retained by health insurers in case medical claims paid out unexpectedly exceed premium revenues. The opportunity cost of holding these surplus funds must be recognized.

Third, it might be the case that health insurance is a relatively risky business. Hence, we can expect health insurance profit rates to be relatively high for that specific reason. Fourth, we may wish to study the operating margins for the entire industry

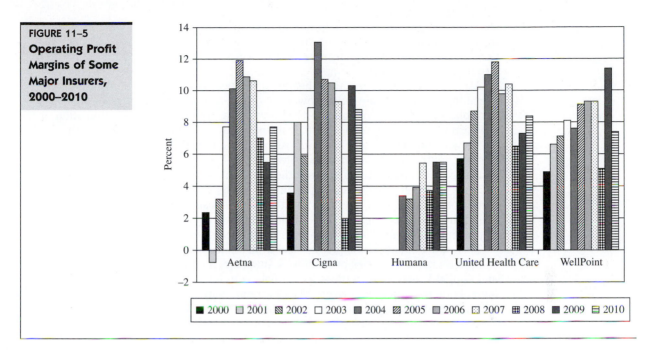

FIGURE 11–5
Operating Profit Margins of Some Major Insurers, 2000–2010

SOURCE: Based on American Hospital Association Chartbook 2011 at http://www.aha.org/aha/research-and-trends/chartbook/ index.html (accessed December 21, 2011).

over time because these five major health insurance companies may simply be efficient at producing health insurance because of their scale, scope of services, or organizational capabilities. Other firms in the industry may not be as efficient. Lastly, the analysis should be conducted at the metropolitan level because health insurance markets are local in nature, as discussed earlier. We would seek to examine if excessive profitability can be linked to high market concentration, while holding constant other determinants of health-insurer profitability.

Provisions of the Patient Protection and Affordable Care Act (PPACA) of 2010 Relating to the Health Insurance Industry

A number of provisions in the PPACA relating to the health insurance industry, such as the insurance mandate, the minimum medical loss ratio requirement, health insurance exchanges, and various taxes and subsidies, have already been discussed at the end of Chapter 6. Here we discuss several additional provisions that likely have more impact on the supply of, rather than demand for, private health insurance.

One can think of PPACA as essentially transforming the private health insurance industry into a federally-regulated entity. This transformation is not a trivial one because state governments, under the McCarran-Ferguson Act of 1945, previously had the responsibility of regulating the private health insurance. The extent, scope, and severity of regulations varied considerably across states, however. For example, some states actively regulated health insurance premium rates for individual and small group policies whereas others did not.

By 2014, the PPACA will eliminate all preexisting condition exclusions, as well as, annual and lifetime limits on how much health insurance companies spend on an individual's medical care. Both of these provisions will likely lead to higher premiums since health insurers will be required to pay out more medical benefits on behalf of its insurance subscribers. When insurers do not exclude coverage for preexisting conditions it is referred to as **guarantee issue** because insurers guarantee a policy will be issued to any individual that applies for one.

Also, PPACA requires that health insurance companies set community-rated premiums. Premiums are only allowed to vary because of geography, family size, age, and tobacco use. The community-rated premiums, coupled with the elimination of the preexisting condition exclusion, means that private health insurance in the United States will take on a new dimension. As pointed out in Chapter 6, private insurance is normally purchased to cover unexpected events. It makes little economic sense to buy insurance for known events because the premium will reflect the known costs plus an expense load. Yet, medical care spending on a preexisting condition cannot be considered unexpected. Also, because of the cross-subsidy implicitly imbedded in the community-rated premiums, those without preexisting conditions will end up helping to pay the known medical care costs of those with preexisting conditions.

This new dimension for private health insurance should not necessarily be judged as promoting inefficiencies or inequities, however. It could represent the most efficient and equitable way to help those individuals with low income to pay for their preexisting condition medical care costs. Also, everyone may face the same chance of possessing a preexisting condition, so requiring its coverage is fair in that sense. Finally, health insurers may find more efficient system-wide methods of using the funds previously directed toward monitoring the prevalence of preexisting conditions such as medical screening costs. Everyone may similarly benefit from systemwide savings.

In addition, PPACA requires health insurers to provide first-dollar preventive care coverage. Economic theory suggests that this preventive care coverage requirement may promote efficiency as long as prevention pays for itself in terms of acute-care medical costs savings in the future. The economic logic goes like this. Without the requirement, individual health insurers face little incentive to invest in preventive care. The reasoning is that any investment in preventive care by an individual health insurer likely leads to higher premiums in the short run. While the preventive care investment may pay for itself in the future, the higher short-run premiums might cause consumers to switch to another insurance company with lower premium because it is not offering preventive care. It follows that the preventive care requirement essentially eliminates a free-rider problem.

Lastly, some provisions of the PPACA are designed to enhance the efficient operation of the health insurance industry. One efficiency enhancement provides consumers with more information about health plans through the world-wide web so they can make better choices. Others provide consumer assistance for complaints against health insurance companies and set uniform standards for the exchange of health information to simplify administration.

Summary

Recent data suggest that the private health insurance industry is relatively concentrated in many local market areas. While a large competitive fringe exists, it appears that intra-industry barriers prevent the fringe firms from entering into the more dominant core of the industry. The reduced level of competition evidently provides the entrenched dominant health insurers with some market power to restrict their output and raise premiums. The quality of health insurance may also suffer as a result of health-insurer market power. These market power effects are likely more pronounced in the individual health insurance market where consumers are relatively uninformed and do not have the alternative of low-risk self-insurance like employees in large firms do.

Empirical evidence finds mixed results regarding the monopsony power of health insurers. Some studies find that health insurers use their market power to bust the monopoly power of hospitals which could benefit consumers through lower hospital prices and premiums. Another study finds that health insurers exercise their market power by reimbursing physicians with below-competitive prices. This exercise of monopsony power may create contrived shortages of physician care and thereby harm consumers.

Considering the empirical findings as a whole, it is unclear how a reduction in health-insurer market power might influence industry performance. On the one hand, reduced health-insurer market concentration may benefit physicians through higher reimbursement rates and remove any contrived shortages of physician care. Also, taken alone, more people may be able to afford health insurance as a result of the lower premiums resulting from reduced health-insurer market concentration. On the other hand, reduced market concentration may mean higher premiums because health insurers are less able to countervail the monopoly power of hospitals. Thus, policy makers must consider this likely trade-off when considering if the market power of health insurers should be constrained or regulated in some manner.

In response to community-rated premiums, health insurers sometimes practice cherry-picking behavior, in which only healthy individuals are offered adequate health insurance coverage. Less-healthy people are denied access to health insurance, are not covered for preexisting conditions, or are charged prohibitively high prices. While this problem is much more pronounced in the individual health insurance market, GR may offer a solution.

In terms of performance, the relative price of private health insurance has tended to rise over the long run. This rise in health insurance premiums may reflect the access value generated by health insurance and the notion that the demand for health insurance is derived from the demand for good health, which tends to be highly valued by consumers. During the short term, the period between 1993 and 1999 witnessed an abrupt slowdown in premium growth because of the successful cost containment efforts of MCOs. However, the backlash against MCOs after 2000 led to less restrictive supply-side policies and consequently a return to rapidly rising health insurance premiums once again.

Some output problems continue to prevail in the market for private health insurance. A significant percentage of Americans lack health insurance coverage. Others are locked into their jobs because of variations in health insurance coverage offered by different employers. People are uninsured for a variety of reasons, so no one single type of policy action can be expected to reduce the uninsurance rate to zero in a voluntary health insurance system.

Finally, the profitability of the private health insurance industry was discussed. We learned that the operating margins of five major health insurers averaged around 7 to 8 percent over the 2000 to 2010 period. Before drawing any conclusions about the relative efficiency of an industry from profits, however, we must make sure that the opportunity cost of all resources, risk, normal rates of return, and the proper time frame are all considered.

Review Questions and Problems

1. Many economists point to moral hazard as the primary reason underlying rising health care costs in the United States.
   A. Explain the general argument behind moral hazard.
   B. Explain the five ways in which moral hazard takes place (explain with a graph when possible).
   C. How does price elasticity of demand influence the moral hazard problem?

D. Explain how an insurer could reduce the scope of the moral hazard problem by introducing a consumer copayment.

E. What two considerations determine the optimal copayment rate?

2. Recent empirical evidence suggests that the health insurance industry is noncompetitive. Based on various determinants of industry structure, explain why drawing that conclusion makes some sense.

3. Explain how health insurance mandates may result in inefficiencies and inequities.

4. Fully explain the two reasons the individual health insurance market may be less competitive than the group health insurance market.

5. Blair et al. (1975) find that substantial economies of scale exist in the administration of health insurance, yet survivor analysis finds no scale economies in the provision of health insurance. How can this inconsistency be explained?

6. Verbally and graphically explain how a profit-maximizing dominant health insurer determines the premium to charge for its policies.

7. Explain how the competitive fringe influences the premiums charged by a dominant health insurer.

8. Explain why someone may make the following seemingly contradictory statement: "High administrative costs are good because they sometimes lead to lower costs of providing health insurance."

9. Private insurers tend to experience three consecutive years of profits followed by three consecutive years of losses. What are the various explanations offered for this profit cycle?

10. Managed care plans tend to lower health care costs, yet the level and growth of managed care premiums are similar to those of traditional fee-for-service insurance plans. How can that be explained?

11. What does *cherry-picking behavior* mean? What does the evidence suggest about this type of behavior? Why is it less troublesome in the group health insurance market?

12. What does *adverse selection* mean? How does this type of behavior impose costs on society?

13. Explain why experience rating may be more efficient and equitable than community rating. Explain why community rating may be more efficient and equitable than experience rating.

14. Explain how the contractual feature of guaranteed renewability may lessen some of the problems that result when risk varies among the insured.

15. What is the best way to measure the price of health insurance? Why? What happened to the price of health insurance from 1987 to 1993? Why? What happened to the price of health insurance from 1993 to 1999? Why? What happened to the price of health insurance since 2000? Why?

16. Explain how a monopsonist determines the price paid for and the quantity purchased of a good or service. According to Feldman and Wholey (2001) and Bates and Santerre (2008), do health insurers have monopsony power? Why or why not? How about the study by Dafny et al. (2009)?

17. Describe the typical uninsured person.

18. Explain the difference between voluntary and involuntary uninsurance and between frictional, structural, and cyclical uninsurance.

19. What were the main reasons behind the HIPAA? What are the main features of the act?

20. Explain why accounting profit rates cannot be used to draw inferences about the market power of real-world firms and industries.

21. Suppose the accounting profit margins reported in Figure 11–5 for the major health insurers are correct from an economic perspective. Use the Lerner index to back out the implied price elasticity of demand facing each health insurer in 2010.

Online Resources

To access Internet links related to the topics in this chapter, please visit our website at **www.cengage.com/economics/santerre**.

References

Adam, Atherly, Curtis Florence, and Kenneth E. Thorpe. "Health Plan Switching among Members of the Federal Employees Health Benefits Program." *Inquiry* 42 (September 2005), pp. 255–65.

Atchinson, Brian K., and Daniel M. Fox. "From the Field: The Politics of the Health Insurance Portability and Accountability Act." *Health Affairs* 16 (May/June 1997), pp. 146–50.

Baker, Laurence C., Joel C. Cantor, Stephen H. Long, and M. Susan Marquis. "HMO Market Penetration and Costs of Employer-Sponsored Health Plans." *Health Affairs* 19 (September/October 2000), pp. 121–28.

Baker, Laurence C., and Kenneth S. Corts. "The Effects of HMOs on Conventional Insurance Premiums: Theory and Evidence." National Bureau of Economic Research (NBER), Working Paper No. 5356. Cambridge, Mass.: November 1995, pp. 1–33.

Bates, Laurie J., James I. Hilliard, and Rexford E. Santerre. "Do Health Insurers Possess Market Power?" *Southern Economic Journal* 78 (April 2012), pp. 1289–1304.

Bates, Laurie J., and Rexford E. Santerre. "Do Health Insurers Possess Monopsony Power in the Hospital Services Industry?" *International Journal of Health Care Finance and Economics* 8 (March 2008), pp. 1–11.

Beauregard, Karen M. *Persons Denied Private Health Insurance Due to Poor Health.* AHCPR Pub. No. 92–0016, 1991.

Blair, Roger D., Jerry R. Jackson, and Ronald J. Vogel. "Economies of Scale in the Administration of Health Insurance." *Review of Economics and Statistics* 57 (May 1975), pp. 185–89.

Blair, Roger D., and Ronald J. Vogel. "A Survivor Analysis of Commercial Health Insurers." *Journal of Business* 51 (July 1978), pp. 521–29.

Born, Patricia, and Rexford E. Santerre. "Unraveling the Health Insurance Underwriting Cycle." *Journal of Insurance Regulation* 26 (spring 2008), pp. 65–84.

Cebul, Randall D., James B. Rebitzer, Lowell J. Taylor, and Mark E. Votruba. "Unhealthy Insurance Markets: Search Frictions and the Cost and Quality of Health Insurance." *American Economic Review* 101 (2011), pp. 1842–71.

Chollet, Deborah J., Fabrice Smieliauskas, and Madeleine Konig. "Mapping State Health Insurance Markets, 2001: Structure and Change." Washington, D.C.: Academy for Health Services Research and Health Policy, September 2003.

Conwell, L. J. "The Role of Health Insurance Brokers." Issue Brief #57. Washington, D.C.: Center for Studying Health System Change, October 2002.

Crew, Michael A. "Coinsurance and the Welfare Economics of Medical Care" *American Economic Review* 59 (1969), pp. 906–8.

Cutler, David M., and Mark McClellan. "Is Technological Change in Medicine Worth It?" *Health Affairs* (September/October 2001), pp. 11–29.

Dafny, Leemore. "Are Health Insurance Markets Competitive? *The American Economic Review* 100 (2010), pp. 1399–431.

Dafny, Leemore, Mark Duggan, and Subramaniam Ramanarayanan. "Paying a Premium on Your Premium? Consolidation in the Health Insurance Industry." NBER Working Paper No. 15334. Cambridge, Mass.: NBER, 2009.

Danzon, Patricia M. "Hidden Overhead Costs: Is Canada's System Really Less Expensive?" *Health Affairs* 11 (spring 1992), pp. 21–43.

Dave, Dhavel, and Robert Kaestner. "Health Insurance and Ex Ante Moral Hazard: Evidence from Medicare." NBER Working Paper No. 12764. Cambridge, Mass.: NBER, 2006.

DeNavas-Walt, Carmen, Bernadette D. Proctor, and Jessica C. Smith. "Income, Poverty, and Health Insurance Coverage in the United States: 2010." U.S. Census Bureau, Current Population Reports, P60-239, U.S. Government Printing Office, Washington, D.C., 2011.

Feldman, Roger, Bryan Dowd, and Gregory Gifford. "The Effect of HMOs on Premiums in Employment-Based Health Plans." *Health Services Research* 27 (February 1993), pp. 779–811.

Feldman, Roger, and Douglas Wholey. "Do HMOs Have Monopsony Power?" *International Journal of Health Care Finance and Economics* 1 (2001), pp. 7–22.

Friedman, Milton. "The Folly of Buying Health Care at the Company Store." *Wall Street Journal*, February 3, 1992, p. A14.

Gabel, Jon, Roger Formisano, Barbara Lohr, and Steven Di Carlo. "Tracing the Cycle of Health Insurance." *Health Affairs* (winter 1991), pp. 49–61.

General Accounting Office. "Private Health Insurance: Number and Market Share of Carriers in the Small Group Health Insurance Market in 2004." 6A0-06-155R. Washington, D.C.: GAO, October 13, 2005.

Grossman, Joy M., and Paul B. Ginsburg. "As the Health Insurance Underwriting Cycle Turns: What Next?" *Health Affairs* 23, no. 6 (2004), pp. 91–102.

Gruber, Jonathan, and Brigette C. Madrian. "Health Insurance, Labor Supply, and Job Mobility: A Critical Review of the Literature." NBER Working Paper no. 8817. Cambridge, Mass.: NBER, March 2002.

Hay, Joel W., and Michael J. Leahy. "Competition among Health Plans: Some Preliminary Evidence." *Southern Economic Journal* 50 (January 1987), pp. 831–46.

Health Insurance Association of America (HIAA). *Source Book of Health Insurance Data 1999/2000*. Washington, D.C.: HIAA, 2001.

Holahan, John. "The 2007–2009 Recession and Health Insurance Coverage." *Health Affairs* 30 (2011), pp. 1145–52.

Iglehart, John K. "The American Health Care System—Private Insurance." *New England Journal of Medicine* 326 (June 18, 1992), pp. 1715–20.

Kenkel, Donald S. "Prevention." In *Handbook in Health Economics*, eds. A. J. Culyer and J. P. Newhouse. Amsterdam: North-Holland, 2000, pp. 1675–720

Kopit, William G. "Is There Evidence that Recent Consolidation in the Health Insurance Industry Has Adversely Affected Premiums?"

Health Affairs 23 (November/December 2004), pp. 29–31.

Lerner, Abba P. "The Concept of Monopoly and the Measurement of Monopoly Power." *Review of Economic Studies* 1 (1934), pp. 157–75.

Long, Stephen H., and Jack Rodgers. "Do Shifts toward Service Industries, Part-Time Work, and Self-Employment Explain the Rising Uninsured Rate?" *Inquiry* 32 (spring 1995), pp. 111–6.

Madrian, B. C. "Health Insurance Portability: The Consequences of COBRA." *Regulation* (winter 1998), pp. 27–33.

Manning, Willard, et al. "A Controlled Trial of the Effect of a Prepaid Group Practice on Use of Services." *New England Journal of Medicine* 310 (June 7, 1984), pp. 1505–10.

McCormack, Lauren A., Peter D. Fox, Thomas Rice, and Marcia L. Graham. "Medigap Reform Legislation of 1990: Have the Objectives Been Met?" *Health Care Financing Review* 18 (fall 1996), pp. 157–74.

McLaughlin, Catherine G. "Market Responses to HMOs. Price Competition or Rivalry?" *Inquiry* (summer 1988), pp. 207–18.

Melnick, Glenn A., Yu-Chu Shen, and Vivian Yaling Wu. "The Increased Concentration of Health Plan Markets Can Benefit Consumers." *Health Affairs* 30 (2011), pp. 1728–33.

Miller, Robert H., and Harold S. Luft. "Managed Care Plan Performance since 1980." *Journal of the American Medical Association* 271 (May 18, 1994), pp. 1512–19.

Miller, W., E. R. Vigdor, and W. G. Manning. "Covering the Uninsured: What Is It Worth?" *Health Affairs*, Web Exclusive (March 31, 2004), pp. w4-157–w4-167.

Modern Healthcare. "Largest Health Insurers. Based on 2009 Healthcare-Related Revenue from Health, Life and Health Statutory Fillings." *Modern Healthcare*, 40 (June 28, 2010), p. 32.

Moriya, Asako S., William B. Vogt, and Martin Gaynor. Hospital prices and market structure in the hospital and insurance industries. *Health Economics, Policy and Law* 5 (2010), pp. 459–79.

Morrisey, Michael A. "Competition in Hospital and Health Insurance Markets: A Review and Research Agenda." *Health Services Research* 36 (April 2001), pp. 191–222.

Nichols, Len M., and Linda Blumberg. "A Different Kind of 'New Federalism'? The Health Insurance Portability and Accountability Act of 1996." *Health Affairs* 17 (May/June 1998), pp. 25–42.

Nyman, J. A. *The Theory of Demand for Health Insurance*. Stanford, Calif.: Stanford University Press, 2003.

Patel, Vip, and Mark V. Pauly. "Guaranteed Renewability and the Problem of Risk Variation in Individual Health Insurance Markets." *Health Affairs*, Web Exclusive (August 28, 2002), pp. w280–w289.

Pauly, Mark V. "The Economics of Moral Hazard: Comment?" *American Economic Review* 58 (June 1968), pp. 531–37.

Pauly, Mark V., Alan L. Hillman, Myoung S. Kim, and Darryl R. Brown. "Competitive Behavior in the HMO Marketplace." *Health Affairs* 21 (January/February 2002), pp. 194–202.

Pauly, Mark V., and Philip J. Held. "Benign Moral Hazard and the Cost Effectiveness of Insurance Coverage." *Journal of Health Economics* 9 (1990), pp. 447–61.

Pollitz, Karen, Richard Sorian, and Kathy Thomas. *How Accessible Is Individual Health Insurance for Consumers in Less-Than-Perfect Health?* Report prepared for the Kaiser Family Foundation, Georgetown University Institute for Health Care Research and Policy, June 2001.

Rapoport, John, et al. "Resource Utilization among Intensive Care Patients." *Archives of Internal Medicine* 152 (November 1992), pp. 2207–12.

Reinhardt, Uwe. "The Market Won't Make Health Insurers Efficient." *Norwich Bulletin*, April 12, 1992, p. A5.

Robinson, James C. "Consolidation and the Transformation of Competition in Health Insurance." *Health Affairs* 23 (November/December 2004), pp. 11–24.

Rothschild, Michael, and Joseph Stiglitz. "Equilibrium in Competitive Insurance Markets: An Essay on the Economics of Imperfect Information." *Quarterly Journal of Economics* 90 (November 1976), pp. 630–49.

Samuelson, Paul A. "Interactions between the Multiplier Analysis and the Principle of Acceleration." *Review of Economics and Statistics* 21, no. 2 (1939), pp. 75–78.

Samuelson, William, and Richard Zeckhauser. "Status Quo Bias in Decision Making." *Journal of Risk and Uncertainty* 1 (1988), pp. 7–59.

Santerre, Rexford E. "Examining the Marginal Access Value of Private Health Insurance." *Risk Management and Insurance Review* 9 (2006), pp. 53–62.

Sapolsky, Harvey M. "Empire and the Business of Health Insurance." *Journal of Health Politics, Policy and Law* 16 (winter 1991), pp. 747–60.

Schlesinger, Harris, and Emilio C. Venezian. "Insurance Markets with Loss-Prevention Activity: Profits, Market Structure, and Consumer Welfare." *Journal of Risk and Insurance* 17 (1986), pp. 227–38.

Schneider, John E., Pengxiang Li, Donald G. Klepser, N. Andrew Peterson, Timothy T. Brown, and Richard M. Scheffler. "The Effect of Physician and Health Plan Market Concentration on Prices in Commercial Health Insurance Markets." *International Journal of Health Care Finance and Economics* 8 (2008), pp, 13–26.

Seidman, Laurence S. "Health Care: Getting the Right Amount at the Right Price." *Business Review*, March–April 1982.

Sheth, Jagdish, and Rajendra Sisodia. "Only the Big Three Will Thrive." *Wall Street Journal*, May 11, 1998, p. A22.

Sindelar, Jody L. "The Declining Price of Health Insurance." In *Health Care in America*, ed. H. E. Frech III. San Francisco: Pacific Institute for Public Policy, 1988, pp. 259–91.

Steinmetz, Greg. "Number of Uninsured Stirs Much Confusion in Health-Care Debate." *Wall Street Journal*, June 9, 1993, p. A1.

Stigler, George J. "The Economies of Scale." *Journal of Law and Economics* 1 (October 1958), pp. 54–71.

Strombom, Bruce A., Thomas C. Buchmueller, and Paul J. Feldstein. "Switching Costs, Price Sensitivity, and Health Plan Choice". *Journal of Health Economics* 21 (2002), pp. 89–116.

Swartz, Katherine. "Dynamics of People without Health Insurance." *Journal of the American Medical Association* 271 (January 5, 1994), pp. 64–66.

Swartz, Katherine, John Marcotte, and Timothy D. McBride. "Personal Characteristics and Spells without Health Insurance." *Inquiry* 30 (spring 1993), pp. 64–76.

Temin, Peter. "An Economic History of American Hospitals." In *Health Care in America*, ed. H. E. Frech III. San Francisco: Pacific Research Institute for Public Policy, 1988, pp. 75–102.

Van De Ven, Wynand P. M. M., and Randall P. Ellis. "Risk Adjustment in Competitive Health Plan Markets." In *Handbook of Health Economics, Volume 1*, eds. A. J. Culyer and J. P. Newhouse. Amsterdam: Elsevier Science, 2000.

Weisbrod, Burton A. "The Health Care Quadrilemma: An Essay on Technological Change, Insurance, Quality of Care, and Cost Containment." *Journal of Economic Literature* 29 (June 1991), pp. 523–52.

Wholey, Douglas, Roger Feldman, and Jon B. Christianson. "The Effect of Market Structure on HMO Premiums." *Journal of Health Economics* 14 (1995), pp. 81–105.

Wholey, Douglas, Roger Feldman, Jon B. Christianson, and John Engberg. "Scale and Scope Economies among Health Maintenance Organizations." *Journal of Health Economics* 15 (1996), pp. 657–84.

Wickizer, Thomas M., and Paul J. Feldstein. "The Impact of HMO Competition on Private Health Insurance Premiums." *Inquiry* 32 (fall 1995), pp. 241–51.

Wroblewski, Michael. "Uniform Health Insurance Information Can Help Consumers Make Informed Purchase Decisions." *Journal of Insurance Regulation* 26 (winter 2007), pp. 21–37.

The Physician Services Industry

Throughout the nineteenth century, the physician services industry was largely unregulated. Many physicians were practicing without proper medical training, primarily because the country was dotted with numerous medical schools of questionable quality. In reaction to this state of affairs, the American Medical Association (AMA) was founded in 1847. At its inception, the organization adopted the improvement of medical education in the United States as its major goal. Although improvements were made over the years, significant changes did not take place until the turn of the twentieth century. The impetus for change was the Flexner Report published in 1910 by the Carnegie Foundation.

Concerned that not enough was being done to improve medical education, the Carnegie Foundation, with the blessing of the AMA, asked Abraham Flexner to conduct a study of the medical schools in Canada and the United States. The final report, commonly referred to as the Flexner Report, was highly critical of the medical training provided by an overwhelming majority of the schools in North America. The report was so controversial that Flexner received threats on his life. As a result of the report, many low-quality medical schools were forced to improve or close their doors. In addition, states began to take the role of licensing physicians more seriously (Raffel and Raffel, 1989). Thus, the formation of the AMA, coupled with the Flexner Report, ushered in the modern regulated physician services industry, which requires an individual to fulfill strict educational and licensing requirements before being allowed to practice medicine.

Over the past quarter century, the scope and complexity of physician services have increased dramatically, and this has had a profound impact on the structure and performance of the industry. Increases in demand for medical services and the introduction of many new, costly technologies have increased expenditures on physician services more than eightyfold since 1960. Nearly gone are the days when an appointment with the doctor meant a visit to a self-employed male physician who owned a solo fee-for-service practice. Today, more than one out of four physicians is female and less than one-third of all physicians are working in solo or two-physician practices. Multiphysician practices are the norm, and physicians who wish to survive are now forced to negotiate with managed care organizations (MCOs) for additional patients, adjust to many new and different fee schedules, and subject themselves to utilization reviews.

In keeping with the methodology laid out in the previous chapter, this chapter employs the structure-conduct-performance paradigm to analyze the ever-changing physician services industry. The first part of the chapter describes the current structure of the industry. In particular, the chapter:

- looks at the number and specialty distribution of physicians, examines the mode of practice, analyzes methods of payment, reviews the reimbursement practices of managed care buyers, and discusses the production and cost of physician services.

- discusses the impact of compensation schemes on physician behavior and examines geographic variations in the use of physician services
- looks at the supplier-induced demand hypothesis, reviews the physician practice hypothesis, and explores the implication of a quantity-setting model on physician behavior
- analyzes the impact of managed care on physician behavior
- traces expenditures on physician services over time, reviews the utilization of physician services, and discusses the growth of physician income over time
- discusses the impact the Patient Protection and Affordable Care Act (PPACA) of 2010 may have on the physician services market.

The Structure of the Physician Services Industry

Because the conduct of buyers and sellers depends directly on the structure of the market, we begin with an analysis of the structure of the physician services market. Among the structural elements, we look at the number and specialty distribution of physicians, along with the organization arrangements adopted by physicians to produce medical services. Next we review the sources of physician revenues and examine the impact of managed care on the physician services market. Finally, we analyze barriers to entry and the production of physician services.

The Number of Physicians in the United States

It seems only logical to begin our analysis of the market for physician services with a look at the supply of physician labor, the primary input in the production of physician services.[1] According to Figure 12–1, the United States experienced a substantial increase in the number of physicians from 1975 to 2009. In 1975, a total of 393,742 physicians operated in the United States; by 2009, that number had more than doubled to 972,376.

To get a clearer picture of the impact of this increase in physician labor on the delivery of patient care, we need to look at a breakdown of physicians by major professional activities. According to Figure 12–1, almost 80 percent of all physicians were involved in direct patient care in 2009. That percentage has remained remarkably stable over time. The remaining 20 percent of the physicians were engaged in other activities such as medical teaching, administration, or research.

Although the absolute supply of physicians in the United States increased in recent years, it is impossible to make inferences regarding the relative supply of physicians without comparing the increase in physician labor to the overall increase in population. One crude measure of the relative supply of physician labor is the physician-to-population ratio. Data supplied by the AMA (2011) indicate that the number of patient care physicians per 100,000 civilians increased substantially from 134 in 1970 to 244 in 2009, an increase of almost 80 percent. Put in other terms, in 1970 there was one patient care physician for every 747 people in the civilian population in the United States and by 2009 that number had dropped to 410 individuals.

It is apparent that the United States experienced a significant increase in physician labor over the last three decades. The increase outpaced the overall increase in the

---

1. As we will see later in the chapter, physician services are produced with a combination of various inputs, including physician labor, nurse labor, clerical staff, physician assistants, and lab technicians.

FIGURE 12–1

Number of Physicians in the United States, 1975–2009

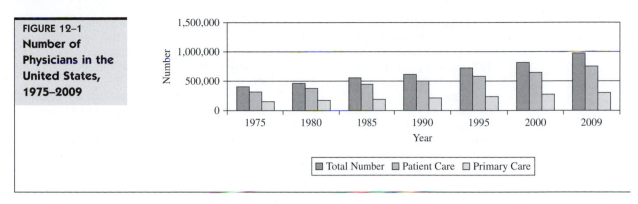

SOURCE: American Medical Association, *Physician Characteristics and Distribution in the U.S. 2011* (Chicago: AMA, 2011).

population and has led to a greater relative supply of labor, as measured by an increase in the physician-to-population ratio. According to a Government Accounting Office study (GAO, 2003b), the growth in physician supply was felt in metropolitan as well as nonmetropolitan areas across the country. Throughout the 1990s, all nonmetropolitan areas and 301 out of 318 metropolitan areas saw increases in the number of physicians per 100,000 people. Of the 17 metropolitan areas that experienced decreases in the relative supply of physicians, only 2 had an absolute decrease in the number of physicians. These results are largely confirmed by Rosenthal et al. (2005), who compare the location patterns of physicians in 1999 and 1979. For example, they find that "even in the most remote categories of counties, with an urban population of less than 2,500 and not adjacent to a metropolitan area, the mean distance to the nearest physician of any type was less than 5 miles" in 1999 (p. 1943).

Shipman et al. (2011) caution that the problem of a geographic maldistribution of physicians still persists and should not be ignored, particularly for certain segments of the population. Despite the growth in the physician workforce, they find millions of children live in areas with an insufficient supply of primary care physicians. As a case in point, they determine that in 2006 nearly "1 million children lived in areas with no local child physician" (p. 19). Together, these findings indicate that while the geographic access to physician services has improved over time in the United States, pockets across the country still remain where access to physician care may be questioned.[2]

Conventional wisdom was that the United States had an overall surplus of physicians and predictions were that the surplus was going to increase over time. For example, in 1992, the Council on Graduate Medical Education (COGME, 1992) issued a report raising concern that the United States may be faced with an overall surplus of physicians. The report also questioned whether the mix of primary care to specialty care physicians was appropriate because too many medical school graduates were electing to practice specialty care rather than primary care.

By the mid-1990s, however, researchers began to question that assertion. For example, Politzer et al. (1996) looked to the future to estimate whether the United States will have an adequate supply of physicians in the year 2020. To establish need, the authors conducted a statistical technique called meta-analysis on five alternative projection methods already developed in the literature. Meta-analysis allows them to establish bands of physician requirements for primary and specialty care physicians.

---

2. We need to keep in mind that these findings do not take into account any local geographic disparities in physician supply that may exist within counties.

Physician supply projections were based on a number of factors, including the number of first-year residency positions likely to exist in the future. The authors conclude that the "future physician supply does appear well-matched with requirements" (p. 181). The authors project a shortage of approximately 33,000 primary care physicians by the year 2020 along with a surplus of specialists.

Cooper et al. (2002) and Cooper (2004) take a very different approach to projecting the adequacy of physician supply and develop a macroeconomic forecast based on four trends that greatly impact the supply of and use of physician services. First and foremost, they consider the strong relationship between the growth of physician supply and economic growth over time. Next, they factor in the impact of population trends, physician work efforts, and the capacity of nonphysician health care professions to provide medical care. Their results are thought-provoking because they contradicted conventional wisdom at the time that the United States has too many physicians. According to their results, a substantial shortfall of approximately 200,000 physicians is likely to exist in the United States by the year 2020.

Subsequently, the COGME (2005) reassessed its position to take into consideration a number of demographic changes and changes in the U.S. health care system. Based on a physician forecasting model that projects the future supply, demand, and need for physician services, the council reversed its earlier estimates and found that by 2020, the United States will face a shortage of around 90,000 physicians. These findings are the result of a number of factors such as an aging population, physicians working fewer hours, and per capita increases in physician visits. Finally, Dill and Salsberg (2008), building on the previous work of the COGME, estimate the physician shortage to expand to 124,000 physicians by 2025.

Distribution of Primary Care and Specialty Care Physicians in the United States

Figure 12–1 also provides information on the number of physicians providing primary care in the United States, as defined by the AMA to include family practice, general practice, internal medicine, obstetrics and gynecology, and pediatrics, but excluding subspecialties within each of these general specialties. While the overall number of active primary care physicians in the United States increased from 144,861 in 1975 to 307,586 in 2009, the proportion of active primary care physicians decreased from approximately 40 percent in 1975 to 32 percent in 2009. The implication is that the number of specialty physicians in the United States over the last three decades increased at a faster pace than the number of primary care physicians.

Many analysts believe the United States has too many specialists and too few primary care physicians, and that the problem has worsened over time. According to Schroeder (1992), the growth in the number of specialists relative to primary care physicians is one reason health costs are so high in the United States. Specialists are more prone to overutilize costly, new, high-technology medical procedures that drive up medical costs. Higher surgery rates and a greater availability of medical technology in the United States, relative to other industrialized nations, are used as evidence to support this hypothesis. To prove his point, Schroeder (1984, 1992) compares the proportion of specialists in the United States to that of various Western European countries in 1980. He finds the proportion of specialists in Belgium, Germany, the Netherlands, and the United Kingdom to lie between 25 and 50 percent. In the United States, the proportion of specialists was slightly more than 60 percent, substantially higher than in most other developed nations.

Whether the United States has more or less than the efficient level of primary care physicians is difficult to determine objectively. One way researchers have attempted to answer this question is by first establishing the medical need for primary care physicians—that is, how many primary care physicians are needed to deliver adequate care to the population.

However, from an economic perspective, demand rather than need is really at issue. Next, the most cost-effective way to deliver physician services must be determined. Only after this has been established can one determine the total number of primary and nonprimary care physicians clinically needed to provide medical services to the entire population. These estimates must then be compared to the actual number of primary and nonprimary care physicians practicing in the United States to determine whether a surplus or a shortage of different specialists exists. Obviously, the process of calculating the optimal number of many specialists is complicated and laced with value judgments.

Weiner (2004) takes on this challenge when he attempts to determine whether the supply of physician labor in the United States is adequate to meet the needs of the population. To establish need, he examines the physician staffing patterns adopted by eight large prepaid group practices (PGPs) at Kaiser Permanente and two other health maintenance organizations (HMOs) that were serving more than eight million enrollees in 2002. Weiner assumes in his analysis that PGPs provide an adequate amount of physician care in the most cost-efficient manner due to the financial incentives they face. In other words, he assumes that large PGPs provide the appropriate amount and type of physician care at least cost.

The goal is to assess the adequacy of the physician workforce in the United States by comparing the physician/population ratios for a select group of PGPs to the overall national average. Before making the comparison, however, Weiner adjusts the PGP physician/population ratios to reflect demographic differences between the PGPs in the sample and the U.S. population as a whole, and to accommodate the use of outside referrals by PGPs. After making these adjustments, he finds that the PGPs in the sample have physician-to-population ratios that are between 22 and 37 percent lower than the overall U.S. ratio. In addition, he finds that the difference in the physician-to-population ratios between the PGPs in the study and the national average for primary care physicians is much less than for specialty care physicians. The major inference from these findings is that PGPs may be able to provide medical care to the general population with far fewer physicians than is currently the case.

While these results are interesting, Salsberg and Forte (2004) caution that we not overextend Weiner's findings and conclude that the United States has too many physicians. Significant differences exist between the ways physician activities are organized in PGPs and in the country as a whole. These differences limit comparisons of physician workforce patterns in PGPs to those of the entire U.S. physician workforce. For one thing, PGPs tend to serve a distinct subset of the U.S. population, which is not adequately accounted for in Weiner's study. For example, enrollees in PGPs are more likely to be employed and therefore have fewer chronic illnesses than the general population. As a result, they require fewer physician services. More important, however, is the fact that the work responsibilities of physicians differ widely across the medical community and are not fully reflected in the staffing patterns of PGPs. As Salsberg and Forte point out, a significant number of physicians conduct clinical research, teach medical students, or provide medical care to individuals with very high needs. These are generally not the duties of PGP physicians. Given these considerations, it is inappropriate to apply the PGP physician staffing ratios to the nation as a whole because they fail to capture the overall scope of physician activities. The challenge, according to the authors, is to determine "which elements of the PGP system contribute to greater efficiencies and effectiveness" (p. 74) in the delivery and financing of medical services, and selectively apply them to other delivery systems.

Clearly, this discussion regarding the number and mix of physicians in the United States points to the need for a better understanding of factors that are likely to impact the demand for and supply of physician services in the coming years. Even more important, we need to more fully understand the relation of physician supply to patient outcomes. As Goodman and Grumbach point out, the "research shows a weak link between patient outcomes and physicians per capita, with the exception of studies of primary care physician supply" (2008, p. 336). These results are not surprising given that the making, or production, of health is influenced by a wide variety of factors including physician services and that the delivery of health care differs dramatically across and within health care systems. As a result, public-policy makers are left to grapple with answering an important question concerning the proper role of the government and market in correcting any imbalances that may exist in the market for physician services.

Mode of Practice

Data from the HSC Community Tracking Study Physician Survey (www.hschange.org) provide a glimpse of the modes of practice utilized by physicians over the last two decades. The survey results indicate that the percent of physicians who were either full or part owners of their practice has been declining modestly over the last two decades. In 1996/1997, slightly more that 60 percent of all physicians were either full or part owners of their practices and by 2008 that percentage had dropped to 56.3 percent. The decrease in ownership has been mirrored by an increase in the proportion of physicians who are not self-employed but are paid on a salary basis. According to figures from the AMA (1998, 2003), 35.1 percent of all physicians were paid on a salary basis by 2001, an increase of approximately 12 percentage points from 1989.

The drop in ownership appears to be matched with a decrease in the proportion of physicians in solo or two-physician practices. According to the HSC Community Tracking Study Physician Survey, in 1996/1997, slightly more than 40 percent of all physicians worked in one or two-physician practices and by 2008 that percent had dropped to 32 percent. At the same time, there also appears to be a movement away from small practices and toward mid-sized practices of between six and fifty physicians. The percent of physicians in mid-sized practices increased from 13.1 percent in 1996/1997 to 19.4 percent in 2008.

Based on this information, there appears to be a trend away from smaller practices toward larger, multidoctor modes of production. This trend might reflect the economies of scope offered by large multidoctor, multispecialty practices or economics of scale in the production of physician services. We review some empirical evidence concerning economies of scale later in this chapter. Other factors that may explain this trend are changes in financial incentives faced by physicians. As the market for physician services moved away from fee-for-service reimbursement environments, physicians reacted by changing their mode of production. This issue is also taken up later in this chapter.

Buyers of Physician Services and Methods of Remuneration

A review of the methods of remuneration provides insight into the number and types of buyers of physician services and the extent to which any one buyer, or group of buyers, may exhibit some degree of market power. In 2010, 38.3 percent of all expenditures on physician and clinical services emanated from the government sector, with Medicare making up 58 percent of that total. This is in sharp contrast to the market for hospital services, in which the government sector accounted for nearly 70 percent of total revenues (see Chapter 13). This suggests that although the government sector is clearly a major player in the physician services market, its ability to influence resource allocation may not be as great as in the market for hospital services.

Rising health care costs have forced politicians to reevaluate the Medicare and Medicaid programs. For example, after much debate, Congress passed the Omnibus Budget Reconciliation Act (OBRA) in 1989, which, among other things, called for major changes in Part B of the Medicare payment system, which provides compensation to physicians for medical services rendered to elderly patients. As of 1992, physicians are now compensated based on resources utilized rather than on the *usual, customary, or reasonable* (UCR) rate. This Medicare reimbursement scheme for physician services, referred to as the *resource-based relative value scale system* (RBRVS), is reviewed in Chapter 10. OBRA 1989 was followed by the Balanced Budget Act of 1997, which extended the resource-based method of payment to include practice and malpractice expenses.

The private sector accounted for about 61.6 percent of physician revenues in 2010, with almost 75 percent coming from private insurance companies. Of the remaining 25 percent, a little more than 15 percent represents out-of-pocket payments and about 10 percent comes from other private sources. This is somewhat different from the hospital services market, in which out-of-pocket payments account for 3.1 percent of total revenues. The relatively higher out-of-pocket expenses for physician services are not too surprising, because insurance theory suggests that insurance coverage is lower for more predictable and lower-magnitude losses.

Overall, the private sector accounts for a much greater share of revenues in the physician services market than it does in the hospital services market. This is largely because out-of-pocket payments are a more important source of funds for physicians than for hospitals. This is not to say, however, that the government plays only a minor role in the physician services market. On the contrary, the recent Medicare reforms indicate that the federal government intends to play a more active role in this market for years to come.

Reimbursement Practices of Managed Care Buyers of Physician Services

Managed care, which embodies a broad set of policies designed by third-party payers to control the utilization and cost of medical care, has had a profound impact on the physician services market. Through the use of alternative compensation schemes, utilization reviews, quality controls, and the like, MCOs hope to modify the behavior of physicians to contain costs. These control mechanisms diminish the autonomy physicians traditionally enjoyed in practicing medicine, and, as a result, many physicians have resisted the movement toward managed care. Despite these reservations, managed care presently has a major impact on the allocation of resources in the physician services market. The strong presence of managed care in the physician services market is reflected in the fact that almost 90 percent of all physicians practicing medicine in 2008 had at least one managed care contract.

Barriers to Entry

It is generally accepted that substantial barriers to entry in the market for physician services impede competition primarily by legally limiting the supply of physicians. Before being allowed to practice medicine, a person must meet a minimum educational requirement (usually a degree from an accredited medical school), participate in an internship or a residency program at a recognized institution, and pass a medical exam. These various requirements entail substantial time and money costs and raise the opportunity cost of becoming a medical doctor. Advocates for these legal restrictions base their argument on the public interest theory. Market failure brought about by an asymmetry of information between patient and physician concerning the appropriateness and quality of medical care justifies the need for government intervention. Because consumers generally have imperfect information concerning the medical care received, given its technical sophistication, they are sometimes unsure about the appropriateness and quality of physician services. As a result, the market cannot be relied on to weed out incompetent doctors or those who would take advantage of their position and prescribe needless and costly medical care.

The necessity of government intervention has also been justified based on the possibility that a negative supply-side externality will occur if incompetent physicians are allowed to practice medicine. For example, if an incompetent physician misdiagnoses a patient infected with the AIDS virus due to a faulty test, others may contract the virus. As a result, government intervention is necessary to ensure that consumers will not become innocent victims of medical malfeasance.

Over the years, proponents of the special interest theory, including Kessel (1958), Moore (1961), Friedman (1962, 1980), and Leffler (1978), have argued that barriers exist primarily to protect the economic interests of physicians. By restricting supply through the creation of educational and training barriers to entry, physicians have succeeded in generating economic profits. As evidence, these analysts point to high physician salaries. Control of medical licensure is the primary mechanism physicians use to restrict their numbers. In the United States, the licensure of physicians is under the control of the states, and most states have medical boards composed of physicians who establish, review, and maintain the criteria for obtaining a license to practice medicine. The fact that these requirements control the process of becoming a physician, rather than encourage the maintenance of medical knowledge, has been used as evidence to support the special interest interpretation of these restrictions.[3]

Control over medical licensure is not the only method physicians use to maintain their market power. Physicians as a group play a critical role in the accreditation of medical schools. For example, the Liaison Committee on Medical Education, the main accrediting body of medical schools, is composed of seventeen people, six of whom are representatives of the AMA (Wilson and Neuhauser, 1985). By maintaining control over the number of medical schools, physicians are in a position to indirectly restrain the supply of their services.

The establishment of limits on the use of physician extenders is yet another method physicians employ to protect their economic interests. Physician extenders, such as physician assistants and nurse practitioners, have the medical training necessary to perform a number of medical tasks traditionally carried out by the physician.[4] Production theory indicates that when more than one variable input is utilized in the production of physician services, a cost-conscious firm combines these inputs to produce in the most cost-efficient manner. For example, let's suppose a staff-model HMO faces an increase in wages for physicians. To counteract this increase, the HMO may attempt to substitute physician extenders for physicians in the production of certain medical services. To limit the possibility of this occurrence, physicians may flex their political muscle to legally limit the duties of physician extenders. The goal would be to legally constrain the marginal rate of technical substitution between physicians and physician extenders to near zero.

Given many of the recent changes in medical care, Svorny (1992) questions the need for medical licensure in the physician market. She believes market incentives can now be relied on to ensure an efficient level of quality. In particular, Svorny points

3. The same argument can be made for lawyers and certified public accountants, who are required to pass the bar exam and Certified Public Accountant exam, respectively.

4. A physician assistant must study for two years in an accredited physician assistant program and pass a certification exam before being allowed to practice. A nurse practitioner is a licensed registered nurse who has received an additional one or two years' training and passed a certification exam. In terms of duties, the difference between the two labor inputs is one of emphasis. Physician assistants concern themselves primarily with the direct application of medical care, whereas nurse practitioners deal mostly in education and wellness.

to changes in medical liability, the rapid growth in for-profit medical care providers, the increased use of brand names, and the growth in employed rather than self-employed physicians as lessening the need for the licensure of physicians.

For example, recent legal decisions have shifted some of the liability for medical malpractice away from physicians and toward institutions, such as hospitals and HMOs. As a result, hospitals and HMOs now have a greater incentive to monitor the behavior of physicians who practice medicine on their premises by assessing the quality of care provided. Institutional liability decreases the need for licensing because it is now in the self-interests of hospitals to weed out incompetent physicians.

The growth in for-profit medical care providers may have the same effect. Because at least one owner has a financial stake in a for-profit medical institution, there may be a greater incentive to oversee the performance of physicians than in a not-for-profit institution, which is run by a board of directors who have no financial commitment to the institution. The expanded use of brand names by hospitals, group practices, and HMOs also increases the incentive for these institutions to more closely monitor the performance of physicians. An incompetent physician can financially hurt the institution by damaging its reputation and tarnishing its image, which took a substantial amount of time and money to establish. Much goodwill is at stake, and hence there is an increased incentive to dismiss incompetent physicians.

The growing use of employed as opposed to self-employed physicians also provides medical institutions with an increased incentive to monitor the activities of physicians. Naturally, it is in the interests of these institutions to eliminate physicians providing low-quality or unnecessary medical care. In addition, because the physician is a salaried employee, the incentive to provide unnecessary care has been diminished. According to Svorny, all these changes have lessened the need for the licensure of physicians because market forces can now be relied on to force doctors to provide quality medical care at least cost.

These institutional and structural changes imply a weakening of barriers to entry into the physician services market. The implication being that the degree of market power in the hands of physicians may have waned over the years.

Production, Costs, and Economies of Scale

Thus far, we have focused primarily on the supply of physicians. In this section, the perspective changes from the physician as an input in the production of medical services to the physician as an entrepreneur: one who makes allocation decisions concerning the most cost-effective way to produce medical services. Unfortunately, the literature on the production and cost of physician services is rather thin compared to the multitude of studies on the hospital services market.

The most comprehensive studies on the production of physician services were carried out by Reinhardt (1972, 1973, 1975), Brown (1988), and Thurston and Libby (2002). These researchers estimate either a production or cost function for physician services and reach a number of conclusions regarding the production characteristics associated with physician services. One, they find that the marginal productivity of physician time is relatively high in comparison to other types of inputs such as nurses or capital equipment. This is not a surprising finding because physicians direct the employment of the other clinical inputs. Two, the typical physician practice could operate more efficiently by using more physician extenders, such as registered nurses and physician assistants. Studies draw this conclusion from the observation that more "bang for the buck" can be derived from physician-extender type inputs by using Equation 7–16 and measures of marginal productivities and input prices. Three, physicians in group practices are more efficient than those in solo practices. Four, the econometric literature suggests moderate economies of scale exist in the production of physician services (Pope and Burge, 1996; Escarce and Pauly, 1998; Gunning and

Sickles, 2011). The literature on survivor analysis also indicates the existence of economies of scale in the production of physician services (Frech and Ginsburg, 1974;
Marder and Zuckerman, 1985). Evidence on economies of scope, however, is lacking.
This means that reasons other than scope economies explain why physicians with different specialties tend to combine into a group practice.

Taken together, this body of research suggests that multiphysician practices have a
cost advantage over solo practices and that economies of scale exist in the production
of physician services, at least up to the three-to-seven physician practice size. However, the ability of physicians to organize across specialties may be limited by scope
diseconomies. Thus, while the average practice size of physicians within specialties
may rise in the future, there is a question as to whether the trend will continue across
specialties.

Summary of the Structure of the Market for Physician Services

Whether the physician services market is measured based on real expenditures or the
number of physicians practicing medicine, it has increased dramatically in size over
the past several decades. Since 1970, the number of physicians and real expenditures
on physician services in the United States has more than doubled. The increase has
outpaced the overall growth in the economy and the general population, as illustrated
by the significant increase in the physician-to-population ratio from 134 in 1970 to 244
in 2009, per 100,000.

The increase in physician labor in the United States has not been without controversy. Some people believe the United States has too many specialists and too few generalists. This issue is likely to play an integral role in any new health care initiatives
over the coming years. There is also some debate as to whether there will be a shortage of physicians in the future.

The mode of practice in the physician services market has also changed significantly
in recent years. There appears to be a movement away from single- and two-physician
practices and toward multiphysician practices with six or more physicians. In addition,
significant growth appears to be occurring in the number of salaried physicians. In all
probability, this trend reflects changing economic conditions in the health care field.
For example, productivity studies and survivor analysis studies indicate the existence
of economies of scale that confer a distinct cost advantage on large multiphysician
practices.

MCOs also appear to play a key role in the physician services market. Almost
90 percent of all physicians have at least one contract with an MCO. The presence
of MCOs in the physician services market may also partly explain the growth of multiphysician practices relative to smaller ones. Since larger practices have a cost advantage over smaller practices, they are in a better position to accept price discounts
from MCOs.

Despite the presence of barriers to entry such as medical licensure, over time, the
physician services market has become even more competitive as large, institutional
buyers challenge the authority of independent physicians. This has caused some policy
makers to call for the elimination of these barriers. As the market for physician services
becomes more competitive, perhaps market forces can be relied on more heavily to dis-
pose of incompetent or unprofessional doctors.

The Conduct of the Physician Services Industry

Now that we have established the market determinants of behavior, or the structure
of the physician services industry, we are in a position to discuss some conduct
issues relating to that market. As you know, market structure interacts with economic

objectives to establish conduct. We look at the supplier-induced demand hypothesis, McGuire's quantity-setting model, the effects of various compensation schemes on physician behavior, geographical variations in the utilization of physician services, and the impact of managed care practices.

The Supplier-Induced Demand Hypothesis

Without a doubt, one of the most talked-about issues in health economics over the years has been whether the **supplier-induced demand (SID) hypothesis** can be used to explain physician behavior. The basic premise of the SID hypothesis is that physicians abuse their role as medical advisors to advance their own economic self-interests. This involves prescribing medical care beyond what is clinically necessary and can include such items as additional follow-up visits, an excessive number of medical tests, or even unnecessary surgery. According to the model, consumers are relatively ill-informed concerning the proper amount of medical care to consume because an asymmetry of information exists regarding the various health care options available. The asymmetry forces consumers to rely heavily on the advice of their physicians for guidance. This implies that physicians are not only suppliers of physician services but also play a major part in determining the level of demand for those services. For example, physicians advise patients about how frequently they should have office visits, medical tests, and appropriate treatments. This situation places physicians in a potentially exploitative position. Physicians may be able to manipulate the demand curves of patients to advance their own economic interests.

For example, assume the market for physician services is initially in equilibrium in Figure 12–2, where equilibrium occurs at point (Q_0, P_0) and Q represents the quantity of physician services. Now assume for some reason an increase occurs in the number of practicing physicians. This increase in the number of physicians causes the supply curve to shift to the right from S_0 to S_1, which in turn forces the average price of physician services to fall from P_0 to P_1. Faced with an increase in competition along with a loss in income, physicians may exercise their ability to influence patients' behavior by inducing them to demand more services. The increased demand may involve more

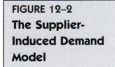

FIGURE 12–2
The Supplier-Induced Demand Model

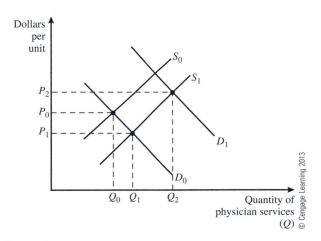

Assume initially that the market for physician services is in equilibrium at point (Q_0, P_0) off the D_0 demand curve and the S_0 supply curve. Now assume that there is an increase in the number of physicians practicing medicine and the supply curve for physician services shifts outward from S_0 to S_1. Under ordinary circumstances, the equilibrium price for physician services would fall to P_1 while the equilibrium quantity would increase to Q_1. In reaction to the decrease in the price of medical services, however, physicians induce the demand for their services and cause the demand curve to shift outward to D_1. The result is that the equilibrium price and quantity for physician services increases to (P_2, Q_2).

office visits, additional tests, or even unnecessary surgery. As a result, the demand for physician services increases from D_0 to D_1. In the end, the price of physician services could actually increase, as shown in Figure 12–2, where the new equilibrium price and quantity equal P_2 and Q_2, respectively.

The SID model can also be described in the context of the principal–agent theory. The principal–agent theory is traditionally used to explain the interaction between the managers of a major corporation, who are the agents, and its stockholders, who are the principals. The fiduciary responsibility of the agent is to manage the firm in the best interest of the principal, and that means maximizing profits. Due to an asymmetry of information between the principal and the agent, the manager is likely to have more information than the stockholders concerning the true operation and performance of the firm. In this situation, the manager has the opportunity to shirk his responsibilities to the stockholders by not seeking to maximize profits. Instead, the manager may use company funds to advance his self-interests. Advancing self-interests may involve such things as higher pay, a large support staff, or a more luxurious office.

Concerning the doctor–patient relationship, the physician is hired to address the health concerns of the patient, the principal. Specifically, the physician, as agent, is given the responsibility of demanding medical services on behalf of the patient, who possesses much less information concerning the appropriateness of medical care. Given that patients are typically covered by health insurance and the physician's personal financial interests are at stake, the physician has the opportunity to exploit the situation by persuading the patient to consume more medical care than is clinically necessary. The increased medical services most likely do no harm, but they do mean increased income for the physician-agent.

The task of reviewing the empirical evidence on the SID hypothesis is daunting given the extensive work on the subject. In one of the earlier studies, Fuchs (1978) uncovers substantial support for the SID hypothesis. In particular, he estimates that a 10 percent increase in the supply of surgeons, as measured by the surgeon-to-population ratio, leads to a 3 percent increase in the per capita surgery rate. Cromwell and Mitchell (1986) also find evidence that surgeons induce demand. However, their estimates are substantially smaller than Fuchs's. They estimate that a 10 percent increase in surgeon density leads to only a 0.9 percent increase in surgeries and a 1.3 percent increase in elective surgeries per capita. Rossiter and Wilensky (1984) and McCarthy (1985) also uncover evidence that substantiates the inducement hypothesis, although the magnitude of the inducement is estimated to be marginal.

A number of more recent studies do not support the supplier-induced demand hypothesis. For example, Escarce (1992) employs Medicare enrollment and physician claims data to test the inducement hypothesis. The results indicate that increases in the supply of surgeons are associated with increases in the demand for initial contacts with surgeons, but have no impact on the demand for services among surgery patients in terms of intensity of use. Thus, the author attributes the greater demand for surgeries to improvements in access, lower time costs, and better quality. These conclusions do not support the inducement hypothesis. Studies by Carlsen and Grytten (1998) and Grytten and Sorensen (2001) also do not support the SID hypothesis.

There are three reasons why empirical support for the SID hypothesis may have waned in recent years. First, older studies tended to rely on aggregate data that made it difficult to discern the extent to which variations in the consumption of physician services can be attributed to induced demand. For example, increased consumption in physician services attributed to induced demand may have resulted from decreased waiting times or travel costs. More recent studies generally employ physician-based practice data. Second, newer studies rely on more sophisticated models and estimating techniques that allow researchers to better control for other market conditions such as time costs and price effects. Finally, newer studies utilize contemporary data sets and all agree that the ability of physicians to manipulate demand has diminished in recent years with the growth of managed care.

In more recent times, the focus has shifted to an examination of whether physicians are self-referring patients to medical facilities they own or where they have a compensation relationship. These medical facilities may contain expensive medical equipment such as magnetic resonance imaging or computed tomography machines. By doing so, physicians stand to gain financially from these self-referrals. At the very least, the self-referring doctors will be able to bill their patients for their services along with a facility fee. While there is nothing inherently wrong with such behavior, the concern is that some physicians may direct healthier patients or those with private insurance to their own facility, and direct those with public insurance or no insurance to other facilities. The motive is obvious given that private insurers tend to pay more than Medicare and Medicaid. There is also concern that self-referral may lead to consumption of medically unnecessary care, thus driving up the overall cost of medical care as physicians try to recoup their financial investments.

On the other hand, an economic argument can be made for self-referrals. First, self-referrals may result in lower health care costs by providing continuity of care to patients, and making it more convenient for patients to schedule appointments and not have to travel between the physician's office and the medical facility. Second, some researchers point out, few individuals, other than local physicians, are in a position to know when a new medical facility is necessary in an area. An investment opportunity provides physicians with an economic incentive to seek out and invest in medical facilities where demand is sufficient.

The concern over self-referrals has increased in recent years with the growth in physician-owned medical facilities (e.g. specialty hospitals and ambulatory surgery centers) and medical equipment (e.g. laboratory testing equipment and MRI scans). For example, Goodell and Casalino (2008) point out that the number of physician-owned specialty hospitals increased by over 100 percent between 2002 and 2007, while Reschovsky et al. (2010) highlight the growing trend of physician ownership or leasing of medical equipment.

In response to the possibility that physicians are driving up the cost of medical care through self-referrals, Congress passed the Stark Act in 1989 that prohibits physician self-referrals of Medicare patients covering a range of "designated health services" such as physical and occupational therapy services. The Act, named after U.S. Representative Pete Stark of California, was later modified and expanded. However, the impact of the Stark Act has been questioned and remains controversial given the wide range of exceptions. For instance, physicians are permitted to self-refer patients for some services offered in their own offices or ambulatory surgery centers (Casalino, 2008).

Research on the impact of self-referral on the quality and cost of medical care is in its infancy. There is evidence, however, indicating that physician ownership impacts referral patterns and the overall utilization of health care services. For example, Gabel et al. (2008) find that physicians with physician-owned facilities are more likely than other physicians to refer well-insured patients to their own facilities and direct Medicaid patients to hospital outpatient clinics. There is much less evidence, however, supporting the possibility that self-referrals are resulting in the consumption of clinically inappropriate medical care. As a result, the question remains open as to whether physician ownership and self-referral are improving access to medical care by fulfilling unmet demand for medical care or are providing medical unnecessary medical care (Casalino, 2008). Overall, the quality of care provided at physician-owned facilities appears to equal that provided by general hospitals.

It is obvious from this brief overview of the literature that the issue of whether physicians possess the ability to induce demand is unlikely to be resolved in the near future. Overall, the evidence suggests that although physicians may possess the ability to induce demand, the extent to which they can do so is much less now than initially thought.

McGuire's Quantity-Setting Model

McGuire (2000) develops an interesting model of physician decision making that is based on monopolistic competition. Recall that many sellers exist in a monopolistically competitive industry, but each seller faces a downward-sloping demand curve because of imperfect substitutability among the products offered by the various sellers. In the case of physicians, imperfect substitutability may simply result from location if consumers value convenience. McGuire's model treats physicians as being quantity setters and shows that physicians respond to a lower-administered price by increasing quantity supplied. Interestingly, the inverse relation between price and quantity supplied is obtained in McGuire's model without resorting to supplier inducement of demand.

Figure 12–3 provides a graphical illustration of McGuire's quantity-setting model. The horizontal axis represents the quantity of physician services and the vertical axis measures the dollar value of cost and benefits. To make the model easier to explain, let's pretend that the analysis represents how a Dr. Maxwell determines price and quantity. The downward-sloping curve, MB, identifies the marginal benefit of the physician services provided by Dr. Maxwell to a typical patient. The horizontal curve, MC, represents Dr. Maxwell's constant marginal cost of producing physician services.

To make this basic model even easier, suppose for now that the patient has no insurance and pays the full price for the physician care. According to McGuire's model, Dr. Maxwell retains a patient by providing at least the amount of net benefits that the patient would receive from an alternative physician. Suppose NB_0, the shaded area, represents the net benefit that the patient would receive from an alternative physician. Dr. Maxwell has to select the price and quantity that maximizes her profits and also provides the patient with at least NB_0 amount of net benefits. In graphical terms, Dr. Maxwell attempts to raise price up vertically above MC and slide quantity over horizontally as much as possible to maximize profits, yet provide at least NB_0 amount of net benefits.

FIGURE 12–3
McGuire's Basic Quantity-Setting Model

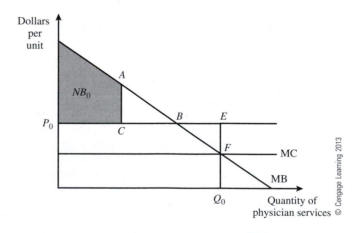

The MB curve represents the marginal benefits the consumer receives from consuming each additional unit of medical care and the MC curve equals the marginal cost of producing physician services. NB_0 represents the net benefit the consumer receives if she visits an alternative physician. Dr. Maxwell chooses P and Q such that profits are maximized and the consumer receives at least NB_0 amount of net benefits. Thus, Dr. Maxwell will require the average consumer to consume no more than Q_0 amount of medical care at price P_0. At this combination of price and quantity, the patient is indifferent between having all or none of the care provided by Dr. Maxwell.

Following this logic, Dr. Maxwell chooses a price no greater than P_0 and a quantity not to exceed Q_0. Notice that at this combination of price and quantity, the consumer is indifferent between having all or none of the care provided by Dr. Maxwell. That is, the patient's net benefits lost by having Dr. Maxwell provide Q_0 amount of care, area *BEF*, is exactly equal to the net benefits not received by the patient if Dr. Maxwell does not provide any care at all, area *ABC*. Any further increase in quantity causes the patient to visit an alternative physician where net benefits are greater.

The model predicts that greater competition causes profits to decline. Notice that Dr. Maxwell's profits equal the rectangular area formed by the difference between price and marginal cost over the range of quantity provided or Q_0. Both price and quantity are influenced by the level of competition in the industry as indicated by NB_0. If the market for physician services becomes more competitive, NB_0 increases. If NB_0 increases, price, quantity, and profits all decline; otherwise Dr. Maxwell loses the patient to a competitor. In a perfectly competitive situation, NB_0 equals the area below MB but above MC and Dr. Maxwell is forced by competition to price and produce the quantity of services at the point where MB equals MC. At the opposite extreme, if NB_0 equals zero, Dr. Maxwell faces no competition and can act like a monopolist, and extract all of the patient's net benefits.

An interesting aspect of the McGuire quantity-setting model concerns how Dr. Maxwell responds to a regulator or third-party administrator with the power to lower price. In McGuire's model, Dr. Maxwell reacts to a lower administered price by increasing quantity supplied because the doctor need only provide a fixed level of net benefits to the patient. Hence, the model predicts that quantity increases in response to a lower regulated price. It is interesting to note that an inverse relationship exists between price and quantity supplied in McGuire's basic model, much as the supplier-induced demand theory also predicts. In this case, however, the inverse relationship occurs without requiring demand inducement.

McGuire extends this basic model to include a third-party administered price and insurance coverage. A graphical illustration of the extended model is provided in Figure 12–4. We suppose that the consumer pays coinsurance equal to $c \times P$, where c represents the coinsurance rate and P equals the fixed price set by the third party. Notice that the third-party payer sets price above marginal cost to encourage Dr. Maxwell to participate in the health plan.

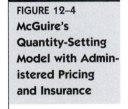

FIGURE 12–4

McGuire's Quantity-Setting Model with Administered Pricing and Insurance

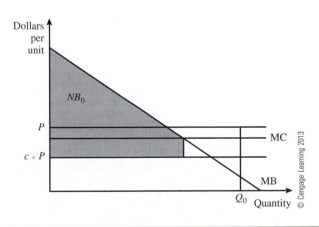

The MB and MC curves represent the marginal benefit and marginal cost curves, respectively. The price ceiling, *P*, which is established by a third party, lies above the MC curve to ensure physician participation in the plan. The *c × P* line represents the out-of-pocket price for physician services. Dr. Maxwell chooses the quantity of services, Q_0, such that the patient is indifferent between receiving all or no care from the doctor and profits are maximized.

The shaded area NB_0 once again represents the net benefit provided to the patient from an alternative physician. Dr. Maxwell no longer chooses price because it is set by the third-party payer, but she does select the quantity of services that maximizes her profits and provides at least NB_0 amount of net benefits to the patient.

The amount Q_0 gives Dr. Maxwell the best choice of quantity. At that quantity of services the patient is indifferent between all or no care provided by Dr. Maxwell and Dr. Maxwell's profits are maximized. Like the basic model, the extended analysis predicts that Dr. Maxwell responds to a lower administered price by increasing quantity supplied as long as price remains above marginal cost.

The Impact of Alternative Compensation Schemes on Physician Behavior

Concern for growing health care costs has caused third-party payers, both private and public, to seek new ways to reimburse physicians. The traditional fee-for-service method of payment has fallen out of favor because it creates an incentive for overutilization of medical care as the SID and McGuire models suggest. The problem becomes particularly acute when the fee-for-service method of reimbursement is combined with a nominal, or zero, consumer copayment, because under these circumstances consumers have little incentive to monitor the behavior of their physicians. To rectify this problem, many managed care providers and private insurance companies have adopted alternative physician reimbursement schemes, commonly referred to as pay-for-performance payment schemes. As a working definition, pay-for-performance payment schemes provide financial incentives to health care providers (in this case, physicians) to improve the quality and/or reduce the cost of medical care provided.

One way to understand the economic rationale for pay-for-performance payment schemes is through the lens of the principal-agent model. As we learned earlier in the chapter, the principal-agent problem results within an organization when ownership and control are disjointed and agents may have some latitude to address their own self-interests rather than those of the principals. In the current context, the principals are the patients who have limited knowledge regarding appropriate medical treatments and the agents are physicians who may take advantage of this asymmetry of information by providing an excessive amount of medical care for the financial reward. We learned in Chapter 4 that the incentive to provide additional high cost, low benefit medical care is enhanced when patients have health insurance that compensates physicians on a variable, or fee-for-service, basis. Thus, the presence of medical insurance exacerbates the principal-agent problem and provides further incentive for physicians to provide an excessive amount of medical care. The goal of pay-for-performance payment schemes is to provide countervailing economic incentives to the physician by directly connecting compensation to the quality and/or cost of medical care provided (Trisolini, 2011a).

A survey conducted by Med-Vantage (2011) illustrates that the use of pay-for-performance payment schemes for physician services has become the norm in the private health insurance industry. This is much different than two decades earlier, when physicians were frequently compensated on a fee-for-service basis. According to the survey results, 96 percent of all private health insurance plans in 2010 have either in place or in development pay-for-performance incentive schemes for physicians. The percentage with pay-for-performance incentive schemes increases to 98 percent for primary care physicians and decreases to 61 percent for specialists. These incentives generally take the form of bonus payments, higher fee schedules, or greater management fees, with the most common form of compensation being bonus payments, based on a set of performance measures. Performance measures may be based on clinical outcomes (e.g. diabetes), clinical processes (e.g. colon cancer screening), patient satisfaction, or cost of care.

The number of empirical studies examining the impact of pay-for-performance payment schemes on physician behavior has grown exponentially in recent years and reflects in large part the growing use of incentive contracts by health care managers and governments to improve the quality of health care provided.[5] Despite their promise, the empirical evidence supporting the use of pay-for-performance contracts has been inconsistent at best. After reviewing the findings of more than 30 studies on the impact of pay-for-performance incentives on physician behavior, Li et al. (2011) conclude: "In general, physicians' response to these financial incentives is of modest size with no evidence of ultimate health improvement for the patients" (p. 8).

Given the widespread use of pay-for-performance schemes, the question remains as to why they have had such minor impact on health outcomes. Economic theory may provide an answer. If the possibility exists that physicians are free to address their own utility functions (because of the principle agent problem), then it can be argued that impact of financial incentives on physician behavior is ambiguous (Li et al., 2011). Some of the variables likely to be included in physicians' utility functions include income, leisure, prestige, patient satisfaction, and work environment. Under these circumstances, utility-maximizing physicians will choose those combinations of these variables that maximize their utility. The upshot is that implementation of a pay-for-performance payment scheme may not Elicit the desired outcome because the added financial incentives may be either ignored or used as a means to address other desires such as additional leisure.

Two examples help illustrate this point. First, a large physician network begins providing financial incentives to its physicians to utilize a new electronic health record system recently put in place. The goal is to improve administrative efficiency and allow physicians to spend more time on patient care. Rather than taking the improvement in efficiency out in terms of added income, however, some physicians may opt for more leisure. Others may take the added efficiency out in terms of enhancing their prestige among peers or the community at large by either attending more professional conferences or serving on additional community boards. As a result, the network may experience only a modest increase in efficiency.

As another example, take the case of a health care organization that puts in place a series of clinical guidelines to improve patient safety and reduce the number of medical errors. Such an initiative is likely to call for some additional documentation. Trisolini (2011b) points out physicians are notorious for their dislike of paperwork. As such, some physicians may ignore guidelines and forego the financial rewards because the additional utility generated from any potential increase in income is more than offset by the disutility of having to fill out more bureaucratic paper work. The upshot is that the health care organization may experience little or no improvement in patient safety.

Another reason that may explain the small effects of pay-for-performance initiatives include the fact that the financial incentives generally provided are just too small to elicit the desired response. Or, that the targeted behaviors are not adequately specified, linked to financial incentives, and/or effectively communicated to health care providers. In conclusion, this is an area that is still in flux and despite the rapid development and implementation of pay-for-performance physician payment schemes, we have much to learn regarding the complex nature of physician duties.

---

5. For a review of the literature, consult either Town et al., 2004; Rosenthal and Frank, 2006; or Li et al., 2011.

Geographical Variations in the Utilization of Physician Services

The phenomenon of **small area variations** in the delivery and consumption of physician services across geographic regions has been documented by an almost limitless number of studies worldwide. For example, Baiker, Buckles, and Chandra (2006) find substantial variation in cesarean deliveries across counties in the United States. In particular, they find that high-use counties have adjusted cesarean delivery rates for births over 2,500 grams that are four times higher than low-use counties. In another study that examines practice variations in the delivery of primary care physician services in Norway during the late 1990s, Grytten and Sorensen (2003) estimate that variations in physician practice style explain between 47 and 66 percent of the variation in expenditures for laboratory tests, and between 41 and 61 percent of the variation in expenditures for specific procedures.

In addition, an extensive body of literature has suggested that selected medical services are overutilized. The estimates regarding the proportion of inappropriate medical care given range from 15 to 30 percent, with a number of more recent studies putting it at about 4 percent.[6] As a result, the public has become fond of blaming high medical costs on physicians who prescribe needless medical tests or perform unnecessary surgery.

The **physician practice hypothesis** has been used to explain these variations in utilization rates across regions. This hypothesis, which is most closely associated with the work of Wennberg (1984, 1985), contends that per capita variations in the use of medical care, particularly surgery, reflect systematic differences in clinical opinions regarding the appropriate amount and type of medical care.

These subjective differences are collectively referred to as "practice style" and exist primarily because of the uncertainty surrounding the practice of medicine. As Eddy (1984) so aptly writes, "Uncertainty creeps into medical practice through every pore. Whether a physician is defining a disease, making a diagnosis, selecting a procedure, observing outcomes, assessing probabilities, assigning preferences or putting it all together, he is walking on very slippery terrain" (p. 75). Physician uncertainty is likely to be greatest when the diagnosis is complicated and the medical procedure is relatively new. As Phelps (1992) writes,

> When the disease is very easy to diagnose, the consequences of not intervening are well understood, and few alternative interventions exist to treat the disease, then observed variability is quite low . . . Hernia repair and removal of an inflamed appendix (appendectomy) provide two good examples. Alternatively, when the "indications" for surgery are less clear, or when alternative treatments exist (such as surgery or bed rest plus therapy for low back injuries) variations increase. (p. 25)

The rate at which medical technology and knowledge are diffused plays a critical role in determining the level of physician uncertainty and degree of practice variations. Other factors also come into play, such as the background and set of beliefs of the individual physician.

Phelps (1992) believes that different local "schools of thought" evolve regarding appropriate practice style. The schools of thought develop as a physician invents a new medical treatment strategy and other doctors in the immediate local community learn and adopt the practice style. Since no property rights are assigned to treatment strategies, the individual physician faces little financial incentive to test and market

---

6. Greenspan et al. (1988) estimate that 20 percent of the permanent pacemakers implanted in Philadelphia County in 1983 were unwarranted, while Chassin et al. (1986) note that 17 percent of coronary angiographies for elderly patients had been unnecessary. However, a more recent group of studies found the level of unnecessary care to be much lower. Leape et al. (1993) find that 2 percent of coronary artery bypass surgeries were inappropriate, while Hilborne et al. (1993) find that 4 percent of percutaneous transluminal coronary angioplasties were inappropriate.

the new idea on a broader basis. Consequently, the treatment strategy or practice style remains confined to the local area. Phelps claims that "allowing doctors to patent treatment strategies offers a tantalizing step into a market economy where 'professionalism' has previously remained. This would be a two-edged sword, however; doctors who produced and patented a strategy for treatment would reap potential profits, but they would also incur liability for subsequent use of that strategy throughout the country" (p. 41).

Addressing the issue of geographic variations from a slightly different but related angle, Chassin (1993) offers the enthusiasm hypothesis. According to him, geographic differences result primarily because certain physicians, for one reason or another, become "enthusiastic" about a particular medical procedure and therefore use it more frequently than other procedures. When the number of enthusiasts in an area becomes sufficiently large, geographic variations occur. Why the number of enthusiasts differs from area to area is open to conjecture. One explanation offered by the author is that a noteworthy teacher from, say, a teaching hospital in an area becomes enamored with a medical technique and persuades residents and other local practicing physicians of its merits. If he convinces enough physicians in the immediate area, geographic variations occur. This is especially true because, as Phelps notes, the new idea is not patentable.

The most interesting element of the enthusiasm hypothesis is the manner in which it differs from the more conventional physician practice hypothesis. Recall that under the physician practice hypothesis, the uncertainty surrounding the efficacy of a particular medical procedure is a primary reason for geographic variations. This is not the case with the enthusiasm hypothesis. Enthusiasts are anything but uncertain because they are thoroughly convinced of the benefits their patients receive from their medical procedure.

Despite the large number of studies on the physician practice hypothesis, it is difficult to determine the extent to which physician practice style explains geographic variations in the utilization of medical services. This is largely because it is very difficult to quantify practice style. One way to get around this problem is to look at studies that use regression analysis to analyze the consumption of medical care and assume that the unexplained variation, or residual, is partly the result of practice style. Because not all of the residual can be explained by any one factor, we can assume that the unexplained variation represents an upper-bound estimate of the impact of practice style on the consumption of medical services.

Utilizing the residual approach, Folland and Stano (1990) and Stano (1991) review numerous studies and conclude that a significant portion of the variation in the consumption of medical services can be explained by traditional supply and demand factors. Although the authors do not dismiss the role of physician practice style, they suggest that it may not play a large role in explaining differences in the aggregate consumption of medical care across geographic regions.

Other studies have attempted to test directly the impact of practice style on the quantity and type of medical care consumed on a micro level. For example, Roos (1989) developed an index that measures physician hospitalization practice style and tested whether it affected the probability that elderly patients would be hospitalized. The results indicate that practice style cannot be ignored when examining the decision to hospitalize elderly patients.

Because physician practice style is difficult to measure, especially at the aggregate level, its impact on the amount and type of medical care consumed is difficult to judge. There is no doubt, however, that the presence of uncertainty means individual physicians will follow different courses of action when treating patients. Insofar as clinical decisions are based on subjective factors, physician practice style is likely to influence medical care.

The Impact of Utilization Review on the Physician Services Market

Various programs under the heading of managed care have been implemented in recent years to contain the cost of medical care. Most of these programs are directed at altering physician behavior primarily because physicians make most of the clinical decisions. As noted earlier, utilization review (UR) is one of the most frequently used methods to contain costs. Programs such as prospective, concurrent, and retrospective reviews evaluate the medical decisions of hospitals and physicians in an attempt to minimize medical costs by eliminating unnecessary medical care and educating patients and physicians concerning proper medical treatments.

Overall, the cost savings from UR programs have been modest. For example, while summarizing Wickizer's work and that of colleagues in this area, Wickizer and Lessler (2002) conclude that pre-admission reviews reduce hospital admissions by 10 percent, while concurrent reviews have only a small impact on length of stay. The combined impact of both UR programs has been to decrease hospital inpatient days by about 12 percent. Scheffler et al. (1991) discovered that Blue Cross and Blue Shield (BCBS) utilization review programs decreased hospital patient days by 4.8 percent and inpatient payments by 4.2 percent. Equally important, Feldstein et al. (1988) find that UR programs have a onetime effect on decreasing utilization and costs. The implication is that UR programs may not significantly decrease the growth of medical expenditures over time. In fact, one can argue that any cost savings from UR programs may erode over time as physicians learn to practice in this new environment. Put another way, as physicians eventually learn to "game the system" and present their diagnoses and treatment plans in a manner that will make them more likely to be approved, UR programs may become increasingly unable to control costs by influencing physician behavior over time.

Recently, a number of MCOs have questioned the value of UR programs and have significantly altered their approach to utilization review. After interviewing administrators from nearly 50 MCOs, Felt-Lisk and Mays (2002) find that many MCOs have reduced or eliminated their reliance on prospective utilization review. Since few pre-approvals were denied, they were deemed too costly to continue. At the same time, many MCOs have enhanced their concurrent and retrospective utilization review policies. The goal of such changes is to reduce "administration costs of operation and improve relationships with consumer and providers" (p. 212). Other strategies include the establishment or enhancement of **disease management** programs that organize care around the patient with a particular disease or condition in the hopes of improving patient satisfaction and containing costs. Whether such programs have the desired effect is open for question.

Second surgical opinion programs constitute another type of UR aimed directly at altering the behavior of physicians, particularly surgeons. These programs, which can be either voluntary or mandatory in nature, have two major objectives. The first is to increase patient knowledge and thereby reduce the asymmetry-of-information problem. The second is to establish a procedure whereby physicians' decisions are routinely scrutinized by their peers. The ultimate goal is to reduce the number of unnecessary or avoidable operations and thereby reduce medical costs.

Empirical evidence suggests that second-opinion programs have failed to significantly reduce medical costs. For one thing, studies have found that voluntary programs have little or no impact on medical cost savings. The evidence on mandatory programs is not much better. For example, Scheffler et al. (1991) find that mandatory second opinions have no impact on hospital utilization or payments. After reviewing the literature on the subject, Lindsey and Newhouse (1990) conclude that because of design flaws, studies fail to provide any conclusive evidence of cost savings from second opinions. The implication is that cost savings from second surgery opinions are likely to be small.

Several studies have examined the impact of MCOs on the utilization of physician services. The question is whether MCOs lead to fewer or more physician office visits than fee-for-service practices. According to the exhaustive review by Miller and Luft (1994), "Most recent data showed either higher rates or little difference in HMO plan office visits per enrollee" compared to fee-for-service plans (p. 1514). Not enough studies were available to enable Miller and Luft to draw a definitive conclusion about the relation between preferred provider organizations and the utilization of physician services, however.

Other efforts to control medical costs have involved the development of clinical practice guidelines for physicians. Numerous medical societies and the Agency for Health Care Policy and Research (AHCPR) are developing and disseminating guidelines that provide physicians and patients with the preferred methods of treating different types of medical conditions. The hope is that guidelines will improve the quality of medical care and at the same time lower costs by providing timely information to physicians concerning the efficacy of various medical procedures. Rice (1993) argues that practice guidelines may backfire and result in higher medical costs. Any cost savings reaped by preventing a few physicians from using an unacceptable medical procedure may be offset by an increase in costs brought about by the adoption of a new, accepted medical procedure by many physicians. Despite the fact that some medical care providers have begun to implement medical guidelines, it is too early to ascertain their overall effect.

Medical Negligence and Malpractice Insurance

Medical malpractice reform has been one of the most contentious health care issues in recent years, and the issue is complicated by the lack of data measuring the amount of medical negligence in the U.S. health care system. In a book highly critical of the U.S. health care system, Barlett and Steele (2004) cite a number of tragic examples of medical negligence. For example, a man from Texas was diagnosed with lung cancer and entered the hospital for lung cancer surgery. Unfortunately, the surgeons mistakenly removed his healthy lung rather than the cancerous one. The patient died shortly thereafter of lung cancer. Also, a healthy woman from Wisconsin needlessly had her breasts removed because her tissue samples were mixed up with another patient who had breast cancer.

While such cases are well documented in the popular press, they provide little guidance as to the number of patients who are victims of medical negligence each year in the U.S. health care system. After evaluating medical claim data and extrapolating to the U.S. population, Shreve et al. (2010) and Van Den Bos (2011) estimate that 1.5 million patients suffered the negative consequences of medical errors in the United States in 2008. The average total cost per error was approximately $13,000 for a total cost of $19.5 billion. Of that total, $17 billion was attributed to a direct increase in medical costs while the remaining $2.5 billion was identified as indirect expenses related to loss productivity due to death ($1.4 billion) and short-term disability claims ($1.1 billion). The authors also estimate that medical errors caused over 2,500 deaths in 2008 and over 10 million days in lost work due to short-term disability claims.

These figures are the root cause of the general frustration that currently exists with our medical malpractice system. When properly designed, malpractice liability law serves two important functions. First, the malpractice legal system, as a type of tort liability law, compensates victims for any damages caused by the negligence of health care providers. Damages include economic losses, pain and suffering costs, and punitive damages (although the latter are rarely awarded). Second, the malpractice system helps deter health care providers from engaging in future acts of negligence. Indeed, the deterrence effect of malpractice liability, by creating incentives for health care providers to offer appropriate medical care, may play a more important role than the compensation function because compensation might be provided more efficiently through other forms of social or private insurance (Danzon, 2000). Stated differently, a malpractice liability system is performing properly when it encourages physicians to provide the socially optimal amount of precautions to guard against medical injuries. That situation occurs when the marginal social benefit derived from the last unit of precautionary care equals the marginal social cost (recall Figure 2–20).

Because of imperfect information and the associated difficulty of establishing properly designed medical liability rules, many people are dissatisfied with the current malpractice system and have called for various types of reforms. Patient advocates are concerned because so few cases of medical negligence translate into malpractice claims and even fewer result in some type of financial settlement. In addition, there is the frustration that health care providers, particularly physicians, are not held accountable for providing inferior medical care. Health care providers are upset because of the large number of frivolous malpractice claims they must contend with, in addition to the excessive jury awards that appear to have little relationship to damages incurred. The result is higher liability premiums and higher practice costs. Physicians are also frustrated because they are encouraged by the current malpractice system to overutilize medical services in an attempt to stave off potential malpractice suits. This phenomenon is known as **defensive medicine**.

Any discussion of the implications of medical malpractice on the physician services market must center on the cost of medical malpractice. Physician liability costs primarily fall into two categories: medical malpractice insurance costs and defensive medical costs. Given the fact that there are wide disparities in liability premiums across states and specialties, it is difficult to make any broad generalizations. For example, according to a 2011 *Medical Liability Monitor* survey, medical liability premiums for internists in Dade County Florida averaged $47,731 in 2011 while the same category of physicians paid only $3,375 in Minnesota. In terms of specialties, obstetrician-gynecologists appear to pay among the highest rates (e.g. $201,808 in Miami and Dade County, Florida) followed closely by general surgeons (Gallegos, 2011).

Recent survey data indicates that for the sixth straight year, medical liability premiums have held steady, if not decreased modestly. According to the *Medical Liability Monitor* 2011 survey, average liability premium rates dropped by 0.2 percent in 2011. Prior to 2006, physicians experienced double increases in premium rates with the average rates of increase topping 20 percent in 2003 and 2004. The rate of increase subsided in 2005 to just under 10 percent and the next two years (2006 and 2007) saw very small increases of less than one percent. Since that time, rates have fallen each year (Karls, 2011).

The issue of state medical malpractice reform has been around since the early 1970s and the recent call to contain medical care costs has only renewed the call for reform. State tort reforms in recent years have included a variety of measures with the most common including the following (Hellinger and Encinosa, 2009; Mello et al. 2011):

- *Damage Caps:* Involves setting a monetary limit on the amount a plaintiff can be awarded in a malpractice lawsuit.
- *Certificate of Merit:* At the point of filing a claim, plaintiffs are required to provide an affidavit from a medical expert that the plaintiff received substandard care.
- *Limits on attorney fees:* Limits the fees charged by the plaintiff's attorney.
- *Pretrial Screening Panels:* Panels of medical experts review potential liability cases at an early stage to determine if a claim has merit to proceed to court.
- *Joint and several liability:* Ensures that the monetary damages awarded are based on the defendant's degree of responsibility and not on the ability to pay.

Using state-level data from 1985 through 2001, Thorpe (2004) estimates the impact that various state reforms have had on premium levels and loss ratios for insurers. The empirical results indicate that damage caps on awards are related to lower premiums and reduced loss ratios. In particular, he finds that states with caps on awards had premiums that were on average 17 percent lower, and loss ratios that were 12 percent lower, than states without caps. Other types of reforms appear to have no impact on premiums or loss ratios. The exception is states with collateral source rules, which appear to have lower loss ratios. Nelson et al. (2007) conclude after reviewing the literature that damage caps reduce premiums somewhere between 6 and 25 percent.

Before leaving the topic of medical malpractice premiums, we need to address the following question: Who has been paying for the increasing cost of malpractice insurance? Doctors say they have been forced to absorb any increase in liability premiums in terms of lower net incomes. However, economic theory suggests that physicians may be able to pass some, or all, of that cost forward to patients, or insurers, by either charging a higher price for medical services or by providing more medical services. Using a large nationwide sample of physician practices, Pauly et al. (2006) find that increasing malpractice premiums cannot be linked to reductions in net income. It appears that physicians have had the ability to pass the cost forward by a combination of greater quantities of medical care and higher prices. In particular, they surmise that more than half of the increase in malpractice premiums has been passed forward in terms of increasing quantities of medical care. Higher prices accounted for the remaining portion. These results may explain why researchers have found only a weak relation at best between rising malpractice premiums and physician location (Mello et al., 2007).

Turning to a discussion of defensive medicine, a number of studies have attempted to estimate the extent to which physicians overutilize medical care to thwart off a malpractice suit. Estimating the cost of defensive medicine poses a unique challenge to researchers because aside from having to precisely define the phenomenon of defensive medicine, they must also distinguish it from the level of clinically justified medical care provided (GAO, 1995). Several studies on the subject find that physicians are encouraged to practice defensive medicine and provide more medical care than is clinically justified. In one of the most widely cited studies, Kessler and McClellan (1996) estimate the cost savings from certain tort reforms to be between 5 and 9 percent without adversely impacting the quality of medical care. In a more recent study which accounts for the presence of managed care, Kessler and McClellen (2002) estimate the cost savings from tort reform to be a more modest 4 percent. A study by Hellinger and Encinosa (2006) support these findings and estimate that state laws limiting malpractice payments caused state health expenditures to decrease by between 3 and 4 percent. More recently, however, Sloan and Shadle (2009) estimate that direct tort reforms have not influenced Medicare payments. The overall evidence suggests that tort reforms have had a modest impact on the incidence of defensive medicine (Kessler, 2011).

Finally, the practice of defensive medicine may encourage physicians to cut back on certain medical services to avoid the possibility of lawsuits. For example, physicians may avoid treating high-risk patients or providing high-risk procedures when the medical outcome is more in doubt and the likelihood of a lawsuit is greater. This behavior is commonly referred to in the literature as negative defensive medicine because it reduces the availability of medical care.[7] The body of evidence either supporting or refuting the practice of negative defensive medicine is sparse. As a result, it is difficult to gauge its economic significance. Dubay et al. (2001) studied the impact of malpractice liability on the utilization of prenatal care and infant health, and their results are consistent with the notion of negative defensive medicine. In particular, they find that higher malpractice premiums resulted in an increase in the incidence of late prenatal

7. At the other extreme is positive defensive medicine of the type discussed earlier that leads to an increase in the utilization of medical care.

care among women. Thus, faced with higher premiums, some obstetricians reacted by holding back on high-risk medical services to decrease the probability of being involved in a costly malpractice suit. Dubay et al. also find the impact of increases in malpractice premiums to differ across income groups and other pertinent demographic factors. For example, they find that unmarried women of lower socioeconomic status are more likely to be impacted by negative defensive medicine than married women of more affluent means. Kessler et al. (2005) find that three years after the adoption of direct malpractice reforms, the supply of physicians increased by slightly more than 3 percent. These findings were only partially supported by the work of Klick and Stratmann (2007) and Matsa (2007). In the case of the former study, they find that the impact of malpractice reform on physician supply to be limited to those specialties facing the highest litigation while the former finds the impact of reform to be limited to physicians located in rural areas.

Research estimating the economic impact of medical liability in the United States suggests that while the cost is high in absolute terms, it is relatively modest when compared to the total cost of health care in the United States. A study by Mello et al. (2010) estimated the overall cost of medical liability in 2008 to equal $55.6 billion. This figure included $5.7 billion in indemnity payments, $4.1 billion in administrative expenses (e.g. legal expenses), and $45.6 billion defensive medicine costs. While a relatively large number, $55.6 billion represented only a modest 2.4 percent of total health care spending in 2008.

This rather brief review of issues surrounding medical malpractice indicates that malpractice reform is likely to be on the public agenda for years to come. While the economic costs of malpractice as measured by malpractice premiums and defensive medical costs are not as high as some would believe, they are significant and have prompted a call for serious medical liability reform. The mismatch between the number of medical injuries resulting from negligence and the number of medical claims has also encouraged many to call for reform.

The Performance of the Physician Services Industry

Now that we have reviewed structure and conduct, we are in a position to examine the overall performance of the physician services market. Although the physician services industry appears to be structurally competitive in terms of the actual number of physicians, some evidence concerning practice variations and supplier-induced demand suggests that behaviorally physicians may act with some market power. An analysis of performance in this industry sheds some light on the net effect of these two contradictory perspectives. This section examines measures of physician price, output, and income over time in the United States.

Expenditures on Physician Services

Expenditures on physician and clinical services increased dramatically over the previous two decades. According to Table 12–1, expenditures on physician and clinical services equaled $158.9 billion in 1990 and then grew to $515.5 billion in 2010. This represents more than a threefold increase over two decades. The annual rate of growth consistently topped 10 percent in the early 1990s, and it was not until the mid-1990s that the rate of increase in expenditures on physician and clinical services began to slow down. Over the period 1993–1999, physician expenditures grew by around 5 percent per year. After that the rate of growth in physician and clinical expenditures was on the rise again and from 2000 to 2008, they grew in excess of 6 percent per year. In the last two years, the rate of increase decreased substantially to 3.99 percent in 2009 and 1.9 percent in 2010.

TABLE 12–1

Expenditures on Physician and Clinical Services for Selected Years (billions of dollars)

Year	Total Expenditures	Annual Rate of Increase	Total Real Expenditures*
1990	$158.9	10.9%	$ 98.8
1995	222.3	4.8	106.5
2000	290.0	7.0	118.5
2005	419.6	6.6	145.9
2010	515.5	1.9	155.6

*Physician expenditures are deflated by the physician services index of the CPI for the December of that year, where 1982–1984 is the base year.

SOURCE: Centers for Medicare and Medicaid Services, www.cms.hhs.gov. Accessed January 12, 2012.

The Physician Services Price Inflation Rate

The most commonly used instrument to measure movements in the average price of physician services is the consumer price index (CPI) for physician services, which is provided for selected years from 1990 to 2010 in Figure 12–5. The data reveal that the average price of physician services increased at an annual rate higher than the general rate of inflation, but slightly less than the overall rate of inflation for medical services. From 1990 to 2010, the CPI for physician services increased from 166.0 to 331.3, an increase of almost 100 percent, while the CPI less medical care increased by a little more than 63 percent. Thus, it appears the average rate of inflation for physician services was almost twice that of the overall rate of inflation less medical care from 1990 through 2010. Figure 12–5 also indicates that the rate of inflation for physician services was slightly less than the rate of inflation for medical care in general and the disparity appears to have grown in recent years.

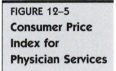

FIGURE 12–5
Consumer Price Index for Physician Services

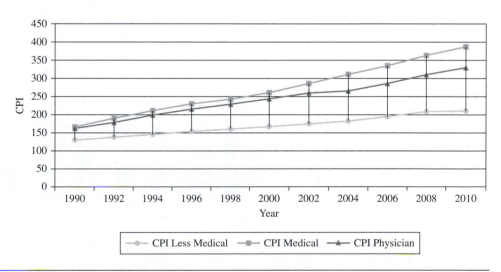

SOURCE: Bureau of Labor Statistics, www.bls.gov.

It should be noted, however, that these figures may overstate the inflation of physician fees for two reasons. First, the figures fail to consider any improvements in the quality of physician services that have taken place over time. Finally, the figures do not adequately reflect many of the technological improvements that have taken place in the production of physician services.

The Utilization of Physician Services

Expenditures on physician services increased significantly during the past few decades, with much of that increase occurring early in the 1990s. From 1990 to 2010, physician expenditures increased by more than threefold while over the same period, the CPI for physician services doubled. Combined, these figures suggest that more than one-half of the average annual increase in physician expenditures was the result of price increases, while the remaining portion was due to increased utilization. The last column in Table 12–1 provides data for real expenditures on physician and clinical services, which is found by dividing nominal values by the relevant CPI. Real expenditures grew by around 3 percent from 1990 to 2010. It is interesting to note that in 2010, nominal expenditures on physician and clinical services increased by less than 2 percent, while real expenditures actually fell modestly.

Physician Income

The last item we examine is changes in physician income over time. Data for nominal and real income (i.e., total physician net income deflated by the CPI in 2002 dollars) for general internists appear in Figure 12–6. Over the period in question, nominal income increased from $158,350 in 2002 to $189,480 in 2010. The data on real income tell a slightly different story. It appears that while nominal increased modestly throughout the period, real income actually declined. From 2002 to 2010, real income

FIGURE 12–6
Nominal and Real Income for Internists, 2002–2010

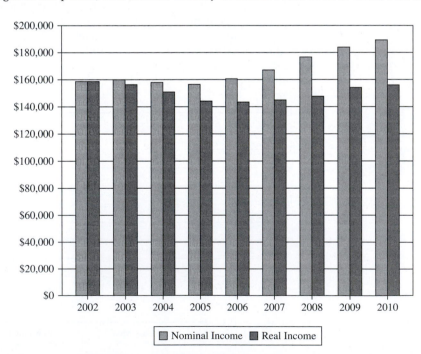

SOURCE: Bureau of Labor Statistics, www.bls.gov.

shrank from $158.4 thousand to $156.3 thousand. No doubt these changes can be attributed to the growth in managed care, the increased use of financial incentives directed toward physicians, and the implementation of tighter fee controls by the Medicare and Medicaid programs. For instance, Hadley and Mitchell (2002) find that the growth of managed care, as measured by HMO penetration in the early 1990s, and the employment of financial incentives to restrict services have a negative effect on physicians' earnings. Specifically, they find that a 10 percent increase in HMO enrollments, from 20 to 22 percent, is associated with a 2.6 percent decrease in physician earnings.

To gauge the relative standing of physician income, we can also compare compensation to the growth in real income sustained by other professionals with extensive graduate training. In particular, consider the ratio of total physician income to total compensation of college faculty at doctoral granting institutions. The ratio remained relatively constant during the early 2000s, hovering between 2.19 and 2.16 from 2002 and 2003. By the mid-2000s, however, that ratio began to fall slightly and by 2007, it equaled 1.99. Since that time, the ratio has inched up to slightly above 2.0. These relative income figures suggest that not only did physicians in general experience a slight decrease in real income throughout the 2000s, they also lost ground relative to other professionals with substantial graduate training.

This conclusion is substantiated by a study that looked at the relative income of physicians from an investment perspective. If expenditures on higher education are treated as an investment in human capital and the increment to earnings received in the job market as a return on that investment, the rate of return received on investments in higher education can be calculated. Utilizing that approach, Weeks et al. (1994) compare the rates of return on educational investments for various professionals, including physicians. According to their results, primary care physicians receive an annual rate of return of 15.9 percent on educational investments over a working life, while specialists receive a 20.9 percent return. As a point of comparison, the authors find that businesspeople and attorneys receive a 29.0 and 25.4 percent rate of return, respectively. These findings imply that physicians receive a rate of return on investments in educational expenditures that is comparable to, if not less than, that of other professionals.

Provisions of the Patient Protection and Affordable Care Act (PPACA) of 2010 Relating to the Physician Services Market

The PPACA of 2010, once fully implemented, has a number of provisions that will significantly impact the market for physician services. Without a doubt the biggest impact should come from expanding the number of people with health insurance by more than 30 million. This should translate into more physician visits and higher practice revenues for most physicians, particularly those serving Medicaid patients. Over half of those who gain health insurance will do so through a major expansion of the Medicaid program.

Such an increase in the number of insured, however, will also exacerbate the looming shortage of physicians, particularly primary care physicians and that may significantly impact patient access to primary care medicine. To counteract this shortage, there are provisions in the PPACA aimed at expanding the primary care workforce. These include expanded scholarship and student-loan forgiveness programs to lure medical students into primary care medicine. Other initiatives include expanding nursing training programs and increasing the number of primary care residency slots across the country.

The PPACA also attempts to address the shortage and improve access to primary care medicine by adjusting the fee payment schedules for Medicaid and Medicare payments. As we learned previously, Medicaid has a lower physician fee payment structure than the private sector and Medicare, which creates little incentive for physicians to care for Medicaid patients. To address this problem, Medicaid payments for certain primary care services will be increased to Medicare payment levels over time. In addition, primary care providers and general surgeons will have the opportunity to receive bonus payments on top of the regular fee payment under Medicare if they provide designated primary care services. Other bonuses will be provided if certain primary care services are provided in designated medically underserved areas.

The PPACA also calls for the formation of the Independent Payment Advisory Board (IPAB) to provide recommendations to Congress regarding Medicare spending. As such, the IPAB is likely to have considerable influence on Medicare fee payments and therefore physician practice revenues over time.

Provisions in the PPACA are also going to profoundly impact physician autonomy and the mode of practice by making it much more difficult for smaller physician practices to compete in the market place. The PPACA calls for the formation of Accountable Care Organizations (ACOs), which are organizations of health care providers (such as physicians) that agree to be collectively accountable for the quality, cost, and overall care provided to Medicare beneficiaries (see Chapter 7). As such, physician practices will be encouraged to form relationships with other professional medical groups including hospitals. Medicare payments may be based on the "total care" provided rather than individual medical services. If successful, this episode-of-care payment system will likely be followed by private insurers. For physicians, this means that emphasis will be placed on assuming responsibility for the care of groups of individuals rather than individual patients. Any savings that occur will be shared among the providers, thus creating a financial incentive for the formation of ACOs. According to a publication of the *Physicians Foundation* (2011), "from a practice standpoint, the ACO model raises issues regarding professional collaboration and internal distribution of savings and risk across primary care physicians and specialists, and the relationship between hospitals and physicians." (p. 58).

There are a number of provisions in the PPACA aimed at enhancing the quality of medical care that will directly impact physicians. For example, under the new law, the Secretary of Health and Human Services is required to develop a separate payment modifier for the Medicare physician fee schedule that takes into account the quality of care provided relative to cost. The legislation also calls for the creation of an Innovation Center with the Centers for Medicare and Medicaid Services to develop, test, and evaluate alternative payment schemes aimed at containing cost and improving the quality of care. Finally, the PPACA will support comparative effectiveness research that will assist physicians in making informed decisions regarding the relative merits or outcomes of alternative treatment choices. The hope is that such research will both enhance the quality of care and curtail the amount of unnecessary care provided. The concern is that such work will reduce physician autonomy and innovation.

The PPACA also provides demonstration project grants to states to develop, implement, and evaluate alternatives to the current tort litigation system for resolving disputes about injuries caused by physicians and other health care providers.

This brief discussion highlights some of the ways the PPACA of 2010 will impact physicians. According to the *Physicians Foundation* (2011), there are more than 40 areas in the legislation that are of direct concern to physicians. Whether physicians gain or lose relative to other health care providers is an open question at this time and will likely be the subject of much research over the coming years.

Summary

The physician services market has experienced profound changes in recent years, with both the size and scope of the market increasing substantially. Since 1990 the size of the market has increased, whether measured on the basis of real physician expenditures or the number of practicing physicians. The mode of production has also changed considerably, with economies of scale forcing physicians into large-group practices as opposed to small-group or solo practices. All these changes, coupled with an erosion of barriers to entry, have intensified the level of structural competition in the physician services market. Most of the market power physicians currently possess appears to result primarily from the asymmetry of information that exists between doctor and patient. Although the level of competition varies across regions, overall the market can be classified as being monopolistically competitive. The physician services industry contains a large number of sellers, moderate barriers to entry, a certain amount of product differentiation, and some information imperfections.

The well-publicized geographic variations in physician utilization rates have been the source of much concern for policy analysts and politicians alike. The empirical evidence indicates that much of this concern may be uncalled for, since most of the variation can be explained by traditional supply and demand factors. Nevertheless, studies uncover dramatic variations in medical care costs across areas of the United States as pointed out in Chapter 13. Moreover, research suggests that greater spending is not always associated with better health outcomes. As a result, practice variations will continue to interest health economists.

Without a doubt, the single greatest change in the physician services market has been the growing presence of managed care. Almost 90 percent of all physicians are involved with at least one MCO. All indications suggest that the intensity of interactions with MCOs will increase in the future. Managed care has ushered in a new set of compensation schemes, along with a host of utilization review programs. The evidence on compensation schemes suggests that clinical decisions are sensitive to the method of payment. For example, the utilization of medical resources is inversely related to whether the physician is compensated on a salary or capitation basis rather than the more traditional fee-for-service system. Findings concerning the impact of utilization review programs on utilization and costs have been mixed, however. For example, second-opinion programs appear to have little impact on the level of medical care. There does appear to be a movement toward the development and use of clinical guidelines for physicians. It remains to be seen whether such efforts will affect the amount and cost of physician care.

Review Questions and Problems

1. Physician assistants have long argued that they have the ability to provide as much as 70 percent of the medical services provided by primary care physicians at a much lower cost. Yet government regulations limit their ability to work independently of physicians. Explain what would happen to the level of competition in the physician services market if all the statutes limiting the activities of physician assistants were eliminated.

2. Discuss how enhanced competition in the physician services market may have affected the ability of physicians to induce the demand for medical services.

3. Analyze the alternative compensation schemes discussed in this chapter that private insurers use to pay physicians. Think in terms of how these different compensation schemes may affect the incentive of physicians to provide an excessive amount of medical services.

4. As you know, various medical groups are in the process of developing medical guidelines. Assuming guidelines are developed and widely adopted by physicians, how will this affect the physician services market?

5. Some argue that practice variations exist because information on practice style is disseminated slowly. Phelps (1992) argues that physicians should be allowed to patent and sell their practice strategies. Explain how this policy might affect practice variations.

6. Discuss the theoretical and empirical issues surrounding the supplier-induced demand theory.

7. Discuss the factors that have contributed to the increase in expenditures on physician services over the past decade.

8. Explain the many institutional and structural changes that might make physician licensing obsolete.

9. Why may the physician inflation rate be exaggerated?

10. According to McGuire (2000), the problem of defensive medicine can be analyzed in the context of the supplier-induced demand model because physicians induced the demand for their services to decrease the chances of a medical malpractice suit. Use the supplier-induced demand model to illustrate McGuire's point.

11. Use each of McGuire's quantity setting models to explain how a physician is likely to react to price controls. In particular, explain how the physician continues to earn economic profits despite the implementation of price controls.

12. As we learned, MRI and CT scanning facilities have been growing at a fast pace over the last decade. Consider the case in which physicians make referrals to facilities in which they have an ownership stake. Identify and describe some of the incentives such arrangements provide to physicians. Are there countervailing forces that may act as controls on those incentives?

Online Resources

To access Internet links related to the topics in this chapter, please visit our website at **www.cengage.com/economics/santerre**.

References

"A Roadmap for Physicians to Health Care Reform." *The Physicians Foundation*, May 2011, http://www.physiciansfoundation.org/Foundation ReportDetails.aspx?id = 288, accessed February 28, 2012.

American Medical Association. *Physician Characteristics and Distribution in the U.S., 2011.* Chicago: AMA, 2011.

American Medical Association. *Physician Characteristics and Distribution in the U.S., 1997/98.* Chicago: AMA Center for Health Policy Research, 1998.

————. *Physician Characteristics and Distribution in the U.S., 2005.* Chicago: AMA, 2005.

————. *Socioeconomic Characteristics of Medical Practice, 2003.* Chicago: AMA, 2003.

Baiker, Katherine, Kasey S. Buckles, and Amitabh Chandra. "Geographic Variation in the Appropriate Use of Cesarean Delivery." *Health Affairs*, Web Exclusive (August 8, 2006).

Barlett, Donald L., and James B. Steele. *Critical Condition*. New York: Doubleday, 2004.

Brown, Douglas M. "Do Physicians Underutilize Aides?" *Journal of Human Resources* 23 (summer 1988), pp. 342–55.

Bureau of Labor Statistics, www.bls.gov, accessed January 10, 2012.

Carlsen, Fredrick, and Jostein Grytten. "More Physicians: Improved Availability or Induced Demand?" *Health Economics* 7 (1998), pp. 495–508.

Casalino, Lawrence P. "Physician Self-Referral and Physician-Owned Specialty Facilities." *The Synthesis Project, Robert Wood Johnson Foundation* 15 (June, 2008).

Centers for Medicare & Medicaid Services, www.cms.hhs.gov, accessed January 12, 2012.

Chassin, Mark R. "Explaining Geographic Variations: The Enthusiasm Hypothesis." *Medical Care* 31 (supplement 1993), pp. YS37–YS44.

Chassin, Mark R., et al. "Variations in the Use of Medical and Surgical Services by the Medicare Population." *New England Journal of Medicine* 314 (January 30, 1986), pp. 285–90.

Cooper, Richard A. "Weighing the Evidence for Expanding Physician Supply." *Annals of Internal Medicine* 141 (November, 2004), pp. 705–14.

Cooper, Richard A., Thomas E. Getzen, Heather J. McKee, and Prakash Laud. "Economic and Demographic Trends Signal an Impeding Physician Shortage." *Health Affairs* 21 (January/February 2002), pp. 140–54.

Council on Graduate Medical Education. *Sixteenth Report: Physician Workforce Policy Guidelines of the United States, 2000–2020.* Rockville, Md.: January, 2005.

Council on Graduate Medical Education (COGME). *Third Report: Improving Access to Health Care through Physician Workforce Reform: Directions for the 21st Century.* Rockville, Md.: 1992.

Cromwell, Jerry, and Janet B. Mitchell. "Physician Induced Demand for Surgery." *Journal of Health Economics* 5 (1986), pp. 293–313.

Danzon, Patricia M. "Liability for Medical Malpractice." In *Handbook of Health Economics*, Volume I, eds. A. J. Culyer and J. P. Newhouse. Amsterdam: Elsevier Science, 2000.

Dill, Michael J, and Edward S. Salsberg. *The Complexities of Physician Supply and Demand Projections through 2025.* Association of American Medical Colleges, Washington, D.C.: November, 2008.

Dubay, Lisa, Robert Kaestner, and Timothy Waidmann. "Medical Malpractice Liability and Its Effect on Prenatal Care Utilization and Infant Health." *Journal of Health Economics* 20 (July 2001), pp. 591–611.

Eddy, David M. "Variations in Physician Practice: The Role of Uncertainty." *Health Affairs* 3 (summer 1984), pp. 74–89.

Escarce, Jose J. "Explaining the Association between Surgeon Supply and Utilization." *Inquiry* 29 (winter 1992), pp. 403–15.

Escarce, Jose J., and Mark V. Pauly. "Physician Opportunity Costs in Physician Practice Cost Functions." *Journal of Health Economics* 17 (April 1998), pp. 129–51.

Feldstein, Paul J., Thomas M. Wickizer, and John R. C. Wheeler. "Private Cost Containment: The Effects of Utilization Review Programs on Health Care Use and Expenditures." *New England Journal of Medicine* 31, 8 (May 19, 1988), pp. 1310–14.

Felt-Lisk, Suzanne, and Glen P. Mays. "Back to the Drawing Board: New Directions in Health Plans' Care Management Strategies." *Health Affairs* 21 (September/October 2002), pp. 210–17.

Folland, Sherman T., and Miron Stano. "Small Area Variations: A Critical Review of Propositions, Methods and Evidence." *Medical Care Review* 47 (winter 1990), pp. 419–65.

Frech, H. E., and Paul B. Ginsburg. "Optimal Scale in Medical Practice: A Survivor Analysis." *Journal of Business* 47 (1974), pp. 23–36.

Friedman, Milton. *Capitalism and Freedom.* Chicago: University of Chicago Press, 1962.

Friedman, Milton. *Free to Choose.* New York: Harcourt Brace Jovanovich, 1980.

Fuchs, Victor R. "The Supply of Surgeons and the Demand for Operations." *Journal of Human Resources* 13 (supplement 1978), pp. 35–56.

Gabel, Jon R., et al. "Where Do I Send Thee? Does Physician Ownership Affect Referral Patterns to Ambulatory Surgery Center." *Health Affairs*, Web Exclusive (March 18, 2008), pp. w165–w174.

Gallegos, Alicia. "Liability Premiums Hold Steady, but State Disparities Linger." *American Medical News*, October 17, 2011, www.amednews.com, accessed January 6, 2012.

Goodell, Sarah, and Lawrence P. Casalino. "Physician Self-Referral and Physician-Owned Specialty Facilities, Policy Brief." *The Synthesis Project, Robert Wood Johnson Foundation* 15 (June, 2008).

Goodman, David C., and Kevin Grumbach. "Does Having More Physicians Lead to Better Health System Performance?" *Journal of the*

American Medical Association 299 (January 23, 2008), pp. 335–37.

Government Accounting Office (GAO). *Medical Liability Impact on Hospital and Physician Costs Extends beyond Insurance.* Washington, D.C.: September 1995.

———. "Medical Malpractice Implications of Rising Premiums on Access to Health Care." Washington, D.C.: August 8, 2003a.

———. "Physician Workforce: Physician Supply Increase in Metropolitan and Nonmetropolitan Areas but Geographic Disparities Persist." Washington, D.C.: October 31, 2003b.

Greenspan, Allan M., et al. "Incidence of Unwarranted Implantation of Permanent Cardiac Pacemakers in a Large Medical Population." *New England Journal of Medicine* 318 (January 21, 1988), pp. 158–63.

Grytten, Jostein, and Rune Sorenson. "Type Contract and Supplier-Induced Demand for Primary Physicians in Norway." *Journal of Health Economics* 20 (2001), pp. 379–93.

———. "Practice Variation and Physician-Specific Effects." *Journal of Health Economics* 22 (2003), pp. 403–81.

Gunning, Timothy S., and Robin C. Sickles. "A Multi-Product Cost Function for Physician Private Practices." *Journal of Production Analysis* 35 (2011), pp. 119–28.

Hadley, Jack, and Jean M. Mitchell. "The Growth of Managed Care and Changes in Physicians' Incomes, Autonomy, and Satisfaction, 1991–1997." *International Journal of Health Care Finance and Economics* 2 (2002), pp. 37–50.

"HCS Community Tracking Study Physician Survey." *Health System Change*, www.hschange.org, accessed January 12, 2012.

Hellinger, Fred J., and William E. Encinosa. "The Impact of State Laws Limiting Malpractice Damage Awards on Health Care Expenditures." *American Journal of Public Health* 96 (August, 2006), pp. 1375–81.

———. "Review of Reforms to Our Medical Liability System." *Agency for Healthcare Research and Quality* (December 31, 2009).

Hilborne, Lee H., et al. "The Appropriateness of the Use of Percutaneous Transluminal Coronary Angioplasty in New York State." *Journal of*

American Medicine 269 (February 10, 1993), pp. 761–65.

Karls, Chad C., "From Crunchy Candy to Simmering Frogs, Waiting and Hoping for a Hardening Market as the Market Trends Slowly, Steadily Softer." *Annual Rate Survey Issue, Medical Liability Monitor* 36 (October, 2011), pp. 1–6.

Kessler, Daniel P. "Evaluating the Medical Malpractice System and Options for Reform." *Journal of Economic Perspectives* 25 (spring 2011), pp. 93–110.

Kessler, Daniel, and Mark McClellan. "Do Doctors Practice Defensive Medicine?" *Quarterly Journal of Economics* 111 (May 1996), pp. 353–90.

———. "Malpractice Law and Health Care Reform: Optimal Liability Policy in an Era of Managed Care." *Journal of Public Economics* 84 (2002), pp. 175–97.

Kessler, Daniel P., William M. Sage, and David J. Becker. "Impact of Malpractice Reforms on the Supply of Physician Services." *Journal of the American Medical Association* 293 (June 1, 2005), pp. 2618–25.

Kessel, Reuben. "Price Discrimination in Medicine." *Journal of Law and Economics* 1 (1958), pp. 20–53.

Klick, Jonathan, and Thomas Stratmann. "Medical Malpractice Reform and Physicians in High-Risk Specialties." *The Journal of Legal Studies* 36, Part 2 (June, 2007), pp. S143–S182.

Leape, Lucian L., et al. "The Appropriateness of Use of Coronary Artery Bypass Graft Surgery in New York State." *Journal of the American Medical Association* 269 (February 10, 1993), pp. 753–60.

Leffler, Keith B. "Physician Licensure: Competition and Monopoly in American Medicine." *Journal of Law and Economics* 21 (1978), pp. 165–86.

Li, Jinhu, et al., "Physician Response to Pay-For-Performance: Evidence from a Natural Experiment." *NBER Working Paper Series.* Cambridge, Mass.: National Bureau of Economic Research, March, 2011.

Lindsey, Phoebe A., and Joseph P. Newhouse. "The Cost and Value of Second Surgical Opinion Programs: A Critical Review of the Literature."

Journal of Health Policy, Politics and Law 15 (fall 1990), pp. 543–70.

Marder, William D., and Stephen Zuckerman. "Competition and Medical Groups." *Journal of Health Economics* 4 (1985), pp. 167–76.

Matsa, David A. "Does Malpractice Liability Keep the Doctor Away? Evidence from Tort Reform Damage Caps." *The Journal of Legal Studies* 36, Part 2 (June, 2007), pp. S121–S142.

McCarthy, Thomas R. "The Competitive Nature of the Primary-Care Physician Services Market." *Journal of Health Economics* 4 (1985), pp. 93–117.

McGuire, Thomas. "Physician Agency." In *Handbook of Health Economics,* Volume I, eds. A. J. Culyer and J. P. Newhouse. Amsterdam: Elsevier Science, 2000.

Med-Vantage. *2010 National P4P Survey Executive Summary.* San Francisco, Calif.: June 2011

Mello, Michelle M., et al. "Changes in Physician Supply and Scope of Practice during a Malpractice Crisis: Evidence from Pennsylvania." *Health Affairs,* Web Exclusive (April 2007).

Mello, Michelle M., et al. "National Cost of the Medical Liability System." *Health Affairs* 29 (September 2010), pp. 1569–68.

————, Allen Kachalia, and Sarah Goodell. "Medical Malpractice Update." *The Synthesis Project, Robert Wood Johnson Foundation* 8 (April, 2011).

Miller, Robert H., and Harold S. Luft. "Managed Care Plan Performance since 1980." *Journal of the American Medical Association* 271 (May 18, 1994), pp. 1512–19.

Moore, Thomas. "The Purpose of Licensing." *Journal of Law and Economics* 4 (1961), pp. 93–117.

Nelson, Leonard J., Michael Morrisey, and Meredith Kilgore. "Damages Caps and Medical Malpractice Cases." *Millbank Quarterly* 85 (2007), pp. 259–286.

Pauly Mark, et al. "Who Pays? The Incidence of High Malpractice Premiums." *Forum for Health Economics and Policy* 9 (2006), pp. 1–19.

Phelps, Charles E. "Diffusion of Information in Medical Care." *Journal of Economic Perspectives* 6 (summer 1992), pp. 23–42.

"*Physician Supply and Demand: Projections to 2020.*" U.S. Department of Health and Human Services, Health Resources and Services Administration (October 2006).

Politzer, Robert M., et al. "Matching Physician Supply and Requirements: Testing Policy Recommendations." *Inquiry* 33 (summer 1996), pp. 181–94.

Pope, Gregory C, and Russel T. Burge. "Economies of Scale in Physician Practice." *Medical Care Research and Review* 53 (December 1996), pp. 417–40.

Raffel, Marshall W, and Norma K. Raffel. *The U.S. Health System: Origins and Functions,* 3rd ed. New York: Wiley, 1989.

Reschovsky, James, Alwyn Cassil, and Hoangmai H. Pham. "Physician Ownership and Medical Equipment." *Health Systems Change Data Bulletin* 36 (December, 2010).

Reinhardt, Uwe E. "Manpower Substitution and Productivity in Medical Practices: Review of Research." *Health Services Research* 8 (1973), pp. 200–27.

————. *Physician Productivity and Demand for Health Manpower.* Cambridge, Mass.: Ballinger, 1975.

————. "A Production Function for Physician Services." *Review of Economics and Statistics* 54 (February 1972), pp. 55–66.

Rice, Thomas H. "An Evaluation of Alternative Policies for Controlling Health Care Costs." In *Building Blocks for Change: How Health Care Reform Affects Our Future,* eds. Jack A. Meyer and Sharon Silow-Carrol. Washington, D.C.: Economic and Social Research Institute, 1993.

Roos, Noralou P. "Predicting Hospital Utilization by the Elderly: The Importance of Patient, Physician, and Hospital Characteristics." *Medical Care* 27 (October 1989), pp. 905–17.

Rosenthal, Meredith B., and Richard G. Frank. "What is the Empirical Basis for Paying for Quality Health Care." *Medical Care Research and Review* 63 (April, 2006), pp. 135–57.

Rosenthal, Meredith B., Alan Zaslavsky, and Joseph P. Newhouse. "The Geographic Distribution of Physicians Revisited." *Health Services Research* 40 (December 2005), pp. 1931–52.

Rosenman, Robert, and Daniel Friesner. "Scope and Scale Inefficiences in Physician Practices." *Health Economics* 13 (2004), pp. 1091–1116.

Rossiter, Louis E, and Gail R. Wilensky. "Identification of Physician Induced Demand." *Journal of Human Resources* 19 (spring 1984), pp. 232–44.

Salsberg, Edward, and Gaetano Forte. "Benefits and Pitfalls in Allying the Experience of Prepaid Group Practices to the U.S. Physician Supply." *Health Affairs,* Web Exclusive, (February 4, 2004).

Scheffler, Richard M., Sean D. Sullivan, and Timothy Hoachung Ko. "The Impact of Blue Cross and Blue Shield Plan Utilization Management Programs, 1980–88." *Inquiry* 28 (fall 1991), pp. 263–75.

Schroeder, Steven A. "Physician Supply and the U.S. Medical Marketplace." *Health Affairs* 11 (spring 1992), pp. 235–54.

————. "Western European Responses to Physician Oversupply." *Journal of the American Medical Association* 252 (July 20, 1984), pp. 373–84.

Shipman, Scott A., Jia Lan, Chiang-Hua Change, and David C. Goodman. "Geographic Maldistibution of Primary Care for Children." *Pediatrics* 127 (January, 2011) pp. 19–27.

Shreve, Jon et al. *The Economic Measurement of Medical Errors.* Society of Actuaries, June 2010, http://www.soa.org/research/research-projects/health/research-econ-measurement.aspx

Sloan, Frank A., and John H. Shadle. "Is There Empirical Evidence for 'Defensive Medicine'? A Reassessment." *Journal of Health Economics* 28 (2009), pp. 481–91.

Stano, Miron. "Further Issues in Small Area Variations Analysis." *Journal of Health Politics, Policy and Law* 16 (fall 1991), pp. 573–88.

Svorny Shirley. "Should We Reconsider Licensing Physicians?" *Contemporary Policy Issues* 10 (January 1992), pp. 31–38.

Thorpe, Kenneth E. "The Medical Malpractice 'Crisis': Recent Trends and the Impact of State Tort Reform." *Health Affairs,* Web Exclusive, (January 21, 2004).

Thurston, Norman K., and Anne M. Libby. "A Production Function for Physician Services Revisited." *Review of Economics and Statistics* 84 (February 2002), pp. 184–91.

Town, Robert, Douglas R. Whole, John Kralewski, and Bryan Dowd. "Assessing the Influence of Incentives on Physicians and Medical Groups." *Medical Care Research and Review* 61 (September, 2004), pp. 80s–118s.

Trisolini, Michael. "Introduction in Pay for Performance." In *Pay for Performance in Health Care Methods and Approaches,* eds. J. Cromwell, et al. Research Triangle Park, N.C.: RTI Press Publication, 2011a.

————. "Theoretical Perspective on Pay for Performance." In *Pay for Performance in Health Care Methods and Approaches,* eds. J. Cromwell, et al. Research Triangle Park, N.C.: RTI Press Publication, 2011b.

Van Den Bos, Jill, et al., "The $17.1 Billion Problem: The Annual Cost of Measurable Medical Errors." *Health Affairs* 30 (April 2011), pp. 596–602.

Weeks, William B., Amy E. Wallace, Myron M. Wallace, and H. Gilbert Welch. "A Comparison of the Educational Costs and Incomes of Physicians and Other Professionals." *New England Journal of Medicine* 330 (May 5, 1994), pp. 1280–86.

Weiner, Jonathan P. "Prepaid Group Practice Staffing and U.S. Physician Supply: Lessons for Workforce Policy." *Health Affairs,* Web Exclusive (February 4, 2004).

Wennberg, John E. "Dealing with Medical Practice Variations: A Proposal for Action." *Health Affairs* 3 (summer 1984), pp. 6–32.

————. "On Patient Need, Equity, Supplier-Induced Demand, and the Need to Assess the Outcome of Common Medical Practices." *Medical Care* 23 (May 1985), pp. 512–20.

Wickizer, Thomas M., and Daniel Lessler. "Utilization Management: Issues, Effects, and Future Prospects." *Annual Review of Public Health* 23 (2002), pp. 233–54.

Wilson, Florence A., and Duncan Neuhauser. *Health Services in the United States,* 2nd ed. Cambridge, Mass.: Ballinger, 1985.

CHAPTER 13

The Hospital Services Industry

Just about everyone, either as a patient, a visitor, or an employee, has had some experience at a hospital. Some people conceive of hospitals as cold, lifeless facilities that spell gloom and doom. Others imagine hospitals as wondrous places where miraculous lifesaving feats, such as human organ transplants, are performed. Regardless of one's view, it is safe to say that the hospital of today bears little resemblance to its early-nineteenth-century predecessor. According to Peter Temin (1988), a noted economic historian,

> Hospitals were primarily nonmedical institutions throughout most of the nineteenth century. They existed for the care of marginal members of society, whether old, poor, or medically or psychologically deviant. Medicine was practiced outside the hospital, and the medical staffs of hospitals were small. Hospitals were charitable institutions, and they looked for moral rather than physical improvement in their patients.... In short, the nineteenth-century hospital was closer to an almshouse than to a modern hospital. (pp. 78–79)

With the development of the germ theory of disease, the advent of new technologies, and increased urbanization, the "modern" hospital replaced the old-style version in the years following 1880. Hospitals have subsequently evolved into vibrant centers of medical and business activities.

Today's hospital is a technological marvel. The once simple hospital bed can now cost up to $10,000 when it includes customized accessories, such as automatically inflating air mattresses for patients with bedsores, voice-activated adjustments for paraplegics, and in-bed weight scales for bedridden patients (Anders, 1993a). Aided by advances in computer and pharmaceutical technologies, the modern hospital has proven capable of offering numerous therapeutic and diagnostic services that extend and improve the quantity and quality of lives. Indeed, one may point to the success of modern medicine as the culprit behind the ever-rising cost of delivering hospital services. Accounting for expenditures of $814 billion and 31 percent of all personal health care expenditures in 2010, the hospital services industry is the largest of the medical care industries.

This chapter explores issues relating to the structure, conduct, and performance of the hospital services industry. Specifically, the chapter:

- *examines the level of market concentration in the hospital services market*
- *studies sources of barriers to entry into the hospital services industry*
- *explores various features regarding the relationship between managed care practices and hospital behavior*
- *focuses on numerous characteristics influencing the interplay between hospital competition, regulation, and pricing behavior*
- *assesses the output, pricing, and profit performance of the hospital services industry*
- *studies how some provisions of the Patient Protection and Affordable Care Act (PPACA) of 2010 may affect the hospital industry in the United States.*

The Structure of the Hospital Services Industry

In the next section, various topics relating to the structure of the hospital services industry are addressed. Some issues relate directly to the nature of competition within the hospital services industry. Others deal with various structural concerns raised by researchers and practitioners within the hospital services industry. The overarching question is whether individual hospitals, and the industry as a whole, are structured properly from an efficiency perspective.

Market Concentration within the Hospital Services Industry

As you know, medical care takes on many different forms. Prescription drugs, office visits to physician clinics, rehabilitation services at nursing homes, and hospital care all represent examples of medical care. While hospitals also offer outpatient services, the distinguishing characteristic of a hospital is the application of acute care within an inpatient setting. Inpatient means that patients receive food and lodging, in addition to medical care. This situation of hospitals contrasts sharply with that of nursing homes and physician clinics which only offer, in comparative terms, food and lodging and acute-care (but less invasive) services, respectively.

Although some hospitals only produce specialized services, such as psychiatric or nose, throat, and eye care services, about 85 percent are classified as community hospitals which simultaneously offer a multitude of diagnostic and therapeutic services. Given the multiproduct nature of community hospitals, the relevant product market (RPM) for hospital services is normally defined as a **cluster of inpatient hospital services**. This definition of the RPM makes sense because many services such as X-rays, blood tests, and surgery, are complements to one another (Frech, 1987). Correspondingly, the size of the hospital services market is generally measured by economists in inpatient terms by beds, admissions, inpatient days, or inpatient revenues.

Of course, not all hospitals are created equal. In particular, some hospitals provide different levels of care in terms of technical sophistication and quality of services rendered or the seriousness and complexity of illnesses treated. Thus, some hospitals located in the same community may not belong to the same RPM because the level of care differs across services. Professionals in the hospital industry generally distinguish among four types of care (U.S. v. Carilion, 1989).

Primary care services involve the prevention, early detection, and treatment of disease. Services of this nature include obstetrics, gynecology, internal medicine, and general surgery. A hospital that limits itself to providing primary care typically has some diagnostic equipment to perform X-ray and laboratory analysis. *Secondary* care involves more sophisticated treatment and may include cardiology, respiratory care, and physical therapy. Equipment and laboratory capabilities are more sophisticated in secondary care hospitals. *Tertiary* care is designed to arrest disease in process, including heart surgery and such cancer treatments as chemotherapy, and requires still more sophisticated equipment than primary or secondary services do. Community hospitals normally provide both primary and secondary care, and some offer tertiary care. Research hospitals associated with university medical schools are argued to provide state-of-the-art *quaternary*-level care. These differences in the level of care may result in specific hospitals, such as academic medical centers, operating in different niches of the overall hospital services industry.

We learned in Chapter 8 that the relevant geographical market (RGM) must also be considered when measuring market concentration. Knowing that two stages of competition exist in hospital markets is crucial for understanding the scope of the RGM (U.S. DOJ/FTC, 2010). At the first stage, hospitals compete among themselves to be included in the provider networks of various health insurers. Hospital prices are negotiated between hospitals and health insurers so the ability of health insurers to switch to hospitals in other areas helps to define the RGM within this stage. At the second stage, hospitals within the same network compete for patients. Patients are likely to consider nonprice factors such as convenience and quality when choosing among hospitals at this stage. The consumers' willingness and ability to travel long distances also factors into defining the RGM within the second stage. Hospitals can acquire market power at one or both stages. In addition, market power established in either stage can sometimes be leveraged to obtain market power in the other.

Not surprising, most health care analysts agree that most real-world hospital markets are fairly small or local in nature. As Judge Posner noted in the *Rockford* antitrust case (U.S. v. Rockford Memorial, 1990), "For highly exotic or highly elective hospital treatment, patients will sometimes travel long distances, of course. But for the most part hospital services are local. People want to be hospitalized near their families and homes, in hospitals in which their own—local—doctors have hospital privileges."

If markets are defined as being local in nature, it appears that many hospital services markets are highly concentrated. For example, Capps and Dranove (2011) report that the Herfindahl-Hirschman index (HHI) for hospital services market concentration exceeded 2,500 in 80 percent of all metropolitan statistical areas (MSAs) in 2009. Recall that 2,500 is the HHI cut-off for a highly-concentrated market as set by the Department of Justice (DOJ) and Federal Trade Commission (see Chapter 8). They further point out that the HHI was below 1,500, the threshold for unconcentrated markets, in only 7 percent of the MSAs. Capps and Dranove also point out that hospital services markets have become increasingly concentrated over time, with the average MSA-level HHI rising from 4,200 in 1997 to 4,700 in 2009. Moreover, they show that the hospital services HHI increased by more than 500 points in 30 MSAs during the 2006 to 2009 period. They argue that the increase in hospital services market concentration is largely due to mergers and consolidations among hospitals and a shift away from independent hospitals to multihospital systems. More specifically, they report that 63 percent of all hospitals located in MSAs belong to a hospital system as of 2009.

However, when assessing the overall competitiveness of a market, economists also consider the degree of potential competition as reflected by any barriers to entry into a market. A high degree of potential competition creates an incentive for aggressive price competition even when only a few firms dominate an industry. We take up entry barriers in the next section.

Barriers to Entry

State certificate of need (CON) laws are often cited as a type of entry barrier into the hospital services industry. CON laws make it more costly for hospitals to enter new markets and/or expand because they must first obtain authorization from the government. During CON hearings, entrenched hospitals are often in a position to oppose entry or expansion and thereby limit the competition they face. In fact, Simpson (1995) shows that after CON laws were removed, the majority of new hospitals in California contained fewer than 100 beds, proving that small hospital entry is otherwise limited because of CON law. In agreement, Santerre and Pepper (2000) use survivor analysis (see Chapter 11) and find empirically that CON laws favor larger-sized hospitals.

Other studies reveal that CON laws limit the entry of specialized health care facilities. For example, Short, Aloia, and Ho (2008) find that states with acute-care CON laws have fewer facilities that perform treatments for cancer. Ho et al. (2007) conclude that the number of hospitals performing coronary artery bypass graft surgery was significantly greater in states without CON laws, demonstrating that CON regulations act as a barrier to entry for cardiac facilities. Ho, Ku-Goto, and Jollis (2009) demonstrate empirically that states eliminating CON laws have more cardiac care providers statewide. As Salkever (2000) notes in his earlier review of regulations that affect hospitals in the United States, CON laws limit competition by restricting both the number of hospital beds and institutions. Thus, it is not surprising that, in 1987, the federal government ended its policy, which began in 1975, of encouraging the development of CON programs. According to Baker (1988), nearly one-quarter of the states abolished their CON laws by the end of 1987.

Baker (1988) argues that even in the absence of CON laws, entry into the hospital industry may be difficult. The technological specifications for modern hospital buildings, including wide corridors and doorways, large elevators, strongly supported flooring, and extensive plumbing, require about four to nine years of planning and construction time. The relatively huge investment in the hospital infrastructure represents a sunk cost that may discourage new hospitals from entering a market in a timely manner.

In addition to sunk costs, other cost conditions, such as scale economies, learning curve effects, and system affiliation, may serve as barriers to entry. With respect to scale economies, empirical analyses that treat hospitals as multiproduct firms and rely on neoclassical cost theory, as discussed in Chapter 7, fail to provide any strong and consistent econometric evidence for the presence of long-run economies of scale in the production of inpatient services (e.g., Cowing and Holtmann, 1983; Grannemann et al., 1986; Eakin and Kniesner, 1988; Vita, 1990; Fournier and Mitchell, 1992). In fact, most of the evidence suggests that the production process for inpatient hospital services exhibits long-run diseconomies of scale, at least for the average-size hospital in the various studies. The implication of these studies is that long-run economies of scale are not a serious deterrent to potential entrants in the hospital services industry.

Recall from Chapter 7 that learning-by-doing is another characteristic associated with the cost structure hospitals face. Studies focusing on learning economies in the hospital industry usually investigate how the volume of output affects the quality of patient outcomes. The econometric difficulty for studies examining learning-by-doing is reverse causation—the so-called selective referral bias. It is entirely possible that patients flock to hospitals that provide higher-quality care; that is, higher quality leads to higher admissions rather than the reverse. After considering selective referral bias, most empirical studies have offered evidence to support learning-by-doing for various hospital services and surgical procedures, but the magnitude varies greatly (Halm et al., 2002).

One exception worth mentioning is a study by Ho (2002) that uses longitudinal data on patients receiving coronary angioplasty, a procedure to widen narrowed arteries, to empirically examine changes in outcomes and costs. Because a panel data set of patient outcomes over a relatively long period of time (1984–1996) is used in the empirical test, Ho is able to differentiate between scale economies (more output at a point in time), learning-by-doing (greater cumulative output over time), and "learning-by-watching" on health outcomes and costs. **Learning-by-watching** refers to productivity or quality improvements that occur over time regardless of production volume. It arises from knowledge or technological change that can be easily transferred from one hospital to another.

Based on data from California hospitals, Ho shows that all hospitals achieved substantial improvements in patient outcomes with respect to coronary angioplasty over time. However, when empirically explaining those improvements using multiple regression analysis and controlling for factors such as case-mix, quality, and hospital characteristics, she finds no evidence that learning-by-doing improves patient outcomes. Rather, evidence is found to support mild scale economies and learning-by-watching. In terms of cost reductions, Ho's empirical findings cannot rule out lower costs of performing coronary angioplasties because of learning-by-doing. Overall, she points out that efforts to regionalize the production of coronary angioplasties may lead to lower costs per patient but only small outcome improvements.

If "practice makes perfect," as most studies seem to suggest, hospitals with greater volume may tend to attract an even larger market share over time. The learning economies, combined with limit-pricing techniques, may discourage new firms from entering the industry. Thus, most evidence suggests that learning-by-doing may act as a barrier to entry into hospital markets and provide existing firms with some market power to raise prices.

Membership in a **multihospital system** or chain may also provide an existing hospital with an absolute cost advantage relative to a potential freestanding hospital that is contemplating whether to enter the market. The American Hospital Association defines a multihospital system as two or more hospitals that are owned, leased, sponsored, or managed by a single corporate entity. Membership in a multihospital system may result in lower costs because the combined hospitals have better access to capital and more highly trained personnel, and through price discounts resulting from a larger market size. Several empirical studies have examined whether system affiliation actually confers any significant cost savings. While minor cost savings have been found by some researchers, Ermann and Gabel's (1984) review of 18 statistical studies suggests no definitive cost savings from membership in a hospital system. More recent studies, such as Menke (1997) and Wilcox-Gok (2002), also fail to produce any conclusive findings regarding any cost savings from belonging to a hospital system.

In sum, CON laws, the high sunk costs associated with constructing new hospitals, and learning-by-doing appear to be significant entry barriers into the hospital services industry. These entry barriers, when combined with high levels of market concentration, mean that existing hospitals may possess the ability to raise price above the competitive level and thereby earn excess economic profits. One potential constraint on their ability to raise price, however, is the power of buyers in the hospital services market. To that topic we now turn our attention.

Buyers of Hospital Services

Another important aspect of market structure is the number, types, and size distribution of buyers. For example, an influential buyer who purchases a sizeable amount of a product from several different sellers may be able to negotiate significant price discounts by playing off one seller against the others. This is especially true when the various sellers face excess capacity. Table 13–1 shows the main sources of hospital funds in 2010. Of the nearly $800 billion spent on personal hospital care services, about 43 percent originates in the private sector. Individual consumers, accounting for only 3.2 percent of all hospital payments, are most often price insensitive and therefore have little impact on the market price of hospital care.

The private insurance category, representing commercial insurance companies, Blue Cross plans, and independent managed care organizations (MCOs), directly accounts for roughly 35 percent of all spending on hospital services. Whether these buyers have the willingness and ability to bargain successfully for low prices and thereby affect the allocation of resources to hospital services depends on a host of considerations, including their goals (profit or not-for-profit objectives), the competitiveness of the health insurance market, and their individual penetration rates in various hospital services market areas. For example, an individual private health insurance plan is more able to negotiate favorable hospital prices when it represents a relatively large market share of insured individuals in a local hospital market and thereby possesses more bargaining power. We already discussed this possibility in Chapter 11 within the context of health-insurer monopsony power. Evidence appears to suggest that health insurers sometimes possess monopoly-busting rather than monopsony power in the hospital services industry.

Governments at all levels are collectively responsible for 57 percent of hospital care spending, with the Medicare program being the main purchaser at 28 percent. Given

TABLE 13–1
Sources of Hospital Funds, 2010

	Dollars (billions)	Percent
Total hospital care expenses	$814.0	100.0%
All private funds	350.0	43.0
Out-of-pocket	25.9	3.2
Private insurance	285.8	35.1
Other	38.2	4.7
Government	464.0	57.0
Medicare	226.5	27.8
Medicaid and CHIP	155.6	19.1
Other	81.9	10.1

SOURCE: Centers for Medicare & Medicaid Services, http://www.cms.gov (accessed January 9, 2012).

this large share of spending in both national and local markets, the Medicare program may wield considerable power concerning how resources are allocated in the hospital services market. For instance, as discussed in Chapter 10, the diagnosis-related group (DRG) system places hospitals "at risk" for the Medicare portion of their operating costs. These at-risk payments may mean that hospitals are more judicious in their choice and use of medical inputs. However, to the extent that the fixed DRG prices act as a price ceiling, and given the highly concentrated nature of most hospital services market areas, more Medicare patients may be treated (recall the analysis of a price ceiling on a monopolist supplier in Chapter 9).

State governments, who are responsible for administering the Medicaid program which accounts for 19 percent of all hospital revenues, may also be able to influence resource allocation in local hospital services market areas. For example, like the federal government, state governments may administer (rather than negotiate) the prices paid for hospital services. If the number of Medicaid patients is relatively large in local market areas, these administered prices, if they are above or below the competitive level, should influence the manner in which hospitals behave and perform. Also, states may indirectly influence how hospitals conduct themselves through selective contracts with MCOs. In particular, many states selectively contract with MCOs which then provide medical service to Medicaid recipients on behalf of the state governments. To the extent that MCOs aggressively negotiate prices with hospital providers or adopt a less hospital-intensive practice style, hospital behavior and performance may be affected in various local hospital market areas.

Type of Product

Whether the hospitals in a market offer a differentiated or standardized product is another determinant of market structure. According to the anticompetitive view, product differentiation causes the demand curve to become less price elastic and enables the firm to restrict output below and raise price above the competitive level. Hospital choice studies confirm that product differences matter in the hospital services industry. For example, from their review of the literature, Lane and Lindquist (1988) cite seven categories of factors—care, staff, physical facilities, clientele, experience, convenience, and institutional—that strongly affect the choice of hospital. Of these factors, quality of care and staff, equipment and technology, and convenient location were found to be among the more important determinants of choice of hospital.

Marketing and advertising also play important roles in the hospital services industry. The typical hospital engaging in promotion activities spends nearly $120,000 annually on marketing, amounting to approximately 0.1 to 0.2 percent of sales (Barro and Chu, 2002). While that percentage figure pales in comparison to the advertising-to-sales ratios of 10 percent or more observed in the pharmaceutical, cosmetics, soft drink, cereal, and other industries, Gray (1986) notes that hospitals devote as much as 5 percent of gross sales to advertising in some highly competitive areas of the country. Gray also notes, "Hospitals plug such things as Saturday surgery (a convenience for patients), referral services, gourmet food, depression clinics—even free transportation" (p. 183).

Dorfman and Steiner (1954) offer a model that provides a useful starting point for thinking about the determinants of hospital advertising expenditures. While the Dorfman-Steiner theory refers to a monopolist, we simply have to consider other strategic aspects of advertising when applying the model to the hospital services industry. As we discussed previously, the hospital services industry more closely conforms to the characteristics of an oligopolistic market structure in many areas. Following the Dorfman-Steiner approach, we begin by supposing that a hospital faces the following market demand for its services:

(13–1)
$$Q = Q(P, A),$$

where Q stands for quantity demanded and P and A represent price and advertising expenditures, respectively.

The quantity demanded of hospital services is expected to decline with an increase in price, as the law of demand suggests, and rise with greater advertising expenditures, *ceteris paribus*. The latter variable affects the quantity demanded of hospital services through a shift in the demand curve to the right. According to theory, demand increases (and may rotate) because of the information signal provided or the brand loyalty created by the advertising message.

Dorfman and Steiner show mathematically that the profit-maximizing amount of advertising relative to total revenues (A/TR), or advertising intensity, results when the following condition holds:

(13–2)
$$\frac{A}{TR} = \frac{E_A}{E_P}.$$

E_A represents the advertising elasticity of demand and identifies the percentage change in quantity demanded resulting from a one-percentage-point change in advertising expenditures. It measures the responsiveness of consumer demand to a change in advertising expenditures. For example, if $E_A = 2.0$, then a 1 percent increase in advertising expenditures results in a 2 percent increase in quantity demanded. E_P represents the price elasticity of market demand in absolute terms.

According to this Dorfman-Steiner condition, the profit-maximizing level of advertising intensity equals the ratio of the two elasticities. For instance, if E_A and E_P equal 1.5 and 4.5, respectively, then the profit-maximizing ratio of advertising to sales equals 0.33. That is, the profit-maximizing hospital spends one-third of its revenues on advertising expenditures. One implication of the analysis is that a profit-maximizing hospital advertises more intensely when the advertising elasticity is higher. As one would expect, hospitals spend more on advertising when consumers are more responsive to the messages financed with the advertising expenditures.

Another implication of the model is that advertising expenditures are greater when demand is less elastic with respect to price. That relation holds in part because increased advertising expenditures generally lead to higher per-unit costs and prices. When demand is less elastic with respect to price, the higher price resulting from the increased advertising expenditures leads to a smaller percentage reduction in quantity demanded.

Using the expression for the Lerner index of monopoly power developed in Chapter 8, the price-cost margin can be substituted for the price elasticity of demand facing a monopolist. Thus, Equation 13–2 can be restated as

(13–3)
$$\frac{A}{TR} = E_A \frac{(P - MC)}{P}.$$

As a result, Equation 13–3 offers the interpretation that advertising intensity is larger when quantity demanded is more responsive to advertising and also when the gap between price and marginal cost is greater. Thus, a third implication of the Dorfman-Steiner condition is that firms with greater market power tend to advertise their products more aggressively, all other factors held constant. In fact, a perfectly competitive firm may not advertise at all, according to Equation 13–3, because the price-cost margin equals zero in the long run.

Recall that the Dorfman-Steiner model is based on a monopolist and that most hospital services markets are oligopolistic in nature. Within an oligopoly setting, previous research suggests that we must consider that advertising could have both an *industry expansion* and a *market share expansion* effect. That is, advertising by a single hospital may expand the size of the entire industry by informing consumers about the general availability of a product or procedure (such as an MRI), or why one product (such as hospital outpatient care) is superior to a substitute product (outpatient care in physician clinics). Notice that all of the hospitals in an area stand to gain from a single hospital's advertising when it leads to industry expansion. In fact, if all of the hospitals in an industry offer fairly standardized products and each individual hospital attempts to free-ride the advertising efforts of others to gain from the industry expansion without incurring costs, economic theory suggests that little advertising may actually take place. This free-rider argument provides another reason why firms in a perfectly competitive market are not likely to spend much on advertisements. In contrast, one of a few hospitals in an oligopolistic market may be able to internalize more of the gains from the industry expansion effect. Hence, advertising expenditures are likely to be greater in an oligopolistic setting than in a perfectly competitive market.

Another consideration is that an individual hospital may gain from the market share effect in an oligopolistic setting. Persuasive advertising may allow a hospital to attract some of its rivals' customers. Using advertising as a nonprice means of competing is further reinforced by the fact that rival hospitals can quickly and easily respond to a price cut by a competitor. Consequently, price competition often does not provide a sustainable method of enlarging market share in an oligopolistic market. A clever advertising campaign, in contrast, can catch rivals off guard and sometimes lead to a sizeable increase in market share for a longer duration than the short-lived market share increase that develops from the initiation of a price war.

The market share expansion effect also implies that diminishing returns may set in with respect to additional advertising expenditures at some point. For example, an oligopolistic hospital with a 65 percent market share may have to spend considerably more on advertising to attract an additional 1 percent of the market from its rivals than is required to capture any previous increments of 1 percent. In addition, the market share effect holds no value for a monopolist, so it may not hold much value for a firm already in possession of 95, 90, or 80 percent of the market. For these reasons, advertising intensity may level off or decline at some level of industry concentration.

Based on the Dorfman-Steiner model, Town and Currim (2002) examine the advertising behavior of a sample of California hospitals from 1991 to 1997. The authors find that the percentage of California hospitals that advertised increased from 16 to 45 percent over the six-year period. These figures compare very closely to those of Barro and Chu (2002), who report that the percentage of hospitals advertising in the nation increased from 36 percent in 1995 to more than 50 percent in 1998. In addition, among hospitals that advertised, Town and Currim explain that inflation-adjusted hospital advertising expenditures in California grew more than sixfold over the period. However, at the national level over the shorter three-year period from 1995 to 1998, hospital expenditures on advertising increased by only 10 percent in real terms according to Barro and Chu.

Following the Dorfman-Steiner model, Town and Currim specify various variables such as the HHI in their multiple regression equation that affect either the advertising or price elasticity of demand. Their analysis offers a number of interesting insights. First, the empirical findings support the Dorfman-Steiner theory by indicating that hospital advertising intensity is greater in more concentrated market areas. Specifically, they find that an increase in the HHI from about 1,470 to 3,310 produces a 72 percent increase in advertising expenditures.

Second, the findings imply that for-profit hospitals did not advertise any differently than their not-for-profit counterparts. We see later in this chapter that for-profit and not-for-profit hospitals share a lot of behavioral similarities. Finally, their results also suggest that hospitals spend more on advertising in an attempt to attract a greater share of the more profitable Medicare and health maintenance organization (HMO) patients as compared to the less profitable Medicaid or charity care patients. The direct empirical relation between the percentage of HMO patients and advertising intensity may also reflect a hypothesis offered by Barro and Chu. They argue that HMOs achieve market power by threatening to leave hospitals out of their networks. Advertising helps hospitals differentiate their products and make themselves indispensable in the eyes of the consumer and thereby reduce the threat and market power of HMOs.

In summary, the data suggest that advertising is beginning to play a greater role in the hospital services industry. The Dorfman-Steiner theory suggests that growing market concentration in the hospital services industry may be one reason for this growing dependence on hospital advertising. Moreover, hospitals may be using advertising to differentiate their products so as to improve their standing with HMO networks for negotiation purposes. Differentiated products, in turn, lower the price elasticity of demand facing an individual hospital and thereby create an additional incentive to spend more on hospital advertising.

If, in the future, hospitals rely more on nonprice methods of competition, such as advertising, price competition may become less aggressive. That is, hospital prices may become relatively rigid as hospitals compete on the basis of advertising, quality, and convenience, for example. The net effect of this trend on consumer welfare is uncertain and depends on a variety of considerations, including whether the nonprice methods promote real or illusory gains for consumers. It also depends on whether oligopolistic hospitals agree to collude on a number of dimensions, including advertising, at some point. For example, five of the six hospitals in Des Moines, Iowa, were accused of agreeing to limit their advertising, an action in violation of antitrust laws. The hospitals involved in the suit eventually settled with the DOJ (Burda, 1993).

Summary of the Structure of the Hospital Services Industry

For all practical purposes, the market for hospital services is best defined as hospitals offering a similar cluster of inpatient services within the same geographical area. The geographical market area of most primary and secondary care hospitals tends to be local in nature. The structural competitiveness of the hospital services market is determined by the number and size distribution of hospitals, number and size distribution of buyers such as insurers, height of any barriers to entry, and type of product. In terms of the supply side, most local hospital markets are characterized by a relatively few large hospitals. Most metropolitan market areas have become more concentrated over time because of consolidations among hospitals.

In addition to the degree of actual competition, the behavior of hospitals depends on the ease of potential entry or the magnitude of any barriers to entry. CON laws, high sunk costs, and learning-by-doing rather than long-run economies of scale or multihospital systems appear to be the major reasons for barriers to entry into the hospital services industry. Hence, based on a relatively few competitors and sizeable barriers to entry in most market areas, the supply side of the hospital services industry can be characterized as being oligopolistic in nature.

Another important structural factor affecting hospital behavior from the demand side of the market is buyer concentration. Simply put, buyer concentration has the ability to negate seller concentration. The federal government, state governments, and some private insurers may possess the appropriate size on the demand side of the market necessary to influence hospital pricing and output behavior. Also, reimbursement policies that place hospitals at risk for high costs have the potential to promote cost-effective medicine.

The Conduct of the Hospital Services Industry

The industrial organization triad predicts that market structure influences the conduct of the hospitals within a given market area. According to traditional microeconomic theory, a large number of sellers and low barriers to entry promote competition. More intense competition usually shows up in increased output, higher quality, and lower prices. The general conduct of real-world hospitals is difficult to predict on a market or an aggregate basis, however. Hospitals pursue different objectives, operate in various market settings, face alternative types of reimbursement methods from third-party payers, and are subject to a variety of government regulations.

Ideally, from a societal point of view, we hope that incentives exist such that hospitals act independently and strive to minimize costs and satisfy consumer wants. However, some structural features of the hospital services industry, such as barriers to entry, product complexity, and asymmetry of information, suggest that such incentives may be lacking in many local markets across the nation. Also, a substantial body of empirical evidence indicates that hospitals sometimes compete on the basis of cost-enhancing quality instead of price in many markets. In this section, we focus on the pricing behavior of hospitals, particularly not-for-profit hospitals. We also discuss what is known empirically about the relation between hospital market structure and various measures of conduct, such as price, costs, and quality. We also examine the effects of ownership structure, managed care, and government regulations on the conduct of hospitals.

Pricing Behavior of Not-For-Profit Hospitals

In Chapter 8, we developed several market models, including perfect competition and monopoly, to analyze the pricing behavior of for-profit organizations. However, most hospitals are organized on a not-for-profit basis. Therefore, the previously discussed market models may be inappropriate for analyzing the conduct of not-for-profit hospitals, which because of their nondistribution constraint may pursue goals other than profit maximization.

Over the years, a number of utility maximization models have been developed to explain the behavior of not-for-profit organizations. In general, utility maximization models assume that managers of a not-for-profit hospital attempt to maximize their own personal utility. Although debate exists over what variables belong in managers' utility functions, most analysts have assumed that managers derive utility either directly or indirectly from things such as organizational size, quality of services, and discretionary profits.

Quantity Maximization. Baumol (1967) argues that rather than pursuing profit maximization, large firms with a substantial amount of market power tend to maximize the size of their output subject to a break-even level of profits. Because executive salaries and prestige are more strongly correlated with firm size than with profits, managers try to expand sales at the expense of profits. Figure 13–1 depicts the situation for a hospital where Q stands for the number of patient-days. An output- or quantity-maximizing hospital produces output up to the point where the average cost of production equals average revenue, or at Q_0 patient-days in the figure. At that point, the hospital is servicing the maximum number of patient-days without incurring an economic loss. If it expands services beyond Q_0, the hospital operates with an economic loss, since AC exceeds AR. A profit-maximizing hospital with the same cost curves produces up to the point where MR = MC and provides Q_1 patient-days and charges P_1. It follows that an output-maximizing hospital produces more output and charges a lower price than a profit-maximizing hospital, *ceteris paribus*.

Davis (1972) points out that most hospitals offer a wide array of services, each with its own price, and it is logical to assume that an output-maximizing hospital follows a pricing strategy that increases the number of patients admitted. The chosen pricing strategy involves a certain degree of cross-subsidization. Specifically, the hospital may charge a price below cost on services for which demand is more elastic to generate more admissions, and then make up for the loss by charging a much higher price for services for which demand is less inelastic. For example, the hospital may charge a price below cost for basic room services to attract more patients and cover the loss by charging a higher price for ancillary services such as pharmaceutical products. The net effect is that the hospital breaks even. In the process, however, the hospital services more patients through cross-subsidization.

The long-run implications of the model are interesting. In the long run, an output-maximizing hospital may generate some profits to acquire the funds it needs for expansion. It obtains the profits by charging a price that is slightly above the average cost of

FIGURE 13–1

The Output Maximization Model

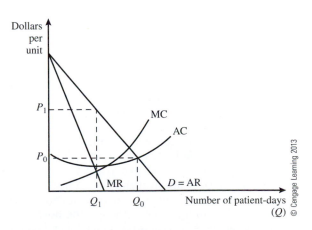

Suppose the typical not-for-profit hospital faces a downward-sloping demand curve and the usually shaped average and marginal cost curves and attempts to maximize the quantity of hospital services subject to a break-even constraint ($P = AC$). If so, the not-for-profit firm produces more services (Q_0) but charges a lower price (P_0) than an otherwise comparable for-profit hospital (P_1, Q_1).

production. As a result, an output-maximizing hospital should not only provide more output than a profit-maximizing hospital at any point in time but should also have a higher rate of expansion over time.

The quantity maximization model can be used to explain the behavior of a not-for-profit organization. Since such a firm is restricted by law from distributing profits, managers may opt to maximize quantity to increase the firm's market share and enhance its prestige in the community. Economists have pointed out that the assumption of output maximization is consistent with the public's perception concerning how a not-for-profit hospital should operate (Newhouse, 1970). From the public's point of view, hospitals are given not-for-profit status because they are expected to provide care to some people in the community who otherwise might not receive care due to profit considerations. If the managers of a not-for-profit hospital maximize quantity, they validate the public's view that their firm plays an important role in the provision of health care to the community at large. That may make it much easier for the hospital to gather community support for such activities as fund-raising.

In the case of a quantity-maximizing not-for-profit hospital, the interests of the managers may also be aligned with the board of trustees, or board of directors, which oversees the general operation of the hospital. Board members, who generally are leading citizens, may also want to maximize quantity to increase their presence in the community. They may wish to be perceived as taking a leading role in the provision of health care to the community.

The quantity maximization model can also explain why in a given community there might be a certain degree of excess capacity in hospital services. A quantity-maximizing hospital may acquire an additional piece of medical equipment even if it does not generate a profit, provided it may attract a sufficient number of additional admittances. Such buying behavior may lead to a duplication of resources and overcapacity as each hospital expands its facility beyond the profit-maximizing point. The quantity maximization model, however, cannot explain why the cost of hospital services has been rising so rapidly over time in recent decades, because it offers only a static rather than a dynamic view of hospital behavior. A static view analyzes behavior or performance at a point in time, whereas a dynamic analysis considers behavior or performance over time. Some other models, discussed next, set quality of services as an attainable goal. Because quality of services is heavily dependent on technology and because medical technology has changed dramatically over time, these models may provide a partial explanation for rising health care costs.

Quality Maximization.   It has been argued that managers derive utility from the quality of hospital care provided. As you know, quality is difficult to measure but can appear in the structure, procedures, or outcomes of an organization. For example, the quality of care is enhanced every time the hospital purchases new equipment, widens the spectrum of services to patients, or retains more specialists on staff. Any increase in the quality of care is also likely to drive up the cost of producing medical services.

Lee's (1971) model of hospital behavior is consistent with the quality maximization argument. The basic premise of the model is that managers of not-for-profit hospitals maximize utility by attempting to enhance the status, or prestige, of their institutions. Since status is defined to be positively related to the "range of services available and the extent to which expensive and highly specialized equipment and personnel (including M.D.'s) are available" (p. 49), the only way managers can achieve their goal is to maximize quality. This quest for status is the force driving the behavior of managers.

According to Lee's theory, the hospital has a desired level of status that it attempts to achieve. The desired status depends on the mission of the hospital and the hospital's relative standing in the medical community. Because the actual level of status tends to be below the desired level, managers are constantly attempting to improve status by increasing the quality of care. The hospital must provide the level of quality of care that is consistent with the desired level of status the managers are trying to achieve. For example, a large teaching hospital with a prestigious reputation is obligated to possess the most technologically sophisticated equipment and have a large number of specialists on staff because the managers view their organization as being on the forefront of medical development. In other words, the reputation and status of the hospital demand that it offers the highest-quality care. A small nonteaching hospital, on the other hand, will try to achieve a much more modest status level. The small nonteaching hospital will offer a quality of care below that of a larger hospital but on a par with hospitals of similar status.

Given a relatively inelastic demand for hospital services, managers can pursue a policy of quality maximization with little concern for costs. Any increase in the cost of hospital services associated with an enhancement in quality can be passed on to the payer through a higher price with minimal impact on output. The quest for status through quality maximization may provide one explanation for rising hospital costs in the years prior to managed care and the Medicare prospective payment system.

Because the physicians on staff at the hospital are also likely to receive utility from any increase in the quality of care, the interests of the managers and medical staff are likely to be aligned in this instance. As the hospital acquires more advanced medical inputs, physicians are given the opportunity to provide more varied and sophisticated medical treatment to their patients. The more sophisticated medical inputs may allow physicians on staff to expand their practices. In addition, the hospital is likely to find it easier to recruit and retain medical personnel if it improves the quality of care. The same argument may apply to the board of trustees. Board members may also receive utility from enhanced hospital status. Finally, don't forget that an enhancement of status may also cause the demand curve to shift to the right.

The quality maximization model suggests that new technology is diffused in a tiered fashion. Any new piece of equipment or medical technology is likely to be adopted first by the most status-conscious institutions, such as research and teaching hospitals. Their lofty status requires that research and teaching hospitals be on the cutting edge of medical technology. Hospitals of lesser status acquire the technology only after it has become a more accepted part of medical treatment and some of the hospitals in that status group have begun to acquire it. The implication is that most hospitals acquire new technology not because it is a prudent investment but because managers do not want to jeopardize the institution's status or relative standing in the medical community. Thus, new technology is acquired primarily for defensive purposes. The quality maximization model may explain why the hospital sector tends toward duplication of resources and overspecialization. Hospitals constantly attempt to expand services to enhance their status, not because profit maximization or efficiency calls for the expansion of services.

Quality and Quantity Maximization. Feldstein (1971) and Newhouse (1970) extend the quality maximization model by combining it with the quantity maximization model. According to Newhouse, management jointly determines the quantity and quality of output and produces the levels that maximize utility. Since any increase in quality comes at the expense of quantity, and vice versa, managers face an important trade-off and must jointly determine the optimal levels of quality and quantity to produce. Figure 13–2 illustrates this trade-off.

Given that quality can be enhanced only by increasing the cost of production (see Chapter 7), every time a hospital attempts to increase quality, its cost curves shift upward. This situation is depicted in Figure 13–3, where initially an output-maximizing hospital produces at point A. If management decides to increase quality, that decision causes the average cost curve to shift upward from AC_0 to AC_1. With no change in demand, the output-maximizing level of output equals Q_1 (point B), and the increase in quality is associated with a decrease in output. In all likelihood, any

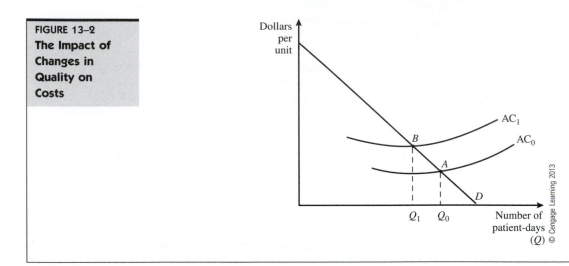

FIGURE 13–2
The Impact of Changes in Quality on Costs

A not-for-profit hospital that chooses to produce with higher quality faces increased costs of AC_1. As a result, the hospital must produce fewer services (Q_1) when faced with a break-even constraint.

increase in quality will lead to an increase in the demand for hospital services. Consumers may be more willing to purchase medical services of higher quality at a higher price. This does not change the analysis, however, provided the increase in demand is relatively small.

If quality is adjusted further, a trade-off curve between quality and quantity can be derived. The trade-off curve appears in Figure 13–3. Points A and B on the graph correspond to points A and B in Figure 13–2. The curve is downward sloping, indicating the trade-off between the quality and quantity of medical care produced.

The quality/quantity maximization model indicates that the managers of not-for-profit hospitals face the dilemma of trying to maximize the level of services provided to the public while at the same time increasing the quality of care to enhance the status of the hospital. Because a trade-off exists between the two, managers must choose that mixture of quantity and quality that maximizes their personal utility.

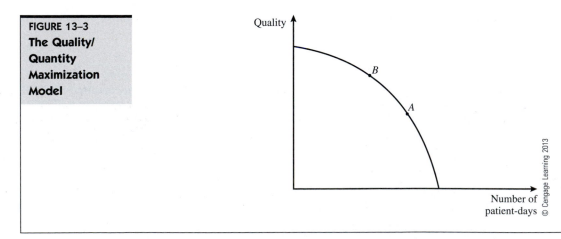

FIGURE 13–3
The Quality/ Quantity Maximization Model

This figure shows the various combinations of quality and quantity of hospital services that can be produced, given a fixed budget constraint. To maximize their utility and given the trade-off, decision makers at a not-for-profit hospital must choose a specific point such as A or B, given their preference weights for the two goods.

The Managerial Expense Preference Model.   The final model discussed in this section is the managerial expense preference model (Williamson, 1963). The model was developed to explain the behavior of large firms that are not directly managed by major stockholders. The basic tenet of the model is that managers use their authority to divert funds away from profits to serve their own self-interests—that is, to enhance their own utility. Among other things, the funds are used to pursue the five Ps of increased pay, perquisites, power, prestige, and patronage. In a sense, managers absorb profits in the process of increasing their own utility by maximizing the amount of discretionary expenditures.

The ability of managers to provide stockholders with less than the maximum amount of profits stems from the existence of an asymmetry of information between the stockholders and the managers regarding firm performance. Stockholders do not always have the means to fully monitor activities of managers and ensure that they are providing the maximum amount of profits. Managers are afforded a certain amount of freedom to run the firm, provided stockholders receive what they consider an acceptable level of profits.

In the context of the model we have been working with, managerial expense preference behavior suggests that managers maximize discretionary expenditures by choosing the profit-maximizing level of output and price and then absorbing the profits through discretionary expenditures. The pursuit of discretionary expenditures can be treated as a kind of rent-seeking behavior because managers are attempting to obtain a bigger slice of the pie for themselves rather than trying to enlarge the size of the pie. Figure 13–4 illustrates this rent-seeking process. For simplicity's sake, assume marginal cost is constant and equals average cost. As such, the marginal and average cost curves are the same and horizontal and represented by MC_{true} in Figure 13–4. The MC_{true} curve reflects the true costs that exhibit production efficiency.

To maximize discretionary expenditures, the difference between revenue and the true cost of production, the firm follows the typical profit maximization rule, producing at the Q_0 level of output and charging P_0. However, instead of reflecting excess profits, the rectangle P_0AEC_{EXP} represents the amount of profits managers absorb as discretionary expenditures or income. In the process of enhancing their own utility, managers drive up the cost of production in the form of discretionary expenditures. The point

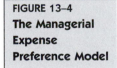

FIGURE 13–4

The Managerial Expense Preference Model

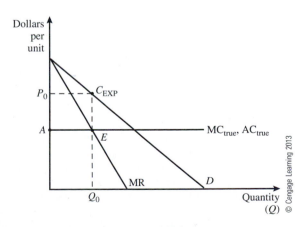

A not-for-profit hospital that maximizes discretionary profits will choose to produce at Q_0 where $MR = MC$ just like an otherwise comparable for-profit hospital. The difference is that the not-for-profit hospital uses the discretionary profits to finance unnecessary expenditures and thereby raises the "observed" costs of production to C_{EXP}, a point above the true costs of production. The not-for-profit hospital reports the same price and quantity of services as the for-profit hospital but shows no economic profit.

C_{EXP} represents the "observed" average cost of production after the expense preference behavior of managers has been taken into account.

The vertical distance between points E and C_{EXP} (or that between A and P_0) represents the inefficiencies brought about by expense preference behavior. The firm reports a normal profit rather than excess profits. In a different context, this type of inefficiency has been referred to as X-inefficiency (Leibenstein, 1966). The inefficiency exists because managers of firms with some market power may not have the incentive to employ inputs efficiently. Inputs are either overemployed or are not used to their fullest potential. In addition, managers may pay input prices beyond the necessary amount.

The managerial expense preference model has some interesting implications. The model suggests that managers consciously drive up the cost of production in an attempt to further their own self-interests. The model can also help explain the behavior of not-for-profit firms. Surprisingly, the expense preference model suggests that managers of not-for-profit firms act much like their counterparts at for-profit firms; that is, they maximize profits. The difference lies in the extent to which managers absorb profits as discretionary income. Since not-for-profit providers are prohibited by law from distributing profits to external parties, all the profits can be diverted by managers. As a result, we should observe not-for-profit firms having higher costs than for-profit firms that are closely controlled by profit-conscious owners, *ceteris paribus*. The cost differential reflects the wider latitude that not-for-profit managers are given to absorb profits. The fact that some of these profits are spent on additional personnel and equipment may help explain the duplication of resources in the health care sector.

In conclusion, utility maximization models have many positive attributes. First, they explain how firm behavior is affected when managers address their own utility functions rather than attempting to maximize profits. Behavior other than profit maximization is important to understand because a significant proportion of health care providers function in not-for-profit settings. Second, the models explain why the health care sector may tend toward duplication of resources and overspecialization, as in the case of the market for hospital services. Third, utility maximization models help explain why health care costs have increased over the years, at least until most recently. Managers who seek to advance their personal goals, such as maximizing the quality of output at the expense of profits, are not likely to be overly concerned with the impact any policy change may have on the financial "bottom line." A lack of concern for the bottom line naturally causes the cost of medical care to increase.

Market Concentration and Hospital Behavior

Another conduct issue of interest to economists and policy makers is the impact of market concentration on the price, cost, and quality of hospital care. The issue is whether lower prices and higher levels of quality result in a market where output is concentrated among a few large firms or dispersed among a relatively large number of smaller firms. In hospital services markets characterized by insured consumers, not-for-profit entities, government-regulated prices, MCOs, and informational asymmetries, economic theory alone cannot predict the impact of increased market concentration on societal welfare, so we must turn our attention to empirical studies on the relationship.

Economists investigating the impact of market concentration on hospital behavior tend to examine the periods before and after the mid-1980s. The mid-1980s acts as the cutoff because, after that period, prospective payment systems like the DRG system began to replace cost-based systems, the market share of for-profit hospital increased in many market areas, and enrollments in MCOs started to explode. In simple terms, health care payers became more price conscious, and hospital competition changed from being patient driven to being payer driven (Dranove et al., 1993).

Studies using data prior to the mid-1980s found evidence to support a "medical arms race" among hospitals in more competitive areas (Robinson and Luft, 1985).

According to the medical arms race hypothesis, hospitals in more competitive areas provide physicians with greater levels of hospital quality in the form of advanced medical technologies, excess bed capacity, and amenities in return for admitting their patients. The higher quality shows up as increased costs of producing hospital services. In support of the medical arms race hypothesis, many studies using data prior to the mid-1980s find empirical evidence linking increased competition (a lower value for the HHI) with increased hospital costs (Hersch, 1984; Robinson and Luft, 1985; White, 1987; Noether, 1988; Fournier and Mitchell, 1992), lower levels of technical efficiency (Wilson and Jadlow, 1982), greater excess bed capacity (Joskow, 1980; Farley, 1985), and a larger number of duplicate specialized services in local markets (Farley, 1985; Dranove et al., 1992).

After the mid-1980s, with heightened payer-driven competition, empirical studies no longer found support for the medical arms race. For example, using data for 1987, Melnick et al. (1992) determine that more hospital competition resulted in a lower Blue Cross preferred provider organization (PPO) negotiated price for hospital services in California. Further studies using data after 1990 find that increased hospital competition improves technical efficiency (Rosko, 2001), reduces excess capacity (Santerre and Adams, 2002), lowers hospital prices (Town and Vistnes, 2001) and hospital costs, and results in lower rates of adverse outcomes (Kessler and McClellan, 2000).[1]

By analyzing the impact of hospital consolidations during the 1990s, we can obtain further information about the effects of market structure on hospital prices, costs, and quality of care. Recall from Chapter 9 that hospital consolidations can have procompetitive or anticompetitive impacts on consumer welfare. Dranove and Lindrooth (2003) provide an insightful analysis of hospital consolidations by distinguishing between hospital acquisitions and mergers. In the case of an acquisition, two hospitals become commonly owned within the same system but have separate licenses for reporting and regulatory purposes. Acquisitions involve hospitals in different areas so clinical consolidations do not take place. In contrast, hospital mergers involve the combination of separate facility licenses into a single license. The merged organization issues a single financial or utilization report and is regulated as a single entity for CON and other purposes. Hospitals that merge together are generally in close geographical proximity and therefore may gain from reorganization and clinical consolidations.

Dranove and Lindrooth compare the costs of real hospital consolidations to equivalent hypothetical consolidations from one year prior to the consolidation to four years after the consolidation. The hypothetical consolidations reflect hospitals that did not combine but had similar characteristics to those that actually did combine over the same period. These researchers use national data for independent hospitals that consolidated some time during 1989 to 1996. They find that consolidation into systems does not generate savings even after four years. Mergers, in contrast, result in savings for two or more years after consolidation. Dranove and Lindrooth argue that system consolidations do "not yield synergistic cost savings, perhaps reflecting the difficulty of achieving efficiencies without combining operations. An actual merger is a big step, requiring giving up a license (with the high cost of going back) and usually senior managers. Hospitals do not merge unless they could confidently pull it off" (p. 996).

But are the cost savings from mergers passed on to the buyers of hospital care? To answer that question, Capps and Dranove (2004) examine the before and after effects of hospital consolidations on actual negotiated PPO prices in four market areas of the United States during the period 1997 to 2001. The results of their multiple regression analysis, which controls for quality of care, patient case-mix, and other factors, suggest that most consolidating hospitals raise price by more than the median price increase in

---

1. But see Dranove, Lindrooth, White, and Zwanziger (2008). For a sample of California and Florida hospitals, they find that increased competition no longer had a dampening effect on price during the 2001 to 2003 period because of the backlash against restrictive managed care plans.

their markets. Overall, they report that their findings do not support the argument that efficiencies from consolidations among competing hospitals lead to lower prices. Rather, their results are broadly consistent with consolidations among competing hospitals leading to higher prices because of enhanced market power.

The empirical literature concerning the impact of hospital consolidations on the quality of care is less extensive. Ho and Hamilton (2000) determine empirically that consolidation has no measurable impact on the inpatient mortality of heart attack and stroke patients but find some evidence linking consolidation to higher hospital readmission rates and early discharges. Cuellar and Gertler (2005) study the effect of consolidation on three types of quality: (1) rates of inpatient mortality following certain hospital conditions and procedures; (2) rates of procedures considered overused; and (3) patient safety indicators. They find that rates of avoidable inpatient mortality and inadequate safety did not change after consolidation for either indemnity or managed care patients. However, for managed care patients, consolidation did reduce the rate of overutilized procedures. Thus, the few existing studies do not find strong evidence suggesting that hospital consolidation significantly improves the quality of care.

Hospital Ownership and Hospital Behavior

Recall that property rights theory argues that for-profit hospitals behave differently from not-for-profit hospitals because the latter face a nondistribution constraint. It is illegal for a not-for-profit hospital to distribute any residual of revenues over costs, which represent profits to a for-profit hospital, to outside parties. The residual must be retained and used to support the purpose for which the not-for-profit hospital was formed. For example, the residual might be used to expand the facilities of the hospital, purchase new equipment, or pay for the hospital care of indigent individuals.

Because of the nondistribution constraint, it is sometimes argued that not-for-profit and government hospitals face less of an incentive than for-profit hospitals to behave efficiently because of the absence of outside owners or residual claimants who face a strong, direct financial incentive to monitor activities and who are able to discipline management when deviations from cost minimization occur. Thus, the property rights theory suggests that not-for-profit hospitals may operate with higher costs than otherwise similar for-profit hospitals, as the previously discussed expense preference model predicts.

Also, public choice theorists point out that public hospitals lack a further incentive to minimize the cost of production. Unlike private hospitals (both for-profit and not-for-profit), public hospitals can rely to some extent on direct funding from the government in addition to patient-driven revenues. As a result, public hospitals are not at the complete mercy of the marketplace to minimize costs, unlike private hospitals. Keep in mind, however, that public hospitals are typically monitored directly by elected or appointed committees and those participating on the committees may wish to be reelected or reappointed to their positions. The threat of losing their position on the committee may give them a stakeholder (rather than stockholder) interest in the efficient operation of the hospital. If so, one type of incentive system and disciplining mechanism simply replaces the other.

Property rights theory also suggests that the quality of care might be lower in for-profit hospitals than otherwise similar not-for-profit and public hospitals. To make greater profits, for-profit hospitals may face an incentive to skimp or cut corners on quality, especially quality of care that cannot be easily monitored by outside individuals. In contrast, not-for-profit hospitals, because of the attenuation of property rights, face less of an incentive to sacrifice quality for the sake of profits. This would be particularly true for situations where quality of care enters the utility function of the managers running the not-for-profit hospitals.

Given the theoretical discussion, it should not be too surprising that a relatively large amount of research has examined whether ownership status affects price, costs, and quality of care. Taken as a whole, most studies do not find any sizeable differences in efficiency across hospitals with different ownership types. The cost differences that are sometimes observed can usually be explained by unmeasurable variations in quality. Although for-profit hospitals tend to charge higher prices, the price differences can often be explained by the fact that not-for-profit hospitals do not pay most taxes, borrow at lower interest rates because interest on their bonds is tax exempt, and receive donations from outside parties.[2]

Other explanations exist for the cost and price similarity observed in hospitals with different types of ownership. Sloan (1988) argues that physicians on the medical staff may act as residual claimants in not-for-profit hospitals and thus "have a financial stake in keeping such hospitals efficient. Inefficient hospitals are candidates for acquisition by for-profit hospitals" (p. 138). Pauly (1987) claims there is little theoretical justification to assert that not-for-profit hospitals do not minimize production costs. Consider a not-for-profit hospital that maximizes output. Although the managers are not maximizing profits, they still face an incentive to produce output as cheaply as possible. An incentive to minimize costs exists because more output can be produced from a given budget if managers keep per-unit costs to a minimum. The similarity of outcomes may also be explained by the fact that hospitals, regardless of ownership, are actually organized as physician cooperatives with the (for-profit) objective of maximizing the combined incomes of staff physicians (Pauly and Redish, 1973). Finally, various analysts note that market competition forces hospitals of all ownership forms to produce as cheaply as possible and charge reasonable prices. High-cost, high priced hospitals do not survive in competitive markets.

Economists have conducted much less research on quality-of-care differences across hospitals of different ownership types (Sloan, 2000). Representative of the few conducted, in terms of empirical results, Sloan et al. (2001) compare probability of death at one month, six months, and one year following admission into public, for-profit, and not-for-profit hospitals. After holding constant other determinants of mortality, the authors find no discernible difference in mortality rates between hospitals with different ownership forms.

While costs, prices, and quality of care tend to be reasonably similar across differently owned hospitals, most studies find that public hospitals are much more likely to provide greater amounts of uncompensated care. Uncompensated care is usually defined as bad debts and charity and is measured as a percent of total hospital expenses. As evidence, Mann et al. (1997) estimate that uncompensated care as a percentage of expenses was 15.4 and 6.3 percent for urban public and rural public hospitals, respectively, in 1994. The comparable figures for not-for-profit and for-profit were 5.0 and 4.2 percent, respectively. Not surprisingly, public hospitals have been dubbed the "hospital provider of last resort" or "safety net" because of their charitable nature. In fact, one study finds that private hospitals provide less uncompensated care when a public general hospital exists in the area (Thorpe and Brecher, 1987).

These figures on uncompensated care help motivate two other interesting questions. First, why do for-profit hospitals provide any uncompensated care at all? Supposedly, the business of for-profit hospitals is business and therefore the maximization of profits or stockholder wealth. Providing care to the indigent subtracts from maximum profits

---

2. But see Sloan et al. (2001), who find that payments on behalf of Medicare patients admitted to for-profit hospitals during the first six months following a health shock were higher than those admitted to not-for-profit and public hospitals. They argue that the higher payment to for-profits "plausibly reflects their greater incentive to maximize reimbursements from payers by various means including formal and informal contractual relationships with other suppliers of health care services" (p. 18).

and reduces the return to owners. However, Herzlinger and Krasker (1987) point out for-profit hospitals may provide some uncompensated care because "hospital costs are mostly fixed and the marginal costs of an additional patient-day, generally low. Even an indigent patient contributes somewhat to covering the hospital's fixed costs" (p. 103). In addition, providing uncompensated care may favorably impact a for-profit hospital's relationship with regulatory agencies and the community at large.

The second question deals with not-for-profit hospitals. One reason not-for-profit hospitals are granted tax-exempt status is because they are supposed to apply any unused revenues (or profits) toward the express purpose for which they were formed. Not-for-profit hospitals are formed to provide medical care to the sick and needy and are responsible to the community at large. Therefore, not-for-profit hospitals are expected to provide charitable care and other community benefits. The fact that their uncompensated care is only 5 percent of expenses and quite close to that of for-profit hospitals raises the question whether the tax-exempt status of not-for-profit hospitals should be revoked. In fact, state and local governments in Texas, Pennsylvania, and Utah, among others, have introduced legislation intended to pressure not-for-profit hospitals into providing more charity care. Not-for-profit hospitals would be required to prove that they benefit their areas or lose their tax exemption.

Morrisey et al. (1996) demonstrate that the concern about the tax-exempt status of not-for-profit hospitals may be warranted. They compare the amount of uncompensated care to the estimated tax subsidy that each not-for-profit hospital receives and find that nearly 20 percent of all not-for-profit hospitals do not provide uncompensated care sufficient to compensate for the tax subsidies they receive.

Taking the analysis a step further, Nicholson et al. (2000) argue that the dollar value of the tax exemption to not-for-profit hospitals should be compared to total community benefits rather than to the value of uncompensated care. Since not-for-profit hospitals do not have to return profits to residual claimants as for-profits do, the authors note that not-for-profits should be expected to provide community benefits equal to those provided by for-profit hospitals plus the profits these hospitals earn. Based on data for the three largest for-profit hospital systems over the period 1996 to 1998, they find that community benefits (taxes plus estimated cost of uncompensated care) and profits as a percentage of equity and assets equaled 30 and 10 percent, respectively. When applied to the equity and assets of an average not-for-profit hospital, these percentages imply that a not-for-profit would be expected to spend $9.1 to $13.2 million on community benefits per year, yet uncompensated care accounts for only about $3.3 million. Even after accounting for a host of other public benefits the typical not-for-profit might provide, such as subsidized medical research and price discounts, the authors write that "not-for-profit hospitals appear to fall far short of providing the expected level of community benefit that would justify current levels of investment" (p. 176).

Managed Care Buyers and Hospital Behavior

Another interesting aspect of hospital conduct is the relation between MCOs, such as HMOs and PPOs, and hospital behavior. The question is whether managed care provides the proper incentives for efficiency without seriously sacrificing quality. Most of the research on the relation between MCOs and hospital behavior has examined the effect of HMOs on hospital costs, utilization rates, or the quality of health outcomes. In general, studies suggest that HMO hospitalization rates are about 15 to 20 percent lower than those of traditional insurance plans after controlling for a host of health-related factors, including ages of the patients, case-mix, severity of illnesses, and hospital-specific influences (Luft, 1981; Manning et al., 1984; Dowd et al., 1991; Miller and Luft, 1994). Moreover, studies imply that the lower hospitalization rates tend to hold for most types of HMOs (Bradbury et al., 1991;

Dowd et al., 1991). Even among intensive care patients, a setting that appears to allow very little room for discretion in treatment decisions, some evidence indicates that managed care results in cost savings when compared to traditional insurance (Rapoport et al., 1992).

Another line of research investigates the effect of MCOs on the degree of technical inefficiency practiced by hospitals. Technical inefficiency occurs when hospitals use more inputs than technically necessary to produce their products, such as inpatient and outpatient care, or fail to produce the maximum amount of products with a given amount of inputs. As mentioned previously, MCOs are supposed to emphasize cost-effective methods of production and use various management strategies and financial incentives to align health care provider interests, such as hospitals, with technical efficiency. Assuming hospitals otherwise face some organizational slack, these cost-effective practices and strategies of MCOs are expected to improve technical efficiency.

Rosko (2001) examines the impact of HMO penetration on technical inefficiency using a national sample of nearly 2,000 urban hospitals in 1997. Rosko finds empirically that increased HMO penetration is associated with less technical inefficiency at the hospital level. Brown (2003) examines the effects of enrollments in both HMOs and PPOs on technical inefficiency using a production function approach and a panel data set of 613 hospitals over the five-year period from 1992 to 1996. Brown shows overall that greater enrollment in both HMOs and PPOs is associated with increased hospital efficiency at the margin. Finally, Bates et al. (2006) find evidence of increased technical efficiency at the industry level in states characterized by more HMO activity and increased health insurer concentration. Taken together, these three studies suggest that greater pressure from HMOs improves the degree of technical efficiency experienced by hospitals.

Research also indicates that inpatient outcomes are not systematically worse (Retchin and Brown, 1991; Carlisle et al., 1992; Retchin et al., 1992; Miller and Luft, 1994; Miller and Luft, 2002) for HMOs compared to traditional insurance coverage, although some disagreement remains about the care of low-income patients in HMOs (compare Ware et al. [1986] and Greenwald and Henke [1992]). Most studies do report worse results on many measures of access to care and lower levels of satisfaction for HMO enrollees (Miller and Luft, 2002). The relatively comparable level of quality has surprised some critics of HMOs because they suspected that the scope and mission of these institutions creates an incentive for an underproduction of care. A number of empirical and theoretical factors may account for the quality-of-care similarity in MCO and non-MCO plans. First, empirically it is very difficult to distinguish among health plans in practice, especially when health insurers have multiple plans and health care providers treat patients belonging to a number of alternative plans. Quality of care may appear similar because the observations are wrongly assigned into MCO and non-MCO plans.

Second, some MCOs are structured as not-for-profit institutions. For example, 42 percent of all HMO enrollees received their care from organizations that were structured as not-for-profit in 1994 (Corrigan et al., 1997). Many researchers argue that not-for-profit institutions pursue goals other than profit maximization, as we discussed earlier in this chapter. If not-for-profit MCOs attempt to maximize some other objective rather than the "bottom line," it is not theoretically apparent why the quality of care in those MCOs should differ from that of traditional indemnity insurers.

Third, like traditional plans, MCOs often invest huge sums of money establishing brand names that can be tarnished by offering inferior care. The prospect of losing repeat buyers and not receiving a proper return on investment can place a considerable amount of pressure on MCOs to provide the proper level of care. Of course, well-informed consumers are necessary for that kind of pressure to materialize. In this regard, it would be interesting to know whether the constant attention given MCOs in the popular press and political arena has had any effect on the behavior and performance of MCOs.

Fourth, physicians that contract with MCOs likely subscribe to the same basic ethical code of conduct (such as the Hippocratic Oath) as the doctors that deal with traditional insurers. In fact, many physicians simultaneously contract with both types of insurers. Although doctors may find themselves pressured by the financial incentives and management strategies of MCOs at the margin, it is not clear theoretically whether these pressures dominate over ethical concerns, on average.

In contrast to HMOs, only a few studies assess the effect of PPOs on hospital utilization rates and expenditures. They fail to reach a consensus on the *overall* cost-containment effectiveness of PPOs. While Zwanziger and Auerbach (1991) report that PPOs lead to a reduction in inpatient expenditures, the increased expenditures stemming from expansions in outpatient benefits tend to swamp these cost savings (Hester et al., 1987; Diehr et al., 1990; Garnick et al., 1990).[3] According to Fielding and Rice (1993), PPOs are ineffective in controlling overall costs because the typical participating physician has only 11 enrollees from a particular PPO. Consequently, an individual PPO has limited ability to exert any buyer power over the prices and utilization practices of physicians.

Price Regulations and Hospital Behavior

Public policies may also affect the conduct of hospitals. In 1972, Congress passed Section 222 of the Social Security Amendments, giving states the authority to establish rate-setting programs (Anderson, 1991). By the late 1970s, more than 30 states had adopted some form of hospital rate-setting program (Coelen and Sullivan, 1981). However, only three of the states had a mandatory "all-payer" program that controlled rates for all patient groups, including private payers, commercially insured patients, patients with public insurance, and Blue Cross plans. By 1996 only one state, Maryland, still had an all-payer rate-setting program.

Proponents of rate-setting programs have argued that these programs can contain health care costs with no concomitant reduction in the quality of care because they view hospitals as operating with organizational slack. The organizational slack, taking form in such factors as higher than necessary hospital salaries, duplication of facilities, and unnecessary hospital amenities, results from imperfect markets or hospital objectives other than cost minimization. When slack is present, price regulations or ceilings may promote lower expenditures without an associated reduction in patient care.

Empirical studies have almost unanimously supported the view that state regulation of hospital fees can lower health care costs. For example, Lanning et al. (1991) find that states with mature rate-setting programs have 14.6 percent lower per capita health care expenditures than otherwise comparable states without such policies.[4] Schneider (2003) investigates the impact of mandatory rate regulation on hospital costs and finds lower hospital operating costs in states with all-payer price regulations but that the effect of rate regulation on hospital costs tended to decline after 1991. He points out that rate regulation may have accomplished its cost-control objective in the early years but the gains were not sustainable over time. At the same time, he discovers that hospitals in more concentrated hospital services markets tend to have increasingly higher operating costs over time. Overall, Schneider's results indicate "that the opportunity costs of hospital rate regulation increased as the cost-control effects of regulation lessened and the cost-control effects of a feasible organizational

---

3. But see Smith (1997/1998), who finds that, on average, PPOs were associated with cost savings of 12 percent per covered life as compared to traditional plans with utilization review. The cost savings result primarily from lower rates of physician visits and hospital admissions.

4. But see Antel et al. (1995). Earlier studies that did not control for the endogeneity of rate setting suggest that the percentage effect is much smaller, at about 2.0 to 4.1 percentage points (see Morrisey et al., 1984). Some empirical evidence (e.g., Romeo et al., 1984) has also linked states' prospective payment systems to a slower diffusion of new medical technologies, although the results are too limited to generalize.

alternative—competitive contracting—increased" (p. 310). As a result, many states abandoned their rate regulation programs and turned to managed care as a method of controlling hospital costs in the 1990s.

The findings of empirical studies focusing on the relation between rate setting and quality of care have been mixed, however. For example, Draper et al. (1990) and Kahn et al. (1990) conclude that the Medicare prospective payment system (PPS), which can be considered a federal rate-setting program, has contained hospital costs without generally lowering the quality of care for Medicare patients. However, a comparable study by Fitzgerald et al. (1988) finds that the overall care for Medicare patients with hip fracture has worsened since the implementation of PPS. Clearly, more studies are needed before we can make any generalizations about the relation between government rate-setting programs and the quality of care.

Cost Shifting Behavior

Because the federal government and various state governments are responsible for setting (rather than negotiating) reimbursement rates under the Medicare and Medicaid programs, some individuals believe that lower reimbursement rates for these public programs lead to higher prices paid by private payers. This practice is referred to as **cost shifting.** Ginsburg (2003) defines cost shifting "as the phenomenon in which changes in administered prices of one payer lead to compensating changes in prices charged to other payers" (p. 473). For example, hospitals raising prices paid by commercial insurers in response to a Medicare payment reduction provides an example of cost shifting.

Not all policy analysts, particularly economists, are convinced that cost shifting actually takes place. That's because private prices are normally set to maximize economic profits. As a result, raising private prices in response to public price cuts produces even lower profits because the quantity demanded for medical services falls as prices increase. The theory behind this view is provided in Figure 13–5. In the figure, the private-pay and public-pay submarkets of a local hospital industry are shown. For simplicity, we suppose that only Medicare patients constitute the public pay category and the marginal (and average) costs, MC, are constant and the same for treating both private-pay and Medicare patients.

In the graphical model on the right in Figure 13–5, the hospital is treated as a price taker with respect to Medicare patients. It is supposed that the federal government initially sets the fixed administered price, R_0, equal to the marginal costs of treating Medicare patients. The hospital is assumed to treat M_0 Medicare patients during the period. The graph on the left shows the initial equilibrium in the private-pay submarket (before cost shifting presumably takes place). It is assumed that the hospital has (or hospitals collectively have) some degree of market power, as reflected in the downward-sloping demand curve, D. It is further assumed (initially) that the hospital maximizes economic profits. As a result, the hospital treats the number of private-pay patients indicated by Q_0 where marginal revenue, MR, equals marginal cost, MC, and charges a price of P_0. Equilibrium in the private-pay submarket is thus represented by point A.

Now suppose the federal government lowers the Medicare reimbursement rate from R_0 to R_1 in the hopes of containing costs. Notice that when the Medicare payment rate declines to R_1, the hospital suffers a loss, L, equal to the rectangular area formed by the difference in per-unit costs and the reimbursement rate, bound by the number of Medicare patients treated. But we cannot rule out the possibility that hospitals respond to the lower Medicare reimbursement rate by releasing Medicare patients quicker and sicker or by dumping these patients onto other hospitals (although this practice is illegal).

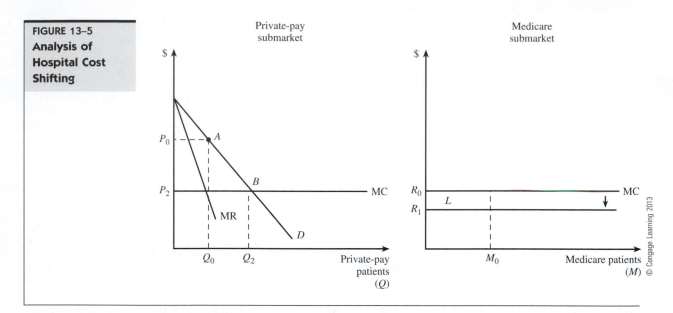

FIGURE 13–5
Analysis of Hospital Cost Shifting

Private-pay submarket

Medicare submarket

© Cengage Learning 2013

Suppose the two submarkets are in an initial equilibrium represented by R_0, the Medicare reimbursement rate, and point A. The latter point reflects that the hospital is initially operating at the profit-maximizing number of private-pay patients. If the government lowers the Medicare reimbursement rate to R_1, the hospital will not raise private price to finance the Medicare loss, L, because price is already at the profit-maximizing level in the private submarket. Hence, cost shifting does not occur in this case. However, if the hospital is initially operating with some unexploited market power, as at point B, where the number of private-pay patients is maximized (rather than profits), hospitals may raise price in response to the Medicare loss. Thus, cost shifting can occur. The ability to raise price in this case depends on the magnitude of the price elasticity of demand.

It is this loss that the hospital may prefer to shift elsewhere. But notice that the hospital faces no incentive to raise price for private payers because profits have already been maximized. That's because a price above P_0 results in fewer private patients treated and lower profits because MR > MC. Hence, cost shifting is irrational under this situation.

To successfully practice cost shifting, Morrisey (2003) explains that hospitals must "have market power that heretofore [they] had not exploited." He goes on to note, "If providers have market power and, indeed, have not charged private insurers 'what the traffic will bear,' then cost shifting can exist—even as a matter of theory" (p. 490). The downward-sloping private-pay demand curve in Figure 13–5 fulfills the first condition that the hospital possesses market power. Now rather than maximizing economic profits, assume that the hospital, as a not-for-profit organization, maximizes the number of patients treated subject to a break-even level of profits. As we saw earlier in this chapter, maximizing an objective other than profits is consistent with the view that not-for-profit organizations face a nondistribution constraint and cannot legally distribute any excess earnings to residual claimants. Maximization of the number of patients is also consistent with the view that not-for-profit hospital administrators and board members may derive personal utility from directing large enterprises.

Point B represents the equilibrium at which the hospital maximizes the number of patients treated subject to a break-even level of profits and therefore initially operates with some unexploited market power. In this case, the hospital treats Q_2 private-pay patients where demand intersects marginal cost and charges a price of P_2. Notice that at Q_2, the chosen number of patients exceeds the number that maximizes economic profits where marginal revenue, MR, equals marginal costs. At point B, the hospital initially earns a normal profit on both private-pay and Medicare patients.

Now suppose the government lowers the Medicare reimbursement rate from R_0 to R_1. In this case, because the hospital initially operates with some unexploited market power, it might respond to the lower Medicare reimbursement rate by raising price above P_2 but not greater than P_0, the price that maximizes profits. It follows theoretically that cost shifting can take place if hospitals initially operate with some amount of unexploited market power.

Curious about the degree to which the practice actually occurs in the United States, researchers have subjected the theory of cost shifting to empirical testing. At best, the empirical evidence regarding hospital cost shifting behavior has been mixed. Two papers by Hadley and Feder (1985) and Zwanziger et al. (2000) attest to the ongoing nature of the cost shifting discussion (from 1985 to 2000) and the general inconclusiveness of the empirical findings. Specifically, Hadley and Feder find that hospital markups on private payers did not vary systematically with revenue pressure in the United States. Instead, hospitals respond to revenue pressure by taking several actions to reduce costs, including reducing personnel, postponing employee pay increases, and limiting charity care. Zwanziger et al. find empirically that both for-profit and not-for-profit hospitals increased private-pay prices in response to Medicare payment rate reductions.

Thus, economic theory suggests that hospital cost shifting can take place under certain limited conditions, and some empirical evidence suggests that it may have occurred in practice. We must remember, however, that hospitals can engage in cost shifting behavior only when they possess a sufficient amount of market power. That is, hospitals must be able to raise their prices above the competitive level when confronted with losses from treating public-pay patients. When private buyers of medical services, such as individual MCOs, also possess market power on the demand side of the market, hospitals may be unable to negotiate higher prices. Thus, many economists believe that cost shifting is less likely to occur in today's health economy because of the buying clout of many MCOs. Frakt (2011) concludes his extensive review of the literature on hospital cost shifting by writing: "Policymakers should view with a degree of skepticism most hospital and insurance industry claims of inevitable, large-scale cost shifting. Although some cost shifting may result from changes in public payment policy, it is just one of many possible effects. Moreover, changes in the balance of market power between hospitals and health care plans also significantly affect private prices. Since they may increase hospitals' market power, provisions of the new health reform law that may encourage greater provider integration and consolidation should be implemented with caution" (pp. 90–91).

Summary of the Conduct of the Hospital Services Market

A number of structural and related factors simultaneously influence the conduct of hospitals in the marketplace. The degree of actual competition, barriers to entry, reimbursement practices of third-party payers, and hospital objectives jointly affect how an individual hospital behaves, and therefore only carefully conceived studies can sort out how any individual factor influences hospital conduct. Most empirical studies using data prior to 1983 have found that hospitals competed on the basis of quality rather than price, but recent evidence suggests that the growing price consciousness among health care payers may be causing increased price competition among hospitals.

Empirical evidence also suggests that efficiency differences are quite small among not-for-profit, public, and for-profit hospitals, especially after controlling for quality and case-mix differences. The reason cited for the similarity is that physicians act as residual claimants in not-for-profit hospitals and thus ensure that the hospitals behave as efficiently as possible. The provision of indigent care has been found to be considerably higher in public hospitals than in otherwise identical not-for-profit and for-profit hospitals. In addition, the amount of indigent care has been found to be quite similar for not-for-profit and for-profit hospitals, raising doubt about the desirability of the tax-exempt status generally conferred on not-for-profit hospitals.

MCOs appear to offer modest hospital cost savings without reducing the quality of patient outcomes compared to traditional fee-for-service medicine. HMOs appear to provide more consistent cost savings than PPOs, however. State rate-review programs have also proven effective in containing hospital care costs. However, studies investigating the effect of state rate review policies on the quality of hospital outcomes have failed to reach a definitive conclusion. In addition, the cost containment effects of rate programs appear to have waned in recent years, at least compared to the same effects from MCOs.

The Performance of the Hospital Services Industry

This final section focuses on the aggregate performance of the hospital services industry. While it might be best to analyze the performance of the hospital industry in each state or, perhaps, in each metropolitan area in the United States given the structural diversity of hospital markets, the analysis would be unwieldy and the necessary data are less widely available at a disaggregated level. As a result, we examine and discuss various trends relating to the growth of hospital expenditures, hospital price inflation rate, and hospital profits over time to get some idea about the aggregate performance of the hospital services industry in the United States.

The Growth in Hospital Expenditures

Over the last few decades, expenditures on hospital services, which include spending on both inpatient and outpatient services, have tended to comprise about 30 to 36 percent of all health care spending, making it the dominant expense of most health care payers. The big-ticket aspect of hospital spending should not be surprising given the fact that the severely ill typically receive hospital care. Also, the technologically intensive method of delivering most types of hospital care requires much spending. Table 13–2 reveals that nominal hospital care expenditures in the United States rose dramatically from $9 billion in 1960 to $814 billion in 2010. As a fraction of gross

---

TABLE 13–2

Hospital Expenditures in the United States, Selected Years, 1960–2010

Year	Total Hospital Expenditures (billions of dollars)	Spending as a Percentage of Gross Domestic Product
1960	$ 9.0	1.7%
1970	27.6	2.6
1980	101.5	3.6
1990	253.9	4.3
1995	343.6	4.6
2000	413.1	4.2
2005	605.5	4.8
2010	814.0	5.6

SOURCE: Center for Medicare & Medicaid Services, http://www.cms.gov (accessed January 12, 2012).

domestic product (GDP), hospital care spending also increased but not steadily throughout the 50-year period. In particular, notice in the table that hospital care spending spurted upward from 1.7 to 4.6 percent of the nation's income over the period from 1960 to the mid-1990s.

However, after that period, hospital care spending declined as a percentage of GDP to 4.2 percent in 2000. As mentioned previously, the middle to late 1990s represents the heyday of managed care. The success of managed care at controlling hospital costs during the heyday shows up in the lower percentage of GDP allocated to health care. But the lower hospital spending could also reflect overall changes in the production of medical care. For example, the push to outpatient care services may have resulted in lost hospital revenues as physician practices took over some of this business. Also, the greater use of skilled nursing homes, rather than hospitals, for rehabilitative care may have reduced the revenues of hospitals.

After 2000, hospital care costs as a percentage of GDP renewed its upward trend, rising to 5.6 percent by 2010. The upward trend may reflect the backlash against restrictive managed care plans as insured individuals moved into less restrictive plans with looser networks of physician and hospital providers. Alternatively, the relative increase in hospital spending may reflect that restrictive managed care plans were only able to squeeze out some short-run inefficiencies and that new medical technologies eventually set in motion a long-term increase in hospital spending.

As you are well aware, hospital expenditures equal the product of the price and quantity of hospital services. As yet, we do not know whether the change in hospital expenditures over time is attributable to higher price changes or an increased quantity of services. This is an important consideration because, first, a greater quantity of hospital services may make people better off, whereas price increases have the opposite effect of reducing real incomes and consumer welfare. Second, as mentioned earlier, various structural elements of health care markets, such as extensive third-party coverage, may give rise to the overproduction of hospital services at the expense of all other goods and services and thereby result in allocative inefficiency. Thus, to get a better understanding of hospital expenditure growth, we next examine trends in the hospital services price inflation rate.

The Hospital Services Price Inflation Rate

Expenditures on many types of products can be easily broken down into their price and quantity components. The decomposition of hospital care expenditures into its quantity and price components is much more complicated because of the intangible and heterogeneous nature of hospital services. Yet conceptually, we know that an implicit price and an implicit quantity of services exist for every amount of hospital care spending.

Beginning in 1997, the Bureau of Labor Statistics (BLS) collected data from hospitals to construct a "hospital services" price index that reflected a hospital visit defined by a date of admission, a date of discharge as documented on a hospital bill, and the specific diagnosis or medical condition.[5] Now, BLS staff members select a sample of hospital bills based on revenues generated by eligible payers (i.e., privately insured and uninsured patients). Then the field staff describes the item in terms of the bundle of goods and services consumed during that visit. The goal of the hospital services index is to follow the transaction prices of selected services over time while keeping constant price-determining characteristics such as length of stay and the medical reason for the visit. The transaction price is the actual amount the hospital receives from the insurance carrier and/or the patient's out-of-pocket payments.

---

5. See the description of the medical price index and its components at the BLS web site, http://www.bls.gov/cpi/cpifact4.htm (accessed January 14, 2012).

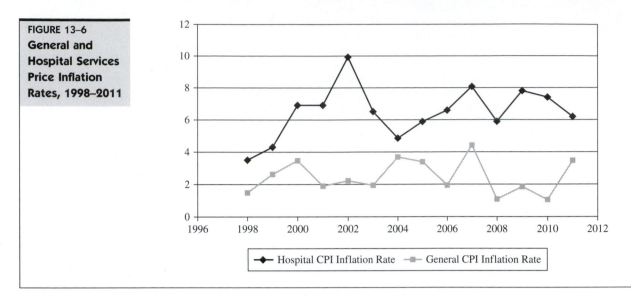

FIGURE 13–6

General and Hospital Services Price Inflation Rates, 1998–2011

SOURCE: U.S. Department of Labor, Bureau of Labor Statistics, http://www.bls.gov (accessed January 12, 2012).

Be aware that adjustments in the price index from one year to the next may be misstated if the quality of goods and services also changes over time. For instance, health outcomes may improve over time as medical care becomes more effective at saving lives, perhaps as health care production moves down the learning curve. The inability to control for quality of outcomes raises concern about the reliability of medical price indices. Nevertheless, the medical price indices reported by BLS continue to be used for private and public policy purposes because they are the best currently available on a systematic basis.

Figure 13–6 shows the general price inflation rate, as measured by the percentage change in the urban consumer price index, and the hospital services price inflation rate over the period from 1998 to 2011. The figure indicates that the hospital services inflation rate exceeded the general price inflation rate in every year, averaging 6.5 percent compared to only 2.4 percent for all goods and services over the entire period. In addition, the hospital services price inflation rate seems much more volatile than the general price inflation rate ranging from a low of 3.5 percent in 1998 to a high of percent of 9.9 percent in 2002. Economists point out that volatile prices tend to make long-run investment planning much more difficult for decision makers. Finally, the figure suggests that the volatility of the hospital services inflation rate has moderated somewhat since 2005, hovering between 6 and 8 percent.

Overall, the time-series data for the hospital services inflation rate suggest that hospital prices have risen more quickly than most other prices in the U.S. economy over the last 13 years. Unfortunately, the data cannot identify the source of the relative price increase in the hospital sector. Lack of a profit motive, fee-for-service medicine, generous insurance coverage, quality competition, and unbridled hospital pricing power could all conceivably contribute to the relatively high and rising hospital inflation rate in the United States. However, the normal functioning of a market economy may also explain rising hospital prices. That is, relative prices normally rise for goods and services that become more highly valued or more costly to produce than others. Information on marginal social benefit and cost is needed before one can determine whether hospital services are efficiently produced or not.

Do Hospitals Provide Flat-of-the-Curve or Ineffective Medicine?

Another way to examine if hospital services are produced efficiently, that doesn't involve a consideration of marginal social costs and benefits, is to study the marginal productivity or the effectiveness of the care that patients receive. A necessary (but not a sufficient) condition for efficiency is that the marginal productivity of hospital care is greater than zero. Recall in Chapter 2 that some studies have provided evidence for flat-of-the-curve medicine as the marginal product of medical care is estimated to be close to zero. Overly-generous health insurance and caring rather than curing is often pointed to as reasons behind the marginal ineffectiveness of medical care.

Several studies have well-documented the wide variation in Medicare spending across different regions of the United States (Congressional Budget Office, 2008). For example, Medicare beneficiaries in high-spending areas are found to receive about 60 percent more services than otherwise comparable Medicare recipients in low-spending areas (Fisher et al., 2003a). Some researchers have used these variations in Medicare spending to explore the relationship between medical spending and health care outcomes. In particular, Fisher et al. (2003a, 2003b) examine whether regions with higher Medicare spending are characterized by better quality of care, better survival chances, improved functional status, or greater satisfaction with care. They focus on differences in costs and outcomes of care separately for hip fracture, colorectal cancer, and myocardial infarction. These two studies by Fisher et al. offer a number of valuable insights into the relation between Medicare spending and health outcomes.

First, the authors find that greater regional spending on Medicare can be largely explained by practice patterns that involve more inpatient services and specialty care. That is, differences in spending primarily result from more frequent physician visits, specialist consultations, tests, and minor procedures, and greater use of the hospital and intensive care units. Second, they note that Medicare enrollees in higher-spending regions tend to receive more care than those in lower-spending regions but do not have better health outcomes or satisfaction with care. Three, neither quality of care nor access to care appear to be better for Medicare enrollees in higher-spending regions, all other factors held constant.

Skinner et al. (2006) argue that these variations exist across regions because each area develops its own local constrained production function relating medical care spending to health outcomes. Health production functions may be constrained, according to these authors, "because lack of knowledge and skills, or poor organizational structure, could prevent health care systems from attaining the efficient (and perhaps hypothetical) 'best practice' production function" (p. W47). Figure 13–7, which depicts three different total product curves for medical spending, helps to shed some light on their argument. (Consult Chapter 2 if you are rusty about total product curves.) We begin by supposing that two regions face the same total product curve, TP_0, at the beginning of some period and that both regions initially choose to operate at point A with M_0 amount of medical spending and its associated level of health outcomes as represented by H_0.

Then, we allow for a different set of new medical technologies to be adopted over time in the two regions. The new medical technologies may simply take the form of different methods of delivering medicine. Specifically, suppose that Region 2 adopts a set of low-cost, highly-effective procedures that shift its total product curve upward to TP_2. Perhaps, these new procedures mean a less hospital-intensive practice style. As a result, Region 2 moves from point A to point C on TP_2 and the level of medical care spending increases by a relatively small amount to M_2 and level of health improves substantially to H_2. Region 1, in contrast, chooses a set of relatively high-cost, less-effective medical procedures. For example, several new hospitals, with lots of modern medical equipment and many unfilled beds, may be constructed in Region 1. If so, Regions 1's total product curve also shifts upward because of the new medical

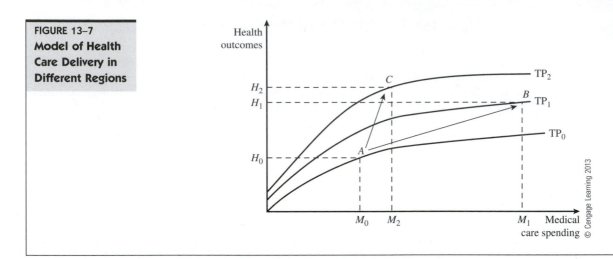

FIGURE 13–7
Model of Health Care Delivery in Different Regions

Suppose two regions initially operate at point A on total product curve TP_0. Both regions subsequently adopt new medical technologies with Region 1 choosing high-cost, low-quality technologies and Region 2 selecting low-cost, high-quality technologies. As a result Region 2's total product curve shifts upward to TP_2, whereas Region 1's total product curve only shifts upward to TP_1. Given the new total product curves, Region 2 moves from point A to point C and Region 1 shifts from point A to point B. While health improves in both areas, it appears that an inverse relationship exists between medical care spending and health outcomes.

technologies, but only to TP_1. Based upon its choice of medical technologies, Region 1 moves from point A to point B with a much increased level of medical spending relative to Region 2 and less of an improvement in health. Skinner et al. note that this model reconciles the cross-sectional evidence that an inverse correlation exists between medical spending and health outcomes, as can be seen by comparing points B and C to point A. At the same time, the model also reconciles the time-series evidence that, on average, everyone is made better off over time because of new medical technologies, but that regional gains are not correlated with regional spending increases.

Fisher et al. (2003a) conclude their study by writing, "These findings call into question the notion that additional growth in health care spending is primarily driven by advances in science and technology and that spending more will inevitably result in improved quality of care" (p. 286). Hence, the authors find some evidence to support "flat-of-the-curve" medicine in the case of additional Medicare spending. The implication is that additional medical care services may not provide important benefits to the population served. As the authors note, the results of their studies underscore the need for research to determine how to safely reduce Medicare spending levels in various regions.

However, Kaestner and Silber (2010) reach the opposite conclusion about the effectiveness of Medicare spending. They use Medicare claim data to study the association between inpatient spending and the 30-day mortality of Medicare patients admitted to hospitals between 2001 and 2005 for specific types of surgeries and medical conditions. These researchers estimate that a 10 percent increase in inpatient spending on nearly all patients was associated with a 3 to 11 percent increase in survival. Kaestner and Silber point out that "although some spending may be inefficient, the results suggest that the amount of waste is less than conventionally believed, at least for inpatient care" (p. 560).

As you can see, evidence regarding the existence of flat-of-the-curve medicine is inconclusive. Indeed, several other studies, cited in Chapter 2, also show a relationship between increased health care spending and better health care outcomes at the margin. This topic will likely be debated for several years to come, if not more. As Kaestner and Silber note, "Clearly, more research is needed, particularly research that provides a credible assessment of the causal relationship between spending and health" (p. 583). Believers in flat-of-the-curve medicine argue that health care spending can be reduced by 20 to 30 percent without harming health outcomes. Others are more skeptical about that assessment and policy action.

Hospital Profit Margins

In addition to measures of expenditures, price, and output, economic profitability also provides information about the performance of an industry, as discussed in earlier chapters. Persistent economic profits typically signal an inefficient allocation of resources. That's because, when entry barriers are absent, additional resources are drawn to markets with economic profits until price equals average costs. In addition, negative economic profits indicate that suppliers are not receiving sufficient revenues to cover costs and therefore may exit the industry if the losses persist. Both of these situations are potentially associated with reductions in consumer well-being.

Figure 13–8 shows the average profit margins for U.S. community hospitals and the U.S. manufacturing sector from 1981 to 2009, by decade. The hospital profit margin reflects payments received for inpatient and outpatient care services from all types of payers (Medicare, Medicaid, private insurers, self-pay, and so on) plus any nonpatient revenues (e.g., interest earnings and cafeteria revenues) less total hospital expenditures. Like most industries, the average profit margin of hospitals has cycled over time. The profit margin averaged nearly 5 percent throughout the period and ranged from a low of 2.6 percent in 2008 to well over 6 percent in 1996, 1997, and 2007.

These hospital margins do not appear to be particularly high or low relative to the manufacturing sector. In fact, the two operating margins are approximately equal over the entire 19-year period. However, operating margins do vary considerably among rural and metropolitan hospitals, nonteaching and teaching hospitals, and hospitals with different payer mixes. In general, private-insurer profit margins tend to be higher than Medicare profit margins which in turn are higher than Medicaid profit margins. About 28 percent of all community hospitals experienced negative total hospital margins each year during the 2000s in part because of their Medicaid-intensive payer mix.

FIGURE 13–8

Average Total Operating Margins for the U.S. Hospital Industry and the Manufacturing Sector, 1981–2009 by Decade

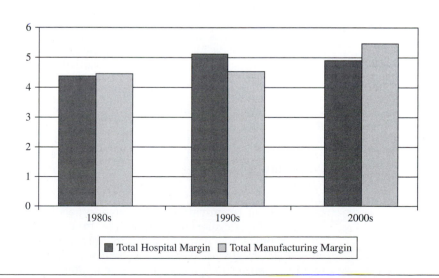

Total Hospital Margin   Total Manufacturing Margin

SOURCE: American Hospital Association Chartbook, 2011 at http://www.AHA.org and Economic Report to the President, 2010 at http://www.gpoaccess.gov/eop/tables10.html (accessed January 12, 2012).

Indeed, from a pricing perspective, the hospital services industry can be viewed as possessing unregulated and regulated segments or submarkets as we saw earlier in our discussion of cost shifting behavior. In the unregulated segment, the private payer price is established through many independent negotiations between private insurers and individual hospitals in various local hospital services markets throughout the United States. In contrast, the Medicare and Medicaid reimbursements rates are administered by the federal and state governments. Some interaction likely exists between the private and public reimbursement rates because the federal and state governments often look at the status of private profit margins when setting their rates. Higher private margins often mean lower public rates.

Provisions of the Patient Protection and Affordable Care Act (PPACA) of 2010 Relating to the Hospital Services Industry

Several provisions of PPACA are likely to affect the hospital services industry in the United States to some extent. One, as discussed in more detail at the end of Chapter 7, the PPACA provides financial incentives to hospitals and other types of medical care providers to establish strong vertical relations and form accountable care organizations (ACOs). Bundled or episodes of care payments may be employed to reimburse these ACOs to better align these vertical relations. The hope that these vertical relations can lower costs and improve the quality and continuity of care represents a key component of the PPACA. However, the development of ACOs may also lead to market power effects. Antitrust authorities may have to continually monitor the hospital services market to ensure that local markets remain reasonably competitive.

Two, we discussed in this chapter how not-for-profit hospitals receive tax breaks from the government. We also mentioned that some economists find empirically that the community benefits not-for-profit hospitals provide do not always justify their tax-exempt status. The PPACA now requires not-for-profit hospitals to conduct or participate in a community health needs assessment every three years. Three, Medicare establishes a value-based purchasing program to incentivize acute care hospitals to provide higher levels of quality, beginning in 2012. Under value-based purchasing, health care providers are rewarded for offering higher levels of efficiency and quality.

Four, the PPACA provides financial incentives to increase the supply of primary care providers. If these incentives work, the greater supply of primary care workers should benefit the hospital services industry through lower wages. Lastly, the increased demand resulting from the health insurance mandate, beginning in 2014, may financially benefit the hospital services industry. The greater insurance availability should cover some of the free emergency care services hospitals are required to offer under the Emergency Medical Treatment and Active Labor Act (EMTALA) of 1986. The EMTALA requires any hospital participating in the Medicare program to provide care to anyone needing emergency treatment regardless of citizenship, legal status, or ability to pay without reimbursement. Hospitals must stabilize the patient, and can only transfer or discharge patients needing emergency treatment under their own informed consent or when their condition requires transfer to a hospital better equipped to administer the treatment. Consequently, less free care should be provided by hospitals because of the health insurance mandate.

Summary

Hospital expenditures represent the largest component of health care spending, accounting for over 5 percent of U.S. GDP. Without a doubt, any realistic cost containment policies must be directed at the hospital sector of the health economy. The hospital services industry is best characterized as being oligopolistic in nature. Most markets have a few competing hospitals, with existing hospitals generally having a cost advantage over new ones due to learning curve economies. Because of limited actual and potential competition, hospitals likely have some ability to raise price above the competitive level, reduce quality, and produce with inefficient methods.

Countervailing the ability of hospitals to raise price is the dominance of some third-party payers in the hospital services market. The federal government sets fixed prices for nearly 30 percent of all hospital revenues under the Medicare program. In addition, large private insurers sometimes have sufficient buyer clout to negotiate sizeable hospital price discounts.

Despite these changes, some evidence suggests that Medicare beneficiaries in regions with high levels of Medicare spending are not better off in terms of health outcomes. In addition, hospital care prices and costs continue to rise in the aggregate. Whether the aggregate hospital price and expenditure increases are due to imperfect hospital markets or normal market forces remains to be determined. Some health policy analysts want the federal government to encourage increased competition in the entire hospital sector so that macro-level cost savings are realizable. Others look to government to adopt blanket regulations, such as an "all-payer" Medicare PPS, as a way to contain aggregate hospital care costs. The merits of market-based and government-based solutions continue to be debated by health policy analysts.

Review Questions and Problems

1. Explain how the relevant product market is typically defined for community hospitals. Why? How is the relevant geographical market defined? Why?
2. Assume there are 10 equally sized hospitals in a market area. Calculate the Herfindahl-Hirschman index. Two hospitals in the market area inform the Department of Justice that they wish to merge. According to the current DOJ merger guidelines, will the merger be contested? Explain.
3. What are some possible sources of barriers to entry into the hospital industry? What has the literature concluded about the severity of these barriers?
4. Explain how you might design a statistical test to examine the presence of a certificate-of-need law on hospital care expenditures. What would be your main hypothesis in this experiment? What would be the unit of analysis in your experiment? What variables would you specify on the right-hand side of the estimation equation to act as control variables? What would be your identification strategy to eliminate any concerns about reverse causation or a third variable affecting both the presence of a CON law and hospital care expenditures?
5. In Chapters 11 and 12, survivor analysis was discussed as a test to determine if larger-sized hospitals are more efficient at producing services than smaller-sized ones. If you were to use national data for hospitals based on bed size, discuss how you would set up the experiment to perform this survivor test for the hospital services industry. Now go to your library and locate various issues of *Hospital Statistics*, which is published by the American Hospital Association and use actual data to complete the analysis. Are larger-sized hospitals more efficient? Explain.
6. According to the text, empirical studies have not uncovered any strong evidence to indicate that cost savings result from a hospital belonging to a multihospital

system. Yet, hospitals continue to consolidate and form multihospital systems. Why do you suppose that is the case?

7. Equation 13–3 in the text shows the Dorfman-Steiner condition for the optimal amount of advertising intensity for a monopoly. For a few nonteaching and teaching hospitals in your community, see if you can find data on advertising expenditures, revenues, and the accounting operating margin (i.e., net income/revenues). Is it true that more profitable hospitals advertise more? Now use Equation 13–3 and those figures to impute the advertising elasticity of demand for those particular hospitals. Does a nonteaching or teaching hospital face a higher advertising elasticity?

8. Given the not-for-profit nature of most hospitals in the United States, do you think advertising and other types of promotion expenditures are warranted from a societal perspective? Explain.

9. Your roommate is working on a paper for a medical sociology class. You are asked by her if the typical hospital in the United States possesses any market power. How would you respond? Use theory and empirical evidence to support your argument.

10. Suppose 15 years from now you find yourself running a nonprofit hospital (apparently not a bad gig according to some of our former students). You make all of the major decisions for the hospital but must reach agreement with your board of directors for most of them. But, of course, you appointed most of them to their positions so the disagreement will likely be minimal. What would be your main goal or goals in running that nonprofit hospital? For example, would you request more pay for yourself or your staff, larger offices, or the acquiring of other hospitals? Could your decisions be construed as contrasting with (social) efficiency?

11. A study by Mark (1996) finds that not-for-profit psychiatric hospitals are no more efficient than their for-profit counterparts after controlling for quality. At the same time, the study finds that not-for-profit psychiatric hospitals provide a higher quality of care as measured by the number of violations and complaints received. Use the quality/quantity maximization model to explain these results.

12. Some economists have suggested that the best way to control medical costs is to remove the profit incentive for health care providers, particularly hospitals. This would involve making all hospitals not-for-profit institutions. Use the utility maximization model to explain the likely impact such a policy would have on the cost of producing hospital services. What would happen if instead a policy was instituted that reduced barriers to entry in the hospital sector and therefore made the market more competitive?

13. Suppose a state attorney challenges the tax-exempt status of ACME Hospital because of a disagreement over the amount of charitable care the hospital has been providing. The attorney general claims that the hospital provided only $25.9 million in charity care over the last five years. Using a much broader definition of charity care that included items that were not reimbursed, such as the costs of community service programs and education, ACME claimed it had provided $191.9 million of charity care over that same period. In addition, ACME was criticized for adding an extravagant, nine-story building called the Wile E. Coyote Tower that included a spacious, two-story lobby, a health club, and a gourmet restaurant. Use the economic theory developed in this chapter to put the debate between the attorney general and ACME in a broader context.

14. Studies using data prior to 1983 found that increased hospital competition led to higher rather than lower hospital prices. How do researchers explain that result? What have more recent studies concluded about the relation between competition and prices in the hospital industry? What accounts for that change?

15. Explain the theoretical reasoning why economists suspect that hospitals with different ownership forms will behave differently with respect to price, quality, and access. Also, explain some of the reasons why most empirical studies have

not found any significant differences between for-profit and not-for-profit hospitals with regards to their performance.

16. Given that empirical studies find that both HMOs and state rate-review programs have been relatively successful at containing costs, would you prefer more managed care competition or a single-payer system? Explain your choice.

17. You learned in this chapter that hospitals expenditures continue to grow and the hospital services price inflation exceeds that of the general price inflation rate. Do you think these increases resulted from imperfections in the hospital services market such as a nonprofit motivation, insurance coverage, CON laws, etc. or because of the normal functioning of supply and demand? Explain.

18. What does cost shifting involve? Why do many economists suspect that cost shifting may not occur in practice? Theoretically, what conditions are necessary for hospitals to practice cost shifting?

19. Explain would you conduct a study to determine if hospitals produce flat-of-the-curve medicine? Does the discussion surrounding Figure 13–7 refer to flat-of-the-curve medicine? Why or why not?

20. Go to the March 2011 MedPAC report to Congress at the following site and learn more about the characteristics of hospitals treating Medicare patients in the United States: http://www.medpac.gov/chapters/Mar11_Ch03.pdf. Also visit the American Hospital Trend Chartbook to learn about various trends concerning and affecting community hospitals: http://www.aha.org/research/reports/tw/chartbook/index.shtml.

Online Resources

To access Internet links related to the topics in this chapter, please visit our website at **www.cengage.com/economics/santerre**.

References

Anders, George. "Medical Luxury: Hospital Beds Go High-Tech, and Some Cost as Much as a Car." *Wall Street Journal*, May 6, 1993a, p. A1.

Anderson, Gerard F. "All-Payer Ratesetting: Down but Not Out." *Health Care Financing Review* (annual supplement, 1991), pp. 35–41.

Antel, John J., Robert L. Ohsfeldt, and Edmund R. Becker. "State Regulation and Hospital Costs." *Review of Economics and Statistics* 77 (August 1995), pp. 416–22.

Baker, Jonathan B. "The Antitrust Analysis of Hospital Mergers and the Transformation of the Hospital Industry." *Law and Contemporary Problems* 51 (spring 1988), pp. 93–164.

Barro, Jason R., and Michael Chu. "HMO Penetration, Ownership Status, and the Rise of Hospital Advertising." NBER Working Paper No. 8899. Cambridge, Mass.: National Bureau of Economic Research, April 2002.

Bates, Laurie J., Kankana Mukherjee, and Rexford E. Santerre. "Market Structure and Technical Efficiency in the Hospital Services Industry: A DEA Approach." *Medical Care Research and Review* 63 (August 2006), pp. 499–524.

Baumol, William. *Business Behavior, Value and Growth*. Englewood Cliffs, N.J.: Prentice Hall, 1967.

Bradbury, R. C., Joseph H. Golec, and Frank E. Stearns. "Comparing Hospital Length of Stay in Independent Practice Association HMOs and Traditional Insurance Programs." *Inquiry* 28 (spring 1991), pp. 87–93.

Brown, H. S. "Managed Care and Technical Efficiency." *Health Economics* 12 (2003), pp. 149–58.

Burda, David. "Flurry of Merger Plans Has Eyes Focused on Iowa." *Modern Healthcare*, April 12, 1993, p. 24.

Capps, Cory, and David Dranove. *Market Concentration of ACOs*. Presentation for America's Health Insurance Plans, June 2011, http://www.ahipcoverage.com/wp-content/uploads/2011/10/

ACOs-Cory-Capps-Hospital-Market-Consolidation-Final.pdf, accessed February 23, 2012.

Capps, Cory, and David Dranove. "Hospital Consolidation and Negotiated PPO Prices." *Health Affairs* 23 (March/April 2004), pp. 175–81.

Carlisle, David M., et al. "HMO vs. Fee-for-Service Care of Older Persons with Acute Myocardial Infarction." *American Journal of Public Health* 82 (December 1992), pp. 1626–30.

Coelen, C., and D. Sullivan. "An Analysis of the Effects of Prospective Reimbursement Programs on Hospital Expenditures." *Health Care Financing Review* 2, no. 3 (1981), pp. 1–40.

Congressional Budget Office. *Geographic Variation in Health Care Spending.* Washington, D.C.: U.S. Government Printing Office, February 2008, at http://www.cbo.gov/ftpdocs/89xx/doc8972/MainText.3.1.shtml.

Corrigan, Janet M., Jill S. Eden, Marsha R. Gold, and Jeremy D. Pickreign. "Trends toward a National Health Care Marketplace." *Inquiry* 34 (spring 1997), pp. 11–28.

Cowing, Thomas G., and Alphonse G. Holtmann. "Multiproduct Short-Run Hospital Cost Functions: Empirical Evidence and Policy Implications from Cross Section Data." *Southern Economic Journal* (January 1983), pp. 637–53.

Cuellar, Alison E., and Paul J. Gertler. "How the Expansion of Hospital Systems has Affected Consumers." *Health Affairs* 24 (January/February 2005), pp. 213–19.

Davis, Karen. "Economic Theories of Behavior in Not-for-profit, Private Hospitals." *Economic and Business Bulletin* (winter 1972), pp. 1–13.

Diehr, Paula, et al. "Use of a Preferred Provider Plan by Employees of the City of Seattle." *Medical Care* 28 (November 1990), pp. 1073–88.

Dorfman, Robert, and Peter O. Steiner. "Optimal Advertising and Optimal Quality." *American Economic Review* 44 (1954), pp. 826–36.

Dowd, B. R., Roger Feldman, Stephen Cassou, and Michael Finch. "Health Plan Choice and the Utilization of Health Care Services." *Review of Economics and Statistics* 73 (February 1991), pp. 85–93.

Dranove, David, Mark Shanley, and Carol Simon. "Is Hospital Competition Wasteful?" *Rand Journal of Economics* 23 (summer 1992), pp. 247–62.

Dranove, David, Mark Shanley, and William D. White. "Price and Concentration in Hospital Markets: The Switch from Patient-Driven to Payer-Driven Competition." *Journal of Law and Economics* 36 (April 1993), pp. 179–204.

Dranove, David, and Richard Lindrooth. "Hospital Consolidation and Costs: Another Look at the Evidence." *Journal of Health Economics* 22 (2003), pp. 983–97.

Dranove, David, Richard Lindrooth, William D. White, and Jack Zwanziger. "Is the Impact of Managed Care on Hospital Prices Decreasing?" *Journal of Health Economics* 27 (2008), pp. 362–376.

Draper, D., et al. "Studying the Effects of the DRG Based Prospective Payment System on the Quality of Care: Design, Sampling, and Fieldwork." *Journal of the American Medical Association* 264 (October 17, 1990), pp. 1956–61.

Eakin, B. Kelly, and Thomas J. Kniesner. "Estimating a Non-Minimum Cost Function for Hospitals." *Southern Economic Journal* (January 1988), pp. 583–97.

Ermann, Dan, and Jon Gabel. "Multihospital Systems: Issues and Empirical Findings." *Health Affairs* 3 (spring 1984), pp. 50–64.

Farley, Dean E. *Competition among Hospitals: Market Structure and Its Relation to Utilization, Costs and Financial Position.* Research note 7, Hospital Studies Program, National Center for Health Services Research and Health Care Technology Assessment, 1985.

Feldstein, Martin S. "Hospital Cost Inflation: A Study of Not-for-profit Price Dynamics." *American Economic Review* 61 (December 1971), pp. 853–72.

Fielding, Jonathan E., and Thomas Rice. "Can Managed Competition Solve the Problems of Market Failure?" *Health Affairs* 12 (supplement, 1993), pp. 216–28.

Fisher, Elliott S., David E. Wennberg, Therese A. Stukel, Daniel J. Gottlieb, F. L. Lucas, and Etoile L. Pinder. "The Implications of Regional Variations in Medicare Spending. Part 1: The Content, Quality, and Accessibility of Care." *Annals of Internal Medicine* 138 (February 18, 2003a), pp. 273–87.

Fisher, Elliott S., David E. Wennberg, Therese A. Stukel, Daniel J. Gottlieb, F. L. Lucas, and Etoile L. Pinder. "The Implications of Regional

Variations in Medicare Spending. Part 2: Health Outcomes and Satisfaction of Care." *Annals of Internal Medicine* 138 (February 18, 2003b), pp. 288–99.

Fitzgerald, John F., Patricia S. Moore, and Robert S. Dittus. "The Care of Elderly Patients with Hip Fracture: Changes since Implementation of the Prospective Payment System." *New England Journal of Medicine* (November 24, 1988), pp. 1392–97.

Fournier, Gary M., and Jean M. Mitchell. "Hospital Costs and Competition for Services: A Multiproduct Analysis." *Review of Economics and Statistics* (November 1992), pp. 627–34.

Frakt, Austin B. "How Much Do Hospitals Cost Shift? A Review of the Evidence." *The Milbank Quarterly* 89 (March 2011), pp. 90–130.

Frech, H. E., III. "Comments on Antitrust Issues." In *Advances in Health Economics and Health Services Research,* vol. 7, eds. Richard M. Scheffler and Louis F. Rossiter. Greenwich, Conn.: JAI Press, 1987, pp. 263–67.

Garnick, Deborah W., et al. "Services and Charges by PPO Physicians for PPO and Indemnity Patients: An Episode of Care Comparison." *Medical Care* 28 (October 1990), pp. 894–906.

Ginsburg, Paul B. "Can Hospitals and Physicians Shift the Effects of Cuts in Medicare Reimbursement to Private Payers?" *Health Affairs,* Web Exclusive (October 8, 2003), pp. 472–9.

Grannemann, Thomas W., Randall S. Brown, and Mark V. Pauly. "Estimating Hospital Costs: A Multiple-Output Analysis." *Journal of Health Economics* 5 (1986), pp. 107–27.

Gray, James. "The Selling of Medicine, 1986." *Medical Economics* (January 20, 1986), pp. 180–94.

Greenwald, Howard P., and Curtis J. Henke. "HMO Membership, Treatment, and Mortality Risk among Prostatic Cancer Patients." *American Journal of Public Health* 82 (August 1992), pp. 1099–1104.

Hadley, Jack, and Judith Feder. "Hospital Cost Shifting and Care for the Uninsured." *Health Affairs* 4 (1985), pp. 67–80.

Halm, Ethan A., Clara Lee, and Mark R. Chassin. "Is Volume Related to Outcome in Health Care? A Systematic Review and Methodologic Critique of the Literature." *Annals of Internal Medicine* 137 (September 2002), pp. 511–20.

Hersch, Philip L. "Competition and the Performance of Hospital Markets." *Review of Industrial Organization* 1 (winter 1984), pp. 324–40.

Herzlinger, Regina E., and William S. Krasker. "Who Profits from Not-for-Profits?" *Harvard Business Review* (January–February 1987), pp. 93–106.

Hester, James A., Anne Marie Wouters, and Norman Wright. "Evaluation of a Preferred Provider Organization." *Milbank Quarterly* 65 (1987), pp. 575–613.

Ho, Vivian. "Learning and the Evolution of Medical Technologies: The Diffusion of Coronary Angioplasty." *Journal of Health Economics* 21 (2002), pp. 873–85.

Ho, Vivian, and Barton H. Hamilton. "Hospital Mergers and Acquisitions: Does Market Consolidation Harm Patients?" *Journal of Health Economics* 19 (2000), pp. 767–91.

Ho, Vivian, Joseph S. Ross, Bramajee K. Nallamothu, and Harlan M. Krumholz. "Cardiac Certificate of Need Regulations and the Availability and Use of Revascularization Services." *American Heart Journal* 154 (2007), pp. 767–757.

Ho, Vivian, Meei-Hsiang Ku-Goto, and James G. Jollis, "Certificate of Need (CON) for Cardiac Care: Controversy over the Contributions of CON." *Health Services Research* 44, no. 3 (2009), pp. 483–500.

Joskow, Paul L. "The Effects of Competition and Regulation on Hospital Bed Supply and the Reservation Quality of Hospitals." *Bell Journal of Economics* (autumn 1980), pp. 421–47.

Kaestner, Robert and Jeffrey H. Silber. "Evidence on the Efficacy of Inpatient Spending on Medicare Patients." *The Milbank Quarterly* 88 (2010), pp. 560–594.

Kahn, K. L., et al. "Comparing Outcomes of Care before and after Implementation of the DRG-Based Prospective Payment System." *Journal of the American Medical Association* 264 (October 17, 1990), pp. 1984–88.

Kessler, Daniel P., and Mark B. McClellan. "Is Hospital Competition Socially Wasteful?" *Quarterly Journal of Economics* (May 2000), pp. 577–615.

Lane, Paul M., and Jay D. Lindquist. "Hospital Choice: A Summary of the Key Empirical and Hypothetical Findings of the 1980s." *Journal of Health Care Marketing* 8 (December 1988), pp. 5–20.

Lanning, Joyce A., Michael A. Morrisey, and Robert L. Ohsfeldt. "Endogenous Hospital Regulation and Its Effects on Hospital and Non-Hospital Expenditures." *Journal of Regulatory Economics* 3 (1991), pp. 137–54.

Lee, Maw Lin. "A Conspicuous Production Theory of Hospital Behavior." *Southern Economic Journal* 38 (July 1971), pp. 48–58.

Leibenstein, Harvey. "Allocative Efficiency vs. X-Efficiency." *American Economic Review* 56 (1966), pp. 392–415.

Luft, Harold S. *Health Maintenance Organizations: Dimensions of Performance*. New York: Wiley Interscience, 1981.

Mann, Joyce M., Glenn A. Melnick, Anil Bamezai, and Jack Zwanziger. "A Profile of Uncompensated Hospital Care, 1983–1995." *Health Affairs* 16 (July/August 1997), pp. 223–32.

Manning, Willard G., et al. "A Controlled Trial of the Effect of a Prepaid Group Practice on Use of Services." *New England Journal of Medicine* 310 (June 7, 1984), pp. 1505–10.

Mark, Tami L. "Psychiatric Hospital Ownership and Performance." *Journal of Human Resources* 31 (summer 1996), pp. 631–49.

Melnick, Glenn A., Jack Zwanziger, Anil Bamezai, and Robert Pattison. "The Effects of Market Structure and Bargaining Position on Hospital Prices." *Journal of Health Economics* 11 (1992), pp. 217–33.

Menke, Terri J. "The Effect of Chain Membership on Hospital Costs." *Health Services Research* 32 (June 1997), pp. 177–96.

Miller, Robert H., and Harold S. Luft. "HMO Plan Performance Update: An Analysis of the Literature, 1997–2000." *Health Affairs* 21 (July/August 2002), pp. 63–86.

Miller, Robert H., and Harold S. Luft. "Managed Care Performance since 1980: A Literature Analysis." *Journal of the American Medical Association* 271 (May 18, 1994), pp. 1512–19.

Morrisey, M. A. "Cost Shifting: New Myths, Old Confusion, and Enduring Reality." *Health Affairs*, Web Exclusive (October 8, 2003), pp. 489–91.

Morrisey, Michael A., Gerald J. Wedig, and Mahmud Hassan. "Do Not-for-Profit Hospitals Pay Their Way?" *Health Affairs* 15 (winter 1996), pp. 132–44.

Newhouse, Joseph. "Toward a Theory of Not-for profit Institutions: An Economic Model of a Hospital." *American Economic Review* 60 (March 1970), pp. 64–74.

Nicholson, Sean, Mark V. Pauly, Lawton R. Burns, Agnieska Baumritter, and David A. Asch. "Measuring Community Benefits Provided by For-Profit and Not-for-profit Hospitals." *Health Affairs* 19 (November/December 2000), pp. 168–77.

Noether, Monica. "Competition among Hospitals." *Journal of Health Economics* 7 (1988), pp. 259–84.

Pauly, M., and M. Redish. "The Not-for-Profit Hospital as a Physicians' Cooperative." *American Economic Review* 63 (1973), pp. 87–99.

Pauly, Mark V. "Not-for-Profit Firms in Medical Markets." *American Economic Review Proceedings* 77 (May 1987), pp. 257–62.

Rapoport, John, Stephen Gehlbach, Stanley Lemeshow, and Daniel Teres. "Resource Utilization among Intensive Care Patients: Managed Care vs. Traditional Insurance." *Archives of Internal Medicine* 152 (November 1992), pp. 2207–12.

Retchin, Sheldon M., and Barbara Brown. "Elderly Patients with Congestive Heart Failure under Prepaid Care." *American Journal of Medicine* 90 (February 1991), pp. 236–42.

Retchin, Sheldon M., et al. "How the Elderly Fare in HMOs: Outcomes from the Medicare Competition Demonstrations." *Health Services Research* 27 (December 1992), pp. 651–69.

Robinson, James C., and Harold S. Luft. "The Impact of Hospital Market Structure on Patient Volume, Average Length of Stay, and the Cost of Care." *Journal of Health Economics* 4 (December 1985), pp. 333–56.

Romeo, Anthony A., Judith L. Wagner, and Robert H. Lee. "Prospective Reimbursement and the Diffusion of New Technologies in Hospitals." *Journal of Health Economics* 3 (1984), pp. 1–24.

Rosko, Michael D. "Impact of HMO Penetration and Other Environmental Factors on Hospital X-Inefficiency." *Medical Care Research and Review* 58 (December 2001), pp. 430–54.

Salkever, David S, "Regulation of Prices and Investment in Hospitals in the United States." In *Handbook of Health Economics*, eds. A. J. Culyer and J. P. Newhouse. Amsterdam: Elsevier Science, 2000, pp. 1489–1535.

Santerre, Rexford E., and Ammon S. Adams. "The Effect of Competition on Reserve Capacity: The Case of California Hospitals in the Late 1990s." *International Journal of Health Care Finance and Economics* 2 (2002), pp. 205–18.

Santerre, Rexford E., and Debra Pepper. "Survivorship in the US Hospital Services Industry." *Managerial and Decision Economics* 21 (2000), pp. 181–89.

Schneider, John E. "Changes in the Effects of Mandatory Rate Regulation on Growth in Hospital Operating Costs, 1980–1996." *Review of Industrial Organization* 22 (2003), pp. 297–312.

Short, M. N., Thomas A. Aloia, and Vivian Ho. "Certificate of Need Regulations and the Availability and Use of Cancer Resection." *Annals of Surgical Oncology* 15 no. 7 (2008), pp. 1837–1845.

Simpson, John. "A Note on Entry by Small Hospitals." *Journal of Health Economics* 14 (1995), pp. 107–13.

Skinner, Jonathan S., Douglas O. Staiger, and Elliott S. Fisher. "Is Technological Change in Medicine Always Worth It? The Case of Acute Myocardial Infarction." *Health Affairs* 25 (2006), pp. W34–W47.

Sloan, Frank A. "Not-for-Profit Ownership and Hospital Behavior." In *Handbook of Health Economics*, Vol. 1B, eds. A. J. Culyer and J. P. Newhouse. Amsterdam: Elsevier Science, 2000, pp. 1141–74.

Sloan, Frank A. "Property Rights in the Hospital Industry." In *Health Care in America*, ed. H. E. Frech III. San Francisco: Pacific Research Institute for Public Policy, 1988, pp. 103–41.

Sloan, Frank A., Gabriel A. Picone, Donald H. Taylor, Jr., and Shin-Yi Chou. "Hospital Ownership and Cost and Quality of Care: Is There a Dime's Worth of Difference?" *Journal of Health Economics* 20 (2001), pp. 1–21.

Smith, Dean. "The Effects of Preferred Provider Organizations on Health Care Use and Costs." *Inquiry* 34 (winter 1997/1998), pp. 278–87.

Temin, Peter. "An Economic History of American Hospitals." In *Health Care in America*, ed. H. E. Frech III. San Francisco: Pacific Research Institute for Public Policy, 1988, pp. 75–102.

Thorpe, Kenneth E., and Charles E. Brecher. "Improved Access for the Uninsured Poor in Large Cities: Do Public Hospitals Make a Difference?" *Journal of Health Politics, Policy and Law* (summer 1987), pp. 313–24.

Town, Robert, and Gregory Vistnes. "Hospital Competition in HMO Networks." *Journal of Health Economics* 20 (2001), pp. 733–53.

Town, Robert J., and Imran Currim. "Hospital Advertising in California, 1991–1997." *Inquiry* 39 (fall 2002), pp. 298–313.

U.S. v. Carilion, 707 F. Supp. 840 (W.D. Va. 1989), 843.

U.S. v. Rockford Memorial, 898 F.2d 1278; 1284 (1990).

U.S. Department of Justice (DOJ) and Federal Trade Commission (FTC). *Horizontal Merger Guidelines*, August 19, 2010.

Vita, Michael G. "Exploring Hospital Production Relationships with Flexible Functional Forms." *Journal of Health Economics* 9 (June 1990), pp. 1–21.

Ware, John E., et al. "Comparison of Health Outcomes at a Health Maintenance Organization with Those of Fee-for-Service Care." *Lancet* (May 3, 1986), pp. 1017–22.

White, Stephen L. "The Effects of Competition on Hospital Costs in Florida." *Policy Studies Journal* 15 (March 1987), pp. 375–93.

Wilcox-Gok, Virginia. "The Effects of For-Profit Status and System Membership on the Financial Performance of Hospitals." *Applied Economics* 34 (2002), pp. 479–89.

Williamson, Oliver E. "Managerial Discretion and Business Behavior." *American Economic Review* 53 (December 1963), pp. 1032–57.

Wilson, George W., and Joseph M. Jadlow. "Competition, Profit Incentives, and Technical Efficiency in the Provision of Nuclear Medicine Services." *Bell Journal of Economics* (autumn 1982), pp. 472–82.

Zwanziger Jack, Glenn A. Melnick, and Anil Bamezai. "Can Cost Shifting Continue in a Price Competitive Environment?" *Health Economics* 9 (2000), pp. 211–255.

Zwanziger, Jack, and Rebecca R. Auerbach. "Evaluating PPO Performance Using Prior Expenditure Data." *Medical Care* 29 (February 1991), pp. 142–51.

The Pharmaceutical Industry

The research-based pharmaceutical industry as it is known today began with the development of sulfanilamide in the mid-1930s and penicillin in 1938.[1] With World War II came an increased demand for sulfa drugs and penicillin to protect soldiers from infection. The pharmaceutical industry quickly responded by replacing handicraft methods of preparing drugs, traditionally required for individual prescriptions, with mass production techniques (Egan et al., 1982). Chemical firms, such as Lederle and Merck, found ways to produce drugs in bulk form, which were then transformed into dosage form (such as powders and tablets) by drug companies, such as Upjohn. Pfizer developed a fermentation process to allow penicillin to be produced in large quantities. Penicillin was soon followed by other antibiotics, and research was stimulated in other therapeutic fields as well (Statman, 1983).

Following the war, the pharmaceutical industry continued to evolve and mature. High potential profits generated further innovation and drew other companies into the pharmaceutical industry. As drug firms expanded many acquired sales forces to market their drugs in finished form. Research and development efforts in the pharmaceutical industry continually expanded during the postwar period.

This chapter provides a contemporary analysis of the pharmaceutical industry. Although the pharmaceutical industry of today closely resembles its postwar antecedent in terms of many supply-side characteristics, we show that several institutional changes on the demand side of the market have had wide-sweeping effects on the conduct of the industry. The chapter studies the structure, conduct, and performance of the pharmaceutical industry. Specifically, it:

- discusses seller concentration, buyer concentration, barriers to entry, and product differentiation to see whether existing drug firms are endowed with some market power.
- examines some topics pertaining to the conduct of the pharmaceutical industry, including price competition, promotional strategies, and product innovation. The important question concerns the actual degree of price and product competition that presently takes place in this industry.
- assesses the performance of the contemporary pharmaceutical industry in terms of aggregate prices, output, and profits. The main query here is whether firms in the pharmaceutical industry have tended to charge high prices and earn excess profits.
- studies how some provisions of the Patient Protection and Affordable Care Act (PPACA) of 2010 may affect the pharmaceutical industry in the United States.

---

1. Statman (1983) points out that the drug trade is very old. The Ebers Papyrus lists 811 prescriptions used in Egypt in 550 BC.

The Structure of the Pharmaceutical Industry

Number and Size Distribution of Sellers

When one thinks about the pharmaceutical industry, the names of a few large companies, such as Pfizer, Johnson & Johnson, and Merck, normally come to mind. But actually a sizeable number of large companies coexist in the drug industry. Table 14–1 lists the total sales and market share of the 10 largest companies selling pharmaceutical products in the United States as of 2010. Pfizer, the leader with an 8.5 percent market share, sells $7.4 billion more of pharmaceuticals than Merck & Company, the next largest domestic seller of drug products. The companies listed produce brand-name pharmaceuticals, although they may manufacture and sell generic versions of these drugs as well. Some of the companies listed, such as Roche, are headquartered outside the United States.

Also, a multitude of lesser-known, smaller firms exist in the pharmaceutical industry. Many of these drug firms primarily manufacture and retail generic drugs and place little, if any, emphasis on new drug discovery. In fact, data from the U.S. Bureau of the Census (2011) show that, as of 2007, 763 firms operated in the domestic pharmaceutical industry with the four largest drug companies accounting for 35 percent of all industry output and the largest eight responsible for 54 percent. The Census data also reveal that the Herfindahl-Hirschman index (HHI) of market concentration equals 457. Considered alone, these figures imply that the pharmaceutical industry contains a considerable number of equally sized firms, and therefore appears to be reasonably competitive from a structural perspective.

These Census estimates of market concentration in the pharmaceutical industry are based on an assumption that the market for all pharmaceuticals, despite the intended use of the many individual drugs, properly constitutes the relevant product market (RPM). A fairly broad definition of the RPM may be desirable if firms can allocate resources to new drug development or expand existing developments in a timely manner without substantial retraining or new hiring of personnel

TABLE 14–1

Ten Largest Pharmaceutical Companies by U.S. Sales, 2010

Corporation	Total Sales (U.S. $Billions)	Market Share (percent)
Pfizer	$26.2	8.5%
Merck & Co.	18.8	6.1
AstraZeneca	18.3	6.0
Novartis	15.7	5.1
Lilly	14.3	4.7
Roche	13.8	4.5
Teva Pharma	13.7	4.5
GlaxoSmithKline	13.6	4.4
Johnson & Johnson	12.9	4.2
Amgen Corp.	12.7	4.1

SOURCE: Based on IMS Health, http://www.imshealth.com (accessed January 17, 2012).

(DiMasi, 2000). If barriers to new development exist within specific product lines, however, a therapeutic-market definition may offer a narrower and more appropriate approach to defining the RPM for drugs.

Given that most drugs are not substitutes in consumption because they have different intended uses, therapeutic markets are defined to include only drugs that treat common diseases or illnesses. For example, a physician looking to relieve a patient's ulcer condition does not choose among various brands of antidepressants and antiulcer drugs. However, the doctor may choose among Tagamet, Zantac, or Pepcid, which are all antiulcer drugs. Data for concentration ratios based on therapeutic markets typically suggest a more concentrated market environment for drugs.

DiMasi (2000) reminds us that market-concentration measures at a point in time, regardless of how the RPM is defined, only represent static indicators of industry structure. To fully understand the likely behavior of firms, it is important to also know whether industries are becoming more or less concentrated. Thus, it is also important to examine trends in market concentration over time. Earlier data from *Census of Manufacturers* suggest that the degree of seller concentration in the pharmaceutical industry has increased moderately over time, based on the aggregate or broad definition of the RPM (http://www.census.gov/econ/concentration.html). While fairly stable at 22 percent during the 1963 to 1992 period, the four-firm concentration ratio (CR_4) shot up to 36 percent in 1997 and has remained stable at that level. (Although not measured in the same manner as the Census figures, notice the CR_4 of 26 percent that can be calculated from the figures reported in Table 14–1 for 2010.) The upward spike in the aggregate level of concentration since 1992 likely resulted from the many mergers involving relatively large drug companies. Some examples of the mergers taking place since 1992 include Pfizer with Warner-Lambert and Pharmacia, Glaxo Wellcome and SmithKline Beecham, and Ciba-Geigy with Sandoz (to form Novartis).

Sales data are unavailable to analyze changes over time in market concentration at the therapeutic level. However, DiMasi (2000) offers some information on the percentage of new molecular entities (NMEs) produced by the largest drug firms over time. Among his findings, he reports HHIs of 1,243, 864, 412, and 328 for cardiovascular NMEs during the 1960s, 1970s, 1980s, and 1990s, respectively. He notes that other therapeutic classes also generally exhibit a downward trend in market concentration, although the specific period at which deconcentration occurred varied by therapeutic class.

Taking all of the information together, today's pharmaceutical industry comes across as being mildly concentrated. While a few drug companies do not account for a majority of all sales in the aggregate market, they tend to dominate most therapeutic markets. However, evidence also indicates that these dominant positions are not very permanent in the pharmaceutical industry. Market shares are reasonably close among the top 10 drug companies, and significant deconcentration has taken place at the therapeutic level for NMEs. In any case, information on market concentration cannot by itself identify whether drug companies possess significant market power. Information on other market structure elements and the market behavior of drug firms must also be considered before drawing conclusions about the market power of firms in the pharmaceutical industry.

The Buyer Side of the Pharmaceutical Market

The degree of buyer concentration is another important element that makes up market structure. For example, we discussed in Chapter 11 how a single buyer may exert monopsony power and force the reimbursement price below the competitive level. As another example, a powerful buyer may be able to offset any market power

TABLE 14–2
Payers for Prescription Drugs, 2010

Source	Expenditures (billions of dollars)	Percentage of Total
Total	$259.1	100.0%
All private	165.8	64.0
Out-of-pocket	48.8	18.8
Private insurance	117.0	45.2
All government	93.3	36.0
Medicare	59.5	23.0
Medicaid and SCHIP	21.8	8.4
Other government	12.0	4.6

SOURCE: Centers for Medicare and Medicaid Services, http://www.cms.gov (accessed January 17, 2012).

otherwise existing on the seller side of the market. Consequently, it is worthwhile to also examine the demand side of the pharmaceutical market in terms of buyer characteristics. Data in Table 14–2 show that the buyer side of the market is relatively fragmented. Unlike spending on hospital and physician services, consumers directly pay for a relatively large percentage of drug costs. In particular, out-of-pocket expenses amount to $49 billion, representing nearly 19 percent of all prescription drug expenses in 2010. Interestingly, that same percentage figure was 63 percent just 20 years earlier. Beginning in the early 1990s, many managed care companies attracted enrollees by offering them prescription drug coverage. Not surprisingly, the percentage of prescription drug costs reimbursed by insurers rose from 24.5 percent in 1993 to 45.2 percent in 2010.

The government, at all levels, currently accounts for 36 percent of all spending on prescription drugs. About 8.4 percent of all pharmaceutical spending falls under Medicaid and the State Children's Health Insurance Program. Medicare picks up about 23 percent of all prescription drug expenditures. As was pointed out in Chapter 10, the Medicare Prescription Drug Improvement and Modernization Act (MMA) of 2003 began in 2006. The Act allows Medicare beneficiaries to enroll in private drug benefit plans that contract with the government. Beneficiaries who join a Medicare drug plan pay a monthly premium equal to 25 percent of the cost of a standard drug plan. As mentioned earlier, the drug benefit is designed with an annual deductible, benefit limits, and a catastrophic threshold, which are all indexed to grow over time. Most Medicare beneficiaries are also responsible for paying a coinsurance amount or a copayment. Medicare provides additional premium and cost-sharing assistance to beneficiaries with limited incomes and financial resources. The private insurers of Part D plans negotiate discounts and rebates with drug companies. The MMA prohibits Medicare from directly negotiating drug prices with pharmaceutical companies.

The Realized Demand for Pharmaceutical Products. Although consumers are responsible for footing a relatively large portion of the drug bill, they generally are not responsible for choosing which specific drug to buy. Since the passage of the Federal Food, Drug, and Cosmetic Act of 1938, consumer access to powerful drugs has been severely restricted (Temin, 1992). The 1938 act gave drug manufacturers the responsibility to assign new drugs to either of two classes: over-the-counter (OTC) or prescription (Rx).[2] Directions for use on the label make a drug available for self-medication. A prescription-only warning makes a drug available only by a physician's prescription. The Food and Drug Administration (FDA) has to approve the manufacturer's proposed label.

Because prescription drugs remain the dominant type sold today, the "realized demands for pharmaceuticals depend not only on ultimate consumer tastes but also on the behavior of physicians who prescribe these drugs and the retail and hospital pharmacists who dispense the prescriptions" (Caves et al., 1991, p. 4). Physicians are not always in a position to serve the best financial interests of consumers, primarily because they are unaffected financially by the choice of prescription and often lack suitable information about the price, effectiveness, and risk of substitute drug products (Temin, 1980). Moreover, customary prescribing behavior minimizes effort and also provides a legal defense if a malpractice suit arises. This customary behavior tends to favor high-priced, brand-name pharmaceutical products, especially because the "trademarked *brand-name* attached to a pioneering product by the innovator is short, and easier to remember than its *generic name*, which in turn is a shorter, simpler version of the *chemical name* that describes the molecular structure of the active chemical entity to scientists" (Caves et al., 1991, p. 5). The point is that physicians are responsible for prescribing medicines, yet may lack a financial incentive to make cost-effective choices. The result is often the selection of high-priced, brand-name drugs when equally effective lower-priced generics are available.

In certain cases, pharmacists are permitted to substitute generic drugs. As Carroll and Wolfgang (1991) write, "while consumers and prescribers have the legal right to request or deny substitution, for the great majority of prescriptions they leave choice to the pharmacists. Thus, for the most part, pharmacists determine the extent to which generic substitution will occur" (p. 110). Grabowski and Vernon (1986) point out generic products generally provide higher profit margins to pharmacists, suggesting that pharmacists face a financial incentive to substitute bioequivalent generic drugs for brand-name drugs. It follows that the realized demand for prescription drugs depends on the incentives facing consumers, physicians, and pharmacists.

Third-Party Influences on the Demand for Pharmaceutical Products. Many third-party payers have turned to formularies, drug utilization review, and required generic substitution as different ways to control the decisions of prescription-writing physicians or pharmacists and rein in pharmaceutical costs. A formulary is a list of selected pharmaceutical products that physicians are required to prescribe. The listed drugs are thought to be medically effective and reasonably priced. Virtually all hospitals use formularies. A majority of managed care organizations (MCOs) and many state Medicaid programs also employ formularies.

Like hospital utilization review, **drug utilization review** is designed to monitor the actions of physicians. By monitoring their actions, third-party payers can ensure that physicians follow the formulary and can single out physicians who inappropriately prescribe medicines. Some third-party payers also require that pharmacists substitute lower-priced generic products for higher-priced brand-name products whenever medically possible. Many MCOs have adopted drug utilization review programs and generic substitution requirements.

The federal Maximum Allowable Cost (MAC) program, which began in 1974, also mandates drug substitution in government health programs, such as Medicare and Medicaid. The MAC program limits reimbursement for multiple-source drugs to the

---

2. According to the *Henry Holt Encyclopedia of Word and Phrase Origins*: "Rx. The Latin 'recipere,' 'take this,' provides the R in the symbol Rx used by pharmacists for centuries, while the slant across the R's leg is a sign of the Roman god Jupiter, patron of medicine. The symbol looks like Rx and is pronounced that way."

lowest cost at which chemically equivalent drugs are generally available, plus a reasonable fee for dispensing a drug (Schwartzman, 1976). If a doctor prescribes a specified drug whose price exceeds the MAC price, the pharmacist can obtain reimbursement only for the MAC price unless the doctor certifies in writing that the drug is medically necessary. Such certification entitles the pharmacist to full reimbursement. Otherwise, the pharmacist must bill the patient for the difference between the price of the drug and MAC reimbursement (Schwartzman, 1976).

Two laws enacted during the 1990s by the federal government effectively impose price controls on drugs sold to Medicaid patients and federal agencies (Price Waterhouse, 1993). First, under the Omnibus Budget Reconciliation Act of 1990, federal matching subsidies are granted to state Medicaid programs only for drugs covered by a manufacturer rebate agreement. The rebate agreement normally contains both a basic and an additional component. The basic rebate per unit dispensed is the difference between the average manufacturer price and the "best price" for a drug, the latter being the lowest price charged to any other private or government buyer. There is also a minimum basic rebate equaling about 15 percent of the average manufacturer price. The additional rebate per unit dispensed equals the excess of the increase in the average manufacturer price over the increase in the urban consumer price index since September 1990.

The second federal law affecting pharmaceutical prices is the Veterans Health Care Act of 1992, which influences the price federal agencies, such as the Veterans Administration and the Department of Defense, pay for pharmaceutical goods. The act mandates that drug manufacturers enter into pricing agreements with the Federal Supply Schedule, the Veterans Administration depot, and the Department of Defense depot as a condition for conducting business with the federal government. The price of a branded drug purchased under these agreements must be no higher than 76 percent of the nonfederal average manufacturer's price during the most recent year. In addition, any increase in the price of a prescription drug is limited to the increase in the urban consumer price index.

In sum, consumers pay relatively high out-of-pocket costs for pharmaceutical products, yet exert only a very small influence over the choice and prices of prescription products. Physicians, pharmacists, and third-party payers have more control over the ultimate choice and price paid. Certain changes, such as required substitution, formulary restrictions, and drug utilization review, suggest that the buyer side of the market has become more cost conscious for those drugs paid for by a third-party payer. Changes such as these most likely increase the elasticity of demand for any one company's pharmaceutical product and make the seller side of the market more price competitive.

Pharmacy Benefit Management Companies. Another influential player in pharmaceutical markets, in addition to the consumer, third-party payer/health plan, physician, manufacturer, and pharmacist, is the pharmacy benefit management company (PBM). In fact, more than 200 million Americans obtain their drugs through a PBM (PricewaterhouseCoopers, 2001). PBMs never physically handle prescription drugs, but only serve as intermediaries between health plans and both drug manufacturers and pharmacies. Health plans pay a fee to PBMs. The fee paid to the PBM may be based on the number of insured individuals or on a fee-for-service basis, whereby the health plan pays the PBM the (reduced) cost of the prescription plus an administration fee. In return, the PBM negotiates rebates from drug manufacturers by offering to include their products on a formulary. PBMs also arrange price discounts from pharmacies by channeling a relatively large volume of consumers/patients to them.

PBMs promote generic substitution through their formularies and also through their interactions with pharmacies. Many PBMs use lower copayments as a financial inducement for consumers to purchase generic as opposed to brand-name drugs and formulary versus nonformulary drugs. In addition to focusing on cost containment, some PBMs have turned their attention to disease management. Disease management involves the assembly of comprehensive databases on current prescribing practices and health outcomes to determine cost-effective methods of treating various diseases. As Cohen (2000) writes:

> Diabetes is a prime candidate for PBM-led disease management, as it is a chronic high-cost illness with multiple symptoms covering a wide range of therapeutic classes, and whose treatment relies heavily on the extended delivery of pharmacotherapy. With the current claims databases at their disposal, PBMs already can identify a number of factors leading to above-average treatment costs and lower-than-average quality of care (for example, inappropriate drug treatment and/or poor patient compliance). (p. 317)

In the early 1990s, several drug manufacturers acquired large PBMs. For example, Eli Lilly purchased PCS in 1994, Merck purchased Medco in 1993, and SmithKline Beecham bought Diversified Pharmaceutical Services in 1994. (Interestingly, all three drug manufacturers eventually divested these PBMs.) If a drug company acquires a PBM, the antitrust concern is that the newly created vertically integrated pharmaceutical organization may give unwarranted favorable treatment to its own drugs and may not include competitor drugs, perhaps some that are even more cost effective, on its formulary. The exclusion of competitors from the market might thereby lessen competition and lead to higher prices and lower quality. Another antitrust concern is that the PBM may share information on drug prices with rival manufacturers and the PBM could be used to facilitate a collusive arrangement among drug manufacturers. These concerns may be valid. According to PricewaterhouseCoopers (2001), the market for pharmacy benefit management (PBM) is relatively concentrated, with four PBMs accounting for more than 80 percent of the market in 2001.

But recall that economic theory also offers an efficiency justification for vertically integrated organizations like PBMs. In Chapter 7, we learned that a supplier might merge with a buyer to minimize the transaction costs associated with market transactions. By producing internally, the combined firm avoids the transaction costs of negotiating, writing, and enforcing contracts. In addition, the combined firm can avoid the opportunistic behavior that results from incomplete contracts. If a vertical arrangement like a PBM results in efficiencies and adequate market competition exists, consumers benefit from the resulting lower prices.

It follows that both the potential benefits and costs must be considered when determining the economic desirability of PBMs owned by drug manufacturers. It is interesting to note that the Federal Trade Commission (FTC) imposed conditions on both of the Medco and Eli Lilly acquisitions of PBMs. Among the conditions, the FTC required that companies maintain "open formularies" that include drugs selected and approved by an independent pharmacy and therapeutics committee. Also, the vertically integrated organizations were not allowed to share proprietary and nonproprietary information they received from competitors, such as prices (FTC, 1998).

Barriers to Entry

Economic theory suggests that barriers to entry may prevent potential competition and confer market power on pharmaceutical companies. Three types of barriers to entry into the pharmaceutical industry are typically cited. The first and most effective source is a *government patent* that gives the innovating firm the right to be the sole producer of a drug product for a legal maximum of 20 years. Patent protection may be necessary to protect the economic profits of the innovating firm over some time period. Otherwise, easy imitation, lower prices, and smaller profits reduce the financial incentive for firms to undertake risky and costly, but socially valuable, research and development activities. The economic rationale underlying the patent system is that even though the patent confers monopoly power on the innovator, the monopoly restriction of output is better than having no product at all. That is, the new drug might not be introduced on the market if not for the patent protection; thus, some of the drug is better than none.

Patent protection does not guarantee that the company will remain perfectly insulated from competition. Lu and Comanor (1994) observe that a pharmaceutical patent is granted for a new drug's *chemical composition*, not its *therapeutic novelty*. This means a new drug may receive patent protection because of a different chemical composition even though it treats the same disease that an established, already patented drug does. For example, SmithKline held a patent on its antiulcer drug, Tagamet, until May 1994. Prior to patent expiration, SmithKline faced competition from Glaxo's Zantac and Merck's Pepcid, which are also antiulcer drugs but have different chemical compositions. In fact, while Tagamet was first to market and was the world's biggest-selling drug at one point, Glaxo's Zantac took over as drug leader for more than six years. While Zantac was considered less of a scientific breakthrough, it was marketed more aggressively (Moore, 1992). Thus, a legal patent does not guarantee a monopoly position. The entry of new brand-name drugs expands the choices of physicians and provides competition for an established drug with a similar indication.[3]

Another point concerning a legal patent for prescription drugs is that its effective duration is often less than 20 years because the FDA takes a number of years to approve a product for commercial introduction. With the passage of the Drug Price Competition and Patent Term Restoration Act of 1984 (Hatch-Waxman Act), the effective life of a new drug patent is extended by a maximum of 5 years, but not beyond 14 years of effective life, if it can be shown that the FDA delayed its introduction into the market by at least that amount of time.

The Hatch-Waxman Act not only increased the effective patent life of new drugs but also quickened the approval process for generic drugs. No longer must producers of generic drugs prove safety and effectiveness; they need only show that the generic is bioequivalent to a brand-name drug (i.e., it contains the same active ingredient[s]). Consequently, the act has made it easier for generics to enter pharmaceutical product markets once the patent period expires. Partly in response to this act and to third-party pressure for drug cost control, the generic share of prescriptions increased sharply as a result. Overall, the impact of the Hatch-Waxman Act is interesting. On the one hand, it increased the market power of the drug innovator by extending the effective patent life. On the other hand, the act enhanced postpatent competition by reducing the cost of generic entry.

The second type of barrier to entry into the pharmaceutical industry is a **first-mover** or **brand-loyalty advantage** (Schmalensee, 1982). A drug innovator can usually acquire and maintain a first-mover advantage because the quality of a substitute generic product is generally unknown and requires one to experience it. Generic drugs can be considered experience goods because consumers normally lack the knowledge they need to judge or experience the drugs' quality. Physicians have little time or financial incentive to seek out information about the efficacy and risk of new generic products. Furthermore, the cost of a bad consumption experience can be particularly harmful in terms of prolonged illness, adverse side effects, or a malpractice suit when switching from a known brand name to an unknown generic drug (Scherer and Ross, 1990). Therefore, unless a generic drug offers different and important therapeutic advantages or a very large discount, physicians and consumers, when faced with the choice, are reluctant to choose generic over brand-name drugs after the patents expire.

---

3. According to the *Mosby Medical Encyclopedia* (1992): "an indication is a reason to prescribe a medication or perform a treatment, as a bacterial infection may be an indication for prescribing a specific antibiotic or as appendicitis is an indication for appendectomy" (p. 411).

Many industrial organization economists believe that a first-mover advantage confers market power on the innovator of a new product. Being first on a market enhances a firm's image which can be further reinforced through persuasive advertising. A first-mover advantage allows pioneer firms to charge high prices and maintain a dominant market share even after the expiration of a patent. It is because of a first-mover advantage that McRae and Tapon (1985) found that compulsory licensing of patented pharmaceuticals was not sufficient to induce more competition in the Canadian pharmaceutical industry. **Compulsory licensing** means that a firm is given legal permission to import or manufacture a patented drug if it pays a stipulated royalty rate (of 4 percent in Canada) to the patent holder. Despite the effective elimination of the patent barrier through the compulsory licensing program, the market power of first entrants, in terms of high prices and market shares, declined only modestly over a six-year period in Quebec. The authors attribute that finding to the high postpatent barrier associated with first-mover brand loyalty.

Finally, *control over a key input*, such as a specific chemical or active ingredient, can also make it difficult for new firms to enter a drug market. New competitors require access to the input, and the originating firm may sell it to the new entrants only if it is profitable to do so. If it is not, and replication is difficult or costly, new firms may find it unprofitable to enter the industry.

In sum, significant barriers to entry exist in the pharmaceutical industry. Legal patents and brand names may give entrenched firms an advantage over potential entrants. Theoretically, the advantage translates into market power and the ability to maintain market share despite high prices. FDA approval lags reduce the effective patent life, but brand-name recognition typically increases the effective monopoly period for a drug product.[4]

Consumer Information and the Role of the FDA

As with most medical goods and services, a substantial amount of technical knowledge is necessary to judge a pharmaceutical product. Because pharmaceutical products are experience goods, or in some cases credence goods that require repeated use, they are difficult to evaluate before purchasing them. Consumers therefore face some risk when directly purchasing pharmaceutical products. Temin (1980) points to three types of risk. First, there is the risk associated with overpaying or receiving a pharmaceutical product of inferior quality. Second, an adverse reaction to a drug may lead to sickness or death. Third, a consumer may purchase the wrong drug or take the wrong dosage and therefore fail to recover from an illness or injury.

In the early 1930s, before prescription-only pharmaceuticals became the norm, drug products were less complex and were limited mainly to anti-infection drugs. Thus, self-medication was more feasible during that time period. Today, however, many substitute drugs are available to treat any given disease, and some are associated with adverse side effects for certain patients. Others cannot be used in combination with other drugs or alcoholic beverages. It is not surprising that physicians, as experts, are assigned the role of prescribing most medicines to consumers as a way to reduce consumer risks.

The FDA also plays an important role in protecting consumers from the risks associated with drug purchases. In addition to determining whether drugs should be assigned over-the-counter or prescription status, the FDA must approve a new drug before it can be sold in the marketplace. Government approval is necessary, it is

---

4. Schwartzman (1976) also examined economies of scale in pharmaceutical manufacturing, promotion, and research and development as barriers to entry. While Schwartzman found no evidence supporting manufacturing economies, he noted that larger firms tend to be associated with promotion and R&D economies. These two economies make it harder for small potential competitors, but not large ones, to compete with entrenched pharmaceutical companies. These and other studies on research economies are taken up in the conduct section.

argued, because drug firms may otherwise perform insufficient testing in an attempt to gain a first-mover advantage or to avoid high costs. The elixir sulfanilamide and thalidomide tragedies in the 1930s and 1960s are two examples where people either died or were harmed by unsafe drug products. The elixir sulfanilamide disaster occurred when Massengill Company used diethylene glycol as a solvent to formulate a liquid form of sulfanilamide without testing it for toxicity. More than 100 children died from the poisonous chemical. The other tragedy happened in Germany and other European countries when thalidomide, a sleeping pill, caused babies to be born without hands or feet.

Because the market may fail in the absence of government intervention and provide either unsafe or ineffective drugs, the FDA has been assigned the role of approving new drugs. Economists, such as Grabowski and Vernon (1983), point out that the FDA tends to err on the side of conservatism, resulting in long FDA approval times and a slower rate of pharmaceutical innovations. The economic argument goes like the following.

An all-knowing FDA approves the drug application when the therapeutic benefits of the drug outweigh its risk. Thus, a correct decision means the FDA approves a safe and effective product or rejects an unsafe or ineffective one. Due to uncertainty, however, the FDA may make two types of errors.

The first error, called *type 1* error, occurs when the FDA rejects the application for a new drug that is truly safe and effective. In contrast, a *type 2* error occurs when the FDA approves a drug that is unsafe or ineffective. As Grabowski and Vernon (1983) write, "Both types of error influence patients' health and well-being since consuming a 'bad' drug or not having access to a 'good' drug can have deleterious effects on health" (p. 10). One would think either type of error is random and therefore equally likely to occur in an uncertain world. However, that is not the case. An FDA member who unknowingly approves an unsafe drug faces personal losses: job loss, political indignation, and the knowledge that some consumers may have been harmed. Moreover, the outcome from approving an unsafe drug is eventually known and highly visible.

The cost associated with rejecting a safe and effective drug, a type 1 error, on the other hand, is borne by a third party (the drug manufacturer or a sick patient) rather than by an FDA member and therefore is less apparent. The rejection of a good drug may never be known. Thus, according to this view, the FDA faces an incentive to reject rather than accept, or at least delay the approval of, a drug more often than is necessary in a perfect world.

Interestingly, an unconstrained market faces incentives to accept "bad" drugs and commit a type 2 error. Profit-seeking drug firms wishing to be the first to market with a new drug may skimp on necessary testing. The FDA faces an incentive to reject or delay "good" drugs and commit a type 1 error. Longer approval periods translate into further testing, higher R&D costs, lower expected profitability, and fewer drug innovations. Thus, both the market and the government potentially make mistakes. The gnawing question is which institution, the market or the government, makes fewer and less costly ones.[5]

The Structure of the Pharmaceutical Industry: A Summary

The structure of an industry reflects whether certain market conditions hold such that firms can, either unilaterally or collectively, exploit their market power and operate inefficiently. Competitive market conditions such as a large number of sellers and

---

5. The Prescription Drug User Fee Act of 1992 and the Food and Drug Administration Modernization Act of 1997 included provisions designed to improve the efficiency of FDA review procedures and the clinical development process. See Reichert et al. (2001) for more information on these laws and their effectiveness in achieving their goals.

buyers, low entry barriers, perfect information, and homogeneous products all point to a situation in which sellers are unable to exert market power. The degree of structural competition in the pharmaceutical industry is not easy to assess, because measures of concentration are sensitive to the definition of the relevant product market and have tended to change significantly over time. Moreover, patents and brand loyalty, by establishing an entry barrier, make it more difficult for new firms to enter various therapeutic markets. Established brand-name firms, however, may not face these obstacles if they have sufficient resources to produce similar drugs but with slightly different chemical compositions.

The demand side of the market remains fairly fragmented, so any market power that drug manufacturers possess is not automatically offset by influential buyers. However, the use of formularies, drug utilization programs, mandated generic substitution, and third-party payer contracts with informed pharmaceutical benefit management companies places greater emphasis on cost-effective medicines, which counteracts seller market power to some extent. Given this ambiguity about the degree of structural competitiveness, we will now turn to a discussion of the conduct of firms in the pharmaceutical industry.

The Conduct of the Pharmaceutical Industry

In this section, we analyze evidence regarding the behavior of pharmaceutical companies. Three practices of drug firms are examined: pricing, promotion, and product innovation. The basic question is whether evidence exists for competitive or noncompetitive behavior in the pharmaceutical industry. For example, we ask the following four questions, among others:

1. Are drug prices lower when drug firms face greater competition?
2. Are newcomers more likely to enter pharmaceutical markets when existing firms' profits are high during the postpatent period, or do postpatent barriers prevent entry?
3. Is drug promotion informative or persuasive? Do the promotion expenditures of established firms impede the entry of new firms?
4. Is a large firm size necessary for product innovation in the pharmaceutical industry?

Pricing Behavior

The relatively high concentration of sales among a few firms and substantial barriers to entry in many therapeutic markets imply that pharmaceutical companies may possess the ability to price their drug products above the marginal costs of production and generate economic profits. In addition, first-mover advantages may mean that leading firms have the power to maintain brand-name prices above costs and still dominate the market over generic companies even after patent expiration. Promotion expenditures by the leading pharmaceutical firms may help reinforce the habit-buying practices of many buyers, especially physicians.

The potential for noncompetitive pricing has motivated several researchers to examine the pricing practices of pharmaceutical companies (Hurwitz and Caves, 1988; Caves et al., 1991; Grabowski and Vernon, 1992; Lu and Comanor, 1994; Wiggins and Maness, 2004; Reiffen and Ward, 2005; Rizzo and Zeckhauser, 2009). Although these seven studies use various empirical methods and data sets, they tend to draw fairly consistent conclusions regarding the competition between branded drugs, generic drugs, and branded and generic drugs.

First, the prices of both brand-name and generic products are found to be lower when a greater number of substitute products are available in the marketplace.[6] This finding should not be surprising because more substitutes mean buyers can more easily switch to alternative drugs when the price of any one drug is raised. Two, prices of branded drugs sometimes rise upon generic entry. That result implies that leading pharmaceutical firms do not engage in limit pricing because they would otherwise set a low price to discourage or limit entry. Grabowski and Vernon note that the higher branded drug price occurs in response to the dynamics of a segmented market. That is, as generics enter the market and satisfy price-sensitive buyers with lower prices, brand-name firms are left with buyers who are relatively price insensitive. As a result, brand-name companies are able to raise their prices, at least in the short run, because they now effectively face a less elastic demand for their pharmaceutical products.

Three, the goodwill established during the patent period plays an important role, allowing established firms to maintain a large market share and relatively high prices despite the huge discounts offered by generic companies. Four, a high brand-name profit margin at the time of generic entry increases the number of entrants fairly quickly, sometimes by the end of first year. This finding means entry of new generic products is sensitive to expected profits in the product market when entry barriers are low, as economic theory suggests. Five, price accounts for most of the variation in a generic company's market share although other factors, such as first- (or second-) mover advantages and perceptions of quality differences among generic suppliers, may also be important in specific circumstances. Six, the therapeutic novelty of a drug influences pricing strategy over time. In particular, therapeutically innovative drugs are generally introduced under a modified price-skimming strategy. A modified price-skimming strategy means that therapeutically innovative drug prices are initially set high and then held relatively constant over time. Imitative drugs, on the other hand, are introduced under a market penetration strategy. The prices of imitative drugs are low at first to enlarge market share, but are then increased over time as information about their availability spreads.

Promotion of Pharmaceutical Products

Medicines are cited as one of the first products advertised in printed form (Leffler, 1981). Timely product information is especially valuable in the pharmaceutical industry due to the continual introduction of new lifesaving drugs. With about 22,000 different drugs on the market, doctors have a great deal to learn and remember (Schwartzman, 1976). Before prescribing, doctors must know the appropriate drug, the correct dosage, and the properties of the drug for different patients, classified by various characteristics such as age, weight, and general health status. Thus, it is not surprising that promotion expenditures can run as high as 20 to 30 percent of sales for many research-based pharmaceutical companies. In 2010, nearly 60 percent of the promotional budget was spent on personal promotion by detailers (pharmaceutical salespeople), and journal advertising (about 3 percent). Direct-to-consumer advertising accounted for the rest of the promotional budget (see Top-Line Market Data at www.IMSHealth.com).

It is theoretically unclear to economists whether pharmaceutical promotion strategies enhance or reduce societal welfare. As we saw in Chapter 8, advertising may promote or impede competition depending on whether informed or habit-buying behavior results. Early studies on this topic by Leffler (1981), Hurwitz and Caves (1988), and Caves et al. (1991) find evidence supporting both the informational and persuasion effects of pharmaceutical promotion.

---

6. Also see Ellison et al. (1997), who find relatively high elasticities between generic substitutes and also significant elasticities between therapeutic substitutes at both the prescribing and dispensing stages.

In terms of informative advertising, Leffler finds that advertising intensity is greater for newer and more important pharmaceutical products, which, he argues, reflects the informational content of the promotion message. Leffler, as well as Hurwitz and Caves, discovers that the new entrants' promotion expenditures helped them expand their market shares. Caves et al. conclude that increased generic competition results in less advertising by the innovator, which, they argue, must reflect the informational rather than persuasive content of the innovator's pharmaceutical advertising during the preentry period.

The evidence for persuasive advertising is equally strong. In particular, Leffler finds that less detailed targeting of younger physicians occurs for older products. That is, advertisers tend to direct their advertisements to the physician age group in medical schools when the drug product was originally introduced. Thus, the creation of brand loyalty and reinforcement of habit buying must be the real purpose behind advertising. Hurwitz and Caves find that the leading firms' promotion expenditures preserved their market share from new generic entrants. Finally, the study by Caves et al. notes that generic firms gain relatively small shares despite their huge discounts, perhaps reflecting the goodwill built up by the innovator's promotion expenditures during the patent period.

Given the inconsistent findings in the literature, Rizzo (1999) investigates the informative versus persuasive aspects of promotional activities in an entirely different manner by examining the impact of promotional expenditures on price elasticity of demand. According to economic theory, demand becomes more elastic, and price declines, when buyers are more fully informed because of promotional activities. In contrast, persuasive promotional activities cause habit buying, less elastic demand, and higher prices according to economic theory. Therefore, we can infer whether promotional activities are persuasive or informative by empirically studying how such activities influence price elasticity of demand.

In support of the persuasive view of promotional activities, Rizzo finds that greater detailing efforts led to a lower price elasticity of demand for antihypertensive drugs. As an example of his findings, Rizzo reports that price elasticity with no detailing equaled -1.98 for one of his models. In contrast, price elasticity of demand equaled -0.48 in the short run as a result of increased current detailing activities. Thus, Rizzo provides direct empirical evidence "that product promotion inhibits price competition in the pharmaceutical industry, lowering price elasticities and leading to higher equilibrium prices" (pp. 112–13).

Like studies examining promotion activities directed toward physicians, research focusing on direct to consumer advertising (DTCA) has also been inconclusive with regards to the efficiency implications of promotion activities in the drug industry. For example, Capella et al. (2011) use data on brand name drugs in five major therapy classes which were marketed in the United States during the 2001 to 2005 period. They test the effect of DTCA and other promotional variables on the price elasticity of demand. The predictions of the two competing theories on the economic effects of advertising, as previously discussed in the context of the Rizzo study, are used as a basis for forming their hypotheses. The empirical findings of Capella et al. indicate that, in general, no significant relationship exists between DTCA and the price elasticity of demand for drugs in the five categories studied. Thus, given the inverse relationship between elasticity of demand and price, their findings do not support the position that consumers pay higher prices as a result of DTCA in the pharmaceutical industry.

In contrast, Dave and Saffer (forthcoming) investigate the separate effects of broadcast and nonbroadcast DTCA on price and demand, using an extended time series of monthly records for all advertised and nonadvertised drugs in four major therapeutic classes (painkillers and cholesterol, heartburn and insomnia medicines) over the period 1994 to 2005. Controlling for the amount of promotion directed at physicians, their results suggest that broadcast DTCA directly impacts own-sales and price, with estimated elasticities of 0.10 and 0.04, respectively. In addition, they find relative to broadcast DTCA, nonbroadcast DTCA had a smaller impact on sales (elasticity of 0.05) and price (elasticity of 0.02). Given the relatively large increase in DTCA expenditures over time, their simulations suggest that the expansion in broadcast DTCA may be responsible for about 19 percent of the overall growth in prescription drug expenditures over the sample period, with over two-thirds of this impact being driven by an increase in demand as a result of the DTCA expansion and the other third because of higher prices.

As mentioned previously, promotion expenditures represent about 20 to 30 percent of the typical drug firm's budget. Whether those expenditures benefit or harm consumers is largely dependent on the persuasive versus informative content of the promotion activities. Empirical research focusing on how drug promotion activities influence consumer and physician behavior has generally been inconclusive. Clearly, more cost and benefit (value of lives saved because of advertising) studies are needed before any solid conclusions can be drawn about the overall efficiency implication of drug promotion activities.

Product Innovation

The most important contribution associated with the pharmaceutical industry is the timely introduction of new drug products that can extend or improve lives. New drug discoveries require a significant amount of research and development activities. The R&D process for new drugs is normally spread over many years, and only a small fraction of new drug discoveries are eventually approved for marketing. R&D costs constitute a sizeable proportion of sales revenues. For example, Figure 14–1 shows that R&D expenditures for research-based pharmaceutical companies ranged from a low of 11 percent of sales in 1974 and 1978 to a high of 22 percent of sales in 1994. The R&D to sales ratio, or R&D intensity, averaged nearly 19 percent during the 2000s.

FIGURE 14–1
R&D Intensity of Major Pharmaceutical Companies, 1970–2009

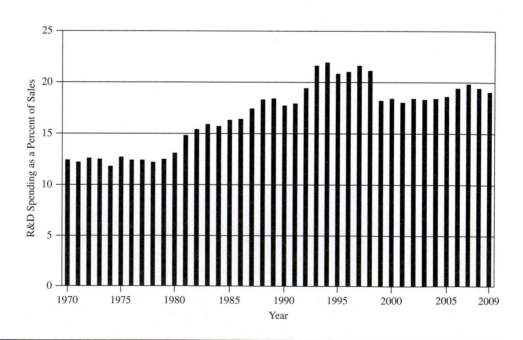

SOURCE: PhRMA (2010).

Due to the high cost and risk associated with R&D, the decision-making process underlying new drug development tends to unfold sequentially. At several points in the R&D process, a company reviews the development status of a drug and makes a decision about continuing or abandoning the project. The decision rests on the expected profitability of the proposed drug and thus considers both expected revenues and costs. Expected revenues depend in part on the therapeutic properties of the drug, the size of the target market, and the number of substitute drugs. Anticipated costs depend on the frequency and severity of adverse reactions to the drug and the projected additional development, marketing, distribution, and production costs (DiMasi et al., 1991).

Researchers generally identify eight stages involved in the R&D process. DiMasi et al. estimate that the clinical period from the initiation of Phase I testing to drug approval lasts about 98.9 months, with the FDA approval process taking about 2½ years, on average. The average time needed to complete the entire process from the discovery stage to marketing approval is estimated at 12 years (with some overlap occurring among the various stages). About 75 percent of the NMEs in Phase I testing enter Phase II testing, and about 36 percent eventually enter Phase III testing. Only 18.3 percent of the drugs that entered clinical trials during 1980 to 1984 were marketed by the mid-1990s (DiMasi, 1995).

Determinants of R&D Spending.   As with any investment, the optimal amount of R&D spending depends on the amount of expected economic profits or the difference between the expected future streams of revenues and costs. Thus, when empirically examining the determinants of pharmaceutical R&D, researchers focus on variables affecting both the expected revenues and costs of investing in new drug development. Variables that increase the rate of return lead to more R&D spending whereas those that raise opportunity cost reduce the level of R&D.

Researchers, such as Grabowski and Vernon (1981), Vernon (2005), and Lichtenberg (2004), have investigated the determinants of pharmaceutical R&D using the expected revenue and cost framework just described. While a variety of variables have been specified in the estimation equations in these various studies, most have relied upon the contemporary profit rate, past R&D success (e.g., number of new drug per R&D dollar over the last few years), or market value of the firm as a measure of expected revenues.

To control for factors influencing the opportunity cost of R&D, these researchers typically specify a variable measuring each firm's cash flow margin during the previous year. The cash flow margin is specified because the opportunity cost of internal funds is less than that of external funds. That is, because of transaction costs, the cost of borrowing external funds (i.e., loans from banks or sales of stocks and bonds) is generally higher than that of using internal funds. Thus, R&D spending is expected to increase with a greater cash flow margin because opportunity costs are lower. In general, researchers find that variables influencing expected revenues, such as the market value of the drug company, and the past value of cash flow are important determinants of drug innovation. These empirical findings are important because they suggest a price ceiling on drug prices, by reducing cash flows and expected revenues, could result in a reduction in pharmaceutical R&D.

In fact, over the recent past, various members of Congress have questioned whether the Medicare program should directly "administer" the drug prices paid to drug manufacturers rather than allow private health insurance companies to "negotiate" prices with drug companies. The argument is that the Medicare program could use its sizeable buyer clout to extract lower drug prices for Medicare recipients. Critics argue, however, that a situation of that kind would be tantamount to a price ceiling regime. Recall from Chapter 9 that under specific circumstances, a price ceiling can lead to quality reductions and shortages, among other effects.

For example, Giaccotto et al. (2005) estimate that pharmaceutical expenditures would have been about 30 percent lower if the federal government had limited drug prices to the same rate of growth as the general price inflation rate during the 1980 to 2001 period. Moreover, while the price ceiling would have produced sizeable cost-savings for consumers during that period, Santerre and Vernon (2006) estimate that the losses would have been much greater in terms of fewer new drugs created and, correspondingly, the value of lives that would have been lost.

Firm Size and Innovation.   Another important issue regarding the conduct of pharmaceutical firms is the relation between firm size and innovative activities. The question is whether large pharmaceutical firms are more likely than small firms to engage in successful innovative ventures. Given the importance of product innovation in this industry, antitrust laws concerning mergers may not be enforced so strictly if larger firms are found to be more innovative than smaller ones.

Economic theory by itself offers only limited insight on the relation between firm size and innovation. Schumpeter (1950) is among the first economists to propose that larger firms may be more successful at innovation than smaller firms because they have the resources necessary to engage in modern large-scale R&D activities. Modern and commercially successful innovations are very expensive to undertake, and therefore small firms may lack the necessary physical and financial resources. In addition, larger firms diversify their R&D efforts among various projects and thus can better absorb the risks associated with innovative activities. Finally, many analysts believe that economies of scale exist in research such that per-unit costs fall with a greater production of R&D activities because more efficient, specialized research inputs are used.

These three factors—resource capability, risk absorption, and research economies—suggest that larger firms tend to face a greater incentive to undertake successful R&D activities than smaller firms. Opposing this tendency, however, is the argument that greater bureaucratic red tape in larger organizations stifles creativity. Since important decisions are normally made at a centralized level in a large, bureaucratic firm, communication flows ultimately break down and decisions take longer to execute. The resulting time lags from this issue delay or discourage new product ideas from being pursued or continued. Using data from 1982, Acs and Audretsch (1988) analyze the innovative contributions of small and large firms, defined as firms having fewer or more than 500 employees, respectively. For the pharmaceutical industry, Acs and Audretsch find that larger firms had 9.23 times the innovations of smaller firms in 1982. However, larger pharmaceutical firms also had 19.41 times the employment of smaller drug firms. Together these results indicate that larger firms generate only half the number of pharmaceutical innovations that smaller firms do on a per-employee basis. Thus, according to their empirical results, large firm size may not be necessary for pharmaceutical innovation.

In a related study, Acs and Audretsch (1987) analyze the specific characteristics affecting the differential innovation rates of large and small firms across different industries. Acs and Audretsch determine that large firms tend to have an innovative advantage in industries that are capital intensive, advertising intensive, and relatively concentrated at the aggregate level. In contrast, small firms are more innovative in industries in which total innovation and the use of skilled labor play a large role and where some, but not many, large firms exist. We mentioned earlier that the pharmaceutical industry is characterized by high advertising intensity. This industry characteristic tends to favor the innovation of large pharmaceutical firms. However, most of the characteristics described previously suggest that small pharmaceutical companies may be more innovative.

First, total innovation plays a very important role in the pharmaceutical industry. In fact, Acs and Audretsch (1988) cite the pharmaceutical industry as the fourth most innovative out of 247 industries in 1982. Second, the skilled labor of pharmacologists, biochemists, and immunologists, among others, is necessary in the drug industry given the high technical sophistication of pharmaceutical R&D. Third, casual empiricism suggests that a number of large, highly visible firms coexist with a much larger number of smaller firms in the pharmaceutical industry. Fourth, Schwartzman (1976) notes that capital requirements for manufacturing are relatively low in the pharmaceutical industry. Finally, we saw that the pharmaceutical industry is characterized by relatively low aggregate seller concentration.

Thus, the safest conclusion to draw is that a mixture of firm sizes is most favorable for fostering pharmaceutical innovation. While smaller drug firms seem to hold a decisive advantage, the preceding results suggest that the innovativeness of smaller firms is greatest when large firms dominate in an industry. Encouraging innovation through a diversity of firm sizes should not be too surprising. Many researchers note that new ideas are relatively cheap to conceive, but the commercial development and successful marketing of new products are costly and risky. Small firms might have the edge at the discovery stage, but large firms possess development and marketing advantages. Greer (1992) contrasts the innovativeness of large and small firms as follows:

> The foot-dragging behavior of leading firms is so common that theorists have dubbed it "the fast-second strategy." Briefly the idea is that, for a large firm, innovation is often costlier, riskier, and less profitable than imitation. A large firm can lie back, let others gamble, then respond quickly with a "fast second" if anything started by their smaller rivals catches fire. (p. 669)

Greer notes that Genentech, an infant firm in the late 1970s, founded biotechnology. Larger pharmaceutical firms, such as Eli Lilly, followed Genentech's lead into biotechnology in the mid-1980s.

The Conduct of the Pharmaceutical Industry: A Summary

The studies discussed in this section show that a considerable amount of competition takes place in the pharmaceutical industry. Drug firms sometimes face price competition during the patent period from other branded products, and prices are lower when more branded competition exists. Branded drugs also compete with generics on the basis of price during the postpatent period. Generics offer huge discounts relative to branded products. Also, product competition is particularly important in the pharmaceutical industry. Incentives for new product development exist because a new drug product, especially a therapeutically important one, can easily supplant others in the market.

However, the degree of competition in the pharmaceutical industry is not perfect. Firms offering single-source drugs are able to raise prices above the marginal cost of production because substitutes are unavailable. Furthermore, evidence shows that pharmaceutical marketing is used partly to reinforce the habit-buying practices of physicians. Hence, some drug buyers still remain price insensitive due to brand loyalty.

The Performance of the Pharmaceutical Industry

In this section, we appraise the performance of the contemporary pharmaceutical industry. Competitive market impediments, such as patents, trademarks, and high promotion expenditures, characterize the pharmaceutical industry and suggest that entrenched companies may possess enough market power to restrict output, raise prices, and earn excessive profits.

First, we compare the prescription drug price inflation rate to the general inflation rate in the United States and identify trends and measurement problems. Second, since product innovation is the true output of the pharmaceutical industry, we discuss studies analyzing the benefits of new drugs and examine historical data on the number of NMEs. Finally, we look at some comparative data on the aggregate profitability of pharmaceutical companies.

The Relative Price Inflation Rate of Pharmaceutical Products

To gauge performance, policy makers often examine how the price of a product changes over time. Prices may change because of imbalances in supply and demand or distortions in the marketplace. For consumers with relatively fixed incomes, higher prices can be particularly harmful in terms of the amounts of other goods and services that must be given up. With that backdrop in mind, let's study how drug prices have tended to change over the last few decades in the United States.

Figure 14–2 compares the prescription drug price and general price inflation rates in the United States for the period 1996 to 2011 (November to November). We start the analysis in 1996 because prior to that year the Bureau of Labor Statistics (BLS), the agency responsible for determining price indices, undersampled new drug products, failed to treat generic products as lower-price substitutes for branded drugs, and used list prices rather than actual transaction prices. These flaws in the method, which have been corrected, tended to overestimate the true pharmaceutical inflation rate.

The figure indicates that the drug price inflation rate exceeded the overall price inflation rate during 13 of the 16 years shown. Indeed, over the entire period the drug price inflation rate averaged 3.8 percent compared to the 2.5 percent overall price inflation rate. Thus, real drug price increased, on average. However, the real drug

FIGURE 14–2
Drug and General Price Inflation Rates, 1996–2011

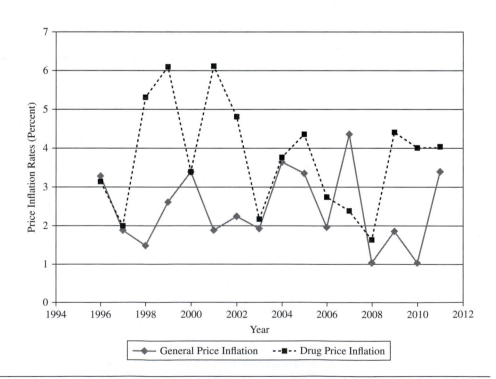

SOURCE: Bureau of Labor Statistics, http://www.bls.gov. (accessed January 20, 2012).

price did not rise continuously throughout the 16-year period. For example, during the period 2004 to 2005 the two inflation rates were virtually equal at 3 percent. In contrast, the drug price inflation rate was twice as high as the overall price inflation rate during the 2009 to 2011 period (4.2 percent compared to 2.1 percent). Overall, it can be concluded that drug prices increased more rapidly than general prices during the 1996 to 2011 period. It stands to reason that the relatively higher drug prices during this period reduced the consumer surplus of those individuals with fixed incomes who were heavily dependent on prescription drugs to maintain their health.

Before moving on to the next section, it should be noted that the BLS faces a difficult task when measuring changes in the quality of products over time. As Scherer (1993) has noted, "some new drugs, by improving the quality of life or making expensive surgery unnecessary, plainly yield enormous increments of consumer surplus" (p. 103). Because new pharmaceutical products are introduced and utilized at such a rapid rate, quality-adjusted price inflation rates may be lower than the BLS reported rates. If pharmaceutical manufacturers adjust new drug prices to compensate for the higher quality, however, no overstating of the true drug price inflation rate occurs.

Output of New Pharmaceutical Products

Another measure of an industry's performance is output. Economic theory tells us that societal welfare is enhanced when goods are produced up to the point where marginal social benefit equals marginal social cost (see Chapter 3). Empirically, costs and benefits are hard to measure, so we must often rely on information regarding industrial structure and conduct, as well as sound judgment, to determine whether the right incentives exist for efficient output levels. Because of some noncompetitive structural conditions (patents, trademarks, promotion) existing in the pharmaceutical industry, one might expect some restrictions on output. The question is whether evidence supports this expectation.

New drugs probably represent the single most important measure of pharmaceutical output. New drugs improve quality of life by relieving pain and have significantly reduced deaths from many diseases including tuberculosis, kidney infection, and hypertension. Pharmaceutical innovations have virtually eliminated diseases such as whooping cough and polio.

An ample amount of academic research supports the argument that new drug products extend or improve the quality of lives. For example, Lichtenberg (2005) performs an econometric analysis of the effect of new drugs on longevity using disease-level data from 52 countries during 1982 to 2001. His empirical analysis allows him to control for other potential determinants of longevity, such as education, income, nutrition, the environment, and lifestyle. He finds historically that new drugs have a strong positive impact on the probability of survival. More specifically, Lichtenberg discovers that new drugs increase life expectancy of the entire population by an average annual increase of one week (based on conservative assumptions). This means that people in society, on average, can expect to live one week longer each year because of new drugs. He also estimates that new drugs, on average, produce an additional life-year at an incremental cost of about $6,750, which is far lower than most estimates of the value of a statistical life-year ($100,000 to $150,000).

Another strand of academic research asks whether new drugs, although expensive, pay for themselves by substituting for more expensive types of invasive surgery. For example, Weidenbaum (1993) notes that "the cost of treating ulcers with H-2 antagonist drug therapy runs about $900 per year. The cost of ulcer surgery, by contrast, averages $28,900" (p. 87). As another example, the use of tranquilizers has substantially reduced the hospitalization of mental patients (Peltzman, 1974). This substitution of new drugs for non-drug therapy is sometimes referred to as the **new drug cost offset theory**.

Unfortunately, academic research on this topic offers inconsistent evidence regarding the new drug cost offset theory. Studies such as Lichtenberg (2001, 2002, and 2009), Civan and Koksal (2010), and Santerre (2011) provide evidence to support the theory when the analysis is conducted at an aggregated level such as for all drugs combined or for states or countries. Others such as Duggan (2005), Miller (2006), Law and Grepin (2010), and Liu and Hsieh (forthcoming 2012) offer no support, perhaps because their studies are performed at a disaggregated level such as for a particular disease. Clearly, more studies are needed before we can draw any strong conclusions regarding whether or not new drugs generally pay their own.

Nevertheless, many recognize the significant and positive effect of new drugs on longevity and quality of lives. Thus, because we are assessing the performance of the drug industry, it is useful to know how the number of NMEs has changed over time. Data on the number of NME approvals in the United States from 1980 to 2009 appear in Figure 14–3.

As Figure 14–3 shows, the number of NMEs increased from an average of 22 per year in the 1980s to 31 per year in the 1990s. Nine more drugs per year represent a sizeable rise in innovative activities. During the 2000s, however, the number of NMEs slipped to an average of 23 per year. This fall in the number of NMEs in the 2000s is somewhat surprising given the relatively high amount of drug sales devoted to R&D during the late 1980s and 1990s (see Figure 14–1). Recall that it takes about 12 years of research to successfully launch a new drug. However, other factors, such as diminishing returns with respect to R&D activities and slower FDA approval times, may account for the recent drop in the number of NME approvals in the United States.

Profits in the Pharmaceutical Industry

Most complaints aimed at the pharmaceutical industry have concerned excessive profits. Patents, brand loyalty, and an inelastic demand for drugs written by physicians are cited as the causes of high pharmaceutical profits. Some comparative data for the after-tax return on equity (ROE) and return on assets (ROA) are shown

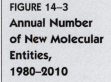

**FIGURE 14–3
Annual Number
of New Molecular
Entities,
1980–2010**

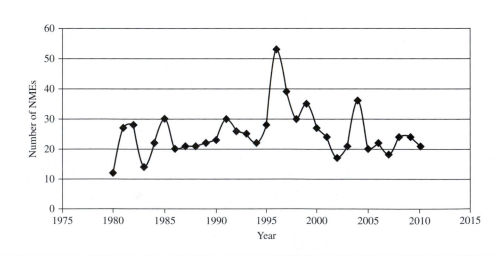

SOURCE: U.S. Food and Drug Administration at http://www.fda.gov/AboutFDA/WhatWeDo/History/ProductRegulation/SummaryofNDAApprovals Receipts1938tothepresent/default.htm from 1980 to 2006 and various popular press reports thereafter. After 2003, the figures also include the number of therapeutic biologic product approvals.

TABLE 14–3

Return on Assets and Stockholder Equity for Drug and All Manufacturing Companies, Various Years

	After-Tax Return on Equity								
	1986	**1989**	**1992**	**1995**	**1997**	**2001**	**2004**	**2007**	**2010**
All manufacturing	9.6%	13.5%	2.6%	16.2%	16.6%	2.0%	15.7%	15.4%	15.1%
Drugs (SIC 283 or NAICS 3254)	24.1	25.3	22.3	27.0	23.2	32.1	14.6	16.3	14.5%

	After-Tax Return on Assets								
	1986	**1989**	**1992**	**1995**	**1997**	**2001**	**2004**	**2007**	**2010**
All manufacturing	4.2%	5.5%	0.9%	6.2%	6.6%	0.8%	6.4%	6.8%	6.6%
Drugs (SIC 283 or NAICS 3254)	11.8	12.5	10.5	10.4	9.5	12.2	7.2	9.0	6.9%

SOURCE: U.S. Bureau of the Census, Quarterly Financial Report (various issues), http://www.census.gov (accessed January 19, 2011).

in Table 14–3 for all manufacturing firms and drug firms for selected years from 1986 to 2010. ROE and ROA are determined by dividing net income (net sales less operating costs and expenses) after taxes by the value of stockholder equity and the firm's assets, respectively. The data illustrate that the profit rate of drug firms, as measured by either ROE or ROA, was much greater than that of the manufacturing industry average for each of the years up to 2001. Specifically, the ROE and ROA for drug firms, on average, were more than twice the manufacturing industry average for the first six years shown.

Beginning in 2004, however, the profit rate situation reversed somewhat. For two of the three years, the ROE average for all manufacturing surpassed that of the pharmaceutical industry, albeit narrowly. In addition, the ROA for all manufacturing and drug companies have been fairly close during the more recent years. Market forces, such as increased competition from generic drugs or government regulations affecting drug manufacturing costs, may account for the declining relative drug profit rates since 2001. These declining drug profit rates may be one reason for the slight slowing of R&D intensity during the 2000s that can be observed in Figure 14–1.

Researchers point out accounting rates of return may be biased upward for drug firms due to unusually high R&D and marketing outlays (see Scherer, 1993). Expenditures on these "intangible assets" are expensed, but should be capitalized and then depreciated over an appropriate time period because they ordinarily yield a long-term flow of benefits to drug manufacturers. Studies have found that pharmaceutical returns are 20 to 25 percent lower when R&D and marketing outlays are treated as intangible assets (Office of Technology Assessment, 1993).

Even after accounting biases have been eliminated, pharmaceutical returns typically remain higher than the manufacturing average (Comanor, 1986). Pharmaceutical industry spokespeople point out that R&D is a risky venture. High R&D risks translate into high pharmaceutical returns, because otherwise risk-averse individuals would be unwilling to invest in drug firms. They note that the successful introduction of a pharmaceutical product costs about $802 million or more because a drug firm encounters a large number of misses before finding a commercial hit which hopefully translates into a blockbuster drug (DiMasi et al., 2002).

The Performance of the Pharmaceutical Industry: A Summary

In this section, we reviewed data concerning the prescription drug price inflation rate, number of new chemical entities, and accounting profits as measures of industry performance. Drug prices were shown to have increased more rapidly than general prices for all but a few years since 1996. Except for a few years, the average profit rate in the pharmaceutical industry was also shown to be higher than the average profit rate in the manufacturing sector. By themselves, these two performance measures suggest that society's scarce resources may be misallocated in the pharmaceutical industry. Data regarding R&D spending and number of NME approvals paint a somewhat different picture of the pharmaceutical industry. Drug R&D spending averaged about 20 percent of sales during the 1990s and 2000s compared to 18 percent during the 1980s. In addition, the number of NMEs averaged 31 and 23 per year during the 1990s and 2000s; more than the 22 per year average of the 1980s.

This discussion implies that a trade-off might exist between "static" and "dynamic" efficiency. Static efficiency refers to the efficiency of firms at a point in time and reflects how successfully firms employ a given technology or produce a given product. In contrast, dynamic efficiency relates to the efficiency of firms over time and captures how successful they are at developing new products and processes. As Berndt (2002) writes:

> *Although this conflict between static efficiency (price new drugs low, near short-run marginal cost) versus dynamic efficiency (price new drugs high, maintain incentives for innovation) is a deep and enduring one, as the costs of bringing new drugs to market have increased sharply in recent years, this tradeoff is becoming more severe. The resolution of this static versus dynamic efficiency conflict is likely the single most important issue facing the pharmaceutical industry over the next decade. (p. 45)*

Provisions of the Patient Protection and Affordable Care Act (PPACA) of 2010 Relating to the Pharmaceutical Industry

This act will likely have a number of direct and indirect effects on the pharmaceutical industry. For example, the pharmaceutical industry is required to offer increased rebates under the Medicaid program (23.1 percent rather than 15.1 percent basic rebate) and to help fill the Medicare donut hole by offering sizeable discounts (see Chapter 10). Also, the drug industry may be affected by any comparative effectiveness research measures adopted by the Patient Centered Outcomes Research Institute (see Chapter 2). Here, we only focus on some provisions having a more direct impact on the pharmaceutical industry, particularly the branded-drug segment of the industry.

First, the increased health insurance coverage resulting from the health insurance mandate should increase the demand for all type of drugs and thereby raise sales in the drug industry. Whether the increased demand largely influences the utilization or price of drugs is difficult to predict and depends on the cost structure that individual drug firms face and any controls, such as formularies and utilization review programs, adopted by drug payers.

Second, firms manufacturing or importing branded drugs will be required to pay an annual fee, which amounts to a tax on branded-drug sales beginning in 2011. The amount of the tax for any one firm is dependent on that firm's share of all branded-drug sales in the United States. For the branded-drug industry as a whole, the aggregate annual fee starts at $2.5 billion in 2011, increases to a maximum of

$4.1 billion in 2018, and then decreases to $2.8 billion in 2019 and onward. As economic theory suggests, the incidence of this tax on branded drugs depends on the relative supply and demand elasticities with respect to price. If generic versions of the branded drugs are available, consumers should pay a smaller percentage of the tax. Manufacturers of generic drugs may benefit from the annual fee on branded drugs.

Finally, the PPACA attempts to increase access to lower-cost generic drugs by preventing brand-name drug companies from delaying approval of generic drugs by making label changes to their brand name or listed drugs. Prior to the act, the labeling of generic drugs was required to match the labeling of the referenced brand name or listed drugs, or they would not be approved. Under the PPACA, a generic drug can be approved despite last-minute changes to the labeling of the listed drug, as long as the labeling change to the listed drug is approved 60 days prior to the date of expiration of the listed drug's patent or exclusivity period, and provided that the labeling change does not affect the "Warnings" section of the listed drug's labeling.

Summary

This chapter assessed the structure, conduct, and performance of the U.S. pharmaceutical industry. Based on aggregate Census data, the pharmaceutical industry was shown to contain a relatively large number of equally sized firms, but disaggregation of the pharmaceutical industry into therapeutic markets showed that only a few major drugs typically compete against one another. Legal patents and brand loyalty built up during the patent period are argued to cause substantial barriers to entry into therapeutic markets. Generic drug companies offering huge discounts are particularly ineffective in influencing the loyalty attached to brand-name drugs because physicians are often responsible for selecting drugs. Physicians are not normally price sensitive since they are effectively spending someone else's money.

Further evidence, however, reveals that considerable deconcentration has taken place in the pharmaceutical industry at the therapeutic level. Studies show that price competition takes place among multisource drugs. Price competition sometimes occurs among branded drugs during the patent period and between generic and brand-name drugs during the postpatent period. Drug prices are usually lower when there are more substitute products.

New product innovation, the major benefit of the pharmaceutical industry, tends to be a risky endeavor and was shown to depend on expected profitability and cash flow. Debate still continues over the relation between firm size and innovation. The safest conclusion to draw from recent studies is that a mixture of firm sizes in the pharmaceutical industry best favors innovation.

Data suggest that real drug prices have risen more quickly than general prices and pharmaceutical firms have experienced relatively high rates of return, at least until the last several years. The resulting cash flow may have helped to finance R&D spending and NMEs during the 1990s and 2000s. All in all, the pharmaceutical industry seems to best fit the model of a "mild to tight differentiated oligopoly." That is, there is some evidence of a few competitors in therapeutic markets, substantial but not perfect barriers to entry based on patents and trademarks, product differentiation, evidence of price and product rivalry rather than cooperation, and evidence of relatively high prices and profits.

The future should witness a continual evolution in the pharmaceutical industry. The demand side of the market will most likely adopt further cost-saving methods, such as formularies, drug review utilization, and generic substitution. As a result of the MMA of 2003, government may be prone to impose price controls if drug prices continue to soar given the greater financial responsibilities of the public sector in pharmaceutical markets. Seller concentration in many therapeutic markets should diminish as many drug patents soon expire and generic competition increases. It will be interesting to follow the effects of these demand- and supply-side changes on the amount of new drug innovation.

Review Questions and Problems

1. Describe three benefits associated with pharmaceutical products. Cite one example of each.

2. As mentioned in the chapter some empirical studies have shown that new drugs improve health status. Does that finding invalidate the flat-of-the-curve medicine discussed in Chapter 2? Why or why not?

3. Suppose a drug has the potential to reduce the use of surgery but the cost of a full-year treatment with that drug costs $15,000. Discuss how you might approach a cost-effectiveness or cost-benefit analysis comparing that drug versus surgery.

4. How do the six-digit North American Industry Classification System (NAICS) and the therapeutic market definition of the pharmaceutical industry differ in terms of seller concentration? Which do you think is a better measure? Why? Think in terms of actual and potential competition.

5. Explain some methods adopted by third-party payers to control drug prices.

6. Explain the purpose and functioning of a PBM company. What are the antitrust concerns about a drug manufacturer purchasing a PBM company? What is the efficiency justification for such an acquisition?

7. The main economic rationale for a patent system is that quick imitation and commercialization reduces the expected profits of drug companies which thereby diminishes innovative activities. Given market realities, do you think a patent system is truly necessary? Can you think of other alternatives to a patent that might maintain innovation but preserve competition?

8. How would you describe the current market structure of the pharmaceutical industry? Do you think that the typical drug firm possesses any market power based on market structure? Why or why not?

9. This chapter argues that the FDA faces an incentive to delay the approval of new drugs, whereas pharmaceutical firms face an incentive to accelerate the introduction of new drugs. Explain some market realities that may force pharmaceutical firms to introduce new drugs at a more efficient pace.

10. What general conclusions have empirical studies reached concerning drug price competition?

11. In this chapter we discussed the information versus persuasive aspect of advertising as a way of inferring the efficiency implication of drug advertising. If you had all of the necessary data available to you, explain how you might conduct a study to determine if drug advertising is cost-effective (as a way of inferring efficiency)? Think in terms of health outcomes.

12. Suppose the Centers for Medicare and Medicaid Services (CMS) began directly negotiating prices with drug manufacturers on behalf of Medicare recipients. Also suppose that CMS decides to pay the same price for branded drugs and generic drugs when the latter are available. Discuss how that practice might affect the creation of new drugs in the future.

13. Do you think drug companies earn excessive profits? Why or why not?

14. Do you think clinical practice guidelines should be relied upon when distinguishing between uses of drugs versus surgery? Why or why not?

15. One suggested remedy for high drug prices in the United States is the re-importation of lower-priced drugs from other countries. Do you think re-importation of drugs is a good idea? Why or why not? What are the costs and benefits of that practice?

16. Some states have considered or implemented tiered copayments for drugs covered by their Medicaid programs. For example, that means low-income Medicaid recipients would have to pay higher copayments for branded drugs versus generic versions and for drugs not on the formulary to ones that are on the formulary. Do you think that is a good policy from an economic perspective? What are some of the trade-offs involved?

Online Resources

To access Internet links related to the topics in this chapter, please visit our website at **www.cengage.com/economics/santerre**.

References

Acs, Zoltan J., and David B. Audretsch. "Innovation in Large and Small Firms: An Empirical Analysis." *American Economic Review* 78 (September 1988), pp. 678–90.

Acs, Zoltan J., and David B. Audretsch. "Innovation, Market Structure, and Firm Size." *Review of Economics and Statistics* 69 (November 1987), pp. 567–74.

Berndt, Ernst B. "Pharmaceuticals in U.S. Health Care: Determinants of Quantity and Price." *Journal of Economic Perspectives* 16 (fall 2002), pp. 45–66.

Capella, Michael L., Charles R. Taylor, Randall C. Campbell, and Lance S. Longwell. "Do Pharmaceutical Marketing Activities Raise Prices? Evidence from Five Major Therapeutic Classes." *Journal of Public Policy & Marketing* 28 (2011), pp. 146–61.

Carroll, Norman V., and Alan P. Wolfgang. "Risks, Benefits, and Generic Substitution." *Journal of Consumer Affairs* 25 (summer 1991), pp. 110–21.

Caves, Richard E., Michael D. Whinston, and Mark A. Hurwitz. "Patent Expiration, Entry, and Competition in the U.S. Pharmaceutical Industry." *Brookings Papers: Microeconomics* (1991), pp. 1–66.

Civan, Abdulkadir, and Bulent Koksal. "The Effect of Newer Drugs on Health Spending: Do They Really Increase the Costs?" *Health Economics* 19 (May 2010), pp. 581–95.

Cohen, Joshua P. "PBMs and a Medicare Prescription Drug Benefit." *Food and Drug Law Journal* 55 (2000), pp. 293–476.

Comanor, William S. "The Political Economy of the Pharmaceutical Industry." *Journal of Economic Literature* (September 1986), pp. 1178–1217.

Dave, Dhaval M., and Henry Saffer. "Impact of Direct-to-Consumer Advertising on Pharmaceutical Prices and Demand." *Southern Economic Journal* (Forthcoming).

DiMasi, Joseph A. "New Drug Innovation and Pharmaceutical Industry Structure: Trends in the Output of Pharmaceutical Firms." *Drug Information Journal* 34 (2000), pp. 1169–94.

DiMasi, Joseph A. "Success Rates for New Drugs Entering Clinical Testing in the United States." *Clinical and Pharmacology Therapeutics* 58 (July 1995), pp. 1–14.

DiMasi, Joseph A., Ronald. W. Hansen, and Henry G. Grabowski. "The Price of Innovation: New Estimates of Drug Development Costs." *Journal of Health Economics* 22 (2002), pp. 151–85.

DiMasi, Joseph A., Ronald W. Hansen, Henry G. Grabowski, and Louis Lasagna. "Cost of Innovation in the Pharmaceutical Industry." *Journal of Health Economics* 10 (1991), pp. 107–42.

Duggan, Mark. "Do New Prescription Drugs Pay for Themselves? The Case of Second Generation Antipsychotics." *Journal of Health Economics* 24 (2005), pp. 1–31.

Egan, John W., Harlow N. Higinbotham, and J. Fred Weston. *Economics of the Pharmaceutical Industry*. New York: Praeger, 1982.

Ellison, Sara F., Ian Cockburn, Zvi Griliches, and Jerry Hausman. "Characteristics of Demand for Pharmaceutical Products: An Examination of Four Cephalosporins." *RAND Journal of Economics* 28 (autumn 1997), pp. 426–46.

Federal Trade Commission (FTC). "Merck Settles FTC Charges That Its Acquisition of Medco Could Cause Higher Prices and Reduced Quality for Prescription Drugs." Press release (August 27, 1998), http://www.ftc.gov.

Giaccotto, Carmelo, Rexford E. Santerre, and John A. Vernon. "Drug Prices and Research and Development Investment Behavior in the Pharmaceutical Industry." *Journal of Law and Economics* 48 (April 2005), pp. 195–214.

Grabowski, Henry G., and John M. Vernon. "Brand Loyalty, Entry, and Price Competition in Pharmaceuticals after the 1984 Drug Act." *Journal of Law and Economics* 35 (October 1992), pp. 331–50.

Grabowski, Henry G., and John M. Vernon. "Longer Patents for Lower Imitation Barriers: The 1984 Drug Act." *American Economic Review Papers and Proceedings* 76 (May 1986), pp. 195–98.

Grabowski, Henry G., and John M. Vernon. *The Regulation of Pharmaceuticals: Balancing the Benefits and Risks.* Washington, D.C.: American Enterprise Institute, 1983.

Grabowski, Henry G., and John M. Vernon. "The Determinants of Research and Development Expenditures in the Pharmaceutical Industry." In *Drugs and Health,* ed. Robert Helms. Washington, D.C.: American Enterprise Institute, 1981, pp. 3–20.

Greer, Douglas F. *Industrial Organization and Public Policy.* New York: Macmillan, 1992.

Hurwitz, Mark A., and Richard E. Caves. "Persuasion or Information? Promotion and the Shares of Brand Name and Generic Pharmaceuticals." *Journal of Law and Economics* 31 (October 1988), pp. 299–320.

Law, Michael R., and Karen A. Grepin. "Is Newer always Better? Re-evaluating the Benefits of Newer Pharmaceuticals." *Journal of Health Economics* 29 (2010), pp. 743–50.

Leffler, Keith B. "Persuasion or Information? The Economics of Prescription Drug Advertising." *Journal of Law and Economics* 24 (April 1981), pp. 45–74.

Lichtenberg, Frank R. "Have Newer Cardiovascular Drugs Reduced Hospitalization? Evidence from Longitudinal Country-Level Data in 20 OECD Countries, 1995–2000." *Health Economics* 18 (May 2009), pp. 519–34.

Lichtenberg, Frank R. "The Impact of New Drug Launches on Longevity: Evidence from Longitudinal, Disease-Level Data from 52 Countries, 1982–2001." *International Journal of Health Care Finance and Economics* 5 (2005), pp. 47–73.

Lichtenberg, Frank R. "Public Policy and Innovation in the U.S. Pharmaceutical Industry." In *Public Policy and the Economics of Entrepreneurship,* eds Holtz-Eakin D, Rosen HS. MIT Press: Cambridge, MA, (2004) pp. 83–113.

Lichtenberg, Frank R. "Are the Benefits of New Drugs Worth Their Cost? Evidence from the 1996 MEPS." *Health Affairs* 20 (September/October 2001), pp. 241–51.

Lichtenberg, Frank R. Benefits and Costs of Newer Drugs: An Update. National Bureau of Economic Research Working Paper No. 8996. Cambridge, Mass.: NBER, 2002.

Liu, Ya-Ming, and Chee-Ruey Hsieh. "New Drugs and the Growth of Health Expenditures: Evidence from Diabetic Patients in Taiwan." *Health Economics* (forthcoming 2012).

Lu, Z. John, and William S. Comanor. "Strategic Pricing and New Pharmaceuticals." Mimeo, University of California at Santa Barbara, 1994.

McRae, James J., and Francis Tapon. "Some Empirical Evidence on Post-Patent Barriers to Entry in the Canadian Pharmaceutical Industry." *Journal of Health Economics* 4 (1985), pp. 43–61.

Miller, G. Edward, John F. Moeller, and Randall S. Stafford. "New Cardiovascular Drugs: Patterns of Use and Association with Non-Drug Health Expenditures." *Inquiry* 42 (2006), pp. 397–412.

Moore, Stephen D. "Glaxo, SmithKline Renew Their Rivalry in Medicines Used to Prevent Vomiting." *Wall Street Journal,* November 19, 1993, p. B4D.

Mosby Medical Encyclopedia. New York: C. V. Mosby, 1992.

Office of Technology Assessment. *Pharmaceutical R and D: Costs, Risks and Rewards.* OTA-11-522. Washington, D.C.: U.S. Government Printing Office, February 1993.

Peltzman, Sam. *Regulation of Pharmaceutical Innovation: The 1962 Amendments.* Washington, D.C.: American Enterprise Institute, 1974.

Pharmaceutical Research and Manufacturers of America (PhRMA). *Profile 2008 Pharmaceutical Industry.* Washington, D.C.: PhRMA, 2008.

Price Waterhouse. *Financial Trends in the Pharmaceutical Industry and Projected Effects of Recent Federal Legislation.* Report prepared for the Pharmaceutical Manufacturers Association, October 21, 1993.

PricewaterhouseCoopers. "Study of Pharmaceutical Benefit Management." HCFA Contract No. 500- 97-0399/0097, June 2001, http://www.pcmanet.org/ research/ostudies/hcfastudy.pdf.

Reichert, Janice M., Jennifer Chee, and Claire S. Kotzampaltiris. "The Effects of the Prescription Drug User Fee Act and the Food and Drug Administration Modernization Act on the Development and Approval of Therapeutic Medicines." *Drug Information Journal* 32 (2001), pp. 85–94.

Reiffen, David, and Michael R. Ward. "Generic Drug Industry Dynamics." *Review of Economics and Statistics* 87 (February 2005), pp. 37–49.

Rizzo, John A. "Advertising and Competition in the Ethical Pharmaceutical Industry: The Case of Antihypertensive Drugs." *Journal of Law and Economics* 42 (April 1999), pp. 89–116.

Rizzo, John A., and Richard Zeckhauser. "Generic Script Share and the Price of Brand-name Drugs: The Role of Consumer Choice." *International Journal of Health Care Finance and Economics* 9 (2009), pp. 291–316.

Santerre, Rexford E. "National and International Tests of the New Drug Cost Offset Theory." *Southern Economic Journal* 77 (April 2011): pp. 1033–1043.

Santerre, Rexford E., and John A. Vernon. "Assessing Consumer Gains from a Drug Price Control Policy in the U.S." *Southern Economics Journal* (July 2006), pp. 233–245.

Scherer, F. M. "Pricing, Profits, and Technological Progress in the Pharmaceutical Industry." *Journal of Economic Perspectives* 7 (summer 1993), pp. 97–115.

Scherer, F. M., and David Ross. *Industrial Market Structure and Economic Performance.* Boston: Houghton Mifflin, 1990.

Schmalensee, Richard. "Product Differentiation Advantages of Pioneering Brands." *American Economic Review* 72 (June 1982), pp. 349–65.

Schumpeter, Joseph. *Capitalism, Socialism and Democracy.* New York: Harper, 1950.

Schwartzman, David. *Innovation in the Pharmaceutical Industry.* Baltimore: Johns Hopkins University Press, 1976.

Statman, Meir. *Competition in the Pharmaceutical Industry: The Declining Profitability of Drug Innovation.* Washington, D.C.: American Enterprise Institute, 1983.

Temin, Peter. "Realized Benefits from Switching Drugs." *Journal of Law and Economics* 35 (October 1992), pp. 351–69.

Temin, Peter. *Taking Your Medicine: Drug Regulation in the United States.* Cambridge, Mass.: Harvard University Press, 1980.

Vernon, John A. "Examining the Link between Price Regulation and Pharmaceutical R&D Investment." *Health Economics* 14 (2005), pp. 1–16.

Weidenbaum, Murray. "Are Drug Prices Too High?" *Public Interest* 112 (summer 1993), pp. 84–89.

Wiggins, Steven N., and Robert Maness. "Price Competition in Pharmaceuticals: The Case of Anti-Infectives." *Economic Inquiry* 42 (April 2004), pp. 247–63.

CHAPTER 15

The Long-Term Care Industry

In a cult movie of the 1970s, Wild in the Streets, Max Frost, a rock star and newly elected 21-year-old president, created an imaginative solution to what was perceived as an "elderly" problem in the United States. He placed all the elderly people into concentration camps and fed them hallucinogens like LSD. Far away in the concentration camps, elderly people were kept out of sight and out of mind (literally so, because of the hallucinogens). To Max and friends, if you were 35 years of age or older, you were elderly. Elderly people, like parents, teachers, and policemen, possessed authority. Max and his followers despised authority. Hence, the concentration camps for the elderly. Hey! What do you expect from a movie that was designed to appeal to the rebellious young adults growing up during the 1960s?

Today, one could rightfully argue that we do have a problem concerning the elderly in the United States. The problem has nothing to do with authority, however. The problem pertains to the delivery and financing of long-term care for individuals incapable of caring for themselves. Elderly people make up a majority of the individuals requiring long-term care, and the number of elderly people has grown both in absolute and relative terms over time. In fact, while only one in ten people in the United States was 65 years of age or older in Max Frost's day (the 1960s), today that number is less than one in eight. And the population is expected to get even older on average in years to come. Projections suggest that by the year 2050 one out of every five people will be a senior citizen. Indeed, nearly 5 percent of the U.S. population is expected to be older than 85 by 2050!

We learned earlier in the text that health capital depreciates more rapidly with age. Consequently, the graying of the United States will likely be associated with a more intensive use of medical services for a growing number of the elderly, all of which will contribute to rising health care costs in the future. Of particular concern is the increasing cost of caring for the chronically ill elderly on a long-term basis. Finding ways of containing long-term care costs without compromising the quality of care or lives will be a tremendous challenge. Society will have to make hard choices and trade-offs are inevitable unless some truly imaginative solutions are found.

With these choices, trade-offs, and imaginative solutions in mind, this chapter investigates the market for long-term care services. Specifically, this chapter:

- studies the structure of the long-term care industry by analyzing the number and size distribution of the various providers of long-term care services such as nursing homes and home health care agencies. We also look at the buyer side and barriers to entry in the long-term care market, among other structural features.
- discusses the conduct of long-term care providers. In particular, the behavior of long-term care providers, mainly nursing homes, in response to market competition; various pricing methods (such as prospective versus retrospective reimbursement); form of ownership; and regulations are extensively studied. Quality issues pertaining to long-term care are also highlighted.

- examines the performance of the long-term care industry by observing and discussing various indicators such as aggregate price, input usage, output, insurance coverage, and expenditures.
- analyzes the implications of the Patient Protection and Affordable Care Act of 2010 regarding the Long-Term Care Industry.

The information obtained will help us understand the structure, operation, and performance of the contemporary long-term care services industry and will be vital in our roles as informed consumers and voters, health care providers, and public policy makers.

The Structure of the Long-Term Care Services Industry

Before we begin our discussion of the industry, it would be useful to define **long-term care**. Long-term care is typically defined as:

> *a set of health care, personal care, and social services delivered over a sustained period of time to persons who have lost, or never acquired, some degree of functional capacity, as measured by an index of functional ability.*

According to this definition, long-term care primarily enhances quality of life rather than cures a particular medical problem. In many instances, patients in need of long-term care have one or more physical limitations that will be with them for the rest of their lives or, at the very least, for an extended period of time. For example, an elderly man may need help with bathing and walking because of a recent stroke. Or a young woman may need continual assistance because of a car accident that left her permanently paralyzed from the neck down. In each instance the need for long-term care is likely to be permanent—the emphasis is on enhancing quality of life and gaining some measure of independence for the patient. Although hospitals and physicians offer some level of long-term care, they primarily provide short-term treatment aimed at curing rather than caring for or rehabilitating a patient.

Scanlon (1980) points out that, unlike the demand for medical services, the demand for nursing home care reflects a basic rather than a derived demand. He goes on to note that nursing homes are long-term substitutes for independent living and that the function of nursing homes is not to restore health, or "cure," but to provide "care" to those with permanent disabilities. Consequently, physicians play only a minor role in the choice process concerning nursing home care, unlike the choice concerning hospital services where they play a dominant role.

Other elements to keep in mind are that the continuum of care and the organizational settings in which care is provided varies widely. The continuum of care varies from the occasional need for assistance to perform various household chores, such as mowing the lawn or shopping for groceries, to the need for around-the-clock nursing care. Or the continuum of care may include a rehabilitation program that involves physical, occupational, and/or speech therapy. The spectrum of organizational settings that provide long-term care also varies extensively. For example, friends and family members may provide long-term care on an informal basis in the elderly person's own home, or long-term care can be provided in a formal, highly intensive setting such as a skilled nursing home. Intermediate care can be provided by a home health care agency or at an assisted living facility. We begin to analyze the structure of the long-term care industry by examining the need for long-term care. This discussion is followed by a review of the major providers of long-term care services.

The Need for Long-Term Care

It is generally recognized that an individual needs long-term care when faced with a long-term physical or mental limitation severe enough to impede the ability to carry out the everyday activities of independent living. One of the most frequently used

TABLE 15–1
A Measurement of the Need for Long-Term Care

Measurement	Examples of Basic Functions
Activities of daily living (ADL)	Bathing
	Dressing
	Eating
	Getting in and out of a chair or bed
Instrumental activities of daily living (IADL)	Going outside the home
	Performing household chores
	Keeping track of household finances
	Cooking and preparing meals
	Using the telephone
	Taking medicine

SOURCE: General Accounting Office, Long-Term Care, Current Issues and Future Directions. GAO/HEHS-95-109. Washington, D.C.: GAO, April 1995

methods to determine whether an individual requires long-term care is to assess whether that individual has the ability to carry out a predetermined list of activities of daily living (ADL), or instrumental activities of daily living (IADL) (see Table 15–1). ADL and IADL are sets of activities used by health care professionals to measure the ability of individuals to perform routine daily living activities. These rating scales are of value because they provide policy analysts with an objective means of establishing the need for long-term health care, both in terms of the number of people who require long-term care and the intensity of care needed.

Using these criteria, estimates from Older Americans (2010) indicate that 42 percent of the elderly population, defined as all individuals age 65 and older, has some limitation of activity and may be in need of some type of long-term care. The elderly are not the only ones in need of long-term care. In 2006, 7.3 percent of the population under age 18 and 5.5 percent of individuals aged 18 to 44 had some limitation of activity attributable to a chronic condition. Clearly, however, the need for long-term care is greatest among the elderly population.

Structure of Informal Care Providers

It is generally agreed that family members and friends provide a substantial amount of long-term care on an informal basis. By its very nature, however, the amount of care provided is difficult to accurately measure. Fortunately, a few recent surveys shed some light on the number of people providing long-term care on an informal basis and the backgrounds of those individuals. For example, Feinberg et al. (2011) estimate that in 2009 approximately 42 million individuals provided informal care in the United States.[1]

Despite wide variations in the estimates concerning the amount of informal care provided, the surveys are in general agreement regarding what types of individuals are providing the care. According to the Feinberg et al. (2011), the representative

---

1. Ho et al. (2005) and Gibson and Howser (2007) reach different conclusions about the number of informal caregivers, in part, because of differences in the manner in which elder care is defined and the timing of the care. In terms of timing, the person being surveyed could be asked, "Are you currently providing long-term care?" or "Have you provided care to anyone in the last year?" Naturally, the latter survey question will generate much higher estimates regarding the amount of informal care provided.

informal caregiver tends to be a woman in her late forties who is providing more than 20 hours of care per week. She is most likely employed full-time, possesses at least a high school degree, and is of relatively modest economic means. Not surprisingly, most caregivers are related to the recipient, usually a relationship involving a daughter and her mother. Finally, in more than 75 percent of the cases, the caregiver lives either with the care recipient or within 20 minutes of the care recipient. These findings are compelling and suggest that "caregiving for an elder has become a 'normative' experience for U.S. families" (Wagner, 1997, p. 2).

Structure of the Nursing Home Care Industry

The structure, conduct, and performance paradigm of industrial organization suggests that the structure of an industry matters. In conjunction with the firm's objectives and various government regulations, structure affects how intensely firms compete and ultimately their performance in the health care sector and overall economy. Among the more critical factors influencing market structure are the number and size distribution of firms, the number and size distribution of buyers, and the height of any barriers to entry into the industry. We next assess each of these structural features with respect to the nursing home industry.

Number and Characteristics of Nursing Home Providers. Table 15–2 provides estimates for the number of facilities, quantity of beds, ownership status, size distribution, and occupancy rate of nursing homes in the United States. According to the data, roughly 16,000 nursing homes function in the United States with approximately 1.7 million beds. These two figures suggest that the typical nursing home facility operates with about 100 beds, roughly half the bed size of the typical hospital in the United States.

Most nursing homes are organized on a for-profit basis and that percentage has been rather stable in recent years. The data in Table 15–2 for Medicare- and Medicaid-certified nursing homes show that the percentage of nursing homes in the

TABLE 15–2
Characteristics of the Nursing Home Industry

	2003	**2006**	**2009**
Nursing Homes	16,779	16,118	15,884
For-profit	65.5%	66.3%	67.5%
Not-for-profit	28.4%	27.7%	26.6%
Government	6.1%	6.1%	5.9%
Nursing Home Beds (per 1,000 residents)	5.91	5.61	5.44
Size Distribution			
Fewer than 50 beds	16.1%	14.8%	13.7%
50–99 beds	36.5%	36.1%	36.4%
100–199 beds	40.8%	42.7%	43.7%
200 beds or more	6.6%	6.4%	6.2%
Occupancy	84.3%	84.4%	83.0%

SOURCE: Nursing Home Data Compendium 2008 and 2010 Editions.

smallest and largest bed-size categories have tended to marginally decline over time. Moreover, the percentage of nursing homes with 50–99 has held stable while the percentage of nursing homes with 100–199 beds has marginally increased over time. As a result, the survivorship principle suggests that the optimal bed-size may hold between 50 and 199 beds given that most nursing homes find it best to operate in this bed-size range over time. We examine later what econometric studies tend to suggest about the existence of scale economies in nursing homes. Finally, the data in Table 15–2 imply that the occupancy rate of the typical nursing home in the United States is roughly 84 percent and that occupancy has declined marginally over time. The 84 percent nursing home occupancy rate is substantially higher than the 60 to 70 percent occupancy rate observed in the hospital services industry.

Taking all of the information together, we can get a clearer picture of the typical nursing home. The representative nursing home is organized on a for-profit basis and contains approximately 100 beds, and 85 of those beds are occupied on a typical day.

Buyers and Users of Nursing Home Services.   Nursing home expenditures were slightly more than $143 billion in 2010. As shown in Figure 15–1, four groups are primarily responsible for paying for nursing home services: the Medicaid program, the Medicare program, consumers, and private health insurers. The single largest payer of nursing home services is the Medicaid program, accounting for approximately 32 percent of nursing home expenditures. The next largest category of government funding is the Medicare program, accounting for about 22 percent of total funding.

Individual consumers represent the second-largest payer group for nursing home care services. Out-of-pocket costs account for 28 percent of nursing home expenditures and largely reflect the amount paid by private payers for long-term care services. Roughly 40 percent of all nursing home residents are private-pay patients. Empirical studies find that the price elasticity of demand for private-pay nursing home care varies widely, ranging from −0.16 to −2.30. Studies also find that the income elasticity of demand for nursing home care varies considerably with estimates ranging from −0.38 to 2.27 (Reschovsky, 1998). As one might expect, price and income elasticities of demand tend to be more elastic for elderly individuals who are either married or less chronically ill (Reschovsky, 1998) because home care represents

FIGURE 15–1
Expenditure Shares for Nursing Home Services, 2010

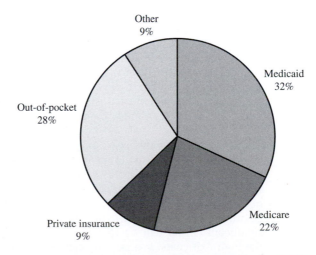

SOURCE: Centers for Medicare & Medicaid Services, National Health Expenditures. www.cms.gov.

a viable alternative in these two cases. The availability of informal care is another determinant of the demand for long-term care by private-pay individuals.

Finally, private insurers represent the next largest payer for nursing home care, at 9 percent of the cost. Most of the reimbursement pays for short-term post-acute nursing home services. Presently, only a small percentage of individuals have private insurance coverage for long-term care. We take up the reasons for the low long-term care insurance coverage rate later in this chapter.

In sum, data suggest that most nursing home care is paid for by federal and state governments, reflecting the large amount of short-term services provided to individuals under the Medicare program and long-term services provided to individuals under the Medicaid program. The government, because of its dominance in the market, may exert some influence on the operation and performance of short-term Medicare and long-term Medicaid nursing home services. Out-of-pocket costs remain sizeable for nursing home care. Studies find that the demand for nursing home care by private payers is more elastic with respect to price and income compared to the demand for medical care. The elastic nature of the private demand for nursing home care services may also limit the ability of an individual nursing home to raise price or reduce quality below the competitive level.

Barriers to Entry.   As discussed throughout the text, entry barriers may play an important role in the structure, conduct, and performance of an industry. Simply put, barriers to entry reduce the degree of potential competition and thereby may provide existing firms with some market power depending on the degree of actual competition in the marketplace. Market power may show up in high prices and/or reduced quality of care. It was also pointed out in earlier chapters that barriers to entry may be government-created (e.g., certificate of need programs, government franchises, or patents) or because of technical considerations (such as economies of scale, high sunk costs, learning curve effects, or exclusive control over a necessary input).

As mentioned in earlier chapters, econometric studies examine the existence of scale economies by estimating cost functions for goods or services. The estimated cost function shows the isolated empirical relationship between total operating costs and some measure of output or size after controlling for other determinants of costs such as input prices, quality of care, and patient case-mix. Taken as a whole, the econometric literature suggests that economies of scale are slight (i.e., the average cost curve is relatively flat in the scale economies range) for nursing home facilities and that the minimum efficient scale occurs at about 50 beds. For example, Christensen (2004) finds that small nursing homes experience some economies of scale while larger nursing homes experience no significant economies and may face some diseconomies of scale. Chen and Shea (2002) find that economies of scale do not exist in the nursing home industry with the exception of the Medicare post-acute care segment of the market, while Knox et al. (2007) find the nursing home industry experiences constant returns to scale. Therefore, it follows that scale economies do not represent a significant entry barrier into nursing home markets.

Sunk or irretrievable costs may cause a barrier to entry into an industry. Recall that irretrievable costs may involve initial investments or assets that cannot be easily salvaged when a firm exits the industry. Contestability theory suggests that markets are more contestable or potentially competitive when sunk costs are low because new entrants realize they can leave an industry relatively costlessly if economic circumstances do not turn out as initially suspected. Conversely, if sunk costs are significant, firms will be reluctant to enter new markets, *ceteris paribus*, because of the high exit costs. We saw in Chapter 13 that hospitals face huge sunk costs because of the immense cost and time involved in hospital construction. Nursing homes, however, are much smaller on average than hospitals. In addition, unlike hospitals with numerous floors and wide elevators, nursing homes tend to have one or two floors to minimize access problems of chronically ill residents. Also, unlike hospitals, very little diagnostic and therapeutic equipment is necessary to provide nursing home care. The upshot is that much less sunk costs are involved in nursing home care than hospital care, with the implication that sunk costs most likely do not seriously inhibit entry into the nursing home marketplace.

Certificate of need (CON) programs may represent a serious entry barrier in the nursing home industry. Recall that CON laws require that new and existing health care providers, like nursing homes, obtain approval before building new medical facilities or purchasing new capital items. CON laws are designed to control the amount of capital devoted to medical care as a way of controlling health care costs. However, if enforced too stringently, CON laws might result in inefficiency if too much capital is discouraged, competition is stymied as a result, and monopoly pricing ensues. Consequently, the effect of CON laws on the behavior and performance of nursing homes remains an empirical issue.

Unfortunately, only a few studies have examined empirically the impact of CON laws on the provision of nursing home care. After controlling for a host of factors such as income, age composition, and the state Medicaid reimbursement rate, Gulley and Santerre (2003) find that the existence of a state CON law program had no impact on the number of nursing homes or the number of nursing home beds relative to the elderly population. Similarly, Grabowski et al. (2003) find that the repeal of CON and moratorium laws had no effect on nursing home or long-term care Medicaid expenditures. As Harrington et al. (1997) note, the ineffectiveness of CON laws in reducing the number of homes and beds may result from the "lack of coordination with other regulatory programs, lack of significant compliance mechanisms, politicized review processes, and high approval rates for most requests" (p. 575).

Focusing on the growth rather than the level of nursing home beds, Harrington et al. (1997) found that the presence of a CON/moratorium program does matter. Specifically, Harrington et al. determined empirically that state regulations measurably slow the growth of nursing home beds. What remains to be determined is whether the reduction in the rate of growth is optimal from a societal perspective. While the reduced growth in nursing home beds may help contain the rising costs from excessive capital creation, it may also provide existing nursing homes with some market power. If so, existing nursing homes may desire CON laws because of the resulting market power. But according to Harrington et al., "the nursing home industry in general has been strongly ideologically opposed to CON and moratorium regulatory controls" (p. 586).

In sum, the nursing home industry contains a relatively large number of nursing homes with low market shares. Barriers to entry are relatively low, especially in areas without binding growth regulations such as CON laws. While the typical nursing home most likely faces a downward-sloping demand curve because most residents prefer locations near friends and relatives, the individual nursing home probably has little control over price since it faces the countervailing power of government and the highly price elastic demand of private buyers. From a structural perspective, the nursing home industry comes closest to resembling a monopolistically competitive industry.

Structure of the Home Health Care Industry

Similar to the nursing home industry, we now analyze the structure of the home health care industry. Once again, the characteristics of the seller and buyer side of the market are discussed to assess the structural competitiveness of the market. These structural features become important when evaluating the conduct and performance of the industry.

Number and Characteristics of Home Health Care Providers. In its broadest definition, home health care encompasses a variety of medical services to "individuals or families in their place of residence to promote, maintain, or restore health or to maximize the level of level of independence while minimizing the effects of disability and illness" (Haupt, 1998, p. 1). As such, home care services can involve a variety of medical services such as nursing care, physical and/or occupational therapy, speech therapy, homemaker services, and certain medical supplies.

The market for home health care has seen some rather dramatic shifts in recent years, largely because of changes in government funding. If you recall, during the mid-1980s the government implemented a prospective payment system for inpatient hospital services, called the diagnosis-related group (DRG) system. This new payment system caused the demand for outpatient services, including home health services, to increase rapidly. This increase in demand, coupled with a cost-based Medicare payment system for home health services, caused the number of home health agencies to grow rapidly during the 1990s. For example, from 1990 to 1995 the number of annual users of home health services increased by 75 percent and the volume of visits more than tripled (MedPAC, 2010). Thereafter, the number of agencies dropped significantly, from 10,917 agencies in 1997 to 7,528 in 2000. The decline was largely because of the Balanced Budget Act of 1997, which called for the implementation of the Interim Payment System that placed stricter limits on the Medicare cost-based reimbursement system.

In 2000, the Prospective Payment System for the payment of Medicare home health services was put in place. It pays home health agencies a predetermined rate for each 60-day episode of home health care. Since 2000, the number of home health agencies has increased dramatically, suggesting that the fixed Medicare payments may be more than adequate to cover costs. More specifically, the number of home health agencies increased from 7,528 in 2000 to 10,422 in 2009 (MedPAC, 2010).

In 2007, for-profit providers accounted for almost 70 percent of all home health agencies, with the remaining 30 percent divided up among not-for-profit (23.5 percent) and government entities. Nearly 30 percent of all agencies were affiliated with a group or chain and the average home health agency serviced 177 patients at any point in time in 2007 (Park-Lee et al., 2010).

Buyers and Users of Home Health Care Services. Home health care expenditures amounted to approximately $70 billion in 2010 and included payments to freestanding home health agencies, payments for certain types of medical equipment and payments to other nonmedical types of home care such as Meals on Wheels. The two largest payers for home health care services, amounting to 82.2 percent of all purchases, were the Medicare and Medicaid programs. Private insurers were responsible for 6.4 percent of total expenditures, while out-of-pocket expenses picked up an additional 7.1 percent. The remaining 4.3 percent came from other public and private sources. Given the significant role the government sectors plays in the home health care sector, we can see why changes in government reimbursement policies have had such a dramatic impact on the home health care services sector over the years.

Barriers to Entry. Entry barriers are most likely minimal in the home care services industry. Since services are provided in the home, very little capital is necessary. Hence, sunk costs play virtually no role. While most home care agencies are Medicaid and Medicare certified, which could cause an entry barrier, some states have as many unlicensed home care agencies as certified.

Economic theory suggests that cost structure characteristics such as scale and scope economies or learning curve effects might prohibit the entry of new firms. Cost characteristics do not appear particularly binding on the entry of new firms, however. For example, Kass (1987), in a study of 1,704 home health agencies, finds that economies of scale and scope are not substantial, while Gonzales (1997) finds similar results, showing that economies of scope are fully exhausted at 9 services (e.g. skilled nursing care, physical therapy, and occupational therapy). Given that most of the home health agencies in the sample normally provided between 7 and 11 services, scope economies do not seem to provide existing home health agencies with a cost advantage over new agencies. While Gonzales provides some evidence for scale economies, the relation between size and total costs does not appear to be particularly sizeable. Specifically, Gonzales finds that a 10 percent increase in size, as measured by home visits, leads to a 7.6 percent increase in costs. Therefore, the average cost curve is relatively flat such that the per-unit cost of production is fairly close for both small- and large-sized home health care agencies, *ceteris paribus*.

The Structure of the Long-Term Care Industry: A Summary

It is difficult to judge the degree of structural competitiveness in the long-term care industry. Long-term care tends to take place in local markets because elderly people wish to remain fairly close to family and friends. Consequently, detailed micro-information on the number and size distribution of nursing home and health care agencies is needed before conclusions can be drawn about the structural competitiveness of the long-term care industry in each local market area.

Having stated this limitation, long-term care most likely can be treated as a monopolistically competitive industry. There appears to be a sufficient number of actual competitors. For example, one nursing home competes against others and also with home health care agencies for patients. Also, for some recipients of long-term care, informal care remains an alternative to formal care. Moreover, most studies find the demand for private-pay long-term care, particularly nursing home care, to be highly elastic with respect to price. In addition, sources of technical barriers to entry, such as economies of scale, sunk costs, and chain organizations, do not seem to reduce the degree of potential competition. Only CON laws, when binding, and other government-created barriers (such as zoning laws), may limit the entry of new firms. We next assess how the conduct of the long-term care industry is influenced by its monopolistically competitive nature.

The Conduct of the Long-Term Care Industry

In this section, we discuss how various external circumstances, such as government regulations, influence the behavior of long-term care providers. The price and quality of long-term care are two of the behavioral issues examined. Virtually all of the discussion focuses on the nursing home industry because that is where most research has been directed. The monopolistically competitive nature of the nursing home industry, and the resulting downward-sloping demand curve, suggest that individual nursing homes may have some latitude in determining the price charged for private long-term care. Up against this framework, we examine the effect of Medicaid reimbursement, as a type of price regulation, on the behavior of nursing homes. We also examine whether type of ownership matters and the impact of market competition on the behavior of nursing home care providers.

The Dual Market Model of Nursing Home Pricing

The nursing home industry provides an interesting but complex setting to examine the pricing behavior of individual firms. Complexities result because, on a routine basis, nursing home decision makers must question the financial consequences of admitting patients who seek care on either a short- or a long-term basis and who may privately pay or receive insurance coverage from public programs such as Medicare or Medicaid. Consequently, decision makers in nursing homes must recognize the trade-offs involved and simultaneously determine the price charged and number of patients for each type of service and payer category. In this chapter we ignore short-term nursing home care because our concern is solely with issues relating to the delivery of long-term nursing home care. Neglecting short-term care is not too problematic because, as we saw when we examined the market structure of long-term care providers, most individuals receive long-term rather than short-term care in nursing homes.

We also saw that the dominant payers for nursing home care are private individuals who pay out of pocket and the Medicaid program. These two purchasers add an interesting twist to the pricing issue. While each state government sets the price paid by its Medicaid program for long-term care, the individual nursing home must still determine how many private-pay and Medicaid patients to treat and the price charged to private payers. Luckily for us, Scanlon (1980) provides an insightful model to investigate this choice-making process of an individual nursing home. A graphical illustration of his dual market model is provided in Figure 15–2.

Dollar values are shown on the vertical axis and the total number of private-pay and Medicaid patients is shown on the horizontal axis. The aggregated demand curve facing the individual health care provider has three distinct segments. The first segment, labeled AB, shows the private demand that lies above the Medicaid reimbursement rate of P_M. The second segment, BC, represents the Medicaid reimbursement rate of P_M for a particular number of Medicaid-eligible individuals in the market area, as measured by the horizontal distance BC. The third segment, CD_P, reflects the remaining portion of the private-pay demand. The curve AMR_P indicates the marginal revenue associated with the first segment of the private-pay demand curve. Given that the Medicaid reimbursement rate is independent of the number of Medicaid patients, P_M also reflects the marginal revenue associated with treating each additional Medicaid patient.

The profit-maximizing nursing home continues to treat additional patients as long as the additional revenues compensate for the added costs, MC. Thus, in equilibrium, the

---

FIGURE 15–2

The Dual Market Model of Nursing Home Behavior

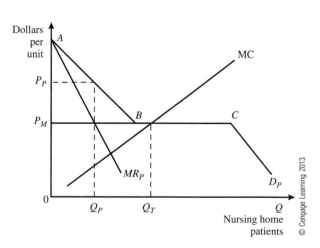

Lines AB and AMR_P represent the demand and marginal revenue curves for private-pay patients. Line segment BC represents the Medicaid reimbursement rate of P_M for the number of individuals eligible for Medicaid coverage in the market area. Line segment CD_P identifies the remainder of the private demand curve. The nursing home admits $0Q_T$ patients because the marginal revenue of $P_M = MC$. Of the total patients, $0Q_P$ are private pay and the remaining portion, Q_PQ_T, represents the number of Medicaid patients. Private-pay patients pay P_P for nursing home care. Because the horizontal distance Q_PQ_T, representing the number of Medicaid patients admitted, is less than the horizontal distance BC, showing the number eligible for Medicaid coverage, an excess demand for Medicaid nursing home care exists in the market area.

nursing home treats a total of $0Q_T$ patients where $P_M = \text{MC}$. Of the $0Q_T$ patients, $0Q_P$ are private-pay patients because they add more to profits over that range (that is, $MR_P > P_M$). The number of Medicaid patients lies between Q_P and Q_T. The theoretical model indicates that private-pay patients pay a higher price than Medicaid patients for the same services. According to the figure, each private-pay patient pays P_P, whereas the health care provider receives P_M for each Medicaid patient. In addition, the figure suggests that excess Medicaid demand exists at the government-established price of P_M because the horizontal distance between Q_P and Q_T, the number of admitted Medicaid patients, is less than the horizontal distance BC, reflecting the number of Medicaid eligible individuals in the market area.

An interesting policy question concerns what the government might do to reduce any excess demand for nursing home care. As one option, the government might raise the Medicaid reimbursement rate. As the Medicaid fee increases, the horizontal segment of the MR curve shifts upward along the MC curve and the nursing home expands its number of Medicaid patients relative to the number of private-pay patients. The exact number of additional Medicaid patients depends on the slopes of the private demand and marginal cost curves. Flatter curves imply that more Medicaid patients are admitted in response to a higher Medicaid reimbursement rate.

Notice, according to Figure 15–2, that private-pay patients are required to pay a higher price if the Medicaid reimbursement rate is increased. Gertler (1989) points out another possible consequence of a higher Medicaid reimbursement rate when a capacity constraint exists such as a CON law. Recall from Chapter 5 that higher quality shifts demand upward to the right, and lower quality shifts it to the left. In response to a higher Medicaid reimbursement rate, Gertler notes that nursing homes may react by lowering quality instead of, or in addition to, raising the private-pay price. Both actions reduce the quantity demanded of nursing home care by private-pay patients and provide additional rooms for the marginally more profitable Medicaid patients.

Consequently, private-pay patients may pay a higher price and/or receive a lower quality of care as a result of the higher Medicaid reimbursement rate if a capacity constraint exists. It should be pointed out that Medicaid patients also face a lower quality of care because it is illegal and also may not be cost effective for nursing homes to provide different levels of care to private-pay and Medicaid patients. For one reason, complementarities exist with respect to providing various activities such as food and laundry services to both private-pay and Medicaid patients. Although reduced, as long as the resulting quality of care is beyond the level of care provided in private homes, both private-pay and Medicaid patients may find it preferable to remain in the nursing home. Thus, when a capacity constraint and excess Medicaid demand jointly exist, higher Medicaid reimbursement rates may be associated with reduced quality. Gertler (1989), Nyman (1985), and Zinn (1994) all find that a higher Medicaid reimbursement rate lowers quality. However, using more recent data, Grabowski (2004) finds that higher Medicaid reimbursement has a positive impact on quality, pointing to a lessening of the capacity constraint over time along with enhanced competition from nursing home substitutes such as assisted-living facilities.

Raising the Medicaid reimbursement rate is likely to be a costly public policy option. Taxes on the general public must be raised to support the increased subsidy, especially if the higher price causes more individuals to become financially eligible for Medicaid coverage. Also, the nursing home may earn excess economic profits if price increases relative to average cost and entry barriers exist. If entry barriers do not exist, however, the greater profitability may create an incentive for new firms to enter the nursing home industry in the long run. Entry will shift down the private demand curve facing each individual nursing home and could result in a lower price paid by private-pay patients.

Another policy option is for the government to directly subsidize the costs of providing nursing home care. The subsidy reduces the marginal costs of production and shifts the MC curve downward. The lower marginal cost, in turn, creates an incentive for the representative nursing home to admit more Medicaid-eligible patients. Once again, however, this may be a costly alternative, as general taxes must be increased to cover the subsidy to nursing homes.

The Effect of Alternative Payment Methods

While useful for predicting the impact of changes in the Medicaid reimbursement rate or marginal costs on the behavior of nursing homes, the static analysis of Figure 15–2 may ignore some dynamic aspects of the reimbursement issue. As discussed in previous chapters, third-party payers may pay health care providers in a number of different ways. For example, the payment from the state government to the nursing home may be based on the actual cost at each nursing facility or some fixed amount based independently on some industry-wide standard. Differences in payment methods matter because they influence how individual nursing homes behave over time in terms of costs, quality of care, and patient case-mix. Some examples may highlight the differences.

First, suppose a state government sets the reimbursement rate for the next period based on the nursing facility's actual costs of servicing Medicaid patients. In fact, many states paid for nursing home care using retrospective cost-based reimbursement systems before 1980 (Coburn et al., 1993). Because of the retrospective and facility-specific nature of the reimbursement method, the nursing home faces less incentive to control costs, realizing it can simply pass on any cost increases to the state government. The higher costs will impose a greater tax burden on the general public. There is a silver lining to this dark cloud, however. If the nursing home can easily pass on any cost increases to the state government, it may be less likely to compromise quality of care and more likely to admit patients in more severe case-mix categories.

Second, suppose a state government sets a flat rate independent of actual facility costs or prospectively sets the reimbursement rate at the industry average projected forward with an automatic annual adjustment for inflation. The important consideration is that no allowance is made for actual costs incurred by the nursing facility for either the flat rate or the prospective payment method. Nursing homes are permitted to keep any profits but must also incur losses if actual costs exceed the Medicaid reimbursement, so they are at financial risk for any cost overruns. In this case the nursing facility faces an incentive to control the costs of servicing patients. Lower nursing home costs imply lower taxes for the general public but also mean that nursing homes may control costs by skimping on the quality of care or by practicing cherry-picking behavior. As a result, patients in the more severe case-mix categories may experience admission discrimination, and those that are admitted may not be provided with the proper quality of care.

As we can see, the government faces a policy dilemma not only when establishing the level of reimbursement but also with the method of reimbursement under Medicaid. Some hybrid forms of reimbursement exist that attempt to rectify some of the weaknesses of pure retrospective or prospective systems. One such method is case-mix adjusted reimbursement, which tries to compensate each nursing facility based on its particular patient case-mix and may include financial penalties and/or rewards to encourage efficient behavior. Price regulations like these, while well intended, can be difficult in practice to design correctly and typically involve substantial administrative costs (e.g., see Nyman and Connor, 1994).

Empirical studies tend to find that reimbursement methods influence the incentives of nursing homes with respect to costs, quality, and patient case-mix. In terms of costs, an early study by Frech and Ginsburg (1981) find that pure cost reimbursement without ceilings was associated with the highest costs. Specifically, compared to simple flat-rate systems, pure cost reimbursement led to costs that were 21 percent higher in the typical home. They also find that prospective reimbursement systems led to costs that were between pure cost and flat-rate reimbursement. The exact outcome depended on whether the prospective rates were established on the basis of the industry or the individual facility's experience in a previous year. When prospective rates are based on a facility's cost experience in the previous period, incentives are diluted and more resemble cost reimbursement. Using cost data for 1978 to 1980, Holahan and Cohen (1987) reach a similar conclusion, that prospective and flat-rate systems generally reduced cost growth more than retrospective payment.

In terms of quality, Zinn (1994) finds that both fixed rate and prospective systems led to fewer RNs per resident and worse process quality (a greater percentage of patients restrained and greater percentage not toileted, respectively) when compared to retrospective reimbursement. Case-mix reimbursement was found to increase the number of RNs per resident and improve process quality (lower percentage not toileted) relative to cost reimbursement. Cohen and Spector (1996) find that in states with fixed reimbursement, nursing homes use more lower-skilled and fewer higher-skilled professional nurses than homes in states with cost-based approaches. Finally, Cohen and Dubay (1990) determine that nursing homes respond to flat-rate systems by decreasing the severity of their case-mixes through admission discrimination and also decrease their staffing levels.

Scale Economies with Respect to Quality

Notice in the previous discussion that nursing homes may respond to changing external circumstances by altering the quality of care. Generally, a trade-off exists between costs and quality of care. The severity of the trade-off depends on whether scale economies hold with respect to producing quality. Figure 15–3, where total costs are shown on the vertical axis and the level of quality is depicted on the horizontal axis, helps clarify this point. Notice that two curves, $0A$ and $0B$, are drawn in the figure. Both curves show how much it costs to provide varying levels of quality at a representative nursing home. Suppose we begin with costs of C_0 and, correspondingly, a quality level of X_0 in each case. Now suppose that policy makers wish to reduce nursing home costs to C_1. Notice the degree to which the level of quality must change to accommodate the reduction in costs in the two cases. In the case of curve $0A$, quality declines by a relatively small amount to X_1^A, but for curve $0B$ quality falls by a

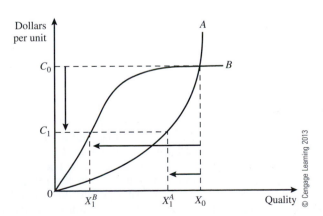

FIGURE 15–3
The Cost Savings from Quality Reductions

Curve $0B$ depicts scale economies with respect to quality whereas curve $0A$ shows diseconomies of scale with respect to quality. The graphical model suggests that quality must be sacrificed a great deal to achieve a given cost savings of C_0C_1 when scale economies hold. Conversely, the model indicates that quality improvements come at a much larger cost when the quality/cost relation exhibits diseconomies of scale.

much larger amount to X_1^B. The difference in the reduction of quality can be explained by scale economies. Curve $0B$ reflects decreasing costs or increasing returns with respect to quality, so costs increase proportionately slower than quality. Consequently, it takes a relatively large change in quality to achieve a given level of cost savings. Curve $0A$, in contrast, reflects increasing costs or decreasing returns, so smaller reductions in quality can attain a given level of cost savings.

In an imaginative paper, Gertler and Waldman (1992) measure scale economies with respect to quality in nursing homes. Based on relatively sophisticated theoretical and empirical modeling techniques, their work finds that the nursing home cost function exhibits diseconomies of scale in quality. As a result the authors point out that policies aimed at improving quality will be very costly. Policies aimed at cost savings, however, can be achieved with very small reductions in quality. For example, the authors determined that an increase in the Medicaid reimbursement rate lowers quality, as the Scanlon model with a capacity constraint predicts. However, the quality reduction was relatively small at 0.02 percent, whereas the cost savings were relatively larger at 0.2 percent given a one standard deviation increase in the Medicaid reimbursement rate. As another example, the authors find that increased market competition improves quality. More specifically, an increase in competition, as measured by a one standard deviation reduction in the Herfindahl-Hirschmann Index (HHI), raised quality by only 2.5 percent but increased costs by a much larger 20 percent.

Ownership and Conduct

According to property rights theory, ownership status may also influence how institutions behave. In for-profit organizations, individuals claim private ownership to any residual profits. In contrast, public and not-for-profit institutions are subject to a nondistribution constraint, meaning that any residual earnings cannot be distributed to those who control the organization, like managers, employees, or directors (Hansmann, 1996). As a result, some theorists believe that the lack of property rights to any residual profits provides less of an incentive for public and not-for-profit organizations to operate with least-cost methods of production. However, other theorists point out that although not-for-profit organizations do not maximize profits, they do pursue goals such as quantity and quality maximization. Alternative goals can be more easily realized when costs are held to a minimum.

Although the theory may be suspect for hospitals as discussed in Chapter 13, a relatively large number of studies have supported the basic prediction of property rights theory in the case of nursing homes. Nyman and Bricker (1989), in one of the more cited studies, compare the technical efficiency of not-for-profit and for-profit nursing homes. Technical efficiency exists when a given amount of output is produced with the fewest inputs. The authors employ a linear programming technique called **data envelopment analysis (DEA)** to determine the factors that influence the technical efficiency of a sample of nursing homes operating in Wisconsin. Briefly, this technique identifies benchmark firms that produce a fixed level of output with the fewest inputs. The inputs used in the Nyman and Bricker study include total nursing hours, total social service worker hours, total therapist hours, and total all other hours in an average day.

The benchmark firms are then used as a reference set to calculate an efficiency score for the remaining firms in the sample. The benchmark of most efficient firms are assigned a score of 1, while the less efficient firms are given scores less than 1 depending on their level of technical inefficiency. The efficiency scores in Nyman and Bricker's sample range from 0.226 to 1.

The efficiency scores are then regressed on a series of independent variables to determine the factors that influence the extent to which nursing homes efficiently utilize inputs. In their study, the factors used in the regression equation include a dummy variable controlling for the ownership status of the nursing home. The dummy variable equals 1 if the nursing home was a for-profit firm and 0 if it is organized on a not-for-profit basis. The hypothesis is that for-profit nursing homes have higher efficiency scores, as the basic property rights theory indicates.

Nyman and Bricker's findings indicate that for-profit nursing homes employed 4.5 percent fewer inputs per patient-day than otherwise comparable not-for-profit nursing homes. The authors' findings are consistent with the predictions of the managerial expense preference model, as discussed in Chapter 13 in the context of not-for-profit hospitals. Because managers of not-for-profit nursing homes are not pressured by owners to operate in an efficient manner, they increase costs by expanding discretionary expenditures and employing more than the minimum amount of inputs. The authors go on to state that if for-profit managers similarly acted in an inefficient manner, the owners would replace them. If the findings of this study are generally indicative of managerial behavior in the nursing home industry, as other studies such as Nyman et al. (1990), Fizel and Nunnikhoven (1992), and Knox et al. (2007) tend to confirm, ownership status does affect the performance of nursing homes. In the absence of an ownership constraint, managers of not-for-profit nursing homes act in an inefficient manner by overemploying labor inputs and operating at a point above the cost curve of otherwise similar for-profit nursing homes.

In their study, Nyman and Bricker attempt to control for quality differences among nursing homes by specifying the number of Medicaid certification code violations and other indirect measures of quality in the regression equation. Controlling for quality is particularly important when it comes to a service such as nursing home care because fewer labor inputs per patient may reflect a lower level of quality rather than greater efficiency. Their approach to holding quality constant is troublesome, however. Like the number and types of patients and inputs, the level of quality is also a variable decided by nursing home administrators. Stated in econometric terms, the level of quality is endogenous to the individual nursing home—a choice variable decided within the model—and not an exogenous variable, a parameter determined outside the model. The failure to properly specify quality as an endogenous variable could have led to improperly drawn conclusions.

In fact, theory suggests that not-for-profit organizations, because of the attenuation of property rights, may provide better quality of service than for-profits do when asymmetric information exists. Without sufficient consumer information, for-profit organizations may have more incentive to engage in opportunistic behavior in the process of maximizing profits. Not-for-profit institutions, in contrast, have less incentive to take advantage of consumers because of the nondistribution constraint. Consequently, not-for-profit status may signal an interest in quality over profits and serve as a guarantee of quality assurance, much as a trademark does.

An article by Hillmer et al. (2005) does a nice job of summarizing the research on the relationship between nursing home ownership status and the quality of care provided. A systematic review of the literature generated 81 results from 38 studies on the subject. Quality measures vary widely and include structure indicators (such as nursing aide turnover), process indicators (such as inappropriate restraints), and outcome indicators (such as infections). Of the 81 results, only 6 indicate that not-for-profit nursing homes deliver a lower quality of care than for-profit nursing homes, while 33 results find just the opposite, that for-profit nursing homes provide inferior care. The remaining results find no significant difference in the quality of care delivered across ownership type. Overall, the results suggest that "residents of for-profit nursing homes were more likely to be the recipients of poor quality compared with similar residents in not-for-profit facilities" (p. 162). These results were supported by a more recent review of the literature by Commondore et al. (2009).

But showing empirically that not-for-profit nursing homes provide higher quality of care than do for-profits does not necessarily offer evidence supporting the theory that for-profits pursue profits over quality when asymmetric information exists or that for-profits provide inefficiently low quality. Quality is just one of the many attributes that make up a good or service. For a given price, more quality generally means less and lower amounts of other types of attributes. In this case, people who value quality highly will be drawn to institutions offering high levels of quality. Decision makers of not-for-profit nursing homes may maximize quality, or quality and quantity, rather than profits, as discussed in Chapter 13. As a result quality may be higher in not-for-profit nursing homes not because of asymmetric information but because of differences in the taste for quality and alternative goals of organizations. It is important to understand the theoretical reason for any disparity in quality. If ownership form by itself results in quality differences, public policy might be directed toward encouraging one type of ownership form over another if quality improvement is an issue. However, if asymmetric information is the cause for quality differences, public policy might be aimed at offering better information to consumers.

Chou (2002) sorts out the differences by comparing the effect of ownership status on the quality of nursing home care in the presence and nonpresence of asymmetric information. For the test, Chou measures quality of care by mortality and several adverse health outcome measures (decubitus ulcers, dehydration, and urinary tract infection). Asymmetric information is defined as existing when nursing residents have no spouse or no child visiting within a month after admission. Chou argues that nursing home residents are usually frail and disabled; therefore, family members often serve as representatives to monitor or evaluate their quality of care.

Chou's empirical findings prove to be very interesting. The results for two of the four quality indicators suggest that not-for-profit nursing homes provide better quality than for-profits when asymmetric information exists. That is, when residents lack family members to monitor the service, for-profit nursing homes face less incentive to maintain the quality of care. Chou's empirical results support the theory that for-profit nursing homes practice opportunistic behavior and sacrifice quality of care for more profits when asymmetric information exists.

Grabowski and Hirth (2003) take the analysis a step further by analyzing whether competitive spillovers from not-for-profits cause for-profit nursing homes to deliver higher quality of care. The authors argue theoretically that patients in for-profit nursing homes will be better informed because not-for-profits attract a greater proportion of uninformed consumers given the quality assurance signal generated by the nondistribution constraint. Grabowski and Hirth test their theory by empirically examining how the market share of not-for-profits affects nursing home quality while holding constant a host of demand and supply side factors. They find that a higher not-for-profit market share improves for-profit and marketwide nursing home quality as measured by several structural, procedural, and outcome indicators. Grabowski and Hirth conclude by noting that if not-for-profits "have a competitive advantage in 'trustworthiness' while for-profits have greater incentives for efficiency, intersectoral competition can yield better outcomes than a market consisting exclusively of one type of firm" (p. 19). That is, competition from not-for-profits raises the quality of nursing home care while competition from for-profits limits inefficiency and the exercise of market power.

Finally, using the Svorney model (see Chapter 9), Santerre and Vernon (2007) compare the likely consumer benefits of higher quality with the potentially greater production costs that result from more not-for-profit activity in a nursing home services market area. Their empirical results indicate that, from a consumer's perspective, too few not-for-profit nursing homes exist in the typical market area of the United States. The policy implication is that more quality of care might be obtained by attracting a greater percentage of not-for-profit nursing homes into many market areas. To encourage more not-for-profits, Santerre and Vernon point out that the government may want to subsidize the not-for-profit conversion of existing for-profit nursing homes and enforce CON laws to the advantage of not-for-profit nursing homes.

Market Concentration and Nursing Home Conduct

Conventional microeconomic theory predicts that more competition results in lower prices and greater quality. Costs of production are unaffected by competition, according to conventional microeconomic theory, because firms are assumed to be motivated by maximum profits. The drive for maximum profits ensures that firms operate on and not purposely above the cost curve.

We have been learning throughout this text that conventional microeconomic theory does not always relate perfectly well to medical care markets. Motivations other than profit maximization, third-party reimbursement, low out-of-pocket prices, and rational consumer ignorance are some of the various features of medical markets that point to that conclusion. It is also important to realize that some of these features apply only to specific medical care markets and not to all of them. For example, we learned in Chapter 13 that hospitals reacted to increased competition by raising quality, costs, and prices prior to the 1980s because of the so-called medical arms race. But the medical arms race does not apply to the care provided by nursing homes. Furthermore, unlike the market for hospital services, the nursing home market may be characterized by excess demand and not excess capacity. That is why it is so important to carefully consider the theoretical relation and review the empirical findings between conditions such as market structure and the conduct of firms in each specific medical care market such as the nursing home industry. To that we now turn our attention.

Market Concentration and the Price of Nursing Home Care. Following in the footsteps of industrial organization (IO) theory, health economists have been interested in the relationship between the degree of competition, as measured by market concentration, and the pricing behavior of medical firms of various kinds, of which nursing homes are no exception. Nyman (1994) was among the first to apply IO theory to an analysis of market behavior in the nursing home industry. Nyman begins by deriving and specifying the price markup function or Lerner (1934) index facing the individual nursing home in the following form:

(15–1)
$$\frac{(P_i - C_i)}{P_i} = \frac{1}{[\alpha|E_m| + (1 - \alpha)|E_i|]}.$$

In Equation 15–1, P_i and C_i stand for the price charged by the individual nursing home and marginal cost, respectively, so the expression on the left-hand side of the equality symbol represents the firm's markup of price above marginal cost expressed as a percentage of price. The expressions $|E_m|$ and $|E_i|$ stand for market demand elasticity and the individual nursing home's price elasticity of demand stated in absolute terms. Because of fewer alternatives, the market demand elasticity is less than the price elasticity of demand faced by the individual nursing home in absolute terms and depends on the availability of other substitutes for nursing home care such as home health agencies and informal care provided in the home.

The α parameter reflects the conjectural variations held by nursing homes in the market and captures whether the typical nursing home facility expects the others to match or offset its output decision. If nursing homes expect matching or coordinated behavior, α equals 1 and the markup depends on market elasticity alone. The markup is the largest and equals that of a monopoly when firms in a market perfectly collude.[2] If firms compete rather than collude, α equals 0, and the individual nursing home's

---

2. The expression on the right-hand side of the equality symbol can be referred to as a modified Lerner index of monopoly power. See Chapter 8 for further discussion of the Lerner index of monopoly power.

markup depends on the degree to which the firm can successfully differentiate its product from others in the same market. A less differentiated product means a higher price elasticity of demand facing the individual nursing home and hence a lower markup of price over the costs of production.

Based on Equation 15–1, Nyman uses multiple regression analysis to investigate the determinants of the markup percentage across a sample of nursing homes in Wisconsin using 1988 data. Since Nyman examines the factors affecting the markup on private payers of nursing home care, he uses the Medicaid reimbursement rate instead of marginal cost in the Lerner index, as the analysis surrounding Figure 15–2 suggests. That is, the opportunity cost of caring for a private-pay patient is the additional revenues that would be received from caring for a Medicaid patient. Nyman specifies a HHI of market concentration with the county defined as the relevant geographical market in the multiple regression equation along with other variables affecting market elasticity and the price elasticity of demand facing the individual firm. Recall from the discussion in Chapter 8 that matching behavior and collusion are more likely to prevail in highly concentrated markets. Thus, one expects a direct relation between the HHI and the markup of private price relative to the Medicaid reimbursement rate.

For Nyman's sample, the markup over the Medicaid fee for a skilled nursing home facility averaged 18.2 percent and the average HHI was 2,240. Although both of these averages are quite high and suggestive of market power, Nyman finds that the estimated positive coefficient on the HHI was not statistically different from zero. The absence of a statistical relationship may reflect that nursing home markets were highly contestable at that time in Wisconsin because of low entry barriers. The threat of potential competition may have forced nursing homes to charge a price independent of the low degree of actual competition, given that matching behavior was not expected because of low entry barriers.

In a follow-up study, Mukamel and Spector (2002) use 1991 data for a sample of for-profit nursing homes in New York to estimate the price elasticity of the private demand facing individual nursing homes to assess their degree of market power. They implicitly assume that the representative nursing home expects offsetting behavior (i.e., α equals 0 in Equation 15–1) and thus $(P_i - MC_i)/P_i = 1/|E_i|$. As noted earlier, lower price elasticities of demand suggest more power to elevate price above the marginal costs of production. Mukamel and Spector consider that CON laws may or may not be binding, different degrees of patient case-mix severity, and the Medicaid reimbursement rate may replace marginal cost in the Lerner index as noted earlier.

Mukamel and Spector calculate that the average price elasticity facing the individual nursing home lies between −3.46 and −3.85, depending on whether estimated marginal costs or the Medicaid rate is used to calculate the Lerner index. The authors note that these elasticities are relatively low and result in comparatively high price markups to private payers. Mukamel and Spector go on to note that the "large price mark ups and the possibility that nursing homes behave as monopolists in the private pay market raise the question of whether this aspect of the market should be regulated" (p. 419). Gulley and Santerre (2007) reach a similar conclusion about the market power of nursing homes based upon their cross-sectional sample of for-profit and nonprofit California nursing homes in 2000.

Market Competition and Quality. Another important issue concerns how the degree of market competition influences the quality of nursing home care. From a theoretical perspective, the impact of market concentration (one aspect of competition) on quality is theoretically ambiguous. On the one hand, when a few for-profit firms command a large share of market sales and competition is thereby diminished, traditional IO theory suggests that the few firms may face an incentive to restrict both output and quality in an attempt to earn greater profits. On the other hand, when few firms exist in the market, consumers may be able to gather better information on potential suppliers, which can promote better quality (Pauly and Satterthwaite, 1981).

Zinn (1994) attempts to clear up the theoretical ambiguity by empirically examining the relationship between various measures of market competition and alternative structural and process measures of the quality of nursing home care. Process measures of quality include the proportion of residents not toileted, the prevalence of urethral catheterization, and the prevalence of physical restraint usage. The number of registered nurses per nursing home resident represents the structural measure of quality. The unit of analysis is the 2,713 counties in the 48 contiguous states of the United States. Among the measures of competition are market share concentration, measured by the HHI based on bed capacity in the county; the presence of an entry barrier, measured by a statewide moratorium on nursing home bed construction; and the availability of substitutes, measured by home health staff per capita and the percentage of women aged 15 to 64 not in the workforce (i.e., availability of informal care).

Zinn uncovers some mixed results. In particular, she finds that increased market concentration (i.e., less actual competition), as indicated by a higher HHI, tends to improve the quality of care, particularly process quality. Hence, the empirical results suggest that better quality of care results when fewer nursing homes exist in a market, *ceteris paribus*, providing support for the Pauly and Satterthwaite (1981) argument that less providers means more-informed choices and greater competition. However, she also finds that the existence of entry barriers (i.e., less potential competition) is associated with reduced quality.

In addition, the empirical results regarding the availability of substitutes on the quality of nursing home care were equally mixed. For example, the availability of home health agencies was found to be associated with higher levels of RN staffing but not with any of the process quality measures. Yet, the proportion of women aged 15 to 64 not in the workforce, representing an informal substitute for nursing home care, was found to lower the proportion of residents not toileted but was associated with greater use of physical restraints and lower RN staffing. Given these conflicting results, more studies are clearly needed before we can safely draw any conclusions about the relationship between market competition and quality of care in the nursing home industry.

Conduct of the Long-Term Care Industry: A Summary

We have examined theoretically and empirically a large number of issues relating to how long-term care providers react to influences such as the level and type of Medicaid reimbursement, form of ownership, and market competition. Because few studies focus on the home health care industry, the analysis focused solely on how these various factors influence the private price of nursing home care, the quality of nursing home care, and patient case-mix. What follows is a brief summary of the findings.

Under normal conditions, the dual market model of nursing home behavior predicts that a greater Medicaid reimbursement rate increases the access of Medicaid recipients to nursing home beds. Interestingly, the dual market model also predicts that the quality of nursing home care suffers if the Medicaid reimbursement rate increases when a capacity constraint exists. According to the model, nursing homes lower quality to reduce the number of private-pay patients and thereby make additional room for the marginally more profitable Medicaid patients. While earlier empirical studies have found an inverse relation between the Medicaid reimbursement rate and nursing home quality, some recent evidence suggests that the relation may no longer hold because an excess demand condition may no longer exist in the nursing home industry. Excess demand may no longer apply because of the elimination of CON laws in some states and a growing availability of alternatives to nursing home care, such as home health care and assisted living arrangements.

The method of Medicaid reimbursement was also found to matter in terms of the incentives faced by nursing homes. Nursing homes face less financial risk when Medicaid payments are more flexible and facility specific. Thus, we can think of the degree of financial risk imposed on nursing homes as ascending from retrospective to facility-specific prospective, class prospective, and flat-rate reimbursement systems. Empirical studies clearly suggest that the reimbursement method matters because of financial incentives. Studies tend to suggest that more restrictive methods are associated with lower nursing home costs and reductions in quality and patient case-mix severity. Chen and Shea (2002) question whether the cost reductions brought on by restrictive payment systems reflect efficiency or simply unwanted cuts in quality. The authors find that costs are unaffected by prospective reimbursement when quality differences among facilities are controlled for and the endogeneity of quality variables is addressed. As a result, like Zinn (1994) and some others, Chen and Shea argue that the level and method of Medicaid reimbursement should be linked to the quality of care.

Next, we addressed the efficiency and quality implications of the type of ownership. Property rights theory suggests that for-profit nursing homes may behave more efficiently than not-for-profits although the precise objective of the latter ownership form is theoretically unclear. Empirical studies indicate that for-profit nursing homes are more technically efficient and produce at a lower cost than not-for-profits. However, many question whether the cost savings associated with for-profit nursing homes reflect lower quality when compared to otherwise similar not-for-profits. Indeed, the theory implies that not-for-profit organizations may provide a higher quality of care than for-profits when an asymmetry of information exists. Chou's (2002) study empirically supports the theory.

We then examined the impact of market competition on the price and quality of nursing home care. The Lerner index of monopoly power tells us that the ability of firms to elevate price above the marginal costs of production depends on market elasticity of demand, the individual firm's elasticity of demand, and the conjectural variations formed by the firms in the industry. Using multiple regression analysis, Nyman (1994) was unable to empirically link the Lerner index to a HHI of market concentration using a sample of nursing homes in Wisconsin in 1975. Directly calculating the Lerner index, Mukamel and Spector (2002) find empirically that the mean price elasticities calculated for nursing homes in New York State in 1991 ranged from -3.46 to -3.85, quite low for an industry professed to be monopolistically competitive. Further evidence is needed on this issue before sweeping conclusions can be drawn about the relative profitability of nursing homes in the private-pay segment of the industry.

Finally, we turned our attention to the impact of market competition on the quality of care and relied on Zinn's (1994) study for empirical insights. With respect to market competition, her study analyzes the impact of market concentration, entry barriers, and the availability of substitutes on various structural and process measures of quality. We discussed how the relation between market concentration and quality of care is theoretically unclear and depends on whether less firms in an industry lead to a restriction of quality or means more informed choices. Unfortunately, Zinn's results are too mixed to draw any strong conclusions about the relationship between market competition and quality in the nursing home industry.

The Performance of the Long-Term Care Industry

We conclude the chapter with an examination of the overall performance of the market for long-term care. This presents a number of interesting challenges because the long-term care industry is unique and differs in three important respects from the previous medical care industries discussed. First, long-term care is generally associated with chronic care and care for those with disabilities rather than acute care. As a result, care is generally provided on a long-term basis, and the cost may be spread out over a number of years, possibly even decades. Second, much of the long-term care provided is informal in nature and provided by family and friends. Since no direct payment is made for the care provided, the cost is indirect and involves forgone wages. Third, the number and types of formal health care providers are diverse and run the gamut from skilled nursing home facilities to assisted-living centers with everything in between, such as meals-on-wheels programs and senior centers. To keep the discussion manageable, we focus primarily on nursing home facilities and home health care agencies. The objective of this section is to assess the overall performance of the long-term care industry by examining such measures as expenditures on long-term care; private insurance for long-term care; the price of nursing home care; and the utilization of nursing home, home health care, and hospice services.

Expenditures on Long-Term Care

Informal Expenditures on Long-Term Care. Calculating the cost of informal care poses an interesting challenge to researchers because they must impute the economic cost of the caregiver's time. For example, what is the economic value of a caregiver's time when she spends all day Saturday helping her mother with some household chores and bringing her to the doctor? Or what is the economic value of the time of a semi-retired man who drives every afternoon to his father's house to help him prepare his meals?

Unfortunately, a lack of precise data regarding the number of informal caregivers and the number of hours of care provided makes it difficult for researchers to come up with exact estimates. For example, according to Gibson and Houser (2007), estimates for the number of informal caregivers vary between 12 and 44 million per year, while the number of hours per week devoted to care fluctuates between 16 and 25 hours. Finally, establishing the economic value of one hour of caregiving time is also open for interpretation. Does one use the federal minimum wage ($7.25 per hour), the cost of hiring a home health aide ($10.46 per hour), or the cost of hiring a health care support worker ($12.94 per hour)? With these challenges in mind, Feinberg (2011) determines the annual economic cost of informal care was $450 billion in 2009. The study estimates that there were 42.1 million caregivers providing care for 18.4 hours a week at an average value of $11.61 per hour. To put this figure in perspective, the United States spent a combined total of $204 billion on nursing home and home health care in 2009.

Overall, studies indicate that a substantial amount of informal care is provided at a significant cost to the U.S. economy. Estimates by Arno give us a glimpse as to how the cost of informal care has changed over time. According to his work (1999, 2002, 2006), the economic cost of informal care equaled $196 billion in 1997, $257 billion in 2000, and $306 billion in 2004. The increase over time was fueled by a mild increase in the amount of informal care provided, both in terms of number of caregivers and hours of care provided, coupled with an increase in the opportunity cost of providing that care in terms of foregone wages.

Formal Expenditures on Long-Term Care

Data in Table 15–3 examine the extent to which formal expenditures on long-term care have changed over time. The analysis focuses exclusively on expenditures for nursing home care provided by freestanding nursing homes and home health care delivered by freestanding home health facilities. We focus on these two types of facilities for two reasons. First, the data are available and consistent, which provides us with the

TABLE 15–3
Nursing Home and Home Health Care Expenditures, Selected Years, 1980–2010

	1980	1990	1995	2000	2005	2010
National health Expenditures (billions of dollars)	$255.7	$724.3	$1,027.5	$1,377.2	$2,029.1	$2,593.6
Annual rate of increase	15.4%	11.9%	5.6%	7.0%	6.8%	3.9%
Nursing home Expenditures (billions of dollars)	$15.3	$44.9	$64.5	$85.1	$112.5	$143.1
Annual rate of increase	14.4%	16.1%	10.0%	5.4%	6.3%	3.1%
Home health care Expenditures (billions of dollars)	$2.4	$12.6	$32.4	$32.4	$48.7	$70.2
Annual rate of increase	25.2%	22.7%	18.2%	−1.4%	11.2%	6.2%

SOURCE: Centers for Medicare & Medicaid Services National Health Expenditures Tables

opportunity to trace expenditures over time. Second, since expenditures on nursing home and home health care represent the bulk of the institutional expenditures on long-term care, they can serve as a reasonably good proxy for total formal expenditures.

In 1980 expenditures on nursing home care and home health care equaled $15.3 billion and $2.4 billion, respectively, and in total they accounted for only 6.9 percent of total national health expenditures. The next decade and a half saw a phenomenal growth in expenditures on nursing home and home health care. As a result, by 1995 nursing home expenditures and home health care represented 9.4 percent of national health care expenditures. The largest increase in percentage terms took place in home health care as expenditures on freestanding home health care facilities increased at an annual rate of about 20 percent from 1980 through 1995. This increase was the direct result of an increase in both the number of individuals receiving home health services and an increase in the number of visits per patient (MedPAC, 1999).

As was the case with national health care expenditures, the rate of increase in nursing home and home health care decelerated in the mid- and late-1990s. For example, in 1997 the rate of increase in expenditures on nursing home care fell to 6.9 percent, which was slightly more than the 5.6 percent increase in overall national health expenditures. Much of the decrease in the rate of growth in nursing home care expenditures can be attributed to a more modest growth in medical prices and increased use of alternative forms of long-term care such as home health care and assisted living facilities (Levit et al., 2002). Changes in the rate of growth of home health care expenditures have been much more volatile. The volatility results because home health care is one of the smallest categories in the national health accounts and even modest changes in spending generate significant changes in rates of growth.

During the late 1990s and early 2000s, expenditures on nursing home and home health care continued to grow, but at a much lower rate. In fact, home health care expenditures actually fell by more than 1.4 percent in 2000. Most of this decrease can be attributed to changes in public policy that brought about a decrease in the proportion of medical expenditures financed through public sources in 1998 for the first time in a decade. The most significant change took place in the Medicare program with the passage of the Balanced Budget Act (BBA) of 1997, which called for significant savings by restraining payments to providers. The slight increase in spending after 2000 resulted from the Balanced Budget Refinement Act (BBRA) of 1999. Faced with the criticism that the BBA of 1997 reduced spending too much and too quickly, Congress passed the BBRA of 1999, which limited or delayed some of new payment provisions (MedPAC, 2000). More recently, nursing home expenditures have continued to increase at a relatively modest pace while home health care expenditures have increased at a much higher rate. In 2010, nursing home expenditures equaled $143.1 billion while home health expenditures reached the $70 billion mark.

Taken together, these figures indicate that the economic cost of long-term care is substantial, with informal caregivers paying for the bulk of the care measured in terms of forgone wages. Using 2009 as a benchmark, it appears that a little more than two-thirds of all long-term care is provided on an informal basis in the United States.[3] Extending the analysis one step further, expenditures for long-term care (both informal and formal) account for slightly more than one-quarter of all health care expenditures in the United States and represent the second-largest spending category behind hospital care. While these percentages can only be considered ballpark at best, they do underscore the importance of long-term care and illustrate that informal caregivers are the mainstay of the U.S. long-term care health system.

Private Insurance for Long-Term Care

Given the high cost of long-term care, researchers have long wondered why so few individuals, particularly those at or approaching retirement age, have not purchased long-term care insurance. According to America's Health Insurance Plans, by 2005 approximately 5 million long-term care policies were active. Although this is an impressive number, one has to keep in mind that at the same point in time there were 109 million people aged 45 years or older in the United States. Among the many factors said to contribute to the relatively small number of long-term insurance policies purchased are adverse selection, moral hazard, Medicaid crowding out, and intertemporal risk (Cutler, 1996; Norton, 2000).

As we learned in Chapter 11, adverse selection occurs because there is an asymmetry of information concerning the health status of potential consumers. When this situation develops, high-risk individuals have the incentive to withhold information concerning their true health status from insurers and purchase long-term care insurance at premiums based on a pool of subscribers with better health. Over time, premiums are driven upward as the high-risk subscribers consume more custodial care than their healthier counterparts. Faced with the choice of paying high premiums, low-risk subscribers may elect not to renew their long-term care policies while potential new customers' may decide to self-insure and not purchase any long-term care insurance. The problem of adverse selection is particularly difficult in the market for long-term care because the potential population is heterogeneous and a relative lack of claims data makes it difficult for insurance companies to accurately assess risk.

For example, Temkin-Greener et al. (2000/2001) estimate that at least one out of seven individuals aged 65 years or older had been rejected for long-term care insurance because of poor health yet posed no greater financial risk to insurers than those who had been accepted. Adverse selection also appears to be impacting the demand side of the long-term care market. For example, Sloan and Norton (1997) find that individuals who reported a high probability that they would need nursing home services in five years were more likely to purchase long-term care insurance, while Mellor (2001) finds self-reported poor health to have a significant, yet marginal, impact on the probability of having long-term care insurance.

---

3. This figure was arrived at by dividing the total dollar amount of formal and informal care provided in 2009 into the cost of informal care as estimated by Feinberg et al. (2011), or [$450 billion/($450 billion + $204.7 billion)] = 69 percent. The amount of formal long-term care provided was assumed to equal the combined value of nursing home expenditures ($138.6 billion) and home health care expenditures ($66.1 billion).

Moral hazard has also been offered as an explanation for the lack of demand for private long-term care insurance. In a now classic article, Pauly (1990) argues that the elderly prefer to receive care from family in their own homes rather than from a staff of health care professionals in a nursing home, all else held constant. As a result, the elderly may shy away from purchasing private health insurance because it lowers the out-of-pocket price of formal care and provides their children with an inducement to institutionalize them if and when they need long-term care, or perhaps even prematurely. The incentive to substitute child-provided informal care with formal care results from the relative decrease in the price of formal care that occurs when long-term care insurance is present.

While the preference for informal care on the part of the elderly may decrease the demand for long-term care insurance, the desire to protect bequests to family and friends may have just the opposite effect. Long-term care can be quite expensive and even a relatively short stay in a nursing home can wipe out a family's savings. To guard against the potential loss of a desired bequest, a risk-averse individual may purchase long-term health insurance. Thus, the desire to leave a specific bequest in a world where long-term care costs are difficult to project should increase the demand for long-term care insurance.

There is little empirical evidence supporting the notion that the elderly substitute child-provided care for long-term care insurance. For example, Mellor (2001) finds that the availability of informal caregivers had no statistical impact on whether an elderly person purchased a long-term care insurance policy or intended to purchase one. Sloan and Norton (1997) find that the existence of children had no impact on the likelihood of purchasing long-term health insurance. In addition, Sloan and Norton also find that the bequest motive had no impact on the decision to purchase long-term care insurance. Specifically, elderly people who responded that leaving an inheritance was somewhat or very important are no more likely to purchase long-term care insurance than the rest of the sample.

Public support for long-term care through the Medicaid program may also dampen the incentive to purchase private long-term care insurance. Faced with the reduced risk of having to privately pay for long-term care because of the Medicaid program, some consumers may elect to forgo the purchase of long-term care insurance. The basic question from an economic perspective is, therefore, whether private long-term care insurance and Medicaid can be considered substitutes. Sloan and Norton (1997) are careful to point out that private insurance and Medicaid can be considered only imperfect substitutes at best. Strict eligibility requirements necessitate that individuals deplete most of their financial assets before becoming eligible for Medicaid coverage. As a result, the Medicaid program offers little opportunity to protect assets that may be consumed in the future or bequeathed to loved ones. Coupled with this, elderly individuals on Medicaid coverage have to contend with the stigma of "going on public assistance."

The empirical evidence appears to support the notion that the demand for long-term care insurance is experiencing crowding out from the Medicaid program. For instance, Brown and Finkelstein (2007) find Medicaid crowding out to be extensive and may explain why the lowest two-thirds of the income distribution do not purchase long-term care insurance.

Cutler (1996) points out that the market for long-term care insurance is limited by the intertemporal risk that comes into play when insurers establish premiums. Recall from the earlier discussion on insurance in Chapter 11 that the insurer is responsible for managing the financial risk associated with establishing premiums. Relying on the law of large numbers, the insurer estimates the expected medical costs for a given population over a specified period of time. With that information in hand, the insurer sets the insurance premium to equal the expected benefits to be paid out plus any marketing and administration costs, taxes, and profits. Overall risk, which is reflected in profits in terms of the classic risk-return trade-off, is minimized through diversification across a given population of potential policyholders.

With long-term care insurance, insurers are forced to assess risk over an extended period of time when the average cost of an insured event is likely to increase over time.[4] With this increase in cost over time comes increasing price risk because the insurer finds it progressively more difficult to predict medical payments well into the future. The problem is that in this situation the insurer cannot diversify risk across policyholders because everyone faces the same potential increase in costs due to higher input prices. Faced with the inability to lower risk through cross-sectional diversification, the insurer has no alternative but to increase premiums in excess of the expected payout or offer an indemnity-type insurance policy. In the first case, the insurer increases the premium to compensate for the added risk of predicting health care costs well into the future by requiring a higher rate of profit. In the second case, the insurer forces policy holders to bear some of the risk of higher long-term care costs. For example, the policy may call for the insurer to pay up to $200 a day if the policy holder enters a nursing home. If the cost of nursing home care is in excess of that amount, then the policy holder must pay the added expense out-of-pocket. To illustrate his point, Cutler notes that for a sample of 73 long-term health care policies in 1991, 72 had indemnity payments. In either case, the demand for long-term care insurance is likely to decrease because of intertemporal risk.

The theoretical and empirical research in this area clearly indicates that the decision to purchase long-term insurance is complex and involves a host of factors. Other variables found to impact the probability of purchasing a long-term health insurance policy include assets, income, age, and education. The positive and significant results for the assets and income variables make sense and suggest that those with greater wealth and income are more likely to purchase insurance because they have a greater incentive to protect against the possibility of spending down to qualify for Medicaid coverage. The positive and significant results for the age variable indicates that as people get older and the possibility of needing long-term care increases, so does the likelihood of purchasing insurance coverage. Finally, more highly educated people are found to be more likely to purchase insurance coverage (Mellor, 2001).

This rather cursory review of literature illustrates that a variety of factors may explain why the long-term care insurance market is rather limited. As Brown et al. (2011) state at the conclusion of their paper, "the market may be small due to 'death by a thousand cuts' rather than by one overwhelming factor" (p. 23).

Prices for Nursing Home Services

Unfortunately, a lack of data prevents a detailed examination of the pricing behavior of nursing homes and home health care facilities over time. What little information there is can be obtained from Bureau of Labor Statistics. According to data in Table 15–4 the consumer price index for Nursing Homes and Adult Day Services increased from 137.8 in 2003 to 184.7 in 2011, for an average annual rate of increase of 4.3 percent. These price increases roughly match the rate of increase of overall medical care over the same period.

The Utilization of Long-Term Care Facilities

Nursing Homes.   Table 15–5 supplies information about the users of nursing home care from the 2010 edition of the *Nursing Home Data Compendium*. Included in Table 15–5 is an age profile of nursing home residents in 2009. In general, the data confirm our earlier point that the need for long-term care is heavily concentrated among the

---

4. Take the case of an individual who purchases a long-term health care policy at age 55. It may be 25 years or more before benefits are paid out for the first time.

TABLE 15–4

Consumer Price Index for Nursing Homes and Adult Day Care, 2002–2011

	2003	**2004**	**2005**	**2006**	**2007**	**2008**	**2009**	**2010**	**2011**
CPI	137.8	142.6	147.6	155.1	162.7	167.9	174.0	179.4	184.7
Annual Rate of Increase	5.8%	3.4%	3.2%	5.4%	4.9%	3.2%	3.6%	3.1%	3.0%

The data are for the December of each year and 1996 = 100.

SOURCE: Bureau of Labor Statistics www.bls.gov.

TABLE 15–5

Distribution of Nursing Home Residents according to Age, Gender, and Functional Status 2009

Number of Patients	**3,277,924**
Age Group	**Percent of Nursing Home Population**
Under 65 years	11.7
65 years and older	88.3
65–74 years	11.7
75–84 years	31.4
85 years and older	45.2
Gender	
Male	34.6
Female	65.4
Functional Status	
Received no help	26
Received help with at least 1 ADL	74

SOURCE: General Accounting Office, Long-Term Care, Current Issues and Future Directions. GAO/HEHS-95-109. Washington, D.C.: GAO, April 1995.

elderly population. According to the table, close to 9 out of 10 nursing home residents were 65 years of age or older. To no one's surprise, data in the table also indicate that the need for nursing home care increases rapidly with age among the elderly population. Almost half of all nursing home residents were aged 85 years or older and more than one of five elderly above age 84 had a nursing home stay in 2009.

Table 15–5 provides additional information about the representative nursing home resident in 2009. Almost two-thirds of all nursing home residents were female. This finding is not surprising given that females tend to outlive their male counterparts and are more likely to require assistance in older age either in nursing homes or in private residences. In addition, about 74 percent of all residents needed assistance with at least one ADL.

While these utilization figures paint an interesting profile of the current users of nursing home services, they do not tell the whole story. Some interesting trends emerging are likely to have a profound impact on the market for long-term services (Bishop, 1999). First, the extent to which the elderly rely on nursing homes for long-term care is diminishing. According to the most recent figures, while the number of elderly nursing home residents increased from slightly more than 2.7 million in 2005 to 2.8 million in 2009, the proportion of elderly in nursing homes has diminished from 460 to 422 per 10,000 population over the same time period. Second, the intensity of care provided to nursing home residents has increased because of an increase in disabilities among elderly residents. In 2005, slightly more than two-thirds of nursing home residents had at least one ADL impairment, and by 2009 that figure had increased to 74%. Bishop (1999) contends that these changes are the result of a decrease in disabilities among the elderly and an increased desire among the elderly to seek care in alternative settings such as home health care, adult day care facilities, or assisted living facilities. According to Cutler (2001), the steady decline in disability among the elderly can be attributed to enhanced medical technology and lifestyle changes. Other contributing factors may be improved socioeconomic status, diminished exposure to diseases, and the development and use of medical aids that allow the elderly to live independently for a longer period of time.

Thus, it appears that the nursing home industry has been simultaneously experiencing a significant decline in its patient population and an increase in the disability rate among those patients who require nursing home care. These trends may help explain some of the changes that have taken place in the nursing home industry over the past decades. For example, the increase in the level of care provided may in part explain the increase in the price of nursing home services that took place from 2003 to 2011. As noted earlier, the CPI for nursing home and adult day care increased by more than one-third from 2003 to 2011. The decrease in the proportion of elderly in need of nursing home facilities may also help explain the drop in number of Medicare- and Medicaid-certified nursing homes from 17,378 in 2000 to 15,889 in 2009. Faced with a shrinking patient base coupled with increased competition from alternative long-term care providers, some nursing homes have been forced to cease operations and potentially merge with other facilities.

Home Health Care. A variety of demographic characteristics for home health care patients appear in Table 15–6. More than 1.4 million patients used some form of

TABLE 15–6
Home Health Care Patient Characteristics, 2007

Number of Patients	1,459,900
	Percentage Distribution
Gender	
Male	36.0
Female	64.0
Age Group	
Under 65	31.3
65 and older	68.7
65–74	17.9
75–84	29.1
85 and older	21.8

SOURCE: Caffrey, Christine et al. "Home Health Care and Discharged Hospice Care Patients: United States, 2000 and 2007." *National Health Statistics Reports* (2011).

home health care in 2007, which is in sharp contrast to the 2.4 million who received home health care in 1996. This decrease likely reflects the cost containment and utilization controls mandated by the Balanced Budget Act of 1997 for home health care.

In total, this means that approximately 4.6 million people used some type of formal long-term care from either a nursing home or a home health agency in the mid-2000s. The data also indicate that females use formal long-term care more frequently than males, with the degree of gender imbalance being greatest for nursing home care. Finally, it appears that the elderly use formal care most intensively, with the heaviest users being between ages 75 and 84 for home care, and over age 84 for nursing home care.

What Do the Demographics Tell Us about the Future of Long-Term Care?

Predicting what the future holds in store for the long-term care market is, as you can imagine, a speculative task. However, longer life expectancies coupled with an aging baby boom generation should translate into a substantial increase in the demand for long-term care services. At the turn of the new millennium, between 12 and 13 percent of the total population was age 65 or older and less than 2 percent was age 85 or older. By 2050 the number of elderly is projected to make up 20 percent of the total population, with 1 out of 20 citizens being over age 85. Keeping in mind that more than 89 percent of nursing home residents were over 65 years old in 2009, these projections indicate that the demand for long-term care is likely to dramatically increase over the next few decades.

These demographic changes notwithstanding, a number of factors may cause the demand for long-term care to increase at a rate lower than otherwise would be the case. For one thing, increased longevity does not appear to have a major impact on health expenditures. Lubitz et al. (1995) estimate the lifetime Medicare expenses for a sample of beneficiaries and find total health expenditures to be only modestly impacted by longevity. Long-term expenditures are also likely to be impacted by overall health, everything else constant. It stands to reason that long-term care expenses will fall as the proportion of life spent in a relatively healthy state increases. Cutler (2001) explains earlier that disability among the elderly has decreased by approximately 1 percent per year since the 1950s. If this trend were to continue into the future, it would have a significant impact on the individual demand for long-term care.

Picking up on this point, Lakdawalla and Philipson (2002) argue that improved health coupled with increased life expectancy will impact the mix of formal and informal care provided along with the total amount spent on formal long-term care. The reason is relatively straightforward: a healthy elderly individual may become an informal supplier of long-term care. What is most interesting, however, is that the authors argue the impact on the supply of informal care depends on the degree to which increases in longevity and health impact men relative to women. If the increase in health and longevity impacts men more than women, then the individual demand for long-term care may diminish, on average. If the opposite occurs, the individual demand for long-term care may increase.

Since women live longer than men on average, they generally spend more years alone and, therefore, have a greater need for formal care. Recall from Table 15–6 that women made up 65 percent of all nursing home residents in 2009. When the relative supply of healthy men increases, elderly couples stay married longer and husbands become informal suppliers of care. As a result, the demand for formal care among women should diminish. If, on the other, hand, the increase in health and longevity is concentrated among women, the demand for formal long-term care should increase because women will spend even more time alone and without a spouse to provide informal care. Lakdawalla and Philipson test their hypothesis using panel data for 1971 through 1991. Their results generally support the contention that healthy aging is inversely related to the per capita demand for formal long-term care. Healthy aging decreases the amount of formal care provided directly by "shrinking the base of people who need care, and indirectly, by raising the supply of healthy elderly who can provide care at home" (p. 305).

Other researchers point to a few demographic trends that may cause the individual demand for long-term care to increase in the coming years. For example, Kramarow et al. (2007) are concerned about the impact of rising levels of obesity and the declining health of middle-aged people (brought on in part by an increase in chronic health conditions such as diabetes) on the health care spending among the elderly in the future. Of course, we cannot ignore the potential impact that increased incomes, enhanced quality of care, and changes in tastes and preferences may have on the individual demand single for long-term care. The increased prevalence of long-term care insurance may also increase demand because it decreases the out-of-pocket price of institutional care.

While improved health and longevity may dampen the individual demand for long-term care, the sheer number of baby boomers reaching retirement age over the next few decades will ensure that the market demand for long-term care increases. One estimate has 76 million baby boomers born between 1946 and 1964 reaching retirement age by 2035 (General Accounting Office, 2002). With this anticipated increase in market demand comes a great many challenges concerning the availability of public and private funding and the relative mix of informal and formal care provided.

Implications of the Patient Protection and Affordable Care Act (PPACA) of 2010 Regarding the Long-Term Care Industry

The Patient Protection and Affordable Care Act (PPACA) of 2010 will impact the market for long-term care in two important ways. First, the PPACA requires skilled nursing home facilities under Medicare and Medicaid to disclose information regarding ownership, accountability requirements, and expenditures. Such information will provide potential nursing home clients with more information to compare facilities.

Second, there are a few changes in the Medicaid program aimed at expanding services to elderly in need of long-term care in home or community-based settings. States will now be given opportunities to offer home and community-based services through Medicaid without having to apply for a waiver. PPACA also calls for the creation of the State Balancing Incentive Program and the Community First Choice Option. The former will provide qualifying states with either a 2 or 5 percentage point increase in their federal match for Medicaid Home- and Community-Based Services costs while the latter will provide community-based support and services to individuals with individuals in need of institutional care.

Summary

Monopolistic competition best describes the market structure of the long-term care industry. A large availability of substitute providers exists in the industry and entry barriers are fairly low. The typical nursing home most likely faces a downward-sloping demand because people prefer convenient locations near former neighbors, relatives, and friends. The buyer side of the market is relatively concentrated, with the federal and state governments representing highly influential buyers of both home health care and nursing home care.

Pricing and quality are two important conduct issues pertaining to long-term care. Empirical studies continue to sort the impact of reimbursement policies on the behavior of nursing homes. Recent studies indicate that there may no longer be an excess demand for nursing home services because of the elimination of CON laws and increased availability of alternative ways to acquire long-term care. Research also points out that reimbursement methods faced by nursing homes influence firm behavior because of financial incentives. It appears that more restrictive reimbursement schemes not only lower costs but also adversely impact the quality of care provided. Finally, the empirical evidence also corroborates the property rights theory as for-profit nursing homes appear to produce care at a lower cost than their not-for-profit counterparts but by providing lower quality of care when asymmetrical information exists.

The impact of market competition on both the price and quality of nursing home care is of interest to health economists and policy makers. Overall, empirical research seems to suggest that nursing home facilities may have some ability to elevate price above costs in areas where market concentration is high and entry barriers exist. The empirical evidence is mixed with respect to how market concentration impacts the quality of nursing home care.

The market for long-term care services has experienced profound changes over the last few decades and these changes are likely to continue into the near future. In the coming years, we are likely to see a significant increase in the demand for long-term care as baby boomers reach retirement age. While improved health and longevity may moderate the overall increase in the demand, the steep increase in the absolute number of retirees will place a significant strain on funding sources for long-term care.

On the supply side of the market, the delivery system for long-term care has become increasingly more diversified and has an almost endless list of community-based and institutional providers. For example, in recent years a host of community-based long-term care programs have been aimed at augmenting the level of informal care provided by assisting patients who have difficulty maintaining an independent lifestyle. Meals on Wheels, home health care, and adult day care are but three examples of such programs. These community-based programs represent a low-cost alternative to skilled nursing home care because they either delay or avert altogether the decision to institutionalize an individual in need of long-term care. Institutional care is now provided in a number of alternative settings aside from skilled nursing homes. For example, assisted-living residences and continuing-care-retirement communities have become very popular in recent years.

While this can be considered only a cursory look at the supply side of the long-term care market, it does indicate that individual providers of long-term care are likely to face increasing competition in the coming years. This increase in competition will likely have an impact on the mix of informal and formal care as well as the total expenditures on long-term care.

Review Questions and Problems

1. Explain the various differences between the demand for long-term care and medical services.
2. List the different types of providers of long-term care.
3. Explain the profile of the typical informal long-term caregiver.
4. Identify the structural characteristics of the typical nursing home. Think in terms of ownership status, size, chain membership, entry barriers, and so on.
5. Who is the main purchaser of nursing home services?
6. Discuss the role that entry barriers play in the nursing home industry.

7. Explain why the number of home health care agencies increased so dramatically in recent years.

8. Who is the largest payer for home health care services?

9. What roles do the Medicare and Medicaid programs serve in the home health care industry?

10. What does the empirical evidence suggest about scale economies in the home health care industry?

11. Use the Scanlon model to identify the impact of an increase of the Medicaid reimbursement rate on the private price for nursing home care and the number of private-pay and Medicaid patients.

12. Use the Scanlon model to identify the impact of an increase of the Medicaid reimbursement rate on the private price for nursing home care and the number of private-pay and Medicaid patients given a completely vertical marginal cost curve.

13. Explain theoretically how the method of reimbursement influences costs, quality, and patient case-mix. Note the trade-offs typically involved.

14. Explain why returns to scale are so important when it comes to quality improvements.

15. Discuss theoretically how a nondistribution constraint may influence costs and quality differences among nursing homes with different ownership structures. What are the general findings of studies examining the relation between ownership status and the costs and quality of nursing home care?

16. Explain why the relation between market concentration and the quality of care is theoretically unclear.

17. Identify and explain the intuition behind the Lerner index of monopoly power.

18. Suppose the price elasticity of market demand for nursing home care equals -3 and the individual nursing home's price elasticity of demand equals -6. The Medicaid reimbursement rate facing the nursing home equals $100 per day. Also suppose that because of a few nursing homes in the market and high barriers, the nursing home expects that other nursing homes will match its behavior with perfect certainty. Calculate the price charged to private payers by the individual nursing home. How would the results change if the individual nursing home expected offsetting behavior with perfect certainty? How about with a 50 percent probability of offsetting behavior?

19. Discuss the factors that researchers must consider when estimating the cost of informal care.

20. Approximately what fraction of long-term care expenditures is informal care?

21. Identify and explain the reasons why so few people purchase long-term care insurance.

22. Provide a profile of the typical nursing home resident. How is this profile likely to change in the future and why?

23. Discuss the demographic changes taking place that are likely to impact the future of long-term care.

24. Consult the Nursing Home Compare web site developed by Medicare at http://www.medicare.gov/NHCompare. Choose two different nursing home markets in the same state as defined by two distinct zip code areas that have both for-profit and not-for-profit nursing homes and compute the four-firm concentration ratio, CR_4, and Herfindahl-Hirschman Index for each market based on the number of licensed beds for a market area of 10 miles. What percentage of the nursing homes is for-profit? What do the figures tell you about the degree of market concentration in each market? What do the figures for CR_4 and HHI tell you about any potential price differences that may exist across the two markets? Now recalculate the CR_4 and HHI for a market area of 25 miles. Have the figures changed? Why?

Online Resources

To access Internet links related to the topics in this chapter, please visit our website at **www.cengage.com/economics/santerre**.

References

Arno, Peter S. "Economic Value of Informal Caregiving, 2000." Presented at the American Association for Geriatric Psychiatry, Orlando, Florida, February 24, 2002.

Arno, Peter. "Prevalence, Hours and Economic Value of Family Caregiving, Updated." National Family Caregivers Association and Family Caregiving Alliance and the Family Caregiver Alliance, 2006.

Arno, Peter S., Carol Levine, and Margaret M. Memmott. "The Economic Value of Informal Caregiving." *Health Affairs* 18 (March/April 1999), pp. 182–88.

Bishop, Christine. "Where Are the Missing Elders? The Decline in Nursing Home Use, 1985 and 1995." *Health Affairs* 18 (July/August 1999), pp. 146–55.

Brown, Jeffrey R., et al. "Why Don't Retirees Insure Against Long-Term Care Expenses? Evidence from Survey Responses." 13th *Annual Joint Conference of the Retirement Research Consortium,* Washington, D.C. (August 4–5, 2011).

Brown, Jeffrey R., and Amy Finkelstein. "The Interaction of Public and Private Insurance: Medicaid and the Long-Term Care insurance Market." *American Economic Review* 98 (2007), pp. 1083–1102.

Chen, Li-Wu, and Dennis G. Shea. "Does Prospective Payment Really Contain Nursing Home Costs?" *Health Services Research* 37 (April 2002), pp. 251–71.

Chou, Shin-Yi. "Asymmetric Information, Ownership and Quality of Care: An Empirical Analysis of Nursing Homes." *Journal of Health Economics* 21 (2002), pp. 293–311.

Christensen, Eric W. "Scale and Scope Economies in Nursing Homes: A Quantile Regression Approach." *Health Economics* 13 (April 2004), pp. 363–77.

Coburn, Andrew F., Richard Fortinsky, Catherine McGuire, and Thomas P. McDonald. "Effect of Prospective Reimbursement on Nursing Home Costs." *Health Services Research* 28 (April 1993), pp. 45–68.

Cohen, Joel W., and L. C. Dubay. "The Effect of Medicaid Reimbursement Method and Ownership on Nursing Home Costs, Case Mix, and Staffing." *Inquiry* 27 (1990), pp. 183–200.

Cohen, Joel W., and William D. Spector. "The Effect of Medicaid Reimbursement on Quality of Care in Nursing Homes." *Journal of Health Economics* 15 (1996), pp. 23–48.

Commondore, Vikram et al. "Quality of Care in For-Profit and Not-For-Profit Nursing Homes: Systematic Review and Meta-Analysis." *British Medical Journal* 339 (2009), pp. 1–15.

Cutler, David M. "Declining Disability among the Elderly." *Health Affairs* 20 (November/December 2001), pp. 11–27

———. "Why Don't Markets Insure Long-Term Risk?" Working paper, *National Bureau of Economic Research*, 1996.

Feinberg et al. "Valuing the Invaluable: 2011 Update: The Growing Contributions and Costs of Family Caregiving" AARP Public Policy Institute: Washington D.C. (2011).

Fizel, J., and T. Nunnikhoven. "Technical Efficiency of For-Profit and Non-Profit Nursing Homes." *Managerial and Decision Economics* (September/October 1992), pp. 429–39.

Frech, H. E., and Paul B. Ginsburg. "The Cost of Nursing Home Care in the United States: Government, Financing, Ownership, and Efficiency." In *Health, Economics, and Health Economics*, eds. J. van der Gang and M. Perlman. Amsterdam: North-Holland, 1981.

General Accounting Office. Long-Term Care Aging Baby Boom Generation Will Increase Demand and Burden on Federal and State Budgets. Washington, D.C.: GAO, March 2002.

Gertler, Paul J. "Subsidies, Quality, and Regulation in Nursing Homes." *Journal of Public Economics* 39 (1989), pp. 33–53.

Gertler, Paul J., and Donald M. Waldman. "Quality-Adjusted Cost Functions and Policy Evaluation in the Nursing Home Industry." *Journal of Political Economy* 100 (1992), pp. 1232–56.

Gibson, May Jo and Ari Houser. "Valuing the Invaluable: A New Look at the Economic Value of Family Caregiving." AARP Public Policy Institute: Washington D.C., June 2007.

Gonzales, Theresa I. "An Empirical Study of Economies of Scope in Home Healthcare." *Health Services Review* 32 (August 1997), pp. 313–24.

Grabowski, David C. "A Longitudinal Study of Medicaid Payment, Private-Pay Price and Nursing Home Quality." *International Journal of Health Care Finance and Economics* 40 (2004), pp. 5–26.

Grabowski, David C., and Richard A. Hirth. "Competitive Spillovers across Nonprofit and For-profit Nursing Homes." *Journal of Health Economics* 22 (January 2003), pp. 1–22.

Gulley, O. David, and Rexford E. Santerre. "Market Structure Elements: The Case of California Nursing Homes." *Journal of Health Care Finance* 33 (summer 2007), pp. 1–16.

Gulley, O. David, and Rexford E. Santerre. "The Effect of Public Policies on the Availability of Nursing Home Care in the United States." *Eastern Economics Journal* 29 (winter 2003), pp. 93–104.

Hansmann, Henry. *The Ownership of Enterprise.* Cambridge, Mass.: Harvard University Press, 1996.

Harrington, Charlene, James H. Swan., John A. Nyman, and Helen Carrillo. "The Effect of Certificate of Need and Moratoria Policy on Change in Nursing Home Beds in the United States." *Medical Care* 35 (1997), pp. 574–88.

Haupt, Barbara J. "An Overview of Home Health and Hospice Care Patients: 1996 National Home and Hospice Care Survey." U.S. Department of Health and Human Services, National Center for Health Statistics, Advance Data No. 297. Atlanta, Ga.: April 16, 1998.

Hillmer, Michael P., Walter P. Wodchis, Sudeep S. Gill, Geoffrey M. Anderson, and Paula A. Rochon. "Nursing Homeprofit Status and Quality of Care: Is There Any Evidence of an Association?" *Medical Care Research and Review* 62 (April 2005), pp. 139–66.

Holahan, John F., and Joel W. Cohen. "Nursing Home Reimbursement: Implications for Cost Containment, Access, and Quality." *Millbank Quarterly* 65 (1987), pp. 112–47.

Kass, D. J. "Economies of Scale and Scope in the Provision of Home Health Services." *Journal of Health Economics* 6 (June 1987), pp. 129–46.

Knox, Kris Joseph et al. "Technical Efficiency in Texas Nursing Facilities: A Stochastic Production Frontier Approach." *Journal of Economic and Finance* 31(spring, 2007), pp. 75–86.

Kramarow, Ellen, James Lubitz, Harold Lentzner, and Yelena Gorina. "Trends in the Health of Older Americans." *Health Affairs* 26 (September/October 2007), pp. 1417–1425.

Lakdawalla, Darius, and Tomas Philipson. "The Rise of Old-Age Longevity and the Market for Long- Term Care." *American Economic Review* 92 (March 2002), pp. 295–306.

Lerner, Abba P. "The Concept of Monopoly and the Measurement of Monopoly Power." *Review of Economic Studies* 1 (1934), pp. 157–75.

Levit, Katherine, et al. "Inflation Spurs Health Spending in 2000." *Health Affairs* 21 (January/February 2002), pp. 172–81.

Lubitz, James, James Beebe, and Colin Baker. "Longevity and Medicare Expenditures." *The New England Journal of Medicine* 332 (April 13, 1995), pp. 999–1003.

Medicare Payment Advisory Commission (MedPAC). *Report to the Congress; Selected Medicare Issues*. Washington, D.C.: Medicare Payment Advisory Commission, June 1999.

————. Medicare Payment Advisory Commission (MedPAC). *Report to the Congress; Medicare. Payment Policy*, Washington, D.C.: Medicare Payment Advisory Commission, March 2000.

————. Medicare Payment Advisory Commission (MedPAC). *Medicare Payment Policy Report to Congress*. Washington D.C.: Medicare Payment Advisory Commission, March 2010.

Mellor, Jennifer C. "Long-Term Care and Nursing Home Coverage: Are Adult Children Substitutes for Insurance Policies?" *Journal of Health Economics* 20 (2001), pp. 527–47.

Mukamel, Dana B., and William D. Spector. "The Competitive Nature of the Nursing Home Industry: Price Mark Ups and Demand

Elasticities." *Applied Economics* 34 (2002), pp. 413–20.

Norton, Edward C. "Long-Term Care." In *Handbook of Health Economics*, Volume 1, eds. A. J. Culyer and J. P. Newhouse. Amsterdam: Elsevier Science, 2000.

Nursing Home Data Compendium, 2010 Edition. Centers for Medicare and Medicaid Services. Baltimore, Md.: 2010.

Nursing Home Data Compendium, 2008 Edition. Centers for Medicare and Medicaid Services, 2008.

Nyman, John A. "Medicaid Reimbursement, Excess Medicaid Demand, and the Quality of Nursing Home Care." *Journal of Health Economics* 4 (1985), pp. 237–59.

————. "The Effects of Market Concentration and Excess Demand on the Price of Nursing Home Care."*Journal of Industrial Economics* 17 (June 1994), pp. 193–204.

Nyman, John A., and Dennis L. Bricker. "Profit Incentives and Technical Efficiency in the Production of Nursing Home Care." *Review of Economics and Statistics* 71 (November 1989), pp. 586–94.

Nyman, John A., Dennis L. Bricker, and D. Link. "Technical Efficiency in Nursing Homes." *Medical Care* 28 (June 1990), pp. 541–51.

Nyman, John A., and Robert A. Connor. "Do Case-Mix Adjusted Nursing Home Reimbursements Actually Reflect Costs? Minnesota's Experience." *Journal of Health Economics* 13 (1994), pp. 145–62.

"Older Americans 2010 Key Indicators of Well-Being." Washington D.C.: The Federal Interagency Forum on Aging-Related Statistics, July 2010.

Park-Lee, Eunice et al. "Comparison of Home Health and Hospice Care Agencies by Organizational Characteristics and Services Provided: United States, 2007." National Health Statistics Reports 30 (November 9, 2010).

Pauly, Mark. "The Rational Nonpurchase of Long- Term-Care Insurance." *Journal of Political Economy* 98 (1990), pp. 153–68.

Pauly, Mark, and M. Satterthwaite. "The Pricing of Primary Care Physician Services: A Test of the Role of Consumer Information." *Bell Journal of Economics* 12 (1981), pp. 488–506.

Reschovsky, James D. "The Roles of Medicaid and Economic Factors in the Demand for Nursing Home Care." *Health Services Research* 33 (October 1998), pp. 787–813.

Santerre, Rexford E., and John A. Vernon. "Ownership Form and Consumer Welfare: Evidence from the Nursing Home Industry." *Inquiry* 44 (winter 2007), pp. 381–399.

Scanlon, William J. "A Theory of the Nursing Home Market." *Inquiry* 17 (spring 1980), pp. 25–41.

Sloan, Frank A., and Edward C. Norton. "Adverse Selection, Bequests, Crowding Out, and Private Demand for Insurance, Evidence from the Long-Term Care Insurance Market." *Journal of Risk and Uncertainty* 15 (1997), pp. 201–9.

Temkin-Greener, Helena, Dana B. Mukamel, and Mark R. Meimers. "Long-Term Care Insurance Underwriting: Understanding Eventual Claims Experience." *Inquiry* 37 (winter 2000/2001), pp. 348–58.

Wagner, Donna A. Comparative Analysis of Caregiver Data for Caregivers to the Elderly 1987 and 1997. Bethesda, Md.: National Alliance for Caregiving, June 1997.

Zinn, Jacqueline S. "Market Competition and the Quality of Nursing Home Care." *Journal of Health Care Politics, Policy and Law* 19 (fall 1994), pp. 555–82.

Health Care System Reform

PART FOUR

Health Care System Reform

The health care systems, which exist in various developed countries across the globe, are not static institutions by any means. Over time, these medical systems have evolved in response to market forces and regulatory initiatives brought on by heightened social pressures or political exigencies. Some changes, such as the implementation of new health care reimbursement practices, may represent small adjustments in the big scheme of things whereas others, like a shift from public to private production of medical care, may have sweeping implications.

Cutler (2002) explains that the health care systems in many developed countries began to change dramatically during the late nineteenth century with equity as the main goal. Universal health insurance programs were designed to ensure that all people had reasonably equal access to medical care. At first, efficiency concerns were ignored given the sharp focus on fairness with respect to medical care access. But as new cost-enhancing medical technologies increased at a rapid pace and tilted the efficiency-equity balance more toward the latter, various countries adopted regulatory approaches to contain their health care costs. While successful initially at containing health care costs, the tighter supply-side regulations eventually led to medical care shortages developing in many countries. As a result, the regulatory approach fell out of favor and now many countries have turned to demand-side solutions hoping that market incentives might bring about cost savings without cuts being so painful. Cutler warns that new medical technologies will likely always invoke the classic tradeoff in economics between equity and efficiency.

In contrast to other developed countries in the world, the United States largely resisted any movement to universal health insurance, at least until most recently. While serious debates involving health insurance reform in the United States took place during the late 1910s, the 1930s, the late 1940s, the 1960s, the 1970s, and the 1990s, only once over those years—during the 1960s, when the Medicaid and Medicare programs were instituted—were proponents successful at implementing some type of universal health insurance coverage. One can only speculate on the reasons why the United States resisted the adoption of universal health insurance. For those interested in such a speculation, Fuchs (1991) points to a general distrust of government, a heterogeneous population, and more of a commitment to individual freedom than to equality as reasons why the United States failed to adopt universal health insurance whereas other countries did not. Others point to our federalist form of government that makes it difficult to enact any sweeping changes in government policy.

Regardless of the reasons in the past, the Patient Protection and Affordable Care Act (PPACA) of 2010, which we discussed, albeit in piecemeal fashion, at the end of various chapters, represents the seventh attempt at major health care system reform in the United States. If not overturned by the U.S. Supreme Court (supposedly we should know by late spring of 2012), the PPACA will also reflect the second time that proponents of greater government have successfully shaped the U.S. medical care system in a major way. What may be unclear to you are some of the specific reasons for health insurance reform in the

United States and the alternative ways in which health insurance reform may have been designed. Thus, this chapter discusses various issues relating to the economics of health insurance reform. Specifically, this chapter:

- compares the performance of the U.S. health care system to the health care systems in Canada, Germany, Switzerland, and the United Kingdom, among other countries
- discusses how high average returns can coexist with low marginal returns to medicine
- examines why so much disagreement exists concerning how a health care system should be designed
- examines various proposals mentioned for health insurance reform at the national level in the United States
- analyzes the experiences of selected states at implementing various types of health care system reform
- provides a general overview of the PPACA of 2010.

The Overall Performance of the U.S. Health Care System: An International Comparison

Any meaningful performance appraisal requires some type of rubric for comparing the outcomes associated with one country's health care system to another. In the following discussion, we utilize the three-legged stool of medicine, previously discussed in Chapter 1, as our rubric. The three-legged medical stool seems highly appropriate given its simplicity in this regard. In fact, Aaron and Ginsburg (2009) write with some sarcasm: "A child trained to say 'Cost, Quality, Access' might pass as a health policy analyst." We note that Aaron and Ginsburg go on to write: "Sustaining the deception would become more difficult if the innocent were asked to define those terms" (p. 1260).

Table 16–1 compares measures of health care cost, quality, and access in the United States to those of Canada, France, Germany, Sweden, Switzerland, and United Kingdom. These six countries all possess highly developed market economies and share many similar circumstances with the United States. In Chapter 4 we discussed the various elements that make up the health care systems in Canada, Germany, Switzerland, and the United Kingdom. Like those four countries, France and Sweden provide nearly universal health insurance coverage and have a single-payer system. Sweden's distinction is that medical care is primarily produced in its public sector.

The figures in columns 2 and 3 suggest that the United States spent much more on medical care in both absolute and relative terms than the other countries in 2009, the most recent year data are available for all of these countries. For example, per capita health care spending in the United States ($7,960) equaled nearly double the average amount spent by the other six countries ($4,154). In fact, the United States spent nearly $3,000 more per capita on health care than Switzerland, the next highest spender on health care not only in the list but also in the world.

The United States also appears to spend more on medical care in relative terms than the other countries. As a fraction of gross domestic product (GDP), medical care expenditures topped 17.4 percent of GDP in the United States in 2009; this is nearly more than 6 percentage points higher than France, the country with the second greatest amount of GDP allocated to medical care. Table 16–1 also shows data on the annual growth of health care spending in the different countries in column 4. Interestingly, the figures indicate that the annual rate of health care spending growth over the last 10 years is fairly similar in all of the countries. Moreover, the 2.5 percent annual growth rate of per capita health care spending in the United States is close to the average of the other six countries (2.45 percent). The similarity is not surprising because research suggests that new medical technologies account for much of the growth in

TABLE 16–1

Comparative Statistics on Costs, Quality, and Access for Seven Developed Countries

	Costs			Quality			Access	
	Health Care Spending Per Capita in 2009 (US$)[1]	Health Care Spending as a Percent of GDP in 2009[1]	Average Annual Growth Rate of Per Capita Health Care Spending over the Last 10 Years[1]	Infant Mortality Rate in 2008 (Deaths per 1,000 Live Births)[1]	Change in Infant Mortality Rate Over the Last 10 Years[1]	Percent Satisfied with Health Care System in 2008[2]	Percent of Adults Confident if Seriously Ill They Would Receive Most Effective Treatment[3] (2010)	Percent of Adults Who Faced Access Problems When Sick in Previous Year (2010)[3]
Canada	$4,363	11.4%	2.6%	5.2[2007]	–0.3	85%	76%	15%
France	3,978	11.8	2.2	3.8	–1.0	85	85	13
Germany	4,218	11.6	2.1	3.5	–1.2	82	82	25
Sweden	3,722	10.0	2.4	2.5	–1.0	80	67	10
Switzerland	5,144	11.4	2.2	4	–0.8	89[2006]	89	10
United Kingdom	3,487	9.8	3.2	4.7	–1.0	85	92	5
United States	7,960	17.4	2.5	6.5	–0.7	83%	70	33

SOURCES:

[1]Organization for Economic Cooperation and Development, www.oecd.org

[2]Gallup Poll at http://www.gallup.com/poll/117205/americans-not-feeling-health-benefits-high-spending.aspx

[3]Schoen (2010)

health care spending over time (Congressional Budget Office, 2008). These countries have tended to develop similar types of medical technologies over the last few decades, although not necessarily with the same rate of adoption or utilization.

Data in the next three columns provide information on the quality of medical care in the different countries as evidenced by the infant mortality rate (IMR) and its change over time and health care system satisfaction rates. In terms of these outcome quality measures, the data imply that the United States performs poorly when compared to the other countries. Not only did the United States possess the highest IMR among the seven countries in 2008 but its IMR declined relatively little over the last 10 years. The only fairly positive signal regarding access is that the health care system satisfaction rate in the United States closely mirrors the average satisfaction rate for the other six countries.

Previous chapters pointed out that roughly 16 percent of the population is currently without health insurance coverage in the United States and this figure hasn't changed much over time. That situation likely means the health of many people in the United States is seriously compromised when it comes to securing effective health care in a reasonable amount of time. The data pertaining to access in the last two columns support this prediction. Specifically, the United States has the second lowest percentage of people who are confident about receiving effective care. Also, a greater percentage of the adult population in the United States faced medical access problems in 2010 compared to similar people in other countries.

Looking again at the data in Table 16–1, it seems paradoxical that the United States spends so much more on health care in both absolute and relative terms yet achieves relatively little in terms of quality of care. One possible explanation for this puzzling finding was already mentioned in the context of Figure 13–7. In particular, it may be the case that the healthcare system of the United States moved over time from point A to B in that figure whereas other countries expanded their production possibilities further by adopting more appropriate technologies and moved from point A to C. Notice the lower quality of care but higher amount of health care spending at point B relative to C. The difference amounts to a lot of wasteful medical care expenditures. Some studies have provided support for this explanation. For example, research shows that greater health care spending in the United States cannot be explained by more medical resources such as a greater number of hospital beds, physicians, or nurses. Rather, most of the available evidence points to higher medical prices in the United States (Anderson et al., 2003; Aaron and Ginsburg, 2009; Laugesen and Glied, 2011).

Health care policy makers and analysts have questioned the overall effectiveness or value added of medical spending in the United States. Taken as a whole, most of the empirical evidence seems to suggest that medical spending generates net benefits on average in terms of the value of lives saved (e.g., Cutler and McClellan, 2001; Cutler et al., 2006; Skinner et al., 2006) yet yields waste at the margin (Baicker and Chandra, 2004). Cutler (2006) notes: "on the one hand, that medical spending is valuable and affordable and, on the other, medical spending is too high and wasteful" (p. w48). Aaron and Ginsburg summarize this literature by referring to the "coexistence of high average returns and low marginal returns per dollar spent on health care" (p. 1266). They point to the example of interventional cardiology procedures that have been shown to yield high value to some heart-attack patients but not to patients showing no symptoms of health disease but who receive worrisome results from diagnostic tests.

How can these two seemingly inconsistent statements about the average and marginal effects of medical care spending in the United States be conceptualized and explained? We use Figure 16–1, which shares some similarities to Figure 3–2, to address that question. In Figure 16–1 notice the downward-sloping marginal social benefit (MSB) and upward-sloping marginal social cost (MSC) curves, reflecting the laws of diminishing marginal utility and increasing opportunity costs, respectively. Notice that the average counterparts to those marginal curves are also drawn in the

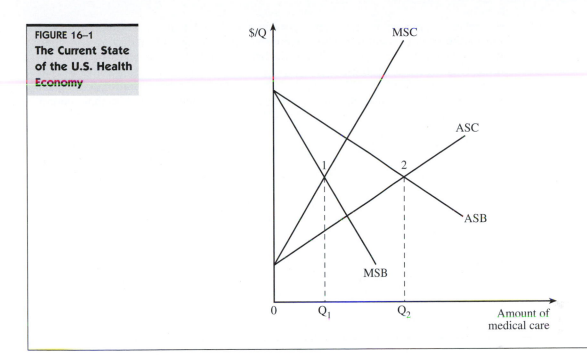

FIGURE 16–1

The Current State of the U.S. Health Economy

Empirical studies find that medical care spending yields positive net benefits on average but negligible net benefits at the margin. That situation happens when the health economy operates between Q_1 and Q_2 in Figure 16-1 because MSC > MSB yet ASB > ASC. It follows that a deadweight loss results from this misallocation of resources in the health economy.

figure. Recall from our discussion regarding cost curves in Chapter 7 that a marginal curve pulls up the average curve when the latter is rising and pulls it down when the average curve is falling. For that reason we know that the average social benefit (ASB) curve lies above the MSB curve and the average social cost (ASC) curve lies below the MSC curve.

We are now in a position to reconcile these seemingly inconsistent statements drawn by analysts about the average net benefit but marginal net loss from medical care spending in the United States. As we know from Chapter 3, allocative efficiency in the figure occurs at Q_1 amount of medical care because MSB = MSC. Beyond Q_1, further increases in the quantity of medical care are associated with marginal net losses because MSC > MSB. But notice between Q_1 and Q_2 units of medical care in Figure 16–1, it is the situation that ASB > ASC such that medical care generates positive net benefits on average. Beyond Q_2, ASB < ASC but contemporary evidence does not support that range of medical care output in the United States. Thus, over the range of medical care between Q_1 and Q_2, it is the case that average net returns are positive but marginal net returns are negative. This is exactly the situation the U.S. health economy faces according to the literature.

Unfortunately, research is silent about exactly where the health economy operates between Q_1 and Q_2 in the figure. The chosen operating point is important. Recall when MSC exceeds MSB, a deadweight loss results. The deadweight loss captures the size of the economic pie or GDP that disappears because society's resources are misallocated. If the actual operating point is closer to Q_1 the deadweight loss is relatively low. But, in the real world, the gap between Q_1 and the chosen operating point may be quite large. Moreover, similar to the managerial expense preference model we discussed in Chapter 13, the "observed" MSC may lie above the "true" MSC, reflecting some amount of X-inefficiency (recall earlier that higher input prices may account for the relatively greater medical care costs in the United States). A situation like that means the health economy is simultaneously experiencing both allocative and production inefficiencies, resulting in the height between the observed MSC and MSB being quite large. If so, a sizable deadweight loss results from a misallocation of resources and waste in the U.S. health economy. Perhaps for this reason, Aaron and Ginsburg (2009) lament: "the margin can be wide, and that spending within that margin is large" (p. 1265).

Why Is There So Much Disagreement Concerning How Health Care System Reform Should Be Designed?

Later in this chapter, we examine various plans for reforming the U.S. health insurance system at the national level and review health care reform taking place in a select group of states. We also discuss in general terms the PPACA of 2010. One may wonder why so much disagreement exists concerning health care system reform. Some advocates for reform argue vehemently for more government controls on health care providers and a greater role for government in the financing of health care. Others shout, "Let the market work!" Musgrave (1993) argues that the disagreement over health care reform can best be explained by the theories X and Y of health economics. Table 16–2 summarizes his arguments, presenting theories X and Y as they pertain to five dimensions of health economics. Notice the essential differences.

On the one hand, theory X views illnesses as occurring randomly. That is, some people get sick or become involved in accidents, and others do not; some live long and healthy lives, whereas others live abnormally short lives plagued with various illnesses. On the other hand, theory Y treats illnesses and accidents as being determined largely by lifestyle choices. Choices concerning cigarette smoking, excessive drinking, safe sex, wearing seat belts, occupation, and the like can affect the probability of entering into a state of sickness or suffering a harmful accident. Individuals who wisely choose healthy lifestyles enjoy long lives free of sickness, according to theory Y.

TABLE 16–2
The X and Y Theories of Health Economics

View of	Theory X	Theory Y
Health	Health and disease occur randomly	Health is determined by people's lifestyle choices
Medical care	Special	No different from any other good or service
The practice of medicine	A science	An art
Economics	Financial rewards reduce the quality of caring	Financial rewards are responsible for generating high-quality medicine
Policy	Regulations are needed to mitigate economic forces	Reduce regulations and encourage market forces
	Tax the healthy; subsidize the sick	Tax the sick, not the healthy
	Discourage new medical technologies	Encourage new medical technologies

SOURCE: Based on Gerald L. Musgrave, "Health Economics Outlook: Two Theories of Health Economics," Business Economics (April 1995), pp. 7–13.

Theory X treats medical care as being special. Necessity, consumer ignorance, the prevalence of not-for-profit medical institutions, highly inelastic demand, and government regulations all make medical care unique. Theory X says that because of uniqueness, medical care "is not and cannot be treated in the same fashion as other economic commodities whose allocation is left to relatively unregulated markets" (Aaron, 1991, p. 6). In fact, greedy, profit-oriented doctors, insurance companies, and pharmaceutical companies as well as the unfettered forces of the marketplace are the root cause of rising health care costs, according to theory X.

Theory Y, in contrast, perceives medical care to be no different from any other good or service. Health care is no more important than food, clothing, or shelter. Consumers probably know more about health care than they do about the engines in their cars, Musgrave asserts, because the benefit of possessing information is greater. Just as no one blames carpenters for homelessness, according to theory Y, health care providers should not be held responsible for the failure of the U.S. health care system. High profits in the health care sector reflect success, not failure. Theory Yers believe that markets have not been allowed to unleash their magic powers because of excessive government regulations.

Theory X also views medicine as a science. Someday experts will arrive at the best way to treat each and every illness. Conversely, theory Y treats medicine as an art. Health care providers will never find the best cure for a given illness, especially because many illnesses are patient-specific, and newer, less painful, and lower-cost treatments will always be in demand.

Regarding economics, theory X proposes that financial rewards diminish the quality of care. Economics and medicine, like oil and water, do not mix. Profit seeking gets in the way of proper patient care. For example, theory Xers claim that personal investments in MRI facilities create an incentive for physicians to overprescribe their diagnostic services to patients. Theory Y, in contrast, views financial rewards as the reason for high-quality medicine in the United States. Health care providers are in the best position to determine the true needs for health care capital. Ownership provides health care providers with an incentive to ensure that needed capital is supplied.

Given the difference between the two views regarding health, medical care, the practice of medicine, and the role of economics, it should not be surprising that theories X and Y take a different stance on policy as well. Table 16–2 lists three policy stances. According to theory X, because financial rewards are the source of system failure, further regulations are needed to curb the profit appetites of health care providers. Government planning is necessary to control the number of hospitals, physicians, and other health care providers and establishments. Government requires more information on health care markets for planning purposes.

Theory Y asserts that health care markets are already overregulated as mentioned earlier. Excessive regulations are partly accountable for some of the observed health care problems. Competitive economic forces should be allowed to function so that health care providers have the incentive to produce with least-cost methods and satisfy consumer wants. Armed with the appropriate information, consumers have the capability to make informed decisions.

Theory X further proposes that taxes should be levied on healthy individuals to pay for the health care costs of unhealthy ones. Because bad health or illness occurs randomly, it is fair to tax the lucky and not the unlucky. In contrast, theory Y argues that subsidizing sickness rewards it. Taxing health reduces the number of people who will remain healthy. It is not efficient to tax the healthy to subsidize the unhealthy.

Finally, theories X and Y differ on their positions concerning new medical technologies. New medical technology and health care spending are undesirable, according to theory X. Global budgets and other spending controls are necessary to curb the application of medical technologies offering high-cost, low-benefit medicine. Theory Y asserts just the opposite. New technologies advance medical care. More health care services, just like more clothing or food, are good. When expenditures rise in the computer or automobile industry, for example, people should point to success, not failure.

Given these two extreme views, it should not be surprising that many issues pertaining to health economics are hotly debated. These two extreme views also account for the disagreement regarding health insurance reform in the U.S. It is constructive to remember that the proper perspectives on most issues, especially as they pertain to a social science field like health economics, are never truly black or white. Hence, many people adopt an intermediate view of health economics somewhere in the XY theory plane.

An Overview of Health Insurance Reform in the United States

The debate over health insurance reform in the United States has been heated, and the volume of the discussion in the popular press attests to the liveliness of the issue. It is not too difficult to figure out why there is so much disagreement with how to fix the health care system in the United States now that we know about theories X and Y of health economics. Also, facing a bewildering number of proposals and counterproposals from every interest group imaginable, health care professionals and consumers alike have a difficult time keeping abreast of the issues. The debate is further complicated by a vast array of new terminology. Terms with which many of us are unfamiliar, such as *accountable care organizations (ACOs), health insurance exchanges,* and *insurance mandates,* are bandied about regularly. This section attempts to help you sort through this maze by reviewing the efficiency and equity implications of four generic health care reform proposals: managed competition, national health insurance, medical savings accounts, and individual mandates. These four proposals were chosen primarily because they include the basic elements of the majority of the proposals typically considered.

Following this discussion, we examine health insurance reform at the state level. State governments are a frequently overlooked player in the health care debate. We review the health insurance reform packages of four states to get a flavor of the various strategies at the state level. Finally, we question, in general terms, how the Obama health care plan, or the PPACA of 2010 may affect medical care costs, quality, and access.

Models of Health Insurance Reform

To bring some consistency to the discussion, each plan is evaluated using four economic criteria:

1. *Universal coverage:* Does the plan achieve universal coverage, and, if so, how?
2. *Financing and budgetary implications:* How is the plan financed, and to what extent does it affect the federal deficit?
3. *Cost containment:* How does the plan contain the growth of medical care expenditures over time?
4. *Employment:* To what extent does the plan influence overall employment opportunities?

Note that the first criterion deals with the issue of vertical equity, while the last two concern efficiency. A summary of how each plan measures up to the four criteria appears in Table 16–3, which the reader is urged to consult throughout the discussion. In addition, the discussion refers to the generalized model of a health care system discussed in Chapter 4.

TABLE 16–3
A Summary of the Four Health Care Plans

	Managed Competition	National Health Insurance
Universal coverage	Employers are required to provide medical coverage to all full-time workers. Subsidies are provided to make it possible for low-income families to purchase medical insurance. Medicaid and Medicare are maintained. Near-universal coverage is possible.	Universal coverage is achieved through a national health insurance plan that covers all citizens.
Financing	Medical coverage is financed primarily through employer mandates so employees most likely pay through forgone wages. Government expenditures are paid through a payroll tax. The impact on the deficit should not be too significant.	Medical coverage is financed out of an income tax. Also, funds for Medicare and Medicaid are diverted to partially offset the cost of the plan. An employer tax equal to the cost of employer-financed medical insurance is also levied.
Cost containment	Cost containment results from the maintenance of a highly competitive private insurance market. A uniform benefit package is offered, and employers are required to pay for 80 percent of the representative plan. The remaining 20 percent provides an incentive for consumers to shop wisely.	Costs are contained through the utilization of a single-payer system that decreases the administration and billing costs that are the by-product of a multipayer system. Also, global budgeting is used to establish a constant relation between gross domestic product and health care expenditures.
Employment	Likely to have a significant effect because employer mandates may create substantial distortions in labor markets, especially among low-wage workers.	Employment effects will be concentrated in the private insurance market and health care administration.

	Medical Savings Accounts	Individual Mandates
Universal coverage	This program is not designed to achieve universal coverage. However, health insurance premiums should become more affordable when they become tax deductible and apply mainly to catastrophic plans. Tax credits and subsidies are used to make health insurance more affordable for poor individuals.	The plan is implemented through mandated insurance coverage and a guarantee by the government that basic medical coverage is available across the country. Tax credits and subsidies are available to make coverage affordable to all. Near-universal coverage is attainable.
Financing	The plan is financed primarily out of individual contributions to medical savings accounts. Because government expenditures on Medicare and Medicaid end, the deficit should diminish.	The plan is financed largely by premium payments by consumers either directly or through employers. A tax increase is necessary. Medicare and Medicaid programs are ended.
Cost containment	Because consumers pay for most health care expenditures out of their own Medisave accounts, they have the incentive to minimize waste and shop around for competitive prices. A reduction in administrative expenses also translates into cost savings.	Costs are contained through the maintenance of a highly competitive medical insurance market. Private insurance vendors are disciplined by the marketplace to provide competitive prices to consumers.
Employment	Minimal impact because labor market distortions are kept to a minimum.	Minor impact because labor market distortions are kept to a minimum.

Managed Competition

The managed-competition plan has received tremendous publicity primarily because it was used as the basis for the Clinton health care plan. The attractive feature of the plan is that it builds on the existing system of employer-provided medical insurance coverage (Enthoven and Kronick, 1989; Enthoven, 1993). Employers are mandated to provide medical coverage for basic medical services and pay, for example, an 8 percent payroll tax on the first $22,500 of wages for employees not covered.[1] Self-employed individuals and early retirees must pay for health care coverage with an 8 percent tax on adjusted income up to a preset maximum. The tax is collected through the income tax system.

The most novel portion of this plan is the creation across the country of government insurance buyer organizations called **health alliances**. These public or not-for-profit agencies use their purchasing power to negotiate competitive prices for health insurance from private insurance companies. Individuals without employer-provided insurance and small employers may purchase competitively priced health insurance through one of these alliances. The alliances also serve as brokers that collect premiums, manage enrollment, and carry out other administrative duties. The intent is to have each alliance offer a number of competing plans to its enrollees.

Universal coverage is ensured through employer mandates and subsidies provided to low-income families to pay for medical coverage. Medicaid and Medicare are maintained and eventually take advantage of the alliances to provide medical insurance coverage. The plan is financed primarily with employer-mandated health insurance premiums and consumer payments. Government expenditures are financed primarily by the payroll tax and other revenues resulting from the plan. The impact on the deficit is not likely to be significant.

Cost containment results from competition among private insurers as they vie for customers through the alliances. This is why the term **managed competition** was coined. The health alliances "manage" the various health care plans to ensure sufficient "competition" at the insurance end of the medical care market. To simplify matters for consumers and intensify competition, all plans must offer a uniform benefit package. This puts consumers in a better position to make informed choices. As further encouragement for cost-conscious behavior, employers are required to make a fixed contribution toward medical coverage for each employee equal to 80 percent of the average plan's cost in the area. The remaining 20 percent is the employee's responsibility. A limit is also placed on the tax deduction employees can take for premium payments. This encourages consumers to pick less expensive health plans that provide less generous benefits, since they must pay for more costly plans with after-tax dollars.

One criticism of managed competition is that rural areas may lack enough private insurance companies. The scarcity of suppliers may make it difficult to promote price competition (Kronick et al., 1993). Another complaint is that the government-sponsored health alliances may result in "one-size-fits-all" health insurance plans, and, as a result, consumers will lose the benefits of variety. Finally, one of the more controversial elements of employer mandates is the fact that they create labor market distortions and lead to unemployment of unskilled workers as the following section explains.

Who Pays for Employer-Mandated Health Insurance? Most proposals for employer-mandated health insurance in the United States call for employers to finance at least 80 percent of the premiums. The remaining 20 percent of the premiums would be paid by employees, presumably in the form of payroll deductions.

---

1. Other health care proposals give employers the option to pay a tax in lieu of providing medical coverage to full-time employees. In the popular literature, this is referred to as the "pay-or-play" option.

Economic principles suggest, however, that the actual economic incidence of a mandate (or tax) may differ from its statutory or legal incidence. For example, in the case of employer-mandated health insurance, it might be the case that the employer may simply pass on their legal share of the mandate to the employee in the form of lower wages. If so, the employee ends up paying the entire cost of the mandate.

Summers (1989) provides a conceptual model that can be used to examine who pays for an employer-mandated health insurance program. The model is presented graphically in Figure 16–2. The figure depicts a competitive labor market in equilibrium where W stands for the annual money wage and L represents the number of full-time workers. Assuming no health insurance benefits are initially provided, equilibrium is at point L_0 where the supply and demand curves intersect at a wage of W_0. We will now compare this initial equilibrium to one with a mandated health insurance program.

According to Summers's analysis, the mandate potentially shifts both the supply and demand curves. The demand curve shifts downward by the amount of the per-employee cost of the insurance program, M. The shift of the demand curve from D_0 to D_1 reflects that any insurance costs must be potentially offset by wage reductions given that each worker generates a particular amount of revenue for a company as discussed at the beginning of Chapter 6. If this confuses you, think in terms of total compensation rather than just wages. With an employer mandate, health premium payments are substituted for wages. The interesting question then becomes: What happens to the supply of labor?

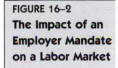

FIGURE 16–2

The Impact of an Employer Mandate on a Labor Market

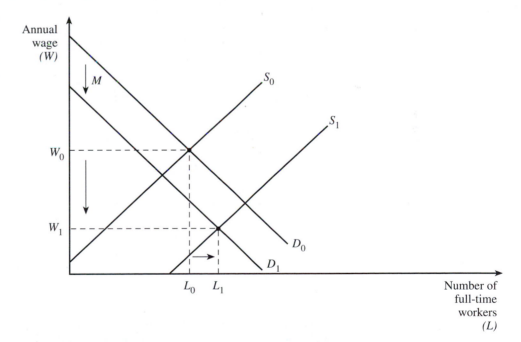

Assuming no health insurance benefits, equilibrium in the labor market initially occurs at point W_0L_0 where the supply and demand curves intersect. Now, assume that government mandates that employers provide health insurance to their employees. In this case, the demand curve shifts downward from D_0 to D_1 because the cost of health insurance must be offset by a lower wage offer. But the supply curve of labor also potentially shifts rightward to reflect the wage income that workers are willing to give up because of the value they attach to health insurance benefits. Supposing that supply shifts from S_0 to S_1 the next equilibrium point is at W_1L_1. Notice that in this case, the wage rate falls by more than the cost of the health insurance because workers perceive that the benefits of health insurance outweigh its cost.

Just as the shift in demand reflects the per-employee cost of the health insurance, the shift in the supply curve captures the benefit of the mandated insurance to the typical employee. If the supply curve shifts downward by the dollar amount of the mandated benefit, it means that the typical employee values the health insurance by exactly the same amount that it costs. That is, the employee is willing to give up wage income equal to the cost of the mandated health insurance. A supply curve that shifts downward by less than the mandated cost suggests that the value of the health insurance to the employee is less than its cost.

For discussion purposes, let us suppose that the supply curve shifts downward by more than demand from S_0 to S_1. That would mean that the new equilibrium wage becomes W_1 and that the employee pays more than the full cost of the mandated benefit in terms of foregone wages. The implication is that the mandated health insurance is efficient since its benefit exceeds its cost. That is, the mandate makes employees better off, and it shows up in the form of a lower wage.

If, on the other hand, the supply curve shifts downward by less than the mandated insurance costs, wages decline but by less than the mandated cost, reflecting that wage income is more important than health insurance at the margin. (You may want to work through this exercise.) Workers would be made worse off by the mandated benefit in this case. In fact, if the supply of labor increases less than demand declines, the analysis suggests that the level of employment decreases in the labor market. Moreover, economic theory indicates that the costs of the resulting unemployment are likely to fall disproportionately upon unskilled workers for three reasons. First, unskilled workers possess low productivity levels. Hence, assuming all other factors remain constant, low skilled workers are the first to be laid off if employers are required to incur higher labor costs (i.e., wages and health insurance costs). Second, unskilled workers, because of their low income, may place less value on the health insurance benefits and assign greater costs to the forgone wages associated with the mandate. The lower net benefits serve as a disincentive for unskilled workers to remain at their jobs. Third, unskilled workers may be paid a government set minimum wage. As a result, their wages cannot legally be adjusted downward to compensate for the added cost of the insurance mandate. In this case, employers have no other recourse than to lay-off workers when faced with the added expense of providing health insurance coverage.

National Health Insurance (NHI)

The NHI plan calls for the implementation of the NHI system similar to the one presently existing in Canada (see Himmelstein and Woolhandler, 1989). As such, the current multipayer system in the United States is replaced by a single-payer public medical insurance program. In terms of the generalized model of a health care system, this means the role of third-party payer is completely taken over by the government sector, and the private market for medical insurance is almost completely eliminated (some specific services, such as dental and optical care, may continue to be covered by private insurance).

Universal coverage is guaranteed with this plan because everyone is covered for all necessary medical services, with no coinsurance, copayments, or deductibles. The plan achieves vertical equity if it is financed out of general taxes, with a heavy reliance on the progressive federal income tax system. A tax increase is necessary to provide the additional funding needed to broaden coverage to uninsured individuals. Since currently funded medical programs, such as Medicare and Medicaid, are no longer needed, funds earmarked for these programs would be used to finance the NHI program. Employer taxes increase by the amount currently spent on health care benefits. The implication is that employer-provided funds are diverted from the private insurance market to a publicly run health insurance program.

Cost containment is based primarily on the efficiencies associated with using a single-payer system. Billing and administration costs are reduced because health care providers no longer need to contend with the complex set of insurance forms and billing procedures that normally result from an uncoordinated multipayer system. In addition, overall expenditures are controlled by establishing a link between GDP and health care costs. Once the proportion between the two is established, overall health care costs are allowed to grow only as fast as the overall economy. Global budgets and simplified fee schedules are utilized to compensate health care providers, such as hospitals and physicians, for services provided. The role of managed care with a national insurance plan is difficult to determine, because most of the impetus for managed care comes from the private health insurance market, which the plan eliminates.

Finally, the employment effects are likely to be most noticeable in the private health insurance market and health care administration. With the elimination of the private health insurance market and the decrease in administrative services, some job displacement is likely to occur, particularly in the short run.

While the NHI plan comes closest to providing universal health insurance, a general criticism has been levied against the plan. The extensive involvement of government and the elimination of private insurers alarm those who believe that government enterprise is monopoly enterprise. Critics claim that the creation of financial innovations to control medical costs would be weakened in a government-run health insurance program. Critics also argue that because a competitive incentive is missing, a public monopoly insurer may offer little variety and be unresponsive to consumer wants.

Medical Savings Accounts (MSAs)

This plan takes a distinctly market-oriented approach to reforming health care by calling for the development of individual tax-free MSAs to pay for routine medical care (Goodman and Musgrave, 1992; Tripoli, 1993). MSAs are similar to the health savings accounts that are discussed in Chapter 6. Proponents of MSAs claim that routine care accounts for a significant fraction of medical expenditures so MSAs may help to contain wasteful spending. The program is purely voluntary in that individuals have the option to make yearly contributions to their MSAs up to a specified amount, and any funds left in the account at the end of the year can be carried over to the next year and earn interest. Catastrophic health insurance plans to finance major medical expenses can also be purchased with pretax income. Premiums for the catastrophic plans are generally cheap due to the high deductibles involved.

An example may help clarify the structure of the MSA proposal. Suppose your employer presently pays $7,000 for your family's major medical and routine care insurance coverage. Under the MSA plan, your employer would purchase catastrophic health insurance coverage worth, say, $3,500 for your family. The catastrophic plan covers expensive major illnesses and has a sizeable deductible. In addition, the employer deposits the remaining $3,500 into a tax-free MSA. Your family can use the funds in the MSA to pay for routine care or to finance the deductible on major medical illnesses during the year. The routine care services could be purchased as needed or on a prepaid basis through a health care provider like a health maintenance organization (HMO). Your family makes the choice by considering relative prices, income, health status, degree of risk aversion, and other demand-side factors. Any unused funds in the MSA are rolled over and used for similar purposes in future years.

The MSA plan does not call for universal health care coverage, but it does give the public freedom of choice. A person can elect to create an MSA and contribute as much as desired up to a preset limit. Because contributions to the MSAs are tax deductible, the price of medical care is reduced, making it affordable for more people. Tax credits also further reduce the price for low-income families, and government subsidies are available for truly needy individuals. Horizontal equity is achieved because all premiums or contributions to the MSAs are tax deductible whether paid by the employee or the employer.[2] Elderly individuals finance health care expenditures with the introduction of medical individual retirement accounts (IRAs). Like traditional IRAs, these accounts grow tax-free and can be used to cover medical expenses during retirement. Eventually they will take the place of Medicare.

Under this plan, consumers individually finance a major proportion of medical expenditures by drawing from the MSAs. The impact on the federal deficit is minimal because the current Medicare and Medicaid programs are eventually ended. The increase in the deficit results primarily from forgone tax revenues because of the tax-exempt nature of the MSAs and because of the tax credits and subsidies to needy individuals.

Cost containment is achieved through enhanced price competition. Since consumers are directly responsible for purchasing medical care out of their MSAs, they have the incentive to reduce waste and comparison shop. Realizing this, health care providers, such as physicians and hospitals, are forced to provide high-quality, competitively priced medical care.

This point is made clear if we look at MSAs in terms of the generalized model of a health care system presented in Chapter 4. It is apparent that MSAs minimize the impact of third-party payers because most transactions take place directly between consumers and health care providers. As a result, fewer market distortions occur because third-party payers play a less influential role in the MSA plan. In addition, costs are reduced due to administrative savings. With high deductibles on catastrophic health care plans, insurance companies are no longer bogged down with thousands of small claims that are relatively expensive to process. Managed care is likely to thrive under the MSA plan as health care providers and insurance companies strive to control costs and remain competitive. The employment effect of this plan is minimal because labor market incentives are not distorted (see the previous discussion on employer mandates).

Several criticisms of MSAs have been raised (Tanner, 1995). First, critics claim that consumers are not sufficiently informed to make cost-conscious decisions regarding medical treatments. Opponents argue that due to the lack of information, physicians will continue to induce the demand for their services and health care costs will continue to rise. Second, critics argue that consumers will forgo necessary or preventive care to save money in the MSAs for other purposes. Less medical care, in turn, will lead to poorer health and higher health care costs in the long run. Third, opponents allege that the plan will lead to adverse selection as healthy people select MSAs while sick individuals choose conventional insurance. Eventually, the price of insurance will increase and create financial access problems as more and sicker members enroll in conventional insurance plans. Fourth, critics point out that the deductible on catastrophic insurance will be insufficient to control expenditures on high-cost, low-benefit medicine. That is, once a person is hospitalized for a major illness, the size of the deductible will not matter. Since critically sick patients account for most of the spending on health care, the MSA plan will be ineffective in containing health care costs. Finally, critics argue that an MSA plan is regressive since the benefits accrue primarily to wealthy individuals.

The advocates of MSAs have responded to each of these criticisms. Basically, proponents point to demand studies showing that consumers are conscious of health care prices, even very small out-of-pocket prices. MSAs will make consumers more responsive and cost conscious, since they will consider the full price of medical services. Further, proponents point to the success of MSA plans currently in use in producing medical cost savings and preventing adverse selection (but see Chapter 6). Finally, advocates claim that the current tax break for employer-provided insurance is far more regressive than MSA plans available for all.

---

2. If only medical premiums paid by employers are tax deductible, horizontal inequities exist because the price of medical coverage depends on employment status rather than income.

Individual Mandates

Like the MSA plan, the individual mandate plan places the responsibility for medical coverage squarely on the shoulders of consumers. Individuals are required by law to purchase a basic medical insurance plan as defined by the government (Pauly et al., 1991). They still have the option to purchase more comprehensive coverage, and nothing precludes employers from providing medical insurance to their employees. As you should now know, mandated health insurance is a provision of the PPACA of 2010.

Universal coverage is achieved through a combination of mandated medical coverage and the government's guarantee that basic medical coverage is available at a competitive price for those unable to pay for a private plan. Tax credits are offered to ensure affordability, and for those who still cannot afford insurance, government vouchers are available. The Medicaid and Medicare programs are eventually phased out.

To make sure competitively priced medical coverage for the basic plan is available to all, the government solicits bids from private insurance vendors throughout the country. At least one basic plan is offered in every geographic region of the country to serve as "fallback" coverage for any consumer who did not purchase a plan in the private market. The plan also moves toward achieving horizontal equity because tax credits depend on income status rather than employment status.

The plan is financed primarily by individual contributions; however, tax credits and subsidies are available for eligible individuals. Although Pauly et al. (1991) do not provide figures, they believe a modest tax increase is necessary to extend medical coverage to the uninsured. The extent of the increase depends on the magnitude of the tax credits and subsidies provided.

Cost containment is ensured through the maintenance of a highly competitive medical insurance market. Private insurance companies find it in their self-interest to provide high-quality, low-cost insurance to consumers who must purchase and pay for their own medical coverage. Competition is also enhanced because the government plays no role as a third-party insurer since the market for medical insurance is completely private. Employment ramifications are likely to be kept to a minimum because labor market incentives are minimally disturbed. In this type of market environment, managed care is likely to be relied on extensively to control costs.

As with the MSA plan, critics of the individual mandate argue that consumers lack the necessary information to shop wisely. Medical insurance plans contain numerous complex terms and conditions, and therefore are difficult for the average person to comprehend. In addition, some argue that the individual mandate provides less incentive than the MSA plan for consumers to consider the full price of the medical services they buy because third-party payers continue to play an influential role under the individual mandate plan. Finally, critics claim that the individual mandate imposes a serious restraint on an individual's freedom of choice (although it should be kept in mind that Social Security and car insurance in many states are presently mandatory).

Attempts at State Health Care and Insurance Reform

The health care systems in most other countries of the world are largely centralized where either the national government or provincial governments make most of the decisions regarding the three basic questions: (1) what medical care to produce; (2) how to produce that medical care; and (3) who receives the medical care? It was the case, until most recently with the passage of the PPACA of 2010, that the United States followed a more decentralized approach to health care policy that allowed individual states a certain degree of latitude in developing their own health care and insurance policies. The reason is largely historic and has its roots in our federalist form of government, which provides states with limited discretion to govern. Coupled with this tradition has been the general belief in the United States that issues relating to health, education, and poverty are best addressed at the local or community level. A case in point is the Medicaid program, which is jointly financed by the federal and state governments. Since states foot a portion of the bill, they have been given latitude as to how those tax dollars are spent. As a result, vastly different Medicaid programs have developed across states over time.

Advocates for a decentralized approach to health care reform point out that this approach is more democratic. This is because states are in a better position than the federal government to address the unique needs of their local population. Another advantage is that states can be seen as "laboratories" or "guinea pigs" where alternative policies can be tried out to see whether they should be adopted at the national level or in other states. Finally, advocates of the decentralized approach are fond of pointing out that the issue of whether health care and insurance reform should take place at the state or federal level is largely moot because our system of government allows states to block any major reforms if they desire. Even with the PPACA of 2010, states are likely to continue playing an important role in the formation of U.S. health care policy especially because states will still be allowed to adopt different health care programs if they demonstrate similar coverage and benefits will be provided to residents.

Confronted with the burden of rising health care costs, a growing number of uninsured individuals, and a citizenry in no mood for further tax increases, most states have been forced to reexamine their health care systems. Many states are aggressively investigating various policy options including new health care reimbursement methods and insurance market reforms. Naturally, space limitations prohibit a discussion of the reforms taking place in each state. With this constraint in mind, we now provide a brief overview of the health care or insurance reform packages that were adopted in Hawaii, Maryland, Massachusetts, and Vermont. These states were chosen because they represent the broad spectrum of policies currently under consideration in other states.

Hawaii: The Case of an Employer Mandate

Hawaii's health insurance system achieved a certain level of recognition a few decades ago, primarily because the state succeeded in achieving near-universal health insurance coverage. When the percentage of nonelderly uninsured in the nation averaged 16.9 percent in 1992, it stood under 7 percent in Hawaii. Even after nearly 20 years, Hawaii's uninsured rate of 9.3 percent lies significantly below the U.S. average of 18.8 percent. Much of Hawaii's success in this regard can likely be attributed to the Prepaid Health Act of 1974, which requires employers to provide health insurance to all full-time employees. In addition, all employers, with few exceptions, are required to provide health insurance coverage to all employees who work a minimum of 20 hours a week. Each medical plan must provide a minimum number of benefits, and the employee's annual premium contribution is limited to 1.5 percent of his maximum salary.

Low-income residents who do not receive employer-provided health insurance may qualify for government-subsidized health insurance. The Fee-for-Service Medicaid Program primarily serves qualifying individuals who are over age 65, or who are blind or disabled. The Hawaii QUEST program offers subsidized health insurance through a variety of managed care plans for those who qualify. The premium payment depends on employment status and asset limits (Pollitz et al., 2005).

The state of Hawaii has also been relatively successful at containing health care costs. Whereas the percentage of GDP in the United States devoted to health care increased from 9.2 percent in 1980 to 17.9 percent in 2009, the similar rate for Hawaii only rose from 7.1 to 13.6 percent. An active population culturally disinclined toward hospitals and a health care market dominated by a few not-for-profit organizations are two of the reasons given for Hawaii's relative success at containing health care costs (Harris, 2009).

But like any health care system, Hawaii's is not perfect. For example, some workers do not qualify for employer-provided health insurance because they work fewer than 20 hours a week. Economic incentives may account for this trend as Lee et al. (2006) found that while private-employer-provided health insurance is more widespread in Hawaii than the rest of the country, there is evidence that some employers try to avoid the requirement by substituting part-time for full-time workers when possible. Some employers duck the law altogether (Harris, 2009).

Despite its relative success, it remains doubtful whether Hawaii's health care system could be transplanted in the rest of the United States. When other states have attempted to implement employer-mandated health insurance, employers threatened to leave the state. Hawaii's isolation may forestall such threats. In addition, Hawaii's paternalistic plantation history made an employer-mandate an easier fit. Also, Hawaii's isolation from the rest of the world means that health care providers are not incentivized to overbuild their facilities with the intention of attracting patients outside the immediate area (Harris, 2009). Finally, people in Hawaii may place a higher value on health insurance coverage and therefore are willing to pay for it through lower wages (see the discussion surrounding Figure 16–2).

Maryland: The Case of Hospital Rate Regulation

Unlike Hawaii, Maryland has focused more of its attention on cost containment rather than the uninsured by regulating hospital rates. Beginning in the 1970s, the Health Services Cost Review Commission (HSCRC) was established and given the responsibility of reviewing and approving the rates hospitals can charge for their services. After receiving a permanent waiver in 1977 from the federal government exempting Maryland from Medicare and Medicaid reimbursement policies, the state was free to implement an "all-payer system" whereby the HSCRC sets the hospital reimbursement rate for all private insurance companies, HMOs, Medicare, and Medicaid based upon a diagnosis-related group type system (Murray, 2009). According to Murray, the "enabling legislation requires the HSCRC to (1) constrain hospital costs; (2) ensure access to hospital care for all citizens; (3) improve the equity and fairness of hospital financing; (4) provide for financial stability; and (5) make all parties accountable to the public" (p. 1369). Note that the HSCRC only determines hospital reimbursement rates and does not set physician fees.

Empirical evidence indicates that hospital rate setting has been relatively successful at containing hospital costs and providing some equity in Maryland. Whereas Maryland's hospital cost per admission was 26 percent above the national average in 1976, it was 2 percent below the national average in 2007 (Murray, 2009). In addition, uncompensated hospital care costs in Maryland rose from 4 percent to more than 8 percent of revenues over the period from 1978 to 2007. This result is notable because the prospectively-set hospital rates in Maryland build in some reimbursement for hospitals to provide uncompensated care. Finally, data suggest that all health care spending as a percentage of GDP in Maryland rose from 8.7 to 14.7 percent from 1980 to 2009, compared to a national trend of 9.2 to 17.9 percent over that same period (www.cms.gov/NationalHealthExpendData/05a_NationalHealthAccountsStateHealth AccountsProvider.asp#TopOfPage).

Massachusetts: The Case of Individual Health Insurance Mandates

In April of 2006 Massachusetts enacted the Massachusetts Health Care Reform Bill with the intent of providing health insurance coverage to all of its residents. At the heart of the bill is an individual mandate that requires all adult residents to purchase health insurance or face substantial tax penalties. To assist those of modest means, the Commonwealth Care Health Insurance Program was created to provide subsidies on a sliding scale basis for the purchase of health insurance. Those individuals with incomes at or below the federal poverty level face no premiums and the subsidies are exhausted once an individual's income reaches 300 percent of the federal poverty level. The legislation also calls for an expansion of Medicaid, or MassHealth, to provide health insurance to children with family incomes up to 300 percent of the federal poverty level.

Employers also play a role in this plan and all employers with more than 10 employees must either provide health insurance coverage or pay a "fair share" contribution of up to $295 per full-time employee per year. These same employers are also required to provide their workers with the ability to pay for health insurance with pretax dollars. As we learned in Chapter 6, this preferential tax treatment serves as a subsidy by effectively lowering the user price of health insurance. Other components of the legislation call for the creation of the Commonwealth Health Insurance Connector, which is an independent public organization responsible for offering individuals and small employers access to affordable health insurance.

Estimates indicate that the reform legislation has significantly diminished the number of uninsured. Based on surveys conducted each year since the health insurance reform occurred in Massachusetts, Long et al. (2012) report that the percentage of nonelderly adults with insurance increased from 86.6 percent in 2006 to 94.2 percent in 2010. Their findings also suggest no evidence of a crowding out of employer-sponsored health insurance coverage as the percentage covered by employer-sponsored health insurance rose from 64.4 to 68 percent over the four-year period. Their survey results also suggest that medical care utilization has improved in Massachusetts since the reform took place. For example, the percentage citing a usual source of care rose 4.7 percentage points and the percentage receiving preventive care rose 5.9 percentage points over the four years. Lastly, it also appears that the greater medical care utilization may have translated into better health outcomes. Specifically, the percentage of survey respondents reporting as being in very good or excellent health increased from 59.7 to 64.9 over the four-year period. Massachusetts must now wrestle with containing health care spending.

Vermont: The Single-Payer Health Care System

In May of 2011, the Governor of Vermont signed the state's single-payer system into law. The reform will be enacted in 2017 when the state expects a waiver from the terms of the PPACA of 2010. Much like the health care system in Canada (see Chapter 4), Vermont's new health care system will result in a publicly-financed health insurance program that provides basic benefits to all of its citizens. In addition, health care providers of each type will be reimbursed similarly in terms of method and rates. By design, the new system guarantees universal coverage and eliminates cost-shifting among providers. Creators of Vermont's single-payer system point to Taiwan where, in 1995, a single-payer system was introduced and insurance coverage grew from 57 to 96 percent of the population in less than two years yet health care spending remained unchanged (Hsaio et al., 2011).

The health insurance benefit package under the new system is based on an established claims database in Vermont and pays, on average, about 87 percent of the actuarial costs of the covered benefits. Out-of-pocket expenses pick up the remaining amount. Financing of the insurance is accomplished through a flat payroll tax (of about 14.2% in the first year) which is split 75/25 between employers and employees. Exemptions are provided for low-income employees. To better ensure efficiency, competitive bidding determines which insurance company becomes responsible for claims administration and health care provider relations. An independent governance board composed of payer (e.g., employers, the state, and families) and beneficiary (e.g., patients and providers) representatives make annual benefit and payment updates and are responsible for any negotiations.

According to Hsiao et al. (2011), savings, of up to 25 percent of current health care spending, are expected through reductions in administrative functions, fraud and abuse controls, malpractice reform, payment reform, and integration of the delivery system. Even after deducting the costs associated with extending coverage to the uninsured and underinsured, providing more comprehensive coverage, and investing in primary care and community hospitals, Hsiao et al. still expect net savings for the state as a whole. Their simulations indicate that a typical household will receive net benefits of $370 (mainly premium cost of old plan less new payroll tax) although higher-income individuals receive less net benefits than lower-income individuals. Most employers should also witness net benefits according to their simulations.

Vermont is certainly embarking on an ambitious undertaking and a bold social experiment. If the law is not challenged and actually implemented, it will be interesting to watch how both medical care utilization and the health of people in Vermont fare under the new system. In particular, the independent governance board will be responsible for updating benefits each year. Lively debate will likely ensue when it comes time to decide, for example, if a new drug should be covered or not by the plan. Some Vermonters may grow tired of "one-size fits all" medicine. Also, examining how health care providers respond to a single-payer system will be interesting. For example, Reinhardt (2012) questions whether the single-payer system in Vermont will be able to control volume. Finally, it will be fascinating to learn if and how other states might benefit from adopting a single-payer system like the one expected in Vermont.

An Overview of the Patient Protection and Affordable Care Act (PPACA) of 2010

Finalizing the most important social legislation since the passage of the Medicare and Medicaid programs in 1965, President Obama signed the PPACA into law in 2010. While the more significant aspects of the legislation relate to the health insurance mandate and health insurance market reforms, some provisions of PPACA are directed at improving the efficiency and quality of health care delivery particularly within the Medicare program. Most of PPACA's provisions have been already discussed where they apply to the material covered in various chapters. Here we simply focus how the PPACA may, in general terms, potentially affect the three-legged stool of medicine by influencing health care costs, quality of care, and access to medical care.

As mentioned previously several times in this book, health care spending in the United Sates increased from 5.2 to 17.9 percent of GDP during the 1960 to 2010 period. Thus, with respect to the first leg, an important question concerns whether or not the PPACA will "bend down the health care cost curve" and help to stop this continual share of GDP being siphoned off to finance health care spending. To accomplish that goal, simply lowering the cost of medical care delivery is not enough; the rising path would continue albeit at a lower level. Rather, the health care spending growth rate must be slowed. As explained previously, new medical technologies primarily account for the rising percentage of health care costs. Consequently, provisions mainly directed at the adoption and dispersion of new medical technologies stand the best chance of bending down the cost curve. However, we don't want to throw out the baby with the bathwater. We have to keep in mind that not all new medical technologies are created equal. Some new medical technologies may be cost-reducing rather than cost-enhancing. For instance we mentioned in Chapter 14 that the new drug cost offset theory argues that new drugs may slow spending on other types of medical goods and services. Also, we don't want to eliminate medical technologies that yield benefits, in terms of lives saved, in excess of their costs as discussed in Chapter 3.

One provision that may slow the growth of new medical technologies is the excise tax on medical device manufacturers. As explained in Chapter 9 this excise tax may provide a disincentive for medical device manufacturers to use their revenues for R&D purposes and thereby reduce the number of new medical devices. Thus, while some people may not live as long as they might have otherwise, health care spending growth may slow. Of course, more people will have the wherewithal to purchase medical devices because of the health insurance mandate, so the negative effects of the excise tax on medical device R&D may be offset to some extent.

Other PPACA provisions that may help slow the growth of new medical technologies are those aimed at stimulating the number of primary care providers. Specialist physicians tend to be the primary adopters and users of new medical technologies. Because of that, it stands to reason that the adoption and dispersion of new medical technologies may slow if more physicians are attracted to primary rather than specialty care in the future. Based upon this same theme, bundled payments may help to bend down the curve if ACOs respond to fixed payments by discovering lower cost, less technology-intensive ways of delivering medical care.

In terms of the second leg, several provisions of PPACA could potentially affect the quality of care, but mostly with respect to the Medicare program. ACOs, value-based purchasing, bundled payments, and financial incentives aimed at enlarging the primary care workforce all stand a chance of improving the quality of care provided to Medicare patients. If private health insurance companies follow some of these same practices, as some policy makers suspect, then quality of care improvements may be even more widespread.

Improving medical care access is certainly the boldest aspect of the PPACA of 2010. The health insurance mandate, subsidies to individuals and small employers, and the expansion of the Medicaid program all point to better access on the demand side of various medical care markets. Moreover, greater subsidies to community health centers and public health services and the community benefit assessment of not-for-profit hospitals all point to better access on the supply side. As about 30 million people transition from uninsured to insured status, economic research indicates the health status of the U.S. population should improve meaningfully.

In sum, if the act is upheld by the Supreme Court and the legislation is not reversed politically, the health care system of the United States will undergo a major transformation because of the PPACA. The act should raise the quality of care and greatly improve access to medical care in the United States. Whether or not the PPACA of 2010 is able to bend down the health care cost curve remains much more doubtful.

Summary

The advanced state of medical technology is possibly the greatest strength of the U.S. health care system. Premature babies, weighing less than 2 pounds, face a relatively good chance of surviving if they are born in the United States because of the state of medical technology. A relatively long life expectancy after age 80 and a high women's 5-year breast cancer survival rate also reflect the advanced state of medical technology in the United States. In addition, the United States continues to be a world leader when it comes to discovering new drug and medical devices.

But as we know, the U.S. health care system is not without weaknesses. Compared to other industrialized countries around the globe, its most glaring weakness is the nearly 16 percent of the population without health insurance. Lack of health insurance creates medical access problems and subjects a family's income to the vagaries of health status. The inability to successfully control costs is another major weakness of the U.S. health care system. The growth of health care costs continues unabated, although the pace has slowed in recent years. Lastly, the quality of care in the United States has been questioned by health care analysts. For example, in many areas of the United States, health care providers continue to adopt relatively high-cost, yet ineffective methods of practicing medicine.

Eliminating weaknesses while maintaining the strengths is a challenge faced by decision makers when it comes to any type of health care reform. Indeed, much of the recent debate on the PPACA of 2010 reflects that dilemma. In the next few years we should learn if this act survives judicial and political challenges. If it does, it will be interesting to see if and how the PPACA transforms the U.S. health care system. Let's hope this act results in medicine that yields positive marginal net benefits, greater access to medical care for those in need, and more consistent and efficient levels of medical care quality throughout the United States.

Review Questions and Problems

1. Data suggest that the United States spends much more on health care than other countries yet health care outcomes are worse. How might one explain that difference in performance?

2. Some empirical studies have found evidence for an inverse relation between costs and quality of care in the United States. Use the discussion in this chapter (hint: and Chapter 13) to provide some economic reasoning for that inverse relationship.

3. Discuss the four generic plans for health insurance reform in terms of the general model of a health care system presented in Chapter 4. Pay particular attention to the role third-party payers play in each plan.

4. Do you think a theory Xer or Yer would support each of the four generic plans for health insurance reform?

5. Which of the four generic plans of health insurance reform appeals to you the most? Substantiate your opinion using economic theory when possible.

6. Which generic health insurance plan would best correct moral hazard? Why? Which generic plan would best achieve scale economies in health insurance administration? Why? Which plan would provide the most variety? Why?

7. Choose a state other than one of the four discussed in the chapter, and research any basic changes in health insurance policy that have been made or are currently being considered.

8. Use economic theory to explain how employees may end up paying for at least a portion of mandated health insurance in terms of forgone wages.

9. Discuss in general terms how the PPACA of 2010 may affect the three-legged stool of medicine.

Online Resources

To access Internet links related to the topics in this chapter, please visit our website at **www.cengage.com/economics/santerre**.

References

Aaron, Henry J. *Serious and Unstable Condition: Financing America's Health Care.* Washington, D.C.: The Brookings Institution, 1991.

Aaron, Henry J. and Paul B. Ginsburg. "Is Health Spending Excessive? If so, What Can We Do about It? *Health Affairs* 28 (September/October, 2009), pp. 1260–1275.

Anderson, Gerard F., Uwe E. Reinhardt, Peter S. Hussey, and Varduhi Petrosyan. "It's the Prices, Stupid: Why the United States is so Different from Other Countries" *Health Affairs* 22 (2003), pp. 89–105.

Baicker, Katherine and Amitabh Chandra. "Medicare Spending, the Physician Workforce, and Beneficiaries' Quality of Care." *Health Affairs* 23 (April 7, 2004), pp. w184–97.

Congressional Budget Office. *Technological Change and the Growth of Health Care Spending.* Washington, D.C.: Congressional Budget Office, January 2008.

Cutler, David M. "Making Sense of Medical Technology." *Health Affairs* (February 7, 2006), pp. w48–w50.

Cutler, David M. "Equality, Efficiency, and Market Fundamentals: The Dynamics of International Medical-Care Reform." *Journal of Economic Literature* 40 (September, 2002), pp. 881–906.

Cutler, David M. and Mark McClellan. "Is Technological Change in Medicine Worth It?" *Health Affairs* 20 (2001), pp. 11–29.

Cutler, David M., Allison B. Rosen, and Sandeep Vijan. "The Value of Medical Spending in the United States, 1960–2000." *The New England Journal of Medicine* 355 (August, 2006), pp. 920–7.

Enthoven, Alain C. "The History and Principles of Managed Competition." *Health Affairs* (supplement 1993), pp. 24–48.

Enthoven, Alain C., and Richard Kronick. "A Consumer-Choice Health Plan for the 1990s." Parts 1 and 2. *New England Journal of Medicine* 320 (January 5, 1989), pp. 29–37, and (January 12, 1989), pp. 94–101.

Fuchs, Victor R. "National Health Insurance Revisited." *Health Affairs* 10 (November, 1991), pp. 7–17.

Goodman, John C., and Gerald L. Musgrave. *Patient Power: Solving America's Health Care Crisis.* Washington, D.C.: Cato Institute, 1992.

Harris, Gardiner. "In Hawaii's Health System, Lessons for Lawmakers" *New York Times*, October 16, 2009.

Himmelstein, David, and Steffie Woolhandler. "A National Health Program for the United States." *New England Journal of Medicine* 320 (January 12, 1989), pp. 102–8.

Hsaio, William C., Anna Gosline Knight, Stephen Kappel, and Nicolae Done. "What Other States Can Learn from Vermont's Bold Experiment: Embracing a Single-Payer Health Care Financing System." *Health Affairs* 30 (July, 2011), pp. 1232–41.

Kronick, Richard, David C. Goodman, John Wennberg, and Edward Wagner. "The Marketplace in Health Care Reform: The Demographic Limitations of Managed Competition." *New England Journal of Medicine* 328 (January 14, 1993), pp. 148–52.

Laugesen, Miriam J. and Sherry A. Glied. "Higher Fees Paid to US Physicians Drive Higher Spending for Physician Services Compared to Other Countries." *Health Affairs* 30 (2011), pp. 1647–56.

Lee Sang-Hyop., et al. "The Effect of Mandatory Employer-Sponsored Health Insurance on the Use of Part-Time versus Full-Time Workers: The Case of Hawaii." *Economics of Population Health: Inaugural Conference of the American Society of Health Economists*. Madison, Wisconsin. (June 4, 2006).

Long, Sharon K., Karen Stockley, and Heather Dahlen. "Massachusetts Health Reforms: Uninsurance Remains Low, Self-Reported Health Status Improves as State Prepares to Tackle Costs." *Health Affairs* 31 (January 2012), pp. forthcoming.

Murray, Robert. "Setting Hospital Rates to Control Costs and Boost Quality: The Maryland Experience." *Health Affairs* 28 (September/October 2009), pp. 1395–1405.

Musgrave, Gerald L. "Health Economics Outlook: Two Theories of Health Economics." *Business Economics* (April 1993), pp. 7–13.

Organization for Economic Cooperation and Development, www.oecd.org.

Pauly, Mark, Patricia Danzon, Paul Feldstein, and John Hoff. "A Plan for Responsible National Health Insurance." *Health Affairs* 10 (spring 1991), pp. 5–25.

Pollitz, Karen, Kevin Lucie, Eliza Bangit, and Mila Kofman. "A Consumer's Guide to Getting and Keeping Health Insurance in Hawaii." Washington, D.C.: Georgetown University Health Policy Institute, October 2005.

Reinhardt, Uwe. "Divide et Impera: Protecting the Growth of Health Care Incomes (Costs)." *Health Economics* 21 (2012), pp. 41–54.

Schoen, Cathy, Robin Osborn, David Squires, Michelle M. Doty, Roz Pierson, and Sandra Applebaum. "How Health Insurance Design affects Access to Care and Costs, By Income, In Eleven Countries". *Health Affairs* 29 (2010), pp. 2323–34.

Skinner, Jonathan S., Douglas O. Staiger, and Elliott S. Fisher. "Is Technological Change in Medicine Always Worth It? The Case of Acute Myocardial Infarction." *Health Affairs* (February 7, 2006), pp. w34–w47.

Summers, Lawrence H. "Some Simple Economics of Mandated Benefits." *American Review* 79 (May 1989), pp. 177–83.

Tanner, Michael. "Medical Savings Accounts: Answering the Critics." *Policy Analysis*, no. 228 (May 25, 1995).

Tripoli, Leigh. "Agoraphobia: What Ails Most of the Conservative Proposals to Reform Health Care." *Business Economics* (April 1993), pp. 30–35.

Accountable care organizations (ACO) Comprise a network of physicians and hospitals that share responsibility for treating patients. These ACOs may be paid on a fee-for-service or capitation basis.

Actual competition The level of competition or rivalry as determined by the number of firms currently operating in the market.

Adverse selection Occurs when an individual with poor health acquires low-risk medical insurance meant for healthy consumers. Results when an asymmetry of information develops between the insurer and the subscriber concerning the subscriber's true health status.

Affordability exception It is given to people who would have to pay more than 8 percent of their annual income for the cheapest health insurance plan.

Agency theory Models a situation in which a principal (say external stockholders) hires a manager (an agent) to run the affairs of the business. Because the principal may be rationally ignorant of the current company policies, the agent may pursue goals that conflict with the objectives of the principal. To better align the interests of the agent with those of the principal, the proper design of the compensation package is an important consideration. For medical care, an important agency relationship holds between the patient and physician.

Allocative efficiency The condition in which the optimal amount of output is produced given the underlying structure of social benefits and costs. (See *production possibilities curve.*)

Bounded rationality The notion that people, in general, have a limited ability to formulate and solve problems at a point in time.

Boycott An agreement among competitors in a given input or output market not to do business with a particular supplier or customer. Boycotting is prohibited by the Sherman Antitrust Act.

Brand-loyalty advantage See *first mover.*

Coinsurance A component of a medical insurance plan in which consumers pay a fixed percentage of the cost of medical care.

Collusive oligopoly An oligopolistic-type market structure in which all the firms in the industry jointly maximize profits as if they all acted collectively as a monopolist.

Community rating A method used by third-party payers to establish insurance premiums based on the average benefits paid out for the total population served. In this case, premiums reflect the average health risk factors for the entire population served.

Comparative static analysis A comparison of the initial and new equilibrium points after an external change alters the model.

Compensating wage differential The increase in wages needed to attract the marginal worker to a given occupation because there is an added cost to entering the occupation, such as a professional license.

Competitive oligopoly A product market characterized by a few dominant sellers that act competitively and do not coordinate their activities. (See *oligopoly.*)

Complements Two goods that are used together in consumption. Two goods are complements in consumption if an increase in the price of one good causes a decrease in the demand for the other.

Compulsory licensing The situation in which one firm is required by law to grant to another firm the opportunity to import or manufacture a patented drug for a royalty.

Conjectural variations The beliefs held by a firm regarding how its rivals will react to its own price and output decisions.

Constant returns to scale Exist when a percentage increase in all factor inputs leads to a proportionately equal increase in output. The long-run average cost curve is horizontal if constant returns to scale exist.

Consumer-driven health care Health care provided to consumers with insurance plans that have high deductibles. Routine health care expenditures are financed out of special tax-exempt accounts such as Health Savings Accounts. With this combination, consumers are made more cost sensitive and, at the same time, avoid the financial risk of a major illness.

Consumer Surplus The difference between the willingness to pay and the actual price paid. It reflects the net benefit to consumers and also equals the dollar value of the utility received from consuming a good and the total expenditures paid for that good.

Copayment A fixed amount paid by consumers for medical care that is independent of the market price.

Cost-benefit analysis A method of analysis used for decision making that estimates the total costs and benefits of an activity.

Cost effectiveness analysis A method of analysis used for decision making that estimates the total costs of achieving a defined health care objective, such as a life-year saved, from a medical treatment or health behavior.

Cost identification studies A study that measures the total costs of a particular medical condition. Cost identification considers direct medical costs, direct nonmedical costs, and indirect costs.

Cost shifting The practice of charging a higher price for a medical service in one market to compensate for a lower administered price.

Cost-utility analysis A method of analysis used to make policy decisions that considers the quantity as well as the quality of life-years saved from a medical intervention. (See *cost effectiveness analysis*.)

Cross-price elasticity An elasticity measure of the extent to which the quantity demanded of one product changes with respect to a change in the price of an alternative product. In precise terms, it equals the percentage change in the quantity demanded of one product divided by the percentage change in the price of another product. If the value of the ratio is negative, the two products are complements; if the ratio is positive, the two products are substitutes.

Cyclical uninsurance The condition of individuals who are uninsured because of variations in the business cycle.

Data envelopment analysis (DEA) A statistical technique used by researchers to estimate the technical efficiency of organizations.

Deadweight loss The social surplus not realized because resources are misallocated.

Decreasing returns to scale Exist when a percentage increase in all factor inputs leads to a less than proportional increase in output.

Defensive medicine The overutilization of medical services by a health care provider in order to prevent a potential medical malpractice suit.

Demand-side subsidy A payment of funds generally directed at consumers to purchase goods and services.

Deselection The termination of a health care provider in a medical network based on an established set of criteria.

Diagnosis-related group (DRG) A prospective reimbursement system developed under Medicare used to compensate hospitals based primarily on the patient's primary diagnosis.

Direct medical care costs All costs incurred by medical care providers resulting from a particular medical intervention.

Direct nonmedical costs All nonmedical costs resulting from a particular medical intervention.

Disease management A program in which health care interventions are coordinated and patients take an active role in their own care.

Diseconomies of scale Exist when the average cost of production increases with the level of output.

Disproportionate share hospital payments Additional reimbursement payments received by states from the federal government for the Medicaid program to defer the high cost of providing medical care to a large number of low-income individuals.

Distributive justice Achieving fairness in the way that goods and services are distributed to members of society. (See *horizontal equity* and *vertical equity*.)

Doughnut hole The portion of the Part D benefit structure in which the enrollee pays 100 percent of the cost of prescription drugs. In 2012, the doughnut hole begins when total annual spending on drugs reaches $2,930 and concludes when total annual spending for drugs surpasses $6,757.5.

Drug utilization review Programs that control costs by reviewing the prescribing behavior of physicians to ensure that formularies are followed and inappropriate medicines are not prescribed.

Economic model A simplified depiction of a complex economic phenomenon used by economists to examine economic behavior.

Economies of scale Exist when the average cost of production decreases with the quantity of output.

Economies of scope Exist when the total cost of jointly producing two or more products is cheaper than the total cost of producing each product individually.

Elastic Describes a situation in which the absolute value of the elasticity is greater than 1, or the percentage change in the dependent variable is greater than the percentage change in the independent variable, in absolute value terms.

Elasticity A measure economists use to gauge the extent to which one variable changes in response to a change in the another variable. It equals the percentage change in the dependent variable divided by the percentage change in an independent variable.

Equity See *Distributive justice.*

Ex ante moral hazard Behavioral changes that occur after becoming insured but take place before the medical illness happens. These actions, such as lack of exercise or improper diet, raise the probability of becoming ill.

Exclusive dealing contract A situation in which a distributor agrees to sell only the manufacturer's products and not the products of a manufacturer's competitors.

Experience rating A method used by third-party payers to establish insurance premiums based on the expected benefits paid out as a result of individual health risk factors.

Ex post moral hazard Behavioral changes that occur after the medical illness happens such as consuming additional units of medical care (e.g., an extra day in the hospital).

Extensive margin The market change in the quantity demanded for a product brought about by a price change because more (fewer) consumers buy the product when its price decreases (increases).

Externality Exists when the actions of a market participant affect another participant in either an adverse or a beneficial fashion and no financial compensation takes place. An externality can emanate from either the demand or the supply side of the market.

Extra billing The situation in which a health care provider bills a patient in excess of a preset fee established by a third party for health care provided.

First-dollar coverage A health insurance plan that reimburses an individual for all medical care expenses, beginning with the first dollar spent on medical care.

First-mover advantage A firm that poses a barrier to entry by being the first to introduce a product to a given market. Potential competitors must overcome the problem of name recognition if they wish to enter the market.

Fixed effects model An identification strategy employed to estimate a causal relationship where a variable or set of variables are included in the model that control for an entity and/or time period.

Formulary A list of low-cost, effective pharmaceutical products that physicians are required to prescribe whenever possible. Hospitals and other health care providers use formularies to control costs.

Frictional uninsurance The condition of individuals who are uninsured because they are temporarily between jobs or searching for a suitable insurance policy.

Gag rules Rules that prohibit a physician in a managed care plan from discussing alternative treatment options not covered by the health insurance plan, providing information on the limitations of the plan, and commenting negatively about the plan to patients.

Government-driven See *National health insurance.*

Guarantee issue Insurers do not exclude coverage for preexisting conditions.

Guaranteed renewability Contractual feature of an insurance policy that requires the insurer to renew the policy on its anniversary date and not charge a premium for that policy based on an individual's personal loss experience.

Health A type of durable human capital that offers a flow of services to an individual. These health services are enjoyed for consumption and investment purposes.

Health alliance A public agency that uses its bargaining power to negotiate competitive prices for health insurance from the private insurance market. (See *managed competition.*)

Health care system The organizational and institutional structures through which an economy makes choices regarding the production, consumption, and distribution of health care services.

Health economics A field of economics that uses economic theory to study how an economy utilizes scarce health care resources to provide and distribute medical care.

Health maintenance organization (HMO) A health care delivery system that combines the insurer and producer functions. HMOs are prepaid and in return provide comprehensive services to enrollees.

Health production function A mathematical expression that shows the relationship between an individual's health and a number of variables, including the amount of health care consumed.

Health-utility index A scale used to measure the quality of life remaining. (See *rating scale, standard gamble model*, and *time trade-off*.)

Horizontal equity Equity that is achieved when, individuals with similar incomes pay equal amounts of taxes and receive the same amounts of subsidies; in other words, equals are treated equally.

Horizontal merger A merger between two firms in the same market.

Human capital approach Equates the value of a human life to the discounted market value of the output produced by an individual over an expected lifetime.

Income elasticity of demand An elasticity measure of the extent to which the quantity demanded changes with a change in income. In precise terms, it equals the percentage change in the quantity demanded divided by the percentage change in income.

Inconsistency Reflects the fact that the composition and quality of medical services vary greatly across points of consumption.

Increasing returns to scale Exist when a percentage increase in all factor inputs leads to a greater percentage increase in output.

Incremental cost effectiveness ratio (ICER) A measure that gauges the relative value of one medical intervention over another. The numerator of the ratio equals the cost of a new medical intervention minus the cost of an established medical intervention, and the denominator of the ratio equals the difference in effectiveness between the new and established medical intervention. (See *cost effectiveness analysis*.)

Indirect costs All nonmonetary costs, such as time costs, incurred from a given medical intervention.

Inelastic Describes a situation in which the absolute value of the elasticity is less than 1, or the percentage change in the dependent variable is less than the percentage change in the independent variable, in absolute value terms.

In-kind Specific goods or vouchers provided to a defined population, such as the needy.

Inseparability Means that production takes place at the time of consumption.

Instrumental variables approach An identification strategy used to estimate causal relationships whereby a variable, or set of variables, independent of the error term are used to estimate the value of an endogenous variable in the model.

Insurance exchange A government-created marketplace in which consumers purchase health insurance with a stipulated minimum benefit package and other plan characteristics as determined by the government.

Intangibility Occurs when a medical service cannot be evaluated by the five senses.

Integrated delivery system (IDS) A legal or contractual combination of buyers and suppliers, such as medical organizations, producing different medical services—for example, physician groups, hospitals, and nursing homes.

Intensive margin The market change in the quantity demanded for a product brought about by a price change because consumers buy more (less) of the product when its price decreases (increases).

Inventory Refers that it is impossible for health care providers to maintain an inventory of medical services.

Law of demand An economic principle stating that the quantity demanded of a good or service is inversely related to its price.

Law of diminishing marginal productivity Health increases at a decreasing rate with respect to additional amounts of medical care, assuming other health-related inputs are held constant.

Law of diminishing marginal utility An economic principle stating that as units of a product are consumed, a point is eventually reached at which total utility increases at a continually smaller rate. In other words, the marginal utility of the product begins to fall.

Law of increasing opportunity cost An economic principle stating that the opportunity cost of an activity increases as more of that activity is undertaken.

Learning-by-doing The economies that result from knowledge or experience gained through the cumulative production of a product.

Learning-by-watching Productivity of quality improvements that occur over time because of knowledge or technological change that can be easily transferred across organizations.

Limit pricing The practice of pricing a product just below the break-even point of a potential entrant as a way to discourage entry.

Loading fee The portion of medical insurance premiums in excess of expected benefits paid out. Its value depends on such items as administrative costs, taxes, and the intensity of competition in the insurance market.

Long-run economies of scale See *economies of scale*.

Managed competition A health care reform plan that calls for the establishment of health alliances that would use their bargaining power to negotiate competitively priced medical coverage from a number of alternative private insurance companies.

Marginal revenue The addition to total revenue brought about by the sale of one more unit of output.

Market allocation A collusive agreement among rival firms not to compete with one another in a given geographical market. This activity is prohibited by the Sherman Antitrust Act.

Market concentration Reflects the number and size distribution of firms in an industry.

Market conduct The second element in the industrial organization triad, which considers firms in terms of pricing, promotion, and research and development activities.

Market performance The third element in the industrial organization triad, which considers firms in terms of production and allocative efficiencies, equity, and technological progress.

Market power The ability of a firm to raise the price above the competitive level.

Market structure The first element in the industrial organization triad, which considers the overall environment within which each firm operates.

Medicaid A jointly financed public program between federal and state governments that provides medical insurance to certain segments of the poor population without private health insurance.

Medicare A federally financed program that provides medical insurance primarily to elderly individuals.

Monopolistic competition A product market characterized by numerous sellers, moderate product differentiation, no barriers to entry, and some imperfections in consumer information.

Moral hazard The situation in which individuals alter their behavior after they have purchased medical insurance because they are no longer liable for the full cost of their actions.

Multihospital system An organization that is made up of two or more hospitals and is managed by a single corporation.

Mutual interdependence The situation in which the behavior of one firm in a given market impacts the pricing and output decisions of other firms in the market.

National health insurance (NHI) A government-sponsored health insurance system covering the entire population and financed by tax revenues. Such a system exists in Canada.

National health service (NHS) A health care system directly operated by the government and financed by general taxes. Such a system exists in Sweden and Finland.

Natural experiment An identification strategy employed to estimate a causal relationship where an exogenous shock takes place that is unrelated to the other variables included in the model.

Negative demand-side externality Exists when the actions of a consumer adversely affect others not directly involved in the market transaction and no financial compensation takes place.

Negative supply-side externality Exists when the actions of a producer adversely affect other market participants and no financial compensation takes place.

New drug cost offset theory The theory that new drugs pay for themselves by lowering the costs of other types of medical care such as hospital or physician services.

Nondistribution constraint Law stating that nonprofit organizations cannot distribute surplus earnings to individuals without regard to the charitable purpose for which the organization was formed.

Normal profits Occurs when revenues are just enough to cover the opportunity cost of each and every resource used in production of a medical good or service. According to economic theory, the typical firm earns a normal profit in the long run when the market is perfectly competitive.

Normative analysis The use of economic theory and empirical analysis to justify whether an economic outcome is desirable.

Oligopoly A product market that is characterized by a few dominant sellers and substantial barriers to entry.

Opportunistic behavior The situation in which an individual pursues his or her own self interests with guile or deceit.

Opportunity cost The value of what is given up by not pursuing the next best alternative.

Outcome quality The quality of medical care as measured by its end result, such as patient satisfaction or postcare morbidity or mortality.

Own-price elasticity of demand An elasticity measure of the responsiveness of quantity demanded to changes in a product's own price. In precise terms, it equals the percentage change in quantity demanded divided by the percentage change in price.

Patient-driven health care Health care provided to patients with health insurance policies that have fairly low out-of-pocket expenses. Such a system provides incentives for health care providers to concentrate on the quality of care provided rather than costs.

Patient dumping The situation in which a private hospital fails to admit a very sick patient because it fears that the medical bills will exceed a preset limit established by a third-party payer. As a result, the patient is forced to acquire medical care services from a public hospital.

Payer-driven health care Health care provided in an environment dominated by managed care providers that control costs by negotiating price reductions with networks of health care providers.

Perfect competition A product market characterized by numerous buyers and sellers, a homogeneous product, no barriers to entry, and perfect consumer information.

Perfectly elastic The special case in which there is an infinite change in the value of the dependent variable when the independent variable changes in value.

Perfectly inelastic The special case in which the value of the dependent variable is unresponsive to changes in the value of the independent variable.

Physician practice hypothesis A hypothesis stating that per capita variations in the use of medical care are explained by systematic differences in clinical opinions concerning the proper type and amount of medical care to prescribe.

Physician profiling The process by which a managed care organization selects and monitors the performance of physicians.

Perfect egalitarian system A system that distributes goods and services equally to all members of a society regardless of their willingness or ability to earn income.

Point-of-service (POS) plan A type of managed care insurance plan that requires subscribers who go outside the network for medical care to pay higher out-of-pocket expenses. The purpose is to contain costs by encouraging subscribers to acquire medical care from a network of providers.

Positive analysis The analysis of economic behavior that uses economic theory along with empirical analysis to explain what is or what happened.

Positive demand-side externality Exists when the actions of a consumer beneficially affect others not directly involved in the market transaction and no financial compensation takes place.

Potential competition The level of competition as determined by the number of firms that may enter a particular market. Potential competition is determined by the height of any barriers to entry.

Practice guidelines A statement concerning the known costs, benefits, and risks of using a particular medical intervention to bring about a given medical outcome.

Preferred provider organization (PPO) A third-party payer that offers financial incentives, such as low out-of-pocket prices, to enrollees who acquire medical care from a preset list of physicians and hospitals.

Present value (PV) A technique used to determine today's value of a future stream of cash payments.

Price discrimination The practice of charging a different price for the same product in two or more market segments.

Price fixing The practice by rival firms in the same market of acting in a collusive manner and setting prices for the purpose of increasing profits. This practice is prohibited by the Sherman Antitrust Act.

Price-payoff contract An insurance contract that compensates the consumer through a price reduction rather than a lump-sum payment.

A price-payoff contract potentially triggers both a substitution and income effect but helps prevent the consumer from engaging in opportunistic behavior.

Price taker A firm that has no influence over the market price of its product and treats the price as a given.

Process quality The quality of medical care as measured by the quality of treatment.

Producer surplus The net benefit producers receive equal to the difference between the price received by the producer and the marginal cost of production.

Production efficiency Achieved when one activity (production or consumption) cannot be increased without a reduction in another activity because the maximum level of output is being produced from a finite amount of inputs. (See *production possibilities curve*.)

Production possibilities curve (PPC) An economic model that shows the various combinations of goods an economy can produce when production efficiency is achieved. Allocative efficiency is obtained when society chooses the point on the cure that maximizes overall as satisfaction. The model illustrates the economic concepts of scarcity, choice, and opportunity costs.

Progressive redistribution scheme The situation in which net taxes as a fraction of income increase with income.

Proportional redistribution scheme The situation in which net taxes as a fraction of income remain constant with income.

Public contracting A health insurance model in which the government contracts with various health care providers for medical services on behalf of the general population.

Public interest theory A theory of government behavior that hypothesizes that government intervenes in a market-based economy to advance the general interest of its citizens.

Pure market system A system that allocates resources and distributes goods and services based on buying and selling decisions made at an individual or decentralized level within a market economy.

Pure monopoly A product market characterized by one seller and perfect barriers to entry.

Quality-adjusted life-year (QALY) A measure that reflects the quantity and quality of life-years saved. It equals the product of life expectancy times a measure of the quality of life-years remaining. (See *cost-utility analysis*.)

Rating scale A technique used to generate a health-utility index that asks individuals to rate various health outcomes.

Rationality The notion that consumers will never purposely make themselves worse off and have the ability to rank preferences and allocate income in a fashion that derives the maximum level of utility.

Rationally ignorant The situation in which consumers have less than perfect information concerning a good or service due to the high cost of acquiring additional information.

Regression analysis A statistical method used to isolate the cause-and-effect relation among variables.

Regressive redistribution scheme The situation in which net taxes as a fraction of income decrease with income.

Relevant geographical market (RGM) Captures the spatial dimension of the relevant market by considering the location of firms that consumers might switch to given a nontrivial and nontemporary change in the price of a product at any one location.

Relevant product market (RPM) Captures the product dimension of the relevant market by considering all of the products that consumers might switch to given a nontrivial and nontemporary change in the price of any one product.

Rule of reason States that courts should weigh the social desirability of a business practice, such as a merger, when determining whether that practice should be allowed to take place. Thus, both the procompetitive and anticompetitive aspects of the business practice are considered.

Search frictions Arise from the imperfections in the process by which employer groups are matched to insurers. Search frictions make it difficult for employers to identify the available policy best suited for the needs and preferences of their workforce.

Selective contracting Occurs when a third party contracts exclusively with a preselected set of medical care providers.

Short-run economies of scale Exist when average variable costs decline with the level of output.

Sickness Funds Private, not-for-profit insurance companies in Germany that collect premiums from employees and employers. (See *socialized health insurance*.)

Small area variations Variations in the per capita utilization of medical services across small geographic regions.

Social experiment An identification strategy employed to estimate a causal relationship whereby subjects are randomly assigned for evaluation purposes.

Socialized health insurance (SI) A health care system in which the government mandates that employers and employees jointly finance the cost of medical care insurance.

Special interest group theory A theory of government behavior that hypothesizes that governments intervene in a market-based economy for the purpose of advancing the economic self-interests of a particular interest group.

Standard gamble A technique used to generate a health-utility index that asks individuals with a given medical condition to choose the probability of dying at which they are indifferent between living a healthy life after having a medical procedure and dying because of the medical procedure.

State health insurance mandates Require that an insurance company or a health plan cover specific benefits, health care providers, or patient populations.

Structural quality The quality of medical services as measured by the quality of the inputs used in production, such as credentials of physicians, education of nurses, and vintage and variety of equipment.

Structurally uninsured The condition of individuals who are uninsured on a long-run basis because of, for example, chronic illnesses, preexisting conditions, or insufficient income.

Substitutes Two goods that are replacements in consumption and fulfill a similar purpose. Two goods are substitutes in consumption if an increase in the price of one good causes an increase in demand for the other.

Sunk costs Costs incurred by a firm that cannot be recovered.

Supplier-induced demand (SID) hypothesis A model of firm behavior that hypothesizes that physicians, to further pursue their own economic self-interests, take advantage of the asymmetry of information about medical care to persuade their patients to consume more medical care than is necessary.

Supply-side subsidy A monetary sum received from a third party directed at reducing the cost of producing a good or service.

Survivor theory A theory that categorizes firms based on size and hypothesizes that any category that includes a growing number of firms over time represents the most efficient producers in comparison to categories in which the number of firms is decreasing.

Technically efficient The condition that exists when the maximum level of output is produced from a given mix of inputs at a point in time.

Time trade-off A technique used to generate a health-utility index that asks individuals to choose the number of years of healthy living at which they are indifferent between living in perfect health followed by death and living a fixed number of years with a given chronic health condition.

Total net social benefit (TNSB) The difference between the total social benefit in consuming and total social cost of producing a good or service.

Total product curve A curve showing the quantity of output produced by different levels of a specific input, such as labor, given that all other inputs are held constant.

Transaction cost economics The costs of searching out the best price and the cost associated with negotiating, writing, and enforcing contracts. Transaction cost economics holds the view that contracts may be incomplete and therefore costly to engage in.

Unit elastic An elasticity with a value of 1 such that the percentage change in the dependent variable equals the percentage change in the independent variable, in absolute value terms.

Utility The level of satisfaction or pleasure an individual or group receives from consuming a good or service.

Utility-maximizing rule A rule stating that a consumer's utility is maximized when the marginal utility received from the last dollar spent on each commodity is equal across all goods and services purchased.

Utilization review program Programs implemented to control medical costs by evaluating the medical decisions of hospitals and physicians. These programs can be carried out on a prospective, concurrent, or retrospective basis.

Vertical equity Achieved when unequal individuals are treated unequally. For example, people with higher incomes pay higher taxes.

Virtual integration A contractual combination of buyers and suppliers.

Willingness-to-pay approach Determines the value of a human life based on a person's willingness to pay for relatively small reductions in the chance of dying.

Page numbers followed by *f* indicate figures; page numbers followed by *t* indicate tables; page numbers followed by *n* indicate footnotes.

Definitions and appropriate page numbers appear in **boldface** type. Page numbers followed by *f* indicate figures; page numbers followed by *t* indicate tables; page numbers followed by *n* indicate footnotes.